T0180387

Lecture Notes in Computer Science 14145

Founding Editors

Gerhard Goos
Juris Hartmanis

Editorial Board Members

Elisa Bertino, *Purdue University, West Lafayette, IN, USA*
Wen Gao, *Peking University, Beijing, China*
Bernhard Steffen ⓘ, *TU Dortmund University, Dortmund, Germany*
Moti Yung ⓘ, *Columbia University, New York, NY, USA*

The series Lecture Notes in Computer Science (LNCS), including its subseries Lecture Notes in Artificial Intelligence (LNAI) and Lecture Notes in Bioinformatics (LNBI), has established itself as a medium for the publication of new developments in computer science and information technology research, teaching, and education.

LNCS enjoys close cooperation with the computer science R & D community, the series counts many renowned academics among its volume editors and paper authors, and collaborates with prestigious societies. Its mission is to serve this international community by providing an invaluable service, mainly focused on the publication of conference and workshop proceedings and postproceedings. LNCS commenced publication in 1973.

José Abdelnour Nocera ·
Marta Kristín Lárusdóttir · Helen Petrie ·
Antonio Piccinno · Marco Winckler
Editors

Human-Computer Interaction – INTERACT 2023

19th IFIP TC13 International Conference
York, UK, August 28 – September 1, 2023
Proceedings, Part IV

 Springer

Editors
José Abdelnour Nocera 🆔
University of West London
London, UK

Helen Petrie 🆔
University of York
York, UK

Marco Winckler 🆔
Université Côte d'Azur
Sophia Antipolis Cedex, France

Marta Kristín Lárusdóttir 🆔
Reykjavik University
Reykjavik, Iceland

Antonio Piccinno 🆔
University of Bari Aldo Moro
Bari, Italy

ISSN 0302-9743   ISSN 1611-3349 (electronic)
Lecture Notes in Computer Science
ISBN 978-3-031-42292-8   ISBN 978-3-031-42293-5 (eBook)
https://doi.org/10.1007/978-3-031-42293-5

© The Editor(s) (if applicable) and The Author(s), under exclusive license
to Springer Nature Switzerland AG 2023

This work is subject to copyright. All rights are reserved by the Publisher, whether the whole or part of the material is concerned, specifically the rights of translation, reprinting, reuse of illustrations, recitation, broadcasting, reproduction on microfilms or in any other physical way, and transmission or information storage and retrieval, electronic adaptation, computer software, or by similar or dissimilar methodology now known or hereafter developed.
The use of general descriptive names, registered names, trademarks, service marks, etc. in this publication does not imply, even in the absence of a specific statement, that such names are exempt from the relevant protective laws and regulations and therefore free for general use.
The publisher, the authors, and the editors are safe to assume that the advice and information in this book are believed to be true and accurate at the date of publication. Neither the publisher nor the authors or the editors give a warranty, expressed or implied, with respect to the material contained herein or for any errors or omissions that may have been made. The publisher remains neutral with regard to jurisdictional claims in published maps and institutional affiliations.

This Springer imprint is published by the registered company Springer Nature Switzerland AG
The registered company address is: Gewerbestrasse 11, 6330 Cham, Switzerland

Foreword

INTERACT 2023 is the 19th International Conference of Technical Committee 13 (Human-Computer Interaction) of IFIP (International Federation for Information Processing). IFIP was created in 1960 under the auspices of UNESCO. The IFIP Technical Committee 13 (TC13) aims at developing the science and technology of human-computer interaction (HCI). TC13 started the series of INTERACT conferences in 1984. These conferences have been an important showcase for researchers and practitioners in the field of HCI. Situated under the open, inclusive umbrella of IFIP, INTERACT has been truly international in its spirit and has attracted researchers from several countries and cultures. The venues of the INTERACT conferences over the years bear testimony to this inclusiveness.

INTERACT 2023 was held from August 28th to September 1st 2023 at the University of York, York, United Kingdom. The INTERACT Conference is held every two years, and is one of the longest-running conferences on Human-Computer Interaction. The INTERACT 2023 Conference was held both in-person and online. It was collocated with the British Computer Society HCI 2023 Conference.

The theme of the 19th conference was "Design for Equality and Justice". Increasingly computer science as a discipline is becoming concerned about issues of justice and equality – from fake news to rights for robots, from the ethics of driverless vehicles to the Gamergate controversy. The HCI community is surely well placed to be at the leading edge of such discussions within the wider computer science community and in the dialogue between computer science and the broader society. Justice and equality are particularly important concepts both for the City of York and for the University of York. The City of York has a long history of working for justice and equality, from the Quakers and their philanthropic chocolate companies, to current initiatives. The City of York is the UK's first Human Rights City, encouraging organizations and citizens to "increasingly think about human rights, talk about human rights issues and stand up for rights whether that's at work, school or home". The City of York has also launched "One Planet York", a network of organizations working towards a more sustainable, resilient and collaborative "one planet" future. York is now working to become the first "Zero emissions" city centre, with much of the medieval centre already car free.

Finally, great research is the heart of a good conference. Like its predecessors, INTERACT 2023 aimed to bring together high-quality research. As a multidisciplinary field, HCI requires interaction and discussion among diverse people with different interests and background. We thank all the authors who chose INTERACT 2023 as the venue to publish their research.

We received a total of 375 submissions distributed in 2 peer-reviewed tracks, 4 curated tracks, and 3 juried tracks. Of these, the following contributions were accepted:

- 71 Full Papers (peer reviewed)
- 58 Short Papers (peer reviewed)
- 6 Courses (curated)

- 2 Industrial Experience papers (curated)
- 10 Interactive Demonstrations (curated)
- 44 Interactive Posters (juried)
- 2 Panels (curated)
- 16 Workshops (juried)
- 15 Doctoral Consortium (juried)

The acceptance rate for contributions received in the peer-reviewed tracks was 32% for full papers and 31% for short papers. In addition to full papers and short papers, the present proceedings feature contributions accepted in the form of industrial experiences, courses, interactive demonstrations, interactive posters, panels, invited keynote papers, and descriptions of accepted workshops. The contributions submitted to workshops were published as an independent post-proceedings volume.

The reviewing process was primary carried out by a panel of international experts organized in subcommittees. Each subcommittee had a chair and a set of associated chairs, who were in charge of coordinating a double-blind reviewing process. Each paper received at least 2 reviews of associated chairs and two reviews from external experts in the HCI field. Hereafter we list the twelve subcommittees of INTERACT 2023:

- Accessibility and assistive technologies
- Design for business and safety/critical interactive systems
- Design of interactive entertainment systems
- HCI Education and Curriculum
- HCI for Justice and Equality
- Human-AI interaction
- Information visualization
- Interaction design for culture and development
- Interactive systems technologies and engineering
- Methodologies for HCI
- Social and ubiquitous Interaction
- Understanding users and human behaviour

The final decision on acceptance or rejection of full papers was taken in a Programme Committee meeting held in London, United Kingdom in March 2023. The full papers chairs, the subcommittee chairs, and the associate chairs participated in this meeting. The meeting discussed a consistent set of criteria to deal with inevitable differences among the large number of reviewers. The final decisions on other tracks were made by the corresponding track chairs and reviewers, often after electronic meetings and discussions.

INTERACT 2023 was made possible by the persistent efforts across several months by 12 subcommittee chairs, 86 associated chairs, 28 track chairs, and 407 reviewers. We thank them all.

September 2023

José Abdelnour Nocera
Helen Petrie
Marco Winckler

IFIP TC13 – http://ifip-tc13.org/

Established in 1989, the International Federation for Information Processing Technical Committee on Human–Computer Interaction (IFIP TC13) is an international committee of 37 IFIP Member national societies and 10 Working Groups, representing specialists of the various disciplines contributing to the field of human-computer interaction (HCI). This field includes, among others, human factors, ergonomics, cognitive science, computer science and design. INTERACT is the flagship conference of IFIP TC13, staged biennially in different countries in the world. The first INTERACT conference was held in 1984, at first running triennially and becoming a biennial event in 1993.

IFIP TC13 aims to develop the science, technology and societal aspects of HCI by encouraging empirical research promoting the use of knowledge and methods from the human sciences in design and evaluation of computing technology systems; promoting better understanding of the relation between formal design methods and system usability and acceptability; developing guidelines, models and methods by which designers may provide better human-oriented computing technology systems; and, cooperating with other groups, inside and outside IFIP, to promote user-orientation and humanization in system design. Thus, TC13 seeks to improve interactions between people and computing technology, to encourage the growth of HCI research and its practice in industry and to disseminate these benefits worldwide.

The main orientation is to place the users at the centre of the development process. Areas of study include: the problems people face when interacting with computing technology; the impact of technology deployment on people in individual and organisational contexts; the determinants of utility, usability, acceptability and user experience; the appropriate allocation of tasks between computing technology and users, especially in the case of autonomous and closed-loop systems; modelling the user, their tasks and the interactive system to aid better system design; and harmonizing the computing technology to user characteristics and needs.

While the scope is thus set wide, with a tendency toward general principles rather than particular systems, it is recognised that progress will only be achieved through both general studies to advance theoretical understanding and specific studies on practical issues (e.g., interface design standards, software system resilience, documentation, training material, appropriateness of alternative interaction technologies, guidelines, the problems of integrating multimedia systems to match system needs and organisational practices, etc.).

IFIP TC13 also stimulates working events and activities through its Working Groups (WGs). The WGs consist of HCI experts from around the world, who seek to expand knowledge and find solutions to HCI issues and concerns within their domains. The list of current TC13 WGs and their area of interest is given below:

- WG 13.1 (Education in HCI and HCI Curricula) aims to improve HCI education at all levels of higher education, coordinate and unite efforts to develop HCI curricula and promote HCI teaching.

- WG 13.2 (Methodology for User-Centred System Design) aims to foster research, dissemination of information and good practice in the methodical application of HCI to software engineering.
- WG 13.3 (Human Computer Interaction, Disability and Aging) aims to make HCI designers aware of the needs of people with disabilities and older people and encourage development of information systems and tools permitting adaptation of interfaces to specific users.
- WG 13.4/WG2.7 (User Interface Engineering) investigates the nature, concepts and construction of user interfaces for software systems, using a framework for reasoning about interactive systems and an engineering model for developing user interfaces.
- WG 13.5 (Resilience, Reliability, Safety and Human Error in System Development) seeks a framework for studying human factors relating to systems failure, develops leading-edge techniques in hazard analysis and safety engineering of computer-based systems, and guides international accreditation activities for safety-critical systems.
- WG 13.6 (Human-Work Interaction Design) aims at establishing relationships between extensive empirical work-domain studies and HCI design. It will promote the use of knowledge, concepts, methods and techniques that enable user studies to procure a better apprehension of the complex interplay between individual, social and organisational contexts and thereby a better understanding of how and why people work in the ways that they do.
- WG 13.7 (Human–Computer Interaction and Visualization) aims to establish a study and research program that will combine both scientific work and practical applications in the fields of Human–Computer Interaction and Visualization. It will integrate several additional aspects of further research areas, such as scientific visualization, data mining, information design, computer graphics, cognition sciences, perception theory, or psychology into this approach.
- WG 13.8 (Interaction Design and International Development) aims to support and develop the research, practice and education capabilities of HCI in institutions and organisations based around the world taking into account their diverse local needs and cultural perspectives.
- WG 13.9 (Interaction Design and Children) aims to support practitioners, regulators and researchers to develop the study of interaction design and children across international contexts.
- WG 13.10 (Human-Centred Technology for Sustainability) aims to promote research, design, development, evaluation, and deployment of human-centred technology to encourage sustainable use of resources in various domains.

IFIP TC13 recognises contributions to HCI through both its Pioneer in HCI Award and various paper awards associated with each INTERACT conference. Since the processes to decide the various awards take place after papers are sent to the publisher for publication, the recipients of the awards are not identified in the proceedings.

The IFIP TC13 Pioneer in Human-Computer Interaction Award recognises the contributions and achievements of pioneers in HCI. An IFIP TC13 Pioneer is one who, through active participation in IFIP Technical Committees or related IFIP groups, has made outstanding contributions to the educational, theoretical, technical, commercial, or professional aspects of analysis, design, construction, evaluation, and use of interactive systems. The IFIP TC13 Pioneer Awards are presented during an awards ceremony at each INTERACT conference.

In 1999, TC13 initiated a special IFIP Award, the Brian Shackel Award, for the most outstanding contribution in the form of a refereed paper submitted to and delivered at each INTERACT Conference, which draws attention to the need for a comprehensive human-centred approach in the design and use of information technology in which the human and social implications have been considered. The IFIP TC13 Accessibility Award, launched in 2007 by IFIP WG 13.3, recognises the most outstanding contribution with international impact in the field of ageing, disability, and inclusive design in the form of a refereed paper submitted to and delivered at the INTERACT Conference. The IFIP TC13 Interaction Design for International Development Award, launched in 2013 by IFIP WG 13.8, recognises the most outstanding contribution to the application of interactive systems for social and economic development of people around the world taking into account their diverse local needs and cultural perspectives. The IFIP TC13 Pioneers' Award for Best Doctoral Student Paper at INTERACT, first awarded in 2019, is selected by the past recipients of the IFIP TC13 Pioneer title. The award is made to the best research paper accepted to the INTERACT Conference which is based on the doctoral research of the student and authored and presented by the student.

In 2015, TC13 approved the creation of a steering committee for the INTERACT conference. The Steering Committee (SC) is currently chaired by Marco Winckler and is responsible for:

- Promoting and maintaining the INTERACT conference as the premiere venue for researchers and practitioners interested in the topics of the conference (this requires a refinement of the topics above).
- Ensuring the highest quality for the contents of the event.
- Setting up the bidding process to handle future INTERACT conferences. Decision is made up at TC13 level.
- Providing advice to the current and future chairs and organizers of the INTERACT conference.
- Providing data, tools, and documents about previous conferences to future conference organizers.
- Selecting the reviewing system to be used throughout the conference (as this impacts the entire set of reviewers).
- Resolving general issues involved with the INTERACT conference.
- Capitalizing on history (good and bad practices).

Further information is available at the IFIP TC13 website: http://ifip-tc13.org/.

IFIP TC13 Members

Officers

Chair

Paula Kotzé, South Africa

Vice-chair for Conferences

Marco Winckler, France

Vice-chair for Equity and Development

José Abdelnour-Nocera, UK

Vice-chair for Media and Communications

Helen Petrie, UK

Vice-chair for Membership and Collaboration

Philippe Palanque, France

Vice-chair for Working Groups

Simone D. J. Barbosa, Brazil

Vice-chair for Finance (Treasurer)

Regina Bernhaupt, The Netherlands

Secretary

Janet Wesson, South Africa

INTERACT Steering Committee Chair

Marco Winckler, France

Country Representatives

Australia

Henry B. L. Duh
Australian Computer Society

Austria

Christopher Frauenberger
Austrian Computer Society

Belgium

Bruno Dumas
IMEC – Interuniversity
Micro-Electronics Center

Brazil

André Freire
Simone D. J. Barbosa (section b)
Sociedade Brasileira de Computação
(SBC)

Bulgaria

Petia Koprinkova-Hristova
Bulgarian Academy of Sciences

Croatia

Andrina Granić
Croatian Information Technology
Association (CITA)

Cyprus

Panayiotis Zaphiris
Cyprus Computer Society

Czech Republic

Zdeněk Míkovec
Czech Society for Cybernetics and
Informatics

Denmark

Jan Stage
Danish Federation for Information
Processing (DANFIP)

Finland

Virpi Roto
Finnish Information Processing
Association

France

Philippe Palanque
Marco Winckler (section b)
Société informatique de France (SIF)

Germany

Tom Gross
Gesellschaft fur Informatik e.V.

Ireland

Liam J. Bannon
Irish Computer Society

Italy

Fabio Paternò
Associazione Italiana per l' Informatica ed
il Calcolo Automatico (AICA)

Japan

Yoshifumi Kitamura
Information Processing Society of Japan

Netherlands

Regina Bernhaupt
Koninklijke Nederlandse Vereniging
van Informatieprofessionals (KNVI)

New Zealand

Mark Apperley
Institute of IT Professionals New Zealand

Norway

Frode Eika Sandnes
Norwegian Computer Society

Poland

Marcin Sikorski
Polish Academy of Sciences (PAS)

Portugal

Pedro Filipe Pereira Campos
Associacão Portuguesa para o
Desenvolvimento da Sociedade da
Informação (APDSI)

Serbia

Aleksandar Jevremovic
Informatics Association of Serbia (IAS)

Singapore

Shengdong Zhao
Singapore Computer Society

Slovakia

Wanda Benešová
Slovak Society for Computer Science

Slovenia

Matjaž Kljun
Slovenian Computer Society
INFORMATIKA

South Africa

Janet L. Wesson
Paula Kotzé (section b)
Institute of Information Technology
Professionals South Africa (IITPSA)

Sri Lanka

Thilina Halloluwa
Computer Society of Sri Lanka (CSSL)

Sweden

Jan Gulliksen
Swedish Interdisciplinary Society for
Human-Computer Interaction
Dataföreningen i Sverige

Switzerland

Denis Lalanne
Schweizer Informatik Gesellschaft (SI)

United Kingdom

José Luis Abdelnour Nocera
Helen Petrie (section b)
British Computer Society (BCS),
Chartered Institute for IT

International Members at Large Representatives

ACM

Gerrit van der Veer
Association for Computing
Machinery

CLEI

César Collazos
Centro Latinoamericano de Estudios en
Informatica

Expert Members

Anirudha Joshi, India
Constantinos Coursaris, Canada
Carmelo Ardito, Italy
Daniel Orwa Ochieng, Kenya
David Lamas, Estonia
Dorian Gorgan, Romania
Eunice Sari, Australia/Indonesia
Fernando Loizides, UK/Cyprus
Geraldine Fitzpatrick, Austria

Ivan Burmistrov, Russia
Julio Abascal, Spain
Kaveh Bazargan, Iran
Marta Kristin Lárusdóttir, Iceland
Nikolaos Avouris, Greece
Peter Forbrig, Germany
Torkil Clemmensen, Denmark
Zhengjie Liu, China

Working Group Chairpersons

WG 13.1 (Education in HCI and HCI Curricula)

Konrad Baumann, Austria

WG 13.2 (Methodologies for User-Centered System Design)

Regina Bernhaupt, Netherlands

WG 13.3 (HCI, Disability and Aging)

Helen Petrie, UK

WG 13.4/2.7 (User Interface Engineering)

Davide Spano, Italy

WG 13.5 (Human Error, Resilience, Reliability, Safety and System Development)

Tilo Mentler, Germany

WG13.6 (Human-Work Interaction Design)

Barbara Rita Barricelli, Italy

WG13.7 (HCI and Visualization)

Gerrit van der Veer, Netherlands

WG 13.8 (Interaction Design and International Development)

José Adbelnour Nocera, UK

WG 13.9 (Interaction Design and Children)

Gavin Sim, UK

WG 13.10 (Human-Centred Technology for Sustainability)

Masood Masoodian, Finland

Organization

General Chairs

Helen Petrie   University of York, UK
Jose Abdelnour-Nocera   University of West London, UK and ITI/Larsys, Portugal

Technical Program Chair

Marco Winckler   Université Côte d'Azur, France

Full Papers Chairs

Antonio Piccinno   University of Bari Aldo Moro, Italy
Marta Kristin Lárusdóttir   Reykjavik University, Iceland

Short Papers Chairs

Marta Rey-Babarro   Zillow, USA
Frode Eika Sandnes   Oslo Metropolitan University, Norway
Grace Eden   University of York, UK

Poster Chairs

Alena Denisova   University of York, UK
Burak Merdenyan   University of York, UK

Workshops Chairs

Jan Stage   Aalborg University, Denmark
Anna Bramwell-Dicks   University of York, UK

Panels Chairs

Effie Lai-Chong Law   Durham University, UK
Massimo Zancanaro   University of Trento, Italy

Student Volunteers Chairs

Sanjit Samaddar   University of York, UK
Daniel Lock   University of York, UK

Interactive Demonstrations Chairs

Barbara Rita Barricelli   University of Brescia, Italy
Jainendra Shukla   Indraprastha Institute of Information Technology,
                               India

Courses Chairs

Nikos Avouris   University of Patras, Greece
André Freire   Federal University of Lavras, Brazil

Doctoral Consortium Chairs

David Lamas   Tallinn University, Estonia
Geraldine Fitzpatrick   TU Wien, Austria
Tariq Zaman   University of Technology Sarawak, Malaysia

Industrial Experiences Chairs

Helen Petrie   University of York, UK
Jose Abdelnour-Nocera   University of West London, UK and ITI/Larsys,
                               Portugal

Publicity Chairs

Delvin Varghese   Monash University, Australia
Lourdes Moreno   Universidad Carlos III de Madrid, Spain

Advisors

Marco Winckler	University of the Côte d'Azur, France
Fernando Loizides	Cardiff University, UK
Carmelo Ardito	LUM Giuseppe Degennaro University, Italy

Web Master

Edmund Wei	University of York, UK

INTERACT Subcommittee Chairs

Anirudha Joshi	Industrial Design Centre, IIT Bombay, India
Célia Martinie	IRIT, Université Toulouse III - Paul Sabatier, France
Fabio Paternò	CNR-ISTI, Pisa, Italy
Frank Steinicke	Universität Hamburg, Germany
Gerhard Weber	TU Dresden, Germany
Helen Petrie	University of York, UK
José Campos	University of Minho, Portugal
Nikolaos Avouris	University of Patras, Greece
Philippe Palanque	IRIT, Université Toulouse III - Paul Sabatier, France
Rosa Lanzilotti	University of Bari, Italy
Rosella Gennari	Free University of Bozen-Bolzano, Switzerland
Simone Barbosa	PUC-Rio, Brazil
Torkil Clemmensen	Copenhagen Business School, Denmark
Yngve Dahl	Norwegian University of Science and Technology, Norway

INTERACT Steering Committee

Anirudha Joshi	Industrial Design Centre, IIT Bombay, India
Antonio Piccinno	University of Bari, Italy
Carmelo Arditto	University of Bari, Italy
Fernando Loizides	University of Cardiff, UK
Frode Sandnes	Oslo Metropolitan University, Norway
Helen Petrie	University of York, UK
Janet Wesson	Nelson Mandela University, South Africa
Marco Winckler (Chair)	Université Côte d'Azur, France
Marta Lárusdóttir	Reykjavik University, Iceland

Paolo Buono	University of Bari, Italy
Paula Kotzé	University of Pretoria, South Africa
Philippe Palanque	IRIT, Université Toulouse III - Paul Sabatier, France
Raquel Oliveira Prates	Universidade Federal de Minas Gerais, Brazil
Tom Gross	University of Bamberg, Germany

Program Committee

Alan Chamberlain	University of Nottingham, UK
Alessandra Melonio	Ca' Foscari University of Venice, Italy
Alessandro Pagano	University of Bari, Italy
Andrea Marrella	Sapienza Università di Roma, Italy
Andrés Lucero	Aalto University, Finland
Anna Sigríður Islind	Reykjavik University, Iceland
Antonio Piccinno	University of Bari, Italy
Ashley Colley	University of Lapland, Finland
Aurora Constantin	University of Edinburgh, UK
Barbara Rita Barricelli	Università degli Studi di Brescia, Italy
Bridget Kane	Karlstad University Business School, Sweden
Bruno Dumas	University of Namur, Belgium
Carla Dal Sasso Freitas	Federal University of Rio Grande do Sul, Brazil
Célia Martinie	Université Toulouse III - Paul Sabatier, France
Chi Vi	University of Sussex, UK
Christopher Power	University of Prince Edward Island, Canada
Christopher Clarke	University of Bath, UK
Cristian Bogdan	KTH, EECS, HCT, Sweden
Cristina Gena	Università di Torino, Italy
Dan Fitton	University of Central Lancashire, UK
Daniela Fogli	University of Brescia, Italy
Daniela Trevisan	Universidade Federal Fluminense, Brazil
Denis Lalanne	University of Fribourg, Switzerland
Dipanjan Chakraborty	BITS Pilani, Hyderabad Campus, India
Fabio Buttussi	University of Udine, Italy
Federico Cabitza	University of Milano-Bicocca, Italy
Fernando Loizides	Cardiff University, UK
Frode Eika Sandnes	Oslo Metropolitan University, Norway
Gerd Bruder	University of Central Florida, USA
Gerhard Weber	TU Dresden, Germany
Giuliana Vitiello	Università di Salerno, Italy
Giuseppe Desolda	University of Bari Aldo Moro, Italy

Helen Petrie	University of York, UK
Jan Van den Bergh	UHasselt - tUL - Flanders Make, Belgium
Jan Gulliksen	KTH Royal Institute of Technology, Sweden
Janet Wesson	Nelson Mandela University, South Africa
Janet Read	University of Central Lancashire, UK
Jens Gerken	Westphalian University of Applied Sciences, Germany
Jo Lumsden	Aston University, UK
Jolanta Mizera-Pietraszko	Military University of Land Forces, Poland
Jonna Häkkilä	University of Lapland, Finland
José Abdelnour Nocera	University of West London, UK
Judy Bowen	University of Waikato, New Zealand
Karen Renaud	University of Strathclyde, UK
Kaveh Bazargan	Allameh Tabataba'i University, Islamic Republic of Iran
Kris Luyten	Hasselt University - tUL - Flanders Make, Belgium
Kshitij Sharma	NTNU, Norway
Lara Piccolo	Open University, UK
Lene Nielsen	IT University of Copenhagen, Denmark
Lucio Davide Spano	University of Cagliari, Italy
Luigi De Russis	Politecnico di Torino, Italy
Manjiri Joshi	Swansea University, UK
Marco Winckler	Université Côte d'Azur, France
Maristella Matera	Politecnico di Milano, Italy
Mark Apperley	University of Waikato, New Zealand
Marta Lárusdóttir	Reykjavik University, Iceland
Netta Iivari	University of Oulu, Finland
Oliver Korn	Offenburg University, Germany
Paloma Diaz	University Carlos III of Madrid, Spain
Paolo Bottoni	Sapienza University of Rome, Italy
Paolo Buono	University of Bari Aldo Moro, Italy
Paula Kotzé	University of Pretoria, South Africa
Pedro Campos	ITI/LARSyS, Portugal
Peter Forbrig	University of Rostock, Germany
Raquel O. Prates	Universidade Federal de Minas Gerais, Brazil
Renaud Blanch	Université Grenoble Alpes, France
Sandy Claes	LUCA School of Arts, Belgium
Sayan Sarcar	Birmingham City University, UK
Shaun Macdonald	University of Glasgow, UK
Simone Kriglstein	Masaryk University, Czech Republic
Sophie Dupuy-Chessa	Université Grenoble Alpes, France

Sumita Sharma	University of Oulu, Finland
Sven Mayer	LMU Munich, Germany
Tania Di Mascio	Università dell'Aquila, Italy
Theodoros Georgiou	Heriot-Watt University, UK
Thilina Halloluwa	University of Colombo, Sri Lanka
Tilo Mentler	Trier University of Applied Sciences, Germany
Timothy Merritt	Aalborg University, Denmark
Tom Gross	University of Bamberg, Germany
Valentin Schwind	Frankfurt University of Applied Sciences, Germany
Virpi Roto	Aalto University, Finland
Vita Santa Barletta	University of Bari Aldo Moro, Italy
Vivian Genaro Motti	George Mason University, USA
Wricha Mishra	MIT Institute of Design, India
Zdeněk Míkovec	Czech Technical University Prague, Czech Republic
Zeynep Yildiz	Koç University, Turkey

Additional Reviewers

Abhishek Shrivastava	Aline Menin
Adalberto Simeone	Alisson Puska
Aditya Prakash Kulkarni	Alma Cantu
Adrien Chaffangeon Caillet	Amy Melniczuk
Adrien Coppens	An Jacobs
Aekaterini Mavri	Ana Serrano
Ahmad Samer Wazan	Anderson Maciel
Aidan Slingsby	André Freire
Aimee Code	Andre Salgado
Aizal Yusrina Idris	Andre Suslik Spritzer
Akihisa Shitara	Andrea Antonio Cantone
Aku Visuri	Andrea Bellucci
Alberto Monge Roffarello	Andrea Esposito
Alessandro Forgiarini	Andreas Fender
Alessio Malizia	Andreas Mallas
Alex Binh Vinh Duc Nguyen	Andreas Sonderegger
Alex Chen	Andres Santos-Torres
Alexander Maedche	Ángel Cuevas
Alexander Meschtscherjakov	Angela Locoro
Alexander Wachtel	Angus Addlesee
Alexandra Voit	Angus Marshall
Alexandre Canny	Anicia Peters
Ali Gheitasy	Anirudh Nagraj

Ankica Barisic
Anna Spagnolli
Annika Schulz
Anthony Perritano
Antigoni Parmaxi
Antje Jacobs
Antonella Varesano
Antonio Bucchiarone
Antonio Piccinno
Anupriya Tuli
Argenis Ramirez Gomez
Arminda Lopes
Arnaud Blouin
Ashwin Singh
Ashwin T. S.
Asim Evren Yantac
Axel Carayon
Aykut Coşkun
Azra Ismail
Barsha Mitra
Basmah Almekhled
Beat Signer
Beenish Chaudhry
Behnaz Norouzi
Benjamin Schnitzer
Benjamin Tag
Benjamin Weyers
Berardina De Carolis
Bharatwaja Namatherdhala
Bhumika Walia
Biju Thankachan
Bram van Deurzen
Çağlar Genç
Canlin Zhang
Carolyn Holter
Céline Coutrix
Chameera De Silva
Charlotte Magnusson
Chiara Ceccarini
Chiara Natali
Chikodi Chima
Christian Frisson
Christophe Kolski
Christopher Frauenberger
Christos Katsanos

Christos Sintoris
Cléber Corrêa
Cleidson de Souza
Daisuke Sato
Damianos Dumi Sigalas
Damon Horowitz
Dan Fitton
Daniel Görlich
Daniel Zielasko
Danielle Langlois
Daphne Chang
Dario Bertero
David Gollasch
David Navarre
Davide D'Adamo
Davide Mulfari
Davide Spallazzo
Debjani Roy
Diana Korka
Diego Morra
Dilrukshi Gamage
Diogo Cabral
Dixie Ching
Domenico Gigante
Dominic Potts
Donald McMillan
Edwige Pissaloux
Edy Portmann
Effie Law
Eike Schneiders
Elisa Mekler
Elise Grevet
Elizabeth Buie
Elodie Bouzbib
Emanuele Pucci
Enes Yigitbas
Eric Barboni
Estela Peralta
Euan Freeman
Evangelia Chrysikou
Evelyn Eika
Fabiana Vernero
Fabio Cassano
Fabrizio Balducci
Fanny Vainionpää

Fausto Medola
Favour Aladesuru
Federica Cena
Federico Botella
Florian Gnadlinger
Francesco Cauteruccio
Francesco Chiossi
Francesco Ferrise
Francesco Greco
Francisco Iniesto
Francisco Maria Calisto
Frank Beruscha
Frank Fischer
Frank Nack
Frida Milella
Funmi Adebesin
Gavin Sim
George Adrian Stoica
George Raptis
Georgios Papadoulis
Gianluca Schiavo
Girish Dalvi
Grischa Liebel
Guanhua Zhang
Guilherme Schardong
Gustavo Rovelo Ruiz
Hanne Sørum
Heidi Hartikainen
Himanshu Verma
Holger Regenbrecht
Hsin-Jou Lin
Hui-Yin Wu
Ikram Ur Rehman
Isabela Gasparini
Ivo Malý
Jack Jamieson
James Simpson
Jan Leusmann
Jana Jost
Jannes Peeters
Jari Kangas
Jayden Khakurel
Jean Hallewell Haslwanter
Jemma König
Jermaine Marshall

Jeroen Ceyssens
Jesper Gaarsdal
Jessica Sehrt
Jiaying Liu
Job Timmermans
Joe Cutting
Jonas Moll
Jonathan Hook
Joni Salminen
Joongi Shin
Jorge Wagner
José Campos
Joseph O'Hagan
Judith Borghouts
Julia Hertel
Julio Reis
Kajetan Enge
Kasper Rodil
Kate Rogers
Katerina Cerna
Katherine Seyama
Kathia Oliveira
Kathrin Gerling
Khyati Priya
Konstantin Biriukov
Kostantinos Moustakas
Krishna Venkatasubramanian
Laden Husamaldin
Lars Lischke
Lars Oestreicher
Laura Helsby
Leena Ventä-Olkkonen
Lele Sha
Leonardo Sandoval
Lorena Riol-Blanco
Lorenzo Torrez
Louise Barkhuus
Luis Leiva
Luis Teran
M. Cristina Vannini
Maälis Lefebvre
Magdaléna Kejstová
Malay Dhamelia
Manik Gupta
Manuel J. Fonseca

Marco de Gemmis
Marco Manca
Marco Romano
Margarita Anastassova
Margault Sacré
Margherita Andrao
Mari Karhu
Maria Fernanda Antunes
María Óskarsdóttir
Marianna Di Gregorio
Marika Jonsson
Marios Constantinides
Mark Apperley
Mark Lochrie
Marko Tkalcic
Markus Löchtefeld
Markus Tatzgern
Marta Serafini
Martin Hedlund
Martin Kocur
Massimo Zancanaro
Mateusz Dubiel
Matthias Baldauf
Matthias Heintz
Max Birk
Maxime Savary-Leblanc
Maximiliano Jeanneret Medina
Mehdi Rizvi
Mengyu Chen
Michael Burch
Michael Rohs
Michalis Xenos
Mihail Terenti
Min Zhang
Mireia Ribera
Mirko De Vincentiis
Miroslav Macík
Mohd Kamal Othman
Monica Divitini
Monisha Pattanaik
Mrim Alnfiai
Murali Balusu
Nada Attar
Nadine Flegel
Nadine Vigouroux

Nadir Weibel
Nahal Norouzi
Najla Aldaraani
Nancy Alajarmeh
Nicholas Vanderschantz
Nicoletta Adamo
Niels van Berkel
Nikolaos Avouris
Nils Beese
Nivan Ferreira
Nurha Yingta
Ohoud Alharbi
Omar Al Hashimi
Pallabi Bhowmick
Pallavi Rao Gadahad
Panayiotis Koutsabasis
Paolo Massa
Parisa Saadati
Pascal Lessel
Patricia Arias-Cabarcos
Paula Alexandra Silva
Pavel Slavik
Peter Bago
Philippe Truillet
Pinar Simsek Caglar
Po-Ming Law
Prabodh Sakhardande
Pranjal Protim Borah
Quynh Nguyen
Radovan Madleňák
Ragad Allwihan
Rahat Jahangir Rony
Rajni Sachdeo
Razan Bamoallem
Rekha Sugandhi
Rishi Vanukuru
Rogério Bordini
Rohan Gaikwad
Romane Dubus
Rosella Gennari
Rui José
Sabrina Burtscher
Sabrina Lakhdhir
Sahar Mirhadi
Saif Hadj Sassi

Salvatore Andolina
Salvatore Sorce
Samangi Wadinambi Arachchi
Sanika Doolani
Sanjit Samaddar
Sara Capecchi
Sarah Hodge
Saumya Pareek
Scott MacKenzie
Scott Trent
Sebastian Feger
Sebastian Günther
Sebastian Weiß
Sébastien Scannella
Shah Rukh Humayoun
Shunyao Wu
Siddharth Gulati
Siiri Paananen
Silvia Espada
Silvia Gabrielli
Simon Ruffieux
Simon Voelker
Simone Barbosa
Siti Haris
Sónia Brito-Costa
Sophie Dupuy-Chessa
Sophie Lepreux
Soraia M. Alarcão
Srishti Gupta
Stefan Johansson
Stéphanie Fleck
Stine Johansen
Subrata Tikadar
Suzanna Schmeelk
Sybille Caffiau
Sylvain Malacria
Taejun Kim
Tahani Alahmadi
Tahani Albalawi
Takumi Yamamoto
Tariq Zaman
Tathagata Ray
Telmo Zarraonandia
Teresa Onorati
Tero Jokela
Theodoros Georgiou

Thomas Kosch
Tilman Dingler
Tom Veuskens
Tomas Alves
Tomáš Pagáč
Tomi Heimonen
Tommaso Turchi
Tong Wu
Tzu-Yang Wang
Valentino Artizzu
Vanessa Cesário
Vanessa Maike
Vania Neris
Vasiliki Mylonopoulou
Vera Memmesheimer
Vickie Nguyen
Victor Adriel de Jesus Oliveira
Vidushani Dhanawansa
Vikas Upadhyay
Vincent Zakka
Vincenzo Dentamaro
Vincenzo Gattulli
Vinitha Gadiraju
Vit Rusnak
Vittoria Frau
Vivek Kant
Way Kiat Bong
Weiqin Chen
Wenchen Guo
William Delamare
Xiying Wang
Yann Savoye
Yao Chen
Yaoli Mao
Yaxiong Lei
Yilin Liu
Ying Ma
Yingying Zhao
Yong-Joon Thoo
Yoselyn Walsh
Yosra Rekik
Yuan Chen
Yubo Kou
Zhiyuan Wang
Zi Wang

Sponsors and Partners

Sponsors

UNIVERSITY OF
WEST LONDON

Partners

International Federation for Information Processing

In-cooperation with ACM

In-cooperation with SIGCHI

Invited Talks

Disability, Design and Innovation for a Fairer World

Catherine Holloway, Ben Hardman, Ben Oldfrey, Daniel Hajas, Jamie Danemayer, Maryam Bandukda, and Tigmanshu Bhatnagar

Global Disability Innovation Hub, University College London, London, E20 2AF, UK
{c.holloway,ben.hardman,b.oldfrey,d.hajas,
j.danemayer.21,m.bandukda,t.bhatnagar.18}@ucl.ac.uk

Abstract. People with disabilities still face many barriers that prevent them from full participation. Some of these barriers can be overcome by innovation. This course aims to introduce the Disability Interaction framework and explore its application at different stages of the innovation process. Participants will learn how to acknowledge the complexities of Disability. In addition, they will get to design new solutions that overcome the barriers faced by people with disabilities in a practical, impactful and creative way.

Keywords: Disability · Design and Innovation

1 Introduction

Many barriers still prevent people with disabilities from fully participating in society. These barriers can be in the form of social issues such as stigma, physical barriers such as inaccessibility and technological barriers causing a lack of appropriate assistive technology (AT). Such barriers prevent people from accessing basic life requirements such as education, employment, and social participation. The situation is particularly severe in the Global South, where most people with disabilities live [1].

Disability innovation breaks down these barriers by developing new technologies, products and services that reach people. In addition, disability innovation can help promote inclusion and diversity in society by ensuring everyone has equitable access to opportunities and resources. However, Disability is complex because it is influenced by many factors that range from individual variability [2] and social interdependence [3] to attitudes [4] and systemic barriers [5]. Addressing disability requires a holistic approach that considers these multiple and multifaceted factors and acknowledges the diversity of experiences of people with disabilities.

This course will introduce practical strategies based on the Disability Interaction framework [2]. Through real case studies, the course will introduce ways to consider and manage the diverse and different needs of the stakeholders on innovation while addressing the multiple confounding factors contributing to a disability, such as social attitudes and environmental barriers. The course will also introduce ways to think and create implementable disability innovations practically. In this hands-on course, we will chart various innovation journeys and discuss the key challenges that HCI can address and pathways to impact that HCI can facilitate.

2 Disability Interactions Framework

The Disability Interactions (DiX) approach combines theories from HCI, disability studies, assistive technology and social development to design disruptive technologies to address the unmet needs of people with disabilities [2]. The central theme of the approach is to acknowledge and include the complexity of Disability in the design process. It motivates the use of participatory design to co-create solutions specific to their use's context. The framework also encourages utilising technological advancements in new ways to make lives with disabilities more accessible and increase the value and usefulness of products. It also positions itself to motivate open innovation that shares ideas, knowledge and resources with external partners to deliver user value. It utilises applied and basic research [6] to address the granular technical and broader societal and attitudinal challenges through design. The course will facilitate the application of Disability Interactions to inclusion, accessibility and technological barriers at different stages of the innovation process.

Fig. 1. The Disability Interaction framework [2]

3 Learning Objectives

This short course aims to introduce the framework of Disability Interactions through the process of innovation, from the exploration of a problem to the construction and validation of its solution to its dissemination and impact. After this learning experience, the participants will be able to understand the ways to work with people with disabilities and to think creatively of solutions to problems that have the potential to create an impact. The learning outcome from this course will be:

1. An understanding of the complex interdependent aspects related to disability in different global contexts.
2. The use of the Disability Interactions framework to design new and meaningful interactions that have the potential to create impact.

By the end of this course, learners will be able to analyse real-world disability issues, understand and identify key challenges, design conceptual solutions to address the solutions and develop a strategic and creative way to create impact.

4 Course Format and Intended Audience

At the core of this course is an effort to implement Disability Interactions so that designer and developers of any new technology can think about accessibility and inclusion in a practical and effective way. The instructional approach will be driven through actionable activities, discussion and problem solving. It will include both individual and group work on specific challenges inspired by real life case studies. We will explore how to innovate in the complex and wicked domain of Disability, while acknowledging the many factors that influence disability innovation at different levels of development towards impact. We will apply the theory of Disability Interactions through different tools and instruments for creative exploration at each stage of the course.

We hope to accommodate up to 20 people. Anyone who is interested in developing disruptive assistive technologies or interested in sustaining and scaling existing technologies to new markets or to make existing systems more efficient is welcome to the course. There is no required submission to participate in the course. The course will run for three hours with a 10-min break in between.

We hope that through the discussions and reflections, we will be able to collect valuable insights and information that will make the theory and tools better and more useful. In addition, participants will be able to use the framework for future projects and allow their students to use them as well.

Table 1 Overview of the course program

Agenda	Time
Overview and Presentation	20 min
Lecture + Group activity 1: Co-creation	40 min
Lecture + Group activity 2: Designing new interactions	30 min
Break	10 min
Lecture + Group activity 3: Nurture open and scalable	30 min
Lecture + Group activity 4: Ensuring sustainable value and use	30 min
Final debriefs and discussion	20 min

5 Reading List

1. Disability Interactions: Creating Inclusive Innovations. Link: https://link.springer.com/book/10.1007/978-3-031-03759-7
2. Global Report on Assistive Technology. Link: https://www.who.int/publications/i/item/9789240049451
3. Ability-Based Design: Concept, Principles and Examples. Link: https://doi.org/10.1145/1952383.1952384
4. What Do We Mean by "Accessibility Research"? Link: https://doi.org/10.1145/3411764.3445412
5. The New ABCs of Research: Achieving Breakthrough Collaborations. Link: https://doi.org/10.1093/acprof:oso/9780198758839.001.0001
6. Interdependence as a Frame for Assistive Technology Research and Design. Link: https://doi.org/10.1145/3234695.3236348

References

1. World Health Organization, Fund (UNICEF) UNC. Global report on assistive technology [Internet]. World Health Organization [cited 2022 Dec 15]. xv, 123 p. (2022). https://apps.who.int/iris/handle/10665/354357
2. Disability Interactions [Internet] [cited 2022 Jul 5]. https://link.springer.com/book/10.1007/978-3-031-03759-7
3. Bennett, C.L., Brady, E., Branham, S.M.: Interdependence as a frame for assistive technology research and design. In: Proceedings of the 20th International ACM SIGACCESS Conference on Computers and Accessibility [Internet] [cited 2020 Sep 17], pp. 161–73. ACM, Galway Ireland (2018). https://dl.acm.org/doi/10.1145/3234695.3236348
4. Shinohara, K., Wobbrock, J.O.: In the shadow of misperception: assistive technology use and social interactions. In: Proceedings of the SIGCHI Conference on Human Factors in Computing Systems [Internet] (CHI 2011) [cited 2020 Jun 24], pp. 705–14.

Association for Computing Machinery, Vancouver (2011). https://doi.org/10.1145/1978942.1979044

5. Wobbrock, J.O., Kane, S.K., Gajos, K.Z., Harada, S., Froehlich, J.: Ability-based design: concept, principles and examples. ACM Trans Access Comput. **3**(3), 9:1–9:27 (2011)
6. Shneiderman, B.: The New ABCs of Research: Achieving Breakthrough Collaborations, 1st edn. Oxford University Press, Inc. (2016)

How to Assess Human Reliance on Artificial Intelligence in Hybrid Decision-Making

Chiara Natali[1] ⓘ, Andrea Campagner[2] ⓘ and Federico Cabitza[2] ⓘ

[1] DISCo, University of Milano-Bicocca, viale Sarca 336, 20126 Milan, Italy
chiara.natali@unimib.it
[2] IRCCS Orthopedic Institute Galeazzi, via Galeazzi, 4, 20161 Milan, Italy

Keywords: Decision Support Systems · Human-AI Interaction · AI Assessment · Hybrid Decision-Making.

1 Learning Objectives

The adoption of AI systems for decision support in sensitive domains has become increasingly normalized and of interest. However, it often relies on the unstated presumption that the accuracy of the AI system is the only relevant element to be considered to ensure a positive impact of AI on human decision-making [2, 6].

This assumption is appealing due to its simplifying consequences, as it allows for the evaluation of an AI system's performance in isolation or by comparing it with the average performance of human decision-makers in the same task. However, this approach has limited applicability in real-world scenarios. It is only reasonable in cases where humans willingly adopt a fully automated decision-making setting and completely delegate decision-making to machines, which is still relatively rare [9]. Instead, in most cases, the automation of classifying tasks is partial and intended as support for human decision-making, for which the human is solely responsible.

In this course, we will emphasize the relevance of taking into consideration the complex socio-technical context [10] in which the system will be embedded after deployment and the emergent phenomena arising from the continuous adjustment and fit between humans, machines, and tasks. The primary learning objective of this course is to enable participants to evaluate AI systems by factoring in both cognitive and socio-psychological determinants and effects, aiming at understanding the role of Decision Support Systems in letting people either avoid or commit incorrect decisions. We will do so by presenting the concepts of *technology dominance* [1], *reliance patterns* [3] and *white-box paradox* [5] and introducing metrics and tools to assess them.

2 Content

In this course, we will focus on the fit between human decision makers and AI support in classification tasks, in order to assess the extent humans *rely* on machines, and the effects of this relationship in the short term of decision efficacy and confidence (purposely neglecting any long-term effect, such as complacency [7] and deskilling [8]). In particular, we will introduce and illustrate a general methodological framework that we recently proposed in [4] to gauge "technology dominance" [1]: the dominating influence that technology may have over the user, which allows the user to take a more subservient position—in essence, the user deferring to the technology in the decision-making process.

To this aim we will present, and discuss the rationales behind, the framework of the reliance patterns (see Table 1, and Fig. 2), that allows to distinguish between positive and negative dominance, and the related biases, such as automation bias, algorithm appreciation, and a phenomenon that deserves more attention: what we defined as the white box paradox (shortly put, whenever automation bias is influenced by the provision of explanations [5]). We will then illustrate a set of methods for the quali-quantitative assessment of technology dominance, which encompass both metrics and data visualizations (see Figs. 1 and 2): we will also distinguish between a standard statistical approach and a causal analysis-based approach that can be applied when additional information is available about the context of interest.

Finally, we apply these methods in case studies from a variety of settings, by also providing open source software and tools that we developed to this purpose to be adopted by the community of interested scholars and researchers.[1] A final roundtable and wrap-up discussion among the participants and organizers will conclude the work of the tutorial about what it means to have a quali-quantitative assessment of human reliance on AI and future research within the INTERACT community.

3 Duration and Intended Audience

Duration. One session (1 h 30 m).
Intended audience. Both scholars and practitioners at all levels of expertise can benefit from this course.

---

[1] Available at: https://dss-quality-assessment.vercel.app.

Table 1 Definition of all possible decision- and reliance-patterns between human decision makers and their AI system (0: incorrect decision, 1: correct decision). We associate the attitude towards the AI in each possible decision pattern which leads to either accepting or discarding the AI advice, to the main related cognitive biases.

Human judgment (H)	AI support (AI)	Final decision (D)	Reliance pattern	Biases and effects
0	0	0	detrimental reliance (dr)	automation complacency
0	0	1	beneficial under-reliance (bur)	extreme algorithmic aversion
0	1	0	detrimental self-reliance (dsr)	conservatism bias
0	1	1	beneficial over-reliance (bor)	algorithm appreciation
1	0	0	detrimental over-reliance (dor)	automation bias
1	0	1	beneficial self-reliance (bsr)	algorithmic aversion
1	1	0	detrimental under-reliance (dur)	extreme algorithmic aversion
1	1	1	beneficial reliance (br)	confirmation bias (in later cases)

4 Reading List

Cabitza, F., Campagner, A., et al. (2023). Rams, hounds and white boxes: Investigating human–AI collaboration protocols in medical diagnosis. Artificial Intelligence in Medicine, 138, 102506.

Cabitza, F., Campagner, A., Natali, C., et al. (2023). Painting the black box white: experimental findings from applying XAI to an ECG reading setting. Machine Learning and Knowledge Extraction, 5(1), 269–286.

Cabitza, F., Campagner, A., Angius, R., et al. (2023). AI Shall Have No Dominion: on How to Measure Technology Dominance in AI-supported Human decision-making. In CHI'23 Proceedings, April 23–28, 2023, Hamburg, Germany.

Cabitza, F., & Natali, C. (2022). Open, multiple, adjunct. Decision support at the time of relational AI. In HHAI2022: Augmenting Human Intellect (pp. 243–245). IOS Press.

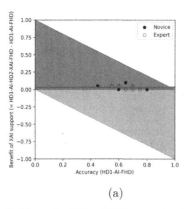
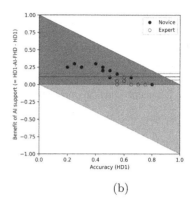

Fig. 1. Example of Benefit Diagrams to visually evaluate the benefit coming from relying on AI (a) and XAI support (b), respectively.

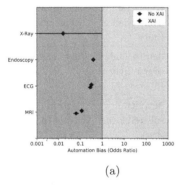
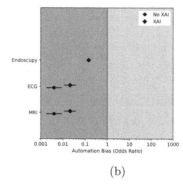

Fig. 2. An example of Automation Bias odds ratios, for the 4 considered case studies: on the left, (a) the frequentist metric; on the right, (b), the causal metric.

References

1. Arnold, V., Sutton, S.G.: The theory of technology dominance: understanding the impact of intelligent decision aids on decision maker's judgments. Adv. Acco. Behav. Res. **1**(3), 175–194 (1998)
2. Birhane, A., Kalluri, P., Card, D., Agnew, W., Dotan, R., Bao, M.: The values encoded in machine learning research. In: Proceedings of the 2022 ACM Conference on Fairness, Accountability, and Transparency, pp. 173–184 (2022)
3. Cabitza, F., Campagner, A., Angius, R., Natali, C., Reverberi, C.: AI shall have no dominion: on how to measure technology dominance in AI-supported human decision-making. In: Proceedings of the 2023 CHI Conference on Human Factors in Computing Systems, pp. 1–20 (2023)
4. Cabitza, F., Campagner, A., Angius, R., Natali, C., Reverberi, C.: AI shall have no dominion: on how to measure technology dominance in AI-supported human

decision-making. In: CHI 2023: The Proceedings of the 2023 CHI Conference on Human Factors in Computing Systems (2023, to be published)

5. Cabitza, F., et al.: Painting the black box white: experimental findings from applying XAI to an ECG reading setting. Mach. Learn. Knowl. Extr. **5**(1), 269–286 (2023)

6. Dignum, V.: Relational artificial intelligence. arXiv preprint arXiv:2202.07446 (2022)

7. Parasuraman, R., Manzey, D.H.: Complacency and bias in human use of automation: an attentional integration. Hum. Factors **52**(3), 381–410 (2010)

8. Rafner, J., et al.: Deskilling, upskilling, and reskilling: a case for hybrid intelligence. Morals Mach. **1**(2), 24–39 (2022)

9. Shrestha, Y.R., Ben-Menahem, S.M., Von Krogh, G.: Organizational decision-making structures in the age of artificial intelligence. Calif. Manage. Rev. **61**(4), 66–83 (2019)

10. Trist, E.L., et al.: On Socio-Technical Systems. Sociotechnical Systems: A Sourcebook, pp. 43–57 (1978)

Introduction to Information Visualisation

Keith Andrews

Graz University of Technology, Austria
kandrews@tugraz.at
https://isds.tugraz.at/keith

Abstract. This course will give participants will an understanding of the principles and methods of information visualisation. The course will start with some basic concepts and a look at human visual perception. Then, it will survey various methods and techniques from information visualisation according to data type. The course will conclude with an overview of tools and toolkits which can be used to produce one's own visualisations.

Keywords: Information visualisation · Introduction · Course

1 Introduction

Information visualisation (InfoVis) is the visual presentation of abstract information spaces and structures together with accompanying interactions, so as to facilitate their rapid assimilation and understanding. In essence, information visualisation techniques harness the visual processing capabilities of the human visual system to amplify cognition.

Interactive data visualisations are used for two main purposes:

1. *Analysis*: Exploratory visualisations help researchers to explore and analyse unfamiliar datasets.
2. *Presentation*: Explanatory visualisations present results and insights to a wider audience.

The visual representation is only half the story. Interaction facilities for navigation and manipulation are equally as important.

The course proposer teaches a graduate-level course on information visualisation at Graz University of Technology every summer semester [1], and has taught short courses on information visualisation at a number of conferences. A short introduction to the field is given in an online slide deck [2]. A full set of course notes (146 pages, PDF) is also available [3]. The course proposer gave a talk about information visualisation at TEDxGraz 2015 [4].

The course will introduce participants to the concepts which underpin information visualisation, guide them through some of the various techniques, and show them some of the more common tools used to produce visualisations.

2 Information Visualisation

Information visualisation (InfoVis) deals with abstract information spaces. Geographic visualisation (GeoVis) deals with spatial, map-based data. Together, these two fields are often called data visualisation (DataVis). The related field of scientific visualisation (SciVis) typically involves concrete (3d) objects and simulations, often depicting flows, volumes, and surfaces in (3d) space.

Different techniques have evolved for visualising different types of data, such as hierarchies, networks, multidimensional (tabular) data, and feature spaces, among others. Figure 1 shows a collage of some of the main techniques for visualising hierarchies. Figure 2 shows a collage of some of the main techniques for visualising multidimensional data.

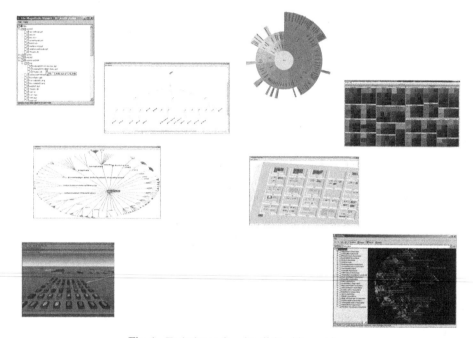

Fig. 1. Techniques for visualising hierarchies.

3 Description of the Course

The course is planned for 3 h and will cover the following topics:

1. Introduction
2. Visual Perception
3. Visualising Hierarchies

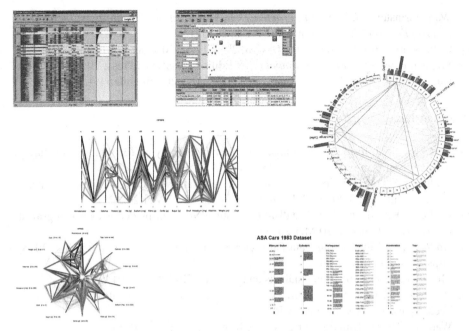

Fig. 2. Techniques for visualising multidimensional data.

4. Visualising Networks and Graphs
5. Visualising Multidimensional Metadata
6. Visualising Text and Object Collections (Feature Spaces)
7. Tools and Toolkits

The topics will be liberally illustrated with live demos and video clips. One or two breaks will be scheduled in accordance with the conference schedule.

4   Intended Audience

The intended audience are lecturers, researchers, professionals, and students attending INTERACT 2023, who have heard about information and data visualisation, and who want to receive a broad introduction to the field.

5   Reading List

The following additional resources are recommended for further reading and viewing:

– Tamara Munzner; *Visualization Analysis and Design*; CRC Press, 2014 [5]. https://cs.ubc.ca/~tmm/vadbook/

- Ward, Grinstein, and Keim; *Interactive Data Visualization: Foundations, Techniques, and Applications*; 2nd Edition, CRC Press, 2015 [6].
- Colin Ware; *Visual Thinking for Design*; 2nd Edition, Morgan Kaufmann, 2021 [7].
- Stephen Few; *Show Me the Numbers*; 2nd Edition, Analytics Press, 2012 [8].
- Hans Rosling; *Stats That Reshape Your World View*; 20-min video [9].

References

1. Andrews, K.: Information Visualisation. Graz University of Technology. https://cou rses.isds.tugraz.at/ivis/. Accessed 25 Apr 2023
2. Andrews, K.: Introduction to Information Visualisation. Slide deck. https://keithandr ews.com/talks/2023/2023-03-15-infovis/. Accessed 15 Mar 2023
3. Andrews, K.: Information Visualisation: Course Notes. https://courses.isds.tugraz.at/ ivis/ivis.pdf. Accessed 10 Mar 2023
4. Andrews, K.: Illuminating Data Through Visualisation, TEDxGraz 2015 Talk (2015). https://youtu.be/fnyKj8r0CN4
5. Munzner, T.: Visualization Analysis and Design. CRC Press (2014)
6. Ward, M., Grinstein, G., Keim, D.: Interactive Data Visualization: Foundations, Techniques, and Applications. CRC Press (2015)
7. Ware, C.: Visual Thinking for Design. Morgan Kaufmann (2021)
8. Few, S.: Show Me the Numbers: Designing Tables and Graphs to Enlighten. Analytics Press (2012)
9. Rosling, H.: The Best Stats You've Ever Seen, TED 2006 Talk (2006). https://ted. com/talks/hans_rosling_the_best_stats_you_ve_ever_seen

Contents – Part IV

Virtual Reality

Virtual Reality and Training

Courses

Industrial Experiences

Interactive Demonstrations

Keynotes

Panels

Posters

Wokshops

User Studies

Comparing Perceived Restorativeness and Stress Reduction in Virtual Reality Environments Using Abstract Fractal Geometries Versus Realistic Natural Landscapes

Diana C. G. Mendes[(⊠)] [iD] and Mónica S. Cameirão [iD]

Faculdade de Ciências Exatas e da Engenharia & NOVA-LINCS, Universidade da Madeira, and Agência Regional para o Desenvolvimento de Investigação, Tecnologia e Inovação (ARDITI), Funchal, Portugal
diana.mendes@nlincs.uma.pt, monica.cameirao@staff.uma.pt

Abstract. Stress and its related mental conditions are an increasing concern in modern societies. Natural settings have been shown to reduce stress and anxiety levels and help restore lost physical-psychological resources. The Perceptual Fluency Account associates this restorative potential with nature's fractal characteristics, which facilitate their visual processing. While many studies have shown the value of Virtual Reality Nature for stress reduction and even treatment, no study of Virtual Reality fractal abstract worlds for restoration has been found. We question whether an abstract fractal-based environment can have similar restorative effects to a realistic nature-based environment in Virtual Reality. A total of 39 participants took part in two studies. In the first one, two groups (N = 19) of participants performed a collecting task in a fractal- or nature-based environment. The results showed that both environments were perceived as restorative and significantly reduced stress. To infer how the existence of a task modulated the results, in the second study, with 20 participants split into two groups, participants were exposed to the same environments, this time without a task. The results showed that the condition was significantly more restorative for the fractal-based environment when no task was performed. To conclude, fractal-based abstract environments show potential to be used for restoration purposes, but the extent to which having a task influences restorativeness needs further research.

Keywords: Virtual Reality · restoration · abstract fractals

1 Introduction

Stress is the physical and psychological response to demanding circumstances in life that threaten our well-being, and it has been recognized as a major challenge worldwide for workers' health and academic performance [1, 2]. Though generally a part of life, it is directly and/or indirectly linked to mental disorders such as PTSD, acute symptoms of stress/acute stress reaction, depression, and anxiety [3]. Stress-related issues will likely increase as the world population in urban areas increases [3, 4].

© The Author(s), under exclusive license to Springer Nature Switzerland AG 2023
J. Abdelnour Nocera et al. (Eds.): INTERACT 2023, LNCS 14145, pp. 3–22, 2023.
https://doi.org/10.1007/978-3-031-42293-5_1

Life in the city is typically tainted with long work hours, mental pressure, and a lack of contact with nature, all associated with reduced levels of happiness and self-satisfaction [5]. Moreover, the characteristic features of urban landscapes (e.g., traffic noise, visual clutter, scarce vegetation) can negatively affect our psychological responses [5, 6]. Au contraire, natural settings (e.g., forests, coasts) have been shown to have very positive psychological effects, reducing stress and anxiety levels and helping to restore or recover the physical and psychological resources lost while adapting to daily demands, a process known as restoration [7, 8].

A few theories have attempted to explain the restorativeness of different environments. The Stress Reduction Theory (SRT) posits that humans subconsciously prefer natural environments as a product of our evolution, feelings of safety and survival that reduce negative thoughts and induce stress recovery [9]. The Attention Restoration Theory (ART) states that urban environments burn out our attention resources for needing constant directed attention, while, the 'soft fascinations' nature provides reduce mental fatigue and stress levels [10]. Other theories associate nature's restorative potential with its mathematical characteristics. The Perceptual Fluency Account (PFA) considers that the fractal characteristics of nature allow us to process it more effectively than human-made non-fractal environments, increasing their healing potential [11]. Fractals are described here as "patterns that repeat at increasingly fine sizes and so create shapes of rich visual complexity" (B. B. Mandelbrot in [12, p. 1]). Studies on fractal art and architecture have shown that they help reduce stress and fatigue and that exposure to abstract non-fractals can have negative effects [12, 13].

Most studies in the field of restorative environments have involved the use of photographs, slides, or videos [14]. Nevertheless, in recent years Virtual Reality (VR) has become a common format for environmental simulations. Some studies using fractals in VR have also shown that they help reduce stress [15, 16]. To the best of our knowledge, no studies have used abstract fractals in a VR setting for restoration purposes. To fill this gap, we conducted two studies to evaluate the restorative potential of abstract fractal landscapes compared to exposure to realistic nature in immersive VR. Both studies explored two base conditions: fractal-abstract and nature-realistic environments. Perceived stress levels and perceived restorativeness of these environments were measured. In the first study, the participants explored the VR environment while collecting crystals. In contrast, in the second study, the participants explored the same environments without crystals to determine to what extent the crystal-collecting task might have influenced the results of our first study. Our results suggested that both environments, with or without a task, significantly reduced perceived stress and showed similar scores of restorativeness.

2   Related Work

2.1   Restorative Features of Nature and Urban Environments

Several studies have shown the restorative potential of nature exposure, even in urban settings [7, 12]. Studies have also suggested features that potentially determine our affective responses to natural environments, such as easily readable spaces with visible pathways, water features, large trees, and sometimes a good balance with man-built elements [6, 7]. Even indoor environments can be restorative as long as there is a greater presence of

trees and forested areas, and indoor views of trees and green landscapes, indoor greenery such as plants and nature walls [5, 6, 12]. The restorative potential of light is also
important to remember, as studies suggest that increased sunlight decreases negative
affect, tiredness, and psychological distress, and increases cognitive performance and
other beneficial effects, as opposed to dark and overcast environments [17].

It has also been suggested that the activities performed in these environments are
equally important, especially if the goal is to create a virtual reality nature environment.
A revision of the literature suggests that contemplative activities (e.g., mindfulness and
interaction with animals) are more restorative than movement-based, cybersickness-
inducing activities (e.g., walking) [18]. However, qualitative data from a study on restorative environments in the automotive context suggested that, since urban users are generally disconnected from nature and more accustomed to active relaxing activities (e.g.,
playing games), these could be more suitable for such users [19].

2.2 Virtual Reality for Restoration

The value of VR nature environments to treat both complicated stress and stress-related
clinical mental illnesses like anxiety or depression has also been studied, being considered a viable alternative whenever in-vivo exposure is not possible or not recommended
[19–21]. The Virtual Therapeutic Garden reduced depression and stress in a sample
of elderly women who had shown no improvement after receiving standard treatment
[22]. The Secret Garden, an at-home 10-min exposure to 360° VR video for dealing
with the psychological distress associated with the COVID-19 lockdown, resulted in
reduced depression and stress symptoms [23]. The Tranquil Cinematic VR, a simulation
of natural landscapes through 360° videos deployed on a Head-Mounted Display, led
to a significant reduction of subjective stress levels in frontline workers employed by
COVID-19 treatment units [24]. Finally, EMMA's World, which uses different natural
scenarios to induce and amplify different emotions, helped patients process stressful
events in several interventions [25, 26].

2.3 The Restorative Potential of Fractals

Studies have also shown that fractal shapes can provide pleasing experiences due to
the effortless attention required [12, 13, 27]. Fractal art and architecture, for instance,
have been shown to reduce stress and fatigue compared to chronic exposure to abstract
non-fractals, which can have negative effects in the long run [12, 13]. A study devoted
to optimizing restoration in a virtual nature environment by emphasizing nature's fractal
geometries showed users' preference for a determined dimension of fractals and a trend,
with no statistically significant results, for stress recovery after exposure to this optimal
fractal dimension [15]. However, up until now, no application of abstract fractal shapes
in a VR environment has been found. Animator Julius Horsthuis has created an application in VR as an artwork that shows abstract fractal landscapes in VR as a cinematic
experience rather than free exploration. Still, no studies on the effect of this particular
experience on people's emotional and psychological well-being have been found [28].
Closer to the use of abstract fractals in VR was the presence of organic abstract art slides

in an immersive virtual environment as a control condition in a study on the restorativeness of natural environments, where it was shown that exposure to these slides also reduced stress [16].

This has led us to question the following: First, would an abstract VR environment based on fractal shapes have restorative effects? We hypothesized that an abstract VR environment using fractal shapes would reduce perceived stress and be considered restorative. Second, does the fact of having a specific activity to perform in the environment influence the results obtained? Based on the literature, we hypothesize that having a task will increase the perceived restorativeness and bring greater levels of perceived stress relief.

3   Study 1. Fractal Abstract Environments for Restoration

This study aims to determine whether a VR environment based on abstract-fractal shapes and geometries reduces perceived stress and is perceived as restorative. It aims to answer our first research question: does an abstract VR environment based on fractal shapes have restorative effects?

3.1   Methods

Experimental Design. This was an independent sample experiment, and the independent variable was the virtual environment the participants were exposed to in two conditions: 1) VR abstract-fractal or 2) VR realistic-nature. There were two dependent variables: perceived levels of stress and perceived restorativeness.

Experimental Environments. The environments have been developed using Unity 3D and were deployed in a high-end Head-Mounted Display (HMD), the Oculus Quest 2. The abstract-fractal setting had an irregular terrain similar to clouds, with abstract shapes and particle systems with fractal characteristics (Fig. 1). The realistic-nature setting depicted a forest-like environment, with spacious paths and areas with trees, bushes, and irregular terrain (Fig. 2). As sound and light have proven to influence stress reduction and perceived restorativeness, both environments had the same daytime cloudless sky and no background music or sound. Despite navigation not being the focus of this study, both environments were characterized by interconnected paths distributed in about 4 Km^2 of virtual terrain, and had some 'built' elements that could work as landmarks (Fig. 1a, 1b and 1c; and 2a and 2b), and their high ground was made non-teleportable to make them as realistic as possible and to avoid reaching its limits. The environments' paths were teleportation areas that the participant used to move around with a pointer (Fig. 1c and 2c), and magic interaction was used (a virtual pointer) to grab objects (Fig. 2d). Some interactable objects were included in both scenes, but to a limited extent (Fig. 1e and 2e). Both environments had crystals instantiated at random points of the terrain (Fig. 1d and 2d), and both groups were assigned to collect these crystals while exploring the environment.

Measures. A demographics questionnaire was used to obtain information about the participant's age, gender, whether they consider themselves a city or country person,

a. b.

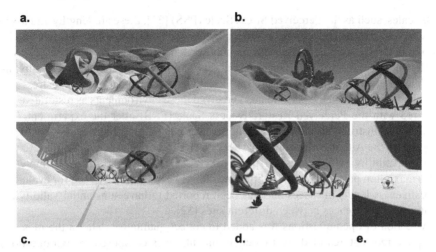

c. d. e.

Fig. 1. Fractal-Abstract virtual environment.

a. b.

c. d. e.

Fig. 2. Nature-Realistic virtual environment.

previous experience with VR using HMDs, and previous video gameplay experience. This was to keep track of possible confounding variables such as their place identity ('dimensions of self that define the individual's personal identity in relation to the physical environment' (Proshansky, 1978, as cited in [29]) and gaming influence.

The Stress Numerical Rating Scale-11 (SNRS-11) was used before and after the experiment to measure stress levels. This test consists of numbers equally spaced across the page from 0 to 10, asking the participants, "On a scale of 0 to 10, with 0 being no stress and 10 being the worst stress possible, what number best describes your level of stress right now?", with participants circling the number that corresponds to their current level of stress [30]. Despite the existence of other more popular and validated subjective stress scales, such as the Perceived Stress Scale (PSS) [31], these are lengthy and assess past stress to estimate current stress, making them not only prone to retrospective bias but also not perfectly suitable for measuring context-dependent stress [30]. The SNRS-11 has shown moderate to strong construct validity and moderate concurrent validity and has shown to be a promising measure for the efficient assessment of current stress.

The extent to which the participants perceived these environments as restorative was measured with the Perceived Restorativeness Scale (PRS) after the experiment. This self-response instrument comprises 26 items that evaluate the four restoration factors proposed by the Attention Restoration Theory (ART): Being away, Fascination, Extent, and Compatibility [10]. It uses a 7-point Likert scale (0: Not at all - 6: Completely) with a maximum possible score of 156 points. It has been frequently used for evaluating restorativeness levels of places and has been reported to have substantial validity and sensitivity to differences between different sites [32].

A section of open questions was added to collect qualitative data on the most and least preferred features of these two environments; it is composed of two questions: What features of this environment did you prefer the most? and What features of this environment did you prefer the least?

Sample. In this study, the inclusion criteria included being over 18 years old and fluent or having intermediate knowledge of English. A convenience sample comprising 21 higher-education students and academic workers participated. However, data from 2 participants in the Fractal-Abstract group were not considered for analysis as technical issues occurred between the first SNRS-11 and exposure to the virtual environment. The first 20 participants were randomly allocated to the two groups using Random.org (https://www.random.org/). Since the invalid results from two participants belonging to the fractal-based group caused an imbalance in the number of participants per group (10 in the nature-based group and 8 in the fractal-based group), the last volunteer participant was allocated to the fractal-based group. They were finally distributed into two groups: 9 (47.4%) in the Fractal-Abstract group and 10 (52.6%) in the Nature-Realistic group.

Experimental Procedure. The experiment took place at the ARDITI facilities, Tecnopolo, Funchal-Madeira. The participants were invited to participate face-to-face by the main researcher and by email. Before the experiment started, the participants were told that the study was about restorative environments: landscapes that increase positive affect and reduce mental fatigue. They were informed about every step and task of the study, were warned about the possibility of dizziness and eyesores immediately after exposure, and were reminded that, as volunteers, they could quit the experiment at any moment. After clarifying any doubts, they signed an Informed Consent. They then completed the demographics questionnaire and did the stress-inducing writing task immediately after. For this task, the participants were asked to recall their most stressful situation within the last six months; whenever they failed to recall such event within the specified timeframe, this was extended to the most recent they could remember. They were informed they had 5 min to write while listening to audio in their headphones (the type of sounds was not specified) and that they could take home or dispose of this text. The headphones would play loud construction site sounds while they wrote. After this, the participants completed the SNRS-11. Once complete, the participants put on the HMD already set up for a stationary area and practiced moving and interacting with the environment using the handheld controllers. When participants felt comfortable using the technology, they were given 10 min to explore the environment and collect the crystals they could find to complete the experimental condition. Once the virtual exploration was complete, the participants filled in the SNRS-11 and the PRS. Immediately after, the participants were exposed to a funny video and were offered chocolate to counteract any possible negative effects of the experience. In the end, we debriefed the participants on the ultimate goal of the study and took notes of their feedback.

Statistical Analyses. Because of the ordinal nature of the data, nonparametric tests were used. Specifically, we used the Wilcoxon match-paired signed-rank test to examine differences in perceived stress before and after exposure to the virtual environment within each group; and the Mann-Whitney U test for between-group comparisons. The threshold for statistical significance was set at 5% ($\alpha = 0.05$). The analyses were conducted in SPSS, version 28.0 [33]. Post-hoc power analyses were carried out using the G*Power software, version 3.1.9.7 [34].

3.2 Results

Demographic Data. The final sample comprised 19 people aged between 20 and 52 years (63.2%, n = 12 male). The participants were distributed evenly in terms of age, with the Fractal-Abstract group having an average age of 31 (SD = 8.0) and the Nature-Realistic group having an average of 30.1 (SD = 8.5). However, females were underrepresented, with most in both groups being men (55.6%, n = 5 of the Fractal-Abstract group and 70.0%, n = 7 of the Nature-Realistic group). Regarding place identity, 66.7% (n = 6) of participants in the Fractal-Abstract group considered themselves country people and 60.0% (n = 6) in the Nature-Realistic one identified themselves as city people. All participants (100%, n = 19) had experience playing video games. Most participants in both groups (77.8%, n = 7 Fractal-Abstract; 90%, n = 9 Nature-Realistic) had previous experience with virtual reality using HMDs.

Perceived Stress. The perceived stress levels between groups before exposure to the experimental environments did not differ significantly, with U = 53.500, p = 0.497 (two-tailed test), a small effect size of r = 0.162, and a post hoc achieved power of 0.112. Comparing perceived stress before and after exposure for each group, reported stress levels from the group exposed to the Fractal-Abstract environment were significantly lower after exposure to the virtual environment, T = 0.000, p = 0.0035 (one-tailed test), with a large effect size of r = 0.893, and a post hoc achieved power of 0.997 (Fig. 3). Reported stress levels from the group exposed to the Nature-Realistic environment were also significantly lower after exposure to the virtual environment, T = 1.000, p = 0.008 (one-tailed test), resulting in a large effect size of r = 0.760, and a post hoc achieved power of 0.964 (Fig. 3). Finally, when comparing between groups, the levels of reported stress reduction between those exposed to the Fractal-Abstract environment did not differ significantly from those exposed to the Nature-Realistic environment, U = 44.000, p = 0.484 (one-tailed test), with a small effect size of r = 0.019, and a post hoc achieved power of 0.060 (Table 1).

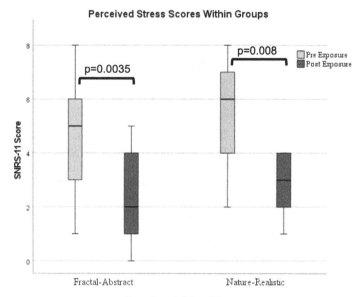

Fig. 3. Boxplot of differences in perceived stress scores before and after exposure to the Nature-Realistic and Fractal-Abstract environments.

Perceived Restorativeness. The levels of perceived restorativeness of those exposed to the Fractal-Abstract environment and the Nature-Realistic environment respectively did not differ significantly, $U = 49.500$, $p = 0.360$ (one-tailed test), with a small effect size of $r = 0.084$, and a post hoc achieved power of 0.057 (Table 1).

Table 1. Comparison of Experimental Environments With-Task.

	Nature-Realistic	Fractal-Abstract	*p-value*
SNRS-11 pre	6 (4)	5 (4)	*p = 0.497[2], r = 0.162*
SNRS-11 post	3 (2)	2 (4)	–
p-value	*p = 0.008[1], r = 0.760*	*p = 0.004[1], r = 0.893*	
Stress reduction	−3 (5)	−2 (3)	*p = 0.484[2], r = 0.019*
PRS	93.5 (44)	95 (31)	*p = 0.360[2], r = 0.084*

Central tendency and dispersion presented as Median (IQR).
[1] P-value results of Wilcoxon signed ranks tests.
[2] P-value results of Mann-Whitney tests.

4 Study 2. Virtual Environments with or without Task

In the previous study, we observed that exposure to the fractal-based abstract VR environment significantly reduced perceived stress levels, the same as the nature-based environment, and that it was perceived as restorative. With this second study, we wanted to analyze to what extent the above results might have been influenced by the fact of having a specific task to perform inside the virtual environment. Basically, it is aimed at answering our second research question: does the fact of having a specific activity to perform in the environment influence the results obtained?

4.1 Methods

Experimental Design. As in the first study, this was a between-group experiment. The independent variable was the virtual environment the participants were exposed to, and it had two levels: 1) Fractal-Abstract Without-Task, and 2) Nature-Realistic Without-Task. The same two dependent variables were recorded: perceived levels of stress and perceived restorativeness.

Experimental Environments. The experimental environments were the same as in the previous study, with the difference that no crystals were instantiated at random points. Hence, participants were not instructed to collect anything but rather explore the environment freely. The few other interactable objects were kept in both scenes but remained to a limited extent (Fig. 1e and 2e).

Measures. We used the same measures as in the previous study: a demographics questionnaire to obtain information about the participant's age, gender, whether they consider themselves a city or country person, previous experience with VR using HMDs, and previous video gameplay experience; the SNRS-11 to measure stress levels at the moment [31]; the PRS to measure to what extent the participants perceive these environments as restorative [33]; and an open questions section to collect qualitative data on the most and least preferred features of these two environments.

Experimental Procedure. The experiment occurred at the exact location as the previous study, and they were also randomly allocated to two groups using Random.org (https://www.random.org/). All participants were sent the same invitation as in Study 1 by e-mail. However, we specified we were looking for volunteers to extend the study, so those who had already participated understood they were not applicable. The steps and tasks of the session were the same as in the previous study: they were introduced to the study, completed a demographic questionnaire, did a 5-min stress-inducing writing task, completed the SNRS-11 questionnaire, went through a 10-min environment exploration, completed the SNRS-11 and PRS questionnaires, and watched a funny video. All materials used for the stress-inducing writing task and funny videos were the same as in Study 1.

Sample. Inclusion criteria included being over 18 years old and fluent or having intermediate knowledge of English. A convenience sample of 21 higher-education students and workers was recruited. Data from 1 participant from the Fractal-Abstract Without-Task group were not considered for analysis as technical issues occurred between the first

SNRS-11 and exposure to the VR environment. They were distributed into two groups: 10 (50%) in the Fractal-Abstract Without-Task and 10 (50%) in the Nature-Realistic Without-Task group.

4.2 Results

Demographic Data. The final sample was composed of 20 people aged 22–47 years old (65%, n = 13 female). The participants were distributed evenly in terms of age, with an average age of 29.50 (SD = 8.8) in the Fractal-Abstract Without-Task group and of 29.40 (SD = 5) in the Nature-Realistic Without-Task group. Regarding sex, the participants were evenly distributed (50/50%) in the Nature-Realistic Without-Task group but not in the Fractal-Abstract Without-Task group, where the majority were female (80%, n = 8). Regarding place identity, in both the Fractal-Abstract Without-Task and the Nature-Realistic Without-Task group, 70% (n = 7) of the participants identified themselves as city people. All participants (100%, n = 20) had experience playing video games, most participants in the Nature-Realistic With-out-Task group (80%, n = 8) had previous experience with VR using HMDs, while most of the Fractal-Abstract Without-Task group (60%, n = 6) did not.

Comparison Between Nature-Realistic and Fractal-Abstract Without-Task Conditions

Perceived Stress. The perceived stress levels between groups before exposure to the experimental Without-Task environments did not differ significantly, with U = 66.000, p = 0.247 (two-tailed test), a medium effect size of r = 0.278, and a post hoc achieved power of 0.084. When comparing the perceived stress before and after exposure for each group, we observed that the reported stress levels of the Fractal-Abstract Without-Task group were significantly lower after exposure to the VR environment, T = 0.000, p = 0.0025 (one-tailed test), with a large effect of r = 0.888, and a post hoc achieved power of 1.00. Reported stress levels provided by the Nature-Realistic Without-Task group were significantly lower after exposure to the VR environment, T = 8.000, p = 0.023 (one-tailed test), a large effect size of r = 0.630, and a post hoc achieved power of 0.993 (Fig. 4). When comparing stress reduction after exposure from groups, the levels of reported stress reduction from the Fractal-Abstract Without-Task group did not differ significantly from the Nature-Realistic Without-Task group, U = 66.000, p = 0.123 (one-tailed test), with a medium effect size of r = 0.273, and a post hoc achieved power of 0.492 (Table 2).

Perceived Restorativeness. The levels of perceived restorativeness reported by the participants in the Fractal-Abstract Without-Task and the Nature-Realistic Without-Task group did not differ significantly, U = 30.000, p = 0.0715 (one-tailed test), with a medium effect size of r = 0.338, and a post hoc achieved power of 0.432 (Table 2).

Comparison Between Nature-Realistic With-Task and Without-Task conditions

Perceived Stress. The perceived stress levels before exposure to the experimental environments between the Nature-Realistic With-Task group (Mdn = 6, IQR = 4) and the

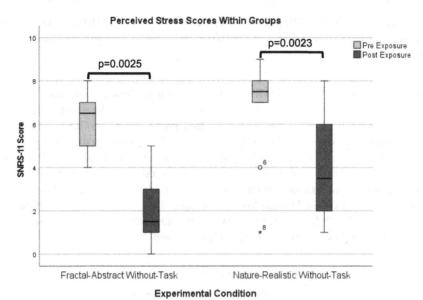

Fig. 4. Boxplot of differences in perceived stress scores before and after exposure to the Nature-Realistic and Fractal-Abstract Without-Task environments.

Table 2. Comparison of Experimental Environments Without-Task.

	Nature-Realistic	Fractal-Abstract	*p-value*
SNRS-11 pre	7.5 (2)	6.5 (2)	$p = 0.247^2$, $r = 0.278$
SNRS-11 post	3.5 (4)	1.5 (3)	–
p-value	$p = 0.023^1$, $r = 0.630$	$p = 0.003^1$, $r = 0.888$	
Stress reduction	−3 (5)	−5 (5)	$p = 0.123^2$, $r = 0.273$
PRS	92 (39)	114 (32)	$p = 0.072^2$, $r = 0.338$

Central tendency and dispersion presented as Median (IQR).
[1] P-value results of Wilcoxon signed ranks tests.
[2] P-value results of Mann-Whitney tests.

Nature-Realistic Without-Task group (Mdn = 7.5, IQR = 2) did not differ significantly, with U = 74.500, p = 0.063 (two-tailed test), and a medium-to-large effect of r = 0.422, and a post hoc achieved power of 0.335. After exposure, the levels of reported stress reduction by the Nature-Realistic With-Task group (Mdn = −3, IQR = 5) did not differ significantly from the Nature-Realistic Without-Task group (Mdn = −3, IQR = 5), with U = 46.500, p = 0.398 (one-tailed test), with a small effect of r = 0.059, and a post hoc achieved power of 0.073 (Tables 1 and 2).

Perceived Restorativeness. The levels of perceived restorativeness of the Nature-Realistic With-Task (Mdn = 93.5, IQR = 44) and the Nature-Realistic Without-Task groups (Mdn = 92, IQR = 39) did not differ significantly, U = 48.000, p = 0.456 (one-tailed test), with a small effect size of r = 0.033, and a post hoc achieved power of 0.078 (Tables 1 and 2).

Comparison Fractal-Abstract With-Task and Without-Task Conditions

Perceived Stress. The perceived stress levels before exposure to the experimental environments between the Fractal-Abstract With-Task group (Mdn = 5, IQR = 4) and the Fractal-Abstract Without-Task group (Mdn = 6.50, IQR = 2) did not differ significantly, with U = 64.500, p = 0.113 (two-tailed test), and a medium effect size of r = 0.370, and a post hoc achieved power of 0.607. Regarding stress reduction, the levels of reported stress reduction by the Fractal-Abstract With-Task group (Mdn = −2, IQR = 3) were significantly lower than the Fractal-Abstract Without-Task group Mdn = −5, IQR = 5), U = 24.500, p = 0.048 (one-tailed test), with a medium effect size of r = 0.389, and a post hoc achieved power of 0.764 (Fig. 5) (Tables 1 and 2).

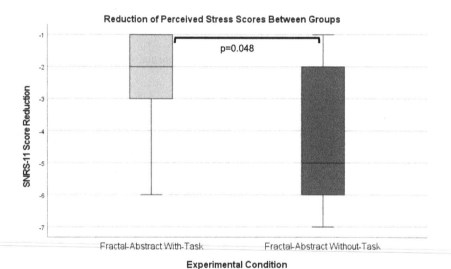

Fig. 5. Boxplot of differences in perceived stress reduction between the Fractal-Abstract With-task and Without-Task conditions.

Perceived Restorativeness. The levels of perceived restorativeness of those exposed to the Fractal-Abstract With-Task environment (Mdn = 95, IQR = 31) were significantly lower than participants in the Fractal-Abstract Without-Task environment (Mdn = 114, IQR = 32), U = 66.500, p = 0.040 (one-tailed test), with a medium-to-large effect size of r = 0.403, and a post hoc achieved power of 0.577 (Fig. 6) (Tables 1 and 2).

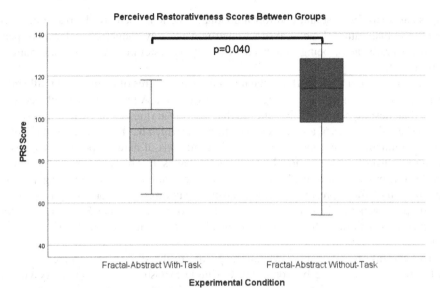

Fig. 6. Boxplot of differences in perceived restorativeness between the Fractal-Abstract With-Task and Without-Task conditions.

5   Discussion

Extensive literature has provided evidence of how beneficial exposure to natural environments is, whether in the real world, through two-dimensional images, or computer-based immersive and non-immersive representations. Exposure to nature has proven to reduce stress and negative affect, increase positive affect, and even reduce symptoms of mental health illnesses like depression. This has translated into several applications using natural landscapes in virtual environments for different purposes, from stress reduction for individuals with limited access to real nature, to supporting treatment for those who have not responded satisfactorily to conventional psychotherapy. However, the number of applications using natural landscapes for restoration purposes also shows the very limited exploration of the restorative potential abstract virtual environments may have. Considering this, we wished to contribute to the literature aimed at designing restorative virtual environments by comparing an abstract world of fractal geometries with a more traditional natural realistic landscape in terms of their potential to reduce stress and their perceived restorativeness.

5.1   Abstract Fractal Environments for Restoration

In our first study, we hypothesized that a fictional VR environment using fractal shapes would help reduce self-reported stress and be perceived as restorative. Our results show a statistically significant perceived stress reduction after exposure to the Fractal-Abstract environment, which supports our main hypothesis. Regarding their perceived restorativeness, the Fractal-Abstract and the Nature-Realistic environments showed no significant differences. Our results suggest that virtual environments based on abstract fractal shapes can spark interest and comfort individuals, reducing perceived stress almost as much as virtual nature. Fractal abstract environments stay caught up in terms of perceived restorativeness, being perceived as nearly as restorative as a realistic natural environment.

Our results seem to support that the mathematical features of nature might influence our physio-psychological well-being more than we think. A review on the subject suggested that, despite being widely believed that the "mysterious vitalistic qualities of the natural scenes" [35, p. 16] are the key to restoration (which has resulted in most restorative environments being mostly realistic representations of nature), positive responses to nature are triggered much more by their fractal shapes than by an accurate representation. A study by Valtchanov et al. comparing free exploration in virtual nature against the visualization of slides presenting organic abstract paintings corroborated that exposure to a computer-generated natural environment leads to an increase in positive affect [16]. However, it also showed that exposure to the abstract-art slideshow had similar effects [16].

The question remains about whether exposure to the studied environments would really differ from relaxing by, for instance, simple exposure to a white empty virtual room. Few studies have been devoted to studying the effect of exposure to an empty environment. However, a study by Browning et al. compared 6 min of sitting and 6 min of walking in a real outdoor natural location, a VR 360^a video captured at the same location, and a control condition where the participants were indoors and instructed to sit in front of a blank white wall [36]. Their main results corroborated that Virtual and outdoor nature led to higher levels of positive affect when compared to the control condition, even though the control condition led to small reductions both in negative and positive affect [36]. Considering this, it is possible that a comparison between our experimental environments and an empty white virtual space would have resulted in the Nature-Realistic and Fractal-Abstract landscapes performing best.

5.2   The Weight of a Task in Virtual Reality-Based Restoration

In our second study, we compared the same opposite environments used in our first study (Fractal-Abstract and Nature-Realistic), but this time without any task to perform. When comparing both environments in the absence of a task, the results were similar to those obtained when the environments had a task: both the Fractal-Abstract and Nature-Realistic Without-Task conditions showed significant reductions of perceived stress when comparing data before and after exposure, and the difference between these two conditions was not significant. Nevertheless, it was still possible that exposure to one environment with a task could be more restorative than exploring the same environment without a task.

To understand if having a specific task to perform influenced the perceived stress reduction and their restorativeness, we compared both environments used in Study 1, where the user had a task to perform (here referred to as With-Task conditions) with their task-less counterparts from Study 2 (here referred to as Without-Task conditions). We hypothesized that having a task would increase the perceived restorativeness and bring greater levels of perceived stress relief. However, our results were unexpected. On the one hand, the Nature-Realistic environment did not obtain significant differences when comparing the With-Task and Without-Task conditions regarding perceived stress reduction or restorativeness. On the other hand, with the Fractal-Abstract environment, when comparing the With-task and Without-Task conditions, significant differences were obtained in both measures. Regardless, the reductions recorded did not go in the expected direction. Instead, they suggested that the Fractal-Abstract environment was more effective in its Without-Task condition. Overall, there is no evidence to suggest that having the crystal-collecting task heavily influenced the results obtained from Study 1.

It is always possible that different activities result in different outcomes. Some authors have considered contemplative activities, such as meditation, more restorative than those requiring movement (e.g., walking or tennis). In contrast, others suggest that active activities, such as playing a game, are more restorative for users who live in a city environment [18, 19]. In our study, we selected the crystal collection activity as we considered it neutral, neither very active nor passive. Therefore, we cannot reject the possibility that our second hypothesis could have proven correct if the activity performed had been meditation or playing a game.

We could also question how different our results could have been had the participants not moved or done anything at all. A study by Rupp et al. compared the effect of a passive break, a relaxation activity, and a casual video game on affect and stress [37]. It showed that, even though all conditions led to some affective restoration, no improvements in positive affect were visible and cognitive resources were still being depleted while the participants were sitting quietly in their thoughts in the passive break condition [37]. We believe that, even though our participants would have obtained some benefit from being exposed to a natural or fractal-based environment while doing nothing, stress recovery would have been reduced.

5.3 Other Modulating Factors

When analyzing the profile of the participants of our studies, some factors could have modulated the results. The participants' age might have determined to some extent the effect of these environments on their perceived stress. A systematic review and meta-analysis suggested that older samples exposed to natural settings had more positive emotions and less negative emotions than when exposed to urban or built environments, so it might not be farfetched to think that the effect these environments had on the current sample are different from those we could have obtained from a majority of participants in, for instance, their 50s or 70s [38].

Their gender could have also influenced perceived stress reduction. Studies have suggested that males demonstrate more stress recovery when cortisol levels are measured than when self-reported [39, 40], and that women are more likely to create stronger associations between greenery and positive health in comparison [41]. Therefore, stress recovery reported in our studies, especially in groups composed of a majority of male participants, could be lower than what their actual physiological state demonstrates.

Another factor could have been environmental preference. Some studies suggest that even though congruence between preference and the type of environment exposed to does not always result in higher perceived restorativeness, it does have some effect in some cases [29]. For instance, most participants exposed to the Nature-Realistic group in both studies were city people. One could argue that city people would be more receptive to abstraction or less naturalistic shapes, so we cannot reject the possibility that had this group been exposed to the Fractal-Abstract environment instead, perceived stress reduction and perceived restorative potential levels could have been higher.

Personality is another important factor, as the 'Big Five' personality traits have been associated with tendencies to choose specific coping styles [42, 43]. A study performed with incarcerated men in Poland suggested that extraversion, openness to experience, consciousness and agreeableness were associated with task-oriented coping strategies [43]. In contrast, men high in neuroticism tended to choose emotion-oriented coping strategies. In other words, it is possible that participants with high extraversion benefited more from having a task to perform in the virtual world than those with high neuroticism, who would have most likely benefited more from emotional support instead.

Exposure time could have also influenced perceived stress reduction. Suppakittpaisarn et al. [44] studied the effect of duration of exposure to virtual natural landscapes in stress recovery, and they concluded that 5 min of exposure was more stress-reducing than 1 or 15 min [44]. Therefore, we cannot reject the possibility that, had our participants been exposed to 5 or 15 min in our environments, stress reduction scores would have been lower or greater.

5.4   Practical Implications and Future Work

We believe this research adds further evidence to a corpus showing the potential of using Virtual Reality to promote mental health in a society that is more and more prone to suffering stress-related morbidities. Immersive Virtual Environments cannot fully imitate real exposure to nature and its inherent fractal geometries. However, we believe that the main contribution of this study lies in adding to a small corpus devoted to studying the potential of fractal geometry in virtual reality environments. Even though fractals and biophilic designs have been widely studied in art and architecture, much more exploration is needed within the vast possibilities of Virtual Reality through Head-Mounted Displays or KAVE systems. Our work will hopefully inspire future interactive media designers for well-being to diverge from the highly established realistic nature pattern and explore the possibilities of using abstract and otherworldly landscapes in their proposals.

Our studies provided answers to our main questions. However, it has also generated further questions. Would our results be significantly different if we had used repeated measures? We believe that carrying out similar studies, but this time exposing participants to both types of environments would complement this research well. In these studies, we did not include soundscape because of the strong restorative effect it has been reported to have, and we focused on the visual aspect. However, it would be interesting to see the degree of stress reduction and perceived restorativeness after exposure to these environments while listening to their respective soundscape: nature sounds, relaxing music, others. We were able to see that, in our case, having a collection task did not influence our environments' potential for restoration significantly. However, similar studies comparing experimental environments with highly active against highly passive tasks (e.g., Nature-Realistic playing golf vs. mindfulness exercises) are needed, especially for designing virtual reality environments for mental health purposes.

It has also been argued that people tend to feel more comfortable with fractal images of nature than non-fractal abstract shapes, and that built elements lacking fractals might cause virtual strain and hence negative physiological effects [12, 13]. Previous studies have suggested that Euclidean shapes have low restorative potential and even increase stress [45]. So, would an immersive VR environment that uses non-fractal or Euclidean geometrical shapes to imitate elements of nature have or not restorative potential? After all, one of our experimental environments is fractal-based but not necessarily free of Euclidean geometries. An area of research that also deserves attention is the potential that abstract environments have for increasing the feeling of 'being away' from our world that immersive VR already offers. It would be interesting to study, regardless of being restorative or not, the level of presence and place illusion [46, p. 3551] felt in a realistic VR environment compared to an abstract environment absent of or with minimal references to reality.

5.5 Limitations

Regarding the limitations of our study, our sample size was small (39 participants, split into 4 different groups), so these results are not generalizable. Furthermore, these environments were tested in a sample mostly of young adults, so we cannot be sure that the benefits of abstract fractal environments would apply to older audiences. This study was also limited to self-reporting measuring tools, which can always be subjected to the influence of cognitive and contextual differences. Data obtained would be better compared, complemented, and corroborated by physiological data such as the participant's heart rate. Moreover, we must remember that the PRS has had different versions and modifications in time, is not completely independent from personal and contextual attributes, and is not specially prepared for VR environments. This means our scores may not consider aspects and features exclusive to the VR realm.

6 Conclusions

We can conclude that exposure to both fractal-abstract and natural-realistic environments seems to be effective for stress reduction and restorativeness, regardless of having a task or not. Hence, the fact of having a task might not be a determinant factor of a VR environment's restorative potential. However, it is important to highlight that this does not mean that those users who explored the environments with no tasks assigned would not have preferred or had had a more enjoyable experience if they had been given any activity to perform. A task might not be essential for restoration in a specially-designed environment, but an appropriate task can always improve the experience and make it more meaningful or memorable.

Acknowledgements. This work was supported by the Fundação para a Ciência e Tecnologia through the scholarship UI/BD/151404/2021, the AViR project (EXPL/CCI-INF/0298/2021) and NOVA LINCS (UIDB/04516/2020), and by MACbioIDi2 (INTERREG program MAC2/1.1b/352).

References

1. Leka, S., Cox, T., Griffiths, A.: Work organization & stress: systematic problem approaches for employers, managers and trade union representatives. In: Protecting workers' health series, no. 3. Geneva, Switzerland: World Health Organization (2003). https://apps.who.int/iris/bitstream/handle/10665/42625/9241590475.pdf
2. Teixeira, R.J., Brandão, T., Dores, A.R.: Academic stress, coping, emotion regulation, affect and psychosomatic symptoms in higher education. Curr. Psychol. 1 (2021). https://doi.org/10.1007/s12144-020-01304-z
3. World Health Organization. Guidelines for the Management of Conditions Specifically Related to Stress, pp. 1–273. WHO, Geneva, Geneva (2013)
4. Abdullah, S.S.S., Rambli, D.R.A., Sulaiman, S., Alyan, E., Merienne, F., Diyana, N.: The impact of virtual nature therapy on stress responses: a systematic qualitative review. Forests 12(12), 1–19 (2021). https://doi.org/10.3390/f12121776
5. Lederbogen, F., et al.: City living and urban upbringing affect neural social stress processing in humans. Nature 474, 498–501 (2011). https://doi.org/10.1038/nature10190
6. Ulrich, R.S.: Human responses to vegetation and landscapes. Landsc. Urban Plan. 13, 29–44 (1986). https://doi.org/10.1016/0169-2046(86)90005-8
7. Weinreb, A.R., Rofè, Y.: Mapping feeling: an approach to the study of emotional response to the built environment and landscape. J. Arch. Plan. Res. 30(2), 127–145 (2013)
8. Simkin, J., Ojala, A., Tyrväinen, L.: Restorative effects of mature and young commercial forests, pristine old-growth forest and urban recreation forest - a field experiment. Urban Forest. Urban Green. 48, 1–12 (2020). https://doi.org/10.1016/j.ufug.2019.126567
9. Ulrich, R.S., Simons, R.F., Losito, B.D., Fiorito, E., Miles, M.A., Zelson, M.: Stress recovery during exposure to natural and urban environments. J. Environ. Psychol. 11(3), 201–230 (1991). https://doi.org/10.1016/S0272-4944(05)80184-7
10. Kaplan, S.: The restorative benefits of nature: toward and integrative framework. J. Environ. Psychol. 15, 169–182 (1995)
11. Joye, Y., van den Berg, A.: Is love for green in our genes? a critical analysis of evolutionary assumptions in restorative environments research. Urban Fores. Urban Green. 10(4), 261–268 (2011). https://doi.org/10.1016/j.ufug.2011.07.004
12. Taylor, R.P.: The potential of biophilic designs to promote health and performance: a review of experiments and applications. Sustainability 13(2), 1–25 (2021). https://doi.org/10.3390/su13020823
13. Wise, J.A., Taylor, R.P.: Fractal design strategies for enhancement of knowledge work environments. In: Proceedings of the Human Factors and Ergonomics Society 46th Annual Meeting, vol. 46, no. 9, pp. 854–858 (2002). https://doi.org/10.1177/154193120204600905
14. Stone, R., Small, C., Knight, J., Qian, C., Shingari, V.: Virtual natural environments for restoration and rehabilitation in healthcare. In: Ma, M., Jain, L.C., Anderson, P. (eds.) Virtual, Augmented Reality and Serious Games for Healthcare 1. ISRL, vol. 68, pp. 497–521. Springer, Heidelberg (2014). https://doi.org/10.1007/978-3-642-54816-1_24
15. van Almkerk, M., Huisman, G.: Virtual nature environments based on fractal geometry for optimizing restorative effects. In: Proceedings of British HCI 2018, pp. 1–11. BCS Learning and Development Ltd., Belfast, UK (2018). https://doi.org/10.14236/ewic/HCI2018.55
16. Valtchanov, D., Barton, K.R., Ellard, C.: Restorative effects of virtual nature settings. Cyberpsychol. Behav. Soc. Netw. 13(5), 503–512 (2010). https://doi.org/10.1089=cyber.2009.0308
17. Beute, F., de Kort, Y.A.W.: Let the Sun Shine! measuring explicit and implicit preference for environments differing in naturalness, weather type and brightness. J. Environ. Psychol. 36, 162–178 (2013). https://doi.org/10.1016/j.jenvp.2013.07.016

18. Nukarinen, T., et al.: Measures and modalities in restorative virtual natural environments: an integrative narrative review. Comput. Hum. Behav. **126**, 1–14 (2022). https://doi.org/10.1016/j.chb.2021.107008

19. Li, J., Ma, Y., Li, P., Butz, A.: A journey through nature: exploring virtual restorative environments as a means to relax in confined spaces. Presented at the Creativity and Cognition (C&C 2021), pp. 1–9. Virtual Event, Italy, Virtual Event, Italy, ACM, New York, NY, USA (2021). https://doi.org/10.1145/3450741.3465248

20. White, M.P., et al.: A prescription for 'nature' - the potential of using virtual nature in therapeutics. Neuropsychiatr. Dis. Treat. **14**, 3001–3013 (2018). https://doi.org/10.2147/NDT.S179038

21. Yu, C.-P., Lee, H.-Y., Luo, X.-Y.: The effect of virtual reality forest and urban environments on physiological and psychological responses. Urban Forestry Urban Green. **35**, 106–114 (2018). https://doi.org/10.1016/j.ufug.2018.08.013

22. Szczepanska-Gieracha, J., Cieslik, B., Serweta, A., Klajs, K.: Virtual therapeutic garden: a promising method supporting the treatment of depressive symptoms in late-life: a randomized pilot study. J. Clin. Med. **10**, 1–13 (2021). https://doi.org/10.3390/jcm10091942

23. Riva, G., et al.: A virtual reality-based self-help intervention for dealing with the psychological distress associated with the COVID-19 lockdown: an effectiveness study with a two-week follow-up. Int. J. Environ. Res. Public Health **18**(8188), 1–19 (2021). https://doi.org/10.3390/ijerph18158188

24. Beverly, E., et al.: A tranquil virtual reality experience to reduce subjective stress among COVID-19 frontline healthcare workers. PLoS ONE **17**(2), 1–13 (2022). https://doi.org/10.1371/journal.pone.0262703

25. Guillén, V., Baños, R.M., Botella, C.: Users' opinion about a virtual reality system as an adjunct to psychological treatment for stress-related disorders: a quantitative and qualitative mixed-methods study. Front. Psychol. **9** (2018). https://doi.org/10.3389/fpsyg.2018.01038

26. Botella, C., Osma, J., Palacios, A.G., Guillén, V., Baños, R.M.: Treatment of complicated grief using virtual reality: a case report. Death Stud. **32**(7), 674–692 (2008). https://doi.org/10.1080/07481180802231319

27. Juliani, A.W., Bies, A.J., Boydston, C.R., Taylor, R.P., Sereno, M.E.: Navigating performance in virtual environments varies with fractal dimension of landscape. J. Environ. Psychol. **47**, 155–165 (2016). https://doi.org/10.1016/j.jenvp.2016.05.011

28. Hayden, S.: Pioneering Fractal Artist Julius Horsthuis is Returning to VR with a New Album Soon. Road to VR (2022). https://www.roadtovr.com/quest-fractal-art-recombination-horsthuis/. Accessed 20 Aug 2022

29. Wilkie, S., Stavridou, A.: Influence of environmental preference and environment type congruence on judgments of restoration potential. Urban Forest. Urban Green. **12**(2), 163–170 (2013). https://doi.org/10.1016/j.ufug.2013.01.004

30. Karvounides, D., Simpson, P.M., Davies, H.H., Khan, K.A., Weisman, S.J., Hainsworth, K.R.: Three studies supporting the initial validation of the stress numerical rating Scale-11 (Stress NRS-11): a single item measure of momentary stress for adolescents and adults. Pediatric Dimen. **1**(4), 105–109 (2016). https://doi.org/10.15761/PD.1000124

31. Cohen, S., Kamarck, T., Merlmelstein, R.: A global measure of perceived stress. J. Health Soc. Behav. **24**(4), 385–396 (1983). https://doi.org/10.2307/2136404

32. Hartig, T., Korpela, K., Evans, G.W., Gärling, T.: A measure of restorative quality in environments. SHPR **14**(4), 175–194 (1997). https://doi.org/10.1080/02815739708730435

33. IBM Corp. IBM SPSS Statistics for Windows. IBM Corp, Armonk, NY (2021)

34. Faul, F.: G*Power. Universität Düsseldorf, Düsseldorf, Germany (2020)

35. Salingaros, N.A.: A 26. Fractal Art and Architecture Reduce Physiological Stress. Unified Architectural Theory: Form, Language, Complexity: A Companion to Christopher Alexander's The Phenomenon of Life-The Nature of Order, vol. Book 1, pp. 11–28 (2017)

36. Browning, M.H.E., Mimnaugh, K.J., van Riper, C.J., Laurent, H.K., LaValle, S.M.: Can simulated nature support mental health? comparing short, single-doses of 360-degree nature videos in virtual reality with the outdoors. Front. Psychol. **10**, 1–14 (2020). https://doi.org/10.3389/fpsyg.2019.02667

37. Rupp, M.A., Sweetman, R., Sosa, A.E., Smither, J.A., McConnell, D.S.: Searching for affective and cognitive restoration: examining the restorative effects of casual video game play. Hum. Factor J. Hum. Fact. Ergon. Soc. **59**(1), 1–12 (2017). https://doi.org/10.1177/001872 0817715360

38. Yao, W., Chen, F., Wang, S., Zhang, X.: Impact of exposure to natural and built environments on positive and negative affect: a systematic review. Front. Public Health **9**, 1–13 (2021). https://doi.org/10.3389/fpubh.2021.758457

39. Jiang, B., Li, D., Larsen, L., Sullivan, W.C.: A dose-response curve describing the relationship between urban tree cover density and self-reported stress recovery. Environ. Behav. (2014). https://doi.org/10.1177/0013916514552321

40. Jiang, B., Chang, C.-Y., Sullivan, W.C.: A dose of nature: tree cover, stress reduction, and gender differences. Landsc. Urban Plan. **132**, 26–36 (2014). https://doi.org/10.1016/j.landur bplan.2014.08.005

41. Sillman, D., Rigolon, A., Browning, m.H.E.M., (Violet) Yoon, H., McAnirlin, O.: Do sex and gender modify the association between green space and physical health? a systematic review. Environ. Res. **209**, 112869 1–13 (2022). https://doi.org/10.1016/j.envres.2022.112869

42. Baumgartner, J.N., Schneider, T.R.: Personality and stress. In: Zeigler-Hill, V., Shackelford, T.K. (eds.) Encyclopedia of Personality and Individual Differences, Springer Reference, pp. 3699–3704. Springer, Switzerland (2020). https://doi.org/10.1007/978-3-319-24612-3

43. Leszco, M., Iwanski, R., Jarzebinska, A.: the relationship between personality traits and coping styles among first-time and recurrent prisoners in Poland. Front. Psychol. **10**(2969), 1–8 (2020). https://doi.org/10.3389/fpsyg.2019.02969

44. Suppakittpalsarn, P., et al.: Duration of virtual exposure to built and natural landscapes impact self-reported stress recovery: evidence from three countries. Landscape Ecol. Eng. **19**, 95–105 (2023). https://doi.org/10.1007/s11355-022-00523-9

45. Trombin, R.: Working with Fractals: A Resource for Practitioners of Biophilic Design. Terrapin Bright Green, New York (2020). https://www.terrapinbrightgreen.com/report/biophilia-fractals-toolkit/

46. Slater, M.: Place illusion and plausibility can lead to realistic behavior in immersive virtual environments. Phil. Trans. R. Soci. B **364**(1535), 3549–3557 (2009). https://doi.org/10.1098/rstb.2009.0138

"I Miss Going to that Place": The Impact of Watching Nature Videos on the Well-Being of Informal Caregivers

Beatriz Peres[1,2,3](✉) ⓘ, Hildegardo Noronha[1,2] ⓘ, Daniel S. Lopes[4,5] ⓘ,
Joaquim Jorge[3,5] ⓘ, and Pedro F. Campos[1,2,6] ⓘ

[1] University of Madeira, Funchal, Portugal
[2] Interactive Technologies Institute, LARSYS, Funchal, Portugal
beatriz.peres@iti.larsys.pt
[3] INESC-ID, Lisbon, Portugal
[4] Interactive Technologies Institute, LARSYS, Lisbon, Portugal
[5] Instituto Superior Técnico, Universidade de Lisboa, Lisbon, Portugal
[6] WoW Systems, Funchal, Portugal

Abstract. Informal caregivers play an essential role in caring for persons who require assistance and in managing the health of their loved ones. Unfortunately, they need more health, leisure, and relaxation time. Nature interaction is one of many kinds of self-care intervention. It has long been regarded as a refreshing break from stressful routines, and research suggests exposure to nature interventions to improve the quality of life of caregivers. Despite not being the real thing, technology allows us alternatives that can still have some beneficial effects. In this preliminary study, we explore the benefits of natural environment videos on informal caregivers as an alternative to exposure to nature. Specifically, we are interested in the effects of their own choices versus a random video. We found that natural environment videos improve the well-being of informal caregivers in at least three key areas: valence, arousal, and negative affect. Furthermore, the effect increases when they choose the video they want to watch instead of a random video. This effect benefits the studied subjects because they need more time and energy to visit real natural environments.

Keywords: Informal caregivers · Self-care · Well-being · Nature videos

1 Introduction

Informal caregivers play an essential role in caring for persons who require assistance and in managing the health of their loved ones. However, coping with heavy responsibilities, like personal care or domestic activities, and securing income may absorb most informal caregivers' time budget, leaving little to no time for them to attend to their health, leisure, and relaxation [19]. This issue is vital as informal caregiving, besides being time-consuming, is also physically and emotionally demanding [13].

© The Author(s), under exclusive license to Springer Nature Switzerland AG 2023
J. Abdelnour Nocera et al. (Eds.): INTERACT 2023, LNCS 14145, pp. 23–32, 2023.
https://doi.org/10.1007/978-3-031-42293-5_2

Self-care is defined by Cook [7] as the process of being aware of and attending to one's basic physical and emotional needs daily through engaging in beneficial behaviors, which may include modifying one's daily routine, relationships, and environment as needed to promote it [7].

Self-care practices are essential to informal caregivers since they positively impact mental health [17]. This matter emphasizes the importance of a build-up of interventions addressing the needs of informal caregivers to reduce stress and improve well-being. Some interventions help reduce the adverse effects of care and enhance caregivers' quality of life. Psychoeducational, psychothera-peutic, self-help, multi-component interventions that give disease or self-care knowledge, problem-solving approaches, communication skills, social support, or mindfulness are examples of these measures [10].

However, these interventions are typically costly and unavailable to everyone, and informal caregivers may need more time for them [5]. Furthermore, interven-tions that incorporate various activities to promote multiple outcomes, such as social support, psychological abilities, and a healthy lifestyle, have been linked to a reduction in burden and an increase in healthy living behaviors [7]. These interventions demonstrate the need to promote and practice self-care, particu-larly among informal caregivers, since it relates to improved physical, emotional, and mental health [7].

Nature interaction is a self-care intervention. It has long been regarded as a refreshing break from stressful routines. For instance, Lehto et al. [13] found that further research is required to support informal cancer caregivers. Neverthe-less, they still suggest exposure to nature interventions, considering the benefits of the natural environment. Human health and well-being have been shown to benefit from interaction with nature and green environments [16].*Shinrin-Yoku* (Forest Bathing) [14], is the practice of spending time in the forest, which pro-motes better health, a more robust immune system, happiness, and calmness. According to Qing Li's research [14], being around trees, filling the home with house plants, and vaporizing essential tree oils can reduce stress and improve health and well-being by interacting with nature.

These interactions have several physiological effects, including decreased sali-vary cortisol, heart rate, diastolic blood pressure, HDL cholesterol, decreased low-frequency heart rate variability (HRV), and increased high-frequency HRV [20]. It also has psychological effects such as positive effects on energy scores, tranquility, heightened levels of happiness, self-transcendent emotions (like awe, gratitude, and wonder), and an increased sense of well-being [2] improved atten-tion levels [2], decreased depression [18], anxiety [2], stress levels [21] and reduced negative emotions such as anger, fatigue, and sadness [2]. Natural environments, such as forests, have been studied extensively, with findings indicating that they benefit human physical and mental health [11,15].

Nature's psychological effects on well-being can also be noticed without direct physical contact with nature. Examples include nature videos [23] and virtual reality nature experiences [1]. In addition there are digital representations of nature in the form of nature videos on digital platforms [23], for example, in online nature activities[1], and webcam travel (i.e., seeing location-based web-cams online) [12]. For people with pre-existing health concerns, digital nature engagement provided a valuable opportunity to access other natural locations, allowing for a sense of escape and fostering nostalgia by establishing linkages to familiar or preferred locales [8].

When in-vivo nature is absent, Darcy et al. [8] findings agree to some extent that digital nature can supplement or serve as a suitable replacement. However, this may not be a sufficient substitute for 'real' nature encounters. For example, a lack of access to specific natural places has resulted in confused sensations or when digital nature fails to deliver a comprehensive sensory experience [8].

Alternatives to real-life nature may improve well-being. However, the impacts of actual [23] are worth noting. Digital nature surrogates (i.e., nature videos, photos, Virtual Reality) can help as they may improve well-being, particularly for informal caregivers who do not have the possibility to experience direct contact with nature.

Informal caregivers may not be able to go to a natural environment. Time constraints due to long working days or immobility may hamper opportunities for physical nature experiences. In addition, only some can access nature easily, as many people may not have the physical constitution or mobility to access nature areas. With this, informal caregivers could use technology to connect with nature without leaving home, such as watching videos that bring natural environments into their homes. However, no study was found using relaxing nature videos with informal caregivers that could allow them to take a break from their caregiving duties and focus on their health and well-being.

1.1 Research Question and Contributions

This preliminary study tries to pull informal caregivers closer to nature through nature environment videos. We aim to analyze whether watching chosen relaxing nature videos can impact the well-being of informal caregivers, as it appears that personal preference can improve well-being. For this reason, we try to answer the following research question:

- Will watching relaxing nature videos of their choice improve informal care-givers' well-being versus watching a random nature video?

The contribution of this paper lies in analysing and interpreting the findings regarding the effects of watching a chosen nature video versus a random video on informal caregivers' well-being.

2 Methods

2.1 Elicitation of Preferences

We used a questionnaire to ascertain the characteristics that informal caregivers like in forest, beach, and mountain environment videos. We then asked the par-

---

[1] Discover Small Moments of Joy in Nature, 2020; The Wildlife Trusts over 1000 Care Homes Sign-Up to Go Wild This June 2020.

ticipants to choose the type of environment videos they wanted to watch. After watching three different videos of the chosen type, we asked what they liked about the videos and what they would change. The answers provided insights into their emotions and feelings during the video visualization. The selected characteristics were: the videos can not have people, the forest and mountain video should be during the day, and the beach environment should have a sunset. This allowed us to preselect three videos for this study, what metrics should be considered, and their possible effects on the informal caregivers' well-being.

2.2 Sample

The subjects of this study are all informal caregivers. A total of thirty participants completed the study, with 49.7 ±9 years old. A significant percentage of the participants were female (86.7%). More than half of the participants (60%) became caregivers because of a family member's disease - 26,7% of them were daughters or sons of the diseased person, and 16.7% were parents. The average time being a caregiver was 9.3 ±6.2 years.

2.3 Data Collection

We used several questionnaires to gather data from the subjects. We started by asking the subjects about their age, gender, why they became informal caregivers, their relationship to the family member they cared for, and how long they had been doing informal caregiving.

We then used the Self-Assessment Manikin (SAM) [3] to measure the emotional states (valence, arousal, and dominance). For this study, we did not measure dominance as it is irrelevant. We also used the Positive and Negative Affect Schedule (PANAS) [22] to measure mood and emotion.

Finally, we administered three *ad hoc* satisfaction questions to assess the user's experience watching the nature environment videos. The questions were: a) What natural environment did you choose and why? b) What feature do you like in the natural environment video? c)What changes would you like to make in the natural environment video?

2.4 Tasks

The participants watched two nature environment YouTube videos in two different conditions from a preselected list based on the feedback of the initial questionnaire. The list had three nature videos (forest, beach, and mountain) [2].

After watching each video, participants had to fill out two self-reported scales.

---

[2] Forest video: https://youtu.be/cm8qZWDjsr4 (starting at min 15); Beach video: https://youtu.be/bCnfORRjaDU (starting at min 15); Mountain video: https://youtu.be/FW5IpeH202s (starting at min 1).

2.5   Procedure

Individuals were invited to participate in the study in their home environment, in a calm environment, and using a mobile phone to watch nature videos. First, they signed the informed consent to participate in the research. Then, they filled out a socio-demographic survey. Then, the study was composed of phases from T0 to T2. In phase T0, and to establish a baseline, they filled out the SAM and PANAS scales.

In phrase T1, the participants were randomly assigned either a choice condition or a random one for the first video, followed by the opposite condition for the second video in phrase T2. In the choice condition, the participant can freely choose the video they want to watch, while on the random condition, the participant gets to watch a randomly selected video. We alternate the conditions (choice and random) to avoid the order effect. After watching the video, participants filled out the SAM and PANAS scales in each condition, administered during phase T0.

In both phrases T1 and T2, participants watched each video for five minutes, as research shows that a 5-minute video can induce positive physiological change [4,6,9]. Therefore, we selected this duration to keep the experiment short but with relevant results.

In the end, the participants answered *post hoc* questions about why they chose that video and what features they liked and disliked in the natural environment video. Figure 1 illustrates each nature video used in this study.

Fig. 1. Screenshots of each nature environment video

2.6   Data Analysis

The data were analyzed using the Friedman test using SPSS Statistics '26'. The Friedman test is a non-parametric test used when measuring an ordinal dependent variable. It is also applied to check for changes within people (repeated measures) and within a group measured in three or more conditions. We applied the Friedman test because we had three conditions, repeated measurements, and ordinal data. Since the Friedman test was significant, we had to examine where the differences occurred. We conducted a separate *post hoc* analysis on each combination using the Wilcoxon pairwise test.

Given that, we needed to adjust the p-value on the Wilcoxon test results since we were performing multiple comparisons. To calculate the p-value adjustment, we divided the previous significant level (0.05) by the number of tests we conducted, yielding a new significant level of 0.017 (0.05/3). If the p-value was higher than 0.017 was not a significant result. The participant's responses to the open-ended question were analyzed by two authors using thematic analysis. Starting by creating initial codes, then grouping codes into themes, reviewing and revising themes, grouping all excerpts associated with a particular theme, and writing the narrative.

3 Results

There was a statistically significant difference in valence, arousal, and negative affect, $X^2(2) = 11.146$ (degrees of freedom = chi-square), $p \leq 0.001$, $X^2(2) = 21.843$, $p \leq 0.001$, $X^2(2) = 34.758$, $p \leq 0.001$, respectively. However, no statistically significant difference was found in positive affect $X^2(2) = 5.845$, $p \geq 0.05$. Wilcoxon's post hoc analysis adjusted the significance level to $p = 0.017$.

Valence showed a statistically significant increase between the baseline and the choice condition ($p \leq 0.001$, $r = 0.54$). However, there was no significant difference between the baseline and the random condition ($p \geq 0.05$ $r = 0.33$). Arousal showed a statistically significant decrease between the baseline and random condition ($p \leq 0.001$, $r = 0.68$) and between the baseline and choice condition ($p \leq 0.001$, $r = 0.58$). Negative Affect showed a statistically significant decrease between the baseline and the random condition ($p \leq 0.001$, $r=0.76$), between baseline and choice condition ($p \leq 0.001$, $r = 0.79$). Figure 2 illustrates the distribution of values for a better understanding of the results.

Most participants ($n = 20$) chose the beach as the environment they preferred to watch, nine chose the forest, and only one chose the mountain. Participants made their choices based on the following reasons: "it brings peace", "it helps to calm down", "it renews energy", "it gives a feeling of freedom", "it relaxes", "it feels light", "it takes away the sadness", "it brings tranquility", and "it makes them feel good". Some participants mentioned that "it is my environment", "I live in the countryside", and "I like contact with nature". Some participants mentioned "a feeling of missing going to that place", "the smell of the sea", "listening to the waves", and "I miss that". Some participants justified that they do not go to this natural environment with: "there is no possibility of great absence", "it is a bit distance from home and I can not leave my family member alone", "lack of time", "lack of money for fuel".

Some participants would like to change the type of environment, the light, the birds' sound, and the green colors of the forest video. They liked the sunset and the sound of the waves in the beach video, but some mentioned they would change the sound to a more relaxing one. In the mountain video, they liked the type of environment and the light but would also change the sound.

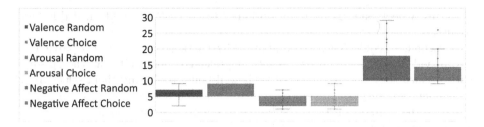

Fig. 2. Box and Whiskers plot of Valence, Arousal and Negative Affect with corresponding Random and Choice

4 Discussion

The main goal of this paper was to explore the impact of natural environment videos on informal caregivers with a focus on the act of choosing. We did find a statistically significant difference in valence, arousal, and negative affect between the baseline and the choice condition. In addition, the negative affect and arousal also have a statistically significant difference between the random and choice conditions.

Having a statistically significant increasing effect on valence seems to indicate a benefit of nature videos. However, in this study, the effect only appears when the subjects choose the video. This may indicate that the choice does matter for valence. Arousal and Negative Affect have a statistically significant decrease. There is a more prominent effect for the random condition for the arousal, while the negative affect has a similar size in both conditions. This finding may indicate that the choice has a small or negligent effect on both arousal and negative affect relative to the base condition.

We surmised that the effects found in valence, arousal, and negative affect might depend on previous feelings and experiences gathered on visitations to similar places. This idea of "gathered experience" highlights how certain places can become emotionally significant. This is supported by how the participants justified the choices with feelings of calmness and peacefulness. In this case, the positive emotional state is associated with an entire scene or specific sensory stimulation, visual or auditory, that evoked familiarity and nostalgia.

5 Study Limitations and Future Work

In this section, we discuss the main shortcomings of our approach and hint at future research opportunities.

Nature Video Selection: We studied only the effect of two nature videos, and anticipated that some videos would appeal more to one than others. Due to this, we requested that participants select the natural video. However, more types of nature videos and giving more options to participants could yield different results.

Researchers could learn more about why participants selected a particular nature video, such as which videos they preferred most and how the specific nature video they selected affected their well-being by letting them select from a broader range of nature videos. Future research should consider this idea, and take the hints given by the subjects to create a better and more extensive selection of videos.

Other Media Types: Although we focused on the effect of watching natural environments, especially on choosing, looking into looking into other media forms, such as visual-only and Virtual Reality, is also essential. Other forms of media should be researched to determine which media the act of choosing has the best effect on the informal caregiver's well-being. These findings could be used to develop other approaches to promote the well-being of informal caregivers.

Regarding the act of choosing, the importance of choice must be further studied to understand its true impact, possibly with additional metrics.

Duration of the Study: Our short-term study provided exciting results. However, a study with more repetitions and a longer duration could provide a stronger case, so we could benefit from doing it in a future study.

6   Conclusion

We conclude that watching a chosen nature video improves the well-being of informal caregivers in at least three key areas: valence, arousal, and negative affect. The choice made by the participants improves the effect on valence. These results are important because many informal caregivers need help entering real natural environments. By viewing chosen nature videos, they can experience the calming effects of nature while in their own homes. By viewing nature videos, informal caregivers can escape caregiving's physical, emotional, and mental fatigue, feel more relaxed and less stressed, and improve their well-being without leaving home. Therefore, providing informal caregivers access to nature videos is an effective and empowering way to provide them with moments of self-care that can positively impact their physical, mental, and emotional health. Caregivers can also find comfort in the choice of nature videos allowing them to take ownership of their caregiving situation and feel empowered to make decisions that promote their physical and emotional health.

Acknowledgments. We are grateful to all the participants that were generous with their time for this study.

This research was funded by the Portuguese Recovery and Resilience Program (PRR), IAPMEI/ANI/FCT under Agenda C645022399-00000057 (eGamesLab) and was supported by PhD FCT grant 2020.08848.BD.

References

1. Bodet-Contentin, L., Letourneur, M., Ehrmann, S.: Virtual reality during work breaks to reduce fatigue of intensive unit caregivers: a crossover, pilot, randomised trial. Aust. Critical Care **36**, 345–349 (2022). https://doi.org/10.1016/j.aucc.2022.01.009, https://www.sciencedirect.com/science/article/pii/S1036731422000108

2. Bowler, D.E., Buyung-Ali, L.M., Knight, T.M., Pullin, A.S.: A systematic review of evidence for the added benefits to health of exposure to natural environments. BMC Public Health **10**, 456 (2010). https://doi.org/10.1186/1471-2458-10-456

3. Bradley, M.M., Lang, P.J.: Measuring emotion: the self-assessment manikin and the semantic differential. J. Behav. Ther. Exp. Psychiatry **25**(1), 49–59 (1994). https://doi.org/10.1016/0005-7916(94)90063-9, https://www.sciencedirect.com/science/article/pii/0005791694900639

4. Brown, D.K., Barton, J.L., Gladwell, V.F.: Viewing nature scenes positively affects recovery of autonomic function following acute-mental stress. Environ. Sci. Technol. **47**(11), 5562–5569 (2013). American Chemical Society. https://doi.org/10.1021/es305019p

5. Brown, E.L., et al.: CareHeroes web and android apps for Dementia caregivers: a feasibility study. Res. Gerontol. Nurs. **9**(4), 193–203 (2016). https://doi.org/10.3928/19404921-20160229-02

6. Chan, S.H.M., Qiu, L., Esposito, G., Mai, K.P., Tam, K.P., Cui, J.: Nature in virtual reality improves mood and reduces stress: evidence from young adults and senior citizens. Virtual Reality (2021). https://doi.org/10.1007/s10055-021-00604-4

7. Cook-Cottone, C.P., Guyker, W.M.: The development and validation of the Mindful Self-Care Scale (MSCS): an assessment of practices that support positive embodiment. Mindfulness **9**(1), 161–175 (2018). https://doi.org/10.1007/s12671-017-0759-1

8. Darcy, P.M., Taylor, J., Mackay, L., Ellis, N.J., Gidlow, C.J.: Understanding the role of nature engagement in supporting health and wellbeing during COVID-19. Int. J. Environ. Res. Public Health **19**(7), 3908 (2022). Number: 7. Multidisciplinary Digital Publishing Institute. https://doi.org/10.3390/ijerph19073908, https://www.mdpi.com/1660-4601/19/7/3908

9. Gladwell, V.F., et al.: The effects of views of nature on autonomic control. Eur. J. Appl. Physiol. **112**(9), 3379–3386 (2012). https://doi.org/10.1007/s00421-012-2318-8

10. Grossman, M.R., Zak, D.K., Zelinski, E.M.: Mobile apps for caregivers of older adults: quantitative content analysis. JMIR Mhealth Uhealth **6**(7), e162 (2018). https://doi.org/10.2196/mhealth.9345

11. Hong, S., Joung, D., Lee, J., Kim, D.Y., Kim, S., Park, B.J.: The effects of watching a virtual reality (VR) forest video on stress reduction in adults. J. People Plants Environ. **22**, 309–319 (2019). https://doi.org/10.11628/ksppe.2019.22.3.309

12. Jarratt, D.: An exploration of webcam-travel: connecting to place and nature through webcams during the Covid-19 lockdown of 2020. Tourism Hospitality Res. **21**(2), 156–168 (2021). https://doi.org/10.1177/1467358420963370

13. Lehto, R.H., Wyatt, G., Sender, J., Miller, S.E.: An evaluation of natural environment interventions for informal cancer caregivers in the community. Int. J. Environ. Res. Public Health **18**(21) (2021). https://doi.org/10.3390/ijerph182111124, https://www.mdpi.com/1660-4601/18/21/11124

14. Li, Q.: Shinrin-Yoku: The Art and Science of Forest Bathing. Penguin UK, London (2018)
15. Li, Q.: The Art and Science of Japanese Forest Bathing. REVOLVE, p. 4 (2019). http://forest-medicine.com/2019/REVOLVEBathing.pdf
16. Mayer, F.S., Frantz, C.M., Bruehlman-Senecal, E., Dolliver, K.: Why is nature beneficial?: The role of connectedness to nature. Environ. Behav. **41**(5), 607–643 (2009). https://doi.org/10.1177/0013916508319745
17. Miller, S., Lee, J.: A self-care framework for social workers: building a strong foundation for practice. Families Soc. J. Contemp. Hum. Serv. **94**, 96–103 (2013). https://doi.org/10.1606/1044-3894.4289
18. Morita, E., et al.: Psychological effects of forest environments on healthy adults: Shinrin-Yoku (forest-air bathing, walking) as a possible method of stress reduction. Public Health **121**(1), 54–63 (2007). https://doi.org/10.1016/j.puhe.2006.05.024, https://www.sciencedirect.com/science/article/pii/S0033350606001466
19. Oliveira, D., Zarit, S.H., Orrell, M.: Health-promoting self-care in family caregivers of people with dementia: the views of multiple stakeholders. Gerontologist **59**, e501–e511 (2019)
20. Twohig-Bennett, C., Jones, A.: The health benefits of the great outdoors: a systematic review and meta-analysis of greenspace exposure and health outcomes. Environ. Res. **166**, 628–637 (2018). https://doi.org/10.1016/j.envres.2018.06.030, https://www.sciencedirect.com/science/article/pii/S0013935118303323
21. Wang, X., Shi, Y., Zhang, B., Chiang, Y.: The influence of forest resting environments on stress using virtual reality. Int. J. Environ. Res. Public Health **16**(18), E3263 (2019). https://doi.org/10.3390/ijerph16183263
22. Watson, D., Clark, L.A., Tellegen, A.: Development and validation of brief measures of positive and negative affect: the PANAS scales. J. Pers. Soc. Psychol. **54**(6), 1063–1070 (1988). https://doi.org/10.1037//0022-3514.54.6.1063
23. Xu, S., et al.: #Springwatch #WildMorningswithChris: engaging with nature via social media and wellbeing during the Covid-19 lockdown. Front. Psychol. **12**, 701769 (2021). https://doi.org/10.3389/fpsyg.2021.701769, https://www.frontiersin.org/article/10.3389/fpsyg.2021.701769

Our Nudges, Our Selves: Tailoring Mobile User Engagement Using Personality

Nima Jamalian[1], Marios Constantinides[2(✉)], Sagar Joglekar[2], Xueni Pan[1], and Daniele Quercia[2]

[1] Goldsmiths, University of London, London, UK
{n.jamalian,x.pan}@gold.ac.uk
[2] Nokia Bell Labs, Cambridge, UK
{marios.constantinides,sagar.joglekar,
daniele.quercia}@nokia-bell-labs.com

Abstract. To increase mobile user engagement, current apps employ a variety of behavioral nudges, but these engagement techniques are applied in a one-size-fits-all approach. Yet the very same techniques may be perceived differently by different individuals. To test this, we developed HarrySpotter, a location-based AR app that embedded six engagement techniques. We deployed it in a 2-week study involving 29 users who also took the Big-Five personality test. Preferences for specific engagement techniques are not only descriptive but also predictive of personality traits. The Adj. R^2 ranges from 0.16 for conscientious users (encouraged by competition) to 0.32 for neurotic users (self-centered and focused on their own achievements), and even up to 0.61 for extroverts (motivated by both exploration of objects and places). These findings suggest that these techniques need to be personalized in the future.

Keywords: mobile engagement · gamification · personality traits · personalization

1 Introduction

User engagement is crucial for the success of mobile apps, especially in modern Internet companies [20]. Mobile apps employ various techniques to capture users' attention and increase their engagement. For example, Foursquare introduced game mechanics to enhance engagement [24]. Users could check-in at venues and inform their friends about their location. However, since not all friends may use the app, incentivizing early adopters became vital for the app's success. To motivate early adopters, Foursquare introduced badges, appealing to their desire for status. By default, the app shared this activity on social media platforms like Twitter, creating a sense of accomplishment and effectively engaging users. In general, engagement strategies, such as badges and rewards [4,32], encompass various mechanisms to increase user engagement [10]. However, most current mobile apps follow a one-size-fits-all approach [23,33], where all users are exposed to the same engagement techniques.

© The Author(s), under exclusive license to Springer Nature Switzerland AG 2023
J. Abdelnour Nocera et al. (Eds.): INTERACT 2023, LNCS 14145, pp. 33–45, 2023.
https://doi.org/10.1007/978-3-031-42293-5_3

While users' personality has been extensively studied in various domains and linked to diverse aspects including online browsing behavior [3,19,30] and patterns of behavior collected with smartphones [35], limited research has investigated its influence on mobile user engagement. To explore the relationship between personality and engagement strategies, we developed and deployed a location-based Augmented Reality (AR) mobile app called HarrySpotter, which incorporates six engagement techniques.

In this study, we made three sets of contributions. First, we developed HarrySpotter, a location-based app that enables users to annotate real-world objects. We conducted a two-week in-the-wild study involving 29 participants, resulting in a collection of 503 annotated objects. Second, we analyzed the engagement techniques chosen by users when capturing these objects and examined their correlation with their Big-Five personality traits. Our findings revealed that competition-based techniques discouraged agreeable users but encouraged conscientious users. Techniques promoting exploration of objects and places were particularly appealing to extroverts and individuals open to new experiences. Additionally, techniques focusing on personal achievements were found to motivate neurotic users. Lastly, we found that these preferences for specific engagement techniques not only correlated with personality traits but also had predictive value. The Adj. R^2 values ranged from 0.16 for conscientious users to 0.32 for neurotic users and as high as 0.61 for extroverts.

2   Related Work

User engagement is a critical factor in the success of various digital experiences, including websites, mobile apps, and online platforms [20]. It refers to the level of involvement, interaction, and interest that users have with a product or service [28], resulting in increased engagement. Similarly, mobile user engagement is described by the level of engagement users have with mobile apps on their smartphones or tablets. Factors such as intuitive user interface design, personalized content delivery, and interactive features play a significant role in fostering mobile user engagement [22,36]. Push notifications, in-app messaging, and social sharing features also contribute to enhancing mobile user engagement [18].

Gamification techniques also play a crucial role in fostering engagement [10, 12]. Gamification involves applying game elements and mechanics to non-game contexts to enhance engagement, motivation, and participation [10]. It taps into people's natural inclination for competition, achievement, and recognition, making it a powerful tool for motivating and incentivizing users [14]. By incorporating game-like features such as points, badges, leaderboards, challenges, and rewards, mobile app developers can transform mundane tasks or activities into more enjoyable and immersive experiences. Rewards can take various forms, such as adding points or levels, to entice users to engage with an app to earn these rewards [24,27]. Badges and leaderboards are also popular gamification elements, which were shown to boost motivation [4]. Additionally, gamification strategies have been used to increase users' physical activity. For example, Althoff et al. [1]

conducted a study on the impact of Pokémon GO [26], an augmented reality (AR) location-based game, and found that the game led to a more than 25% increase in users' physical activity.

While previous studies have explored the use of gamification strategies to engage mobile app users in a variety of tasks or games, the relationship between these strategies and a user's personality remains relatively unexplored. The purpose of this study is to investigate whether different individuals perceive the same gamification strategies differently.

3   The Big-Five Personality

The Big-Five personality model assigns individuals scores [11], representing the main personality traits of Openness, Conscientiousness, Extroversion, Agreeableness, and Neuroticism. We hypothesized the relationship between these traits and our six engagement strategies, and summarized the positive and negative relationships of these hypotheses in Table 1.

Table 1. Question statements assessing HarrySpotter's six engagement strategies. Positive and negative signs indicate the association of these engagement strategies with each personality trait as found in prior literature, and empty cells indicate that no reference has been found. O: Openness; C: Conscientiousness; E: Extraversion; A: Agreeableness; and N: Neuroticism.

Strategy	Question Statement	O	C	E	A	N
Q1 (Point Rewards)	I pay attention to others' spell energy scores				–	
Q2 (Place Rewards)	I am proud of my mayorships				–	+
Q3 (Game with Yourself)	When I play the game, I feel I am representing my house					+
Q4 (Social Connection)	With HarrySpotter, I track the competition among the four houses			+	–	
Q5 (Object Discovery)	HarrySpotter motivated me to discover new objects	+		+		
Q6 (Place Discovery)	HarrySpotter motivated me to visit new places	+		+		

Openness is associated with descriptive terms such as imaginative, spontaneous, and adventurous. Individuals high in Openness are more likely to try new methods of communication, including social networking sites or mobile apps. For example, studies have reported that individuals high in Openness tend to utilize a greater number of features that facilitate exploration in such technologies [31].

Conscientiousness is associated with traits like ambition, resourcefulness, and persistence. Individuals high in Conscientiousness are less likely to engage in mobile content generation. They often view computer-mediated communication as a distraction from their daily tasks [2]. However, when they do engage in such communication, they tend to approach it in a highly methodical and competitive manner. Their motivation is often driven by a desire for positive competition [13].

Extraversion is associated with descriptive terms such as sociability, activity, and excitement seeking. Individuals high in Extraversion typically prefer face-to-face interactions and are less inclined to utilize social networking sites or mobile apps. However, if they do join such platforms, they often participate in multiple groups, contribute content, and are motivated by the positive aspect of exploration as a means of social stimulation [29].

Agreeableness is associated with descriptive terms such as trusting, altruistic and tender-minded. Individuals high in Agreeableness, who are less competitive [13] and less likely to share content [2], are more likely to be negatively motivated by rewards or competition.

Neuroticism is associated with descriptive terms such as emotional liability and impulsiveness. Individuals with high levels of Neuroticism exhibit diverse behaviors across different media platforms. They tend to use the Internet and mobile apps as a means to alleviate loneliness, share accurate personal information in anonymous online forums (e.g., chat rooms), exercise control over their shared information on mobile devices [5], and focus on their own achievements in positive ways [21].

4   HarrySpotter

We developed a mobile app called HarrySpotter, which incorporates gameplay elements inspired by the popular Harry Potter series. Authored by J.K. Rowling, the Harry Potter series revolves around the adventures of a young wizard named Harry Potter, his friends, and their quest to defeat the dark wizard Lord Voldemort. Our app draws inspiration from the series' concept of affiliation through four houses, namely Gryffindor (known for courage and bravery), Hufflepuff (emphasizing hard work and patience), Ravenclaw (highlighting intelligence and learning), and Slytherin (representing ambitions and cunning). HarrySpotter was developed using the Unity game engine for both Android and iOS platforms. The app uses the Mapbox SDK for location-based features, and Vuforia SDK to deliver an augmented reality experience, particularly during the process of claiming a mayorship.

HarrySpotter employs six strategies to engage users in the task of annotating objects: Point Rewards, Places Rewards, Game with Yourself, Social Connection, Object Discovery, and Place Discovery. These strategies were initially derived from the work of Lindqvist et al. [24], but were modified to align with our gameplay's requirements. For example, the effectiveness of badges in Lindqvist's study was evaluated using the question statement: "I pay attention to the badges that others earn." In our case, to assess the effectiveness of point rewards (which function as a type of badge), we adapted the statement to: "I pay attention to others' spell energy scores" (Table 1). Additionally, as our gameplay includes

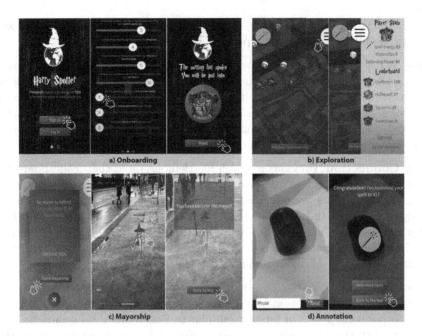

Fig. 1. HarrySpotter's gameplay elements: *a) Onboarding*: set up account and complete the sorting hat quiz; *b) Exploration*: location-based features (e.g., keeping track of mayorship around you), and leaderboard; *c) Mayorship*: AR experience for claiming mayorship (a mage would appear to challenge the user for mayorship); and *d) Annotation:* capture and annotate objects.

two types of rewards—points and place rewards—we categorized them separately, resulting in a total of six strategies, contrasting with the five strategies described in [24].

Point and Place Rewards: Previous research has demonstrated the effectiveness of reward systems, such as points, in engaging users with mobile apps [4]. In HarrySpotter, users are rewarded with spell energy for annotating new objects (Fig. 1d), which reflects their ability to claim mayorships of places. When a user annotates an object, the app compares the user-generated label (object name) with the label automatically detected by an image classifier running on our server. The classifier used is a deep-learning ResNet-162 model with a top 5% accuracy of 94.2% on ImageNet classes. The semantic distance between the user-generated label and the automatically detected label is computed using WordNet [25]. If they match, the user receives extra spell energy. Additionally, the app tracks previously scanned object types and rewards the user when they scan a new type for the first time. However, if the user scans the same object type repeatedly, the reward amount decreases until it reaches the minimum of 10 points. This design choice ensures that the user's score does not reach zero and maintains a balance between engagement and avoiding penalization, such as providing incorrect labels or repetitive images.

Game With Yourself: Users have the option to play the game alone, engaging in various single-player elements such as object annotation, places, and challenging mayorships (Fig. 1b–d). When it comes to mayorships, a user can become the mayor of a place. Subsequently, other users have the opportunity to visit that place and challenge the current mayor. This feature adds a competitive aspect to the game, even when playing individually.

Social Connection: Previous research has demonstrated that leaderboards are effective in enhancing user performance in various tasks [4]. In HarrySpotter, during the onboarding process, users respond to a series of questions inspired by the Harry Potter sorting hat quiz (Fig. 1a) and are sorted into one of the Harry Potter houses [15]. Through the leaderboard, we encourage users to actively participate in the game and contribute to their respective houses' efforts in claiming mayorships of different places.

Object Discovery: Enabling users to explore and discover new places or objects is a crucial aspect of location-based apps. Previous research has demonstrated that incorporating points of interest (similar to Pokémon GO) encourages users to engage with the app while on the move and at various locations [1]. In HarrySpotter, we motivate users to explore different locations by allowing them to become mayors of real places (Fig. 1c). When a user is within the mayorship location range, an AR mage appears and challenges the user for mayorship. The user's spell energy (points) plays a significant role in their chances of claiming the mayorship. To strike the right balance, we set the mayorship range to an 80-meter radius based on empirical evidence. Lower ranges limited accessibility, while higher ranges diminished proximity and overall engagement. Through this strategy, we encourage users to discover and scan objects they may have overlooked in new locations, fostering exploration and engagement.

Place Discovery: Previous research on the motivations behind using location-based apps has revealed that users are driven by their curiosity to obtain information about specific points of interest [24]. This curiosity acts as an incentive for users to actively pursue becoming the mayor of those places. In HarrySpotter, when a user successfully claims mayorships of places, their map visually represents a sense of territorial ownership (Fig. 1b). For example, if a user belongs to Hufflepuff house and becomes a mayor, their map pins will be displayed in yellow, symbolizing their affiliation with Hufflepuff.

5   User Study

Participants and Ethical Considerations. We deployed HarrySpotter in a 2-week study with 29 users (13 female), aged between 18–49 years (median = 34). To be eligible for the study, participants were required to own an Android or iOS smartphone and be located in London, UK. In compliance with GDPR and the Data Protection Act, all individual user data were anonymized to ensure the privacy and confidentiality of the participants. The study was approved by the Ethics Committee of Goldsmiths, University of London.

Procedure. All participants underwent a pre-screening process where we collected demographic information and obtained the unique identifier of their device for generating the app download link. After installing the app, participants were prompted to grant access to the camera and location. Basic instructions were provided on how to use the app, such as annotating objects, with no specific guidelines on what to annotate or how frequently. To maintain study integrity, no information regarding the relationship between personality and engagement techniques was revealed to the participants.

Materials and Apparatus. At the end of the study, we administered a 6-item questionnaire (Table 1) and the 10-item TIPI personality questionnaire [11]. The 6-item questionnaire included statements derived from [24] and had previously been validated in the context of the Foursquare app to assess users' motivations for engagement. Participants rated both questionnaires using a 7-point Likert scale (1: Strongly Disagree; 7: Strongly Agree).

Self-reports and Big-Five Personality Traits. We coded the Likert-scale answers to the 6-item questionnaire and the TIPI [11]. On average, our participants scored as follows on a 1–7 scale: average in Openness ($\mu = 5.14$, $\sigma = 0.8$), high in Conscientiousness ($\mu = 5.12$, $\sigma = 0.85$), average in Neuroticism ($\mu = 4.59$, $\sigma = 0.85$), average in Agreeableness ($\mu = 4.5$, $\sigma = 0.71$), and low in Extraversion ($\mu = 4.43$, $\sigma = 0.94$). These trait distributions aligned with the normative personality values derived from a large sample of the U.S. population [34].

Annotations. Each annotation in our study involved storing the raw image and its corresponding label in a database. To ensure data quality, we implemented checks for image duplication and semantic correctness. To prevent duplication, we utilized FAISS [17], a framework for indexing images based on visual similarity. This allowed us to retrieve the most visually similar images for comparison. We penalized scores for each annotation based on visual similarity to the user's previously uploaded images. For instance, if an image closely resembled a previously captured one, the user would not receive a reward in the form of spell energy. To assess semantic correctness, we first subjected the uploaded image to an off-the-shelf object detector [6]. We then calculated the WordNet semantic distance [25] between the detected label and the user-generated label. The awarded spell energy was proportional to the semantic similarity, discouraging grossly inaccurate or garbled labels. Regarding annotation quantity, we recorded the total number of annotations n_k uploaded by each user k along with their respective images. For annotation quality, three independent annotators rated each annotation on a 1–5 Likert scale, with 5 indicating a perfect match between the image and the user-generated label. For example, if an image depicted a "computer mouse" and the user's label was "mouse," the annotator would assign a score of 5. To ensure reliable results, we calculated a Fleiss kappa score of 0.57, indicating moderate to good agreement among the three annotators. We compiled a set of n images I annotated by each user k as $I_1, I_2, ..., I_n$. The quality score for user k was determined by the median of the quality scores assigned to their n annotated images.

Before using the six self-reports and the quantity and quality of annotation metrics into our regression models, we conducted a Shapiro-Wilk test for normality. As the eight variables exhibited skewed distributions, we applied a log transformation to them. Among the five personality traits, only Extraversion showed a slight skewness, so we also applied a log transformation to it.

6   Results

To ease the interpretation of our results, we applied a min-max transformation to scale our variables within the range of [0–100]. We first examined the pairwise correlation among personality traits, the six self-reports, and the quantity and quality of annotations metrics. We found that neurotic users discovered fewer objects ($r = --0.37, p < 0.1$). Additionally, these users tended to take pride in their mayorships ($r = 0.44, p < 0.05$) and their affiliation with their respective Harry Potter house ($r = 0.47, p < 0.05$). Conversely, Extroverts and those high in Openness liked to discover new objects ($r = 0.44, p < 0.05$ and $r = 0.39, p < 0.05$, respectively) and new places ($r = 0.38, p < 0.05$ and $r = 0.35, p < 0.1$, respectively).

Considering these significant correlations, one might wonder whether it is possible to predict users' personality traits based on their self-reports and the quantity and quality annotation metrics. Using these metrics as predictors, we fitted five linear regression models (Table 2) to predict the Big-Five personality dimensions and determined the best set of predictors using the stepAIC function [37]. Overall, our findings indicate that predicting certain personality dimensions, such as Extraversion (Adj. $R^2 = 0.61$), was relatively easier compared to others like Conscientiousness (Adj. $R^2 = 0.16$).

As expected, users with non-competitive traits (high in Agreeableness) demonstrated a lack of motivation for competing with others ($\beta_{(Q1(\text{Point Rewards}))} = -0.45$). On the other hand, conscientious users, known for their organizational skills, exhibited motivation for competition ($\beta_{(Q1(\text{Point Rewards}))} = 0.59$) among the four houses but moderately predicted their personality trait (Adj. $R^2 = 0.16$). Individuals open to new experiences and extroverts were primarily motivated by the discovery of new objects ($\beta_{(Q5(\text{Object Discovery}))} = 0.84$ and $\beta_{(Q5(\text{Object Discovery}))} = 0.53$, respectively). Moreover, individuals open to new experiences did not find motivation in competing with others ($\beta_{(Q1)} = -1.08$), while extroverts were not motivated by mayorships ($\beta_{(Q2(\text{Place Rewards}))} = -0.60$) or representing their own house ($\beta_{(Q1(\text{Point Rewards}))} = -0.72$). Emotionally unstable users (neurotics) found motivation in representing their own house ($\beta_{(Q4(\text{Social Connection}))} = 0.58$) but not in the discovery of new places ($\beta_{(Q6(\text{Place Discovery}))} = -0.58$), leading them to discover fewer objects ($\beta_{(\text{Quantity})} = -0.32$).

Table 2. Linear regressions that predict the Big-Five personality traits from the six self-reports and the quantity and quality of annotations. Significant predictors with p values $< .05$ are marked in bold. The most predictable personality trait was Extraversion (M_E), while the least predictable was Conscientiousness (M_C).

M_O: Adj $R^2 = 0.28$, Durbin-Watson = 1.96, AIC = 0.47			
Predictor	β	std. error	p-value
Intercept	0.42	0.13	0.005
Q1 (Point Rewards)	−1.08	0.36	**0.01**
Q2 (Place Rewards)	0.42	0.35	0.23
Q5 (Object Discover)	0.84	0.27	**0.01**
M_C: Adj $R^2 = 0.16$, Durbin-Watson = 1.15, AIC = −7.48			
Predictor	β	std. error	p-value
Intercept	0.57	0.12	0.00
Q3 (Game with Yourself)	0.59	0.22	**0.01**
Q6 (Place Discovery)	−0.48	0.23	**0.04**
M_E: Adj $R^2 = 0.61$, Durbin-Watson = 1.88, AIC = −14			
Predictor	β	std. error	p-value
Intercept	0.48	0.19	0.02
Q2 (Place Rewards)	−0.60	0.22	**0.01**
Q4 (Social Connection)	−0.72	0.22	**0.00**
Q5 (Object Discovery)	0.53	0.22	**0.02**
Q6 (Place Discovery)	0.99	0.28	**0.00**
Quantity	−0.37	0.12	**0.00**
Quality	0.18	0.16	0.27
M_A: Adj $R^2 = 0.21$, Durbin-Watson = 1.84, AIC = −12.86			
Predictor	β	std. error	p-value
Intercept	0.57	0.11	0.00
Q1 (Point Rewards)	−0.45	0.24	0.07
Q3 (Game with Yourself)	0.21	0.21	0.31
Q5 (Object Discovery)	−0.37	0.24	0.13
Q6 (Place Discovery)	0.71	0.29	**0.02**
M_N: Adj $R^2 = 0.32$, Durbin-Watson = 2.79, AIC = −3.68			
Predictor	β	std. error	p-value
Intercept	0.36	0.14	0.02
Q2 (Place Rewards)	0.37	0.26	0.17
Q4 (Social Connection)	0.58	0.27	**0.04**
Q6 (Place Discovery)	−0.58	0.29	0.06
Quantity	−0.32	0.14	**0.03**

7   Discussion and Conclusion

Mobile user engagement is commonly pursued through a range of techniques; however, there is a tendency to apply these techniques uniformly to all users, adopting a one-size-fits-all approach. To investigate the possibility that individuals may perceive engagement techniques differently, we created HarrySpotter, a location-based augmented reality (AR) app that enables users to annotate real-world objects using six distinct engagement techniques. By deploying HarrySpotter and analyzing data from 29 users, we found that agreeable users were not motivated by competition, while conscientious users were motivated by it to a greater extent. As expected, individuals open to new experiences and extroverts were motivated by exploration, while neurotics exhibited a stronger drive towards personal achievements. These preferences for specific engagement techniques also predicted personality traits to different extents (e.g., Extraversion with an Adj. R^2 of 0.61, while Conscientiousness with an Adj. R^2 of 0.16), suggesting that engagement strategies should be tailored to one's personality.

From a theoretical perspective, our work is situated within the domain of adaptive user interfaces (AUI). The effectiveness of an AUI hinges on the ability to construct and utilize individual user profiles, allowing for the delivery of personalized versions of the user interface [7–9, 16]. Building upon this foundation, we envision that our methodology could be employed to enhance user models with specific characteristics, such as personality traits. This, in turn, could facilitate the personalization of user interfaces in various contexts, such as advancing levels in a gamified app or completing tasks. From a practical standpoint, our findings can inform the design of personalized engagement strategies. To illustrate, let us consider the scenario of mobile crowdsourcing systems, where a one-size-fits-all approach has proven ineffective in engaging users for specific tasks, such as object annotation [33]. By incorporating brief personality questionnaires, for example during account setup (e.g., the TIPI [11] questionnaire, which can be completed in a minute), mobile developers can implement in-app mechanisms to dynamically infer personality traits, thereby adapting engagement strategies based on users' interactions.

Our work has three limitations that warrant further research efforts. Firstly, our findings are specific to the HarrySpotter game and this particular cohort. Future studies could extend our methodology to different types of mobile apps. For example, developing tailored strategies for Conscientiousness could enhance prediction accuracy by incorporating logging mechanisms for organized individuals. Secondly, the slight skew in Extraversion may be due to self-selection bias, as introverted individuals are less likely to engage with such apps. Future studies should replicate our methodology with larger and culturally diverse populations. Lastly, while our two-week study provided ample data, longer deployments can explore user retention and preferences more comprehensively, thereby enhancing our understanding of personalized engagement strategies.

References

1. Althoff, T., White, R.W., Horvitz, E.: Influence of pokémon go on physical activity: study and implications. J. Med. Internet Res. **18**(12), e315 (2016). https://doi.org/10.2196/jmir.6759
2. Amichai-Hamburger, Y., Vinitzky, G.: Social network use and personality. Comput. Hum. Behav. **26**(6), 1289–1295 (2010). https://doi.org/10.1016/j.chb.2010.03.018
3. Bachrach, Y., Kosinski, M., Graepel, T., Kohli, P., Stillwell, D.: Personality and patterns of facebook usage. In: Proceedings of the ACM Web Science Conference, pp. 24–32 (2012). https://doi.org/10.1145/2380718.2380722
4. Bräuer, P., Mazarakis, A.: Badges or a leaderboard? How to gamify an augmented reality warehouse setting. In: GamiFIN, pp. 229–240 (2019). https://ceur-ws.org/Vol-2359/paper20.pdf
5. Butt, S., Phillips, J.G.: Personality and self reported mobile phone use. Comput. Hum. Behav. **24**(2), 346–360 (2008). https://doi.org/10.1016/j.chb.2007.01.019
6. Cheng, B., et al.: Panoptic-deeplab. In: ICCV COCO + Mapillary Joint Recognition Challenge Workshop (2019)
7. Constantinides, M., Dowell, J.: User interface personalization in news apps. In: CEUR Workshop Proceedings, vol. 1618 (2016). https://ceur-ws.org/Vol-1618/INRA_paper2.pdf
8. Constantinides, M., Dowell, J.: A framework for interaction-driven user modeling of mobile news reading behaviour. In: Proceedings of the 26th Conference on User Modeling, Adaptation and Personalization, pp. 33–41 (2018). https://doi.org/10.1145/3209219.3209229
9. Constantinides, M., Dowell, J., Johnson, D., Malacria, S.: Exploring mobile news reading interactions for news app personalisation. In: Proceedings of the ACM International Conference on Human-Computer Interaction with Mobile Devices and Services, pp. 457–462 (2015). https://doi.org/10.1145/2785830.2785860
10. Deterding, S.: Gamification: designing for motivation. Interactions **19**(4), 14–17 (2012). https://doi.org/10.1145/2212877.2212883
11. Gosling, S.D., Rentfrow, P.J., Swann, W.B., Jr.: A very brief measure of the big-five personality domains. J. Res. Personal. **37**(6), 504–528 (2003). https://doi.org/10.1016/S0092-6566(03)00046-1
12. Hakulinen, L., Auvinen, T., Korhonen, A.: The effect of achievement badges on students' behavior: an empirical study in a university-level computer science course. Int. J. Emerg. Technol. Learn. **10**(1) (2015). https://doi.org/10.3991/ijet.v10i1.4221
13. Halko, S., Kientz, J.A.: Personality and persuasive technology: an exploratory study on health-promoting mobile applications. In: Ploug, T., Hasle, P., Oinas-Kukkonen, H. (eds.) Persuasive 2010. LNCS, vol. 6137, pp. 150–161. Springer, Heidelberg (2010). https://doi.org/10.1007/978-3-642-13226-1_16
14. Hamari, J., Koivisto, J., Sarsa, H.: Does gamification work?-a literature review of empirical studies on gamification. In: 2014 47th Hawaii International Conference on System Sciences, pp. 3025–3034. IEEE (2014). https://doi.org/10.1109/HICSS.2014.377
15. Jakob, L., Garcia-Garzon, E., Jarke, H., Dablander, F.: The science behind the magic? The relation of the harry potter "sorting hat quiz" to personality and human values. Collabra: Psychol. **5**(1) (2019). https://doi.org/10.1525/collabra.240

16. Jameson, A.: Adaptive interfaces and agents. In: The Human-Computer Interaction Handbook, pp. 459–484. CRC Press (2007)

17. Johnson, J., Douze, M., Jégou, H.: Billion-scale similarity search with gpus. IEEE Trans. Big Data (2019). https://doi.org/10.1109/TBDATA.2019.2921572

18. Kim, S., Baek, T.H.: Examining the antecedents and consequences of mobile app engagement. Telemat. Informat. **35**(1), 148–158 (2018). https://doi.org/10.1016/j.tele.2017.10.008

19. Kosinski, M., Bachrach, Y., Kohli, P., Stillwell, D., Graepel, T.: Manifestations of user personality in website choice and behaviour on online social networks. Mach. Learn. **95**(3), 357–380 (2013). https://doi.org/10.1007/s10994-013-5415-y

20. Lalmas, M., O'Brien, H., Yom-Tov, E.: Measuring user engagement. Synth. Lect. Inf. Concept. Retriev. Serv. **6**(4), 1–132 (2014). https://doi.org/10.2200/S00605ED1V01Y201410ICR038

21. Lane, W.: The influence of personality traits on mobile phone application preferences. J. Econ. Behav. Stud. **4**(5), 252–260 (2012). https://doi.org/10.22610/jebs.v4i5.325

22. Leiras, M.: Mobile User Engagement: New Apps versus Mainstream Apps. Ph.D. thesis, Universidade do Porto (Portugal) (2017)

23. Levitas, D.: There is no one-size-fits-all approach to mobile apps (2017). https://www.adexchanger.com/data-driven-thinking/no-one-size-fits-approach-mobile-apps/. Accessed June 2023

24. Lindqvist, J., Cranshaw, J., Wiese, J., Hong, J., Zimmerman, J.: I'm the mayor of my house: examining why people use foursquare-a social-driven location sharing application. In: Proceedings of the ACM CHI Conference on Human Factors in Computing Systems, pp. 2409–2418 (2011). https://doi.org/10.1145/1978942.1979295

25. Miller, G.A.: WordNet: An Electronic Lexical Database. MIT Press (1998)

26. Niantic: PokemonGo (2016). https://pokemongolive.com. Accessed April 2023

27. Nicholson, S.: A RECIPE for meaningful gamification. In: Reiners, T., Wood, L.C. (eds.) Gamification in Education and Business, pp. 1–20. Springer, Cham (2015). https://doi.org/10.1007/978-3-319-10208-5_1

28. O'Brien, H.L., Toms, E.G.: What is user engagement? A conceptual framework for defining user engagement with technology. J. Am. Soc. Inf. Sci. Technol. **59**(6), 938–955 (2008). https://doi.org/10.1002/asi.20801

29. Phillips, J.G., Butt, S., Blaszczynski, A.: Personality and self-reported use of mobile phones for games. CyberPsychol. Behav. **9**(6), 753–758 (2006). https://doi.org/10.1089/cpb.2006.9.753

30. Quercia, D., Kosinski, M., Stillwell, D., Crowcroft, J.: Our twitter profiles, our selves: predicting personality with twitter. In: Proccedings of the 2011 IEEE Third International Conference on Privacy, Security, Risk and Trust and 2011 IEEE Third International Conference on Social Computing, pp. 180–185. IEEE (2011). https://doi.org/10.1109/PASSAT/SocialCom.2011.26

31. Ross, C., Orr, E.S., Sisic, M., Arseneault, J.M., Simmering, M.G., Orr, R.R.: Personality and motivations associated with Facebook use. Comput. Hum. Behav. **25**(2), 578–586 (2009). https://doi.org/10.1016/j.chb.2008.12.024

32. van Roy, R., Deterding, S., Zaman, B.: Collecting pokémon or receiving rewards? how people functionalise badges in gamified online learning environments in the wild. Int. J. Hum. Comput. Stud. **127**, 62–80 (2019). https://doi.org/10.1016/j.ijhcs.2018.09.003

33. Rula, J.P., Navda, V., Bustamante, F.E., Bhagwan, R., Guha, S.: No "one-size fits all" towards a principled approach for incentives in mobile crowdsourcing. In: Proceedings of the Workshop on Mobile Computing Systems and Applications, pp. 1–5 (2014). https://doi.org/10.1145/2565585.2565603
34. Soto, C.J., John, O.P., Gosling, S.D., Potter, J.: Age differences in personality traits from 10 to 65: big five domains and facets in a large cross-sectional sample. J. Personal. Soc. Psychol. **100**(2), 330 (2011). https://doi.org/10.1037/a0021717
35. Stachl, C., et al.: Predicting personality from patterns of behavior collected with smartphones. Proc. Natl. Acad. Sci. **117**(30), 17680–17687 (2020). https://doi.org/10.1073/pnas.1920484117
36. Sutcliffe, A.: Designing for user experience and engagement. In: Why Engagement Matters: Cross-Disciplinary Perspectives of User Engagement in Digital Media, pp. 105–126 (2016). https://doi.org/10.1007/978-3-319-27446-1_5
37. Zhang, Z.: Variable selection with stepwise and best subset approaches. Ann. Transl. Med. **4**(7) (2016). https://doi.org/10.21037/atm.2016.03.35

Turn & Slide: Designing a Puzzle Game to Elicit the Visualizer-Verbalizer Cognitive Style

Sotirios Petsas[1], George E. Raptis[2(✉)], and Christos Katsanos[1]

[1] Aristotle University of Thessaloniki, Thessaloniki, Greece
{petsassg,ckatsanos}@csd.auth.gr
[2] Human Opsis, Patras, Greece
graptis@humanopsis.com

Abstract. Cognitive theories suggest that people differ in processing information, reflecting their different cognitive styles. Research in Human-Computer Interaction has revealed that people with different cognitive styles develop different strategies, achieve different performances, and have different experiences when interacting with information systems. Aiming to provide unique experiences, we need to personalize such systems to support their users' cognitive styles. However, eliciting users' cognitive styles is a time-consuming and non-practical process requiring human intervention. To overcome this, we present the design of *Turn & Slide*. This web-based puzzle game aims to elicit Visualizer-Verbalizer, a well-established cognitive style, implicitly and with no human intervention. We also report the results of an evaluation user study, which revealed that the elicitation is feasible. Such results could increase the practicability and applicability of elicitation techniques, enabling designers to deliver tailored experiences, adapted to their users' cognitive styles.

Keywords: Cognitive styles · Visualizer-Verbalizer · Elicitation · Machine Learning · Classification · Games · User study

1 Introduction

People have different cognitive characteristics, resulting in different strategies to seek, represent, process, and retrieve information. These strategies often reflect *cognitive styles*. Cognitive styles describe an individual's preferred mode of processing and recalling information, tackling information retrieval problems, and regulating and controlling their cognitive functioning [15]; they also influence collaboration and communication interactions [1]. Various cognitive styles can be utilized during different phases of cognitive processing, such as perception, information organization, and inductive reasoning.

A well-established cognitive style is the Visualizer-Verbalizer (VV) cognitive style [15], which refers to an individual's preference for processing and representing information visually or verbally. People with strong visual preferences

© The Author(s), under exclusive license to Springer Nature Switzerland AG 2023
J. Abdelnour Nocera et al. (Eds.): INTERACT 2023, LNCS 14145, pp. 46–56, 2023.
https://doi.org/10.1007/978-3-031-42293-5_4

use mental images and spatial representations, while those with strong verbal preferences use words and linguistic representations. The Visualizer dimension can be further divided into spatial and object dimensions. The spatial dimension reflects the preference for visual or spatial representation, while the object dimension reflects the preference for concrete or abstract representation.

Research works have shown that VV influences several dimensions of human-computer interaction (HCI), such as performance and satisfaction [12,16,17]; thus, it is important to deliver users with VV personalized experiences [24]. To deliver such personalized experiences, eliciting the VV cognitive style is crucial. Eliciting VV traditionally involves non-technological approaches (e.g., questionnaires), which can be time-consuming. Moreover, they typically require a facilitator to administer the questionnaire and an evaluator to analyze the provided answers. Such requirements make delivering personalized experiences tailored to users' cognitive styles non-practical.

In this paper, we tackle the challenges of eliciting the VV cognitive style through a gameful approach. Our proposed game, *Turn & Slide*, aims to accurately and efficiently predict the VV cognitive style without human intervention. We utilized supervised machine learning techniques and conducted an evaluation study to measure their performance. The rest of the paper is organized as follows: i) we provide the theoretical background and review related work, ii) we present the game's design, iii) we describe the evaluation study we conducted, and iv) we discuss the implications of our findings.

2 Background, Related Work, and Research Question

This section discusses the Visualizer-Verbalizer (VV) cognitive style and synthesizes prior research on VV elicitation techniques and games.

2.1 Visualizer-Verbalizer (VV)

The VV cognitive style is based on the dual-coding theory [21] and describes individual preferences for processing visual versus verbal information. Visualizers tend to think concretely and personalize information. On the other hand, verbalizers prefer to process information through words and are more objective [10]. High-imagery ability is linked to visualizers, while low-imagery ability is linked to verbalizers [4,14]. Verbalizers excel at reading and sequential information-processing tasks, while visualizers excel at visual search and structured information-processing tasks [12]. Recent research [3,15] divides visualizers to object- and spatial-visualizers. Object-visualizers have a strong ability to visualize and manipulate images of objects, such as shapes, figures, and patterns and may excel at tasks that require mental manipulation of objects, such as jigsaw puzzles or assembling models. On the other hand, spatial-visualizers have a strong ability to visualize and manipulate spatial information, such as maps, graphs, and three-dimensional (3D) objects. They tend to think in terms of pictures and mental images and may use strategies such as mental rotation to solve spatial problems.

2.2   Elicitation Techniques for VV

Several tools have been proposed for the VV elicitation, including Verbal-Visual Learning Style Rating (VVLSR) [19], Individual Differences Questionnaire - Visual Scale [22], Santa Barbara Learning Style Questionnaire (SBLSQ) [19], Vividness of Visual Imagery Questionnaire (VVIQ) [18], Verbalizer-Visualizer Questionnaire (VVQ) [26], and Object-Spatial Imagery and Verbal Questionnaire (OSIVQ) [3]. They are all based on questionnaires; thus, they follow non-technological and explicit methods. Such tests are typically time-consuming, must be performed before the users interact with the system, and require human intervention (e.g., a supervisor to invigilate the users during the questionnaires session, a facilitator to assess the users' answers and classify them in one of the VV classes).

The explicit elicitation of VV and issues like the aforementioned ones challenge the delivery of personalized experiences. Recent research provides evidence that the VV cognitive style can be inferred implicitly through interactive and eye-tracking data analysis when users view visual and textual stimuli [16], when they visually explore artworks [24], etc. These mechanisms are highly dependent on activity-specific parameters and/or require expensive and specialized equipment (e.g., head-mounted eye-tracking devices); thus, providing a generally applicable elicitation solution is difficult. Hence, it is crucial to enhance the real-time implicit elicitation of the VV cognitive style by employing easily deployable and integrable activities that utilize conventional tools and offer an enjoyable experience to the user. A promising way to achieve this is through playing games.

2.3   Games as Elicitation Tools

In recent years, games and gamification have gained popularity as they provide users with a fun and enjoyable alternative to achieving their objectives in various domains (e.g., education, training) while enhancing their performance and experience [11]. Games and gamification have been utilized in various contexts to elicit users' characteristics and behaviors, including emergency situations [2], requirements collection [5], disaster risk scenarios [6], software engineering [7], distributed requirements elicitation [8], and entertainment, where the elicitation focuses on experience factors such as awe [23]. Focusing on the cognitive styles, games and gamification techniques have been used to infer cognitive styles, such as Field Dependence-Independence [24,27]. However, the use of games to elicit the VV cognitive style has not been explored yet.

2.4   Synthesis of Prior Work

In summary of the preceding discussion, it is crucial to implicitly elicit the VV cognitive style in real-time through easy-to-use, affordable, and entertaining means like games. As such, this paper introduces the design and evaluation of *Turn & Slide*, a spatial puzzle game designed to implicitly elicit the VV cognitive style of its users.

3   *Turn & Slide*

We followed the Kaleidoscope framework [13] to design *Turn & Slide*. The following sections discuss the design decisions that reflect the framework's dimensions: type, game experience, supporting motivated behavior, perceived layer of fun, and workflow. We also briefly discuss the deployment of the game.

Type. *Turn & Slide* is a spatial puzzle game, inspired by *Paper Mario: The Origami King*. We selected this type of game, considering that such games could favor visualizers over verbalizers in identifying visual elements as parts of the puzzle and also favor spatial visualizers over object visualizers in handling game elements, such as rotate and slide rings. Hence, such a game would be a good fit for eliciting the VV cognitive style.

Building the Game Experience. *Turn & Slide* requires various skills, including strategic thinking, problem solving, spatial awareness, patience, and persistence. Each game puzzle consists of concentric regular polygons and looks like a spider's web. Line segments starting from each vertex of the polygon and ending at the center (of the circle circumscribed in each polygon) divide each polygon into areas equal to the number of its sides. The number of polygons (hereafter "rings") as well as the number of their areas (hereafter "slices") varies according to the puzzle's difficulty. Each ring has "balls" that the player must bring to the appropriate position so that they form either *straight lines* or *squares* (e.g., 4×1 or 2×2 respectively for 4 balls placed on 4 rings). To do so, the players can either rotate (turn) a ring or slide the balls (Fig. 1). The game has four different difficulty levels, which are characterized by the type of valid actions, number of rings, number of slices, and maximum number of actions. They are: easy (only turns, 10 slices, 4 rings, 2 actions), normal (only turns or only slides, 12 slices, 4 rings, 2 actions), hard (all types, 12 slices, 4 rings, 2 actions) and, super hard (all types, 14 slices, 5 rings, 3 actions).

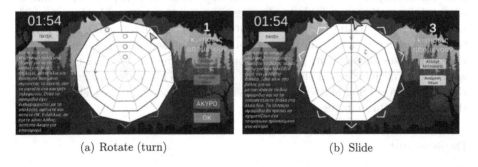

(a) Rotate (turn)   (b) Slide

Fig. 1. *Turn & Slide* supports two types of action: (a) the player can rotate (turn) each ring clockwise or counterclockwise, and (b) slide the balls across a slice.

Supporting Motivated Behavior. We introduced features based on rankings and leaderboards, as they keep players motivated [9, 25]. The players earn points while playing, and after the game, they can view their position against other players. The more difficult the level is, the more points the player earns.

Building the Perceived Layer of Fun. We incorporated various elements to enhance the players' experience and create a sense of fun in the game. These elements include exciting and surprising features, such as animations, transitional screens with visualization effects, and background music. By introducing these attributes, we aimed to create an immersive gaming experience that would enhance player engagement and enjoyment.

Workflow. The workflow of the game is the following: i) The users log in to the game by entering their e-mail address; ii) The main menu is displayed, which provides the users with several options, including instructions on how to play the game, a leaderboard that displays the high scores, a score section that shows the user's score, and the "PLAY" button that the user can click to start playing the game; iii) When the users click the "PLAY" button, they are presented with an interactive tutorial that educates them on how to play the game. This tutorial is specifically designed for first-time users to ensure that they have a smooth and easy start to the game. Once the user has completed the tutorial, the game is ready to start; iv) The game begins, and the main screen (as shown in Fig. 1) displays the rings, slices, and balls that make up the puzzle. In addition to these puzzle elements, there are several buttons available to the user for additional options. These buttons include the "PAUSE" button, which allows the user to pause the game at any time, the "CHANGE MODE" button, which enables the user to switch between the "rotate" and "slice" action modes, the "RESET" button, which starts the puzzle over from the beginning, the "CANCEL" button, which allows the user to undo their last action, and the "OK" button, which confirms the user's action. Additionally, the top left of the screen displays the time remaining for the puzzle, while the top right part displays the number of remaining actions available to the user. These features provide the user with important information to help them strategize and complete the puzzle; v) After the user completes a puzzle, the next puzzle in the sequence is loaded. As the user progresses through the game, the puzzles become increasingly challenging, with a gradual increase in the degree of difficulty. This allows users to develop their problem-solving skills and progressively face more complex challenges as they advance through the game.

Deployment

We used the Unity game engine to develop the game, as it provides cross-platform compatibility, seamless integration with mobile and web features, and supports various programming languages (we used C#). We deployed *Turn & Slide* as a web application and delivered it through the Firebase platform.

4   Study

4.1   Method

Hypothesis. *Turn & Slide* can be used as an implicit elicitation mechanism for the VV cognitive style.

Participants. We recruited 85 study participants (58 men and 27 women) of varying age (minimum: 18 years, maximum: 57 years, $M = 24$, $SD = 7$) and educational background. Most of them had experience playing games. We used OSIVQ [3] to classify them as verbalizers, object visualizers, or spatial visualizers. Our sample consisted of 15 verbalizers, 47 object visualizers, and 23 spatial visualizers.

Tools and Apparatus. Aiming to have an increased ecological validity, the participants played the game on their own computer devices; they reported no issues. For the implicit VV classification, we used `Python` and `Scikit-learn` library; we tested several machine learning techniques, including Logistic Regression, k-Nearest Neighbors (kNN), Naive Bayes, Decision Trees, and Support Vector Machine and Classification (SVM, SVC).

Data. We collected data throughout the gameplay. For each puzzle, we recorded several key metrics, including the number of actions (`actions`), number of rotations/turns (`turns`), number of slides (`slides`), time required for the first action (`fist_action_time`), average time between actions (`avg_action_time`), number of cancellations (`cancels`), number of resets (`manual_rev`), number of automatic resets because of time limitations (`auto_rev`), time needed to solve the puzzle (`time`), result: win or loss (`win`), score (`score`), and total time needed to solve all puzzles up to that point (`total_time`). These metrics were used as features for the VV classification, providing valuable insights into how players interacted with and progressed through the game.

Procedure. To investigate our hypothesis, we conducted a between-subjects study with the following procedure: i) we recruited the study participants using varying methods, including personal contacts and social media announcements; ii) the participants undertook OSIVQ and were classified as verbalizers, object visualizers, or spatial visualizers; iii) each participant played *Turn & Slide*; to avoid bias, the sequence of puzzles remained the same for all participants; iv) during the game-playing session, we collected various data (discussed before), which then we used to analyze, train, and test our machine learning models. v) we performed the implicit classification procedure based on machine learning techniques. We followed a three-step approach: feature selection, classifier selection, and classifier optimization. We followed various approaches to prevent overfitting, including removing features and early stopping.

4.2   Results

We present the best results regarding each difficulty level's mean accuracy and standard deviation with the automatically selected parameter values, using the five best features (Table 1). The analysis performed across a range of classification models, using cross-validation with $k = 5$.

Table 1. Best results derived for VV classification for each difficulty level.

Difficulty	Model	Features	Parameters	Accuracy M	SD
Easy	SVC	slides, cancels, auto_rev, time, total_time	"C": 10, "degree": 3, "gamma": "auto", "kernel": "poly"	.560	.026
Normal	Decision Tree	moves, slides, first_action_time avg_action_time, total_time	"criterion": "gini", "max_depth": 2	.560	.026
Hard	Decision Tree	turns, slides, avg_action_time cancels, total_time	"criterion": "gini", "max_depth": 2	.571	.058
Super hard	SVC	first_action_time, avg_action_time, manual_rev, time, win	"C": 0.1, "gamma": "auto", "kernel": "rbf"	.560	.026

The average accuracy of the models is close to 56%, which is an improvement over the baseline accuracy set by the three classes (33.3%). However, these results still fall short of our desired performance level. To address this issue, we allowed each model to accept all possible combinations of features from the set, up to a maximum of 8. We then selected the best results, favoring to those achieved with fewer features in case of a tie. This approach allowed us to identify the most effective feature combinations and improve the accuracy of our VV classification model up to approximately 68% for the hard difficulty level (see Table 2).

Table 2. Best results derived for VV classification after optimization.

Difficulty	Model	Features	Parameters	Accuracy M	SD
Easy	SVC	turns, cancels, avg_action_time, manual_rev, win, score	gamma="auto" C=10	.643	.029
Normal	kNN	auto_rev, total_time	algorithm="ball_tree" leaf_size=20, n_neighbors=5	.667	.118
Hard	SVC	turns, slides, avg_action_time, cancels, auto_rev, manual_rev	gamma="auto" C=10	.679	.113
Super hard	SVC	moves, turns, first_action_time, avg_action_time, manual_rev, time	gamma="auto" C=10	.668	.085

The per-class analysis shows that the model favors the elicitation of spatial visualizers ($TP = 20$, $ACC = .870$, $F_1 = .851$). Elicitation of verbalizers ($TP = 9$, $ACC = .600$, $F_1 = .690$) and object visualizers ($TP = 29$, $ACC = .617$, $F_1 = .587$) is above baseline, but still low. Future work should optimize these two classes' classification to improve overall performance.

5   Discussion, Limitations, and Future Work

In this paper, we introduced *Turn & Slide*, a spatial puzzle game designed to implicitly elicit the VV cognitive style without human intervention. We conducted a user study with 85 participants who played the game, and their data were used to train and test machine learning models to predict the VV cognitive style. Our classification experiments showed that the VV cognitive style could be predicted with an accuracy of 68% for the hard difficulty level. The best performance was achieved using an SVC classifier and six features derived from the gameplay, as shown in Table 2. Our approach allows for the transparent elicitation of the VV cognitive style in real-time while the user plays the game's hard difficulty level, without requiring human intervention. Our findings offer practical support for considering cognitive factors in the design of personalized experiences. Designers can leverage easy-to-integrate gameful methods to elicit the VV cognitive style without relying on conventional and explicit techniques such as administering questionnaires or tests. This study provides empirical evidence for the feasibility of the implicit VV elicitation, which can help facilitate the development of personalized experiences that cater to users' cognitive styles.

Although our study shows promising results for predicting the VV cognitive style using gameplay data, the accuracy achieved by our models is relatively low. One reason could be the limited sample size used in our study. We acknowledge this limitation and plan to increase the sample size in future studies. Additionally, we believe that incorporating additional metrics, such as eye-tracking data, could improve the accuracy of our predictions, as has been shown in other studies [24]. Furthermore, our sample is skewed toward men. Given the controversy surrounding the relationship between cognitive style and gender [20, 28], we should consider a more balanced sample to avoid potential biases. We found no correlation between gender and VV cognitive style or OSIVQ scores in our sample. Our sample is also skewed towards object visualizers (47/85), which might limit the generalizability of our findings. Therefore, our next steps include increasing the sample size, exploring the use of additional data, and ensuring a more balanced sample.

6   Conclusion

In this paper, we presented the design of *Turn & Slide*, a puzzle game that triggers users' strategic thinking and spatial awareness and can be used to elicit their Visualizer-Verbalizer cognitive style. We also performed an evaluation study in which we employed machine learning techniques. The study's results revealed that the users' cognitive style can be identified while interacting with the game. The results are promising for considering cognitive styles as a human factor when developing personalized interactive applications.

References

1. Alharthi, S.A., Raptis, G.E., Katsini, C., Dolgov, I., Nacke, L.E., Toups, Z.O.: Investigating the effects of individual cognitive styles on collaborative gameplay. ACM Trans. Comput. Hum. Interact. **28**(4) (2021). https://doi.org/10.1145/3445792
2. Almeida, J.E., Jacob, J.T.P.N., Faria, B.M., Rossetti, R.J.F., Leça Coelho, A.: Serious games for the elicitation of way-finding behaviours in emergency situations. In: 2014 9th Iberian Conference on Information Systems and Technologies (CISTI), pp. 1–7. IEEE, Red Hook (2014). https://doi.org/10.1109/CISTI.2014.6876951
3. Blazhenkova, O., Kozhevnikov, M.: The new object-spatial-verbal cognitive style model: theory and measurement. Appl. Cognit. Psychol. **23**(5), 638–663 (2009). https://doi.org/10.1002/acp.1473
4. Di Vesta, F.J., Ingersoll, G., Sunshine, P.: A factor analysis of imagery tests. J. Verb. Learn. Verb. Behav. **10**(5), 471–479 (1971). https://doi.org/10.1016/s0022-5371(71)80017-8
5. Fernandes, J., Duarte, D., Ribeiro, C., Farinha, C., Pereira, J.M., da Silva, M.M.: iThink: a game-based towards improving collaboration and participation in requirement elicitation. Proc. Comput. Sci. **15**, 66–77 (2012). https://doi.org/10.1016/j.procs.2012.10.059
6. Fleming, K., et al.: The use of serious games in engaging stakeholders for disaster risk reduction, management and climate change adaption information elicitation. Int. J. Disast. Risk Reduct. **49**, 101669 (2020). https://doi.org/10.1016/j.ijdrr.2020.101669
7. Garcia, I., Pacheco, C., León, A., Calvo-Manzano, J.A.: Experiences of using a game for improving learning in software requirements elicitation. Comput. Appl. Eng. Educ. **27**(1), 249–265 (2018). https://doi.org/10.1002/cae.22072
8. Ghanbari, H., Similä, J., Markkula, J.: Utilizing online serious games to facilitate distributed requirements elicitation. J. Syst. Softw. **109**, 32–49 (2015). https://doi.org/10.1016/j.jss.2015.07.017
9. Halan, S., Rossen, B., Cendan, J., Lok, B.: High Score! - Motivation strategies for user participation in virtual human development. In: Allbeck, J., Badler, N., Bickmore, T., Pelachaud, C., Safonova, A. (eds.) IVA 2010. LNCS (LNAI), vol. 6356, pp. 482–488. Springer, Heidelberg (2010). https://doi.org/10.1007/978-3-642-15892-6_52
10. Hollenberg, C.K.: Functions of visual imagery in the learning and concept formation of children. Child Develop. **41**(4), 1003 (1970). https://doi.org/10.2307/1127328
11. Iacovides, I., Cox, A.L.: Moving beyond fun: evaluating serious experience in digital games. In: Proceedings of the 33rd Annual ACM Conference on Human Factors in Computing Systems (CHI 2015), pp. 2245–2254. Association for Computing Machinery, New York (2015). https://doi.org/10.1145/2702123.2702204
12. Jonassen, D.H., Grabowski, B.L.: Handbook of Individual Differences, Learning, and Instruction. Routledge (2012)

13. Kappen, D.L., Nacke, L.E.: The kaleidoscope of effective gamification: deconstructing gamification in business applications. In: Proceedings of the First International Conference on Gameful Design, Research, and Applications (Gamification 2013), pp. 119–122. Association for Computing Machinery, New York (2013). https://doi.org/10.1145/2583008.2583029

14. Kirby, J.R., Moore, P.J., Schofield, N.J.: Verbal and visual learning styles. Contemp. Educ. Psychol. **13**(2), 169–184 (1988). https://doi.org/10.1016/0361-476x(88)90017-3

15. Kozhevnikov, M.: Cognitive styles in the context of modern psychology: toward an integrated framework of cognitive style. Psychol. Bullet. **133**(3) (2007)

16. Koć-Januchta, M., Höffler, T., Thoma, G.B., Prechtl, H., Leutner, D.: Visualizers versus verbalizers: effects of cognitive style on learning with texts and pictures - an eye tracking study. Comput. Hum. Behav. **68**, 170–179 (2017). https://doi.org/10.1016/j.chb.2016.11.028

17. Luo, Z., Wang, Y.: Eye-tracking technology in identifying visualizers and verbalizers: data on eye-movement differences and detection accuracy. Data Brief **26**, 104447 (2019). https://doi.org/10.1016/j.dib.2019.104447

18. Marks, D.F.: Visual mental imagery in the recall of pictures. Br. J. Psychol. **64**, 17–24 (1973). https://doi.org/10.1111/j.2044-8295.1973.tb01322.x

19. Mayer, R.E., Massa, L.J.: Three facets of visual and verbal learners: cognitive ability, cognitive style, and learning preference. J. Educ. Psychol. **95**(4), 833–846 (2003). https://doi.org/10.1037/0022-0663.95.4.833

20. Onyekuru, B.U.: Field dependence-field independence cognitive style, gender, career choice and academic achievement of secondary school students in emohua local government area of rivers state. J. Educ. Pract. **6**(10), 76–85 (2015)

21. Paivio, A.: Mental representations: a dual-coding approach. Oxford University Press, New York (1986). https://doi.org/10.1093/acprof:oso/9780195066661.001.0001

22. Paivio, A., Harshman, R.: Factor analysis of a questionnaire on imagery and verbal habits and skills. Canadian J. Psychol. Rev. Canad. Psychol. **37**(4), 461 (1983). https://doi.org/10.1037/h0080749

23. Possler, D., Klimmt, C., Raney, A.A.: Gaming is awesome! a theoretical model on cognitive demands and the elicitation of awe during video game play. In: Bowman, N.D. (ed.) Video Games: A Medium That Demands Our Attention, pp. 74–91. Routledge (2018). https://doi.org/10.4324/9781351235266-5

24. Raptis, G.E., Fidas, C., Katsini, C., Avouris, N.: A cognition-centered personalization framework for cultural-heritage content. User Model. User-Adapt. Interact. **29**(1), 9–65 (2019). https://doi.org/10.1007/s11257-019-09226-7

25. Raptis, G.E., Katsini, C., Cen, A.J.l., Arachchilage, N.A.G., Nacke, L.E.: Better, funner, stronger: a gameful approach to nudge people into making less predictable graphical password choices. In: Proceedings of the 2021 CHI Conference on Human Factors in Computing Systems. Association for Computing Machinery, New York (2021). https://doi.org/10.1145/3411764.3445658

26. Richardson, A.: Verbalizer-visualizer: a cognitive style dimension. J. Mental Imagery **1**(1), 109–125 (1977)

27. Tremopoulos, A., Raptis, G.E., Katsanos, C.: WhatShapeWhatColor: designing a puzzle game to elicit the field dependence-independence cognitive style. In: Proceedings of the 25th Pan-Hellenic Conference on Informatics (PCI 2021), pp. 200–205. Association for Computing Machinery, New York (2022). https://doi.org/10.1145/3503823.3503861

28. Witkin, H.A., Goodenough, D.R.: Cognitive Styles: Essence and Origins. International Universities Press, Madison (1981)

User Studies, Eye-Tracking, and Physiological Data

Electroencephalographic (EEG) Correlates of Visually Induced Motion Sickness (VIMS) in the Virtual Reality (VR) Based Simulations

Jan K. Argasiński[1,2,3]([✉]) [ID], Natalia Lipp[1,2] [ID], and Szymon Mazurek[1] [ID]

[1] Sano Centre for Computational Medicine, Kraków, Poland
{j.argasinski,n.lipp,s.mazurek}@sanoscience.org
[2] Jagiellonian University, Kraków, Poland
[3] Simpro sp. z o.o., Krakow, Poland

Abstract. In the presented study, the possibility of detecting Visually Induced Motion Sickness (VIMS) in Virtual Reality (VR) simulations using electroencephalographic (EEG) recordings was investigated. 31 adult participants were tested with VR and EEG in both VIMS and non-VIMS conditions. A correlation between EEG signals and the Simulation Sickness Questionnaire (SSQ) scores was shown, indicating that VIMS can be detected through EEG recordings.

Keywords: Electroencephalography · EEG · Visually Induced Motion Sickness · VIMS · Virtual Reality · VR · simulations

1 Motivation

Virtual Reality (VR) simulations are increasingly becoming pervasive and essential, particularly in training of remote operations such as piloting Unmanned Aerial Vehicles (UAVs), where simulations closely emulate actual conditions. However, it is crucial to evaluate these simulations for Visually Induced Motion Sickness (VIMS), a common issue experienced by users due to conflicting sensory signals between the visual and vestibular systems. Electroencephalography (EEG) is an essential method for interpreting VIMS, as it provides means of monitoring brain activity and detecting changes associated with motion sickness. However, results of past research are contradictory. Some studies reported changes in alpha, delta and theta band powers mainly in frontal and central areas [6,7,9]. Whereas other suggest that EEG may not be suited to measure VIMS symptoms as they may stem from activity in deeper located structures of a brain [10]. One possible explanation of inconsistent conclusions is different level of immersion in mentioned studies. On the one hand, studies in which significant differences were found, used curved monitors or projection screen. On the other hand, in the study in which CAVE Automatic Virtual Environment-viewed VR was used no neural correlates of VIMS were found. The problem

© The Author(s), under exclusive license to Springer Nature Switzerland AG 2023
J. Abdelnour Nocera et al. (Eds.): INTERACT 2023, LNCS 14145, pp. 59–67, 2023.
https://doi.org/10.1007/978-3-031-42293-5_5

seems to be especially interesting considering the growing popularity of VR systems with a higher level of immersion, that is head-mounted display (HMD). To the best of our knowledge, number of previous studies on neural correlates of VIMS did not use HMDs mostly because in the past it was difficult to use EEG cap together with VR headset. Additionally, it was assumed that HMD-viewed virtual environments may evoke more severe symptoms of motion sickness than desktop-viewed VR. However, it is important to note that HMD-viewed VR provides users with more engaging experience that can redirect their attention from conflicting sensory signals to more pleasant stimuli [2].

The presented study provides an example of how electroencephalographic correlates of simulator sickness can be identified using a simple simulation viewed through HMD to which factors that may cause operator discomfort have been added. With the advent of new VR headsets equipped with EEGs, it will soon be possible to alert operators about the onset of VIMS symptoms before they occur, thus improving the overall experience and effectiveness of VR simulations in remote operations.

The presented study was a part of a larger project aimed at creating an interface and application for controlling semi-autonomous aircraft using virtual reality and eye-tracking technology. One of the key features of the developed interface was to facilitate its long-term use as virtual observational environment without inducing simulator sickness in operator.

2   Materials and Methods

2.1   Participants

The study involved 31 participants (18 male and 13 female) aged from 18 to 42 (M = 28.10, SD = 5.61). Of all participants, 10 had no previous experience with VR, 17 used VR once or twice, and 4 of them indicated regular usage of VR. Additionally, the majority of participants (n = 23) had no previous experience with piloting UAV, four participants indicated that they had moderate experience and the others (n = 4) that they had a lot of experience.

2.2   Measures and Equipment

Task. Participants were immersed in the VR with a stereoscopic head-mounted display. In particular, we used HTC Vive Pro Eye with built-in Tobii eye tracker. The VR application was developed using Unity engine (by Unity Technologies) and Mission Planner (by ArduPilot).

In the first part of the procedure (i.e., non-VIMS session) the participants' task was to navigate the drone with the gaze-based system. They were asked to follow voice instructions that concerned control over drone maneuvers (e.g., directing to new waypoint, giving the current height) and answer questions about simulator sickness symptoms. In the second part (i.e., VIMS session) in addition to the aforementioned task, we included stimuli designed to induce symptoms of simulator sickness. Rotations of the environment in three axes: roll, pitch, and yaw at different speeds appeared every 20 s during performing the main task. The sequence of rotations was randomly generated, and it was the same for all subjects.

EEG Recording Device Setup. The EEG data were collected using g.Nautilius 32-channel equipment and the g.Recorder app. The electrodes were placed accoring to the International 10/20 electrode system. The electrode layout is presented in the Fig. 1. The data was sampled with 500 Hz frequency and then low pass filtered by the device at 250 Hz. Additionally, notch filter was applied at the device level at 50 Hz to automatically remove the power line noise.

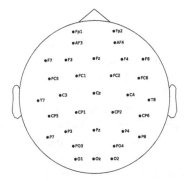

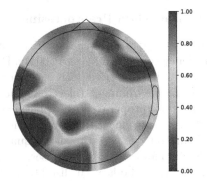

Fig. 1. Electrode layout used in the recording

Fig. 2. Relative difference in VIMS and non-VIMS theta band power across the example subject's scalp

Symptoms of Simulator Sickness. We used Simulator Sickness Questionnaire (SSQ, Kennedy, Lane, Berbaum, Lilienthal, 1994) to measure the intensity of VIMS symptoms. The questionnaire consists of 17 items rated from 0 ('*I do not experience this symptom at all*') to 3 ('*I am significantly affected by this symptom*'). It allows for the calculation of the general factor of VIMS intensity and its three aspects: nausea (N), oculomotor (O), and disorientation (D). The items of SSQ were prerecorded and given to participants' headphones. Participants answered aloud and their answers were recorded during the sessions.

2.3 Procedure

First, participants provided signed consent and answered a set of demographic questions. Next, participants were prepared for EEG measurement and instructed on how to use the VR application, after which they were asked to wear a VR headset and a 5-minute training session started. Next, participants performed the main task in two consecutive sessions (i.e., non-VIMS and VIMS).

Both sessions were designed to last 30 min, but participants could withdraw at any time. Participants were asked to answer to SSQ items every 5 min during both sessions. Participants heard the items in headphones and they answered aloud. That way, collecting their responses did not require interruption of the VR sessions.

The procedure was positively opinionated by the Ethical Committee of the Jagiellonian University at the Institute of Applied Psychology. The experimental sessions were conducted in the morning during two weeks. Throughout the experiment the temperature in the lab was kept at 26 C, and the humidity at 44–50%. All experimental sessions were monitored outside of the experimental room using a video camera.

2.4   Raw Data Preprocessing

Raw EEG signals are characterized by amplitudes in range of µV and contain frequency components up to 300 Hz. Due to these, the reading is prone to various artifacts that interfere with the brain activity signals. The artifacts can come from the environment (electromagnetic fields), the measuring device and it's application (proper electrode placement on the scalp) and also from the patient's body (eye movement, heartbeat, muscular activity). These artifacts can cause a significant decrease the signal quality, leading to difficulties in using the raw EEG data for analytical purposes. To mitigate these negative effects, various pre-processing methods are utilized to increase the signal-to-noise ratio in EEG data. There exist a significant body of work on utilization of filters, decomposition and interpolation techniques to remove artefactual activity components from the recordings. These methods are chosen accordingly to the performed task and the EEG data examined.

After initial data examination, the following pre-processing procedure was performed:

- setting average reference,
- high-pass filtering at 50 Hz using 4-th order Butterworth filter,
- low-pass filtering at 0.1 Hz using 4-th order Butterworth filter,
- remaining artifact removal using WICA method [1].

The frequencies for the filtering were chosen to cover the frequency bands related to simulator sickness described in [5]. The power line noise removal was performed at the measurement level by the g.Nautilius by notch filtering at 50 Hz. Lastly, the artifact removal method WICA was used. This method allows for automated removal of the noise components guided by the recordings. The results of WICA were compared with standard ICA [3] and manual component removal procedure. The effects of both filtering methods were satisfying, therefore WICA was chosen due to time inefficiency of manual component removal.

2.5 Frequency Domain Feature Extraction

For further analysis, the data was extracted from time windows centered at the beginning of every subsequent SSQ readings. The questionnaire was read every 5 min, and the window ranged 180 s before and after the reading has started. The procedure of frequency analysis was created accordingly to the guidelines presented by [5,8]. The following frequency bands were extracted:

- delta (0.2 Hz to 4 Hz),
- theta (4 Hz to 8 Hz),
- alpha (8 Hz to 13 Hz),
  divided further into slow (8 Hz to 10 Hz) and fast (10 Hz to 13 Hz),
- beta (13 Hz to 30 Hz),
  divided further into slow (13 Hz to 20 Hz) and fast (20 Hz to 30 Hz),
- gamma (30 Hz to 45 Hz).

The high end gamma frequency was lowered from commonly used 50 Hz value due to the noise in the 45 Hz - 55 Hz frequency range caused by the g.Nautilius notch filter at 50 Hz.

Finally, the power for every electrode was calculated. It was done using Welch's method, with 10 s time windows, 50% window overlap and median averaging. The window length was chosen to 10 s, as it allows to contain at least two full periods of the slowest waves analyzed in the window (in this case, 0.2 Hz for low end delta frequency). The median averaging was chosen as it is less prone to noise inherent even in the pre-processed EEG signals. The power was represented both as absolute value of a frequency band and relative to the overall power in the given window. Additionally, to compare VIMS and non-VIMS sessions, the same power values were computed for entire lengths of the sessions.

2.6 SSQ Results Processing

The results of every SSQ were processed to obtain unified scoring for nausea (N), oculomotor (O) and disorientation (D) symptoms. To achieve that, the scores of questions related to a given symptoms group were summed. Also, overall SSQ score was computed as a sum of every symptom group scores. The scores of the specific symptoms groups as well as total score were multiplied by the factors presented in [4].

3 Results

In the first step, we checked how many participants finished both sessions (non-VIMS and VIMS). Out of 31 participants: two withdrew after completing only non-VIMS session, two, three, five, and four others after 10, 15, 20, 25 min of VIMS session, respectively. As we mentioned before, participants were told that they can withdraw at any point, especially when they feel unwell. What is important, despite the withdrawal of further participation, they allowed us to use their data collected earlier.

To verify the stated hypotheses, two regression models and a paired t-test were performed. The regression models were fitted using generalized least squares method. In the first regression model, the explained variable was the overall SSQ score and explaining variables were the relative power of chosen frequency bands on given electrode. Every tested model was statistically significant. The results with the R^2 values above 35% are shown in the Table 1.

Table 1. Results of the first regression analysis.

Electr.	Freq. band	Coeff.	Std err.	z	P>|z|	Confidence intvl 0.025	0.975
T8	theta	726.735	51.934	13.993	<.001	624.945	828.524
O2	theta	697.974	50.541	13.81	<.001	598.915	797.033
T8	alpha	941.823	68.697	13.71	< .001	807.178	1076.467
T8	slow alpha	2123.909	155.37	13.67	<.001	1819.389	2428.429
Oz	theta	653.584	48.35	13.518	<.001	558.821	748.347
FC5	theta	718.789	53.108	13.534	<.001	614.699	822.879
T8	fast alpha	1653.101	122.558	13.488	<.001	1412.891	1893.311
T7	theta	750.200	56.812	13.205	<.001	638.85	861.55
F4	theta	731.860	55.412	13.208	<.001	623.255	840.465
FC5	fast alpha	1734.593	132.323	13.109	<.001	1475.244	1993.941
FC5	alpha	965.382	73.77	13.086	<.001	820.795	1109.969
T7	alpha	943.843	72.335	13.048	<.001	802.068	1085.617
T7	slow alpha	2163.223	165.756	13.051	<.001	1838.347	2488.099
F3	slow beta	1194.597	91.746	13.021	<.001	1014.778	1374.415

In the second regression model, where the explained variable was once again overall SSQ score and explaining variables were electrode, frequency band, relative power of chosen frequency bands on given electrode and all these variables combined. The results for variables that were shown to have statistical significance are shown in Table 2.

The last analysis was a series of t-tests for comparison between non-VIMS and VIMS relative power of given frequency bands on given electrodes. The subjects 6, 11 and 15 were omitted due to the missing data from non-VIMS sessions. The comparisons that have shown statistical significance and effect sizes above 0.8 are show in the Table 3.

4 Discussion

The following conclusions can be drawn from the conducted analyses:

Table 2. Results of the second regression analysis.

	Coeff.	Std err.	z	P>|z|	Confidence intvl	
					0.025	0.975
Intercept	19.7363	4.16	4.744	<0.001	11.583	27.89
Band[T.delta]	30.1604	9.534	3.164	0.002	11.475	48.846
Electrode[T.P8]: Band[T.delta]	−30.5873	14.114	−2.167	0.03	−58.251	−2.923
Relative Power	438.1133	137.424	3.188	0.001	168.766	707.46
Band[T.delta]:Relative Power	−476.1319	138.387	−3.441	0.001	−747.366	−204.898
Electrode[T.P7]: Band[T.delta]: Relative Power	381.0233	187.907	2.028	0.043	12.733	749.313

Theta waves are the most differentiating factor between VIMS and non-VIMS. Significant differences were also indicated for **alpha** waves and **delta** waves at selected electrodes.

The most significant electrodes are **F3, F4, FC5, T7, T8, O2, Oz, P7, P8** - these results are consistent with the literature that highlights the significance of electrodes: F3 (in the reported study, FC5 was additionally identified as significant, which is located nearby, and F4, the electrode located symmetrically on the other hemisphere), O1 (in the reported study, Oz and O2 electrodes were identified, which are located nearby the O1 electrode; Oz is on the midline of the head, O2 is symmetrical, but electrodes O1, Oz, and O2 are very close to each other and all represent the occipital lobe, where visual information is processed - this seems to be the appropriate relation), T3 (in our study, T7 and T8 electrodes were identified - the T7 electrode is located nearby T3 representing a similar area; the T8 electrode additionally indicates an area located symmetrically on the other hemisphere), P3 (analogously to the above case of the T3 electrode - in the reported study, P7 and P8 electrodes were identified, located nearby and symmetrically, respectively).

As can be observed, similar areas were identified in the reported study, but systematic changes are visible compared to the literature: in the reported study, activity was often detected further from the axis of the head (in the literature the higher the electrode number, the further away from the head axis, i.e. the T7 electrode is further away than the T3) - this may result from, for example, the construction of the cap - a smaller size cap was usually chosen so that it would fit tightly to the head - on a smaller cap, the distances between electrodes are correspondingly smaller, in the reported study, symmetrical activations in both hemispheres were more frequently detected.

An interesting observed effect that did not appear in the literature is a significant difference in theta wave power on (almost) the entire head (27 out of 32 electrodes) between the VIMS and non-VIMS condition (see Fig. 2).

In conclusion, the obtained results are consistent with the state-of-the-art [6,7,9,10], and the observed effect related to theta waves may contribute to an interesting scientific discussion with other researchers resulting in further scientific hypotheses and studies.

Table 3. Results of the t-tests comparing non-VIMS and VIMS session.

Electr.	Freq.band	nVIMS mean	VIMS mean	t	p	df	Eff. Size
PO3	theta	0.042 ± 0.02	0.032 ± 0.017	5.626	<.001	27	1.083
FC5	theta	0.039 ± 0.018	0.03 ± 0.015	5.493	<.001	27	1.057
C4	theta	0.04 ± 0.018	0.031 ± 0.016	5.455	<.001	27	1.050
CP5	theta	0.041 ± 0.019	0.031 ± 0.016	5.448	<.001	27	1.048
Pz	theta	0.039 ± 0.018	0.029 ± 0.014	5.424	<.001	27	1.044
C3	theta	0.04 ± 0.017	0.031 ± 0.015	5.356	<.001	27	1.031
P3	theta	0.041 ± 0.018	0.031 ± 0.016	5.333	<.001	27	1.026
O2	theta	0.039 ± 0.02	0.029 ± 0.016	5.234	<.001	27	1.007
CP1	theta	0.039 ± 0.017	0.03 ± 0.015	5.217	<.001	27	1.004
FC6	theta	0.037 ± 0.017	0.029 ± 0.014	5.123	<.001	27	0.986
P4	theta	0.041 ± 0.019	0.031 ± 0.016	5.108	<.001	27	0.983
FC1	theta	0.038 ± 0.017	0.029 ± 0.014	5.099	<.001	27	0.981
T8	theta	0.038 ± 0.02	0.03 ± 0.016	5.023	<.001	27	0.967
CP6	theta	0.041 ± 0.019	0.032 ± 0.016	5.018	<.001	27	0.966
Cz	theta	0.039 ± 0.018	0.03 ± 0.015	4.972	<.001	27	0.957
PO4	theta	0.041 ± 0.019	0.031 ± 0.016	4.97	<.001	27	0.956
FC2	theta	0.039 ± 0.016	0.03 ± 0.014	4.906	<.001	27	0.944
Fz	theta	0.039 ± 0.017	0.03 ± 0.015	4.833	<.001	27	0.93
O1	theta	0.039 ± 0.017	0.03 ±0.015	4.777	<.001	27	0.919
F7	theta	0.036 ± 0.018	0.028 ± 0.015	4.763	<.001	27	0.917
AF3	theta	0.038 ± 0.017	0.03 ± 0.015	4.711	<.001	27	0.907
CP2	theta	0.04 ± 0.018	0.031 ± 0.015	4.697	<.001	27	0.904
F4	theta	0.037 ± 0.016	0.029 ± 0.014	4.618	<.001	27	0.889
T7	theta	0.037 ± 0.018	0.029 ± 0.016	4.598	<.001	27	0.885
s F3	theta	0.038 ± 0.016	0.03 ± 0.014	4.575	<.001	27	0.88
P8	theta	0.041 ± 0.021	0.032 ± 0.018	4.562	<.001	27	0.878
P7	theta	0.037 ± 0.017	0.029 ± 0.014	4.475	<.001	27	0.861
F8	theta	0.038 ± 0.019	0.029 ± 0.016	4.244	<.001	27	0.817

A highly interesting and productive next step in research - with direct practical significance for VR simulation users - would be an attempt to replicate the study using one of the popular consumer-grade EEG devices. Subsequently, one could attempt to detect the aforementioned states and alert the user to the need for an immediate break from VR work **before** the onset of very unpleasant symptoms of simulator sickness.

Acknowledgements. This research was funded by the Polish National Center for Research and Development (NCBiR) under project DOB-BIO9/26/04/2018 "Controlling an autonomous drone using goggles (monocular)". This publication is supported by the European Union's Horizon 2020 research and innovation programme under grant agreement Sano No 857533. This publication is supported by Sano project carried out within the International Research Agendas programme of the Foundation for Polish Science, co-financed by the European Union under the European Regional Development Fund.

References

1. Castellanos, N.P., Makarov, V.A.: Recovering EEG brain signals: artifact suppression with wavelet enhanced independent component analysis. J. Neurosci. Methods **158**, 300–312 (2006)
2. Dużmańska, N., Strojny, P., Strojny, A.: Can simulator sickness be avoided? a review on temporal aspects of simulator sickness. Front. Psychol. **9**, 2132 (2018)
3. Hyvärinen, A., Oja, E.: Independent component analysis: algorithms and applications. Neural Netw. Off. J. Int. Neural Netw. Soc. **13**(4–5) (2000)
4. Kennedy, R.S., Lane, N.E., Berbaum, K.S., Lilienthal, M.G.: Simulator sickness questionnaire: an enhanced method for quantifying simulator sickness. Int. J. Aviat. Psychol. **3**(3), 203–220 (1993)
5. Kim, Y.Y., Kim, H.J., Kim, E.N., Ko, H.D., Kim, H.T.: Characteristic changes in the physiological components of cybersickness. Psychophysiology **42**(5), 616–625 (2005)
6. Lim, H.K., et al.: Test-retest reliability of the virtual reality sickness evaluation using electroencephalography (EEG). Neurosci. Lett. **743**, 135589 (2021)
7. Min, B.C., Chung, S.C., Min, Y.K., Sakamoto, K.: Psychophysiological evaluation of simulator sickness evoked by a graphic simulator. Appl. Ergon. **35**(6), 549–556 (2004)
8. Naqvi, S., Badruddin, N., Jatoi, M., Malik, A., Wan Hitam, W.H., Abdullah, B.: EEG based time and frequency dynamics analysis of visually induced motion sickness (VIMS). Australasian Physical & Engineering Sciences in Medicine, Supported by the Australasian College of Physical Scientists in Medicine and the Australasian Association of Physical Sciences in Medicine, pp. 1–9 (2015)
9. Naqvi, S.A.A., Badruddin, N., Jatoi, M.A., Malik, A.S., Hazabbah, W., Abdullah, B.: EEG based time and frequency dynamics analysis of visually induced motion sickness (VIMS). Australas. Phys. Eng. Sci. Med. **38**, 721–729 (2015)
10. Tauscher, J.P., et al.: Exploring neural and peripheral physiological correlates of simulator sickness. Comput. Anim. Virtual Worlds **31**(4–5), e1953 (2020)

Exploring Eye Expressions for Enhancing EOG-Based Interaction

Joshua Newn$^{(\boxtimes)}$, Sophia Quesada , Baosheng James Hou ,
Anam Ahmad Khan , Florian Weidner , and Hans Gellersen

Lancaster University, Lancaster, UK
{j.newn,s.quesada,b.hou2,a.a.khan7,f.weidner,
h.gellersen}@lancaster.ac.uk

Abstract. This paper explores the classification of eye expressions for EOG-based interaction using JINS MEME, an off-the-shelf eye-tracking device. Previous studies have demonstrated the potential for using electrooculography (EOG) for hands-free human-computer interaction using eye movements (directional, smooth pursuit) and eye expressions (blinking, winking). We collected a comprehensive set of 14 eye gestures to explore how well both types of eye gestures be classified together in a machine learning model. Using a Random Forest classifier trained on our collected data using 15 engineered features, we obtained an overall classification performance of 0.77 (AUC). Our results show that we can reliably classify eye expressions, enhancing the range of available eye gestures for hands-free interaction. With continued development and refinement in EOG-based technology, our findings have long-term implications for improving the usability of the technology in general and for individuals who require a richer vocabulary of eye gestures to interact hands-free.

Keywords: Eye Gesture Recognition · Eye Expressions · Electrooculography (EOG) · EOG-Based Interaction · Wearable Computing

1 Introduction

Eye expressions refer to the facial expressions and movements that individuals can produce and manipulate through their eye muscles [15]—examples include squinting (narrowing of the eyes), blinking, winking, and raising eyebrows. Previous studies have relied on vision-based methods for detecting eye expressions [15–17]. Recent work has shown that commercially available off-the-shelf devices that measure electrooculography (EOG) signals, such as the JINS MEME, can measure facial expressions with high fidelity [23]. EOG is a technique that measures the electrical potential difference between the cornea and retina of the eye [3], which varies with eye movements. Given that facial expressions are comprised of complex muscular movements, including those surrounding the ocular region, EOG could serve as an effective method for detecting eye expressions [8].

© The Author(s), under exclusive license to Springer Nature Switzerland AG 2023
J. Abdelnour Nocera et al. (Eds.): INTERACT 2023, LNCS 14145, pp. 68–79, 2023.
https://doi.org/10.1007/978-3-031-42293-5_6

One of the key advantages of using EOG-based is their ability to detect subtle changes in movement robustly—making it a compelling input for interaction [6].

This paper explores the potential for incorporating eye expressions with existing EOG-based interaction methods, which often rely on the movement of the eyes alone [13,25] or with a single eye expression (e.g. blinking [4]). To do this, we collected data from 12 participants as they performed a non-exhaustive subset of eye movement and eye expressions for classification. In total, we collected data on six eye expressions (squint, enlarge, left wink, right wink, blink, stare) and eight directional eye movements: single-stroke (look up, look down, look left, look right) and four multi-stroke (glance up, glance down, glance left, glance right). We aim to assess the effectiveness of utilising both forms of eye gestures together as a first step. Our dataset consists of 14 different classes of eye gestures, which has a high number of classes for classification compared to previous EOG-based eye gesture recognition research to our knowledge.

Using the dataset that was collected under two conditions GUIDED and UNGUIDED, we trained a Random Forest classifier to classify the eye gestures based on 15 prevalent shape- and noise-based features. Our classifier obtained an overall classification performance of 0.77 (AUC).

The contribution of this paper lies in demonstrating the reliable classification of eye expressions with eye movements for interaction. The ability to distinguish a more extensive vocabulary of eye gestures using EOG would facilitate more opportunities for hands-free interaction. Hence, we conclude the paper by discussing our findings and providing future directions for EOG-based interaction.

2   Data Collection

We designed a procedure and tool to collect data on 14 different eye gestures for classification under two conditions, GUIDED and UNGUIDED, in which we recorded 102,772 and 58,917 rows of data, respectively. For each participant, we collected a total of 140 data points (14 eye gestures × 5 trials × 2 conditions).

2.1   Eye Gestures

This paper distinguishes two types of eye gestures: *eye movements* and *eye expressions*. Eye movement refers to the physical movement of the eyeball or eye muscles that control the movement of the eye (e.g. saccades, smooth pursuit, and vergence movement). Eye movements for interaction have long been adopted for interaction [12]. Eye expressions, on the other hand, are often communicative signals conveyed through the eyes. Narrowing of the eyes, also known as squinting, can be associated with emotions such as anger, suspicion, or concentration, while widening of the eyes can indicate surprise, fear, or interest. Closing one eye or both are also eye expressions, a slow blink as an involuntary can signal boredom, while a wink can signal flirtation or humour when used voluntarily.

We selected a total of fourteen eye gestures that represent both types for classification. The set compromised of six eye expressions (blink, left wink, right wink, squint, enlarge, and stare), and the remaining are two variants of up-down-left-right eye movements: looks and glances. Looks are single directional shifts from a centre position (single-stroke), while glances record a directional shift in one direction, followed by a shift in the opposite direction back to the centre (multi-stroke). We selected the eye gestures from various relevant literature sources (e.g. [5,15,19,22]), covering both single-stroke [19] and multi-stroke eye gestures [5], as well as eye expressions such as winks and blinks [18].

2.2 Experimental Setup

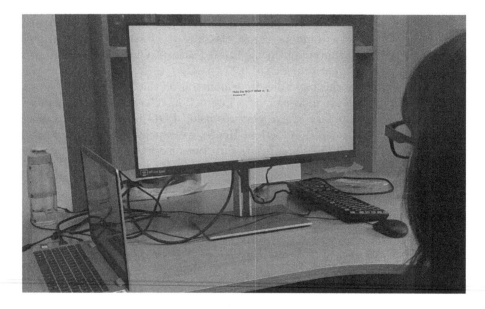

Fig. 1. Experimental setup. Participants sat in front of a 27-inch screen at a distance of 40cm while the experimenter sat adjacent to be able to observe both the screen and the eyes of the participant. The height of the screen was adjusted to ensure that the participant's eyes were aligned with the centre of the screen.

Figure 1 shows our experimental setup. We used the JINS MEME ES_R (100 Hz) smart eyewear with the Academic Pack (SDK)[1] for data collection. The device allows for non-intrusive measurement of EOG signals via three electrodes — one at the bridge of the nose and one on each side of the nose on the upper nasal wings. We built a simple data collection tool with a graphical user interface using pygame library to guide the data collection. The tool displays on-screen

---

[1] https://jinsmeme.com/.

instructions and automatically labels each eye gesture. For each trial, the inter-face displayed specific instructions (e.g. Look →, Right Wink), and included a 3-second countdown timer to signal the start of the trial. We streamed the data from the SDK to the backend of the tool and logged both the EOG signals (horizontal and vertical channels) and corresponding labels together.

2.3   Conditions

We collected data under two conditions, GUIDED and UNGUIDED. In the GUIDED condition, participants were presented with a visual stimulus in the centre of the screen, represented by a red target with a diameter of 1° (equivalent to 7mm on the physical screen). During trials that required participants to make eye movements, the target would move towards the respective edge of the screen, covering approximately ±37° horizontally and ±23° vertically from the centre. The movement duration of the target for each stroke was set at 1 s. Thus, for a glance eye gesture, the target would move in one direction to the edge of the screen for 1 s and then return to the centre in 1 s. For stationary gestures like blinks and winks, participants were instructed to maintain their gaze at the centre of the screen, where the red target remained static, and were also given a 1-second time window to perform the gesture.

In the UNGUIDED condition, participants were instructed to perform the gesture independently without the presence of a visual stimulus. The instructions for the gesture would be displayed on the screen, and after a three-second count-down, a stationary grey target (1°) would appear. This target served as a visual reference, representing the centre of the screen and indicating that participants should execute the gesture instead of fixating on a blank screen.

Previous studies have yielded promising results under each condition, making it unclear which method is more suitable. However, incorporating both condi-tions in our data collection process allows us to mitigate potential issues related to overfitting by introducing greater variation into the dataset. Solely collecting data under the GUIDED condition could limit the generalisability of the machine learning model, as it may not account for the full range of real-world scenar-ios. Conversely, collecting data exclusively under the UNGUIDED condition may result in a lack of control over the experimental setup, making it challenging to establish consistent performance benchmarks. By encompassing both conditions, we can strike a balance between generalisability and control, allowing for a more comprehensive evaluation of our eye gesture classification model. We analysed the mean ranges of eye movements for all participants and observed that the UNGUIDED condition exhibited greater ranges, with a 42% increase in horizontal movement and a 46% increase in vertical movement compared to the GUIDED condition. This finding further supports the notion that the UNGUIDED condition contributes to a broader range of eye movements during data collection.

2.4   Participants

Participants must be able to wink with both eyes, which we made explicit during the recruitment process. Participants who do not have access to contact lenses could still take part in the study if they were short-sighted and could read the instructions on the screen. We collected data from 12 participants (6F, 6M), aged 20–29 (M = 22, SD = 3.1 years), recruited from Lancaster University through word-of-mouth. Among the participants, eight had their vision corrected to normal using either glasses or contact lenses, while two participants were short-sighted but could still read the on-screen instructions.

2.5   Procedure

Upon arrival, participants were asked to sit comfortably in front of a desk facing the screen, given a written overview of the study, and to fill in the consent form and a basic demographic questionnaire to complete. Participants were verbally briefed on the study procedure before proceeding to perform a short practice. The purpose of the practice was three threefold: to familiarise participants with performing all fourteen eye gestures, to ensure that they are able to perform them, and to review whether the EOG signals from the glasses are recording correctly for them (via live plot observation provided by the JINS MEME SDK).

If there were no issues, the experimenter proceeded to remind participants to keep their heads and bodies still during the study, not to talk, and only move their eyes to complete the gestures to minimise the noise in the EOG signal. Further, the experimenter instructed participants to be mindful of the position of the glasses throughout the data collection session and requested participants in advance to readjust the glasses to their original placement if they shifted or moved. This is because the sensors on the glasses need to touch the bridge and sides of their nose. Participants were also requested to avoid blinking while performing a gesture, but could blink if they had dry eyes during the instructions screen or if the screen was blank. This was to mitigate unintentional blinks in the dataset. Lastly, the experimenter made known to participants that they could pause the data collection at any time when an instruction screen was visible.

Participants were positioned in accordance with our experimental setup, with the experimenter seated adjacent to each participant. In the UNGUIDED condition, the experimenter visually monitored whether the participant performed the gesture, which was followed by a key press to proceed to the next instruction screen. The data collection was counterbalanced. Hence, half of the participants began with the UNGUIDED condition, followed by a short break before proceeding to the GUIDED condition, while the other half followed the reverse order. The UNGUIDED condition lasted approximately 5 min, while the GUIDED condition required between 8 to 10 min to complete. The entire study lasted less than an hour for each participant. Participants did not receive any compensation for their involvement. The study was conducted in compliance with the ethical regulations of the research institution.

3   Classification

Using the data collected, we engineered features and built the machine learning model for classifying eye gestures. We first pre-processed the raw data by removing noise generated during the experiment from external factors, for example, head and body movements [10]. Thus, we applied a low pass filter with a cutoff frequency of 15 Hz and a high pass filter with a cutoff frequency of 0.3 Hz to smooth and eliminate most of the EOG signal noise [14]. Drawing from previous research [1,7,14,20,24], we engineered 15 prevalent shape- and noise-based features from the processed EOG signal for eye-gesture classification (Table 1).

Table 1. Features for eye gesture classification.

Category	Features
Shape-based	Slope, Mean, Trimmed mean, Range, Peak Energy, Wavelength, Variance, Kurtosis, Z-Score
Noise-based	RMS, RMS-diff, Standard deviation, Standard deviation-diff, Rayleightest

Table 2. Random Forest classification performance results.

Evaluation Measure	Unguided	Guided	Guided + Unguided
AUC	0.84 ± 0.05	0.73 ± 0.02	0.77 ± 0.03
F_1-Score	0.71 ± 0.01	0.53 ± 0.06	0.60 ± 0.08

We combined the engineered feature vector in the machine learning model to predict the eye gesture classes. We modelled this task as a multi-class classification problem. For each trial, the selected features were fed into a model to predict the label of the eye gesture. As the choice of algorithm can affect the performance of the machine learning model, we experimented with k-nearest neighbours (KNN), Support Vector Machine (SVM) and Random Forest algorithms. Among these options, Random Forest demonstrated the highest classification performance on the testing fold, prompting us to select it for training the machine learning model. We experimented with window lengths and selected 120ms as it gave the highest performance over the testing fold. We fine-tuned the model with 100 trees, using entropy as the splitting criteria and a maximum tree depth of 80 for tree construction. To ensure a thorough evaluation of the model, we conducted 5-fold cross-validation on the complete dataset. In the subsequent section, we present the averaged results across the five folds.

To evaluate the performance of our proposed eye-gesture classification approach, we first separately built and evaluated a Random Forest model using the data obtained in GUIDED and UNGUIDED conditions. Lastly, we built and evaluated the model on the entire data by combining data from both conditions. We evaluate the performance of our classifier using F_1-Score and AUC (area under the receiver operating characteristic curve).

4   Results

Table 2 shows the feasibility of classifying eye movements and eye expressions together in a machine-learning model. Our classifier achieved an average AUC score of 0.77 using the combined data from both conditions, which suggests that 14 eye gestures can be classified accurately to enhance an EOG-based interaction. We observed that the proposed classification model attained the highest performance (AUC=0.84) in the UNGUIDED condition. However, a drop in model performance occurs in the GUIDED condition to an AUC score of 0.73.

To identify the performance of the proposed model for classifying individual eye gestures, we report the confusion matrix of the Random Forest model trained on the combined dataset of GUIDED and UNGUIDED conditions (see Fig. 2). We

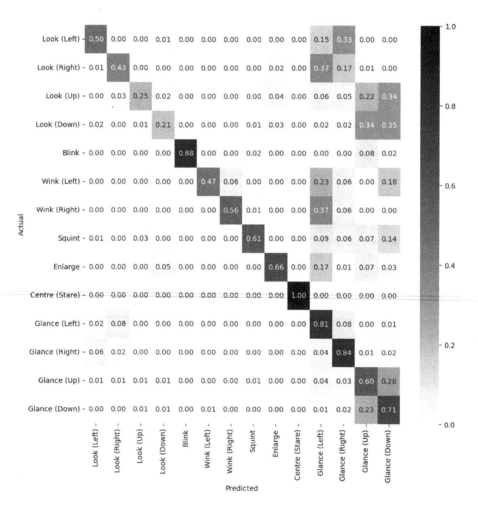

Fig. 2. Average confusion matrix for identifying eye gestures.

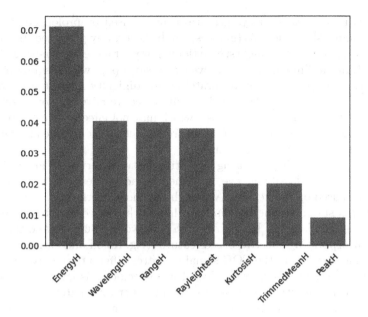

Fig. 3. Top 8 features contributing towards the Random Forest classification models.

observed that the classification model generally classifies eye expressions. This is because eye expression classes are very distinct among themselves. However, eye movements have similarities among themselves, which may result in similar features for different movements leading to misclassification. For instance, we observed that the model occasionally confuses between look and glance classes due to the similarities between these two eye movements, even though there are differences in the number of strokes.

Further, we explored the importance of the engineered feature set for training the model for classifying eye gestures. We employed the Random Forest importance score to observe the top-eight essential features for the classification task (see Fig. 3). We observed that mostly shape-based features (e.g. energy, peak, and wavelength) contributed to predicting the labels of eye gestures. However, some noise-based features, for instance, Rayleightest, also influenced the decision of the classification model.

5   Discussion

This paper explores how well eye movements and expressions can be classified together in a machine-learning model. To achieve this, we engineered shape- and noise-based from the EOG signals and built a Random Forest classifier to predict the different eye gestures. Our method achieved an overall performance of 0.77 (AUC), demonstrating the feasibility of combining both types of eye gestures. Our research differs from previous research, where researchers have mainly classified directional eye movements for hands-free interaction.

Our findings reveal that eye gestures characterised by prolonged eye movements and multi-stroke actions (glances) can be accurately predicted. In contrast, shorter movements with a single stroke (looks) present a greater challenge for correct classification. Similarly, certain eye expressions (e.g. winks, squints) proved to be more difficult to classify accurately. This difficulty may be attributed to the electrode placement on the off-the-shelf device we have employed, where all three electrodes are placed on the nose, which may not effectively capture muscle movements occurring in the surrounding areas, such as the temple and forehead, during these specific eye expressions.

Our proposed method utilising primitive features serves as an initial step toward accurately classifying eye movements and expressions in EOG-based interactions based on our results. Although our model performance for identifying 14 classes surpasses the baseline, further work is necessary to enhance the robustness of our classifier. Future research endeavours could expand the feature space by incorporating spectral-based features (e.g. rolloff and entropy [11]) and correlation features from the EOG signal to better differentiate between distinct eye gestures. Moreover, exploring deep learning models is encouraged as they generally excel in multi-class classification and offer automated feature extraction capabilities [9], which is especially useful in eye gesture classification where the raw signal of different classes (e.g. look and glance) does not have high variability.

6   Future Directions

To conclude this paper, we contribute three future research directions based on our current findings.

First, previous research on EOG has shown the potential for human-computer interaction, particularly for context-awareness applications (e.g. [7]). However, explicit EOG-based interaction remains limited, typically used to replace physical keys such as for steering mobility aids [4] and dwell-free typing [2]. Our findings show the potential for a richer vocabulary use of eye gestures for interface control, where users can map eye expressions to continuous inputs. For example, squinting can activate a function to bring up a magnifying glass to where a cursor is currently positioned. Hence, we can explore new mapping types for EOG-based interaction, especially for eye expressions.

The second research direction attempts to classify a more extensive eye gesture set. As a first step, we employed a subset from each eye gesture type for initial exploration. From our current findings, we better understand how to classify a large EOG-based eye gesture set. In the discussion section, we outlined the reasoning behind our results and potential ways to improve them from a technical standpoint. As we continue to build our understanding, the natural step in our work is to attempt a more exhaustive dataset of eye gestures. This can include variations of eye expressions, such as variations of winking and blinking—single, double, and long [16]—as well as other variations of multi-stroke gestures.

The final research direction is the exploration of EOG-based interactions that combine both eye expressions with eye movements. An example could be similar to Gaze+Hold [21], where one eye can perform an eye expression while the other performs an eye movement. In our case, a long wink would be a "hold", and this gesture can be combined with a discrete directional eye movement.

Acknowledgements. This work was supported by the European Research Council (ERC) under the European Union's Horizon 2020 research and innovation programme (Grant No. 101021229, GEMINI: Gaze and Eye Movement in Interaction).

References

1. Alam, M.M., Raihan, M.M.S., Chowdhury, M.R., Shams, A.B.: High precision eye tracking based on electrooculography (EOG) signal using artificial neural network (ANN) for smart technology application. In: 2021 24th International Conference on Computer and Information Technology (ICCIT) (2021). https://doi.org/10.1109/ICCIT54785.2021.9689821

2. Barbara, N., Camilleri, T.A., Camilleri, K.P.: EOG-based eye movement detection and gaze estimation for an asynchronous virtual keyboard. Biomed. Signal Process. Control **47**, 159–167 (2019). https://doi.org/10.1016/j.bspc.2018.07.005

3. Belkhiria, C., Boudir, A., Hurter, C., Peysakhovich, V.: EOG-based human-computer interface: 2000–2020 review. Sensors **22**(13) (2022). https://doi.org/10.3390/s22134914

4. Bhuyain, M.F., Kabir Shawon, M.A.U., Sakib, N., Faruk, T., Islam, M.K., Salim, K.M.: Design and development of an EOG-based system to control electric wheelchair for people suffering from quadriplegia or quadriparesis. In: International Conference on Robotics, Electrical and Signal Processing Techniques (ICREST) (2019). https://doi.org/10.1109/ICREST.2019.8644378

5. Bulling, A., Roggen, D., Tröster, G.: It's in your eyes: towards context-awareness and mobile HCI using wearable EOG goggles. In: Proceedings of the 10th International Conference on Ubiquitous Computing (2008). https://doi.org/10.1145/1409635.1409647

6. Bulling, A., Roggen, D., Tröster, G.: Wearable EOG goggles: eye-based interaction in everyday environments. In: CHI 2009 Extended Abstracts on Human Factors in Computing Systems (CHI EA 2009), pp. 3259–3264. ACM, New York (2009). https://doi.org/10.1145/1520340.1520468

7. Bulling, A., Ward, J.A., Gellersen, H., Tröster, G.: Eye movement analysis for activity recognition. In: Proceedings of the 11th International Conference on Ubiquitous Computing (2009). https://doi.org/10.1145/1620545.1620552

8. Chang, W.D.: Electrooculograms for human-computer interaction: a review. Sensors **19**(12) (2019). https://doi.org/10.3390/s19122690

9. Daniel, C., Loganathan, S.: A comparison of machine learning and deep learning methods with rule based features for mixed emotion analysis. Int. J. Intell. Eng. Syst. **14**(1), 42–53 (2021)

10. Díaz, D., Yee, N., Daum, C., Stroulia, E., Liu, L.: Activity classification in independent living environment with JINS MEME eyewear. In: IEEE International Conference on Pervasive Computing and Communications (PerCom) (2018). https://doi.org/10.1109/PERCOM.2018.8444580

11. Dietz, M., Schork, D., Damian, I., Steinert, A., Haesner, M., André, E.: Automatic detection of visual search for the elderly using eye and head tracking data. KI - Künstliche Intelligenz **31**(4), 339–348 (2017). https://doi.org/10.1007/s13218-017-0502-z

12. Drewes, H., Schmidt, A.: Interacting with the computer using gaze gestures. In: Baranauskas, C., Palanque, P., Abascal, J., Barbosa, S.D.J. (eds.) INTERACT 2007. LNCS, vol. 4663, pp. 475–488. Springer, Heidelberg (2007). https://doi.org/10.1007/978-3-540-74800-7_43

13. Findling, R.D., Quddus, T., Sigg, S.: Hide my gaze with EOG! Towards closed-eye gaze gesture passwords that resist observation-attacks with electrooculography in smart glasses. In: Proceedings of the 17th International Conference on Advances in Mobile Computing & Multimedia (MoMM2019), pp. 107–116. ACM, New York (2020). https://doi.org/10.1145/3365921.3365922

14. Hossain, Z., Shuvo, M., Sarker, P.: Hardware and software implementation of real time electrooculogram (EOG) acquisition system to control computer cursor with eyeball movement. In: 4th International Conference on Advances in Electrical Engineering. vol. 2018-January, pp. 132–137 (2017). https://doi.org/10.1109/ICAEE.2017.8255341

15. Ku, P.S., Wu, T.Y., Chen, M.Y.: EyeExpression: exploring the use of eye expressions as hands-free input for virtual and augmented reality devices. In: Proceedings of the 23rd ACM Symposium on Virtual Reality Software and Technology (VRST 2017), New York (2017). https://doi.org/10.1145/3139131.3141206

16. Ku, P.S., Wu, T.Y., Bastias, E.A.V., Chen, M.Y.: Wink it: investigating wink-based interactions for smartphones. In: Proceedings of the 20th International Conference on Human-Computer Interaction with Mobile Devices and Services Adjunct (2018). https://doi.org/10.1145/3236112.3236133

17. Ku, P.S., Wu, T.Y., Chen, M.Y.: EyeExpress: expanding hands-free input vocabulary using eye expressions. In: Adjunct Proceedings of the 31st Annual ACM Symposium on User Interface Software and Technology (2018). https://doi.org/10.1145/3266037.3266123

18. Kumar, D., Sharma, A.: Electrooculogram-based virtual reality game control using blink detection and gaze calibration. In: 2016 International Conference on Advances in Computing, Communications and Informatics (ICACCI), pp. 2358–2362 (2016). https://doi.org/10.1109/ICACCI.2016.7732407

19. Lin, C.T., et al.: EOG-based eye movement classification and application on HCI baseball game. In: IEEE Access: Practical Inovations, Open Solutions (2019). https://doi.org/10.1109/ACCESS.2019.2927755

20. Mala, S., Latha, K.: Feature selection in categorizing activities by eye movements using electrooculograph signals. In: International Conference on Science Engineering and Management Research (ICSEMR) (2014). https://doi.org/10.1109/ICSEMR.2014.7043559

21. Ramirez Gomez, A.R., Clarke, C., Sidenmark, L., Gellersen, H.: Gaze+hold: eyes-only direct manipulation with continuous gaze modulated by closure of one eye. In: ACM Symposium on Eye Tracking Research and Applications, Virtual Event, Germany (2021). https://doi.org/10.1145/3448017.3457381

22. Ramkumar, S., Sathesh Kumar, K., Emayavaramban, G.: EOG signal classification using neural network for human computer interaction. Int. J. Control Theory Appl. **9**(24), 223–231 (2016)

23. Rostaminia, S., Lamson, A., Maji, S., Rahman, T., Ganesan, D.: W!NCE: unobtrusive sensing of upper facial action units with EOG-Based eyewear. Proc. ACM Interact. Mob. Wearable Ubiquitous Technol. **3**(1) (2019). https://doi.org/10.1145/3314410
24. Vidal, M., Bulling, A., Gellersen, H.: Analysing EOG signal features for the discrimination of eye movements with wearable devices. In: Proceedings of the 1st International Workshop on Pervasive Eye Tracking & Mobile Eye-Based Interaction (PETMEI 2011), pp. 15–20. ACM, New York (2011). https://doi.org/10.1145/2029956.2029962
25. Wu, S.L., Liao, L.D., Lu, S.W., Jiang, W.L., Chen, S.A., Lin, C.T.: Controlling a human-computer interface system with a novel classification method that uses electrooculography signals. IEEE Trans. Biomed. Eng. **60**(8), 2133–2141 (2013). https://doi.org/10.1109/TBME.2013.2248154

How Many Participants Do You Need for an Open Card Sort? A Case Study of E-commerce Websites

Christos Pechlevanoudis, Grigorios Zilidis, and Christos Katsanos(✉)

Department of Informatics, Aristotle University of Thessaloniki, Thessaloniki, Greece
{pechlevan,gzilidis,ckatsanos}@csd.auth.gr

Abstract. Open card sorting is the most used method for developing user-centered information architectures. One important question for every HCI method is how many users to involve. Existing studies that address this question for open card sorts have involved trained professionals sorting content items of rather specialized domains. In addition, they employ data analysis approaches that might decrease the confidence one can place on the reported findings. This paper investigates the minimum number of participants for open card sorts performed on a general public website domain (e-commerce). In specific, it involves 203 and 210 participants sorting content items of two real-world e-commerce websites. Results from all the participants were compared with those of different-sized and randomly selected samples of the participants. It was found that 15 to 20 participants is a cost-effective way to obtain reliable open card sort data for general public websites.

Keywords: Card Sorting · Information Architecture · Sample size

1 Introduction

Open card sorting is a method that helps in understanding how participants might arrange and organize information that is meaningful to them. In an open card sort, participants sort content items (cards) into groups and then label these groups.

Open card sorting is a valuable method to support the design or evaluation of website Information Architecture (IA) [1, 2]. IA refers to the way the content is structured and interconnected [1]. However, card sorting is a general knowledge elicitation method and thus it has proved useful in many other contexts, such as to understand how designers group guidelines for robot teleoperation [3] and age-friendly websites [4], how children categorize games in app stores [5] or perceive cybersecurity warnings [6], how health professionals perceive self-tracking for mental wellness [7], and to validate HCI tools for interactive system design [8–10].

Previous studies looked at a range of methodological issues on how to conduct an open card sort and analyze the data. Card sorting can be done by hand using physical cards or by using software. The results obtained from manual and software-mediated card sorting are fairly similar [11, 12]. Usability of card sorting tools has been also examined

© The Author(s), under exclusive license to Springer Nature Switzerland AG 2023
J. Abdelnour Nocera et al. (Eds.): INTERACT 2023, LNCS 14145, pp. 80–89, 2023.
https://doi.org/10.1007/978-3-031-42293-5_7

[13]. However, most tools in this study are no longer maintained or have significantly changed and new tools, such as the open source CardSorter [14], have also appeared. Regarding the session time, participants may need from 20 min for 30 cards to 60 min for 100 cards [15]. In terms of the number of cards to sort, it should be neither less than 30 because forming groups might be problematic, nor more than 100 because participants may become tired or confused [2]. In addition, recent research provides support for the validity [16] and reliability [17, 18] of the open card sorting method and how the results are affected by user characteristics, such as sense of direction [19] and self-efficacy [20]. Regarding analysis of open card sort data, various approaches have been proposed [21], such as tabulations of data [2], graph visualizations [22], hierarchical cluster analysis [2, 12], k-means clustering [2], multidimensional scaling [2], factor analysis [23] and recent algorithms developed specifically for the purpose of analyzing card sort data [24, 25].

One important question for every HCI method is how many participants to involve. One study [26] recommends involving 20 to 30 users in open card sorts. Based on the same study data, Nielsen [27] argues that 15 users are enough as a cost-effective solution. One other study [28] suggests involving 10–15 participants. However, existing studies focus on a very specific context, that of trained professionals categorizing content items from rather specialized domain fields. In specific, the Tullis and Wood study [26] involved IT employees grouping cards from the Intranet website of their company's usability department. The Lantz et al. study [28] involved mental health professionals organizing well-established mental disorders into categories.

This paper investigates the minimum number of participants required for the cost-effective collection of reliable data from open card sorts for websites. Our research contributes to the existing HCI literature by adding two studies, involving more than 200 participants per study, on a general public website domain (e-commerce). In addition, our work uses 100 samples of each size, instead of 10 used in the existing studies [26, 28], which increases the confidence one can place on the obtained results. Finally, we conduct comparisons for all possible sample sizes (e.g., for $N = 1$ to the max number of participants with a step of 1), instead of arbitrarily-chosen sample sizes; $N = \{2, 5, 8, 12, 15, 20, 30, 40, 50, 60, 70\}$ in [26] and $N = \{1, 5, 10, 15, 20, 25, 30, 35, 40, 45, 50\}$ in [28]. This results in increased accuracy of the reported values as no interpolation is performed. Based on our findings, we recommend involving 15–20 participants in an open card sort study for a general public website.

2   Methodology

2.1   Participants

Two open card sort studies were conducted for two e-commerce websites, hereafter referred to as Eshop1 and Eshop2. Eshop1 offers a large variety of products, such as electronics, equipment for sports and hobbies, clothes, health and beauty products, and office supplies. Eshop2 is a women's clothes shop. Eshop2 is smaller in size and more homogenous in terms of content compared to Eshop 1.

Participants were recruited through calls in university courses, social media, and personal contacts. The Eshop1 study involved 203 participants, 136 males and 67 females, with a mean age of 22.5 years (SD = 5.2). The Eshop2 study involved 210 participants, 137 males and 73 females, with a mean age of 22.8 years (SD = 6.4). All of the participants were native speakers of the language used in the cards.

2.2 Selection of Cards

E-commerce websites are typically large in size. Research suggests that a card sort should involve from 30 to 100 cards [2] and that the maximum session time for the sort should not exceed 20–30 min. Following Spencer's [2] recommendations, a total of 54 and 59 cards were chosen for the Eshop1 and Eshop2 respectively. Examples of the selected cards for the Eshop1 are the following: "Wearables", "Home appliances", "Gardening", "Jewelry", "Camping", "Perfumes", "Fishing", and "Books". Examples of the selected cards for the Eshop2 are the following: "Shirts", "Belts", "Socks", "Hats", "Earrings", "Perfumes", "Necklaces", "Boots", and "Jeans".

2.3 Instruments and Procedures

Each open card sort was remotely mediated using OptimalSort by Optimal Workshop (https://www.optimalworkshop.com), an online card sorting tool. The URL to the OptimalSort study was supplied to the participants and they completed an electronic informed consent form inside the OptimalSort environment. Next, each participant performed an individual open card sort using the OptimalSort drag-and-drop environment. Participants were allowed to place each given card in only one group. They required on average 22 min 30 s and 19 min 4 s to sort the cards for Eshop1 and Eshop2 respectively. Finally, participants completed an electronic questionnaire inside the OptimalSort environment that captured their gender and age.

2.4 Data Analysis Methodology

For each open card sort study, we wanted to compare the results obtained when using a sample of participants to the ones obtained when using the full set of participants.

Previous research [26, 28] has used 10 random samples for each size value examined; sizes of 2, 5, 8, 12, 15, 20, 30, 40, 50, 60, and 70 participants in [26] and 1, 5, 10, 15, 20, 25, 30, 35, 40, 45, and 50 participants in [28]. We used 100 random samples for each possible sample size (i.e., from 1 to max N with a step of 1). We developed a custom-built tool in Python to support our data analysis approach. This tool uses as input the raw open card sort data extracted from the OptimalSort environment as spreadsheet files. For each comparison between the whole dataset and a randomly selected sample, the tool performs two types of analysis: a) distance matrices comparison, which compares the raw open card sort data, b) clusterings comparison, which compares the clusters produced after employing hierarchical cluster analysis.

The first analysis compared the distance matrices produced by all participants against the distance matrices produced by samples. A cards × cards distance or dissimilarity matrix is typically used to summarize card sort data [21]. The dissimilarity between two cards is measured by each cell value in this matrix, which spans from 0 (cards always grouped together) to 1 (cards never grouped together). We used the Mantel test [29] to check the null hypothesis that there is no correlation between the distance matrix produced by all participants and the distance matrix produced by each random subset of participants. This test is a kind of permutation test and, unlike traditional correlation analysis used in existing studies [26, 28], it does not presuppose observation independence or homogeneity of variance, both of which are typically violated for a distance matrix [12, 18]. We used 10000 permutations for the Mantel test when the minimum suggested number is 1000 [30]. Our tool used the Python implementation of the Mantel test available at https://github.com/jwcarr/mantel.

Card sorting data analysis typically involves using clustering algorithms to support the process of creating an IA. The most popular algorithm for this purpose is agglomerative hierarchical clustering [15, 21, 31]. Our second analysis aimed to compare the dendrograms produced after applying average-linkage hierarchical clustering on the full open card sort dataset and the different-sized samples. To this end, out analysis tool uses Clusim [32], an open-source Python toolkit that can be used to compare split, overlapping and hierarchical groupings. In specific, we used the Element-centric Clustering Similarity (Elsim) [33] to compare the hierarchical groupings produced by all the participants and the ones produced by the different-sized samples of participants. This similarity metric is interpreted like a correlation index.

3 Results

3.1 First Study: Eshop1

Distance Matrices Comparison. Table 1 presents the Mantel r correlations between the distance matrix produced by all 203 participants and the distance matrices produced by 100 samples of the following sizes: 2, 5, 8, 12, 15, 20, 30, 40, 50, 60, 70. Due to space constraints, we present results only for the sample sizes used by Tullis and Wood [26]. However, we have results for each sample size from 1 to 203.

Figure 1 is a line chart of the mean Mantel r correlation between the distance matrix produced by all participants and the ones produced by the aforementioned sample sizes. The association between sample size and average correlation is a negatively rising function, as seen in the line chart. As expected, the rise is steeper at smaller sample sizes. Also, as illustrated by the error bars, the variation of the results is substantially higher for the smaller samples. The line chart shows that there is very little increase in the value of the correlation coefficient as the sample size grows above 15–20. Nielsen [27] argues that a correlation coefficient of 0.90 is good enough for most projects because they have very limited resources for user research. Based on this recommendation and our results from this analysis, 9 users (mean Mantel r = 0.903) would be a cost-effective choice.

Hierarchical Clusterings Comparison. Table 1 also presents the Elsim similarity scores between the hierarchical clusterings from all 203 participants and hierarchical clusterings produced by 100 samples of the aforementioned selected sizes.

Figure 2 is a line chart of the mean Elsim similarity score between these groupings as a function of sample size. As seen in the line chart, the relationship between sample size and mean similarity score is a negatively increasing function. The increase is higher

Table 1. Descriptive statistics for the metrics used to compare the data from all participants (N = 203) with the data from 100 random samples of selected sample sizes for the Eshop1 study.

Size	Mantel r correlations				Elsim similarity scores			
N	Mean	Sd	Min	Max	Mean	Sd	Min	Max
2	0.699	0.126	0.146	0.879	0.761	0.032	0.655	0.825
5	0.843	0.054	0.686	0.920	0.807	0.026	0.750	0.868
8	0.891	0.028	0.807	0.944	0.830	0.030	0.764	0.879
12	0.929	0.016	0.882	0.957	0.851	0.026	0.790	0.929
15	0.942	0.013	0.898	0.965	0.861	0.030	0.777	0.932
20	0.956	0.010	0.921	0.974	0.868	0.027	0.793	0.917
30	0.971	0.006	0.947	0.981	0.887	0.027	0.807	0.952
40	0.980	0.003	0.970	0.986	0.897	0.023	0.825	0.956
50	0.985	0.002	0.979	0.989	0.907	0.027	0.853	0.963
60	0.985	0.002	0.979	0.989	0.907	0.023	0.864	0.948
70	0.990	0.002	0.986	0.994	0.914	0.031	0.865	0.994

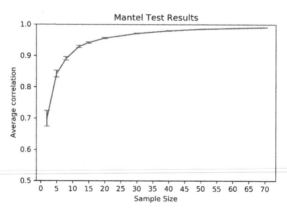

Fig. 1. Line chart of the mean Mantel r correlation coefficients between data from all 203 participants and data from 100 samples of selected sizes for the Eshop1 study. Error bars represent the 95% confidence interval.

with lower sample sizes. In addition, the error bars show that the variation of the results is relatively low even for small sample sizes. Figure 2 shows that there is very little increase in the value of the similarity score as the sample number grows above 15–20. Based on Nielsen's recommendation [27] and our results from this analysis, 44 users (mean Elsim score = 0.899) would be required to reach a mean similarity score close to 0.90. However, in this case, a good compromise for cost-efficiency would probably be a sample size between 12 (mean Elsim score = 0.851) and 26 (mean Elsim score = 0.880).

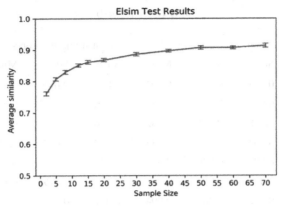

Fig. 2. Line chart of the mean Elsim similarity score between hierarchical clusterings from all 203 participants and hierarchical clusterings from 100 samples of selected sizes for the Eshop1 study. Error bars represent the 95% confidence interval.

3.2 Second Study: Eshop2

Distance Matrices Comparison. For the distance matrices comparison of the Eshop2 study, Table 2 and Fig. 3 present descriptive statistics and a line chart, as it was done for the first study. Figure 3 shows that when the sample size increases beyond 15–20, the correlation coefficient's value increases relatively little. According to the Nielsen [27] recommendation and the results of this analysis for the Eshop2 study, one could choose a sample size of as low as 9 users (mean Mantel r = 0.901).

Hierarchical Clusterings Comparison. For the hierarchical clusterings comparison of the Eshop2 study, Table 2 and Fig. 4 present descriptive statistics and a line chart, as it was done for the first study. Figure 4 shows that when the sample size increases beyond 15–20, the mean Elsim similarity score increases relatively little. According to the Nielsen [27] recommendation and the results of this analysis for the Eshop2 study, one would choose a sample size of 17 users (Elsim r = 0.899).

Table 2. Descriptive statistics for the metrics used to compare the data from all participants (N = 210) with the data from 100 random samples of selected sample sizes for the Eshop2 study.

Size	Mantel r correlations				Elsim similarity scores			
N	Mean	Sd	Min	Max	Mean	Sd	Min	Max
2	0.703	0.131	0.333	0.900	0.781	0.037	0.669	0.863
5	0.834	0.073	0.526	0.928	0.842	0.033	0.715	0.915
8	0.889	0.044	0.716	0.946	0.862	0.029	0.788	0.922
12	0.927	0.027	0.844	0.965	0.889	0.028	0.803	0.931

(continued)

Table 2. (*continued*)

Size	Mantel r correlations				Elsim similarity scores			
N	Mean	Sd	Min	Max	Mean	Sd	Min	Max
15	0.941	0.017	0.876	0.964	0.897	0.027	0.807	0.946
20	0.957	0.010	0.914	0.971	0.910	0.023	0.865	0.946
30	0.970	0.008	0.923	0.982	0.926	0.020	0.870	0.960
40	0.979	0.005	0.961	0.987	0.923	0.024	0.856	0.957
50	0.984	0.004	0.970	0.990	0.939	0.017	0.876	0.967
60	0.988	0.003	0.978	0.992	0.941	0.019	0.873	0.974
70	0.990	0.002	0.981	0.994	0.947	0.013	0.887	0.978

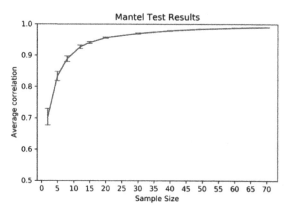

Fig. 3. Line chart of the mean Mantel r correlation coefficients between data from all 210 participants and data from 100 samples of selected sizes for the Eshop2 study. Error bars represent the 95% confidence interval.

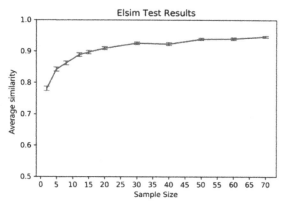

Fig. 4. Line chart of the mean Elsim similarity score between hierarchical clusterings from all 210 participants and hierarchical clusterings from 100 samples of selected sizes for the Eshop2 study. Error bars represent the 95% confidence interval.

4 Discussion and Conclusion

This paper investigates the number of participants required for an open card sort study for general content websites. Specifically, two studies for e-commerce websites were presented. Analysis of the collected data compared the raw groupings and dendrograms of all the participants with the ones produced by randomly selected samples of different sizes. In specific, the Mantel test was used for the distance matrices and the Elsim similarity score for the dendrograms analysis.

Regarding the first study (Eshop1), the mean Mantel correlation reached the value of 0.90 for 9 participants, 0.93 for 14 participants and 0.95 for 18 participants. The mean Elsim similarity score reached the value of 0.85 for 12 participants and up to 26 participants the score ranged from 0.86 to 0.88. Regarding the second study (Eshop2), the mean Mantel correlation reached the value of 0.90 again for 9 participants, 0.93 again for 14 participants and 0.95 for 19 participants. Unlike the Eshop1 study, the mean Elsim similarity score reached the value of 0.85 for only 6 participants, 0.90 for 17 participants and for 18 to 38 participants the score ranged from 0.90 to 0.93.

In general, Mantel correlations were larger than Elsim similarity scores. Thus, a very high correlation value (0.90) was quickly reached for a sample size as small as 9 participants. By contrast, the sample size required for the mean Elsim similarity score to reach 0.90 is almost double (17 participants for Eshop2) or even almost quintuple (44 participants for Eshop1). This may be attributed to the fact that the Elsim analysis works on clusterings, which are a transformation of the raw dataset that may result in loss of information as each card must be placed in only one cluster. However, hierarchical clustering is typically used to analyze card sort data and support IA-related decisions, thus it is important to consider it when recommending the minimum number of participants for open card sorts. Previous work either compares only the distance matrices [28] or employs exemplary comparisons based on visual inspection of dendrograms produced by all participants and some subsamples [26].

In addition, while the results of the Mantel tests share a highly similar pattern for both studies, the results of the Elsim analysis does not. Eshop1 required a sample size that was approximately 2.5 times larger in order to reach a similarity score of 0.90 compared to Eshop2. Eshop1 sells items that are far more heterogeneous, which might have resulted in more heterogenous groupings in general, and thus it might be harder to reach high similarity scores with smaller sample sizes compared to Eshop2.

One important limitation of this research is that it focuses only on quantitative data related to participants' groupings of cards and ignores qualitative data, such as users' terminology in the provided labels for the groups or comments. In addition, more studies in different contexts, such as website domains or number of cards, would be beneficial for the generalizability of the findings. To this end, we are already running similar studies for travel websites.

In conclusion, we recommend involving 15–20 participants in open card sorts of general public websites. This is because samples of 15–20 participants produced raw groupings and cluster analysis results that were already highly similar to the ones produced for all participants; mean Mantel r from 0.94 to 0.95 and mean Elsim similarity score from 0.86 to 0.91 respectively. For more than 20 users, both metrics increased at a very low rate. Thus, it does not make sense resource-wise to involve more than 20 participants in the same open card sort. It should be noted that if one wants to learn whether there are differences between discrete groups of users then 15–20 participants for each discrete group of users should be involved.

Acknowledgments. We would like to thank Optimal Workshop for kindly proving a free license to their OptimalSort software for conducting the open card sort studies reported in this paper.

References

1. Rosenfeld, L., Morville, P., Arango, J.: Information Architecture: For the Web And Beyond. O'Reilly Media, Sebastopol, CA (2015)
2. Spencer, D.: Card Sorting: Designing Usable Categories. Rosenfeld Media, Brooklyn, N.Y. (2009)
3. Adamides, G., Christou, G., Katsanos, C., Xenos, M., Hadzilacos, T.: Usability guidelines for the design of robot teleoperation: a taxonomy. IEEE Trans. Hum. Mach. Syst. **45**, 256–262 (2015)
4. Zaphiris, P., Ghiawadwala, M., Mughal, S.: Age-centered research-based web design guidelines. In: CHI 2005 Extended Abstracts on Human Factors in Computing Systems, pp. 1897–1900. ACM, New York, NY, USA (2005)
5. Cassidy, B., Antani, D.S., Read, J.C.C.: Using an open card sort with children to categorize games in a mobile phone application store. In: Proceedings of the 2013 CHI Conference on Human Factors in Computing Systems, pp. 2287–2290. ACM, New York, NY, USA (2013)
6. Jeong, R., Chiasson, S.: "Lime", "open lock", and "blocked": children's perception of colors, symbols, and words in cybersecurity warnings. In: Proceedings of the 2020 CHI Conference on Human Factors in Computing Systems, p. 14 pages. ACM, New York, NY, USA (2020)
7. Kelley, C., Lee, B., Wilcox, L.: Self-tracking for mental wellness: understanding expert perspectives and student experiences. In: Proceedings of the 2017 CHI Conference on Human Factors in Computing Systems, pp. 629–641. ACM, New York, NY, USA (2017)
8. Katsanos, C., Tselios, N., Goncalves, J., Juntunen, T., Kostakos, V.: Multipurpose public displays: can automated grouping of applications and services enhance user experience? Int. J. Hum. Comput. Interact. **30**, 237–249 (2014)
9. Katsanos, C., Tselios, N., Avouris, N.: Automated semantic elaboration of web site information architecture. Interact. Comput. **20**, 535–544 (2008)
10. Katsanos, C., Tselios, N., Avouris, N.: AutoCardSorter: designing the information architecture of a web site using latent semantic analysis. In: Proceedings of the Twenty-Sixth Annual SIGCHI Conference on Human Factors in Computing Systems, CHI 2008, pp. 875–878. ACM, Florence, Italy (2008)
11. Harper, M.E., Jentsch, F., Van Duyne, L.R., Smith-Jentsch, K., Sanchez, A.D.: Computerized card sort training tool: is it comparable to manual card sorting? In: Proceedings of the Human Factors and Ergonomics Society Annual Meeting, pp. 2049–2053. SAGE (2002)
12. Petrie, H., Power, C., Cairns, P., Seneler, C.: Using card sorts for understanding website information architectures: technological, methodological and cultural issues. In: Campos, P., Graham, N., Jorge, J., Nunes, N., Palanque, P., Winckler, M. (eds.) INTERACT 2011. LNCS, vol. 6949, pp. 309–322. Springer, Heidelberg (2011). https://doi.org/10.1007/978-3-642-23768-3_26
13. Chaparro, B.S., Hinkle, V.D., Riley, S.K.: The usability of computerized card sorting: a comparison of three applications by researchers and end users. J. Usability Stud. **4**, 31–48 (2008)

14. Melissourgos, G., Katsanos, C.: CardSorter: towards an open source tool for online card sorts. In: Proceedings of the 24th Pan-Hellenic Conference on Informatics, pp. 77–81. ACM, New York, NY, USA (2020)
15. Hudson, W.: Card sorting. In: Soegaard, M. and Dam, R.F. (eds.) The Encyclopedia of Human-Computer Interaction, 2nd edn. Interaction Design Foundation (2013)
16. Ntouvaleti, M., Katsanos, C.: Validity of the open card sorting method for producing website information structures. In: Extended Abstracts of the 2022 CHI Conference on Human Factors in Computing Systems, p. Article374:1-Article374:7. ACM, New York, NY, USA (2022)
17. Pampoukidou, S., Katsanos, C.: Test-retest reliability of the open card sorting method. In: Extended Abstracts of the 2021 CHI Conference on Human Factors in Computing Systems, p. Article330:1-Article330:7. ACM, New York, NY, USA (2021)
18. Katsanos, C., Tselios, N., Avouris, N., Demetriadis, S., Stamelos, I., Angelis, L.: Cross-study reliability of the open card sorting method. In: Extended Abstracts of the 2019 CHI Conference on Human Factors in Computing Systems, p. LBW2718:1-LBW2718:6. ACM, New York, NY, USA (2019)
19. Zafeiriou, G., Katsanos, C., Liapis, A.: Effect of sense of direction on open card sorts for websites. In: CHI Greece 2021: 1st International Conference of the ACM Greek SIGCHI Chapter, p. Article6:1-Article6:8. ACM, New York, NY, USA (2021)
20. Katsanos, C., Zafeiriou, G., Liapis, A.: Effect of self-efficacy on open card sorts for websites. In: Proceedings of the 24th International Conference on Human-Computer Interaction, HCI International 2022, pp. 75–87. Springer, Gothenburg, Sweden (2022)
21. Righi, C., et al.: Card sort analysis best practices. J. Usabil. Stud. **8**, 69–89 (2013)
22. Paul, C.: Analyzing card-sorting data using graph visualization. J. Usabil. Stud. **9**, 87–104 (2014)
23. Capra, M.G.: Factor analysis of card sort data: an alternative to hierarchical cluster analysis. In: Proceedings of the Human Factors and Ergonomics Society 49th Annual Meeting, pp. 691–695. HFES, Santa Monica, CA (2005)
24. Paea, S., Katsanos, C., Bulivou, G.: Information architecture: Using k-means clustering and the best merge method for open card sorting data analysis. Interact. Comput. **33**, 670–689 (2021)
25. Paea, S., Katsanos, C., Bulivou, G.: Information architecture: using best merge method, category validity, and multidimensional scaling for open card sort data analysis. Int. J. Hum. Comput. Interact. Forthcoming (2022)
26. Tullis, T., Wood, L.: How many users are enough for a card-sorting study? In: Usability Professionals Association (UPA) 2004 Conference (2004)
27. Nielsen, J.: Card Sorting: How many users to test. https://www.nngroup.com/articles/how-many-test-users/
28. Lantz, E., Keeley, J.W., Roberts, M.C., Medina-Mora, M.E., Sharan, P., Reed, G.M.: Card sorting data collection methodology: how many participants is most efficient? J. Classif. **36**, 649–658 (2019)
29. Mantel, N.: The detection of disease clustering and a generalized regression approach. Can. Res. **27**, 209–220 (1967)
30. Manly, B.F.J.: Randomization, Bootstrap and Monte Carlo Methods in Biology. Chapman & Hall, London (1997)
31. Wood, J., Wood, L.: Card sorting: current practices and beyond. J. Usabil. Stud. **4**, 1–6 (2008)
32. Gates, A.J., Ahn, Y.-Y.: CluSim: a Python package for the comparison of clusterings and dendrograms. bioRxiv. 410084 (2018)
33. Gates, A.J., Wood, I.B., Hetrick, W.P., Ahn, Y.-Y.: Element-centric clustering comparison unifies overlaps and hierarchy. Sci. Rep. **9**, 8574 (2019)

Quantifying Device Usefulness - How Useful is an Obsolete Device?

Craig Goodwin[1]([⊠]) [iD], Sandra Woolley[1] [iD], Ed de Quincey[1] [iD], and Tim Collins[2] [iD]

[1] Keele University, Staffordshire, UK
c.goodwin@keele.ac.uk
[2] Manchester Metropolitan University, Manchester, UK

Abstract. Obsolete devices add to the rising levels of electronic waste, a major environmental concern, and a contributing factor to climate change. In recent years, device manufacturers have established environmental commitments and launched initiatives such as supporting the recycling of obsolete devices by making more ways available for consumers to safely dispose of their old devices. However, little support is available for individuals who want to continue using legacy or 'end-of-life' devices and few studies have explored the usefulness of these older devices, the barriers to their continued use and the associated user experiences. With a human-computer interaction lens, this paper reflects on device usefulness as a function of utility and usability, and on the barriers to continued device use and app installation. Additionally, the paper contributes insights from a sequel study that extends on prior work evaluating app functionality of a 'vintage' Apple device with new empirical data on app downloadability and functionality for the same device when newly classified as 'obsolete'. A total of 230 apps, comprising the top 10 free App Store apps for each of 23 categories, were assessed for downloadability and functionality on an Apple iPad Mini tablet. Although only 20 apps (8.7%) could be downloaded directly onto the newly obsolete device, 143 apps (62.2%) could be downloaded with the use of a different non-legacy device. Of these 163 downloadable apps, 131 apps (comprising 57% of all 230 apps and 80.4% of the downloadable apps) successfully installed, opened, and functioned. This was a decrease of only 4.3% in functional apps (of the 230 total apps) compared to the performance of the device when previously classified as 'vintage'.

Keywords: Device obsolescence · Application obsolescence · Usefulness · Digital sustainability · Electronic waste

1 Introduction

Sustainable HCI [6, 14, 26, 28] and the study of device longevity and usefulness are particularly important whilst the number of obsolete devices and the levels of global e-waste continue to rise. The "Internet of Trash" [7, 15] has been used to describe the billions of end-of-life mobile and Internet-connected devices [9, 18] that contribute to the 53 million tons of e-waste generated per year [10]. In a review of the literature, Mellal [21] compares and contrasts different definitions of 'obsolete' and 'obsolescence' and

© The Author(s), under exclusive license to Springer Nature Switzerland AG 2023
J. Abdelnour Nocera et al. (Eds.): INTERACT 2023, LNCS 14145, pp. 90–99, 2023.
https://doi.org/10.1007/978-3-031-42293-5_8

distinguishes between types of obsolescence such as 'technological', 'functional', 'style' and 'planned'. Planned obsolescence is a contentious issue [4, 8, 20]. Though it has been argued to be a consequence of competitive forces in a free and technological society [31] it contributes to increasing sustainability concerns and to consumer dissatisfaction [8, 19, 29] particularly amongst users of not-so-new devices. However, it is not unusual for device manufacturers to launch new device models and variants on an annual basis [30].

Apple has made a commitment to carbon neutrality by 2030 [2] and has committed to improving product recycling and the use of recycled materials. Currently, however, little is known, in general, about where obsolete products go after being sent for recycling [13]. In terms of definitions, Apple defines products as 'vintage' when "Apple stopped distributing them for sale more than 5 and less than 7 years ago" and defines them as 'obsolete' when "Apple stopped distributing them for sale more than 7 years ago" [3]. When devices are 'vintage' (but not 'obsolete') they are in a transitional state, where support from app developers declines, updates reduce, and users may receive warnings that apps will no longer be supported [1]. When devices become 'obsolete' their warranties expire and the services that Apple were legally obliged to provide previously will no longer be available [3].

Often obsolete or 'end-of-life' devices hold little or no value in terms of serving their original purpose [25, 33] and, to date, few studies have focused on the assessment of the usefulness of vintage or obsolete devices. Where legacy devices are reused, their applications are often limited in scope (at least compared to their original lives as more general-purpose computing devices) and can be trivial compared to their original capability. For example, a legacy iPad used as a shopping list, or an iPhone used as a music player [27]. While this sort of repurposing extends the lifespan of devices and delays their disposal, if we think about usefulness with an HCI lens as a function of utility and usability [16, 24] then the limited nature of this type of repurposed utility inevitably reduces the device usefulness [5]. So how useful can a legacy device be? Can we quantify its usefulness? If utility relates to the scope of device use, then the ability to continue installing and updating apps must be significant to its usefulness. In this paper we investigate device usefulness by exploring the barriers to software installation and analyzing the functionality of downloadable apps. The work extends on a prior study that evaluated app functionality of a 'vintage' device [12] and it contributes new empirical results that quantify app downloadability and functionality for the same device when newly 'obsolete'. The study results are compared, and the usefulness and user experiences of vintage and obsolete devices are reflected upon.

2   Methods

Attempts were made to install popular free Apple App Store apps onto an obsolete device. The study device was an Apple iPad Mini Tablet, first manufactured in 2012, discontinued in 2015, received the last OS update (iOS 9.3.5) in 2016 and classed as 'obsolete' by Apple in 2022 [3]. The study took place in a three-day period between 4th and 6th May 2022. This allowed just enough time to attempt downloads for all top 10 free apps from 23 App Store categories and minimized the risk of apps having a newer pushed update, meaning the last supported versions could be removed from the Apple App Store.

For apps that cannot be downloaded directly, a current non-legacy Apple device must be used to obtain a "purchase history" on an Apple account that is shared with the legacy device. An attempt can then be made to download the "last previously supported" app for the obsolete device. Alternatively, users can connect their device to a computer and use an older version of Apple's "iTunes" to download the required app. But, either way, another device is necessary for the app installation process and these methods are not well-known and feature only infrequently on Apple forums [22]. For simplicity, we refer to this somewhat complicated workaround to downloading as 'Download via Another Device' (DvAD). To obtain a purchase history on a shared Apple account, a current non-vintage iPhone SE was used.

2.1 App Selection Criteria

A total of 230 apps were selected comprising the top 10 free App Store apps from 23 categories. App categories requiring modern features such as AR mode and extensions for the Apple Watch were excluded due to their incompatibility with the study device.

As shown in Fig. 1, each of the top ten apps for each of the categories was tested to determine whether it could be downloaded directly. Apps that did download were tested to determine whether they installed, opened, and functioned. Attempts were made to download apps via another device (as summarized earlier) if they did not download directly. Apps that downloaded successfully in this way were then tested to determine whether they installed, opened, and functioned.

3 Results

As shown in Fig. 1, only 20 (8.7%) of the total 230 top apps could be directly downloaded and of these, only 16 apps (7%) functioned. However, 143 apps (62.2%) of the total 230 top free apps could be downloaded with the help of another device, making a total of 163 apps (70.1% of all apps) that could be downloaded either directly or via another device. Of the 163 apps that did download, 115 (80.4% of the 163 apps) installed, opened, and functioned.

In total, 131 out of the 230 (57%) total apps could either be downloaded directly or via another device and were capable of functioning. This was a decrease of only 4.3% in functional apps (of the 230 total apps) compared to the performance of the device when previously classified as 'vintage'. In total, 67 (29.1% of the 230 apps) were not downloadable, however, 27 (40.3% of the 67 non-downloadable apps) were never previously supported by the device. For example, these included apps that had a release date long after the device was originally released. In total, 99 out of 230 (43%) apps were unsuccessful in download, installation, opening and/or functioning. However, of the 163 apps that did download, 131 apps (80.4%) successfully installed, opened, and functioned.

3.1 Result Breakdown by Category

A breakdown of functional apps by category is shown in Fig. 2. Although dominated by apps that required download via another device, at least half of the apps in 18 of

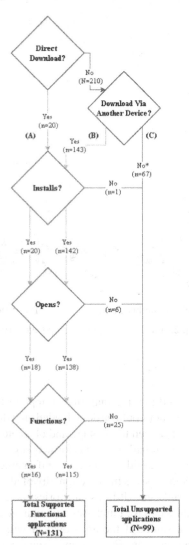

Fig. 1. A summary of the study method and app results. (A): Apps downloaded directly (green). (B): Apps downloaded via another device (yellow). (C): Apps that could not be downloaded directly or via another device (*including the 27 apps were never previously supported by the device iOS version) or that failed "Installs?", "Opens?" or "Functions?" (red). (Color figure online)

the 23 categories successfully functioned and more than half (i.e., at least 6 out of 10) apps successfully functioned for 14 of the 23 categories. Of the apps that could be downloaded, six failed to open and 25 failed to function but only one (Google maps in the 'Navigation' category) failed to install.

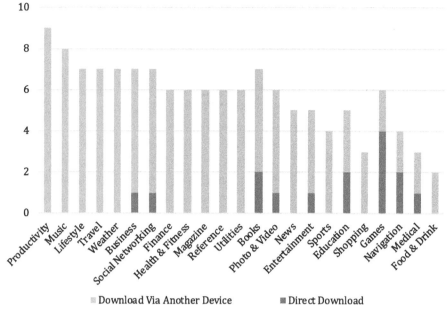

Fig. 2. Functional Apps by App Category

4 Analysis and Discussion

Overall, the study demonstrated that the majority of apps installed, opened and functioned on the obsolete device if they could be downloaded, and that only a small reduction in functioning apps occurred between the vintage and obsolete studies.

Apps were considered 'functional' if they performed key functions as intended. For example, if a video streaming app could play a video, or if a game was playable. However, it was not possible to confidently assess the functionality of all apps. For example, some apps in Finance, Food & Drink and Utilities categories require logins to pre-existing user accounts to unlock features, make purchases and manage accounts. In these cases, minimal functionality was assumed if the apps opened with a login screen with no warning or incompatibly notification. For example, some apps in the Entertainment category successfully downloaded, installed, and opened but with a notification that the app was no longer compatible and an upgrade was recommended.

4.1 Comparing 'Vintage' and 'Obsolete' Device Results

A summarized performance comparison of the two studies is provided in Table 1. The number of apps that could be downloaded directly reduced from 29 apps (12.6% of the top 230 apps) in Sept 2021 when the device was vintage down to 20 apps (8.7% of the top 230 apps) when the device was newly obsolete. Also, the number of apps that could be downloaded (either directly or via another device) increased slightly from 140 apps (60.9%) to 143 apps (62.2%). However, the number of apps that functioned (having been downloaded by either method) reduced from 141 apps (61.3%) when the device was vintage to 131 apps (57%) when the device was newly obsolete. This small decrease in functional apps might be expected as a device enters its obsolete phase.

Between the two studies there were some variations in the contemporary rankings and memberships of the free top 10 apps, and there were some variations in the performances of apps in each category. However, in both studies, all top 10 'Productivity' category of apps (e.g., email and calendar apps) failed to download directly yet 9 of the 10 apps functioned on the obsolete device and all 10 functioned on the vintage device after successful download via another device. Similarly, for the 'Health and Fitness' and 'Travel' categories of apps there were no changes in performance between the two studies yet 6 out of the 10 apps on the vintage device and 7 out of 10 apps on the obsolete device, functioned after successful download via another device. In contrast the number of functional 'Games' apps increased by 5 from 2 to 7 on the obsolete device (four being directly downloadable) which was not anticipated due to i) the release dates of popular games being rather more recent than the device, and ii) the minimum hardware requirements of games might often be expected to exceed those of a legacy device.

Table 1. Comparison of the results from each study

	Sept 2021	May 2022	Percentage Change
Direct Download	12.6%	8.7%	−3.9%
Download via Another Device	60.9%	62.2%	+1.3%
Non-Downloadable	26.5%	29.1%	+2.6%
Direct Download and Functions	10.4%	7.0%	−3.4%
Download via Another Device and Functions	50.9%	50%	−0.9%
Total Functional Apps	61.3%	57%	−4.3%
Total Non-functional* Apps	38.7%	43%	+4.3%

* 'non-functional' apps are apps that did not download (either directly or indirectly) or did not install, open or function.

4.2 The Usefulness of an 'Obsolete' Device

Labels like "vintage" and "obsolete" may make consumers perceive devices as no longer functional, usable or useful and, therefore, ready for disposal. However, as the study results demonstrate, this is not the case. Legacy devices, whether 'vintage' or 'obsolete' devices, can be capable of extended and useful function that includes the installation of many new apps. But at what point do consumers give up on efforts to continue making use of their devices? Perhaps another decrease in functioning apps at this boundary between vintage and obsolete classifications is the point at which all but the most determined users with the necessary app download know-how and access to a non-vintage device, will give up on new app installations and further use of their device.

Ideally, manufacturers would promote device longevity and assist consumers in avoiding barriers to extending the lifespans and usefulness of their devices [17, 23].

As illustrated in the percentage of functional apps in Fig. 3, if we consider that useful-ness correlates with apps capable of functioning (not only via direct download but by either method) then vintage and obsolete devices clearly have potential for longer, useful lifespans.

We cannot forget, however, that security is a key consideration for all devices. It could be argued that obsolete devices are not viable platforms given current challenges to safe and secure systems. Certainly, apps where security is critical, for example, banking apps, should not be used on obsolete devices. However, many useful apps like games, calculators, media players and other tools may present relatively little, or no, security concerns.

Graceful degradation could be a method that manufacturers adopt in future iterations of their device ranges as a way of being more inclusive to legacy device users [32]. This would reduce barriers to device longevity and avoid sudden reductions in device usefulness. A gradual decline would likely be preferred by legacy device users but quantifying or being aware of this decline (see Fig. 3) is difficult for consumers to follow.

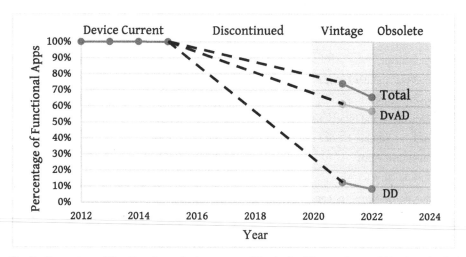

Fig. 3. Percentage of functional apps in the context of the device lifespan that could be downloaded directly (DD) or downloaded via another device (DvAD).

4.3 Study Limitations and Future Work

The study was limited to 230 popular free apps (10 from each of 23 categories). Increasing the number of apps and categories could provide more insights, however, there is an inherent time pressure to download apps because apps are updated regularly. Future work could extend the functionality assessments of apps and include assessments of their performance and usability which could include a more thorough evaluation of application functionality. Also, future work could apply a similar study methodology (as illustrated in Fig. 1) for the assessment of other Apple devices. As more devices become vintage and obsolete, a larger and more comprehensive comparative study could be conducted to assess and 'rank' changes in performance and usefulness across multiple systems. Furthermore, a similar study methodology could potentially be applied to other smartphone and tablet devices such as Android devices with "download via another device" replaced by the "sideloading" of apps [11]. This device compared to a similar era Android device has much less developer support and has a higher probability of becoming e-waste sooner as the limitations on usage become more prevalent.

5   Conclusion

The study demonstrated that most of the apps installed, opened, and functioned on the obsolete device if they could be downloaded, and that only a small reduction in functioning apps occurred between vintage and obsolete stages.

Continued efforts to improve product recycling must be made but, to reduce the mounting levels of electronic waste, new strategies are needed. As more devices become obsolete on an annual basis, new initiatives are needed to support users improve the longevity and usefulness of their old devices. It is recommended that device manufacturers remove the barriers to lifecycle extensions for obsolete devices by releasing patches to allow direct download of apps still compatible with legacy devices.

References

1. Apple. Apple Lifecycle Management, Apple (2020). https://www.apple.com/ie/business/docs/resources/Apple_Lifecycle_Management.pdf. Accessed 11 Jan 2023
2. Apple. Apple charges forward to 2030 carbon neutral goal, adding 9 gigawatts of Clean Power and doubling supplier commitments, Apple Newsroom (2021). https://www.apple.com/newsroom/2021/10/apple-charges-forward-to-2030-carbon-neutral-goal-adding-9-gigawatts-of-clean-power-and-doubling-supplier-commitments/. Accessed 11 Jan 2023
3. Apple. Obtaining service for your Apple product after an expired warranty, Apple Support (2023). https://support.apple.com/en-us/HT201624. Accessed 12 Jan 2023
4. Barros, M., Dimla, E.: From planned obsolescence to the circular economy in the smartphone industry: an evolution of strategies embodied in product features. Proc. Design Soc. 1, 1607–1616 (2021). https://doi.org/10.1017/pds.2021.422
5. Bieser, J., et al.: Lifetime Extension of Mobile Internet-Enabled Devices: Measures, Challenges and Environmental Implications, University of Zurich. University of Limerick Institutional Repository (2021). https://www.zora.uzh.ch/id/eprint/204774/. Accessed 12 Jan 2023
6. Blevis, E.: Sustainable interaction design. In: Proceedings of the SIGCHI Conference on Human Factors in Computing Systems, pp. 503–512 (2007). https://doi.org/10.1145/1240624.1240705
7. Boano, C.A.: Enabling support of legacy devices for a more sustainable internet of things. In: Proceedings of the Conference on Information Technology for Social Good [Preprint] (2021). https://doi.org/10.1145/3462203.3475883
8. Malinauskaite, J., Erdem, F.B.: Planned obsolescence in the context of a holistic legal sphere and the circular economy. Oxf. J. Leg. Stud. 41(3), 719–749 (2021). https://doi.org/10.1093/ojls/gqaa061

9. Chirumamilla, P.: The unused and the unusable: repair, rejection, and obsolescence. In Refusing, Limiting, Departing, In: CHI 2014 Workshop Considering Why We Should Study Technology Non-Use, Toronto (2014). http://nonuse.jedbrubaker.com/wp-content/uploads/2014/03/2014_position_paper.pdf

10. Forti, V., et al.: The global E-waste monitor 2020: Quantities, flows and the circular economy potential, UNU Collections. United Nations University/United Nations Institute for Training and Research, International Telecommunication Union, and International Solid Waste Association (2020). https://collections.unu.edu/view/UNU:7737. Accessed 12 Jan 2023

11. Goodwin, C.: 'Why Sideload?' user behaviours, interactions and accessibility issues around mobile app installation. Electronic Workshops in Computing (2020). https://doi.org/10.14236/ewic/hci20dc.5

12. Goodwin, C., Woolley, S.: Barriers to device longevity and reuse: an analysis of application download, installation and functionality on a vintage device. Reuse Software Qual. **13297**, 138–145 (2022). https://doi.org/10.1007/978-3-031-08129-3_9

13. Gravier, M.J., Swartz, S.M.: The Dark Side of Innovation: exploring obsolescence and supply chain evolution for sustainment-dominated systems. J. High Technol. Manage. Res. **20**(2), 87–102 (2009). https://doi.org/10.1016/j.hitech.2009.09.001

14. Hansson, L.Å., Cerratto Pargman, T., Pargman, D.S.: A decade of sustainable HCI. In: Proceedings of the 2021 CHI Conference on Human Factors in Computing Systems (2021). https://doi.org/10.1145/3411764.3445069

15. Higginbotham, S.: The internet of trash [internet of everything]. IEEE Spectrum **55**(6), 17 (2018). https://doi.org/10.1109/mspec.2018.8362218

16. Interaction Design Foundation. What is usefulness?, The Interaction Design Foundation (2017). https://www.interaction-design.org/literature/topics/usefulness. Accessed 11 Jan 2023

17. Jensen, P.B., Laursen, L.N., Haase, L.M.: Barriers to product longevity: a review of business, product development and user perspectives. J. Clean. Prod. **313**, 127951 (2021). https://doi.org/10.1016/j.jclepro.2021.127951

18. Jobin, M., et al.: Extending the lifetime of mobile devices to reduce their environmental impact: a glimpse on the project lifesaving (2021). SocietyByte. Marilou Jobin https://www.societybyte.swiss/wp-content/uploads/2022/02/SocietyByte_Logo_EN_plus_1030x94.png. Available at: https://www.societybyte.swiss/en/2020/05/20/extending-the-lifetime-of-mobile-devices-to-reduce-their-environmental-impact-a-glimpse-on-the-project-lifesaving/. Accessed 12 Jan 2023

19. Kuppelwieser, V.G., et al.: Consumer responses to planned obsolescence. J. Retail. Consum. Serv. **47**, 157–165 (2019). https://doi.org/10.1016/j.jretconser.2018.11.014

20. Makov, T., Fitzpatrick, C.: Is repairability enough? big data insights into smartphone obsolescence and consumer interest in repair. J. Clean. Prod. **313**, 127561 (2021). https://doi.org/10.1016/j.jclepro.2021.127561

21. Mellal, M.A.: Obsolescence – a review of the literature. Technol. Soc. **63**, 101347 (2020). https://doi.org/10.1016/j.techsoc.2020.101347

22. MichelPM. Downloading older IOS 9.3.5 versions of apps only available now for IOS 10 or later, Downloading Older iOS 9.3.5 Versions of A... - Apple Community (2020). https://discussions.apple.com/docs/DOC-13282. Accessed 11 Jan 2023

23. Møller, K.P., Frydkjær, N.S., Haase, L.M.: Smartphone updates as a longevity barrier for Electronic Consumer Products, Aalborg University's Research Portal. LUT Scientific and Expertise Publications (2021). https://vbn.aau.dk/en/publications/smartphone-updates-as-a-longevity-barrier-for-electronic-consumer. Accessed 12 Jan 2023

24. Nielsen, J.: Usefulness, utility, usability: 3 goals of UX Design (Jakob Nielsen), YouTube. YouTube (2017). https://www.youtube.com/watch?v=VwgZtqTQzg8. Accessed 11 Jan 2023

25. Proske, M., et al.: Obsolescence of electronics - the example of smartphones. 2016 Electronics Goes Green 2016+ (EGG) [Preprint] (2016). https://doi.org/10.1109/egg.2016.7829852

26. Remy, C.: Addressing obsolescence of consumer electronics through Sustainable Interaction Design. In: Proceedings of the 33rd Annual ACM Conference Extended Abstracts on Human Factors in Computing Systems (2015). https://doi.org/10.1145/2702613.2702621

27. Rogerson, J.: What to do when your old iPhone or iPad doesn't run iOS 14 or iPadOS 14, Techradar (2022). https://www.techradar.com/how-to/what-to-do-when-your-old-iphone-or-ipad-doesnt-run-ios-14-or-ipados-14. Accessed 11 Jan 2023

28. Silberman, M.S., et al.: Next steps for sustainable HCI. Interactions **21**(5), 66–69 (2014). https://doi.org/10.1145/2651820

29. Strausz, R.: Planned obsolescence as an incentive device for unobservable quality. Econ. J. **119**(540), 1405–1421 (2009). https://doi.org/10.1111/j.1468-0297.2009.02290.x

30. Taffel, S.: AirPods and the earth: digital technologies, planned obsolescence and the Capitalocene. Environ. Plan. E: Nat. Space **6**(1), 433–454 (2023)

31. The Economist. Planned obsolescence, The Economist. The Economist Newspaper (2009). https://www.economist.com/news/2009/03/23/planned-obsolescence. Accessed 11 Jan 2023

32. W3. Graceful degradation versus progressive enhancement, Graceful degradation versus progressive enhancement - W3C Wiki (2015). https://www.w3.org/wiki/Graceful_degradation_versus_progressive_enhancement. Accessed 11 Jan 2023

33. Wiche, P., Pequeño, F., Granato, D.: Life cycle analysis of a refurbished smartphone in Chile. E3S Web Conf. **349** (2022). https://doi.org/10.1051/e3sconf/202234901011

Usability Evaluation of a Brazilian Dam Safety Data Exploration Platform: A Consolidation of Results from User Tests and Heuristic Evaluation

Bruna Santana Capeleti[1]([✉]), Caroline Queiroz Santos[2],
Jaqueline Isabel de Souza[3], and André Pimenta Freire[1]

[1] Universidade Federal de Lavras, Lavras, MG 37200-900, Brazil
brunacapeleti@gmail.com, apfreire@ufla.br
[2] Universidade Federal dos Vales do Jequitinhonha e Mucuri,
Diamantina, MG 39100-000, Brazil
caroline.queiroz@ufvjm.edu.br
[3] Fundação de Desenvolvimento Científico e Cultural, Lavras, MG 37200-900, Brazil
jaquelinesouza.ti@fundecc.org.br

Abstract. Data-driven decision-making has gained paramount importance and has become indispensable to learning new knowledge and gaining insights in various contexts. Specifically, in critical and security contexts, interactive systems are imperative to support decision-making. However, for systems that enable data exploration, good usability is essential to facilitate effective data exploration for experts and laypeople. This study aimed to evaluate the usability of a system containing information regarding Brazilian dams, with a panel and an information filter, by consolidating the results obtained from user evaluations and a set of Human-Data Interaction heuristics proposed in the literature. The user evaluations involved 18 participants aged between 22 and 45 years, with previous knowledge about dam safety. Three specialists in Human-Computer Interaction performed the heuristic evaluation. The results from user evaluations and heuristic evaluation facilitated the analysis of the main problems encountered by users and their relationship with recently-proposed heuristics. User evaluations revealed the need for usability improvements related to the affordance of interactive map elements and information filters. The paper discusses the impact of the problems faced by users in the map-based dam data exploration platform and how the Human-Data Interaction heuristics aided the identification of different types of problems. These results provide crucial input for enhancing critical data exploration platforms and methodological reflections on the different contributions brought by different usability evaluation methods applied to Human-Data Interaction.

Keywords: User tests · Usability · Dam safety · Human data interaction

© The Author(s), under exclusive license to Springer Nature Switzerland AG 2023
J. Abdelnour Nocera et al. (Eds.): INTERACT 2023, LNCS 14145, pp. 100–119, 2023.
https://doi.org/10.1007/978-3-031-42293-5_9

1   Introduction

Data plays a fundamental role in the communication and acquisition of knowledge. Users gain insights into various topics through their interaction with data. Initially, the field of Human-Data Interaction focused solely on analyzing the data itself. However, over time, it became apparent that understanding how users interpret the presented information was equally crucial [22], particularly given the ever-growing size and intricacy of data resulting from advancements in data collection and dissemination technologies [12].

Human-Data Interaction plays a critical role in all domains involving information transmission, as it serves as a conduit for knowledge acquisition, as outlined in the research conducted by Victorelli and Reis [20]. This study also highlights the contributions of methods employing tools to support the data life cycle [20]. In environmental studies, the ability to access data accurately and concisely is of utmost importance, particularly in accident prevention and monitoring.

Dams have received substantial attention in the Brazilian environment. The country has numerous water dams connected to hydroelectric plants and mining tailings dams. Many major accidents have occurred in some dams, leading to severe environmental and human impacts. In Brazil, the National Dam Safety Policy was established by Law 12,334/2010 [2] to safeguard lives and nature during dam accidents. The Brazilian National Water Agency [1] defines dam accidents as situations in which there is a "compromise of the structural integrity of a dam, leading to the uncontrolled release of the reservoir contents".

When conducted appropriately, the interaction with data related to the state of preservation of a dam is of great significance in preventing accidents, and in more severe cases, it enables experts to leverage their knowledge to predict risks and evacuate the area before the event occurs. Additionally, data availability allows lay users to access information about nearby dams and their danger levels.

Human-Computer Interaction concepts can be employed to measure interaction aspects [14,22], to assess whether users can comprehend the data as intended. Such evaluation may be conducted using methods like user tests or heuristics focused on data, as proposed by Victorelli and Reis [21].

Despite the increased attention to studies on Human-Data Interaction [14,22], specific areas of knowledge have not been subjected to a detailed analysis that can derive implications for design. In the environmental field, there is insufficient understanding of the outcomes obtained through applying Human-Computer Interaction techniques aimed at data exploration platforms via inspections utilizing heuristic evaluations or user tests, for instance.

The objective of this research was to evaluate an environmental data exploration platform that aims to centralize information about Brazilian dams using a combination of two methods: 1) tests with users who know the environmental and technological areas and 2) a collaborative heuristic evaluation conducted by three specialists in Human-Computer Interaction. The usability heuristics defined by Nielsen and Molich [15] and the specialized usability heuristics for Human-Data Interaction defined by Victorelli and Reis [21] were used in the evaluation. In addition to identifying issues through these heuristics, the study also developed categories to group the most significant problems to facilitate improvement.

The paper is structured as follows: Sect. 2 provides the theoretical background, defining essential terms related to dam safety and human-data interaction. Section 3 discusses related studies. Section 4 outlines the methods employed in this study. Section 5 presents the results obtained from the applied methods. Finally, Sect. 6 summarizes the contributions of this work and outlines avenues for future research.

2 Theoretical Background

This section introduces definitions relevant to dam safety in the Brazilian context and human-data interaction. This section lays the foundation for the research presented in this paper by providing these definitions. Additionally, this section discusses related works and their findings.

2.1 Context of Dam Safety in Brazil

Law 12,334 [2] was enacted in Brazil in 2010, establishing the National Policy on Dam Safety. Its main objective was to preserve life and nature by anticipating accidents involving dams before their occurrence [17]. According to the Brazilian National Water Agency - [1], a "dam" is defined as "a structure for the retention or accumulation of liquid substances or mixtures of liquids and solids".

Dam safety is closely tied to monitoring existing dams to maintain their integrity and preserve life and the environment around them. Additionally, according to the Brazilian National Water Agency [1], an accident involving a dam can be defined as "the structural integrity compromise with the uncontrollable release of reservoir contents".

In 2015 and 2019, the Brazilian population witnessed accidents involving dams. The first accident in Mariana, in the state of Minas Gerais, resulted in the release of about 40 million cubic meters of tailings, causing the loss of life and a significant environmental imbalance [13]. The second accident occurred in the municipality of Brumadinho, also in Minas Gerais, in 2019. It involved the release of about 12 million cubic meters of tailings, resulting in a higher number of fatalities than the 2015 incident and a smaller environmental impact [5].

Thus, in the Brazilian context, dam safety requires conducting suitable inspections and verifications of erected dams to anticipate and forestall accidents.

2.2 Human-Data Interaction

Knaflic [7] states that in human-data interaction, it is crucial to determine the intended audience to whom the presenter will communicate. This approach establishes the context for the data presentation. Explaining what will be presented is necessary while avoiding excessive information to prevent user confusion. This information is particularly relevant in the context of the evaluated data since users often access it independently without assistance or supervision.

In their article, Mortier *et al.* [14] have identified three main aspects of human-data interaction. The first aspect is readability, which focuses on presenting data more transparently and understandably for readers. The second aspect is action, which relates to users' actions based on the information absorbed from the data. The third and final aspect is negotiability, which concerns visualizing changes in individuals and society resulting from the interpretation of data over time.

In their study, Victorelli and Reis [21] proposed a set of heuristics related to the design of elements that utilize human-data interaction, including:

1. Human-data interaction design guidelines for visualization systems
   1.1. Self-evidence in coordinated views
   1.2. Consistency between coordinated visualizations
   1.3. Reversible operations in visualizations
2. Use smooth animated transitions between visualizations states when they can help the user to notice the difference between the data
3. Immediately provide visual feedback on the interaction
4. Maximize direct manipulation with data
5. Minimize information overload
   5.1. Show information context
   5.2. Avoid requiring data memorization
6. Semantically enrich the interaction
   6.1. Semantically enrich search interaction
   6.2. Enriched feedback from humans incorporated into the system
   6.3. Refine and train models through user feedback

3   Related Work

This section presents related work concerning improving dam monitoring systems, mapping questions asked by users, adapting architecture to perform dam simulations, and analysis focused on human-data interaction.

The study performed by Law, Lai-Chong, and Ebba Thora Hvannberg [9] investigated the complementary nature and convergence of heuristic evaluation and usability testing in evaluating the usability of a universal brokerage platform. The case study explores how these two evaluation methods can be integrated to provide a more comprehensive assessment of the platform's usability. The results from both methods were compared and synthesized to reveal the complementarity and convergence between heuristic evaluation and usability testing. The findings demonstrated that heuristic evaluation identified high-level usability issues and provided valuable design suggestions, while usability testing uncovered specific and contextual usability problems encountered by users during task execution. Integrating heuristic evaluation and usability testing provided a more holistic evaluation of the universal brokerage platform's usability, with each method offering unique perspectives and insights.

Ekşioğlu, Mahmut, *et al.* [4] investigated the efficacy of combining heuristic evaluation and user testing to assess user interface usability. The presented case study involved evaluating a real-world web application. Initially, heuristic evaluations were conducted, wherein usability experts analyzed the interface based on predefined heuristics. This phase identified several potential usability issues within the interface. Subsequently, user testing was performed, involving participants completing specific tasks while their behaviours and perceptions were observed. User testing helped validate and further explore the findings from the heuristic evaluation, uncovering additional problems not identified through expert analysis alone. The results suggest combining heuristic evaluation and user testing can be a powerful approach to evaluating interface usability, enabling more effective identification and resolution of problems. This highlights the significance of utilizing a multi-method approach in usability evaluation, leveraging the strengths of different approaches to achieve comprehensive and reliable insights into the quality of the user experience.

Komarkova, Jitka, *et al.* [8] presents a study that focuses on the usability evaluation of the Prague Geoportal, a web-based geographic information system (GIS). The study aims to assess the usability of the Geoportal and identify potential improvements to enhance the user experience. The evaluation process involved a combination of heuristic evaluation and usability testing. Usability experts performed heuristic evaluations, applying established usability heuristics to analyze the interface design and functionality. Additionally, usability testing was conducted with real users who performed specific tasks on the Geoportal while their interactions were observed. The study found several usability issues and provided recommendations for improving the interface's navigation, information presentation, and overall user interaction. The findings highlight the importance of considering usability principles in GIS design and development to ensure efficient access to spatial data and enhance user satisfaction. By integrating heuristic evaluation and usability testing, the study contributes to a better understanding of usability challenges and offers valuable insights for optimizing GIS interfaces.

The study by Jeon *et al.* [6] starts from the principle of seeking to increase the safety of dams in South Korea because of the risks involved in accidents. Therefore, a dam safety monitoring system was created to seek data from water systems, dams, instrumentation, hydrological information, inspection, and dam information. Having a more robust system with more information than the system currently used in Korea made it possible to conclude that decisions and actions can be taken faster with more detailed and easily visualized data.

Rodrigues *et al.* [16] conducted a study to understand which questions users ask during their interaction with the data. Twenty-two users participated in the study, totalling 1058 questions, divided into two groups for analysis: the first group was related to straightforward questions, and the second group to questions with some problem. As a result, the authors categorize the questions into five categories, described according to the author's definition:

1. ERR - questions containing conceptual errors (88 occurrences);

2. AMB - questions that contain some ambiguity (41);
3. DTA - questions that are technically answerable, but are difficult to answer with the visualization, i.e., questions for which the visualization was not appropriate (43);
4. DNA - questions the visualization does not answer (28);
5. INS - failures to follow the instructions when filling out the questionnaire (79).

The study can be used in learning about data visualization since it can map questions and errors raised by users during the analysis, also helping in a better view of the questions that can be asked by users and how to cover them in the presentation of data better.

The study carried out by Liu *et al.* [11] consisted of adapting an architecture so that dam information could collaborate more with a simulation focused on verifying possibilities of dam failure and its impacts. The data flows used in this research focused on experienced users reading this type of data and inexperienced users to ensure that several users could access the remodelling of the tool already used.

Leskens *et al.* [10] bring a system for analyzing flooding scenarios in their study. Despite the complexity involved in the data, the developed tool aims to be accessible to professionals and people who have no contact with the area. This objective is facilitated by the 3D tool used by the system. It helps better estimate the scale and impact of a flood.

According to Calvetti *et al.* [3], they were conducting a study using use cases that often have a large amount of information and generating a detailed view of the data. In this way, the existing processes were improved by specialists. Thus, they concluded that monitoring human activities deserves to be highlighted, indicating as accurately as possible what data will be collected and the expected results.

The study carried out by Trajkova *et al.* [18] sought to understand which aspects related to interaction would be necessary to ensure that museum visitors understood how to use the system and how to attract people to interact with the screen, keeping their attention.

The studies mentioned in this section bring views on mapping impressions about interaction with data and which methodologies worked, especially in the context of dam safety. In this sense, this study aims to complement the information already in the literature to bring an approach containing the junction of human-data interaction with user tests for a dam safety context.

4   Methods

This study aimed to investigate aspects of the interaction between humans and data in exploring environmental issues. The investigation employed user testing techniques and heuristic evaluation to assess an application that explores a dataset on the safety of Brazilian dams.

The overseeing agency responsible for monitoring Brazilian dams maintains a comprehensive database containing all relevant dam-related information. This dataset is utilized to develop a dashboard that enhances data visualization and comprehension, ultimately contributing to establishing a national repository of records concerning Brazilian dams.

Concerning the user tests, the research involved 18 participants assigned specific tasks to interact with the data. Their perceptions and opinions were solicited, and upon completion of the tasks, they were asked to complete a questionnaire and participate in a brief post-test interview.

The heuristic evaluation was conducted by three experts specializing in human-computer interaction, employing the collaborative heuristic evaluation method. This approach involved the evaluators performing the same tasks as the users and collaboratively identifying any issues or problems encountered during the evaluation process.

4.1   Task Performed in Evaluations

The objective of the study was to examine the usability of a webpage that featured a dashboard presenting data related to dam safety, accompanied by search filters.

During the execution of the assigned task, participants were instructed to interact with both the dashboard and the search filters, expressing their understanding of the provided information and articulating any inquiries that arose.

4.2   Procedures for Heuristic Evaluation

The evaluation aimed to appraise the performance of the data presented within the dashboard, along with its associated filters. The issues identified in the application were assessed and compared against general-purpose usability heuristics proposed by Molich and Nielsen [15] and specific heuristics for human-data interaction put forth by Victorelli and Reis [21], as described in Sect. 2.2. The Nielsen and Molich's heuristics [15] were: 1) Visibility of system status, 2) Match between system and the real world, 3) User control and freedom, 4) Consistency and standards, 5) Error prevention, 6) Recognition rather than recall, 7) Flexibility and efficiency of use, 8) Aesthetic and minimalist design, 9) Help users recognize, diagnose, and recover from errors and 10) Help and documentation.

The inspection was conducted by three Human-Computer Interaction specialists through a collaborative heuristic evaluation conducted remotely. This approach sought to facilitate evaluators' joint identification of issues and their assignment of corresponding heuristics.

4.3   Procedures for User Tests

The testing phase involved 18 participants aged between 22 and 45 years, possessing prior knowledge in dam safety and technology, primarily from disciplines such as Environmental and Sanitary Engineering and Computer Science, with experience in technology and environmental management. User recruitment was conducted through invitation-based selection, where interested individuals were included as participants upon acceptance. In the event of non-acceptance, researchers proceeded to the following potential user. Each user was assigned the same task to evaluate their comprehension of the presented data. Due to the Covid-19 pandemic, the tests were conducted remotely via a videoconferencing platform. The testing protocol and post-test user interviews were approved by the Research Ethics Committee, with the code CAAE 55663422.8.0000.5148.

During the test phase, upon initial contact with the user, the researcher introduced themselves and provided an overview of the research objectives. The user was then given an explanation of the nature and procedures of the usability tests, emphasising the confidentiality of their personal information. We clarified that the purpose of the test was to assess the platform's performance rather than the user's ability to comprehend the dashboard. Additionally, users were informed of their right to discontinue the test at any point. Following this initial briefing, the user was presented with the assigned task and instructed to employ the Think-Aloud protocol [19] to verbalize their impressions and experiences while using the platform. Subsequently, the test session commenced. After completing the test, participants were asked to provide demographic information through a questionnaire, including their age, computer experience, and familiarity with dam safety information. Additionally, a usability questionnaire was administered, comprising a series of statements with response options ranging from "Totally disagree" to "Completely agree", presented as follows:

1. Overall, I was able to understand the information presented in the data;
2. In general, the reading of the data was easy to carry out;
3. I would use the data presented to carry out studies;
4. I would recommend the page containing the data to friends;
5. I believe the presentation of the data was easy to understand;
6. I believe the information is useful in my life.

After the completion of the questionnaire, users were invited to participate in a concise interview aimed at eliciting their perceptions regarding their interaction with the platform. The interview questions were as follows:

1. Were you able to understand the information presented in the data?;
2. Did you have any questions while interpreting the data?;
3. In your opinion, what is the best way to perform a data presentation?;
4. If you want to mention any other point you deem necessary, feel free to expose it.

4.4 The Evaluated System

The system under evaluation represents an enhanced version of the existing Brazilian dam information system, with a heightened emphasis on data presentation and consolidation. The objective is to facilitate even easier access to information for users compared to the currently utilized system.

It is important to note that the release of the updated product has not occurred as of yet. User testing is being conducted at an intermediate stage of the development process to leverage the obtained results as a tool for implementing enhancements and refining the already developed features and functionalities. An example of a screen used in the evaluation is shown in Fig. 1.

4.5   Analysis

The problems encountered during user testing were categorized as unique issues to avoid repeating an error identified by multiple users. There was no repetition of the same problem during each test; therefore, the analysis considered only the number of users who identified a specific problem.

Based on the previous outcome, the next step involved cross-referencing the results identified through heuristic evaluation and user testing to determine which issues were exclusively identified by one of the methods and which were identified by both. This analysis allowed for a comprehensive understanding of the aspects of interaction that were addressed by each approach.

5   Results and Discussion

This section describes the findings derived from the analysis of information obtained through user testing and the outcomes yielded from the heuristic evaluation.

5.1   Heuristic Evaluation Results

The heuristic evaluation successfully identified 41 issues by simulating the same task assigned in the user tests. Out of the 41 problems identified, 28 did not yield a similar outcome in the user testing. Among the critical problems, one significant issue involved comprehending the data due to its scattered presentation across the dashboard, leading to a disconnection between the titles and the corresponding data. Additionally, the interaction was hindered by the utilization of closely related colour scales for the presented data, frequently impeding the comparison of information when seeking specific details. The problems identified solely through heuristic evaluation are displayed in Table 1.

Specialists also encountered a different category of problems related to technical terminology. Given that the system caters to diverse audiences, an expectation was to provide a "translation" of the technical terms into a more accessible language.

Furthermore, the presence of a Spanish translation option on the page did not result in the dashboard being updated when selected.

Table 1. Issues found only by the heuristic evaluation

Issues found only by heuristic evaluation	Related Heuristics
It was not clear if the dams registered in 2022 were part of the total (make it clear that among the registered dams, x were in 2022)	V6, N8
Purple buttons do not make it clear that they are inactive	V3, N7, N8
It is not clear what will be shared - the entire page? Only one piece of data?	V3, N1, N7
"Last update" - the last time the page was loaded or the last update that was entered into the system? - ambiguous information	V3, N1, N7, N8
"Last update" should not be there - it seems outdated - it would be better to have one for each chart	V5, N6, N7
Dams with good or excellent completeness - You are viewing the entire Brazil - large blank space - is it below or to the right? - one chart or all of them?	V2, N1, N7, N8
When hovering, it shows - state, class, number of dams - but are those with good or excellent completeness?	V4, V5, N7
The only indication of the current state is through color - it would need to be shown in another way (text, for example)	V6, N5, N6, N9, N10
There is no feedback that there has been a change in the charts on the right when clicking on a state	V3, N1, N7, N8
There is no consistent font type and size (filter, illustrations)	N8
When clicking on a bar, the data changes, and it does not show the status to verify what happened	V3, N6, N7
There is no indication that the bars are clickable	V3, N7, N8
The map and bar charts do not facilitate establishing connections between the data	V6, N1, N6
The list of dams is out of the field of view	V3, N4, N6
There are no instructions on how to obtain more information about a dam	V6, N6, N7
Some terms are specific and difficult to understand for non-experts, without an explanation of their "main use"	V5, V6, N6, N7
The expand button does not have an obvious meaning	V6, N6, N7, N8
"You are viewing the profile of the entire Brazil" even after applying a filter	V5, N6, N7, N8
After filtering, it is not possible to know the location of the dams - only in the final list	V5, N6, N7, N8
The heatmap map does not change after filtering	V3, N1, N6, N7, N8
There is no legend identifying the classifications of dams	V3, N1, N6
A "?" is missing to indicate explanations in other points, not just technical items	V6, N2, N6
Only the menu is translated into Spanish, but not the data visualization	V3, N2, N4, N6, N7, N8
It should be available in English	V6, N2, N5, N8
Before the name, a chart with the dams and the timeline could be included	V5, N1, N7
Risk category: Not applicable - can accidents really not occur?	V6, N5, N6, N7
There is no explanation or label to indicate what each item represents	V6, N6, N9, N10
There should be an outline for the map of Brazil when applying filters, not just removing the states	N7, N8

5.2   User Tests Results

In total, 27 problems were found by users. An identical problem encountered by multiple users was consolidated to prevent the duplication of problem analysis. Nonetheless, the number of users who reported the issue was included in the results and examined.

The problems identified during user tests were systematically categorized into individual issues, with their frequency of occurrence meticulously recorded, and subsequently linked to the heuristics proposed by Victorelli and Reis [21], and Molich and Nielsen [15] (Table 2).

In this particular context, most of the issues experienced by users were directly associated with the use of search filters, which demonstrated considerable complexity in terms of comprehensibility, primarily owing to the extensive array of information available for selection and the disparities, as mentioned earlier with the dashboard.

5.3   The Outcomes Derived from the Consolidation of User Tests and Heuristic Evaluation

Upon defining the task at hand, various usability issues were identified, which were found to be associated with the heuristics outlined by Victorelli and Reis [21], specifically centred around human-data interaction, as well as the heuristics proposed by Molich and Nielsen [15].

Following the execution of the application utilizing both methods for the identical task within the system, a comparative analysis was conducted to determine the prevalence of specific heuristics in each method and the insights they yielded.

The most prevalent issue encountered during interaction with the dashboard was the perceived lack of interactivity in the map of Brazil (reported by 14 users), where the ability to select and isolate data about a specific state by clicking on it was absent (Table 3).

As evidenced by related works, the combined approach of user testing and heuristic evaluation provides complementary insights into the issues that require attention. Furthermore, based on the obtained results, it was possible to confirm that heuristic evaluation also encompasses aspects of design suggestions, as Law, Lai-Chong, and Ebba Thora Hvannberg [9]. The integration of these two aspects yielded a comprehensive overview of improvements and problem categories that can be encountered in applications like the one under evaluation.

Among the heuristics proposed by Victorelli and Reis [21], the ones most closely associated with the issues encountered by users and identified during the heuristic evaluation were as follows: 3. Immediately provide visual feedback on the interaction due to lack of feedback and confusion caused to users at certain moments of the interaction, and 6. Semantically enrich the interaction, focusing on its sub-item 6.1 Semantically enrich search interaction, since search filters were applied and often did not have adequate feedback.

Table 2. Issues found by user tests

Issues found only by user tests	Related Heuristics	Number of users who have reported the issue
The filter icon only shows which filters have been selected, when in fact it gives the impression that it is possible to select a filter through it	V3, N1, N3	1
When expanding the 'Dam Name' filter, the dam codes were listed	V3, N1, N4	1
Depending on the selected filter, the charts displayed on the dashboard overlap with the titles	V2, V5, N8	1
When opening a filter listing for selection, the system gives the impression that it is possible to select multiple pieces of information from the same filter, when in reality only one can be selected	V4, N6	1
When reviewing the data presented in the table (which can be extensive), there is no option to return to the top of the table display	V6, N7	1
The map is too small, making interaction more difficult. It would be easier if it were larger	V3, N8	1
The functioning of the filters causes a lot of confusion about how to use them	V5, N3, N6, N7	8
The filter does not close after selecting an option	V2, N7	1
Clicking on the dashboard gives the impression that the filters will also be updated	V4, N4, N6, N7	1
The filter information is cut off when opening the options	V6, N8	2
When hovering over the title of a piece of information, it disappears	V6, N7, N8	1
Filter icons (such as focus mode) overlap with the filter information itself	V5, N8	2
When selecting an option on the map, it is not updated in the filters	V3, N1, N4, N6, N7, N8	2
In the 'Find dams by' option, it gave the impression that it was a search field	V6, N1, N8	1

Table 3. Issues found by both methods

Issues Found by Both User Tests and Heuristic Evaluations	Related Heuristics	Number of users who have reported the issue
Cleaning filters is out of the field of view	V1, N1, N3, N6, N7, N8	2
Does not increase font size of filters with CTRL +	N8	7
It is not clear that the map is clickable, which can display data for a particular state	V3, N1, N6, N7	14
What is good or excellent completeness? Will people without knowledge of dams understand? It is necessary to explain what it means in terms of data	V5, N7	3
Registered dams - total and dams in 2022 are far away	N1, N8, V6	1
When there is no data, it shows "blank" instead of "not registered" or something similar	V6, N6, N8, N9	1
The 'Most Accessed Dams' do not make it clear what parameter is used for counting (year, months)	V6, N2, N6	1
Search results - but what if I haven't performed any search? What type of search is it?	V6, N6, N7, N8, N10	1
By looking only at the dashboard, it is not possible to know which filters are active	V3, N3, N6, N7	1
When interacting with the map and clicking on a specific state, it does not always appear selected on the map due to the color scheme of the heat map	V3, V4, N1, N8	1
It is not clear that filters cannot be selected together (checkbox affordance)	V3, N7	1
The 'Focus Mode' of the filter sometimes opens in the middle of the screen, giving the impression that the screen is blank	V3, N1, N5, N7, N8	2

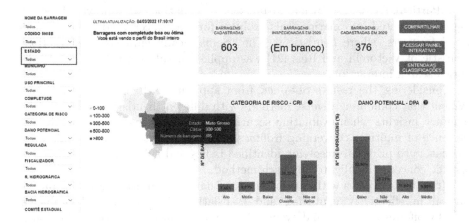

Fig. 1. Example of an issue with the information contained in the dashboard, where "Em branco" means "Blank space"

Regarding the heuristics of Molich and Nielsen [15], the two heuristics most closely linked to user problems were: 7. Flexibility and efficiency of use, and 8. Aesthetic and minimalist design, since the arrangement of elements and the pattern of colours used (mainly in heat maps), end up causing user confusion and hindering interaction. Regarding the problems found in the heuristic evaluation, the heuristics related the most were: 6. Recognition rather than recall, 7. Flexibility and efficiency of use, and 8. Aesthetic and minimalist design, once the interaction became harder because it did not have a pattern of the data presented, confusing the evaluators.

Regarding the heuristic 1 - Human-data interaction design guidelines for visualization systems from Victorelli and Reis [21], the subcategory applicable to the problem found was 1.3 - Reversible operations in visualizations. One of the issues identified during the evaluation was users having difficulty locating the button to clear their previous selections after applying filters and attempting to initiate a new search. This lack of immediate visibility led users to believe there was no option to remove the previously selected data.

During the task execution in the conducted tests, we observed that the presented information lacked fundamental contextualization on multiple occasions. For instance, within the system, updates were displayed without an accompanying explanation, thereby impeding a clear understanding of whether the updates were derived from real-time data or sourced directly from the underlying database along with the existing information. This issue was considered in the heuristic of Victorelli and Reis [21] 5. Minimize information overload, more precisely in subitem 5.1 - Show information context.

Another frequently encountered problem in the interaction involved the excessive spacing or scattered arrangement of substantial amounts of information on the screen. This particular issue hindered users from discerning the context and purpose of each case, thereby impeding the search process within the application. Particularly in cases where insufficient explanations were provided regarding the presented information, this problem further exacerbated the challenges faced by users, where heuristic 6. The "Semantically enrich the interaction" heuristic of Victorelli and Reis [21] was applied in subitem 6.1 - Semantically enrich search interaction.

Considering the results obtained from applying each method, it becomes evident that combining diverse methods with different heuristics yields complementary insights when evaluating security-focused systems. Consequently, the presence of multiple converging fronts, presenting similar outcomes empowers evaluators to prioritize resolving identified issues and subsequently address the specific concerns highlighted by each method.

Utilizing heuristics within the context of data presentation usability proved pivotal in effectively capturing and translating the encountered problems, thereby offering solutions and avenues for improved interpretation of the issues, subsequent rectification, and standardization.

The application of the heuristics proposed by Victorelli and Reis [21] proved beneficial within this project's scope. Specifically, the broader set of six upper-level heuristics demonstrated significant relevance in addressing many encountered issues. However, when utilizing these heuristics in a context different from the case studies analyzed in the initial study, it became evident that there exist gaps that require more precise guidance tailored to specific domains and data contexts, thereby enhancing the efficacy of the broader heuristics.

5.4   Categories Proposed to Represent the Issues Related to Interaction with Data

The identified problems were categorized to represent the various issues encountered during the interactions. The resultant categories derived from this analysis offer valuable insights into the nature of the identified problems and their implications on the design of data exploration systems within dam safety.

Visibility About How to Interact with Data. When data requires a specific path to be accessed, it is imperative for the steps involved in obtaining the information to be transparent. The category "Visibility about how to interact with data" encompasses issues about quickly locating and comprehending the pathway to access data and its corresponding details. This category is proposed to facilitate user interaction with the data application, enabling efficient data exploration.

An instance illustrating an issue within this category was observed in both inspections, wherein the heatmap displayed on the dashboard failed to convey its interactive nature. Despite the intended functionality of optimizing searches beyond Brazilian states, it did not function as anticipated. Furthermore, upon users' realization that the map could be interacted with and an area was selected, the remaining parts of the map disappeared, lacking a clear option to reset the previously made selection.

Position of Key Elements to Interact with Data. In order to interact with data, certain elements serve as keys to unlock specific information. Hence, these keys must be easily discernible and prominently visible to users. For instance, when working with data visualization accompanied by filters that necessitate parameter adjustments, the key for initiating this transition should be within the user's visual field.

An illustrative example, identified during user testing and heuristic evaluation within this category, pertains to the button's location to clear search filters ("Limpar filtro" in Portuguese). This button is situated in an inconspicuous position, erasing the selected filters and initiating a new search more challenging. Furthermore, depending on the user's computer screen size, the button may not be immediately visible until the user scrolls down the page.

Data Presentation Pattern. Another facet of data interaction pertains to the presentation of information. Is there a discernible pattern in data presentation, or is it seemingly random? This category aims to capture this aspect, encompassing information clarity and its organisational structure's comprehensibility. Additionally, the pattern must be coherent, enhancing understanding and ease of interaction with the data narrative.

The evaluated application allows users to employ filters to locate the desired dam. However, in each filter category, the application conveys that multiple pieces of information can be selected. Nonetheless, in practice, only one item from each filter category can be selected, leading to user frustration when choosing two items within the same parameter.

Operating Error to Achieve the Expectation of Interaction with the Data. Several malfunctioning issues were identified during the evaluations in the context of a recently released system. This category is introduced to address functional errors that can detrimentally impact the quality of data interaction, as the expected behaviour may not be fulfilled within the system, thus hindering the completion of the data interaction process.

It is important to acknowledge that systems generally are not exempt from malfunctions in specific functionalities. Within this application, an issue related to this category was observed concerning the zoom-in or zoom-out functionality of the dashboard. Despite the user's attempts to increase the font size, no visible changes occurred.

Lack of Clarity in Terms that Explain the Data Presented. Certain domains necessitate the use of technical terminology to describe the presented data. Dam safety, for instance, employs specific terms to denote safety levels and risks associated with dam failure. These terms are commonly familiar to professionals engaged in daily dam safety management activities. However, considering that the system's target audience encompasses the entire population, it is crucial to acknowledge that they may not be familiar with these terminologies.

In Brazil, dam safety policies incorporate specific terms to indicate the risk level of a potential dam failure, the associated risks in case of a breach, and the completeness of information about a particular dam. While these terms were devised to enhance safety inspection management, they may be unfamiliar to users. Hence, it is imperative to "translate" this information for users, ensuring their comprehension and alleviating concerns arising from potential misinterpretation.

5.5 Relation Between Issues Found in the Approaches and the Categories Proposed

The category with the fewest number of related issues was "Operating error to achieve the expectation of data interaction" (4 issues), which is expected in a system that has already been released, where malfunctions should ideally be minimized. The second-lowest category was "Position of key elements to interact with data" (6 issues), indicating that users encountered minimal difficulties locating the necessary elements to interact with the data.

The comparison between the category with the highest frequency and the category with the second-lowest frequency indicates that specialists perceive users to have a greater ability to navigate and interact with the system than comprehend the data itself. This observation raises questions regarding potential improvements in data presentation to convey the intended information.

The category exhibiting the highest number of related issues was also "Visibility about how to interact with data," with nine associated problems. These nine issues were observed by users in at least 30 instances during the tests, indicating that they were consistently perplexing and caught users' attention in the majority of the evaluations. The second most prevalent category linked to the issues encountered by users was "Data presentation pattern" (8 issues with 15 instances), underscoring the difficulties users faced in visualizing how to interact with the data application and the employed presentation patterns. Consequently, it is crucial to contemplate how data can be presented effectively, enabling users to better understand the narrative conveyed by the data.

6   Final Considerations

This study aimed to contribute to comprehending data exploration platform interaction within environmental systems focused on dam safety. The evaluation encompassed the usability assessment of a platform featuring information regarding the safety of Brazilian dams, a matter of paramount importance for accident prevention. The study identified categories of usability problems concerning human-data interaction in this context, elucidating the primary issues encountered during the evaluations.

The evaluation involved 18 participants aged between 22 and 45 years who interacted with the dashboard and utilised the filters to access the presented data. Throughout this process, a total of 27 problems were identified. Additionally, a collaborative heuristic evaluation was conducted to compare the results derived from user feedback with those provided by experts in the field of human-computer interaction, leading to the identification of 41 problems.

The outcomes achieved through each method can be associated with the heuristics and subsequently subjected to comparison. For the heuristics of Victorelli and Reis [21], both methods indicated the use of the heuristics 3 - Immediately provide visual feedback on the interaction due to lack of feedback and confusion caused to users at certain moments of the interaction, and 6 - Semantically enrich the interaction, focusing on its sub-item 6.1 - Semantically enrich search interaction. As for the heuristics of Nielsen [15], the user tests provided a view of mainly two heuristics: 7 - Flexibility and efficiency of use, and 8 - Aesthetic and minimalist design, while the heuristic evaluation highlighted, in addition to those mentioned, also the heuristic 6. Recognition rather than recall.

The categories established to encapsulate the issues encountered in both methods, namely heuristic evaluation and user tests, revealed "Visibility about how to interact with data" and "Data presentation pattern" as the most prominent. These categories shed light on the challenges users face when attempting to comprehend the interaction process for accessing or comprehending data, indicating that current designs lack appropriate patterns. In terms of data presentation, participants expressed in interviews that an optimal approach involves amalgamating various tools, such as dashboards, tables, and texts. The problems identified during the heuristic evaluation exhibited similarities to the issues reported by users, with emphasis on the interaction with dashboard information, which failed to clearly indicate the parameter employed for each presentation.

Thus, it becomes feasible not only to assess the usability of the application itself but also to comprehend that, within this particular context, user tests and heuristic evaluation mutually complement each other in inspecting the quality of a product with an environmental focus that necessitates thorough examination for safety reasons. Moreover, it is also possible to establish a correlation between the encountered problems and the existing heuristics in the literature.

For future studies, the attained results will be utilized by the responsible agency in charge of the system's development to ensure the continuous enhancement and evolution of the application employed in this study. Subsequent tests can be conducted during the developmental process. Our objective is to deepen the understanding of the interaction issues identified in the evaluations and expand the knowledge in this domain, thereby elucidating the implications for design by scrutinizing other systems pertinent to human-data interaction in the environmental context.

Acknowledgments. We would like to thank all participants for their most valuable contribution to this study. We also thank Agência Zetta and the Agência Nacional de Águas e Saneamento Básico (ANA) for the financial support. André Pimenta Freire thanks CNPq for a research fellowship.

References

1. Agência Nacional de Águas e Saneamento Básico ANA (Brazilian National Water Agency): Definições importantes sobre segurança de barragens (important definitions concerning dam safety) (2022). https://www.snisb.gov.br/Entenda_Mais/outros/definicoes-importantes-sobre-seguranca-de-barragem.pdf. Accessed 31 Jan 2023

2. Brazil: Lei 12.344/2010 - national dam safety policy (2010). https://www.planalto.gov.br/ccivil_03/_ato2007-2010/2010/lei/l12334.htm. Accessed 31 Jan 2023

3. Calvetti, D., Mêda, P., Sousa, H., Gonçalves, M.C.: Human data interaction in sensored sites, challenges of the craft workforce dimension. In: Proceedings of the 2021 European Conference on Computing in Construction (2021 EC3), Rhodes, Greece, pp. 26–28 (2021)

4. Ekşioğlu, M., Kiris, E., Çapar, B., Selçuk, M.N., Ouzeir, S.: Heuristic evaluation and usability testing: case study. In: Rau, P.L.P. (ed.) IDGD 2011. LNCS, vol. 6775, pp. 143–151. Springer, Heidelberg (2011). https://doi.org/10.1007/978-3-642-21660-2_16

5. G1: Barragem da vale se rompe em brumadinho, mg. encurtador.com.br/aKR14 (2019)

6. Jeon, J., Lee, J., Shin, D., Park, H.: Development of dam safety management system. Adv. Eng. Softw. **40**(8), 554–563 (2009)

7. Knaflic, C.N.: Storytelling with Data: A Data Visualization Guide for Business Professionals. Wiley, New York (2015)

8. Komarkova, J., Sedlak, P., Struska, S., Dymakova, A.: Usability evaluation the Prague geoportal: comparison of methods. In: 2019 International Conference on Information and Digital Technologies (IDT), pp. 223–228. IEEE (2019)

9. Law, L.C., Hvannberg, E.T.: Complementarity and convergence of heuristic evaluation and usability test: a case study of universal brokerage platform. In: Proceedings of the Second Nordic Conference on Human-Computer Interaction, pp. 71–80 (2002)

10. Leskens, J.G., et al.: An interactive simulation and visualization tool for flood analysis usable for practitioners. Mitig. Adapt. Strat. Global Change **22**(2), 307–324 (2017)

11. Liu, M., et al.: Optimization of simulation and visualization analysis of dam-failure flood disaster for diverse computing systems. Int. J. Geogr. Inf. Sci. **31**(9), 1891–1906 (2017)

12. Matteson, N., Keoborakot, D., Grodek, M., Celone, C.: ATLAS: a framework for geospatial visualization. In: Proceedings of the 36th ACM International Conference on the Design of Communication, pp. 1–2 (2018)

13. Ministério Público Federal: Caso samarco. encurtador.com.br/iBOP1 (2022)

14. Mortier, R., Haddadi, H., Henderson, T., McAuley, D., Crowcroft, J.: Human-data interaction: the human face of the data-driven society. Available at SSRN 2508051 (2014)

15. Nielsen, J., Molich, R.: Heuristic evaluation of user interfaces. In: Proceedings of the SIGCHI Conference on Human Factors in Computing Systems, pp. 249–256 (1990)

16. Rodrigues, A.M.B., Barbosa, G.D.J., Lopes, H.C.V., Barbosa, S.D.J.: What questions reveal about novices' attempts to make sense of data visualizations: patterns and misconceptions. Comput. Graph. **94**, 32–42 (2021)

17. da Costa e Silva, D.C., Fais, L.M.C.F., Freiria, R.C.: Seguraná de barragens: Panorama histórico da legislação brasileira. encurtador.com.br/cpsA9 (2020)
18. Trajkova, M., Alhakamy, A., Cafaro, F., Mallappa, R., Kankara, S.R.: Move your body: engaging museum visitors with human-data interaction. In: Proceedings of the 2020 CHI Conference on Human Factors in Computing Systems, pp. 1–13 (2020)
19. Van Someren, M., Barnard, Y.F., Sandberg, J.: The Think Aloud Method: A Practical Approach to Modelling Cognitive, p. 11. Academic Press, London (1994)
20. Victorelli, E.Z., Dos Reis, J.C., Hornung, H., Prado, A.B.: Understanding human-data interaction: literature review and recommendations for design. Int. J. Hum. Comput. Stud. **134**, 13–32 (2020)
21. Victorelli, E.Z., Reis, J.C.D.: Human-data interaction design guidelines for visualization systems. In: Proceedings of the 19th Brazilian Symposium on Human Factors in Computing Systems, pp. 1–10 (2020)
22. Werman, T.: Human data interaction (HDI): the new information frontier (2021). Interaction Design Foundation. shorturl.at/ijlmP. Accessed 31 Jan 2023

Virtual Reality

Asymmetric Communication in Virtual Reality: Designing for Presence, Effectiveness, and Enjoyment

Markus Kirjonen$^{(\boxtimes)}$ and Mika P. Nieminen

Department of Computer Science, Aalto University, Konemiehentie 2, 02150 Espoo, Finland

Abstract. This paper investigates the design of multi-user virtual reality (VR) communication and collaboration, focusing on asymmetric VR where one user is immersed in the virtual environment while the other interacts from the external world. Through an exploratory user study (n = 16), we examine how users experience different asymmetric VR communication methods and how these experiences inform the design of effective communication systems. We identify key factors that influence the effectiveness of different styles of asymmetric VR communication and highlight the benefits and limitations of these styles. Our thematic analysis of the participants' responses and experiences sheds light on the importance of considering communication methods and their impact on users' experiences in asymmetric virtual environments. Our study provides insights into how communication methods can be designed to enhance presence, social presence, communication effectiveness, and enjoyment. These findings can inform the design and development of more engaging and effective asymmetric communication methods for multi-user collaboration.

Keywords: Virtual reality · Asymmetric virtual reality · Collaboration

1 Introduction

Communication and collaboration are important activities in multi-user virtual reality. These activities typically occur with both users wearing head-mounted-displays and experiencing equal levels of immersion in the virtual environment. An alternative approach is asymmetric virtual reality, where one user (the VR user) is immersed in the virtual environment, while the other (non-VR user) interacts with them from the external world. In such a setup, the VR user and non-VR users often communicate and collaborate on a shared task. Asymmetric communication has been seen in the context of games [16–18], research [1–3, 12], and commercial applications.

How asymmetric communication is implemented has been shown to affect numerous user-related factors. These include the immersed user's sense of presence [4–6], enjoyment [3], and autonomy [12], as well as the social dynamic that exists between the two users [12]. In this paper, we complement existing works by comparing how users react to different implementations of asymmetric communication. Unlike prior works, which

© The Author(s), under exclusive license to Springer Nature Switzerland AG 2023
J. Abdelnour Nocera et al. (Eds.): INTERACT 2023, LNCS 14145, pp. 123–132, 2023.
https://doi.org/10.1007/978-3-031-42293-5_10

have typically focused on a single method at a time, we seek to investigate multiple interaction methods in the same study. By examining how users respond to a range of interaction methods, we aim to provide a more nuanced understanding of the strengths and limitations of various approaches, as well as insights into how different methods can be combined and integrated to enhance the effectiveness of communication and collaboration in asymmetric settings. Furthermore, by using the same set of users for all interaction methods, we can control for individual differences and contextual factors that may impact users' experiences and provide a more direct comparison of the methods under investigation.

In our exploratory user study (n = 16), we investigated how users experienced and perceived different asymmetric communication methods. A thematic analysis revealed key themes related to sense of presence in the virtual environment, communication effectiveness, and social presence. Each theme is explored and illustrated with relevant participant quotes. Based on these themes, we provide design suggestions for implementing asymmetric VR communication and discuss trade-offs such as communication effectiveness versus enjoyment and presence in the virtual environment versus social presence. This examination of identified themes and ensuing design recommendations offers insights for informed decision-making regarding the selection and implementation of asymmetric communication methods.

2   Literature Review

Literature on asymmetric virtual reality features numerous examples of asymmetric communication styles. Here, we explore several prominent approaches. These approaches serve as inspiration for the design of our study.

Direct verbal communication is commonly used in asymmetric VR. In such a setup, the non-VR and VR users interact directly through spoken word. This style of communication can be remote [1, 11, 14] or co-located [3]. During remote communication the non-VR user's voice is heard through the headset, while co-located verbal communication has both users sharing the same physical space and no additional hardware is necessary.

How to represent the non-VR user in the virtual environment during communication has been explored in various works. Forms of embodiment range from full body avatars [1, 14] to abstract representations [2, 6]. For instance, Ibayashi et al.'s DollhouseVR system represents the non-VR user as a giant floating hand pointing at objects in the virtual environment [2]. In Koller's work on treating patient's fear of public speaking in VR, the non-VR user, a trained psychiatrist, can take over virtual audience members at will in order to communicate with the immersed patient as they practice delivering a speech [1].

Non-verbal asymmetric communication methods have also been explored. One important function of non-verbal communication is pointing (directing the user's attention to objects in the virtual environment). Kumaravel et al. highlighted this style of communication as being a primary activity in asymmetric VR [10]. Approaches to directing the VR user's attention include Duval & Fleury's work on representing a non-VR user's 2D pointer input as a 3D ray in the virtual environment for the VR user to see [7], Oda et al.'s use of spatial annotations such as 3D arrows [8], Ibayashi et al.'s aforementioned giant pointing hand, and having external text messages appear on a diegetic virtual screen [6]. Peter, Horst, & Dörner compare two approaches to directing user's attention using non-verbal communication: highlighting objects using a diegetic beam of light, and outlining objects with white glowing borders [4]. We follow a similar approach in our study.

Several works have discussed user-related factors relating to asymmetric VR, showing that how users experience and perceive asymmetric communication is highly affected by how it is implemented. For instance, Gugenheimer et al. showed how the design of an asymmetric communication method can have an impact on the user's perceived dominance in the interaction [12]. Likewise, Wang et al. found that having the non-VR user appear in the virtual environment served as a social affordance, indicating that two-way verbal communication is now possible [9]. They also pointed out that this seemed to shift the user's attention from the virtual scene to the social interaction. This in turn relates to the concept of presence, the experience of "being there" in a virtual environment [19, 21]. Several works have broken presence into sub-components: spatial and social presence [19, 20, 22]. We use a similar distinction in this work.

In this work, we compare several styles of asymmetric communication based on the features discussed here. Participant comments reflected several user-related factors discussed in these prior works, as well as introducing new unexplored dynamics.

3 Methodology

The communication methods implemented in our study incorporated various design features from prior literature, including disembodied verbal communication, embodied verbal communication, and non-verbal communication. Based on these features, we implemented 6 communication methods:

Co-located Speech with No Hardware: This method involves the user speaking with other users who are physically in the same location, without the need for any additional hardware such as headsets or microphones. The communication is based on the user's physical presence and their ability to project their voice to the other users.

Remote Speech That the User Heard Through their Headset: This method involves the user hearing speech from other users who are in a remote location, through their VR headset. The speech is transmitted to the user's headset through directional speakers and spatial audio.

Walkie-Talkie: In this method, the user communicates with the moderator through a virtual Walkie-Talkie. The user needs to press a button to speak. While the communication is two-way, the user must initiate the interaction by answering the beeping Walkie-Talkie or by picking it up and making a call to the moderator.

2D Video Feed Similar to a Skype Call: This method involves the user communicating with other users through a 2D video feed, similar to a Skype call. The user can see the non-VR user's face and hear their voices, but the non-VR user is not fully immersed in the VR environment. A similar method was described in [5].

Outlines: This method uses white glowing outlines around objects of interest to guide the user's attention. The outlines serve as a non-verbal form of communication and are used to draw the user's attention to specific objects or areas in the VR environment. A similar method was described in [4].

Beam of Light: This method involves a beam of light shining through a window and guiding the player's attention to objects of interest. The beam of light serves as a non-verbal form of communication, similar to the outlines, and is used to draw the user's attention to specific objects or areas in the VR environment. It was intended to offer a more "lifelike," less gamified nonverbal approach compared to Outlines. A similar method was described in [4].

3.1 Study Design

We conducted a user study (n = 16) to investigate how users experience and perceive different implementations of asymmetric VR communication. Participants solved a series of puzzles in a virtual environment designed as a rustic cabin in the mountains. Each puzzle used a different asymmetric communication method, inspired by prior literature and including both verbal and non-verbal methods. The puzzles included arranging lettered blocks in the correct order based on clues in the virtual cabin, finding numbered cards in the cabin, and finding a hidden key in the cabin. Feedback was collected from participants and post-session interviews were conducted to explore their thoughts and perceptions. The study followed a within-subjects design, with each participant trying out all six communication methods. The communication methods were counterbalanced between sessions. Each session lasted between 20–40 min. The participants played the role of the VR-user, while the researchers played the role of the non-VR user in all six tasks. One of the two researchers carried out five of the six conditions remotely, while the other remained in the room with the participant and carried out the co-located condition. A backend tool similar to the VRGuides system described by Peter, Horst, & Dörner [4] was implemented for running the sessions and controlling the remote communication methods. The virtual environment was implemented in the Unity game engine, and hardware included an HTC Vive Pro 2.0 headset and a VIVE Wireless adapter for untethered movement in the virtual environment.

3.2 Data Analysis

All interviews were audio-recorded, transcribed, and analyzed using a thematic analysis approach. During this process, the researchers began with a close reading of the interview transcripts, noting important or interesting passages. These were then labeled with codes based on their content. As more codes emerged, patterns and connections began to emerge between them. For example, when looking at the codes related to the user's sense of presence in the VR experience, the researchers noted that many users talked about feeling fully immersed in the environment and feeling like they were actually present in the virtual world. These codes were then grouped together and a theme of "sense of presence" emerged. In total, 92 codes were identified, which were structured into 4 overarching themes: sense of presence, communication effectiveness, social presence, and user preference. These themes were then used to inform the development of design drivers for asymmetric VR communication methods.

4 Findings

The themes that emerged during our analysis of participant interviews are described here.

Sense of Presence in the Virtual Environment: When discussing the theme of sense of presence in relation to the different asymmetric VR communication methods, we found that some methods led to a greater sense of immersion and presence in the virtual environment than others. For example, users described feeling more present and engaged when using methods that involved non-verbal cues: *"Yeah it was quite nice when everything was so quiet. I could hear the bird which I didn't hear before. And the fire. And at some point I was feeling like I should sit down at the table. And the window! The window scene was... I know it was VR, but I almost felt like 'uuuu it's cold.'"* (P5); Another user described it by stating *"Collaboration was nice, it was fun talking to someone, but when I was looking for clues by myself, I definitely paid more attention to what was in the cabin and explored it a bit more than I had earlier."* (P4); Although users received less instruction and guidance during these portions of the session, leaving them to figure out the puzzles for themselves with subtle environmental cues wasn't necessarily a bad thing, as it shifted their attention from the social interaction to the virtual environment. This attention-shifting is similar to Wang et al.'s description in [9].

Communication Effectiveness: Our analysis of user interviews revealed that certain types of asymmetric VR communication methods were perceived as more effective for communicating information than others. In particular, methods that involved direct speech allowed for efficient back-and-forth between the VR and non-VR user. Most participants found this direct verbal communication to be useful: *"The most helpful was the audio, I needed clues for the whole puzzle."* (P7); *"I felt like I had this constant companionship, and I wasn't bothering you by asking questions"* (P8). On the other hand, we found that it was somewhat common for users to not immediately notice or understand the non-verbal cues (Outlines, Beam of Light): *"I initially assumed it was part of the environment."* (P9); *"At first I didn't understand that it was helping me, but I enjoyed it once I did."* (P5); *"Wait, is this a hint?"* (P10); *"Are you turning that light on?"* (P4); *"That glowing outline would have been very easy to miss, if I hadn't been looking for all the possible places a key is supposed to go. I saw it out of the corner of my eye."* (P6).

Interestingly, the communication effectiveness of certain communication methods also influenced the power dynamic between the participant and non-VR user acting as the moderator. Whereas the other communication methods were initiated by the non-VR user, the Walkie-Talkie relied on the participant answering before dialogue began. Several users talked about a temptation to not answer: *"You offered me the option of making contact at one point, calling me on the Walkie-Talkie... and I was so tempted to not do that, because I want to figure this out on my own."* (P14); Others actually did ignore the incoming calls: *"Yeah, yeah, I know, I know, but I'm not gonna. I can do it by myself."* (P8); One participant described using it at their discretion when they needed help: *"Ok I'm getting too impatient, I need to give you a call. Got any hints for me? Over."* (P11). This shift in power is similar to Gugenheimer et al.'s concept of dominance in the interaction [12].

Social Presence and Collaboration: Social presence emerged as a key theme in our analysis of user interviews. Users reported that some methods facilitated a sense of social presence and connection with the external user far more than others. During the non-verbal cues, participants often described themselves as being "alone." Even though the Outlines and Beam of Light helped guide them through their respective puzzles, participants often did not conceptualize this as a social interaction, but rather, as part of the gameplay: *"Oh that's true, it didn't feel like that. I thought it was part of the design of the game. Like you're playing a game and certain objects blink. It's very different to talking to someone about how to solve this puzzle"* (P8); *"I didn't realize it was a cue from you guys, I thought it was just me being smart."* (P12).

Moving from non-verbal to verbal, participants reported appreciating the straight-forward nature of direct verbal communication, although this too was often treated as more of a gameplay element than a social interaction: *"Whereas your voice through the headphones felt like it was part of the game."* (P3); *"Just speaking to me through the headphones feels like a video game, like a narrator."* (P11); *"I thought it was like in a military environment, you just receive commands from the headset, you don't talk back to the headset."* (P12).

When switching to the two most visually apparent communication methods, the Walkie-Talkie and 2D Video Call, participant's descriptions of the interactions immediately shifted to focusing on the social element. Discussing the Walkie-Talkie, participants reported: *"I'd say the Walkie-Talkie one was probably the most immersive. It's like you're somewhat in that virtual environment talking to me. That's how I felt."* (P11); This was even more apparent with the video feed, where the non-VR user appeared on screen: *"When you showed up on the screen that was a bit different because then I had, you, I was very aware of your presence at that time."* (P8); *"You were present, not with me in the cabin, but on the screen in the cabin, so you were there."* (P1); *"I felt very connected, I think's it's like having a phone call versus a Skype call, you feel more connected with the person and more immersed."* (P14); *"You're getting that feedback that someone is listening to you that I didn't get with the other ways."* (P12).

User Preference: User preferences emerged as an important theme in our analysis. Users reported that their individual communication styles and preferences influenced their perceptions of the different methods. For example, most participants commented on the Beam of Light positively: *"It was helpful and subtle, not directly telling me to do something. It was nice to be helped like that."* (P4); Others found it to be too obvious, or even condescending: *"It was funny but annoying at the same time. It was like yeah, you won't solve this, let this holy light guide you to your next piece."* (P10); *"Yeah, it was more undermining in a sense."* (P2); Similarly, reactions to Co-Located Speech were mixed and depended on the individual user. Some participants found the guidance generally useful and did not think much about it: *"It felt the same [as remote voice], just a voice."* (P9); Others did not: *"You being in the same room but not interacting with me through the environment but actually just talking to me, and not even through headphones, to me that was... the least believable" (P1); "I guess that it was a reminder about the real world, that you're talking to me from the real word, whereas with others it felt like you were in that world with me." (P4); "You talking right next to me, that didn't really... I didn't want to have that in the experience. If I could have chosen, I would rather be without that." (P14).

User preferences also came into play when reacting to the 2D video call. While that communication method fostered the most social presence, some participants found that it was too much social presence: "Seeing your face... I felt like instead of creating closeness it felt like I was under some onus to take help, so I'd rate it lower." (P8); "You'd rather just hear a voice in that space. It's kind of weird, like oh don't come see me, I'm in this... this cabin now, don't intrude on my experience." (P3); "It felt like you're being watched. But then again I guess you were watching the whole time anyways. But yeah that definitely felt like, like you were watching everything I was doing, and it felt weird." (P11); These comments echo the sentiments of Willich et al.'s participants in [5] when reacting to a similar communication format.

Sometimes, individual's ways of interpreting the design of communication methods were quite amusing. One participant described the disembodied Co-Located voice as follows: "Yeah, that was also like the godly voice. [laughing] Because at first the light lights up the right place, and then there's this like, like, older male voice, you know, stereotypical god with a beard, something like that. [laughing] It's a nice cabin we have here, really high up!" (P10); Another participant associated the 2D Video Call with horror movie connotations, saying: "It was straight from the Saw movies, you weren't the helper in my mind anymore, you were the captor." (P10).

5 Discussion

As we have seen, the design of asymmetric communication methods can have a strong impact on the user experience. Based on the themes that emerged from the analysis of our interview data, we derived design drivers for implementing effective asymmetric VR communication methods. Design drivers can be thought of as specific goals or outcomes that inform the design and implementation of asymmetric VR communication. As you will notice, these design drivers can either work in unison or detract from each other. These design drivers are:

Creating a Sense of Presence in the Virtual Environment: The design of asymmetric communication can enhance the user's sense of presence in the VR environment to increase immersion and engagement. Low-distraction communication methods such as non-verbal pointing allow the user to retain their focus on the virtual environment's sounds, props, and tasks. We also observed that communication methods with less social presence can encourage users to pause and think through things more, rather than immediately seeking advice.

Fostering Social Presence: Asymmetric communication methods can be designed to promote social presence and enhance the feeling of being in a shared space with the non-VR user. This can be achieved by incorporating communication into the virtual environment itself, rather than using disembodied methods. Additionally, allowing for continuous two-way verbal communication between the VR user and non-VR user, and providing social affordances such as the Walkie-Talkie that beeps when activated, can enhance social presence.

Maximizing Communication Effectiveness: Asymmetric communication methods should be designed to support task performance and minimize distractions when social and environmental presence are secondary objectives. In such a case, clear and direct communication methods are preferred to minimize confusion and errors. For example, direct two-way verbal communication can be effective in supporting task performance and maximizing communication effectiveness.

Increasing Enjoyment: Promoting enjoyment and engagement with the virtual environment can be another important design driver for asymmetric communication. Designing communication methods that fit well with the virtual environment's theme and setting can enhance the user's overall enjoyment, even if it may not maximize communication effectiveness.

The design drivers discussed here may be more or less important depending on the context and specific goals of the VR experience and should be weighed carefully.

6 Limitations and Future Research

One potential limitation of this study is that it was conducted in a laboratory setting, which may not be representative of the real-world use of asymmetric communication methods in VR. Participants may have behaved differently than they would in a natural environment, which could affect the results. Additionally, the small sample size and the use of the same two moderators for all sessions could introduce bias into the study. Furthermore, the puzzles used in the study were designed to be similar in nature and difficulty, which may not accurately reflect the range of tasks that users may encounter in VR applications. Finally, it should be noted that the study focused solely on the user's subjective experiences and did not measure objective metrics such as task completion time or accuracy.

7 Conclusion

Our study compared six approaches to asymmetric VR communication. These approaches were based on common design styles in asymmetric VR literature. A thematically analysed was conducted to understand how participants experienced our asymmetric communication approaches. We found four design drivers (creating a sense of presence in the virtual environment, fostering social presence, maximizing communication effectiveness, and increasing enjoyment), which the designer of asymmetric VR should balance and prioritize based on the goals of the VR experience.

Acknowledgements. The authors thank Aalto University School of Science, Department of Computer Science for funding this research.

References

1. Koller, M., Schäfer, P., Lochner, D., Meixner, G.: Rich interactions in virtual reality exposure therapy: a pilot-study evaluating a system for presentation training. In: 2019 IEEE International Conference on Healthcare Informatics (ICHI), pp. 1–11 (2019). https://doi.org/10.1109/ICHI.2019.8904768
2. Ibayashi, H., Sugiura, Y., Sakamoto, D., Miyata, N.: Dollhouse VR: a multi view, multi-user collaborative design workspace with VR technology. SIGGRAPH Asia 2015 Posters (2015). https://doi.org/10.1145/2820926.2820948
3. Gugenheimer, J., Stemasov, E., Frommel, J., Rukzio, E.: ShareVR: enabling co-located experiences for virtual reality between HMD and non-HMD users. In: Proceedings of the 2017 CHI Conference on Human Factors in Computing Systems – CHI, pp. 4021–4033. ACM Press, Denver, Colorado, USA (2017). https://doi.org/10.1145/3025453.3025683
4. Peter, M., Horst, R., Dörner, R.: Vr-guide: a specific user role for asymmetric virtual reality setups in distributed virtual reality applications. In: Proceedings of the 10th Workshop Virtual and Augmented Reality of the GI Group VR/AR. Gesellschaft fur Informatik (2018)
5. von Willich, J., Funk, M., Müller, F., Marky, K., Riemann, J. Mühlhäuser, M.: You invaded my tracking space! using augmented virtuality for spotting passersby in room-scale virtual reality. In: Proceedings of the 2019 on Designing Interactive Systems Conference (2019)
6. Zenner, A., Speicher, M., Klingner, S., Degraen, D., Daiber, F., Krüger, A.: Immersive notification framework: adaptive & plausible notifications in virtual reality. Extended Abstracts of the 2018 CHI Conference on Human Factors in Computing Systems, pp. 1–6. Association for Computing Machinery, Montreal QC, Canada (2018). https://doi.org/10.1145/3170427.3188505
7. Duval, T., Fleury, C.: An asymmetric 2D Pointer/3D Ray for 3D Interaction within Collaborative Virtual Environments. Web3D 2009 33–41 (2009). https://doi.org/10.1145/1559764.1559769
8. Oda, O., Elvezio, C., Sukan, M., Feiner, S., Tversky, B.: Virtual replicas for remote assistance in virtual and augmented reality. In: Proceedings of the 28th Annual ACM Symposium on User Interface Software and Technology (2015)
9. Wang, C., Yong, S., Chen, H., Ye, Y., Chan, L.: HMD light: sharing in-VR experience via head-mounted projector for asymmetric interaction. In: Proceedings of the 33rd Annual ACM Symposium on User Interface Software and Technology (2020)
10. Kumaravel, B., Nguyen, C., DiVerdi, S., Hartmann, B.: TransceiVR: bridging asymmetrical communication between vr users and external collaborators. In: Proceedings of the 33rd Annual ACM Symposium on User Interface Software and Technology, pp. 182–195 (2020)
11. Kumaravel, B., Anderson, F., Fitzmaurice, G., Hartmann, B., Grossman, T.: Loki. In: Proceedings of the 32nd Annual ACM Symposium on User Interface Software and Technology (2019)
12. Gugenheimer, J., Stemasov, E., Sareen, H., Rukzio, E.: FaceDisplay. In: Proceedings of the 2018 CHI Conference on Human Factors in Computing Systems. (2018)
13. Slater, M. and Anthony Steed, A.: A virtual presence counter. Presence 9, 413–434 (2000). https://doi.org/10.1162/105474600566925
14. Furukawa, T., Yamamoto, D., Sugawa, M., Peiris, R., Minamizawa, K.: TeleSight. ACM SIGGRAPH 2019 Emerging Technologies (2019)
15. Hartmann, J., Holz, C., Ofek, E., Wilson, A.: RealityCheck. In: Proceedings of the 2019 CHI Conference on Human Factors in Computing Systems (2019)
16. Keep Talking and Nobody Explodes on Steam. https://store.steampowered.com/app/341800/Keep_Talking_and_Nobody_Explodes/. Accessed 25 April 2023

17. Black Hat Cooperative on Steam. Store.steampowered.com. https://store.steampowered.com/app/503100/Black_Hat_Cooperative/. Accessed 25 April 2023

18. Eye in the Sky on Steam. Store.steampowered.com. https://store.steampowered.com/app/566700/Eye_in_the_Sky/. Accessed 25 April 2023

19. Heeter, C.: Being there: the subjective experience of presence. Presence: Teleoper. Virtual Environ. 1(2), 262–271 (1992). https://doi.org/10.1162/pres.1992.1.2.262

20. Lee, K.M.: Presence, explicated. Commun. Theory 14(1), 27–50 (2004). https://doi.org/10.1111/j.1468-2885.2004.tb00302.x (1992)

21. Lombard, M., Ditton, T.: At the heart of it all: the concept of presence. J. Comput.-Mediat. Commun. 3(2), 1997 (1997). https://doi.org/10.1111/j.1083-6101.1997.tb00072.x

22. Tamborini, R., Bowman, N.D.: Chaper 5 presence in video games. In: Immersed in Media, pp. 105–128. Routledge. (2010)

Digital Modeling for Everyone: Exploring How Novices Approach Voice-Based 3D Modeling

Giuseppe Desolda[1]([✉])(ID), Andrea Esposito[1](ID), Florian Müller[2](ID), and Sebastian Feger[2](ID)

[1] Department of Computer Science, University of Bari Aldo Moro, Bari, Italy
{giuseppe.desolda,andrea.esposito}@uniba.it
[2] LMU Munich, Munich, Germany
{florian.mueller,sebastian.feger}@um.ifi.lmu.de

Abstract. Manufacturing tools like 3D printers have become accessible to the wider society, making the promise of digital fabrication for everyone seemingly reachable. While the actual manufacturing process is largely automated today, users still require knowledge of complex design applications to produce ready-designed objects and adapt them to their needs or design new objects from scratch. To lower the barrier to the design and customization of personalized 3D models, we explored novice mental models in voice-based 3D modeling by conducting a high-fidelity Wizard of Oz study with 22 participants. We performed a thematic analysis of the collected data to understand how the mental model of novices translates into voice-based 3D modeling. We conclude with design implications for voice assistants. For example, they have to: deal with vague, incomplete and wrong commands; provide a set of straightforward commands to shape simple and composite objects; and offer different strategies to select 3D objects.

Keywords: Digital Fabrication · 3D Design · Voice Interaction · Wizard of Oz Study

1 Introduction

The digital fabrication revolution aims to democratize the way people create tangible objects [13]. With the widespread availability of 3D printing together with many other digital fabrication technologies such as laser cutters or Numerical Control (CNC) routers, end users are moving from passive consumers to active producers. While the actual manufacturing process is largely automated today, users are still required to have a profound knowledge of complex 3D modeling applications, when they adapt models to their needs or even design new objects from scratch [53]. Thus, even if the introduction of technologies such as 3D printers has revolutionized the hobbyist community, lowering the barrier of entry to manufacturing

---

Supplementary Information The online version contains supplementary material available at https://doi.org/10.1007/978-3-031-42293-5_11.

© The Author(s), under exclusive license to Springer Nature Switzerland AG 2023
J. Abdelnour Nocera et al. (Eds.): INTERACT 2023, LNCS 14145, pp. 133–155, 2023.
https://doi.org/10.1007/978-3-031-42293-5_11

even for novices (who can now put their hands in the process of creating artifacts without relying on third parties), we argue that the design of the 3D objects to be manufactured still requires a high level of knowledge and expertise.

These limitations have pushed researchers to investigate natural interaction techniques to simplify 3D modeling tools [36]. For example, research explored gestures [46,50], virtual/augmented reality [10,45], eye tracking [20,54], brain-computer interface [17,44] and their combination [12,21,22,33] as a multimodal approach. However, their adoption is reserved for technical users and it is strongly limited by hardware costs and excessive size/weight that can make the users easily fatigued [36]. As another possible solution, voice-based interaction has been explored, to both integrate the traditional Graphical User Interface (GUI) interface (e.g., to enable shortcuts via voice commands) [47,53]) or as the primary interaction paradigm (e.g., see [24,38,52]). Although voice-based interaction requires only a microphone, it does not yet provide adequate digital modeling support for everyone: existing solutions either do not consider final users at all [52,53], or only target 3D experts [21,24,38,51], and novices are not considered potential target beneficiaries of the proposed innovations.

To lower the barrier to the design and customization of personalized 3D models by exploiting the potential of voice-based interaction, this study aims to understand how the mental model of novices translates into voice-based 3D modeling. We conducted a high-fidelity Wizard of Oz (WoZ) study to elicit novices' mental model, for example, their expectation, beliefs, needs, and abilities. We recruited a total of 22 participants without skills in 3D modeling, who performed 14 tasks revolving around some basic concepts of 3D modeling like the creation of objects, the manipulation of objects (e.g., scaling, rotating, and/or moving objects), and the creation of composite objects. All the WoZ sessions' recordings were analyzed through thematic analysis. The findings of the study have been distilled in the form of lessons learned. For example, we found that: voice assistants must manage the corrections the novices do during and after the commands; deal with vague and incomplete commands; consider the prior novices' knowledge; provide only a simplified set of operations for creating simple and composite 3D objects; design a workflow similar to what novices would do if they were building real objects; understand chained commands; understand commands that are relative to the users' point of view.

The contribution of this paper is two-fold. First, we report the results of our WoZ study presenting the themes that emerged from the thematic analysis. Second, based on these results, we provide a set of design implications for the future design of voice-based interaction paradigms for 3D modeling for novices.

2   Background and Related Work

This study revolves around the concept of voice-based 3D modeling as a key factor for enabling the democratization of digital fabrication. This section starts by illustrating some of the existing solutions based on natural interaction that try to address the complexity of 3D modeling (Sect. 2.1). Next, we provide an overview of the requirements for interacting with voice assistants (Sect. 2.2).

Finally, we provide a brief summary of the motivation of this study and introduce the research question that guided our work (Sect. 2.3).

2.1 Addressing the Complexity of 3D Modeling

To mitigate the issues of traditional GUI-based Computer-Aided Design (CAD), researchers explored natural interaction paradigms like eye tracking [20,54], brain-computer interface [17,44], gestures [46,50], virtual/augmented reality [10,45] and their combination [12,21,22] as a multimodal approach for 3D modeling. The goal of natural interactions with CAD systems is to increase their *usability* for both expert users and, especially, novice users. Specifically, they aim to: i) reduce the learning curve of the system; ii) allow a more intuitive interaction process; iii) enhance the design abilities of the designers [36].

An example of a multimodal system is "3D Palette" by Billinghurst et al.: a mix of tablet and pen inputs, electromagnetic sensors and voice commands are used to support the digital design process [1]. Similarly, Nanjundaswamy et al. explored a mix of gesture-based interaction, speech recognition, and brain-computer interfaces to reduce the initial learning curve of the design system [33]. A complete overview of the multimodal solutions for CAD is reported by Niu et al. [36]. Despite these potential benefits, such multimodal techniques require the adoption of specialized hardware (e.g., depth-sensing cameras for gesture recognition, headsets to recognize brain signals), which use can be limited by their prices, sizes, weight, and complexity of use [33]. Thus, it is still hard for novice users to really adopt them in real and daily contexts [36].

To overcome these limitations, researchers also investigated voice-based interaction because of its intuitive nature and the simplicity of the required hardware, i.e., a microphone, which nowadays is embedded in any laptop, tablet, or webcam [41]. Furthermore, considering the ubiquity of smartphones and the rise of AR and VR glasses, voice-based interaction can be generalized to technologies where other interaction modalities are not available options. Attempts of integrating voice-based interaction to CAD systems date as back as 1985 [40]. A more recent work suggests the use of voice commands to allow users to either quickly search commands by simply stating their intention [47,53], or to annotate 3D models [38]. Systems, where the entire modeling process is carried out by voice commands, have also been explored. An example is the solution presented by Kou and Tan, where voice commands related to a CAD-specific lexicon and grammar are understood by a context-aware algorithm [23]. A similar example was proposed by Xue et al., which improves the previous solution by allowing free-form sentences in [52]. Another example of a fully-working system is the one presented by Grigor et al.: it follows the same ideas as the previous ones but uses Artificial Intelligence (AI) to understand the users' inputs, thus allowing for more freedom in the commands, [14]. Similarly, Kou et al. proposed a flexible voice-enabled CAD system, where users are no longer constrained by predefined commands by exploiting a knowledge-guided approach to infer the semantics of voice input [24].

Among all the previous examples, it must be highlighted that the design of their paradigm was made without any kind of involvement of the final users

[23,40,47,53] or by solely involving experts in the final testing phase [14]. For example, the study by Nanjundaswamy et al. evaluates a multimodal system using gestures, speech and a brain-computer interface by involving a group of five skilled people [33]. Similarly, Khan et al. involve a total of 41 skilled users from an architecture or engineering background to elicit the requirements of a CAD system based on gestures and speech commands [21]. As another example, Vyas et al. test the usability of a speech-based CAD system involving 6 students with backgrounds in engineering, architecture and visualization [51].

The work proposed by Cuadra et al. investigated how novices use voice assistants to design 3D objects [5]. They performed a WoZ study to compare voice assistants with and without the use of a video channel showing the design in progress, investigating how the two approaches impact users' accuracy and satisfaction. Cuadra et al. validate the idea of using voice assistants, as participants are more satisfied with their objects and suffer less from cognitive overload when the design process is supported by video, but it does not provide any insight on the mental model of novices approaching the digital modeling task [5].

2.2 Interacting with Voice Assistants

The first solution of voice interaction implementing speech recognition dates as back as 1952, when Davis et al. proposed a prototype able to recognize digits [7]. In recent years, the evolution of machine learning and AI fostered the spreading of powerful commercial voice assistants, often based on deep neural networks trained on a plethora of data. However, such powerful speech recognition models alone are not sufficient to build an effective voice assistant, since the interaction with such systems must be considered in the design of the whole system [30]. This need, together with the growing availability of commercial voice assistants, has fostered a sharp uptick of studies on user interaction with voice assistants [41]. Aspects like the cues that drive the conversation [49], the properties that a voice assistant should have [48], the user's mental model [15], emotions felt during the conversation [19], conversational design patterns [30] have been investigated. In addition, solutions to design and evaluate interaction with voice assistants are beginning to be proposed (see, for example, [18,25,30–32,37,48]). Careful consideration of these design aspects gains importance when voice assistants aim to simplify challenging or technical operations (e.g., see [3]). Since 3D modeling represents such a demanding task for novices, the elicitation of the novices' mental model is crucial to lower the barrier for 3D modeling.

2.3 Summary and Research Question

The analysis of the literature highlights that to simplify the 3D modeling, often the existing solutions are based on multimodal techniques such as gestures, eye tracking, or brain-computer interfaces; however, their adoption in real contexts is strongly limited by the adoption of specialized hardware and, overall, they target technical users.

Voice interaction seems a promising paradigm that can overcome the limitations of multimodal solutions, but the existing voice-based solutions are still lacking for three important reasons: i) users are often not considered throughout the design phase, or they are only involved too late in testing phases; ii) to the best of our knowledge, novices are never considered as target users; iii) the voice-based interaction is built on top of the existing CAD systems (and their complexity), instead of designing from scratch the voice paradigm and the whole system.

Considering these limitations, to really democratize digital fabrication considering novices, users should be able to access 3D modeling tools even without special skills. All these motivations pushed us to explore novices' mental model in voice-based 3D modeling, in order to reduce the cost of their entry in the digital fabrication era. This is an aspect that has never been explored before and that deserves attention to really democratize digital fabrication. Therefore, our work addresses the following research question: **How does the mental model of novices translate into voice-based 3D modeling?**

3   Method

To answer our research question, we performed a high-fidelity Wizard of Oz (WoZ) study [42] because it has been proven successful in eliciting the user's mental model for voice-based interaction (e.g., see [5,11,28,49]). Then, we carried out an inductive thematic analysis [4] on the qualitative data, i.e., the transcriptions of the WoZ sessions and the answers of the participants to the open questions.

3.1   Participants

A total of 22 participants (F = 15, M =7) have been recruited through convenience sampling [8] on the social circles of the authors of this article. This number of participants is in line with other similar studies (e.g., see [26,49]). Half of the participants were Italians while the other half were Germans. Their mean age was 24.1 years ($\sigma = 3.7$, min = 21, max = 34). The entire study was performed in English so as not to have results related to specific languages, which is out of the scope of this study. To ensure that the collected data is not biased toward knowledgeable users, we only recruited participants without any kind of experience with 3D modeling. Regarding the participants' level of education, around 45.45% already have a High School Diploma or a German A-level, 36.36% have a Bachelor's Degree, 13.64% have a Master's Degree, and only one participant (representing the remaining 4.55%) has not provided any information. Most participants (15 out of 22) do not have a STEM education, while 6 of the remaining 7 do not have any computational thinking skills, as they studied or worked in non-IT scientific fields (e.g., pharmaceutical and nutrition sciences). Regarding the participants' skills, they had an average level of IT knowledge ($\bar{x} = 6.5/10$; $\sigma = 2.1$), a medium-low level of knowledge of voice assistants ($\bar{x} = 3.1/10$; $\sigma = 2.0$) and very low knowledge of 3D modeling ($\bar{x} = 1.6/10$; $\sigma = 1.1$).

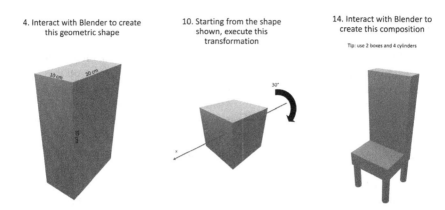

4. Interact with Blender to create this geometric shape

10. Starting from the shape shown, execute this transformation

14. Interact with Blender to create this composition

Tip: use 2 boxes and 4 cylinders

(a) Creation of a simple object

(b) Transformation of an object (rotation)

(c) Creation of a composite object

Fig. 1. Examples of graphical tasks: a brief prompt is reported on top of each task and below a diagram shows the participants the 3D object to create (a, c) or the transformation to be performed (b).

3.2 Tasks

A total of 14 tasks have been designed by two authors of this paper, both experts in 3D modeling, taking into account the most common and useful activities that are required to create simple and composite 3D objects. The resulting tasks revolve around basic concepts of 3D modeling, like the creation of simple objects, the manipulation of objects (e.g., scaling, rotating, and/or moving objects), and the creation of composite geometries. The details of the tasks are reported in the task table in the attached appendix (the list of all the graphical tasks is available in the attached appendix, sub-folder *tasks*). To reduce the impact of the primer effect [8] that providing a textual description of a task would have on the participants, we chose to provide the participants with graphical tasks: each task is composed of a brief prompt and a diagram showing the participants a 3D object or a 3D transformation that should be recreated (an example of graphical tasks is provided in Fig. 1). The representations chosen for each task were validated during a pilot study with 3 novices that were not considered in the final WoZ study.

3.3 Apparatus

We carried out the WoZ study remotely by using Zoom[1]. Four researchers have been involved: two Italians acted respectively as conductors and wizards for the Italian participants, while two German researchers acted as conductors and wizards for the German participants. In both groups, researchers switched roles to minimize the risk of bias introduced when conducting the test.

---

[1] https://zoom.us.

To create the illusion for participants that they are interacting with a real voice-based system for 3D modeling, we decided to use Blender[2], explaining to participants that they can interact with it through voice commands. Blender has been selected since it is a free and open-source software that, among other features like sculpting or rendering, allows one to design and visualize 3D objects. One of the main features that made Blender the perfect choice for our WoZ study is the availability of APIs for the Python language[3] that can be used inside a shell-like environment: this allows the Wizard to immediately create and modify the objects programmatically when the participants provide voice commands, thus preventing the participants from noticing anything odd and increasing the speed at which the Wizard is capable of satisfying the participants' requests. Taking advantage of this feature, we pre-defined a set of functions in a Python module to simplify the use of Blender's APIs for the purpose of this study (the module is available in the supplementary materials, sub-folder *python module*).

To show the participants the task they had to complete, we overlaid the graphical tasks on the bottom-right side of the Blender's window. To this aim, we used Open Broadcaster Software (or, more commonly, OBS)[4], a free and open-source software for video recording and live streaming. Using OBS, it was also possible to define animations and transitions to show when users are moving to the next task and to signal to the participants that the "voice assistant" (i.e., the Wizard) is listening to the user's command or it is actually performing it. In particular, for each task, both the Blender window and the graphical task are visible (see Fig. 2a). When the participants activate the Blender voice assistant by saying "Hey Blender", the "I'm listening" label indicates that participants can provide the command to solve the task (see Fig. 2b). Then, when the voice command has been issued, a rotating icon indicates that the voice assistant is analyzing it, creating the illusion that there is a real voice assistant (see Fig. 2c). During the loading, the Wizard writes the Python statements related to the user commands and the result is finally shown in Blender (see Fig. 2d).

3.4   Procedure

For each participant, when the Zoom session started, both the conductor and the Wizard were connected on Zoom but the latter never appeared or interacted with the participant. While the conductor introduced the participant to the study, the Wizard shared his screen, in particular the window created by using OBS. The sessions were recorded using Zoom's built-in recorder. Before starting the recordings, participants were asked to sign (either in digital or in verbal form) a privacy policy. It is worth mentioning that our universities require approval by an ethics committee only in the case of medical and clinical studies. For other studies like ours, they require that test participants give consent in a written or digital form; thus, we informed participants about all the details of the study and asked them to agree before starting the study. All of them agreed.

---

[2] https://www.blender.org.

[3] https://docs.blender.org/api/current/.

[4] https://obsproject.com.

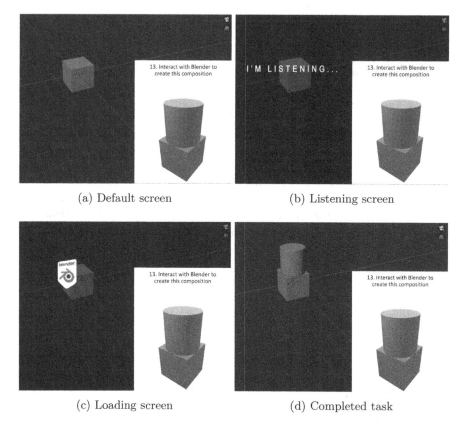

(a) Default screen

(b) Listening screen

(c) Loading screen

(d) Completed task

Fig. 2. The graphical task is overlaid on the bottom-right side of the Blender's window from the beginning of the task (a); when the participants activate the voice assistant by saying "Hey Blender", the "I'm listening" label indicates that they can provide the command to solve the task (b); a rotating icon indicates that the voice assistant is elaborating the user commands (c); the results is shown after the command elaboration (c).

As soon as the participant agreed to attend the study, the conductor invited the participant to complete a set of tasks. The webcam of the conductor was turned off during task execution to avoid disturbing the participant. To reduce the variability between sessions and between the Italian and German participants, the same introductory script was defined (available in the attached appendix, sub-folder "introductory script"). In summary, the conductor explains that the goal of the study was to validate a new voice assistant called Blender, which we created to assist novices in 3D modeling. Then, the conductor asks to complete a set of tasks and that, for each of them, a graphical representation appears on the right-bottom side of their screen. The conductor also specifies that the participant had to first activate the voice assistant by saying "Hey Blender" and then, once the "I'm listening" label appears, the participant can provide a sequence of voice commands that, in their opinion, is the best to solve the task (for example "create a cube"). No examples of voice commands have been provided to avoid introducing bias. At the end of each task, the participants had to communicate with the conductor to move on to the next task.

At the end of the session, each participant filled in a questionnaire that includes questions on demographics, as well as some usability-related questions to evaluate the effectiveness of the Blender voice assistant. Furthermore, since (to the extent of our knowledge) there were no previous examples of graphical tasks for a Wizard of Oz study, we have also chosen to add some questions to evaluate how easy it was for the user to understand the tasks (available in attached appendix, sub-folder *questionnaire*). The entire procedure lasted around 30 minutes for each participant. A graphical synthesis of the entire procedure and the data collected is shown in Fig. 3.

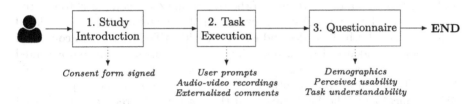

Fig. 3. Phases of the study and data collected at each phase

3.5   Data Analysis

The first analysis regarded the questionnaire answers that evaluate the choice of providing the tasks in graphical format. Specifically, we included a question that asked *"How easy it was to understand the graphical tasks?"* and it ranges from 1 (not simple at all) to 10 (very simple). Both the median and average scores are 8.2/10, with a standard deviation of 1.0. These results seem to validate the idea of presenting the tasks graphically, but it also highlights that for some tasks (the ones with an ambiguous representation) the conductor of the study must be able to guide the participants to the right interpretation (without the use of words that may introduce a primer effect [8]). In our study, this issue impacted only the 11th task for four participants and it was solved by turning the webcam on and mimicking the action depicted in the task, in case the user was showing difficulties in understanding a task or if he/she explicitly requested help.

After ensuring the quality of the graphical tasks, we analyzed the qualitative data collected during the study, which helped us answer the research question, i.e., video transcriptions, questionnaire responses and participants' comments. All the video recordings (a total of about 11 hours) were first transcribed and expanded by including the annotations that identify pauses, the start and the end of the processing by the WoZ, and eventual errors or over-correction by the WoZ. This dataset was completed by reporting the participants comments and the answers to the three open questions we included in the questionnaire: i) What did you like the most about the system used and the interaction with it? ii) What did you like less about the system and the interaction with it? and iii) Would you use a system like Blender to model in 3D? Please motivate your answer.

This data was analyzed in a systematic qualitative interpretation using Inductive Thematic Analysis [4]. The initial coding was conducted independently by four researchers, who are co-authors of this article and are experienced in qualitative data analysis: two of them analyzed the Italian results while the other two the German results. The two couples of researchers began with open coding independently. Once all the data was coded, the set of initial codes was further refined by merging the different codes. This first filtering phase allowed us to obtain a set of code groups that capture meaning at a higher level. The identified code groups were then used by each group to extract the main themes. At the end, both the codes and the themes of the two groups were compared to identify similarities and differences. With the exception of some minor differences related to their naming, both the codes and the themes identified by the two couples of researchers were identical in meaning. The final themes that will be presented here derive from a joint naming session carried out by all four researchers. Only a few small differences were identified, and they will be discussed as part of the design implications. The final codes and themes with the relationships among them are available in the attached appendix, sub-folder *Codes and Themes*.

4   Results

The thematic analysis resulted in the description of five themes reported in the following sub-sections. For each theme, significant participant quotes are reported. For the sake of conciseness, we will refer to participants as "P" followed by the participant number, and to the WoZ system as simply "system".

4.1   Basic Operations

This theme frames the strategies of interactions that novices have when they approach the 3D modeling activities of creation and manipulation.

Creation. Novices tend to provide simple commands in the form "<verb> a <shape>", where the used verbs are typically "create", "draw", "build", and examples of shape names are "cube", "box", or "cylinder". This behavior has been observed in tasks that required the creation of simple or composite objects. Strictly related to this is the object duplication. Novices usually keep the requests simple by asking them to duplicate a precise object, as P4 did in task 12 when he said "duplicate the cube". When the novices, instead, have to face the creation of multiple identical objects, without using the duplication requests (for example, because there was no previous copy in the scene), they simply use a basic creation request by also providing the number of copies: this is clearly exemplified by P5 in task 14 in "create four cylinders".

Manipulation The manipulation operations used by novices during the study are *translation*, *rotation*, and *scaling*. It is worth mentioning that the manipulation operations require some kind of reference frame to be performed; to this aim, novices often use relative references (for more details see theme THE GULF OF EXECUTION where the references used by the novices are discussed).

In more complex cases, novices provided commands containing both a creation request and an implicit manipulation request, where the manipulation is often expressed as a set of constraints on the final object. As an example, in task 14, P8 asked the system to "create four cylinders on the corners of the lower rectangle": in this example, the multiple creation request is clearly visible, and it is put alongside a relative positioning request.

Finally, one of the most interesting identified open codes is the one that relates to moving objects with respect to *implicit construction shapes*. As an example, P4 during the last task asked "place the four cylinders at the four corners of a square." In this example, the participant did not have a square in the scene but implicitly requested the system to create a square, place the cylinders at its corners, and delete the square once the operation was completed. This kind of operation was pretty common throughout the last task: around 45% of the participants provided a command that used a construction shape like the one previously cited.

4.2 Selection of Objects

This theme covers the strategies adopted to identify and select objects, specifically, *absolute* selection, *relative* selection, or *implicit* selection. In the case of absolute selection, most participants explicitly refer to the entire scene, or to a single object in a scene by using its name (the one shown in the "inspector" view in Blender, as P11 asked during task 14 by saying "should I call it Box 0001 if I want to move it?") or by its shape (as P1 did during task 6 by saying "move the cube 20 cm downwards"). A specialization of the latter case is the reference to a shape using a 2D approximation. One example is echoed by P8 during task 14: "Hey blender, move the upper rectangle on the side of the lower one". Here, the user referred to two 3D boxes by their 2D approximation (rectangles).

The relative selection resulted in four commonly used strategies to select objects, namely:

- their relative time of creation (e.g., P3 in task 14: "Blender, place the second box under the first");
- their relative position (e.g., P8 in task 14: "Hey Blender, create four cylinders in the corners of the lower rectangle");
- their dimensions (e.g., P11 in task 14: "Hey Blender, move the tallest box attaching it to the side of the other box");
- by inverting the current selection, eventually applying additional filters (e.g., P3 in task 14: "Blender, place the other two cylinders like you placed the previous ones").

Finally, users also often performed implicit selections of the objects in the scene, for example, by referring to a single object in the scene or by referring to the last edited object, either explicitly or implicitly (e.g., P1 in task 8 implicitly referred to the last edited object by saying "increase the volume by three times").

It is worth remarking that novices do not differentiate nor have preferences between the various methods, and actually, often mix them to be sure that the selection is clear and precise (e.g.: in a previously shown example by P8 in task 14, "Hey blender, move the upper rectangle on the side of the lower one", the user performs the selection by using both an absolute reference to the 2D approximation of the shape of an object, and a relative reference to the positioning of another object).

4.3   Errors

Due to the lack of geometry knowledge and/or 3D modeling expertise, often novices commit *errors of which the users are aware of*, and *errors of which the users are not aware of*. In the first case, they try to prevent or correct the errors. For this reason, we named it "error correction". In the second case, when a user is either not aware of an error or if they do not care about trying to fix it, then the error simply represents a mistake made during the task execution. For this reason, we named it "execution errors". We analyze the details of each thread in the following paragraphs.

Error correction. Different behaviors for correcting the errors have been observed, specifically *during* and *after* the command. Regarding the error correction made during the command, some novices try to prevent their own errors when they recognize one while stating the command, by providing a correction in the same command. For example, P9 during the chair construction task says "Hey blender, create a rectangle over the quadrilateral of length – I mean, height 30 centimeters, depth 5 and side 20–22...". This command contains multiple corrections, starting from the correction of the name of the dimension that the user wants to set to 30 centimeters, and then correcting the actual size of the side of the rectangle to 22 centimeters

Regarding the corrections made after the commands, most of the participants expected some utility commands that are typically available in GUI-based software, like the "undo" and "redo" functions. As an example, P3 during task 14 provided both the command "Blender, undo the last operation", and "place the other two cylinders as you've placed the previous ones." This highlights how, although novices may not be familiar with the task of 3D modeling or voice-based interaction, they were able to transfer the knowledge of other software they may have used in the past, expecting that their previous experience would be applicable to the new, unknown system.

Execution errors. Some of the mistakes committed by the novices are strictly related to *lapsus, lack of knowledge,* or *system shortcomings.* In the case of lapsus, some participants referred to shapes and objects using the wrong name (e.g., P10 was trying to refer to a box by calling it "cylinder" during task 14). In case of lack of knowledge, errors range from wrong names used for dimensions and primitives, to being unaware of the direction of the axis, perhaps by referring to previous knowledge obtained in school. For example, the Y axis in a 2D plane is usually the vertical one, thus some novices expect the Y axis to be the vertical one also in 3D. Finally, we identified system shortcomings, i.e. errors made by the wizard during the execution of the commands: all of these errors can be traced back to the incomprehension of the command, often due to its intrinsic vagueness (see the theme of "THE GULF OF EXECUTION").

4.4   The Gulf of Execution

This theme represents the way novices translate their goals into commands. Throughout the sessions, before providing specific commands, we immediately noticed that novices often think aloud to understand what they have to do and how they can translate it to commands like P16 said during task 14 by saying "so, the picture has a different point of view. I should move it a little bit. Ok. Hey Blender, make the cylinder bigger." Then, by analyzing their commands, we identified three main aspects of the commands where the gulf of execution becomes critical, specifically: i) relativity ii) vagueness iii) abstraction.

Relativity. Here we summarize how novices think about positions, scale, rotation, and selection relative to other parts of the scene. Two main overall frames of reference are used by the novices: the axes and other objects.

To select an axis, novices adopt three approaches, namely: i) *axis relative direction:* a common way of selecting axes is through their relative direction (depending on the user's point of view), as echoed by P9 during task 11, by saying "move the geometric shape 20 cm to the right"; ii) *the axis color:* as an example, during the execution of the last task (the one of creating a chair), P2 referred to the Y axis by its color stating "turn of 180 degrees the box on the green axis"; iii) *axis name:* some novices also refer to axes by their actual name, as P19 did during the 12th task by asking the system to "move the right cube 10 centimeters along the X axis.".

When referring to objects' dimensions, novices adopted two main approaches for selection. A first approach consists of using the dimensions' name, as P3 has done in the task of chair creation by saying *"move along the y axis of a length equal to the base of the second box the last cylinder".* A second approach used a relative comparison to other dimensions; for example, P3 during task 14 selected an object by stating *"move the third cylinder under the highest box [...]".*

Vagueness. It encloses a lack of information in the commands provided to reach the goals. In general, the lack of information is caused by:

- *chaining of multiple commands* to describe at a high level a composite shape, as shown by P22 during the chair creation task, by asking "create four cylinders with the same distance to each other.";
- *missing data* that the system needs to execute the requests; as an example, novices forget to provide some or all dimensions of a shape (e.g., P1 in task 1 stated "create a cube" without providing any dimension), they forget to specify a parameter for a transformation (e.g., P7 in task 10 asked to "rotate of 30 degrees the figure" without specifying a direction).

Abstraction. We noticed two behaviors related to the abstraction of the commands. The first one relates a general abstraction over the process to reach the desired goal, as exemplified by P2 that tried to solve task 14 by saying "create a chair using two boxes and four cylinders". The second one refers to how novices translate the desired 3D shapes into words. For example, shapes are created by providing a general description (e.g., P10 in task 4 by saying "create a 3D rectangle 30 cm high, 20 cm deep, and long 10 cm", referred to a box as a "3D rectangle", thus simply describing the shape) or by approximating the desired shape with a similar 2D shape (e.g., P8 during task 4 used "rectangle" instead of "box" by saying "create a rectangle of height 30, width 20, depth 10"). Furthermore, especially German participants, novices also refer to the 3D shapes by using similar real-world objects (e.g., P17 during task 3 stated "create a dice with an edge length of 30 centimeters", using "dice" instead of "cube").

4.5   Users' Requests

We collected requests and suggestions provided by the participants, which provide useful insights on novices' mental model.

Among the most common requests, participants often asked to rotate the camera and change their point of view. As an example, P11 during the last task of creating a chair, asked "can I see it from below?" and "can I see it from above" to perform some minor adjustments and corrections to the positions of the 3D objects. This behavior underlines the need to provide a way to allow novices to rotate their point of view. This functional requirement is strictly related to the theme of SELECTION OF OBJECTS as it may benefit from different interaction modalities that could be explored (e.g., using Augmented Reality).

Another common request is related to the actual dimensions: when novices explicitly set size in the command (for example, in the third task), they want to check that the system created an object of the right size. This is exemplified by P10 which explicitly asked if "can I ask it to check the dimensions?" in the third task. This suggestion does not translate to an additional requirement for the AI model that recognizes users' commands, but it rather provides some insights on the requirements of the whole 3D modeling tool.

Other minor suggestions regarded the customization of the axis: some participants expected the Y axis to be the "vertical" one as it usually happens in 2D drawings, rather than the Z axis as it happens in 3D modeling tools like

Blender. Providing such a customization option would surely reduce the error rate in a final system, as the novices could adapt it to their own knowledge.

5   Discussion and Implications

Based on the findings of the WoZ study, in the following we present design implications for the development of future voice-based 3D modeling tools for novice designers and relate them to the wider research literature around voice assistants and general user experience principles.

Understand User Corrections and Adapt to Them. This requirement stems from the errors the users are aware of (see theme ERRORS). It poses requirements that impact two different facets of future voice-based digital modeling tools: the Natural Language Understanding (NLU) layer and the conversation flow. Regarding the NLU layer, systems must be able to intercept user corrections and aborted commands. Based on our findings, we note that *recognizing uncertainty, hesitation, doubt, and error awareness early on is particularly crucial in the digital modeling context*, as users displayed them frequently due to their unfamiliarity with 3D modeling [2].

Regarding the conversation flow, after intercepting the error correction, it is important to design a dialog that helps users understand the error and recover from it [18]. Moore and Arar [30] provide valuable pointers through their *Natural Conversation Framework* which proposes a set of conversational patterns. Some of these patterns relate to *user corrections* and can be applied to voice-based digital modeling. An example inspired by this framework that relates to errors that users correct while they issue a 3D modeling command might be:

> *User:* Hey blender, increase of 10 centimeters -no- of 20 centimeters the sides of the geometric figure
> *Agent:* I'm sorry, I didn't understand. Do you mean an increase of 10 or 20 centimeters?
> *User:* 20 centimeters.
> *Agent:* Ok, I'm increasing of 20 centimeters the sides of the geometric figure.

Deal with Vague and Incomplete Commands. We have identified numerous ERRORS by the lack of knowledge and the system's shortcomings that users were unaware of. These errors are related to incomprehension due to the vagueness and abstraction of some commands. Self-repair strategies should be introduced to improve interaction [6]. To this aim, we identified two possible solutions. The first one consists of *sensible defaults*: in case of a vague command, the voice assistant fixes it by *selecting a relevant parameter from a list of alternatives*. For example, if the user says "create a cylinder on top of the cube", the cylinder diameter is not specified. In this case, the system can assume that the diameter is equal to the side of the cube. This solution can also benefit from the dialog context: as suggested by Jain et al., *resolving and maintaining the dialog context* can help select the most appropriate sensible default from a list of alternatives [18]. For example, if other cylinders have been previously created with a given diameter on top of cubes the same can be applied to the new ones in case of vague commands. This allows the system to be proactive, anticipating the users' requests as suggested by Völkel et al. [48].

The second solution consists of *interactively guiding the user* by providing the missing information. With reference to the previous command of the box and cylinder, instead of using defaults, the voice assistant can explicitly ask the user for the desired radius. The strategy adopted by the voice assistant is informed by the degree of system autonomy or desired user control. A hybrid solution can also benefit from both approaches: the selected sensible default can be used by the voice assistant to ask the user if the default is right, for example, with reference to the previous case the voice assistant can reply: "OK, I'm creating a cylinder with a diameter equal to the side of the cube. Is it OK?"

Translate Interaction Conventions to Voice-Based Digital Modeling. Users commonly apply their experience with software applications to other applications or even different domains. As an example, some participants expected to execute "undo" or "redo" commands, which are common across applications and domains. This is in line with the traditional Nielsen heuristics of "user control and freedom" and "consistency and standard" [35]. The latter states that "users should not have to wonder whether different words, situations, or actions mean the same thing", thus the system should "follow platform and industry conventions" (from Nielsen [34]). For this reason, a voice-based 3D modeling system should provide such common operations, like the aforementioned "undo" and "redo" commands. Further exploration may be required to clearly define and match the set of expected commands to voice-based digital modeling.

Adopt Simple Operations Even for the Creation of Composite 3D Models . Based on the theme BASIC OPERATIONS, we note that most users follow similar and simple approaches even in complex tasks. For example, by analyzing task 13 (which consisted of creating a figure having a cylinder on top of the cube), multiple approaches might be adopted, but novices used only basic operations (creation and translation) to create both a simple cube and a cylinder and then moving the latter on top of the former. This highlights that, although many technical operations may be implemented in voice assistants for digital modeling, it is important to provide novices with simple operations to create and compose 3D objects, rather than prescribing more complex operations like "extrusion" and "insetting", which are most adequate for skilled users [33].

Match Digital Modeling Workflows with Novices' Expectations and Experiences from Building Physical Objects. Related to the

Basic Operations, but by focusing on the last task (that consisted of the creation of a chair), we noticed that the majority of the users started by creating the base cylinders (almost all users started with a phrase like *"create four cylinders"*). This surely provides an interesting insight on how people approach the creation of composite 3D objects. By creating the base cylinders first, users are basically following an approach that starts from the bottom and proceeds upwards. This is not different from the approach that users should follow if they were composing physical shapes: by starting from the bottom, they are able to stack the various shapes without the risk of their composition to "fall down". This indication can be useful if wizard procedures are introduced to guide the creation of composite 3D objects; for example, the voice assistants can start the interaction by asking which is the shape, with its features, that must be placed at the bottom, then going on guiding the user to create other shapes on top of the previous ones.

Provide Alternatives for the Selection of 3D Objects. By reflecting on the theme of SELECTION OF OBJECTS, we argue that it is among the most critical ones: most of the 3D modeling revolves around the selection of objects to be composed. We found that several and different techniques have been adopted by the novices. For example, a common solution is represented by commands to select an object by referring to the entire scene, in other words in an absolute way. We also documented commands that use relative references, for example, their relative time of creation, their relative position, their dimensions, and by inverting the current selection. The last approach is represented by the implicit selection of the objects in the scene. These strategies represent different solutions the users can adopt to select a 3D object, and thus the voice assistant should accommodate all of them. To simplify the interaction, future voice assistants can be complemented with additional interaction modalities like gestures or eye tracking, where users could simply point [12, 21, 22] or gaze [27] at the object or surface they want to select.

Understand Commands that Are Relative to the User's Point of View. As described in the themes THE GULF OF EXECUTION and SELECTION OF OBJECTS, users often execute commands that are related to their point of view, in particular, to change the camera perspective, to select an axis, and to select a 3D object. In other words, we found that a common way for novices to issue commands is through the "screen" coordinate system [43], as provided by some professional 3D modeling systems[5], by using common words such as "left" and "right", as P9 did during task 11 with the command "move the geometric shape 20 cm to the right". Furthermore, novices often provided commands relative to both their point of view and other objects (as P10 did during task 13: "insert a cylinder on top of the cube"). This implies that future voice assistants must be equipped with some way of understanding the 3D context into which the command is provided, and they must take into account the user's point of view during the intent-matching process.

---

[5] https://shorturl.at/fGLRZ.

Grant Multiple Ways to Refer to the Axes. Users referred to the axes of the 3D scene by adopting different approaches: by indicating the axis color, by referring to the user's relative direction, by using the axis name (see themes THE GULF OF EXECUTION) or some users also preferred to switch the Y and Z axes as the "vertical" axis (see theme newin-linkSec17theme:usersspssuggestionsUSERS' REQUESTS). This ambiguity is also found in professional systems, as some of them use the Z axis as vertical while others use the Y axis instead [16]. This behavior should be considered in the design of voice assistants for 3D modeling, since this is a core activity that, if not adequately supported, might lead to ineffective user interaction.

Design for Complex Commands. Multiple chained commands have often been prompted to execute various actions. In our study, it was possible to accommodate the multiple users commands thanks to the WoZ but voice assistants are typically restricted to simple standalone commands. Similar to what Fast et al. already proposed for complex tasks [9], also voice-based systems for 3D modeling should address this requirement, which strongly impacts the design of its NLU layer that must be able to understand and execute multiple chained commands.

Favor Explicit Trigger Words. Previous work by Vtyurina et al. argued that forcing the use of explicit trigger words would constrain user interactions, suggesting the use of implicit conversation cues for driving the dialog [49]. On the contrary, during our experiments novices used implicit conversational cues while thinking about their workflow and as a natural reaction after a successful command execution (see THE GULF OF EXECUTION): this highlights the need for future voice-based systems to provide clear explicit activation cues and trigger words, to avoid any unintentional activation that would disrupt users' workflow.

Embrace Diversity in Naming Approaches. As novices usually have little to no knowledge of the 3D modeling domain, they often have to resort to different naming approaches when dealing with shapes for which they do not recall the "right" name. As already highlighted in THE GULF OF EXECUTION, novices can refer to shapes by providing high-level descriptions (e.g., "3D rectangle" instead of "box"), 2D approximations ("rectangle" instead of "box"), or by associating them to a real-world object (e.g., "dice" instead of "cube"). For this reason, future systems must be able to understand both analogies and descriptions of shapes. A concrete solution might be the adoption of a lexical ontology like WordNet [29] to infer the shape name related to the real object.

6   Limitations of the Study

Our study is an initial step toward understanding how novices approach voice-based 3D modeling. We have identified some limitations of our work. First, the novices' languages deserve a wider exploration: our study highlights very small differences between Germans and Italians because of their culture; however, a similar study where participants use their native languages might be useful to understand how language might impact the resulting mental model. Similarly, this study does not focus on how aspects like ethnicity, socio-economic status, and age might impact the novice's mental model. Another limitation regards the tasks: the ones used in the study are representative of the most common operations to design 3D models but digital fabrication often implies the design of objects that are more complex than a chair. In addition, the set of proposed tasks does not cover all possible operations (e.g., selecting textures and making holes). Future work may also study differences between the mental model of lay users (target of this study) and novices in 3D modeling that are domain experts (e.g., they have expertise in sculpting or 3D world composition, but do not know how to model). Similarly, the proposed voice-based interaction approach may be compared with alternative solutions based on mouse and keyboard or multi-modal approaches, to explore the pros and cons of each solution. Finally, Blender has been selected as the 3D modeling tool because of the advantages reported in Sect. 3.3; however, its UI is designed for a WIMP interaction thus it presents commands, buttons, functions, etc., that might bias or confuse novices. Despite carefully hiding all the useless parts of the Blender UI, the adoption of a system purposely designed to better fit the voice interaction might be adopted to elicit the mental model.

7   Conclusion

Voice interaction is emerging as a promising paradigm that can simplify 3D modeling for digital fabrication. However, novices' mental model is never considered when designing voice-based 3D modeling systems. In addition, voice interaction is usually built on top of WIMP systems instead of designing the voice paradigm and the whole system from scratch. This study addresses these limitations by investigating the novices' mental model in 3D modeling and contributes to the state-of-the-art by identifying a set of design implications that support the definition of voice-based interaction paradigms for the design and customization of personalized 3D models. This contribution aims to lower the barrier to 3D modeling thus supporting the wider democratization of digital fabrication.

As future work, we are now addressing the limitations reported in the previous section. We are also working on the development of a prototype of a voice assistant integrated into Blender: it is currently being developed in DialogFlow [39] and it has been designed considering the design implications proposed in this study. The aim is to study novices' behavior when interacting with real systems, also exploring if and how the design indications suggested in this study also accommodate the design of more complex objects in more realistic situations, for example, by proposing scenarios instead of tasks.

Acknowledgements. This work has been funded by the European Union's Horizon 2020 research and innovation program under grant agreement No. 952026 (https:// www.humane-ai.eu/). The research of Andrea Esposito is funded by a Ph.D. fellowship within the framework of the Italian "D.M. n. 352, April 9, 2022' - under the National Recovery and Resilience Plan, Mission 4, Component 2, Investment 3.3 - Ph.D. Project "Human-Centered Artificial Intelligence (HCAI) techniques for supporting end users interacting with AI systems", co-supported by "Eusoft S.r.l." (CUP H91I22000410007).

References

1. Billinghurst, M., Baldis, S., Matheson, L., Philips, M.: 3d palette: a virtual reality content creation tool. In: Proceedings of the ACM Symposium on Virtual Reality Software and Technology, VRST 1997, pp. 155–156. Association for Computing Machinery, Lausanne, Switzerland (1997). https://doi.org/10.1145/261135.261163

2. Bonner, S.E.: A model of the effects of audit task complexity. Acc. Organ. Soc. **19**(3), 213–234 (1994). https://doi.org/10.1016/0361-3682(94)90033-7

3. Braun, M., Mainz, A., Chadowitz, R., Pfleging, B., Alt, F.: At your service: designing voice assistant personalities to improve automotive user interfaces. In: Proceedings of the 2019 CHI Conference on Human Factors in Computing Systems, CHI 2019, pp. 1–11. Association for Computing Machinery, New York (2019). https://doi.org/10.1145/3290605.3300270

4. Braun, V., Clarke, V.: Using thematic analysis in psychology. Qual. Res. Psychol. **3**(2), 77–101 (2006). https://doi.org/10.1191/1478088706qp063oa

5. Cuadra, A., Goedicke, D., Zamfirescu-Pereira, J.: Democratizing design and fabrication using speech: Exploring co-design with a voice assistant. In: CUI 2021–3rd Conference on Conversational User Interfaces, CUI 2021, Association for Computing Machinery, Bilbao (online), Spain (2021). https://doi.org/10.1145/3469595.3469624

6. Cuadra, A., Li, S., Lee, H., Cho, J., Ju, W.: My bad! repairing intelligent voice assistant errors improves interaction. Proc. ACM Hum.-Comput. Interact. **5**(CSCW1) (2021). https://doi.org/10.1145/3449101

7. Davis, K.H., Biddulph, R., Balashek, S.: Automatic recognition of spoken digits. J. Acoustical Soc. Am. **24**(6), 637–642 (1952). https://doi.org/10.1121/1.1906946

8. Etikan, I., Musa, S.A., Alkassim, R.S.: Comparison of convenience sampling and purposive sampling. Am. J. Theoret. Appli. Stat. **5**(1), 1–4 (2016). https://doi.org/10.11648/j.ajtas.20160501.11

9. Fast, E., Chen, B., Mendelsohn, J., Bassen, J., Bernstein, M.S.: Iris: a conversational agent for complex tasks. CoRR abs/ arXiv: 1707.05015 (2017)

10. Feeman, S.M., Wright, L.B., Salmon, J.L.: Exploration and evaluation of cad modeling in virtual reality. Comput.-Aided Design Appli. **15**(6), 892–904 (2018). https://doi.org/10.1080/16864360.2018.1462570

11. Fialho, P., Coheur, L.: Chatwoz: chatting through a wizard of oz. In: Proceedings of the 17th International ACM SIGACCESS Conference on Computers & Accessibility, ASSETS 2015, pp. 423–424. , Association for Computing Machinery, Lisbon, Portugal (2015). https://doi.org/10.1145/2700648.2811334

12. Friedrich, M., Langer, S., Frey, F.: Combining gesture and voice control for mid-air manipulation of cad models in vr environments. In: Proceedings of the 16th International Joint Conference on Computer Vision, Imaging and Computer Graphics Theory and Applications, vol. 1: HUCAPP, pp. 119–127. INSTICC, SciTePress, Online Streaming (2021). https://doi.org/10.5220/0010170501190127

13. Gershenfeld, N.: How to make almost anything: the digital fabrication revolution. Foreign Aff. **91**, 43 (2012)

14. Grigor, S., Nandra, C., Gorgan, D.: Voice-controlled 3d modelling with an intelligent personal assistant. Int. J. User-Syst. Interaction **13**, 73–88 (2020). https://doi.org/10.37789/ijusi.2020.13.2.2

15. Grimes, G.M., Schuetzler, R.M., Giboney, J.S.: Mental models and expectation violations in conversational AI interactions. Decis. Support Syst. **144**, 113515 (2021). https://doi.org/10.1016/j.dss.2021.113515

16. van Gumster, J.: Blender For Dummies, 2nd edn. For Dummies, USA (2011)

17. Huang, Y.-C., Chen, K.-L.: Brain-computer interfaces (BCI) based 3D computer-aided design (CAD): to improve the efficiency of 3D modeling for new users. In: Schmorrow, D.D., Fidopiastis, C.M. (eds.) AC 2017. LNCS (LNAI), vol. 10285, pp. 333–344. Springer, Cham (2017). https://doi.org/10.1007/978-3-319-58625-0_24

18. Jain, M., Kumar, P., Kota, R., Patel, S.N.: Evaluating and informing the design of chatbots. In: Proceedings of the 2018 Designing Interactive Systems Conference, DIS 2018, pp. 895–906. Association for Computing Machinery, New York (2018). https://doi.org/10.1145/3196709.3196735

19. James, J., Watson, C.I., MacDonald, B.: Artificial empathy in social robots: an analysis of emotions in speech. In: Proceedings of the 27th IEEE International Symposium on Robot and Human Interactive Communication, RO-MAN 2018, pp. 632–637. IEEE Press, Nanjing, China (2018). https://doi.org/10.1109/ROMAN.2018.8525652

20. Jowers, I., Prats, M., McKay, A., Garner, S.: Evaluating an eye tracking interface for a two-dimensional sketch editor. Comput. Aided Des. **45**(5), 923–936 (2013). https://doi.org/10.1016/j.cad.2013.01.006

21. Khan, S., Tunçer, B.: Gesture and speech elicitation for 3d cad modeling in conceptual design. Autom. Constr. **106**, 102847 (2019). https://doi.org/10.1016/j.autcon.2019.102847

22. Khan, S., Tuncer, B., Subramanian, R., Blessing, L.: 3d cad modeling using gestures and speech: investigating cad legacy and non-legacy procedures. In: Lee, J.H. (ed.) Proceedings of the 18th International Conference on Computer Aided Architectural Design Futures, CAAD Futures 2019, pp. 347–366. CUMINCAD, Daejeon, Republic of Korea (2019). http://papers.cumincad.org/cgi-bin/works/paper/cf2019_042

23. Kou, X.Y., Tan, S.T.: Design by talking with computers. Comput.-Aided Design Appli. **5**(1–4), 266–277 (2008). https://doi.org/10.3722/cadaps.2008.266-277

24. Kou, X., Xue, S., Tan, S.: Knowledge-guided inference for voice-enabled cad. Comput. Aided Des. **42**(6), 545–557 (2010). https://doi.org/10.1016/j.cad.2010.02.002

25. Langevin, R., Lordon, R.J., Avrahami, T., Cowan, B.R., Hirsch, T., Hsieh, G.: Heuristic evaluation of conversational agents. In: Proceedings of the 2021 CHI Conference on Human Factors in Computing Systems, CHI 2021. Association for Computing Machinery, New York (2021). https://doi.org/10.1145/3411764.3445312

26. Lee, M., Billinghurst, M.: A wizard of oz study for an ar multimodal interface. In: Proceedings of the 10th International Conference on Multimodal Interfaces, ICMI 2008, pp. 249–256. Association for Computing Machinery, Chania, Crete, Greece (2008). https://doi.org/10.1145/1452392.1452444

27. Mayer, S., Laput, G., Harrison, C.: Enhancing mobile voice assistants with worldgaze. In: Proceedings of the 2020 CHI Conference on Human Factors in Computing Systems, CHI 2020, pp. 1–10. Association for Computing Machinery, Honolulu, HI, USA (2020). https://doi.org/10.1145/3313831.3376479

28. Medhi Thies, I., Menon, N., Magapu, S., Subramony, M., O'Neill, J.: How do you want your Chatbot? an exploratory Wizard-of-Oz study with young, Urban Indians. In: Bernhaupt, R., Dalvi, G., Joshi, A., Balkrishan, D.K., O'Neill, J., Winckler, M. (eds.) INTERACT 2017. LNCS, vol. 10513, pp. 441–459. Springer, Cham (2017). https://doi.org/10.1007/978-3-319-67744-6_28

29. Miller, G.A.: Wordnet: a lexical database for English. Commun. ACM **38**(11), 39–41 (1995). https://doi.org/10.1145/219717.219748

30. Moore, R.J., Arar, R.: Conversational UX Design: A Practitioner's Guide to the Natural Conversation Framework. Association for Computing Machinery, New York (2019)

31. Murad, C., Munteanu, C., Cowan, B.R., Clark, L.: Revolution or evolution? speech interaction and HCI design guidelines. IEEE Pervasive Comput. **18**(2), 33–45 (2019). https://doi.org/10.1109/MPRV.2019.2906991

32. Murad, C., Munteanu, C., Cowan, B.R., Clark, L.: Finding a new voice: transitioning designers from gui to vui design. In: CUI 2021–3rd Conference on Conversational User Interfaces, CUI 2021. Association for Computing Machinery, New York (2021). https://doi.org/10.1145/3469595.3469617

33. Nanjundaswamy, V.G., et al.: Intuitive 3D computer-aided design (CAD) system with multimodal interfaces. In: Proceedings of the ASME 2013 International Design Engineering Technical Conferences and Computers and Information in Engineering Conference, vol. 2A: 33rd Computers and Information in Engineering Conference. ASME, Portland, Oregon, USA (08 2013). https://doi.org/10.1115/DETC2013-12277, v02AT02A037

34. Nielsen, J.: 10 usability heuristics for user interface design (1994). https://www.nngroup.com/articles/ten-usability-heuristics/

35. Nielsen, J.: Enhancing the explanatory power of usability heuristics. In: Proceedings of the SIGCHI Conference on Human Factors in Computing Systems, CHI 1994, pp. 152–158. Association for Computing Machinery, Boston, Massachusetts, USA (1994). https://doi.org/10.1145/191666.191729

36. Niu, H., Van Leeuwen, C., Hao, J., Wang, G., Lachmann, T.: Multimodal natural human-computer interfaces for computer-aided design: A review paper. Appl. Sci. **12**(13), 6510 (2022)

37. Nowacki, C., Gordeeva, A., Lizé, A.H.: Improving the usability of voice user interfaces: a new set of ergonomic criteria. In: Marcus, A., Rosenzweig, E. (eds.) Design, User Experience, and Usability. Design for Contemporary Interactive Environments, pp. 117–133. Springer International Publishing, Cham (2020)

38. Plumed, R., González-Lluch, C., Pérez-López, D., Contero, M., Camba, J.D.: A voice-based annotation system for collaborative computer-aided design. J. Comput. Design Eng. **8**(2), 536–546 (2021). https://doi.org/10.1093/jcde/qwaa092

39. Sabharwal, N., Agrawal, A.: Introduction to Google Dialogflow, pp. 13–54. Apress, Berkeley, CA (2020). https://doi.org/10.1007/978-1-4842-5741-8_2

40. Samad, T., Director, S.W.: Towards a natural language interface for cad. In: Proceedings of the 22nd ACM/IEEE Design Automation Conference, pp. 2–8. DAC '85, IEEE Press, Las Vegas, Nevada, USA (1985)

41. Seaborn, K., Miyake, N.P., Pennefather, P., Otake-Matsuura, M.: Voice in human-agent interaction: a survey. ACM Comput. Surv. (CSUR) **54**(4), 1–43 (2021)

42. Sharp, H., Rogers, Y., Preece, J.: Interaction Design: Beyond Human Computer Interaction. John Wiley & Sons Inc., Hoboken, NJ, USA (2007)

43. Shum, H.Y., Han, M., Szeliski, R.: Interactive construction of 3d models from panoramic mosaics. In: Proceedings. 1998 IEEE Computer Society Conference on Computer Vision and Pattern Recognition (Cat. No.98CB36231), pp. 427–433. IEEE, Santa Barbara, California (1998). https://doi.org/10.1109/CVPR.1998.698641

44. Sree Shankar, S., Rai, R.: Human factors study on the usage of BCI headset for 3d cad modeling. Comput.-Aided Design **54**, 51–55 (2014). https://doi.org/10.1016/j.cad.2014.01.006, application of brain-computer interfaces in cad/e systems

45. Stark, R., Israel, J., Wöhler, T.: Towards hybrid modelling environments–merging desktop-cad and virtual reality-technologies. CIRP Ann. **59**(1), 179–182 (2010). https://doi.org/10.1016/j.cirp.2010.03.102

46. Thakur, A., Rai, R.: User study of hand gestures for gesture based 3D CAD modeling. In: Proceedings of the ASME 2015 International Design Engineering Technical Conferences and Computers and Information in Engineering Conference, vol. 1B: 35th Computers and Information in Engineering Conference. ASME, Boston, Massachusetts, USA (Aug 2015). https://doi.org/10.1115/DETC2015-46086, v01BT02A017

47. Voice2CAD: Voice2CAD (2022). https://voice2cad.com/

48. Völkel, S.T., Buschek, D., Eiband, M., Cowan, B.R., Hussmann, H.: Eliciting and analysing users' envisioned dialogues with perfect voice assistants. In: Proceedings of the 2021 CHI Conference on Human Factors in Computing Systems, CHI 2021. Association for Computing Machinery, Yokohama, Japan (2021). https://doi.org/10.1145/3411764.3445536

49. Vtyurina, A., Fourney, A.: Exploring the role of conversational cues in guided task support with virtual assistants. In: Proceedings of the 2018 CHI Conference on Human Factors in Computing Systems, CHI 2018, pp. 1–7. Association for Computing Machinery, Montreal QC, Canada (2018). https://doi.org/10.1145/3173574.3173782

50. Vuletic, T., et al.: A novel user-based gesture vocabulary for conceptual design. Int. J. Hum Comput Stud. **150**, 102609 (2021). https://doi.org/10.1016/j.ijhcs.2021.102609

51. Vyas, S., Chen, T.J., Mohanty, R., Krishnamurthy, V.: Making-a-scene: a preliminary case study on speech-based 3D shape exploration through scene modeling. J. Comput. Inform. Sci. Eng. 1–11 (2022). https://doi.org/10.1115/1.4055239

52. Xue, S., Kou, X., Tan, S.: Natural voice-enabled cad: modeling via natural discourse. Comput.-Aided Design Appli. **6**(1), 125–136 (2009)

53. Xue, S., Kou, X., Tan, S.: Command search for CAD system. Comput.-Aided Design Appli. **7**(6), 899–910 (2010)

54. Yoon, S.M., Graf, H.: Eye tracking based interaction with 3d reconstructed objects. In: Proceedings of the 16th ACM International Conference on Multimedia, MM 2008, pp. 841–844. Association for Computing Machinery, Vancouver, British Columbia, Canada (2008). https://doi.org/10.1145/1459359.1459501

Exploring the Potential of Metaverse Apps for Real-World Applications: A Case Study with CALEND_AR

Konstantinos Tsomokos[(✉)] [iD], Christos Sintoris[iD], Christos Fidas[iD], and Nikolaos Avouris[iD]

Department of Electrical and Computer Engineering, University of Patras, Campus Rio 26504, Greece
tsom1047010@gmail.com, {sintoris,fidas,avouris}@upatras.gr

Abstract. This paper presents CALEND_AR, a hybrid calendar application that uses augmented reality technologies to blend physical and digital calendars. The study investigates user preferences and motivations for using physical or digital calendars and explores the need for a hybrid solution that incorporates both. It comprehensively describes the application's implementation process, including technological background, design considerations, and a user study. Evaluation results show that the hybrid approach combining the benefits of paper-based and digital calendars was appreciated by participants, despite limitations such as inconsistent accuracy of text recognition and mixed user reception of the augmented reality feature. The contributions of the work include the development of a unique and innovative hybrid approach to calendar management and demonstrating the potential of metaverse apps to address real-world problems and enhance people's lives. Future research could explore ways to improve text recognition accuracy and make the augmented reality feature more user-friendly. Overall, CALEND_AR represents an important step forward in designing augmented and mixed reality applications.

Keywords: Augmented Reality · Text Recognition · Paper-Based Calendar · Digital Calendar · Hybrid Calendar · User Evaluation · Calendar Management

1 Introduction

In the modern era, individuals use physical and digital tools to manage their daily schedules. While physical calendars provide a tangible way to view appointments and keep track of schedules, digital calendars offer the convenience of accessing information from anywhere and setting reminders and notifications. However, current calendar management solutions fail to integrate physical and digital calendars effectively, underscoring the need for innovative solutions.

© The Author(s), under exclusive license to Springer Nature Switzerland AG 2023
J. Abdelnour Nocera et al. (Eds.): INTERACT 2023, LNCS 14145, pp. 156–165, 2023.
https://doi.org/10.1007/978-3-031-42293-5_12

The CALEND_AR app presented here combines features of both physical and digital calendars to cater to the needs and preferences of individuals who use both types of calendars. By combining handwriting recognition with augmented reality, the approach presented here allows users to transfer information between the digital and physical worlds seamlessly.

The research began with a comprehensive review of existing applications that serve similar purposes, followed by an investigation of the motivations and needs of individuals who use physical or digital calendars or both. These individuals form the core user base of the application, and their needs and preferences are the primary focus of the design.

2   Related Work

To design an application that effectively combines physical and digital calendars, it is essential to understand the challenges and issues that arise in designing digital calendars as well as, more generally, computer-supported cooperative work applications. Grudin [9] discusses some of these challenges and provides insights into the design and evaluation of organizational interfaces, while Payne [14] investigates digital calendars and compares them to their paper-based counterparts. With the advent of mobile devices and the respective increase in the use of digital calendars, arose the issue of calendar synchronization across a single user's devices [17]. Despite the popularity of digital calendars, users exhibit a lasting preference for paper-based ones, which has led to the exploration of alternative interfaces for digital calendars [10].

Therefore, this paper aims to explore the potential usefulness of metaverse apps [13], using the CALEND_AR app as an example, by taking into account the insights provided by Grudin and other relevant literature. These apps bridge the gap between the digital and real worlds and provide users with new ways to interact with technology.

Digital calendars have been around for decades, and many different calendar applications are available. Some popular examples include Google Calendar [8], Apple Calendar [2], and Microsoft Outlook [11]. These offer a range of features, such as event scheduling, reminder notifications, and integration with other productivity tools. However, most are purely digital and do not offer a solution for users who still rely on paper-based calendars for some tasks.

Some applications attempt to bridge the gap between traditional and digital calendars, such as the Rocketbook Wave [16] and the Moleskine Smart Writing Set [12]. These use handwriting recognition technology, allowing users to transfer their written notes and events to a digital platform. Earlier, Plaisant et al. [15] investigated the digitization of handwritten calendar entries into a shared family calendar, although without handwriting recognition. However, they do not offer functionality that would help transfer scheduled events from the digital to the paper-based calendar. Compared to current solutions, CALEND_AR offers a hybrid approach, allowing users to input information into the digital calendar using handwriting recognition. Additionally, with the help of augmented reality, it allows users to transfer information back to the real world.

3 Motivation

The use of digital calendars has become widespread in organizing personal schedules, offering flexibility and convenience for tracking appointments and events. However, digital calendars also have some limitations [7]. Some individuals find it challenging to switch from a paper-based calendar to a digital one, missing the tangible sensation of handwriting and handling events on a physical calendar. This is particularly true for long-time paper calendar users accustomed to their format and features.

Moreover, some users prefer digital calendars but still need to transfer information between their digital and traditional calendars for different purposes, such as sharing their schedule with others who use physical calendars or having a backup copy of their events. This process can be time-consuming, leading to mistakes and missed events [1].

To address these issues, our approach attempts to merge the benefits of paper-based and digital calendars. Using handwriting recognition, users can enter information into the digital calendar using their handwriting [4], preserving the tactile experience of writing on a paper calendar. Additionally, the transfer of information from the digital calendar to the physical world is possible.

4 Design Rationale

Users who rely on both digital and paper-based calendars may find an augmented reality calendar particularly useful. They can use it to transfer their digital tasks to their paper-based calendar and to manage any conflicts between the two, allowing digital and handwritten tasks to coexist. Users can transfer their handwritten tasks to the digital calendar by using text recognition, while they can use the augmented reality feature to view their entire schedule, digital and paper-based, in a real-world context eliminating the risk of double entries or scheduling conflicts.

The approach followed in the design of CALEND_AR focuses on allowing users to transition back and forth between paper-based and digital calendars and to transfer information between the two modes. An augmented reality calendar should then provide augmented visualization by overlaying digital information onto a physical, paper-based, calendar, provide visual cues, highlight important events, and enhance the overall visibility and comprehension of the calendar data. Users should be able to view, create, reschedule, or delete calendar data in either the paper-based or the digital component of the augmented reality calendar. A user would expect calendar data to be synchronized between the paper-based and digital interfaces, ensuring that changes made on either one are reflected in the augmented reality interface. Consequently, the calendar should be able to incorporate contextual information relating to the paper-based calendar, such as the date and time information relating to the page the user is viewing through the augmented reality interface as well as the events marked on it.

A use case scenario for the task of viewing a scheduled event in CALEND_AR would then entail the following steps: The user activates the augmented reality interface by launching the CALEND_AR application and gazes through it to the open page of her paper-based calendar, where some of the events of her schedule for tomorrow are written. The application recognizes the date of the open page of the paper calendar and pulls the relevant tasks from the online digital calendar. The app also updates the digital calendar with the events written on the paper-based one, by digitizing and recognizing the handwritten tasks. A conflict is recognized in the schedule. The application displays an overlay showing the entries on the digital calendar that have no corresponding entry in the paper-based one, while the entries that are present on both calendars are omitted since they are visible on the paper. The recognized conflict is highlighted (Fig. 2), prompting the user to resolve it by choosing which of the conflicting entries is correct.

To support the above scenario and user needs, when users utilize the augmented reality feature to view their entire schedule on their real-world calendar, each task is seamlessly placed on the correct date without obstructing the date or task. This has been accomplished in CALEND_AR by using an (x,z) coordinate for each task (Fig. 1). If the user wants to modify a task, the (x,z) coordinate will also change, ensuring the task takes its correct position on the real calendar in the augmented reality interface. After the handwritten text is recognized, the system provides to the interface, not only the digitized text but also the position (x,y) of each word's four corners on the photograph. However, in the Unity [20] environment, which was used for the augmented reality feature, the positions of GameObjects [19] that will contain the tasks are based on the position of the target image [22]. Therefore, to ensure seamless interaction between Unity and the text recognition environment, it's essential to establish a correlation between their design scales. The "remap" method [6] was employed to achieve this.

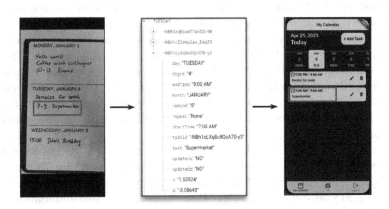

Fig. 1. The digitization process: A visual representation of how handwritten tasks are transformed into digital data within the app's database.

If a handwritten task is transferred to the digital calendar app and is subsequently deleted or altered, the user will be alerted in the augmented reality interface by striking the original handwritten task with a red line, indicating to her that it has been deleted or edited, and the corrected task will be displayed at its new position on the calendar (Fig. 2). This guarantees that users have an accurate and up-to-date representation of their schedule.

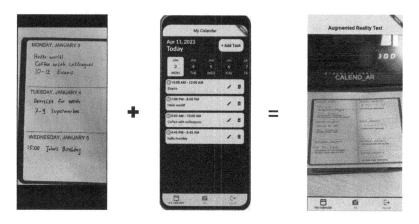

Fig. 2. Harmonious coexistence: Combining digital and handwritten tasks Using augmented reality in CALEND_AR.

5   User Study

Billinghurst et al. [3] emphasize the need for increased user studies and evaluations in AR research and development, as only a small percentage of previous papers included formal evaluations. They identify three main areas for user studies: Perception, Performance/Interaction, and Collaboration. To evaluate the effectiveness of the CALEND_AR app, this study focused on assessing its user-friendliness and comprehensibility through task completion, observation, and participant feedback. The evaluation also collected suggestions for improvement, in line with the recommendation of Billinghurst et al. [3] to use multiple evaluation techniques for AR system design.

To evaluate the CALEND_AR mobile app, a test was conducted for a period of three weeks. The evaluation involved a group of five participants varying in age and profession, including Participant 1, a 30-year-old female architect; Participant 2, a 20-year-old male student; Participant 3, a 37-year-old male chemical engineer; Participant 4, a 25-year-old male software engineer, and Participant 5, a 32-year-old female teacher.

On the first day of the three-week user evaluation period, participants were asked to complete a series of tasks using the app. The first task was to "create a new account and log in to the application." Then, the participants were instructed in the use of the application. To do this, they were first asked to use it to manage a set of dummy tasks scheduled for the first of the three-week period, with the support of the evaluator. Participants' interactions with the app while completing these tasks were observed and recorded, and interviews were conducted to gather additional insights. For the remainder of the evaluation period, the participants were asked to use the app regularly in their daily lives and report any issues or suggestions for improvement. A print calendar to use along the CALENDAR_AR app was hand-delivered to each participant.

After the three-week evaluation period, participants took part in a remote focus group session, where they were asked to provide their viewpoints and discuss facets of their experience of using CALEND_AR. The focus group session allowed participants to engage in group discussions, enabling a broader range of perspectives and in-depth insights to be gathered.

6 Analysis of Results

At the end of the three-week evaluation period, participants were asked to provide feedback on their experience using the app. They were asked to rate CAL-END_AR's user-friendliness on a scale from 1 to 5, with five being the most user-friendly. Four out of five participants rated the app with a 4 or 5, indicating that they found it highly user-friendly. One participant reported that she faced minor challenges in navigating the app.

Participants were also asked about the comprehensibility of the app's features. Four participants found the app's features straightforward and easy to use. In contrast, one participant reported having trouble understanding the instructions and found it difficult to operate the app's augmented reality features.

Based on the analysis of data, participants' engagement with the app's features was measured for the three-week evaluation period. Four out of five participants consistently utilized the app by creating an average of 2.4 entries in the digital calendar per day, while one participant used it only a couple of times throughout the three weeks. These results suggest that the hybrid calendar features of CALEND_AR were engaging enough for most participants to incorporate it into their daily routine in order to manage events and schedule tasks.

The hybrid calendar feature, which includes both text recognition and augmented reality, was highly appreciated by the participants. This suggests that the integration of real-world elements into a digital calendar can be useful for managing schedules and events. The handwritten text recognition feature garnered mixed reviews, with some users finding it very accurate and reliable, while others found it to be somewhat inconsistent. However, the users did agree that it saved them a lot of time, and those who found it time-consuming appreciated the assistance in correcting inaccuracies.

On the other hand, the augmented reality feature was found to be helpful by three users, as it made it easier to see their appointments and to-do lists in a real-world context. These users also found it useful for visualizing their schedules in a real-world setting. They noted that it was convenient for them to be able to see the hybrid weekly schedule at once. However, the remaining two users reported that they preferred viewing their appointments directly in the app, instead of using the augmented reality feature, while one of them reported that it was somewhat finicky and difficult to use.

Overall, the results (Table 1) of the user evaluation suggest that the CALEND_AR app was well-received by the participants, with some areas for improvement.

Table 1. Participant Feedback on App Usability and Features

Feedback Aspect	Average Rating
User-Friendliness	4.2/5.0
Comprehensibility	4.6/5.0
Usage Frequency	4.1/5.0
Timely Notifications	4.8/5.0
Text Recognition Feature	3.4/5.0
Augmented Reality Feature	4.2/5.0

Participant feedback, provided in the form of transcripts from the focus group session, further enriched the findings. Participant 1, for instance, emphasized the seamless transition between paper-based and digital calendars, highlighting the convenience of maintaining a preferred tactile experience while benefiting from the organization and reminder functionality of a digital calendar. Similarly, Participant 2 praised the convenience and flexibility offered by the app and emphasized the ability to transfer information between physical and digital calendars without conflicts, providing the best of both worlds. Additionally, Participant 3 expressed satisfaction with the augmented reality feature, which ensured an accurate and up-to-date schedule by visually indicating changes from the digital calendar to the physical calendar. However, Participant 4 raised concerns about occasional inaccuracies in handwriting recognition, suggesting that improving its accuracy would enhance the overall user experience. Finally, Participant 5 pointed out the learning curve associated with the app and suggested the inclusion of more user-friendly instructions or tutorials to cater to participants who may not be proficient with technology.

7   Conclusions

In line with previous studies on digital calendars [5,18], the user evaluation results of CALEND_AR suggest that the hybrid approach to calendar management, which combines the benefits of both paper-based and digital calendars, was appreciated by the participants. The app's augmented reality feature was well-received by some users, while some experienced difficulties with the accuracy of the text recognition feature. Despite these limitations, CALEND_AR represents a definite advancement in the development of metaverse apps and has the potential to be an effective and user-friendly tool for managing schedules and events [21].

One of the significant advantages of CALEND_AR over other existing solutions is its ability to combine the benefits of paper-based and digital calendars, providing users with a familiar and intuitive experience. The app's augmented reality feature is also a unique and innovative approach to visualizing events in a real-world context.

The user evaluation revealed several compelling use cases that highlight the seamless transition between the paper-based and digital calendar facilitated by the CALEND_AR app. The ability to transfer handwritten tasks from a paper-based calendar to the digital realm using the app caters to users who appreciate the tactile experience of writing on paper while still benefiting from the convenience and organization offered by a digital calendar. Another use case that garnered positive feedback is the augmented reality overlays feature. Participants found this feature particularly useful as it allowed them to view their digital events overlaid onto their paper-based calendar, effectively bridging the gap between the digital and physical worlds. Furthermore, the approach presented in this paper enables the coexistence of digital and handwritten tasks, accommodating users who rely on both mediums for their scheduling needs. The augmented reality function facilitates the seamless transfer of digital tasks to the physical calendar without conflicts or duplication, providing flexibility and convenience. Additionally, the app ensures an accurate and up-to-date schedule by detecting and alerting users about changes during the augmented reality experience. When modifications are made to the digital calendar, a visual indicator, such as a red line, appears over the corresponding handwritten task, promoting reliability and minimizing discrepancies between the physical and digital calendars.

While CALEND_AR has some limitations, including the inconsistent accuracy of the text recognition feature and the mixed user reception of the augmented reality feature, these issues can be addressed in future updates. The contributions of the work are the development of a unique and innovative hybrid approach to calendar management that could benefit individuals and professionals alike. The work also demonstrates the potential of metaverse apps to address real-world problems and enhance people's lives.

Future research in this area could explore ways to improve the accuracy of text recognition and make the augmented reality feature more user-friendly. It would also be interesting to investigate the potential benefits of CALEND_AR for specific professions, such as event planners and educators. Furthermore, the emergence of augmented reality calendars, such as CALEND_AR, opens up possibilities for exploring alternative designs in calendar user interfaces [10]. The integration of augmented reality technology in calendar applications presents an opportunity to reimagine how users interact with their schedules and visualize events in a more immersive and intuitive manner. In conclusion, CALEND_AR has the potential to be a useful and innovative tool for managing schedules and events. The hybrid approach, which combines the best of both paper-based and digital calendars, provides a familiar and intuitive experience for users. Overall, it is believed that this work represents a step forward in the development of metaverse apps.

References

1. Akoumianakis, D., Ktistakis, G.: Digital calendars for flexible organizational routines. J. Enterp. Inf. Manag. **30**(3), 476–502 (2017). https://doi.org/10.1108/JEIM-01-2016-0023
2. Apple: Calendar (nd). https://www.icloud.com/calendar
3. Billinghurst, M., Clark, A., Lee, G.: A survey of augmented reality. Found. Trends Hum. Comput. Interact. **8**(2–3), 73–272 (2015). https://doi.org/10.1561/1100000049
4. Bousbahi, F.: From poster to mobile calendar: an event reminder using mobile ocr. Int. J. Adv. Comput. Sci. Appli. **10**(10) (2019). https://doi.org/10.14569/IJACSA.2019.0101075
5. Buzzo, D., Merendino, N.: Not all days are equal: investigating the meaning in the digital calendar. In: Proceedings of the 33rd Annual ACM Conference Extended Abstracts on Human Factors in Computing Systems, CHI EA 2015, pp. 489–501. Association for Computing Machinery, New York (2015). https://doi.org/10.1145/2702613.2732512
6. Cormen, T.H., Leiserson, C.E., Rivest, R.L., Stein, C.: Introduction to Algorithms. MIT Press, Cambridge (2009)
7. ECAL: 70 percent of adults rely on digital calendar (May 2021). https://ecal.com/70-percent-of-adults-rely-on-digital-calendar
8. Google: Google calendar (nd). https://calendar.google.com/
9. Grudin, J.: Why CSCW applications fail: problems in the design and evaluation of organizational interfaces. ACM Press, New York (1988). https://doi.org/10.1145/62266.62273
10. Hund, P.M., Dowell, J., Mueller, K.: Representation of time in digital calendars: an argument for a unified, continuous and multi-granular calendar view. Int. J. Hum Comput Stud. **72**(1), 1–11 (2014). https://doi.org/10.1016/j.ijhcs.2013.09.005
11. Microsoft: Outlook (nd). https://www.microsoft.com/en-us/microsoft-365/outlook/email-and-calendar-software-microsoft-outlook
12. Moleskine: Smart writing set (nd). https://us.moleskine.com/smart-writing-set/p0690
13. Mystakidis, S.: Metaverse. Encyclopedia **2**(1), 486–497 (2022). https://doi.org/10.3390/encyclopedia2010031
14. Payne, S.J.: Understanding calendar use. Hum.-Comput. Interact. **8**(2), 83–100 (1993)
15. Plaisant, C., Clamage, A., Hutchinson, H.B., Bederson, B.B., Druin, A.: Shared family calendars: Promoting symmetry and accessibility. ACM Trans. Comput.-Hum. Interact. **13**(3), 313–346 (2006). https://doi.org/10.1145/1183456.1183458
16. Rocketbook: Wave (nd). https://getrocketbook.com/products/wave
17. Sell, A., Walden, P.: Mobile digital calendars: An interview study. In: Proceedings of the 39th Annual Hawaii International Conference on System Sciences (HICSS 2006), vol. 1, pp. 23b–23b (2006). https://doi.org/10.1109/HICSS.2006.349

18. Tungare, M., Perez-Quinones, M., Sams, A.: An exploratory study of calendar use (2008). https://doi.org/10.48550/arXiv.0809.3447
19. Unity: Gameobject (nd). https://docs.unity3d.com/ScriptReference/GameObject.html
20. Unity: Unity (nd). https://unity.com/
21. Van Krevelen, D., Poelman, R.: A survey of augmented reality technologies, applications and limitations. Int. J. Virtual Reality 9(2), 1–20 (2010). https://doi.org/10.20870/IJVR.2010.9.2.2767
22. Vuforia: Image targets (nd). https://library.vuforia.com/objects/image-targets

PeriFocus - Training Peripheral Color- and Shape Detection in Virtual Reality

Mads Thomsen, Mathias Halilovic, Alexandru Giuran,
and Markus Löchtefeld(✉)

Aalborg University, Aalborg, Denmark
mloc@create.aau.dk

Abstract. Peripheral vision plays an important role in monitoring and detection of peripheral events not only in our daily life but also in complex and time-demanding situations. For example athletes in team sports such as Football or Handball, that require to not only keep track of one's own team but also the opponents around oneself, benefit greatly from good peripheral vision. This paper examines the possibilities of training peripheral color and shape detection in virtual reality (VR). To this end we created an application called PeriFocus, a simple shooter game in VR that requires users to use their peripheral vision for object identification of the features color, size and shape. Our initial evaluation with six participants over 12 days revealed a statistical significant increase in peripheral color detection measured by an analog visual acuity test. This not only validates prior work conducted in a desktop setting but also highlights potential for future VR applications.

Keywords: Peripheral Vision · Eye-Tracking · Virtual Reality

1 Introduction

Peripheral vision is our ability to detect elements in the corner of our eyes. This means that we're able to identify objects outside of our point of fixation. As humans we utilize peripheral vision in our daily lives, e.g. to detect objects that could result in tripping or falling when walking. Training peripheral vision can be an advantage in for example sports that require the monitoring and detection of peripheral events in complex and time-demanding situations [7]. Handball players have been found to have a faster reaction time to stimuli in their peripheral vision when compared to non-athletes [24]. This can most likely be attributed to the athletes concurrent training, and Yu et al. also demonstrate that peripheral vision can be more actively trained [23]. However, training the peripheral vision specifically can be a boring and time consuming task, here games could help making the training more interesting.

Recently we saw a drastic decrease in cost of eye tracking devices, which has lead to the proliferation of eye-tracking technologies as consumer goods. This means that gaze has become a more compelling method to be integrated into

© The Author(s), under exclusive license to Springer Nature Switzerland AG 2023
J. Abdelnour Nocera et al. (Eds.): INTERACT 2023, LNCS 14145, pp. 166–175, 2023.
https://doi.org/10.1007/978-3-031-42293-5_13

the gameplay of videogames. A variety of different ways [15,17,20] - ranging from simple replacement of controls [3,6] to integration of social gaze [10,22] - have been explored in the past. Lately, using gaze interaction in the unexpected way of not looking at the main elements has been demonstrated to be a viable game mechanic [9,11–14,21]. While this is on first glance a rather non-intuitive way of using gaze, it opens up new possibilities with respect to peripheral interaction [4]. Gomez & Gellersen found evidence that this kind of interaction can affect the players visual skills with greater peripheral awareness [12]. Using an eye-tracking an enabled desktop computer game, they found that their participants demonstrated a significant higher ability to detect objects in their peripheral vision after playing for two weeks every day.

In this work, we follow up on Gomez & Gellersen's findings [12] extending it to Virtual Reality (VR) training of peripheral color- and shape detection with a simple game called PeriFocus. VR headsets with integrated eye-tracking have become more obtainable with devices such as the HTC Vive Pro Eye or Meta Quest Pro. Furthermore, using VR with integrated eye-tracking allows to control factors such as angles between focus points and peripheral targets much more accurate compared to the desktop setup of Gomez & Gellersen [12], which could be helpful for more detailed analysis and training in the future.

2 PeriFocus

The aim of PeriFocus is to replicate the results of Gomez & Gellersen's SuperVision [12] in VR and with a different game. While Gomez & Gellersen used three different mini games, we opted to use a single game to test the different conditions. We want to examine the possibility to train peripheral color and shape detection in VR. Therefore, we developed a simple VR shooting game with three slightly different tasks. The participant has to shoot one of four targets shown to them. In order to select the target, the participants use a gun with a laser pointer (compare Fig. 1) controlled using a VR controller. The different tasks are the changing appearance of the targets to train different aspects of peripheral feature identification. The game gives participants audio cues telling them what targets to identify. The goal for the participant in each task is to make as many correct selections as possible before a timer ends. A single play-through consists of playing all three tasks which are each two minutes long. The time was experimentally determined in a pilot study, in order to reduce the severity of eye-strain caused by the vergence-accommodation conflict [5]. In between tasks, there is a brief break to let the participants relax their eyes.

PeriFocus is separated into three tasks, each training detection of a specific visual feature. These tasks are:

- **Color Task:** Targets are shaped like cubes and colored differently: red, blue, green, yellow. The audio cue will announce one of these four colors. Furthermore, each color is fully saturated as to create a stronger contrast between the targets (see Fig. 1 left).

- **Shape Task:** Targets are shaped after four distinct shapes, specifically, cube, sphere, heart and diamond, and colored red. The audio cue will announce one of the four shapes (see Fig. 1 middle).
- **Size Task:** Targets are shaped like cubes and colored red. The sizes vary, having the size of 80%, 100%, 120% and 140% of the default target size. The audio cue will announce either "biggest" or "smallest" to signify the participants to select either the 140% or the 80% sized target, respectively. The sizes were determined in a pilot study and were chosen in order to challenge the participants without frustrating them (see Fig. 1 right).

To ensure that the participant is using peripheral vision, in each task, they must fixate on one central point - called the fixation point - while trying to find the target they are supposed to shoot in their periphery. If the participants switch their gaze away from the fixation point for more than 100 milliseconds, all targets would turn black, the 2 min duration of the task would be paused and the participants would not be able to select any targets. To continue the experiment, the participant would need to fixate on the fixation point again; targets would then reshuffle and a new audio cue would be given. The 100 ms duration was determined in a pilot study, and proved to be enough to stop participants from switching their gaze away from the fixation point, while also allowing involuntary blinking. The fixation point visual appearance is based on the pattern that Thaler et al. [16] found to be optimal at reducing involuntary eye movements. This is beneficial, since involuntary eye movements might otherwise disrupt the participants efforts. With the fixation point being in the central vision, the four targets are each positioned at 45° angles, as seen in Fig. 1. This arrangement is made so that the participants have to utilize the entirety of their peripheral vision, while reducing size and shape distortion as explored by Baldwin et al. [1]. To make it easier for the participants to fixate on the fixation point, it is important to reduce visual distractions as much as possible. Therefore, as already mentioned, most of the feedback and communication is audio-based and the visuals are kept very simple (see Fig. 1). Furthermore, shadows were removed from the targets to avoid them influencing the detection of features, as participants may otherwise detect contrasts rather than the intended feature.

In case the participant's selection is correct, the targets will reshuffle positions and a new audio cue will be given. If the selection is wrong, the selected target will switch it's color to black for half a second and audio feedback indicating that a wrong target has been hit will be heard. Additionally, to reduce the chance of e.g. fatigue influencing participants' performance for a specific task, their order is randomized. At the end of the three tasks, a score is shown to the participants, based on how many correct selections they had throughout the game. Furthermore, their score is ranked compared to all previous participants to encourage competition.

Fig. 1. A participant using their gun to aim in the three different tasks of PeriFocus. Left: the Color task, Middle: the Shape task, Right: the Size task.

2.1   Hardware and Software

PeriFocus is implemented for the HTC Vive HMD and Unity [18]. As the HTC Vive HMD does not come with eye-tracking functionality, external hardware is needed. For this purpose a binocular add-on from Pupil Labs [8] is used. The add-on consists of two 200hz low latency eye-tracking cameras with IR illuminators [8], as well as clip-on rings to attach it to the HMD. The eye-tracking cameras and a Valve Index controller [19] is used for participants' input.

3   Preliminary Evaluation

Following the example of Gomez & Gellersen's SuperVision [12] we conducted a longitudinal study with 8 sessions divided over the course of 12 days to determine if peripheral vision can be trained in VR. Similarly to Gomez & Gellersen [12] we were interested in peripheral color and shape detection. To measure this we use a visual acuity test (VAT). The following hypothesis will be investigated:

H1$_0$: The experiment will have no effect on peripheral color detection. **H1** states that there will be a statistically significant difference in participants' peripheral color detection between the first and last VAT.

H2$_0$: The experiment will have no effect on peripheral shape detection. **H2** states that there will be a statistically significant difference in participants' peripheral shape detection between the first and last VAT.

3.1   Apparatus

Besides the above described implementation of PeriFocus, we followed the same VAT procedure as [12]. The apparatus used in the VAT was comprised of plywood protractor (including a cut-out for the nose) with a 30 cm radius. A small black piece of wood, with a white dot in the middle was placed at the 90° angle of the protractor, creating a fixation point for the participants [2] (compare Fig. 2). 27 Different slips of paper were used: Nine different shapes (circle, triangle and square, the letters A, B and C, and the numbers 1, 2 and 3) each in three different colors (red, green and blue). The shapes were placed at the top of the slips which had a height of 10 cm and a width of two cm. Following the same procedure as Gomez & Gellersen [12].

Fig. 2. Left: the protractor used for the VAT, made out of cardboard with a radius of 30 cm including a fixation point. Right: Participant undergoing a VAT - notice the red slip being moved along the protractor. (Color figure online)

3.2   Participants

A total of six participants were recruited from our local university for the experiment. All participants identified as male. The mean age of the participants was 25 (SD = 1.63), with an age range of 23–28. These results were gathered as part of a demographics questionnaire, taken at the start of the experiment. Two more questions were included in the questionnaire, which evaluated the participants experience with computer games, as well as their previous experience with VR.

3.3   Procedure

The experiment was done in 8 sessions over 12 days where on Day 2, 6,7 and 9 no sessions were held. This was due to the schedule of the participants and weekends. Each session consisted of a complete play-through of the PeriFocus, which would take around ten minutes, two minutes for each task, as well as around one minute for eye-tracking calibration before and breaks between the different task. On the first day of testing, PeriFocus included a narrated tutorial, which explained the controls and a short description of the tasks. Participants had to do additional steps on the following days: **Day 1**: Participants were asked to complete a demographics questionnaire, as well as a VAT and the tutorial. **Day 5**: Upon completing PeriFocus, participants had to take another VAT. **Day 12**: Upon completing PeriFocus, participants had to take a final VAT.

When doing the VAT, the participant would position the protractor horizontally in front of their face, fitting their nose in the nose hole and were asked to fixate on the focus point, for which can be seen in Fig. 2. A researcher would start slowly moving a paper slip towards the center of the protractor. They were asked to note when they started to notice the slip, at which point the researcher would stop moving it. The participant was then asked to identify either the color or the shape that was drawn on the slip. If either was not identified, the researcher would continue to move the slip until both color and shape were correctly identified and their angles recorded. We did not test in this VAT for size detection, this is left for future work.

Besides the VAT results we also logged performance in PeriFocus, to gauge participants' performance over time and to examine the differences between the three tasks. Score, which is a number that increments each time the correct target is shot. Error rate, which is the percentage of incorrect targets shot during a session. Task time, which is calculated as: (A), the time from when targets are presented, to (B), when a target is shot in seconds.

4   Results

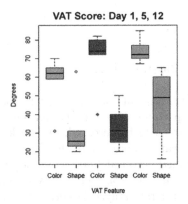

Fig. 3. Boxplots showcasing the VAT scores for both shape and color, including outliers. From left to right: day 1 (orange), day 5 (purple) and day 12 (blue) (Color figure online)

Hypothesis 1 and **Hypothesis 2** were tested comparing the VAT score for day 1 against day 12 using a Wilcoxon Signed-Rank Test. It was found that the experiment had a statistically significant effect on participants' peripheral color detection ($p < .012$). $H1_0$ can thus be rejected and $H1$ accepted. $H2_0$ can not be rejected as the experiment did not have a statistically significant effect on participants' peripheral shape detection ($p < .15$). Similarly, comparing the VAT scores for day 1 and day 5 shows a significant increase in the participant color detection score ($p < .036$) while the participant shape detection score does not significantly increase ($p < .590$). Comparing day 5 with day 12 shows no significant increase in both VAT color score (V = 10, p = 1) and shape score (p < .313). See Fig. 3 for a VAT score comparison between day 1, day 5 and day 12. Comparing participants' measurement logs between day 1 and day 12, it can be seen that they scored significantly higher in all tasks on day 12, see Fig. 4 (left). It can be seen that participants reduced their task time significantly in all challenges, see Fig. 4 (middle). Participants' error rates for the size and color task were similar, with the shape tasks having a higher variability and no statistically significant difference could be found (p < .05) as can be seen in Fig. 4 (right).

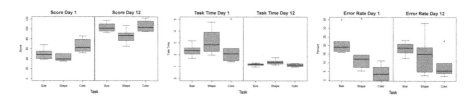

Fig. 4. Boxplots showcasing a comparison between scores, task times, and errorrate on day 1, 5, 12

5 Discussion and Conclusion

H1$_0$ can be rejected, while **H2$_0$** can not, which means that we did find a statistically significant effect on peripheral color detection but not on peripheral shape detection. Both game score, which increased, and task time, which decreased, showed statistically significant differences in the three tasks. This suggests that when participants' performed better at PeriFocus, they also scored higher in the VAT. While the task time and SD was reduced by a significant amount for the size and color task, the error rate stayed largely consistent. However, the error rate variability for the shape task increased over time. This may be due to participants putting more emphasis on scoring higher in the time given and relying more on guesswork to choose the correct shape. For future iterations of PeriFocus it may be advantageous to penalize wrong targets more, e.g. by deducting points, which would shift the focus towards accuracy. Another option would be to remove time as a factor from PeriFocus and instead give participants a set amount of targets per session. Either way, participants may be more inclined to spend more time to identify the shapes in their peripheral and potentially reduce their error rate.

In general it can be stated that the results achieved in our small scale study in VR are overall similar to Gomez & Gellersen's [12]. So our study to a certain extend replicates their findings and extends it to VR. However, we also see some interesting differences. While Gomez & Gellersen's [12] VAT results showed a statistically significant difference in their one-day study, their VAT shape detection score had a SD around 3 times higher than their VAT color detection SD (similarly to our SD). They opted not measure VAT shape detection in their follow-up 2 week study. Given the high SD in their one-day study and the results of the study presented here, it might indicate that peripheral shape detection is not as easily trainable. We also encountered high variability in VAT shape detection, with an SD three times higher than that of VAT color detection. This might be a result of the procedure used for the VAT. The results recorded for identifying primitive shapes (Circle, Square, Triangle) were generally higher than the ones recorded which had either a number (1, 2, 3) or a letter (A, B, C) as the chosen shape. The similarities between letters and numbers might be too small to reliable distinguish them in the peripheral vision compared to primitive shapes. For example, we noticed a couple of participants mistaken the letter "C" for a circle, or the letter "A" for a triangle. Both this study and Gomez & Gellersen's [12] follow this procedure, however the source material for which the VAT procedure was derived from does not draw the shapes on the slips [2]. Rather, the slips are cut with scissors to form the shapes, e.g. cutting the corners of the slip to form a triangle. In this way, perceiving contrast between the shape and the slip color would not be a factor, which may affect the VAT shape detection results. It could be interesting to only use primitive shapes, which may lead to less variability and a statistically significant difference.

Furthermore, looking at Gomez & Gellersen's [12] VAT color detection mean score for the first day (mean = 81.20, SD = 4.08) and last day (mean = 87.90, SD = 2.73), we comparatively had a much lower mean score for day 1 (mean = 58.16, SD = 13.88) and day 12 (mean = 73.83, SD = 6.49). We are unsure as to why there is such a large difference; it may be due to both experiments having a small sample size. Furthermore it is difficult to compare our experiment with Gomez & Gellersen's [12], as they are not stating how they created the VAT slips in terms of size, color and how the shapes were drawn on them. For our study we followed the size recommendation of the original procedure [2]. Another variable not considered for the VAT is the lighting conditions of the experiment room, which may influence color detection in the periphery. While it was consistent in our experiment, it might be vastly different from Gomez & Gellersen's which could have an influence on the ability of peripheral object identification. The biggest limitation of our study at this point is that we only were able to recruit six participants. Furthermore, all of our participants identified as male, which further limits the ability to generalize our results to the population.

The training was found to have a statistically significant effect on peripheral color detection, thereby confirming Gomez & Gellersen's findings as well as opening the possibility of applying it to VR environments. However, the training did not show a statistically significant effect on peripheral shape detection, with a high variability, which increased by the end of the study. The preliminary study conducted here however, has also multiple limitations, besides a small amount of participants, which identified all as male, the overall VAT for shape detection could be optimized as well. Further studies with a modified procedure might show results with a lower variability and a potentially statistically significant effect in shape detection, and are therefore needed.

References

1. Baldwin, J., Burleigh, A., Pepperell, R., Ruta, N.: The perceived size and shape of objects in peripheral vision. i-Perception **7**(4), 2041669516661900 (2016)
2. Buddies, S.: Put your peripheral vision to the test, March 2016. https://www.scientificamerican.com/article/put-your-peripheral-vision-to-the-test/
3. Dorr, M., Böhme, M., Martinetz, T., Barth, E.: Gaze beats mouse: a case study. In: Proceedings of COGAIN, pp. 16–19 (2007)
4. Hausen, D.: Peripheral interaction: facilitating interaction with secondary tasks. In: Proceedings of the Sixth International Conference on Tangible, Embedded and Embodied Interaction, TEI 2012, pp. 387–388. Association for Computing Machinery, New York, NY, USA (2012). https://doi.org/10.1145/2148131.2148227
5. Hoffman, D.M., Girshick, A.R., Akeley, K., Banks, M.S.: Vergence-accommodation conflicts hinder visual performance and cause visual fatigue. J. Vis. **8**(3), 33–33 (2008)
6. Istance, H., Hyrskykari, A., Vickers, S., Chaves, T.: For your eyes only: controlling 3D online games by eye-gaze. In: Gross, T., et al. (eds.) INTERACT 2009. LNCS, vol. 5726, pp. 314–327. Springer, Heidelberg (2009). https://doi.org/10.1007/978-3-642-03655-2_36
7. Klostermann, A., Vater, C., Kredel, R., Hossner, E.J.: Perception and action in sports. On the functionality of foveal and peripheral vision. Front. Sports Active Living **1**, 66 (2020)
8. Labs, P.: Pupil labs products/VR AR (2021). https://pupil-labs.com/products/vr-ar/
9. Lankes, M., Berger, F.: Blind spot: an interactive gaze-aware experience. In: Extended Abstracts of the 2021 CHI Conference on Human Factors in Computing Systems, CHI EA 2021. Association for Computing Machinery, New York, NY, USA (2021). https://doi.org/10.1145/3411763.3451570
10. Pfeuffer, K., Alexander, J., Gellersen, H.: GazeArchers: playing with individual and shared attention in a two-player look & shoot tabletop game. In: Proceedings of the 15th International Conference on Mobile and Ubiquitous Multimedia, MUM 2016, pp. 213–216. Association for Computing Machinery, New York, NY, USA (2016). https://doi.org/10.1145/3012709.3012717
11. Ramirez Gomez, A., Gellersen, H.: Exploring the sensed and unexpected: not looking in gaze interaction. In: Proceedings of the Halfway to the Future Symposium 2019, pp. 1–7 (2019)
12. Ramirez Gomez, A., Gellersen, H.: Supervision: playing with gaze aversion and peripheral vision. In: Proceedings of the 2019 CHI Conference on Human Factors in Computing Systems, pp. 1–12 (2019)
13. Ramirez Gomez, A., Gellersen, H.: KryptonEyed: playing with gaze without looking. In: Proceedings of the 15th International Conference on the Foundations of Digital Games, FDG 2020. Association for Computing Machinery, New York, NY, USA (2020). https://doi.org/10.1145/3402942.3403017

14. Ramirez Gomez, A., Gellersen, H.: More than looking: using eye movements behind the eyelids as a new game mechanic. In: Proceedings of the Annual Symposium on Computer-Human Interaction in Play, CHI PLAY 2020, pp. 362–373. Association for Computing Machinery, New York, NY, USA (2020). https://doi.org/10.1145/3410404.3414240

15. Smith, J.D., Graham, T.C.N.: Use of eye movements for video game control. In: Proceedings of the 2006 ACM SIGCHI International Conference on Advances in Computer Entertainment Technology, ACE 2006, p. 20-es. Association for Computing Machinery, New York, NY, USA (2006). https://doi.org/10.1145/1178823.1178847

16. Thaler, L., Schütz, A.C., Goodale, M.A., Gegenfurtner, K.R.: What is the best fixation target? The effect of target shape on stability of fixational eye movements. Vision. Res. **76**, 31–42 (2013)

17. Turner, J., Velloso, E., Gellersen, H., Sundstedt, V.: EyePlay: applications for gaze in games. In: Proceedings of the First ACM SIGCHI Annual Symposium on Computer-Human Interaction in Play, CHI PLAY 2014, pp. 465–468. Association for Computing Machinery, New York, NY, USA (2014). https://doi.org/10.1145/2658537.2659016

18. Unity: Unity development platform (2021). https://unity.com/

19. Valve: Valve index: Controllers (2021). https://www.valvesoftware.com/en/index/controllers

20. Velloso, E., Carter, M.: The emergence of EyePlay: a survey of eye interaction in games. In: Proceedings of the 2016 Annual Symposium on Computer-Human Interaction in Play, CHI PLAY 2016, pp. 171–185. Association for Computing Machinery, New York, NY, USA (2016). https://doi.org/10.1145/2967934.2968084

21. Vidal, M.: Shynosaurs: a game of attention dilemma. In: Proceedings of the First ACM SIGCHI Annual Symposium on Computer-Human Interaction in Play, CHI PLAY 2014, pp. 391–394. Association for Computing Machinery, New York, NY, USA (2014). https://doi.org/10.1145/2658537.2662979

22. Vidal, M., Bismuth, R., Bulling, A., Gellersen, H.: The royal Corgi: exploring social gaze interaction for immersive gameplay. In: Proceedings of the 33rd Annual ACM Conference on Human Factors in Computing Systems, CHI 2015, pp. 115–124. Association for Computing Machinery, New York, NY, USA (2015). https://doi.org/10.1145/2702123.2702163

23. Yu, D., Legge, G.E., Park, H., Gage, E., Chung, S.T.: Development of a training protocol to improve reading performance in peripheral vision. Vision Res. **50**(1), 36–45 (2010)

24. Zwierko, T.: Differences in peripheral perception between athletes and nonathletes. J. Hum. Kinet. **19**(2008), 53–62 (2007)

Supporting Resilience Through Virtual Reality: Design and Preliminary Evaluation of a VR Experience Based on Viktor Frankl's Logotherapy

Quynh Nguyen[(✉)] (iD), Rodrigo Gutierrez (iD), Lukas Kröninger (iD), and Ulrike Kretzer (iD)

Austrian Institute of Technology GmbH, 1210 Vienna, Austria
quynh-huong.nguyen@ait.ac.at

Abstract. Promoting resilience is crucial to support people in the face of traumatic experiences caused by existential crises. Virtual Reality (VR) can support resilience as it allows for embodied experiences and experiential learning. We present the design and initial user evaluation of an immersive VR experience for strengthening resilience, inspired by Viktor Frankl's psychotherapy, 'logotherapy and existential analysis' (LTEA). The prototype immerses users in two experiences related to guilt or suffering and guides them through an interactive reflection, encouraging them to consider their potential for finding meaning even in adverse circumstances. Although the self-reported resilience measures did not indicate increased resilience, qualitative data suggest that the users were able to use the prototype to reflect on meaning in life. This paper contributes to the field of VR for well-being by introducing the under-explored approach of LTEA to facilitate resilience. We discuss aspects of resilience support in VR by addressing the relevance of identifying and utilising technology-specific affordances to enhance reflective practice and the potential of peer support for promoting resilience.

Keywords: Virtual Reality · Resilience · Reflection · Existential HCI · Logotherapy and Existential Analysis

1 Introduction

With the rise of existential crises arising from e.g., climate change, populism or socioeconomic instabilities, most people will be confronted with at least one potentially life-threatening traumatic experience [12]. As a response, there has been a rise in HCI research focused on well-being and mental health [20]. Resilience, the "healthy, adaptive, or integrated positive functioning over the

Supplementary Information The online version contains supplementary material available at https://doi.org/10.1007/978-3-031-42293-5_14.

© The Author(s), under exclusive license to Springer Nature Switzerland AG 2023
J. Abdelnour Nocera et al. (Eds.): INTERACT 2023, LNCS 14145, pp. 176–186, 2023.
https://doi.org/10.1007/978-3-031-42293-5_14

passage of time in the aftermath of adversity" [24, p. 2], can protect people against existential crises. Virtual Reality (VR) has been found to be useful for resilience interventions through stress inoculation and therapeutic treatments [18]. Because VR enables embodied experiences [3], increases immersion [18], and enhances learning by invoking a state of flow [15], it is a promising tool for facilitating reflection and supporting resilience.

According to Viktor Frankl who founded the meaning-centred psychotherapy 'logotherapy and existential analysis' (LTEA), resilience needs self-transcendence, the ability to move *beyond* oneself to find meaning in the outside world, e.g., through dedicated service to a cause or another person [8]. To do so, a change in perspective and the creation of awareness of one's freedom in life despite all adversity are essential [8]. Thus, we investigate an as-of-yet under-explored approach to support the well-being and resilience of people through a VR experience inspired by LTEA, aiming to answer three sub-research questions (RQs):

RQ1a: To what extent can a VR experience inspired by LTEA positively affect resilience?

RQ1b: How can reflection be integrated into the VR experience to support resilience?

RQ1c: How do the degree of engagement and the narrative storytelling within the VR experience affect users' ability for reflection?

To answer the RQs, we developed a VR prototype to let users immerse themselves in and reflect on aspects of the tragic triad. The tragic triad describes three tragic, yet unavoidable experiences in human life that often lead to an existential crisis: guilt, suffering, and death [8]. We aimed to sensitise users on two of these topics, guilt and suffering, and support the users in reflection based on LTEA principles so that they can think about the potential for seeking meaning in such experiences. The prototype was tested in an explorative user evaluation (N = 12).

This paper offers a new approach to enhancing resilience in VR through concepts and methods of LTEA. It, thereby, contributes to the field of VR for well-being. We explore aspects of resilience support in VR, such as the importance of utilising technology-specific affordances to enhance reflective practice and the potential of peer support to promote resilience in VR.

Fig. 1. Bird's eye view of the "Room of Possibilities", a virtual space that facilitates (de)reflection after an interactive VR experience.

2   Related Work

With the rapid developments and decrease in cost, interest in Extended Reality (XR) technologies for psychological interventions is gradually growing [4]. One factor these interventions aim to support is resilience (see [18] for a scoping review). Though there is no universal definition of resilience, the majority of definitions describe it as "healthy, adaptive, or integrated positive functioning over the passage of time in the aftermath of adversity" [24]. We also understand resilience as a context-dependent dynamic process to eschew the dichotomy of resilience as solely a state or a trait [14].

Recent literature suggests a positive correlation between reflection and resilience [2,6]. For example, teachers who engage in reflection demonstrate a greater capacity to overcome challenges in their professional and educational pursuits [2]. Stress resilience can also be strengthened through reflection on stressors and one's coping with them [6]. In HCI, reflective practice is frequently used to aid technology users in understanding themselves better and motivating them to take measures to adopt healthier behaviours [28]. Meanwhile, in LTEA, reflection is superseded by *de*reflection. With this distinction, Frankl aimed to reorient his patients away from neurotic hyper-fixation manifesting in perpetual self-examination towards reflection to seek external meaning to one's experiences and behaviours [19]. This is supported by research on the importance of self-distance for reflection [1]. Thus, dereflection can also be considered as a transformative reflection for fundamental change or critical reflection to consider the wider scope (cf. [7]).

One design challenge to consider when using immersive VR for reflection is its ability to create high immersion and flow which may paradoxically limit opportunities for self-awareness and critical reflection [10,13]. To address this challenge, Jiang and Ahmadpour [10] developed the RIOR (Readiness for reflection, Immersive estrangement, Observation and re-examination, Repatterning of knowledge) framework for reflection in VR. Based on a scoping review of VR reflection tools, they suggest design choices that support and scaffold reflection, such as hyper-narration through a diegetic narrator.

3   Methods

This section outlines the co-design and iterative evaluation process and the elements of the VR experience as a user story.

3.1   Iterative Co-design and Evaluation

Recent HCI research [11,17] emphasises the need to design *meaningful* technologies. To achieve this, we followed a co-design approach that involves users as situated, meaning-seeking, and active partners in the design process and aims to create technologies that support them in their search for meaning and self-transcendence [17]. Hence, we engaged in a sustained co-design collaboration with future users (N = 6) at three time points, while working with two LTEA experts to translate theoretical work and methods into VR experiences in parallel. Throughout the development, we presented various system elements (e.g., interaction patterns and environmental layouts) to internal test participants (N = 8), incorporating their qualitative feedback into our design cycles.

The first virtually held workshop introduced resilience and technologies for supporting resilience, discussed requirements and limits of technology-aided resilience support and aimed to familiarise participants and researchers with each other. In the second workshop, held two months later in person, the co-designers collaborated on a speculative design fiction about a future resilience-strengthening tool and explored the expectations, attitudes, and values towards technology-aided resilience training. These two workshops provided the foundation of our mutual understanding of technology-supported resilience, aimed to empower co-designers to understand the topic [23]. The third workshop aimed to let them have a say in the ReSolVE prototype. They provided feedback on interactions, environmental designs, and 'gameplays' through Think Aloud and group discussions on the first version of the prototype. Further, they guided our understanding of the interplay between privacy and security concerns and the required benefits of well-being technologies.

The prototype was finally tested in an explorative user evaluation with three measurement points (MPs) (N = 12), see Fig. 2 for an overview of used methods at three measurement points: MP1 (before first contact with the prototype), MP2 (after the individual VR experience), and MP3 (after the group session).

Observation protocols and semi-structured interviews were deductively analysed, and quotes in Sect. 4 were translated from German to English. Questionnaires (Brief Resilience Scale (BRS) for state resilience [5]; Resilience Scale 25 (RS25) for trait resilience [21]; K10 for psychological distress [9]) were analysed.

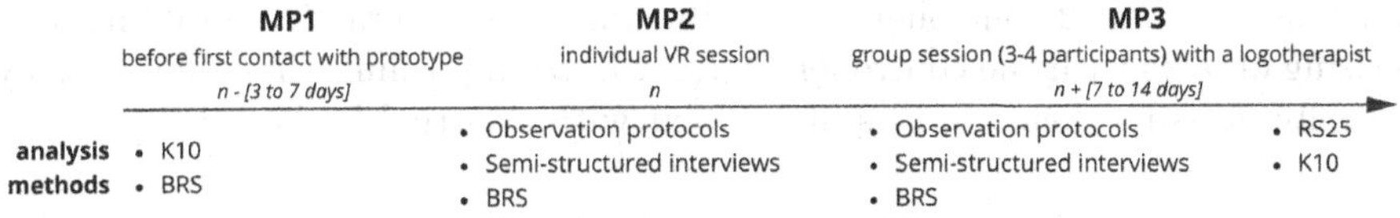

	MP1 before first contact with prototype $n - [3\ to\ 7\ days]$	MP2 individual VR session n	MP3 group session (3-4 participants) with a logotherapist $n + [7\ to\ 14\ days]$	
analysis methods	• K10 • BRS	• Observation protocols • Semi-structured interviews • BRS	• Observation protocols • Semi-structured interviews • BRS	• RS25 • K10

Fig. 2. Methods used in the first evaluation of the ResolVE prototype.

3.2   Description of the ReSolVE VR Experience

Figure 3 describes our design choices to create opportunities for reflection in all four scaffolding phases of the framework based on the RIOR framework [10]: (1) readying participants for reflection (1.1 and 1.2), (2) providing immersive estrangement (2a and 2b) in the two experienced stories aspects of the tragic triad (handling guilt (2a) and suffering (2b)). Lastly, the Room of Possibilities (RoP) (3/4) allowed for both observation and re-examination (3) and supported a re-patterning of knowledge (4) by explicitly asking for reflections on the user's behavioural attitudes (e.g., towards their freedom of choice). To illustrate the VR experience and the opportunities for reflection in more detail, we now describe the user journey of one participant, V.

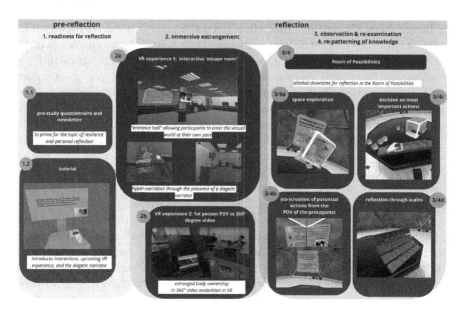

Fig. 3. Overview of the VR experience viewed through the RIOR framework [10].

Priming and Introduction. V receives a newsletter on resilience and LTEA before the study. At the lab, V is informed about the study and fills out a questionnaire (MP1). V is then introduced to the Meta Quest 2 headset and controllers. In the tutorial on the necessary VR interactions, V learns to freely walk within a $3\,\mathrm{m}^2$ area with proximity-visualised boundaries and to use the controllers' teleportation ray for longer distances. The virtual hands show a 3D model of the Quest 2 controller for tangible mapping. V practices grabbing and releasing objects with the controller's trigger button, pushing virtual buttons by naturally pressing them, and inputting text with a virtual keyboard.

VR Experience 1: Interactive Escape Room on Guilt. V enters an escape room-like scene. V plays the role of a person who has inadvertently caused a bicycle accident (Fig. 3, 2a) and is tasked to learn more about the accident and its impact on the injured party. V explores the victim's hospital room to uncover audio-visual interactive artefacts related to the victim (e.g., a medical chart, mobile phone with text messages) that helps V understand the story. After the exploration, V moves to the RoP.

VR Experience 2: 360° Video on Suffering. V takes on the role of a person getting dismissed from work in the first-person perspective in a 360° video embedded in VR (Fig. 3, 2b). V discovers the private struggles and working situation of the embodied story protagonist. After observing the immediate job loss and suffering of the protagonist, V is again guided towards the RoP.

Room of Possibilities (RoP). V walks towards the RoP from the VR experiences (see Fig. 1) and explores the room before approaching the table in the middle of the RoP where a see-through cube filled with smaller cubes floats down (see Fig. 3, 3/4a). V then follows the task instructions on the table (see Fig. 3, 3/4b). The RoP uses customisable cubes to help users (de)reflect on their freedom of choice and attitude despite adversity. V selects pre-written ideas for potential actions and adds their own ideas to empty cubes. This interaction makes V's scope of action and freedom of choice tangible and encourages reflection on both behaviour and attitude modulations. V selects their five most meaningful cubes and reflects on each choice by using boards depicting Likert scales (see Fig. 3, 3/4d) which ask: 1. *typical (for me) – untypical (for me)*, 2. *easy (for me) – challenging (for me)*, and 3. *I cannot/do not want to/should not/do not have to – I can/want/should/have to*. These scales, developed with an LTEA therapist, and based on the principles of Socratic dialogue [19], guide users to take responsibility for their life's meaning and constitute a type of reflection-in-action [22].

Group Session. As the prototype does not support multi-user VR, the VR scenes for MP3 were approximated in two ways. First, one participant went through VR Experience 1 and 2 as a proxy for the whole group, guided by comments and directions of the group. The view of the group proxy was cast to a large screen for the group to view in real time. Second, the RoP was replicated in a physical space with paper cubes and scales. New choices were added through sticky notes attached to the cubes. This session explored the effects of integrating group interactions and dynamics into the process.

4   Preliminary Results

This section presents the main findings concerning the prototype's impact on resilience (RQ1a), its ability to enable (de)reflection on the tragic triad (RQ1b), and on the impact of the degree of interactivity and (non-)linearity in storytelling within the VR experience (RQ1c).

Effects on Resilience Measures. The interventions significantly affected psychological distress (Wilcoxon test; $z = -2.568$, $p = 0.01$). The psychological distress of one participant even improved from 'mid' to 'well' psychological distress after the interventions. There was no significant change in resilience based on BRS ($p_{MP1-MP2} = 0.285$, $p_{MP2-MP3} = 0.181$, $p_{MP1-MP3} = 0.894$) or RS25 ($p_{MP1-T3} = 0.953$).

Perceptions of VR Experience 1 and 2. Participants perceived a qualitative difference between both VR experiences. Experience 2 allowed for relaxed and passive consumption. Participants reported that it was easier to grasp the story than in Experience 1, which consisted not only of finding clues and puzzling together hints to understand the story, but also of operating the novel VR proto-type ad-hoc. The content of Experience 2 was reproduced more consistently by the participants. Interactions in Experience 1 were initially perceived as slightly distracting, especially for participants with limited VR experience. This effect decreased with time spent in the VR.

Empathy emerged more easily with the protagonist of the job loss scenario (VR Experience 2) as it was relatable to the participants and their life experiences ("*[I felt emotionally affected] because I know from my own work experience what it's like not to be valued*" (P10)). In contrast, the accident scenario (Experience 1) was deemed less likely but made participants reflect on the ephemeral nature of life. Last, Experience 1 engendered more creative interpretations: The story explicitly mentions the accident victim's daughter currently staying with her grandparents who struggle with taking care of her and that he asked his sister to go to a parent conference in his stead. P04 created an embellished interpretation: "*[The victim] does not have a good social network besides the aunt. Little other family, few close friends who can help out with the daughter.*"

Room of Possibilities. All participants rated the RoP as a good tool to reflect on possible options for how to handle the experienced situations and one's emerging feelings and thoughts, regardless of the degree of emotional identification. The scales for evaluating one's chosen options were viewed as helpful for dealing with one's choice and understanding one's underlying motivation. This was reported to be very helpful and eye-opening by most participants. Participants also found the cubes helpful for visualising options. The direct interaction with the cubes was reported as essential for the reflection process. However, the participants also saw the potential for improvement in the handling and presentation of information. Specifically, they criticised keyboard input as tedious and suggested other interaction forms such as speech-to-text input.

Collaborative Session. Participants in a more homogeneous group reported that they confirmed impressions, memories, and opinions but also questioned and re-oriented them in the group setting. For example, the group discovered for VR Experience 1 that legal counsel could apply to both themselves *and* the injured party. This led to discussions about subjective culpability. Another group with rather heterogeneous opinions and approaches reported to perceive new insights and perspectives within the group as enriching.

5   Discussion

The results indicate a mixed picture regarding RQ1a. On the one hand, the self-reported resilience measures (RS25 and BRS scales) did not indicate a quantitative resilience change. However, resilience is enacted through ordinary everyday practices [27]. Any quantifiable impact on resilience likely requires a long-term engagement with the prototype which was not achievable through two intervention points. More sustained engagement may be needed to significantly impact resilience. In future work, we, thus, aim to expand our prototype, explore its long-term impact and investigate how VR tools can be designed to provide sustained engagement and support. We also plan to investigate the potential of AI-controlled adaptive support, which could provide personalised feedback and support based on user behaviour, qualitative feedback, or bio-data.

On the other hand, qualitative data suggest that the experiences effectively conveyed the story and underlying message (e.g., the importance of one's attitude towards the inevitable experience of the tragic triad). In addition, linear storytelling and a passive role (VR Experience 2) enhanced the understanding of the story. In line with research on interactive storytelling [26], we found that non-linear, interactive storytelling (VR Experience 1) enabled more creative, diverging interpretations. Further, the reported difference in the ability to relate to the protagonist of VR Experiences 1 and 2 depended on the familiarity and likelihood of the scenario happening to oneself. However, this did not seem to affect the depth of reflection and, thus, the RoP's ability to support self-transcendence through reflection (RQ1c). This, together with the improvement in psychological distress levels, shows the potential of LTEA-based VR resilience support.

To answer RQ1b, we drew on the RIOR framework [10] to create the RoP for reflection-in-action which encourages users to re-examine their experiences and reorganise their knowledge. Based on qualitative results, users viewed reflection in the RoP as beneficial. Particularly beneficial is the interaction with the cubes and scales for transformative reflection [7] so that users view themselves as self-determined actors who can take responsibility for their own meaning in life.

In line with work on social, collaborative reflection [16] we suggest further exploring the potential of collaborative VR resilience training using reflection. Our collaborative sessions showed how participants benefited from discussing their thoughts with others by broadening and contextualising their viewpoints for a change of perspective. This is also supported by research on collaborative reflection to support well-being [25].

6   Conclusion

The presented work showcases how VR for strengthening resilience can be guided by meaning-centred LTEA. It also showcases how considering technology-specific affordances of VR (such as the paradox of high immersion inhibiting critical reflection and self-awareness) needs to be considered in practice to achieve the aims of the VR experience, such as enabling reflection or supporting resilience. This work, thus, contributes to research in VR for well-being by showing a use case of a VR experience for enhancing resilience by presenting stories connected to the tragic triad and facilitating (de-)reflection. Overall, our work showcases the potential of immersive VR for reflection as part of supporting resilience.

Acknowledgement. We thank Alexander Vesely and Katharina Ratheiser for contributing their vast LTEA experience. This research was part of *ReSolVE* (*Resilience Strengthening in Virtual Environments*) (grant agreement no. FO999887481) and *Co-Creation Methods* (grant agreement no. 879324), both partly funded by the Austrian Research Promotion Agency.

References

1. Ayduk, Ö., Kross, E.: Analyzing negative experiences without ruminating: the role of self-distancing in enabling adaptive self-reflection. Soc. Personality Psychol. Compass **4**(10), 841–854 (2010). https://doi.org/10.1111/j.1751-9004.2010.00301.x

2. Ayoobiyan, H., Rashidi, N.: Can reflective teaching promote resilience among Iranian EFL teachers? A mixed-method design. Reflective Pract. **22**(3), 293–305 (2021). https://doi.org/10.1080/14623943.2021.1873758

3. Belisle, B., Roquet, P.: Guest editors' introduction: virtual reality: immersion and empathy. J. Vis. Cult. **19**(1), 3–10 (2020). https://doi.org/10.1177/1470412920906258

4. Bouchard, S., Rizzo, A.: Virtual Reality for Psychological and Neurocognitive Interventions. Springer, New York (2019). https://doi.org/10.1007/978-1-4939-9482-3

5. Chmitorz, A., et al.: German version of the Brief Resilience Scale, February 2018. https://doi.org/10.1371/journal.pone.0192761.s001

6. Crane, M.F., Searle, B.J., Kangas, M., Nwiran, Y.: How resilience is strengthened by exposure to stressors: the systematic self-reflection model of resilience strengthening. Anxiety Stress Coping **32**(1), 1–17 (2019). https://doi.org/10.1080/10615806.2018.1506640

7. Fleck, R., Fitzpatrick, G.: Reflecting on reflection: framing a design landscape. In: Proceedings of the 22nd Conference of the Computer-Human Interaction Special Interest Group of Australia on Computer-Human Interaction, OZCHI 2010, pp. 216–223. Association for Computing Machinery, New York, NY, USA (2010). https://doi.org/10.1145/1952222.1952269

8. Frankl, V.E.: Man's Search for Meaning. Simon and Schuster, New York (1985). ISBN: 9780671834654

9. Giesinger, J., Rumpold, G., Schüßler, G.: German version of the K10 screening scale for psychological distress. Psychosomatik Und Konsiliarpsychiatrie **2**, 104–111 (2008)

10. Jiang, J., Ahmadpour, N.: Beyond immersion: designing for reflection in virtual reality. In: Proceedings of the 33rd Australian Conference on Human-Computer Interaction, OzCHI 2021, pp. 208–220. Association for Computing Machinery, New York, NY, USA (2022). https://doi.org/10.1145/3520495.3520501

11. Kaptelinin, V.: Technology and the givens of existence: toward an existential inquiry framework in HCI research. In: Proceedings of the 2018 CHI Conference on Human Factors in Computing Systems, CHI 2018, pp. 1–14. Association for Computing Machinery, New York, NY, USA (2018). https://doi.org/10.1145/3173574.3173844

12. Karam, E.G., et al.: Cumulative traumas and risk thresholds: 12-month PTSD in the World Mental Health (WMH) surveys. Depress Anxiety **31**(2), 130–142 (2014). https://doi.org/10.1002/da.22169

13. Kors, M.J., Ferri, G., van der Spek, E.D., Ketel, C., Schouten, B.A.: A breathtaking journey. On the design of an empathy-arousing mixed-reality game. In: Proceedings of the 2016 Annual Symposium on Computer-Human Interaction in Play, CHI PLAY 2016, pp. 91–104. Association for Computing Machinery, New York, NY, USA (2016). https://doi.org/10.1145/2967934.2968110

14. Kuldas, S., Foody, M.: Neither resiliency-trait nor resilience-state: transactional resiliency/e. Youth Soc. **54**(8), 1352–1376 (2022). https://doi.org/10.1177/0044118X211029309

15. Kwon, C.: Verification of the possibility and effectiveness of experiential learning using HMD-based immersive VR technologies. Virtual Reality **23**(1), 101–118 (2019). https://doi.org/10.1007/s10055-018-0364-1

16. Mols, I., van den Hoven, E., Eggen, B.: Informing design for reflection: an overview of current everyday practices. In: Proceedings of the 9th Nordic Conference on Human-Computer Interaction, NordiCHI 2016. Association for Computing Machinery, New York, NY, USA (2016). https://doi.org/10.1145/2971485.2971494

17. Nguyen, Q., Himmelsbach, J., Bertel, D., Zechner, O., Tscheligi, M.: What is meaningful human-computer interaction? Understanding freedom, responsibility, and Noos in HCI based on Viktor Frankl's existential philosophy. In: Designing Interactive Systems Conference, DIS 2022, pp. 654–665. Association for Computing Machinery, New York, NY, USA (2022). https://doi.org/10.1145/3532106.3533484

18. Pusey, M., Wong, K.W., Rappa, N.A.: Resilience interventions using interactive technology: a scoping review. Interact. Learn. Environ. **30**(10), 1940–1955 (2022). https://doi.org/10.1080/10494820.2020.1772837

19. Rahgozar, S., Giménez-Llort, L.: Foundations and applications of logotherapy to improve mental health of immigrant populations in the third millennium. Front. Psychiatry **11**, 451 (2020). https://doi.org/10.3389/fpsyt.2020.00451

20. Sanches, P., et al.: HCI and affective health: taking stock of a decade of studies and charting future research directions. In: Proceedings of the 2019 CHI Conference on Human Factors in Computing Systems, CHI 2019, pp. 1–17. Association for Computing Machinery, New York, NY, USA (2019). https://doi.org/10.1145/3290605.3300475

21. Schumacher, J., Leppert, K., Gunzelmann, T., Strauß, B., Brähler, E.: Die Resilienzskala-ein Fragebogen zur Erfassung der psychischen Widerstandsfähigkeit als Personmerkmal. Z. Klin. Psychol. Psychiatr. Psychother. **53**(1), 16–39 (2005)

22. Schön, D.A.: Educating the Reflective Practitioner: Toward a New Design for Teaching and Learning in the Professions. Jossey-Bass, San Francisco (1987). ISBN: 978-1555422202

23. Simonsen, J., Robertson, T.: Routledge International Handbook of Participatory Design, vol. 711. Routledge, New York (2013). ISBN: 9780415720212

24. Southwick, S.M., Bonanno, G.A., Masten, A.S., Panter-Brick, C., Yehuda, R.: Resilience definitions, theory, and challenges: interdisciplinary perspectives. Eur. J. Psychotraumatol. **5**(1), 25338 (2014). https://doi.org/10.3402/ejpt.v5.25338

25. Stefanidi, E., Schöning, J., Rogers, Y., Niess, J.: Children with ADHD and their care ecosystem: designing beyond symptoms. In: Proceedings of the 2023 CHI Conference on Human Factors in Computing Systems, CHI 2023. Association for Computing Machinery, New York, NY, USA (2023). https://doi.org/10.1145/3544548.3581216

26. Sumi, K., Yahata, N.: Interactive storytelling system for enhancing children's creativity. In: Nunes, N., Oakley, I., Nisi, V. (eds.) Interactive Storytelling, pp. 308–312. Springer, Cham (2017). https://doi.org/10.1007/978-3-319-71027-3_32

27. Vyas, D., Dillahunt, T.: Everyday resilience: supporting resilient strategies among low socioeconomic status communities. Proc. ACM Hum.-Comput. Interact. 1(CSCW), 1–21 (2017). https://doi.org/10.1145/3134740
28. Wang, L., et al.: mirrorU: scaffolding emotional reflection via in-situ assessment and interactive feedback. In: Extended Abstracts of the 2018 CHI Conference on Human Factors in Computing Systems, CHI EA 2018, pp. 1–6. Association for Computing Machinery, New York, NY, USA (2018). https://doi.org/10.1145/3170427.3188517

Virtual Reality and Training

A Case Study Using Virtual Reality to Prime Knowledge for Procedural Medical Training

Paul W. L. Watson[1,4](✉) ⓘ, Samuel House[1], Robert Hart[1],
Jonathan Abbas[2]ⓘ, Sheena Asthana[1]ⓘ, and Swen E. Gaudl[1,3]ⓘ

[1] University of Plymouth, Plymouth, UK
{robert.hart,s.asthana}@plymouth.ac.uk
[2] University of Manchester, Manchester, UK
jonathan.abbas@doctors.org.uk
[3] University of Gothenburg, Gothenburg, Sweden
swen.gaudl@ait.gu.se
[4] University of Bolton, Bolton, UK
paul.watson@bolton.ac.uk

Abstract. Procedural training within medical education relies heavily on skill practice. This training requires developing a cognitive understanding of a procedure to prime learners before motor skill trials. With the high demand and costs of specialist equipment, virtual reality (VR) is poised to provide accessible content to develop cognitive understanding, and bridge the gap between knowledge and practice outside of dedicated training centres. Previous work in this field has focused on knowledge transfer, which is important yet insufficient to understand the interplay of instruction, usability, presence, and experience. All of which could impact learning outcomes and frequency of use. To have a more nuanced view of VR medical training beyond its knowledge transfer capability, we integrate HCI & games perspectives into our evaluation approach appraising the VR Bronchoscope Assembly (VR-Bronch) training.

Keywords: Design Process · Usability Testing · Edutainment · Education · Training · Virtual Reality

1 Introduction

The work we present in this paper explores the use of virtual reality to prime cognitive knowledge for procedural tool training [29]. We employ methods from HCI and games research to evaluate a VR training tool. We suggest they are both essential for assessing and furthering VR approaches to aid in medical and educational contexts.

Professional training requires access to an array of equipment, spaces, instruction, and practice scenarios. In medicine, for example, practitioners need to be

© The Author(s), under exclusive license to Springer Nature Switzerland AG 2023
J. Abdelnour Nocera et al. (Eds.): INTERACT 2023, LNCS 14145, pp. 189–208, 2023.
https://doi.org/10.1007/978-3-031-42293-5_15

well-versed in various instruments that require training in assembly and application. As practitioners specialise, their training will involve more bespoke tools and exposure to scenarios that may have a high risk of patient harm. However, access to tools, instruction, or authentic experience may be more limited due to the cost of the equipment, fewer individuals with the required knowledge, or competition for real-world practice within working hours [15]. The recent global pandemic has also highlighted the need for more remote access to specialised equipment and training due to restrictions on personnel gatherings or the need for individuals to isolate themselves. Therefore, training and tool exposure could benefit from more flexibility outside of specific training centres. One common training scenario in medical education is procedural tool training. For effective procedural training, the learner must gather knowledge of appropriate tools and procedure steps. Once obtained, the learner can develop the required motor skills through practice. Broadly speaking, these elements could be considered the cognitive and psycho-motor aspects of training. Both require practice to develop but also revision to maintain knowledge and skills [30].

Virtual reality (VR) immerses the user in a computer-generated world. This allows the user then to focus their attention on a given context. VR can simulate equipment behaviour, interactions, environmental context, and instructional activities. We believe it can complement procedural training by providing a space to prime cognitive understanding and revise tool knowledge outside real-world practice. Thus, supporting cognitive development and maintenance of a procedural skill-set. Consumer-grade VR gear (Meta Quest, HTC Vive etc.) can be used within or outside specialised centres, reducing accessibility barriers within a training program. Therefore, VR has the potential to help bridge the gap between the mental model of a procedure, and the experience gained through real-world interactions.

This study evaluates VR-bronch, a VR procedural training resource developed to prime students before they take part in real-world bronchoscopy tool training, and revise its knowledge post-tool training. Assessing knowledge transfer is an important metric to inform efficacy when evaluating training resources but insufficient for understanding the shortcomings/development needs of a training tool. A broader understanding of usability, perceived experience, and cognitive load is also required to understand what supports or inhibits training performance.

2   Background

Procedural skills can be defined as the cognitive and physical activities required to complete a manual task [30]. In medicine, this would cover a wide range of procedures requiring knowledge and practice of physical tools. Well-documented, traditional approaches to postgraduate medical education are based on "see one, do one, teach one" [28]. However, concerns with potential safety issues, with 28–42% of doctors in training not feeling safe to perform a procedure after only observing it once [18] and the cancellation of medical student's clinical placements during the Covid-19 pandemic [10] highlight that broader more flexible approaches are required.

One approach is through simulation-based training where trainees practice their procedural competency without risk of harm to patients. It has been argued that simulation is required, not just for accessibility of training, but also as part of a robust curriculum. Building on the "see one, do one, teach one", Sawyer et al. [30] argue that procedural skills training must include cognitive, psycho-motor, and maintenance phases. In this framework, learners must "learn" and "see" the tool, procedure, and associated theory to build a cognitive representation and context. In the psycho-motor phase, learners must "practice, prove, & do" to develop competency. Lastly, learners must find ways to maintain and avoid *de-skilling*.

A procedure can be simulated through real-world objects and virtual content. For example, first aid training can use life-size mannequins to practice patient care [33]. Surgeons can use box trainers that approximate the range of motion available to practitioners when applying procedures to patient physiology. In the field of surgery, the use of virtual content to visualise procedures combined with bespoke haptic devices to replicate the required motor skills has seen significant attention [16,27]. These "simulators" will often use a non-immersive display (normal desktop monitor) to visualise virtual interactions. The combination of haptic devices and virtual visualisation is considered an effective procedural training approach for surgery [11].

Access to virtual simulation training equipment outside of specific training centres is still limited due to the size and cost of these machines. One approach to improving accessibility to simulation training is to use commercially available virtual reality (VR) hardware [1]. VR will immerse the user's visual and audio senses so that the presented virtual content becomes their new reality. This technology can create authentic environments and scenario contexts that engage users, deliver instruction, and enable quasi-practice. Compared to dedicated simulators, consumer-grade gear for VR training provides visual and audio immersion but lacks the bespoke haptic devices for accurate motor skill training as hand actions are normally abstracted through held controllers. The lack of bespoke haptic devices and the high cost of creating relevant content may be key drivers to why there has been limited work exploring the use of VR for procedural training, instead focusing on 3d visualisation of body scans and anatomy training [27].

Feasibility studies that have investigated the use of commercial grade VR for medical procedural training observe that task understanding (order of steps within a procedure, insertion placement etc.) can be attained [24] and transferred to real-world practice [7]. However, evaluating educational VR simulations requires more insight than knowledge transfer or skill acquisition alone. A noted trend in virtual reality for education and training is reliance on knowledge transfer and perception of satisfaction for evaluations [8]. Solely focusing on those can be seen as a limitation as this can miss identifying relationships between a vast array of design decisions and learning goals [9] which are crucial for developing better tools. Perceptions of immersion and usability are key to understanding the extent to which VR captures user attention and how intuitively they can engage with the learning tasks. Both immersion and perceived experience have

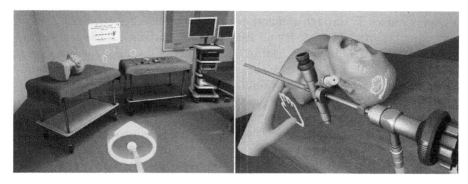

Fig. 1: Screenshots are taken from VR-Bronch training. LEFT: room aesthetic and teleportation arc with the destination target. The floating menu describes a task area; RIGHT: tool parts being assembled through hand interactions

been key focuses of games research. Poor usability or negative associated perceptions could lead to a tool not being properly engaged with or used. Breaks in immersion can lead to user distraction impacting the learning outcomes. Cognitive load of the learning instruction may have greater significance when using a VR platform, especially outside of educational environments. Understanding the impact of cognitive load can help to manage information delivery and learning outcomes better. Additionally, broadening metrics for evaluation can help expand the general understanding of virtual reality and its impact on broader human cognition.

2.1   Case Study

Virtual Reality Bronchoscope Assembly (VR-Bronch) is a simulation and training prototype created by a team of two developers. The goal of the prototype is to develop students' virtual competence in assembly [12], cognitive representation for this assembly, and identification of components of the tracheobronchoscopy, but not in its surgical application. As part of a broader curriculum, this prototype was designed to bridge the gap between the cognitive stage and psycho-motor phase similar to procedural pedagogical frameworks like Sawyer et al. [30]. VR-Bronch requires students to familiarise themselves with the components and associated information of the tracheobronchoscopy. They are then guided through the assembly of the tool for practice before seeing how far they can recall the assembly procedure without guidance.

Tracheobronchial foreign body in the paediatric population can be an urgent, life-threatening condition [25], requiring prompt specialist input to ensure the safe resolution of an associated emergency. Rigid tracheobronchoscopy under anaesthesia is the gold standard for visualisation and manipulation of the foreign body important to re-establish the safe, effective paediatric airway [23,26]. The assembly and deployment of the rigid paediatric bronchoscope can be somewhat challenging, and a lack of training in this specific field of operative ENT can lead to delayed diagnosis and adverse outcomes [13]. Paediatric rigid tracheobronchoscopy is a core competence in UK Ear-Nose-Throat (ENT) training. However, access to the required equipment for simulation can be limited with centres only owning one set of equipment.

The presented work, based on the above case study, explores VR-Bronch through the lenses of knowledge transfer, system usability, perceived experience, and cognitive load to evaluate the efficacy of current design choices. Guided surveys are used to explore these concepts so that development teams could also employ the presented approach with little extra training or adjustments to inform their development.

3 Method

This study received ethical approval from the Faculty Research Ethics & Integrity Committee at the University of Plymouth (UoP). In total, 30 (14 female) participants were recruited. Participants were selected if they were current medical students at UoP, and could confidently read, speak and understand English. Recruitment was done through email communications, digital billboards, social media posts, and word of mouth. Participants did not receive any reward for taking part in this study.

3.1 Experimental Setup

Experimental trials took place in two locations, Main Campus & SciencePark, which were chosen to make study attendance more attractive to a wider cohort. Multiple rooms were used at each location so that survey completion and VR-Bronch training could run concurrently. Surveys were created using the JISC online surveys tool and completed by participants on desktop PCs or tablets with an attached keyboard. The Oculus Rift S VR headset was used [6] as it provides good resolution (1280X1440 per eye), sufficient refresh rate (80 Hz) & field of view (88° in both horizontal/vertical). Additionally, the platform is technically mature and supported by all modern game engines. It uses two controllers that are tracked in 3D space via the headset. Open broadcast software [2] was used to record screen/audio of participant's Oculus Rift head-mounted display.

The VR-Bronch training took place within one virtual room, see Fig. 2. A generic surgical theatre inspired the aesthetic of the room, see Fig. 1 LEFT. Participants always start in the northwest corner where they are shown a floating menu of interaction information. Subjects will always start in the same area and are asked to move between each task every five minutes. The dotted lines in Fig. 2 RIGHT, represent the general areas of interaction and navigation for each task. Task areas are identifiable from the room layout and also the floating menu at each station. These menus provide information on what is expected by the participant for each task. Participants can navigate larger distances through teleportation. To teleport participants press the thumbstick on a controller to

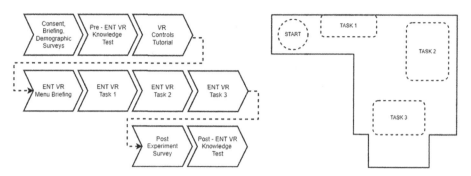

Fig. 2: LEFT: Study procedure flow of events; RIGHT: Room layout for the VR-Bronch training space

generate a line arc and target for aiming their teleportation, see Fig. 1. By releasing the thumbstick, the participants will then teleport to the target. Once at the chosen location, they can walk normally within the confines of the real-world floor space. This allows natural navigation when exploring tasks and teleportation between locations when the virtual world does not match the physical restraints of the real world. Participants can press the "trigger" button on the controllers with their index fingers to pick up an object. This activates a grabbing animation for their virtual hands. Any interactable object caught in this action will be held by the virtual hand until the trigger button is released, see Fig. 1. This mechanism allows for the pick up and placement of instrument parts.

3.2   System Evaluation

A series of questionnaires were administered before and after using VR-Bronch to evaluate the system. These questionnaires were designed to explore knowledge transfer, usability, presence, cognitive load, and perceived experience. Figure 3 highlights the focus of metrics within these categories.

A set of knowledge and recognition tests were administered to each participant before exposure to VR-Bronch training and afterwards. The knowledge and recognition tests had the same questions in both attempts but the order of the questions was different. The difference in recall to these questions will help evaluate knowledge gain. The aim of the knowledge tests is to evaluate the mental representation (what they are and what they are used for) of the components and the order in which they are assembled. Of interest to this training is whether the virtual objects facilitate recognition of real-world components too. The questions covered four test sections.

1. Recognition and assembly understanding of the 3D optical forceps.
2. Recognition purpose understanding for each 3D component introduced.
3. Identification of real-world components that 3D models are based upon.
4. Identification of where to place real-world components onto an image of a real-world paediatric bronchoscope.

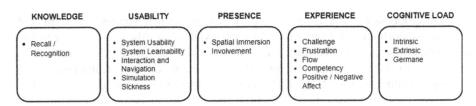

| KNOWLEDGE | USABILITY | PRESENCE | EXPERIENCE | COGNITIVE LOAD |

Fig. 3: Overview of observed metrics contained within our system evaluation to highlight how they align to knowledge transfer, usability, presence, cognitive load, and perceived experience.

Images of 3D objects and real-world components were provided by the medical practitioner involved with the development of VR-Bronch. 3D object renders from the VR-Bronch prototype are used in the recognition tests to directly reflect the imagery participants are exposed to when using VR-Bronch. To facilitate objective and consistent marking of the knowledge test scores, the correct answers were provided and discussed between the researcher and the medical practitioner prior to the evaluation. To avoid developer bias, the scoring was only conducted by the researcher. The majority of questions had two components, unless specified otherwise. These would be identify object X, and describe its use. One mark would be given for each correct choice, half marks were awarded if type of object was recognised but not the specific version, or if some of its use was identified but not all. Half marks were discussed with a medical practitioner involved in making VR-Bronch. On the question of tool assembly, one mark was given for each correctly described step. When identifying placement of real-world objects, one mark was given for each correct placement.

Usability broadly evaluates how effective and satisfying a digital tool can be for reaching desired goals. Poor usability may lead to frustration and confusion when achieving these goals. Evaluating usability for a VR tool can therefore highlight issues that may interfere with the VR training, but also help establish what elements of the prototype are fit for purpose. To evaluate the usability, the Systems Usability Scale (SUS) questionnaire was used [5]. SUS provides an overall score out of 100 and can be broken down into sub-categories that describe how "usable" and "learnable" the system is [4,21]. Typically, individual items should not be fixated upon when interpreting the overall usability level. However, these questions are good points of reflection for a developer and item-level approaches exist for the SUS [22]. Therefore, both the overall score and individual questions are displayed to inform usability and assert where improvements can be made. For this study, we adjusted the term "system" to "VR training" for a better context which does not alter the validity of the tool [4]. SUS is still a popular and widely used tool for assessing usability [20] that is flexible, yet robust in the face of adjustments [4,20]. It is also freely available without requiring a licensing fee, an important feature for commercial development. Extra questions were added for more clarity on design decisions specific to VR-Bronch. These extra questions were not used to calculate the SUS score.

Simulation sickness is a type of motion sickness that describes any feelings of nausea or disorientation from interacting with virtual worlds. Its often attributed to mixed messages between the brain from the eyes and inner ears (what we see and what we feel is the movement). It is not expected that much simulation sickness would occur in this study as the general movement and interaction paradigms closely match real-world body movement. However, any simulation sickness caused could interfere with training and needs to be accounted for. To capture simulation sickness data, the Virtual Reality Simulation Sickness (VRSQ) questionnaire was used [17]. This questionnaire asks a series of questions to help describe any negative oculomotor and disorientation responses to the VR experience. These are then pooled to give an overall simulation sickness score out of 100.

Presence describes the psychological immersion within a virtual world, the subjective acceptance that the virtual world is the current reality. When *present* in an immersive VR world, the user's attention is on the virtual world, not the real world. Poor presence may indicate that individuals are not engaged with the virtual reality and, therefore, the task at hand. Therefore, it is important to quantify if the hardware and software provide a stable experience of presence. To evaluate presence, the Igroup Presence Questionnaire (IPQ) [31] was used. IPQ allows some breakdown of how an experience's interactive and spatial elements create a sense of presence. This helps to identify issues with hardware, software, and interactions concerning presence.

Cognitive load describes attention and working memory resources used when achieving the goals of a task [32]. Cognitive load is often evaluated with educational material as it can inform which elements of a task require cognitive effort. Overall cognitive load is commonly derived from three factors: Intrinsic, extraneous, and germane loads. Intrinsic load describes the complexity of elements from interactions and subject matter. Extraneous load refers to external factors that may distract from learning (how the material is presented, distractions from the real world outside of the VR experience etc.) Germane load refers to the effort required for learning. For example, adding new information to current understanding. The balance of these loads is important as high intrinsic and extraneous loads will leave few cognitive resources to learn from the training. To evaluate the cognitive load for VR-Bronch, a survey developed by Leppink et al. [19] was administered. this survey allows for the analysis of intrinsic, extraneous, and germane loads in a relatively short ten-item survey. The language of the questions was altered to reflect the training topic. A five-point agreement/disagreement Likert scale for each survey question was used instead of rating the statements between zero and ten.

To explore the general experience of participants when using VR-Bronch, the Game Experience Questionnaire (GEQ) [14] was also administered. This questionnaire asks for one of four responses to indicate an individual's agreement with an experience statement: 0 = "not at all", 1 = "slightly", 2 = "moderately", 3 = "fairly", and 4 = "extremely". Responses to these questions are then grouped into experience categories. This questionnaire probes positive and negative experiences during and after the play-through of virtual content. It additionally explores concepts of immersion, challenge and perception of competence. Additionally looking at those concepts not only focuses on evaluating overall experience but also validating presence, influences on cognitive load, and engagement of the tasks.

3.3 Procedure

Participants were inducted through a written briefing and consent form with the opportunity to discuss any questions. They then completed the demographic survey and pre-experiment knowledge test. Participants then put on the Oculus Rift VR hardware and took part in the "First Steps" tutorial. This introduced the participants to the general VR controls and navigation concepts that were reflected in the VR-Bronch Training. It also acted as an acclimatisation period for the VR hardware. Once this tutorial was completed, the VR-Bronch training level was loaded. Next, participants were given information by the experimenter on the menu interaction paradigm and used the title menu to practice these interactions. Participants were then informed that there are three "stations" they would need to navigate to, and each one had a task for them to complete. They would have five minutes at each station before they would be told to move to the next one. The short time at each station was to give participants enough exposure to evaluate their experience whilst maintaining efficiency in the testing process. Task one had participants observe and pick up the various components of the bronchoscopy tool. As they did, information about the items appeared on the floating menu located at the station. Participants were asked to absorb as much information as they could. Task two had subjects taken through the assembly of the bronchoscopy tool. Images and descriptions of the procedure were detailed on this station's floating menu. As subjects completed the assembly, more instruction would be given through this menu. Task three asked the participants to assemble a part of the bronchoscopy tool as presented in an image on the station's floating menu. No other guidance was given and participants had a selection of components in front of them to achieve this task. Once the time for this task had finished, participants were asked to stop what they were doing and then helped out of the VR hardware. They then took part in a post-experiment survey to assess simulation sickness, usability, presence, cognitive load, and game experience questionnaire. Finally, participants were given the post-VR-Bronch training knowledge test. Four variations of the knowledge test were created, they had the same questions but in a different order to counterbalance the knowledge test question order between participants (See Table 1c for details).

Timings for this procedure are as follows (40 min - 1 h):

- Consent, Briefing, demographic + knowledge survey (five minutes)
- Introduction to the equipment + First Steps tutorial (five minutes)
- Menu introduction and task instructions (three minutes)
- Task 1: Component description and interaction (five minutes)
- Task 2: Guided step-by-step assembly of the equipment (five minutes)

- Task 3:Unguided assembly of the equipment (five minutes)
- Post-experiment survey (5–10) minutes
- Post-VR-Bronch training knowledge test (5–10) minutes

4 Results

Of the 30 participants (females = 14), the majority (28/30) were between the age of 18 and 30 (See Table 1a). The average age across all participants was 22.3. All participants studied for the Bachelor of Medicine, Bachelor of Surgery degree. The sample spanned all years of this degree (1–5) but with a bias towards second-year students (10/30). Half of the participants had used VR before (15/30). Of the 15 participants who had used VR before, 13 claimed to have last used VR a year or longer ago. Two participants recalled using VR 6 months ago. All reported low regularity of VR use with one claiming to use VR a couple of times a year and 14 less than once a year.

Table 1: Survey results for (a) participant demographics, (b) Cognitive Load & (c) counterbalanced knowledge test.

Demographic Information

N	Gender	Age	Year of Study	Used VR Before
	M/F	18-30/31-50	1/2/3/4/5	Yes
30	16/14	28/2	4/10/5/4/7	15

(a) Participant Demographics

Cognitive load Survey

CL Cat.	Mid-Point	Mean ± SD	df	t-value	p
Intrinsic	3.00	3.45 ± 0.66	29	3.77	< .001
Extrinsic	3.00	2.14 ± 0.86	29	−5.49	< .001
Germane	3.00	3.97 ± 0.62	29	8.59	< .001

(b) Mean scores with significance testing against the scale mid-point.

Knowledge Test Variation

Group	Pre - Training	Post - Training	N
01	1	2	3
02	1	3	3
03	1	4	2
04	2	1	3
05	2	2	2
06	2	3	2
07	2	4	1
08	3	1	3
09	3	2	2
10	3	4	2
11	4	1	2
12	4	2	1
13	4	3	2
14	4	4	2

(c) Counterbalancing of training groups

Knowledge test scores observed a significant increase in recognition of bronchoscopy tool, components, and assembly steps after exposure to the VR-Bronch training Fig. 4a. Overall mean knowledge test observed a far greater accuracy score after exposure to the VR-Bronch training (M = 0.33, SD = 0.14) compared to before the training (M = 0.10, SD = 0.07). This difference was significant (t(29) = 9.580, p = <.001). To explore if the year of study as a medical student mediated the effectiveness of the VR-Bronch training, participant knowledge test scores were categorised into two groups. Year one and two into one group, representing participants early in their medical studies, and years three, four, and five into a group representing the students that have already gained a significant amount of medical knowledge. An ANOVA was administered using the pre and post scores as factors and the grouped year as a between subject variable. The year of study did not significantly mediate the knowledge test scores before and after exposure to the VR-Bronch training (F(1,28) = 0.199, p = .659).

Presence survey scores (See Table 3b) suggest a positive perception of spatial presence (5.38) and a positive perception of involvement (4.69) within the VR training. The sense of realism of the VR training is lower with a mean score of 3.84. A closer examination of the survey questions suggests that this is due to disagreement with question RL4, see Fig. 4b, "The virtual world seemed more realistic than the real world."

No participants reported feeling simulation sickness (nausea) after using the VR training. Based on the VRSQ survey, the mean total simulation sickness score was 7.22/100 (Oculomotor 10/100, Disorientation 4.44/100). This score would be considered low.

The overall SUS score [5] was 74.25 (SD = 11.36) out of 100. Using adjective criteria described by [3], this can be described as "good" usability overall. To assess the positive or negative perception of each question in the usability survey, the average point scale response (1–5) was compared against the midpoint in the scale with a one sample t-test (Table 2). All questions except one scored statistically higher than the midpoint, evidencing a generally positive perception across the usability questions. Question four ("I think that I would need the support of a technical person to be able to use the VR training") did not score significantly above or below the mid-point which evidences a neutral response. Analysis of the SUS "usable" and "learnable" factors observed significantly higher scores above the midpoint value of three. This indicates a positive perception of these factors. However, "learnable" achieved an average of 3.38 suggesting a positive, but not strong, bias.

Project-specific questions also observed a significantly higher score than the mid value of three. This suggests that interaction, menu, and navigation paradigms were perceived positively by the subjects. Additionally, the question "I would use this application as a learning resource" scored 4.6/5 which suggests a very positive attitude to the use of this project within an educational pipeline.

The Game Experience Questionnaire (GEQ) was used to examine the perceived user experience during and after exposure to the VR Training. Table 3c reports the mean score for each category within the GEQ.

Scores for negative affect (M = 0.18, SD = 0.27) during, and negative experience (M = 0.10, SD = 0.19) after using VR-Bronch training were low. On average these two categories scored closest to "not at all" present. The category

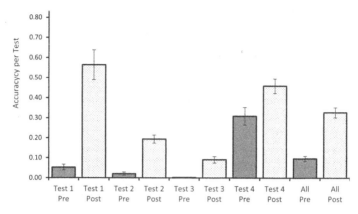

(a) Knowledge Tests 1-4: Mean accuracy for knowledge tests delivered before & after training.

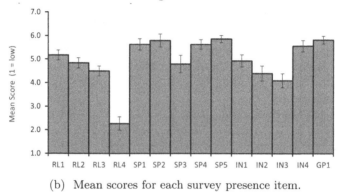

(b) Mean scores for each survey presence item.

Fig. 4: Means for (a) VR-Bronch knowledge tests and (b) presence items.

tension/annoyance also scored low (M = 0.32, SD = 0.64). Low scores in these three categories indicate that feelings of frustration, boredom and regret were much less experienced by users.

Positive affect explores the experience of enjoyment whilst using the VR-Bronch training and positive experience probes how the participant feels after (satisfaction, energised etc.). The positive experience was moderate (M = 1.97, SD = 1.26), and the positive affect scored fairly to extremely high (M = 3.50, SD = 0.46). Categories of flow (M = 2.84, SD = 0.75) and immersion (M = 3.08, SD = 0.70) can be interpreted as "fair" based on the GEQ scoring. This suggests that the activities presented were engaging, but neither the hardware nor software broke the participants' immersion in the VR world or tasks presented. The "Challenge" category investigates ideas of effort, learning, and difficulty. This was reported as moderate (M = 1.83, SD = 0.81). Tiredness scored closest to "not at all" present (M = 0.23, SD = 0.39) which suggests that the activities, hardware and software did not physically or emotionally drain the participants.

Table 2: SUS mean score mid-point, $mid = 3.00$, comparison. ([a] Negative scores reversed to align with positive items [b].)

Usability Survey				
Question	Mean ± SD	df	t-value	p
SUS items				
1. Use VR training frequently	4.50 ± 0.68	29	12.04	<.001
2. Unnecessarily complex[a]	4.00 ± 0.87	29	6.29	<.001
3. Easy to use	4.07 ± 0.87	29	6.73	<.001
4. Support of a technical person[a]	2.77 ± 1.01	29	−1.27	0.214
5. Functions were well integrated	4.37 ± 0.72	29	10.42	<.001
6. Too much inconsistency[a]	4.07 ± 0.87	29	6.73	<.001
7. Learn to use this very quickly	4.13 ± 0.78	29	8.00	<.001
8. Cumbersome to use[a]	3.97 ± 1.03	29	5.12	<.001
9. Confident in use	3.83 ± 0.95	29	4.81	<.001
10. Learn a lot of things before use[a]	4.00 ± 0.83	29	6.60	<.001
Usable	4.12 ± 0.48	29	12.67	<.001
Learnable	3.38 ± 0.73	29	2.89	0.007
Project specific items				
11. I would use this application as a learning resource	4.60 ± 0.68	29	12.99	<.001
12. Comfortable with controls by the time I started the activities	4.07 ± 0.87	29	6.728	<.001
13. The navigation confused me[a]	3.73 ± 1.08	29	3.717	<.001
14. The menus were confusing to use[a]	3.90 ± 0.66	29	7.449	<.001
15. Time to understand interactions	4.17 ± 0.87	29	7.309	<.001
16. Controls were intuitive	4.20 ± 0.66	29	9.893	<.001
17. Practice in object placement [a]	3.87 ± 0.97	29	4.878	<.001
18. Navigation ease	4.10 ± 0.76	29	7.94	<.001
19. Menu ease of use	3.93 ± 0.69	29	7.393	<.001

Participants felt moderately competent in completing the goals set before them (M = 2.22, SD = 1.02). On average, the subjects also felt a slight (M = 1.03, SD = 0.73) re-adjustment period was needed to attune back to the real world after spending time training in VR-Bronch.

Perceived cognitive load was assessed across three categories: intrinsic, extraneous, and germane (A Likert scale was used for the scoring but also to gain some understanding of the extent of whether participants agreed or disagreed with the presence of cognitive load (See Table 1b). Intrinsic load mean scored 3.45 which places perception between neutral and agreement.

Table 3: Survey results for (a) bronchoscopy tool knowledge accuracy, (b) IPQ survey means for presence analysis, (c) Game Experience statistics.

Knowledge gain

Pre/post score	M-diff	t	df	p
Test 1	0.511	−7.089	29	<.001
Test 2	0.172	−10.489	29	<.001
Test 3	0.088	−5.757	29	<.001
Test 4	0.150	−2.983	29	0.006
All	0.230	−9.58	29	<.001

(a) Knowledge accuracy: paired sampled T-Tests before & after training

IPQ Mean Scores

Presence Category	N	Mean ± SD
Spatial Presence	30	5.55 ± 0.81
Involvement	30	4.75 ± 1.16
Realness	30	4.19 ± 0.80
Presence	30	5.08 ± 0.72

(b) IPQ survey mean scores for each category of presence analysis. Scores were obtained through a 7-point Likert scale, 4.00 = midpoint

Game Experience Questionnaire	
GEQ category	Mean ± SD
Competence	2.22± 1.02
Immersion	3.08± 0.70
Flow	2.84± 0.75
Tension/Annoyance	0.32± 0.64
Challenge	1.83± 0.81
Positive affect	3.50± 0.46
Negative affect	0.18± 0.27
Positive Experience	1.97± 1.26
Negative experience	0.10± 0.19
Tiredness	0.23± 0.39
Returning to Reality	1.03± 0.73

(c) GEQ Descriptive Statistics. 0 = "not at all", 1 = "slightly", 2 = "moderately", 3 = "fairly", and 4 = "extremely"

Given that the intrinsic load was significantly higher than the midpoint of the scoring scale, it is likely that participants perceived a moderate amount of intrinsic cognitive load during the required training activities. Extraneous load scored significantly lower than the midpoint (M = 2.14, SD = 0.86). Germane load scored (M = 3.97, SD = 0.62) significantly higher than the midpoint value and reported the highest value among the cognitive load categories.

5   Discussion

We evaluated the VR-Bronch training prototype through the lenses of knowledge transfer, system usability, perceived experience, and cognitive load. Our aim was to inform further development of the VR-Bronch prototype. To align with our target domain, our sample included only medical students. The cohort had limited exposure to VR-Bronch content and low experience with VR platforms.

Knowledge tests observed a significant increase in tool and component recognition after using VR-Bronch. Additionally, recall of assembly steps was significantly greater. The magnitude of the difference between knowledge test sections varied significantly. Knowledge of tool assembly increased by 51%, recognition of 3D components increased by 17%, and recognition of real-world components increased by 9%. This suggests that a general understanding of the tool was developed, but participants were less able to increase their knowledge of individual components. Real-world object recognition did significantly improve, which suggests some transfer from the 3D objects used during training. However, the recognition test for real-world components was framed around object placement and not component use. This might explain some differences in recognition scores between the 3D and real-world tests. It also suggests that some content dedicated to a real-world procedure may help align the 3D models with real-world tools, ie. 360 videos of the bronchoscopy assembly. Overall, the knowledge tests observed a 23% increase in knowledge accuracy after a relatively short exposure to the training. This suggests that VR-Bronch can establish a mental representation of a tool, its assembly and component knowledge. It has potential as a revision tool within a broader curriculum, or a primer before the real-world training commences. Longer exposure needs to be explored to assess the development of mental representation over time.

In this study, the usability of the system has been assessed using an expanded System Usability Scale (SUS) survey. Simulation sickness was also considered to be an aspect of usability and measured with a post-training survey. Participants that feel nauseous will find it more difficult to take part in learning and would find it hard to use the system. For this reason, it can be considered a key aspect of usability for VR content. The overall SUS was measured as "good", with positive perceptions of being both a usable and learnable system. The question "I think I would need the help of a technical person" trended a negative perception, but not significantly so. This suggests that participants felt they might need technical support when using this system. This is an important aspect to consider when developing an educational system outside of a specialist centre and training times. If technical support is not on hand, any built-up frustration in the system may reduce learning outcomes and appetite to use the system further. Therefore, this tool may require better onboarding (in-game tutorials and support material). A need for technical support may also be due to general inexperience with VR prevalent in the cohort. This would suggest that tutorials should also consider covering good practices when using VR. Levels of simulation sickness were low, and no participants reported feeling symptoms of sickness. This suggests that the specific hardware and software design does not cause undue simulation sickness and therefore has not interfered with learning goals.

Presence scores suggest a good level of psychological immersion was established. Spatial presence was high, indicating that the generated reality was the focus of spatial cognition. The presence associated with user involvement in the virtual world was satisfactory, highlighting that user interactions were more salient to the user within the virtual world than in the physical world. But this could be improved. Users who reach the boundaries of the physical space will be reminded of the real world. Being able to keep your own body within the centre of the space whilst teleporting between locations is part of the skill set required for this type of VR navigation paradigm. Therefore, more practice with VR, in general, may improve this metric. Additionally, reducing the need for teleporting by not having the user navigate a large space would reduce contact with real-world boundaries. Any bugs with interactions and objects may also reduce cognition of involvement. As soon as an interaction acts differently from the expected laws of physics (objects becoming unpickable, falling through the floor etc.), the user may be reminded that they are in an artificial construct. Therefore, improving interactions and reducing bugs may also improve this metric. Lastly, participants could also hear the sounds of the real-world building (people walking down corridors, doors closing etc.), which may also draw attention away from the virtual world. Introducing background noise in the simulation may help reduce real-world audio distractions. Concepts of realism and presence scored the lowest. The average was reduced with the question, "The virtual world seemed more realistic than the real world". This scored significantly lower than all other questions suggesting that this question potentially needs refining. Participants know they are in a virtual construct but are willing to suspend their disbelief. So to ask if the virtual world is more real than normal reality is to presume that a user has cognitively succumbed to the virtual world and completely forgotten they are physically placed in the real world using virtual technology. The answer to this will often be no.

Participants' subjective experience was measured through the Game Experience Questionnaire (GEQ). This allows for the evaluation of the experiential effect that VR-Bronch generates. The GEQ results observed a very positive sensory and imaginative immersion score, supporting the presence scores observed in the IPQ survey. Together, these scores suggest that the hardware, activities and environmental context helped establish a sense of presence and successfully drew participants' attention to the virtual world; a sense of flow was established. Those in a state of flow are said to be absorbed by the tasks at hand and, in such states, may be unaware of time passing. To achieve a state of flow there needs to be a sufficient challenge without it being beyond the user's current ability, which is reflected in the GEQ scores. The challenge is observed as moderate, and the sense of annoyance is low. A low sense of annoyance may also suggest that any bugs that were present did not create systemic issues with the experience. Additionally, participants felt moderately competent, which suggests that the interactions and challenges were perceived to be achieved by the participants. But there is variation in this response which ranges from slightly competent to fairly competent. The range in feelings of competence and involvement presence may suggest that participants did not feel as though they mastered the navigation and interaction paradigm without error. Overall, these metrics suggest that the general design of the content, the context of training, and the usability of the controls were sufficient to achieve a state of flow for novice users. However, some competency improvement may be required. Implementing tutorials, refining interactions, and reducing the need for teleportation may be an area of focus to increase perceptions of competency.

Through the GEQ, positive and negative perceptions of the experience both during and after using VR-Bronch can be observed. These metrics can be used to give some insight into the sum of the parts concerning the participant's cognitive state when taking on the challenge of the training. Both during and after the VR-Bronch training, negative experiences were low, suggesting that feelings of boredom and disinterest were not present. Post-training, participants did not feel weary or regretful. Conversely, the post-training positive experience was moderate and during training, fair to high. This suggests that participants felt enjoyment, empowerment, and a sense of fun during training. Post-training participants felt energised and victorious. These positive sentiments are reflected in one of the adjusted usability questions, which asks if the participants would use VR-Bronch as a learning resource, and the majority of participants agreed that they would. Positive and negative experiences suggest there is coherence in the current design of VR-Bronch. The experience is rated good enough and the context of the training makes sense to medical students to the extent that they see its value in their learning. However, since this was a brief exposure to VR training, and subjects had little prior VR experience, there could also be a novelty effect biasing the perceptions more favourably. Understanding which parts create positive experiences will be crucial for motivating training outside of educational centres and flexible learning approaches.

Cognitive load was assessed to help evaluate how cognitive resources were being used. A moderate amount of intrinsic cognitive load was observed, and likely a mix of subject matter and adjustment to the VR interactions. The usability scores suggest that participants viewed the navigation and interaction paradigm positively, but the involvement presence scores and competency scores could be higher. Together these observations suggest that the intrinsic load is likely increased by an individual adjusting to the VR controls and interactions. Intrinsic load is also associated with absorbing new information across a new tool. Given that participants had a relatively short duration with the training, and were exposed to the tool, its assembly, and the individual components, they would have had a lot of new information to digest. The challenge, flow, and competency scores from the GEQ would suggest that the content was not beyond the understanding of the participants. It seems that the time they had with the content was too short to absorb more information. This is also reflected in the knowledge test scores, where individual components were recognised far worse in the knowledge test compared to overall tool recognition and assembly. It suggests that subject matter, and interacting with the information took a moderate amount of working memory resources. The balance of this could be better managed with chunking of delivered information and more time devoted to user onboarding. The extraneous load was low but still observable. This suggests that instructions for the tasks were clear and that the representation of information was good. However, this could most likely be improved. By segmenting practice with interactions from information delivery, the extraneous load could be reduced. The germane load was highest suggesting a strong perception that cognitive resources were focused on learning during the activities. This is not surprising as VR-Bronch would focus on a tool unknown to the participants. This suggests that task choice was satisfactory in presenting both assembly information and knowledge of components. The high germane and intrinsic cognitive load provide additional support that more chunking of information is required. Essentially reduce information delivery with more granular goals. More granular goals may also aid feelings of competency with the platform and subject matter.

6   Conclusion

We evaluated the VR-Bronch training prototype using a set of guided questionnaires that informed knowledge transfer, system usability, perceived experience, and cognitive load. We could then speculate on the interplay between these measured items in the context of the created educational VR content. The selected tools can give valuable information to development teams on the extent to which their system or content is fit for purpose, and what areas require further exploration. Since this approach uses guided surveys, it can be utilised out of the box by small development teams with minimal training.

Learner perceptions of the VR-Bronch prototype suggest that the overall system design and implementation are to a good standard and cohesively come together to form a positive experience. However, some recommendations based on this evaluation are as follows:

- Involvement presence could be improved by reducing the need for teleportation, increasing onboarding, and greater use of environment sound (to hide real-world audio)
- Feelings of competency could be increased by more granular achievements at the beginning of training through onboarding, greater chunking of information, and a reduction in teleportation.
- Greater balance of intrinsic and germane cognitive load could be achieved through chunking of instructional activities and pauses for reflection on own understanding.
- Recognition of real-world objects could be increased with real-world media shown alongside 3D objects.

For our use case, to fully evaluate the gained knowledge it might be worthwhile to validate the knowledge on real-world use of the tool to see what can be transferred. The current evaluation is only able to suggest that the 3d representation has been better known and that procedural steps are understood in the simulation. Participants had a short exposure to the VR-Bronch training, thus, knowledge transfer could be higher if used within a more contextual time period. Additionally, due to participants having low experience with VR as a platform before this study there may be some novelty effect increasing the positivity of the reported experience. The real-world transfer is limited to the recognition of images. Improvements to the depth of this transfer would be to test knowledge from a selection of media or real-world tools.

During our study, we focused on a single use case as a starting point. With future work, we aim to design a broader methodology around our current method for educational VR, flow for engagement, knowledge test for efficacy, presence for platform experience stability, usability to monitor system and interaction frustrations, and also encompassing cognitive load. By doing so, developers could employ our method to evaluate their prototypes beyond focusing on either knowledge or usability but a more integrated approach looking also closer at aspects that could impact long-term usage.

Acknowledgement. For the purpose of Open Access, the authors have applied a CC BY public copyright licence to any Author Accepted Manuscript (AAM) version arising from this submission. This work was supported by the eHealth Productivity and Innovation in Cornwall and the Isle of Scilly project, which was partly funded by the European Regional Development Fund (grant 05R18P02814).

References

1. Abbas, J., Kenth, J., Bruce, I.: The role of virtual reality in the changing landscape of surgical training. J. Laryngol. Otol. **134**(10), 863–866 (2020)
2. Baily, H.: Open broadcaster software | obs (2022). https://obsproject.com/
3. Bangor, A., Kortum, P., Miller, J.: Determining what individual SUS scores mean: adding an adjective rating scale. J. Usabil. Stud. **4**(3), 114–123 (2009)
4. Brooke, J.: Sus: a retrospective. J. Usabil. Stud. **8**(2), 29–40 (2013)
5. Brooke, J., et al.: Sus-a quick and dirty usability scale. Usabil. Evaluat. Indust. **189**(194), 4–7 (1996)
6. Brown, R.: Oculus rifts: Full specification - vrcompare (2022). https://vr-compare.com/headset/oculusrifts
7. Cevallos, N., Zukotynski, B., Greig, D., Silva, M., Thompson, R.M.: The utility of virtual reality in orthopedic surgical training. J. Surg. Educ. **79**(6), 1516–1525 (2022)
8. Checa, D., Bustillo, A.: A review of immersive virtual reality serious games to enhance learning and training. Multim. Tools Appl. **79**(9), 5501–5527 (2020)
9. Ch'ng, E., Li, Y., Cai, S., Leow, F.T.: The effects of VR environments on the acceptance, experience, and expectations of cultural heritage learning. J. Comput. Cult. Heritage (JOCCH) **13**(1), 1–21 (2020)
10. Choi, B., Jegatheeswaran, L., Minocha, A., Alhilani, M., Nakhoul, M., Mutengesa, E.: The impact of the covid-19 pandemic on final year medical students in the united kingdom: a national survey. BMC Med. Educ. **20**(1), 1–11 (2020)
11. Fiani, B., De Stefano, F., Kondilis, A., Covarrubias, C., Reier, L., Sarhadi, K.: Virtual reality in neurosurgery: "can you see it?"-a review of the current applications and future potential. World Neurosurg. **141**, 291–298 (2020)
12. Frank, J.R., et al.: Competency-based medical education: theory to practice. Med. Teacher **32**(8), 638–645 (2010)
13. Huang, Z., Liu, D., Zhong, J., Zhou, J.: Delayed diagnosis and treatment of foreign body aspiration in china: the roles played by physician inexperience and lack of bronchoscopy facilities at local treatment centers. Int. J. Pediatr. Otorhinolaryngol. **77**(12), 2019–2022 (2013)
14. IJsselsteijn, W.A., De Kort, Y.A., Poels, K.: The game experience questionnaire (2013)
15. Jackson, G.P., Tarpley, J.L.: How long does it take to train a surgeon? BMJ **339** (2009)
16. Jiang, H., Vimalesvaran, S., Wang, J.K., Lim, K.B., Mogali, S.R., Car, L.T.: Virtual reality in medical students' education: scoping review. JMIR Med. Educ. **8**(1), e34860 (2022)
17. Kim, H.K., Park, J., Choi, Y., Choe, M.: Virtual reality sickness questionnaire (VRSQ): motion sickness measurement index in a virtual reality environment. Appl. Ergon. **69**, 66–73 (2018)
18. Kotsis, S.V., Chung, K.C.: Application of see one, do one, teach one concept in surgical training. Plastic Reconstruct. Surg. **131**(5), 1194 (2013)

19. Leppink, J., Paas, F., Van der Vleuten, C.P.M., Van Gog, T., Van Merriënboer, J.J.G.: Development of an instrument for measuring different types of cognitive load. Behav. Res. Methods **45**(4), 1058–1072 (2013). https://doi.org/10.3758/s13428-013-0334-1

20. Lewis, J.R.: The system usability scale: past, present, and future. Int. J. Hum. Comput. Interact. **34**(7), 577–590 (2018). https://doi.org/10.1080/10447318.2018.1455307

21. Lewis, J.R., Sauro, J.: The factor structure of the system usability scale. In: Kurosu, M. (ed.) HCD 2009. LNCS, vol. 5619, pp. 94–103. Springer, Heidelberg (2009). https://doi.org/10.1007/978-3-642-02806-9_12

22. Lewis, J.R., Sauro, J.: Item benchmarks for the system usability scale. J. Usabil. Stud. **13**(3) (2018)

23. Maddali, M.M., Mathew, M., Chandwani, J., Alsajwani, M.J., Ganguly, S.S.: Outcomes after rigid bronchoscopy in children with suspected or confirmed foreign body aspiration: a retrospective study. J. Cardiothor. Vascul. Anesth. **25**(6), 1005–1008 (2011)

24. McKinney, B., Dbeis, A., Lamb, A., Frousiakis, P., Sweet, S.: Virtual reality training in unicompartmental knee arthroplasty: A randomized, blinded trial. J. Surg. Educ. **79**(6), 1526–1535 (2022)

25. Oncel, M., Sunam, G.S., Ceran, S.: Tracheobronchial aspiration of foreign bodies and rigid bronchoscopy in children. Pediatr. Int. **54**(4), 532–535 (2012)

26. Paradis, T.J., Dixon, J., Tieu, B.H.: The role of bronchoscopy in the diagnosis of airway disease. J. Thoracic Dis. **8**(12), 3826 (2016)

27. Portelli, M., Bianco, S., Bezzina, T., Abela, J.: Virtual reality training compared with apprenticeship training in laparoscopic surgery: a meta-analysis. Annal. Roy. Coll. Surg. England **102**(9), 672–684 (2020)

28. Rodriguez-Paz, J., et al.: Beyond "see one, do one, teach one": toward a different training paradigm. BMJ Qual. Safety **18**(1), 63–68 (2009)

29. Sawyer, T., Gray, M.M.: Procedural training and assessment of competency utilizing simulation. Semin. Perinatol. **40**(7), 438–446 (2016). https://doi.org/10.1053/j.semperi.2016.08.004

30. Sawyer, T., et al.: Learn, see, practice, prove, do, maintain: an evidence-based pedagogical framework for procedural skill training in medicine. Acad. Med. **90**(8), 1025–1033 (2015)

31. Schubert, T., Friedmann, F., Regenbrecht, H.: The experience of presence: factor analytic insights. Pres. Teleoper. Virt. Environ. **10**(3), 266–281 (2001)

32. Van Merrienboer, J.J., Sweller, J.: Cognitive load theory and complex learning: recent developments and future directions. Educ. Psychol. Rev. **17**(2), 147–177 (2005). https://doi.org/10.1007/s10648-005-3951-0

33. Watson, P., Gaudl, S.E.: Walking through virtual doors: a study on the effects of virtual location changes on memory. In: Orlosky, J., Reiners, D., Weyers, B. (eds.) ICAT-EGVE 2021 - International Conference on Artificial Reality and Telexistence and Eurographics Symposium on Virtual Environments. The Eurographics Association (2021). https://doi.org/10.2312/egve.20211321

Mind the Heart: Designing a Stress Dashboard Based on Physiological Data for Training Highly Stressful Situations in Virtual Reality

Olivia Zechner[1,2]([✉]) [iD], Helmut Schrom-Feiertag[1] [iD], Jakob Uhl[1,2] [iD],
Quynh Nguyen[1,2] [iD], Lisanne Kleygrewe[3,4] [iD], and Manfred Tscheligi[1,2] [iD]

[1] Austrian Institute of Technology, 1210 Vienna, Austria
olivia.zechner@ait.ac.at
[2] University of Salzburg, 5020 Salzburg, Austria
[3] Vrije Universiteit Amsterdam, 1081 HV Amsterdam, The Netherlands
[4] Amsterdam Movement Sciences, 1081 HV Amsterdam, The Netherlands

Abstract. Virtual Reality is becoming increasingly popular to serve as training ground for challenging environments, which often involve making decisions in cognitive demanding and stressful situations. It has become common practice to analyze bio-signals to determine our current physiological status and fitness. However, we continue to rely on subjective feedback obtained through self-rated questionnaires, when it comes to assessing cognitive states. In this paper we describe the user-centered design process of building a stress dashboard prototype and testing it in a field trial to fully understand its potential. We report on mixed-method studies exploring the interplay between the trainer and the VR system. Our findings demonstrate that integrating a stress dashboard, based on objective bio-signal data, can enhance the VR training process, providing trainers with actionable insights that have the potential to shape trainee behavior and learning outcomes.

Keywords: Virtual reality · Immersive technologies · Contextual experience · Training experience · Biofeedback · High stress · Police training · Challenging Environments

1 Introduction

The use of Virtual Reality (VR) for training purposes is on the rise, accelerated by advancements in technology and increasing accessibility of affordable devices. Aligned is the research interest, with the number of publications found in the ACM Digital Library more than doubling from 7,359 in 2010 to 16,585 in 2020 (search term "VR training"). VR provides a robust platform for immersive simulation training [53]. Unlike real-world training, VR enables flexible scenario design and controlled exposure to challenging environments, including high-risk

© The Author(s), under exclusive license to Springer Nature Switzerland AG 2023
J. Abdelnour Nocera et al. (Eds.): INTERACT 2023, LNCS 14145, pp. 209–230, 2023.
https://doi.org/10.1007/978-3-031-42293-5_16

situations or interacting with vulnerable groups and unpredictable subjects. This makes VR an ideal platform for police officers to repeatedly practice decision making and acting (DMA) in stressful situations without being exposed to life-threatening circumstances.

Training of police officers has been a topic of continuous research because of its complexity and importance to society [22]. Incidents in which police officers act as first responders in critical situations range from violent mass shootings at schools (e.g. USA 2022[1]), poisoning and acid attacks (e.g. UK 2018[2]), violent riots (e.g. USA 2021[3], Netherlands 2021[4]) to terror attacks (e.g. France 2015[5] or Germany 2016[6]). In such situations, police officers are often required to make split-second decisions under conditions of severe psycho-physiological stress. Deficits in performance can have tragic outcomes, including serious injury or death [1]. In this article we will explore how manipulation of trainees' stress levels can enhance VR training for law enforcement agencies (LEAs).

According to the seminal work on stress appraisal by Lazarus & Folkman [24], stress occurs when a discrepancy between the perceptions of the situational demands and the coping resources to meet these demands exists. Thus, if an officer perceives his/her abilities to cope with the demands of a situation to be insufficient, stress responses ensue and trigger a cascade of psychological and physiological reactions (e.g. see [43]) which may lead to a decline in performance.

Particularly in police work, where the outcome of an action can have lethal consequences, the influence of stress on performance has considerable implications. Studies in the field of police performance have shown that stress responses can lead to decrements in perception (e.g. tunnel vision), cognition (e.g. dissociation), and skilled motor performance (e.g. shooting skills, self-defense and arrest skills) [33]. For instance, Nieuwenhuys & Oudejans [33] demonstrated that during a shooting task, police officers in a stressful, high-threat condition had faster reaction times and decreased shooting accuracy compared to officers in a low-threat condition. To improve performance under stress, police utilize scenario-based training that resembles the on-duty situations as realistically as possible [22]. Scenario-based training allows police officers to experience occupationally relevant levels of acute stress in a training setting and familiarize themselves with their stress responses, leading to improvements in performance of on-duty tasks [8]. Utilizing VR training, police trainers have the possibilities to steer the training scenarios more specifically to induce and manipulate the stress responses that police officers experience during the training. Several research groups have illustrated how realistic and immersive scenario-based training can improve police officers' skills such as situational awareness and decision-making [8].

---

[1] https://abcnews.go.com/US/timeline-shooting-texas-elementary-school-unfolded/story?id=84966910.

[2] https://www.statista.com/statistics/888324/acid-attacks-in-london/.

[3] https://en.wikipedia.org/wiki/January_6_United_States_Capitol_attack.

[4] https://en.wikipedia.org/wiki/2021_Dutch_curfew_riots.

[5] https://www.bbc.com/news/world-europe-34818994.

[6] https://en.wikipedia.org/wiki/2016_Berlin_truck_attack.

However, implementing innovative and technology-based forms of training comes with its challenges. Current police trainers have limited experience with digital training solutions. Therefore, tools provided need to be simple to use while addressing current real-world training limitations such as quick replication of a variety of training scenarios and fact-based performance indicators (e.g. visual field, stress level) [12]. The possibility to adapt a scenario and stress level in real-time has been another highly desired feature by police trainers, to provide trainees an ideal training experience.

In previous research, Nguyen et al. [32] have presented a user-centered approach based on iterative co-creation events to identify relevant stressors for first responders of LEAs. Among the 40 stressors collected in this process, ten were identified to be the most relevant (including weapons, crowds, items unexpectedly used as weapons such as an ashtray or vase, aggressive dogs and traces of blood). These stressors were developed in VR as audio-visual elements to provide trainers with a library of stress cues to dynamically increase trainee's stress levels when needed. Stress cues give trainers the opportunity to add complexity and thereby increase difficulty of a scenario, for trainees that are not challenged enough by the standard scenario.

In this article we will describe the process of designing a prototype stress dashboard to test the ecological validity of virtual stress cues in realistic VR training with police officers. We will discuss bio-signal measurement options, specific requirements from end-users and results from a field trial. Our aim is to answer the following research questions:

- RQ1: What information or parameters do the trainers need for a real-time analysis of a VR training session?
- RQ2: How can current stress levels of the trainees be visualised in a VR training?
- RQ3: How can trainers interact with trainees to increase or decrease the level of challenge a VR training session provides?

Furthermore, we hypothesize that our stress dashboard will exhibit distinct stress levels corresponding to operational training scenarios specifically designed to induce varying degrees of stress (low, medium, high) in trainees.

Although measurement and identification of stress has been extensively covered in current literature, as discussed in Sect. 2, the majority of contributions focus on controlled lab-based studies rather than application "in the wild" and often do not consider the translation into actionable feedback. With increasing demands for immersive technologies and the adaptation of living, working and training in hybrid worlds, the need for objective evaluation mechanisms is emerging within the Human-Computer Interaction (HCI) community. This article illustrate a practical example of how bio-signal derived stress measurements can enhance VR training systems. While the application is demonstrated within the context of law enforcement, its implications are applicable to a wider range of industries. These principles can be adopted across multiple domains, especially in industries where stress and training stress resilience (e.g. health care, medical first responders, sports performance, serious gaming, driver's safety) plays a significant role. The growth in immersive technologies is expanding the potential applications of this work, not only in traditional simulation training but also in emerging fields like hybrid workspaces or educational platforms. As the HCI community continues to explore these immersive experiences, understanding and managing user stress responses will play a crucial role in enhancing overall engagement and efficacy.

In the following chapters we will present related work (Sect. 2), elaborate on requirements and challenges regarding the concept, design and implementation of such a stress dashboard (Sect. 3), present initial results from a field trial (Sect. 4) and discuss the opportunities, challenges and limitations (Sect. 5) we encountered and foresee for others considering to apply our methods.

2   Related Work

The connection of VR training, real-time stress induction and measurement, as well as possibilities of stress level visualisation as a feedback tool to enhance training performance, are the core aspects of the stress dashboard presented in this paper. Related work in these areas will be addressed in the following.

2.1   Virtual Reality Training in Challenging Environments

The development and application of VR training solutions is an emerging topic [37]. Research on its efficacy and applicability covers a range of application fields and industries. We focus on training solutions for environments that are challenging to train in the real world and that can demonstrate a benefit that is transferable to first-responder and police training. Previous research has investigated the opportunities collaborative Virtual Environments (VE) present to train decision making in evacuation drills and emergency response [46] or VR training in an automotive factory that reports a positive outcome in terms of knowledge transfer from VE to the real factory [44]. Using VR training in one of the most dangerous industries in terms of work-related accidents, underground coal mining, has reported positive effects of long-term acquisition of learned behavior and successful transfer into real coal mines [13]. A participatory approach to urban planning that utilizes multi-modal traffic simulation has been presented, aiming to bolster road safety, appraise urban design alternatives and assist regulations and environmental policies [42]. VR has also been explored as an innovative learning tool, to address current challenges in the health-care education and training industry, that has the potential to enhance current training methods [27]. All above-mentioned research is relevant to virtual police training by demonstrating the possibility of training cognitive skills and decision making, knowledge transfer to the real world, the opportunity to create ecologically valid but safe and controlled environments and to address the challenges of ever changing training needs.

2.2 Stress Measurement and Induction

When a person experiences stress, their body reacts by going through physiological changes that act to reorient the individual's cognitive and physiological capacities to deal with the stressor. These physiological changes can be quantified by stress markers on three levels: 1) activation of the sympathetic nervous system (SNS), also known as the "fight-or-flight" response, 2) withdrawal of the parasympathetic nervous system (PNS), which drives the relaxation response and 3) activation of the hypothalamic-pituitary-adrenal (HPA) axis, which ensures our body has enough energy and resources, such as glucocorticoids, to deal with the stressful situation [54]. A physiological response to acute stress includes an increase in heart rate (HR), respiration rate (RR), blood pressure (BP), skin temperature (SKT), muscle contraction, electrodermal activity (EDA) and decreased heart rate variability (HRV). Giannakakis et al. [11] offer a broad literature overview of stress detection methods using a variety of bio-signals. Advantages and disadvantages of a variety of sensors and wearables are discussed in articles by Can [6] and Gradl [14]. Results from lab-based studies [20], lab-based VR studies [46] and in-the-wild studies [15] have been published. However, most studies use standardized tests to induce stress, such as public speaking or mental arithmetic exercises [21] instead of contextual, scenario based stressors.

Virtual Reality applications are becoming increasingly popular to train resilience against stress, practice coping techniques and improve overall performance in stressful situations because of their ability to produce realistic and immersive situations yet in controlled environments [3]. Domains in which realistic simulation of stressful environments are important, such as first responders [40], military [35] or aviation and space travel [9,50] have started investigating such stress inoculation and measurement methods. However, the majority of studies are analyzing stress levels after the training and to our current knowledge, none of the existing solutions have a real-time stress level visualization method implemented.

2.3 Stress Visualization as Feedback Tool

Visualization of stress can be used as biofeedback tool to support medical interventions, train resilience against stress or explain certain behavior or reactions. Application of such tools in the work environment have been studied by Xue et al. [52] who applied a HRV-based stress-level indicator to investigate how group workers reflect on their own stress levels as well as organizational stress in the workplace. In their study, participants were asked to gauge their perception of the stress visualization tool, such as the clarity of the information, the impact on their work, their opinions on anonymity and their thoughts on the design. The results showed that the traffic light color scheme (red, yellow, green) made the visualization easy to read and understand and did not interrupt the participants' work. This finding is particularly relevant to our research, as it suggests that a similarly designed stress visualization tool might be easily understood by trainers and not disrupt the complex task of conducting training sessions. However, it is important to note that the context of this study was an office setting, which may differ significantly from the training environment we are focusing on. Sanches et al [39] developed a real-time stress level indicator to give participants the opportunity to reflect on the influence of stress on their behavior pattern. The authors acknowledge that making a robust analysis of stress symptoms based on biosensors outside the laboratory environment can be difficult and suggest such visualizations should be designed with transparency towards the user. For our research this is important and suggests that while stress indicators can be valuable tools to support trainer-trainee interaction, they should not be solely relied upon and trainers must consider the broader context when interpreting stress levels. The potential to use VR as a tool to train coping skills for stress has been established by Gaggioli et al. [10] in the context of medical interventions for nurses and teachers, who perceive their work environment as highly stressful. Although our research is applying such training tools for a different target group and work environment, it provides evidence that immersive technology can be used to mimic stressful work environments and successfully train stress management skills.

Furthermore, various research provides evidence that closed-loop biofeedback systems, which automatically adapt content based on the user's physiological data, can positively impact stress management skills in athletes [38] or provide motivation for physical activity in sports gaming, where, for example, the user's heart rate is used to adjust the game's difficulty [47]. Design and implementation considerations for a stress management bio-feedback system have been explored by Tellez et al. who emphasize the importance of using relevant stressors that are similar to the ones they are exposed to in their day-to-day activities [49]. Munoz et al. [30] propose an approach to a) modulate difficulty levels to increase stress and b) provide visual feedback to practice self-regulation of psycho-physiological effects of stress (e.g. breathing) during a virtual shooting exercise. Quintero et al. [36] have developed a software framework for the VR development platform Unity to display real-time cardiovascular data and companies within the biosignal space (e.g. [4]) have started to develop plug-ins for VR development applications.

Our research prototype will differ in two factors from the ones mentioned above: (a) we have designed a fully integrated user (trainer) experience into a current state-of-the-art training solution and (b) the biofeedback is visualized only in the trainer view to not interrupt the immersion of trainees. Hence representing a training environment that is as realistic as possible.

3   Prototype Concept and Design

To determine if a stress dashboard could improve the overall performance and effectiveness of VR training for DMA, we augmented the project's current virtual training environment with the necessary features and displays. The SHOTPROS project aims to investigate the impact of psychological and contextual human factors (HFs) on the decision-making and acting behavior of police officers under stress and in high-risk operational situations, with the ultimate goal to design better VR training solutions for police officers. The goal of our real-time stress dashboard was to give trainers information on trainees' current stress levels as well as the opportunity to dynamically introduce psychological stress cues (e.g. audio-visual) during the training session. A challenge in designing user-oriented features had been the fact that trainers have a variety of tasks to fulfill during a training session and cannot spend much time or attention on the stress dashboard. In this research, user-centered design methods (see e.g. [2]) played a pivotal role in the development and evaluation of the stress visualization system for VR training. The process began with identifying the needs of end-users', which included trainers and trainees, followed by an iterative design and evaluation approach that incorporated their inputs. Throughout the design process, various prototyping techniques were employed to create mock-ups of the stress visualization dashboard, allowing users to interact with the system and provide constructive feedback. This iterative process of refining the design, based on end-user input, ensured that the final stress visualization system was both functional and user-friendly.

3.1   Requirements Workshop with End-Users and Experts

In the beginning of the SHOTPROS project requirements workshops with six LEAs, including 60 police officers and trainers across Europe, were organized to discuss current training practices, training needs and expert advice from existing VR training systems [53]. Stress measurement and real-time display of trainee's stress levels was considered a must have feature amongst all LEAs and real-time stress manipulation during the training was highly desired.

However, several concerns and restrictions were raised regarding the usability of such a stress dashboard during the training. Especially trainers were concerned with the time and attention needed to interact with a digital device on the training field and the background knowledge needed to interpret bio-signals into meaningful levels of stress. Trainers preferred pre-defined categories such as low, medium and high over a contiguous scale because they did not feel comfortable interpreting a number during the training. A simple "stressed" or "not stressed" categorization was considered as too basic. Three to four categories, ideally distinguishable by colors were considered as helpful.

Furthermore, concerns were raised about the display space such stress indicators and interaction possibilities would take away from their current viewing options. Having to switch between different windows or a separate screen to indicate stress levels (or other performance indicators) was rejected and an unobtrusive integration into current user interfaces a clear requirement. Although the majority of trainers had little experience with VR training at this point, the time available to spend handling a digital device was considered low.

From a trainee's perspective, police officers requested a bio-signal measurement device that would not interfere with their movement or handling their gear (e.g. weapon, handcuffs, radio). Must-have requirements included no loose cabling, nothing on their hands and no experts needed to apply.

Technical experts participating in the workshop raised concerns over the computing power needed to process bio-signals of multiple trainees and their categorization in real-time as well as data transfer protocols potentially interfering with the wireless network needed to operate the VR training environment on a 30×30 m field.

3.2   Stress Level Assessment Panel

Fig. 1. Stress Dashboard: Stress Level Assessment panel (bottom left), Stress Control panel (top left) and Live VR view (center)

Although there is currently no accepted standard evaluation method for acute mental stress [20], HRV is one of the most commonly used biomarkers [11] which has been tested and evaluated in a multitude of studies and systematic reviews [6]. It also has the advantage that it can be measured with a consumer-friendly chest belt instead of complicated electrode systems that need to be placed by experts, as it would be the case for electromyography (EMG) [51] and electrodermal activity (EDA) measurements [17]. To ensure reliable sensor data, the Zephyr bioharness[7] was selected because it is easy to use (chest strap that can be applied by the user), comfortable to wear and provides reliable data, even under movement [31].

To provide users a simple and quick overview of the current status, as highlighted in requirement workshops, the stress level was divided into four plus one categories: normal, increased, high, very high and a label indicating the signal is faulty (Fig. 1 - bottom of left panel). These colors evoke an intuitive reaction in police officers, as they are associated with traffic lights, where red represents

---

[7] https://www.zephyranywhere.com/.

stop, yellow and orange a warning to varying degrees and green go. For easy stress monitoring of individuals as well as group dynamics an icon has been introduced on top of each avatar representing a trainee. The selection of icons (siren, exclamation mark in a triangle, bar chart increasing, thumbs up) represent graphics that police officers are familiar with from their line of work and therefore easy to interpret. The stress score formula and thresholds used for this field trial was calculated based on results from a previous study conducted as part of the SHOTPROS project [41].

3.3   Stress Control Panel

The Stress Control panel (see top left box in Fig. 1) gives trainers the possibility to add or remove stress cues, either ad-hoc with instant playback or trigger zone-based with activation once the trainee passes a certain terrain. These stress cues are activated in the VR scenario as concrete, observable audio and/or visual stimuli (e.g. a dog starts barking, child screaming or phone ringing).

Fig. 2. After Action Review: VR view - bird eye (a), VR view - shoulder view (b), individual statistics (c) and timeline view (d) including event marker (e)

3.4   After Action Review

The visualization of stress needs to be simple enough to quickly grasp for the trainer during the training but detailed enough to be meaningful in the de-briefing after the training, the so-called After Action Review (AAR). Hence the different visualizations as icons above the trainee in the "map view" (see Fig. 2a), "VR view" (Fig. 2b) and detailed numerical information for each trainee (Fig. 2c). In addition, the AAR (Fig. 2) provides the opportunity to show the stress level on a detailed timeline (Fig. 2d) with a playback, fast forward and fast backward button as well as the option to adjust playback speed (bottom left slider) for easy navigation through the review videos in 3D. At the very bottom (Fig. 2e) important events (such as shots fired, stress cue active) are clearly marked on a timeline so trainers can easily jump back and forth between crucial events.

4   User Study and Results

For an initial evaluation of the stress dashboard, a field trial was conducted with the following aims: (a) investigate the feasibility of implementing a real-time stress indicator based on bio-signals into a real VR training environment (b) observe the interaction between the user (trainer) and the prototype dashboard and (c) get feedback from trainers on their user experience.

For the field trial the stress dashboard has been integrated into the SHOT-PROS VR training system. The VR system was developed and provided by RE-liON[8] and set up in a gym hall on the premises of Police North Rhine-Westphalia (LAFP NRW). The training field consisted of a 30×30 m field where trainees, commonly in teams of three to four, train in a full-body VR suit and the trainer watches and instructs them from "the real world". Next to the field is a trainer station (used for the AAR and interaction during the training) and the operator station (the operator steers the training by manipulating the VE and non-player characters, communicates with trainees as the dispatcher and leads them through the initial calibration and tutorial process - see Fig. 3).

Fig. 3. Trainer station (left), Operator station (right)

4.1   Procedure

37 active police officers (12 female, 25 male) age 23 to 44 years (Mean $= 29$, SD $= 5$) participated in the field trial. Their average years of service as a

---

[8] https://www.re-lion.com.

police officer was 7.32 (SD = 4.66) and their current rank police superintendent (Polizeikommissar:in). Seven of the 37 police officers also served as current trainers with a minimum of three years trainer experience. They participated in the study as trainees but received additional questionnaires and interviews to provide their trainer perspective. The VR training sessions was conducted by a senior trainer and two assistant trainers. Training was conducted in teams of three resembling how the officers operate in real life. All studies within the SHOT-PROS project were approved by the Social and Societal Ethics Committee of KU LEUVEN (protocol code G-2019 08 1712, August 27, 2019).

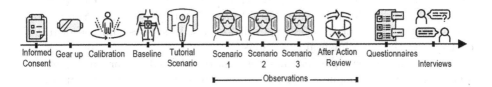

Fig. 4. Infographic Study Procedure

After being introduced to the study and signing the informed consent form, participants filled out a demographic questionnaire and were equipped with a Zephyr chest belt. The belt allowed us to capture participants' heart rate (HR), heart rate variability (HRV) as well as the respiration rate (RR). For HRV, we calculated the root mean square of differences between successive heart-beat intervals (RMSSD). This is a metric for short-term heart rate variation. Lower values of the RMSSD indicate higher stress. These physiological indicators vary amongst individuals [48] and it is therefore necessary to record a baseline for each individual prior to the training. To record the baseline, participants looked at a plain white wall for two minutes with the instruction to breathe normally and not think about anything upsetting [45].

Although the idea was to give trainers the opportunity to manipulate training scenarios on the spot, all trainees went through the same three scenarios, with an increasing amount of stress cues, to create a comparable test environment for this study. In order to use a training procedure that closely resembles a real-world training, scenarios were not randomized but started with the least stressful and ended with the most stressful [5]. Scenarios were designed by an experienced police trainer, using stressors that trainee's would encounter in real-life situations.

All three scenarios were based in the same virtual furniture shop the police officers had been called to, with the task to investigate a disturbance caused by an aggressive person the shop owner reported to the police station. No further information was given to the police officers and the major difference of the three scenarios was the amount and type of stressors placed in the VE. The scenarios started with police officers "virtually" arriving in front of the furniture shop from where they enter and search the shop. Stress cues in the first scenario include a perpetrator with a knife, a slightly injured person and a small amount of blood. In the second scenario the victim's injuries are a lot more severe with more blood spread around the shop. Additionally, a confused bystander is in the shop and screams can be heard in the back of the shop. The third scenario, designed to be highly stressful, include several injured victims and bystanders, screams coming from several different directions, a phone ringing constantly and the perpetrator holding and shooting a gun. The perpetrator was played by a human role-player that reacted to police officers in a realistic manner. Bystanders were represented by non-player characters. The lengths each group required to take control of the situation and complete the scenario varied greatly (between two and eight minutes) from team to team and scenario (scenario 1 (M = 2.29, SD = 0.42), scenario 2 (M = 2.61, SD = 1.08), scenario 3 (M = 4.5, SD = 1.63)), demonstrating some of the challenges of in-the-wild studies and the degree of control over the experimental conditions [7].

After each scenario, participants were asked to fill out a short questionnaire, including Visual Analogue Scales (VAS) for stress [18]. Once participants completed all three scenarios the group moved on to the AAR at the trainer station, where they reviewed each scenario and discussed trainee's individual and group performance. The stress dashboard was explained in the beginning of the AAR and stress levels were continuously monitored throughout the review process. All trainees were in overall agreement with their individual stress level displayed throughout the training session. After AAR was completed, all participants filled out questionnaires related to overall usability and technology acceptance. The seven participating trainers were asked to fill out additional questions asking for feedback on the perception of the stress dashboard, specifically the stress monitoring and manipulation features.

4.2   Data Analysis and Results

Table 1 provides the descriptive statistic of VAS for stress, HR (mean & max), HRV (mean & min) for each scenario. HR and HRV values are the numbers relative to each trainee's baseline. For the baseline the mean of the full two minutes was taken [23]. Change in HR and HRV were calculated over 30-second windows, moving every second, as recommended in the literature for short-term stress measurements [45].

To investigate if there is a difference in the duration trainees manifest in each stress category across the three different scenarios, we calculated the percentage of time each trainee exhibited each stress level for each scenario (see Fig. 5).

The results of the Repeated Measures ANOVA show that there are statistically significant differences in the amount of time different levels of stress (green, yellow, orange, red) were displayed ($F(3, 69) = 15.27$, $p < 0.0001$), across different conditions (scenario 1, scenario 2, scenario 3) ($F(2, 46) = 23.00$, $p < 0.0001$), and the interaction between stress level (color) and condition (scenario) is significant ($F(6, 138) = 4.50$, $p < 0.001$). The post-hoc Tukey HSD test revealed a significant difference in time displayed as "green" between condition scenario 1 and scenario 3 ($p = .016$), with condition scenario1 having a higher mean time

Table 1. Descriptive statistics of subjective and physiological measurements for three scenarios with different stress levels.

		Scenario 1	Scenario 2	Scenario 3
VAS Stress	n	37	36	35
	mean	25.50	39.50	52.12
	SD	16.59	20.86	24.13
% change in HR (mean values)	n	24	24	24
	mean	0.12	0.18	0.20
	SD	0.10	0.13	0.15
% change in HR (max values)	mean	0.28	0.37	0.41
	SD	0.11	0.16	0.17
% change in HRV (min values)	mean	−0.59	−0.68	−0.73
	SD	0.22	0.14	0.15
% change in HRV (mean values)	mean	−0.08	−0.11	0.04
	SD	0.32	0.52	1.01

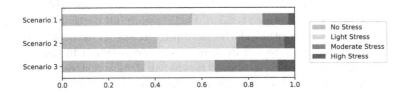

Fig. 5. Percentage of time spent in each stress level by scenario. (Color figure online)

displayed in "green". The differences between other conditions (scenario 1 and scenario 2, scenario 2 and scenario 3) and stress levels (green, yellow, orange, red) were not statistically significant.

Figures 6(a)–(d) show the trajectories of the stress score for four of the participants in each of the three scenarios. As can be seen in Fig. 6, the stress level varies between the three scenarios, with scenario 3 exhibiting the highest values.

4.3   Observations and Feedback from Trainers

Feedback and observations mentioned in the following paragraph were collected from the seven participating trainers through questionnaires and interviews. Each trainer actively participated in a training session and observed other groups train.

Observations showed that the person conducting the VR training spends most of the training time on the field to ensure trainees don't accidentally bump into each other. Therefore not much time to interact with the stress dashboard at the trainer station is available. Feedback from participating trainers suggested it would be useful to have two trainers (one on the field and one at the trainer

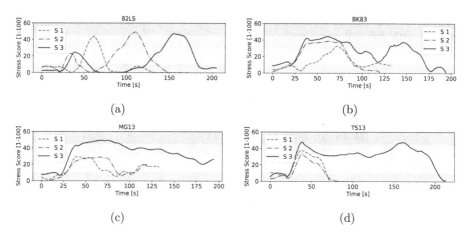

Fig. 6. Examples of stress level (represented by colors) for four trainees. Each trainee completed three different scenarios as indicated by the different lines.

station) or a mobile device that can be carried around to be able to engage with trainees during the training session. Furthermore, all participating trainers indicated a positive perception of the flexibility to add or remove stress cues, even though this was only tested in form of a demonstration in the field trial. Four trainers expressed concerns about tracking all deployed stress cues within a scenario, suggesting a feature that allows trainers to locate them could improve the system's effectiveness and user experience.

During the AAR, where trainer and trainees gather around the trainer station to review and de-brief the training, the stress dashboard was frequently used to point out stress levels in situations where trainee's made mistakes or reacted irrationally. Trainers as well as trainees reported seeing a correlation between the onset of a stress cues and the stress level of themselves and other trainees, when reviewing the training sessions in the AAR.

5 Discussion

A field trial was undertaken to assess various facets of employing a prototype stress dashboard within an operational virtual reality training context for law enforcement officers. This evaluation included considerations such as data and analytical requirements to give trainers the possibility to interpret and monitor trainee's stress levels in real-time, preferences regarding data visualization and the subsequent impact these elements have on the dynamics of trainer-trainee interactions. The primary objective was to elucidate the functional efficacy and potential enhancements of the stress dashboard tool in a practical training environment.

5.1   Real-Time Stress Analysis of a VR Training and Stress Level Visualization

A current challenge in analysing and visualizing trainee's stress levels in real-time is identifying the appropriate bio-signals and classifying them into meaningful categories indicating trainee's current level of stress. In this study we have applied a stress score developed during a lab-based study based on a combination of HR and HRV [41]. Although HRV is considered to be one of the most important indicators of stress [20] other measurements such as EDA [17] have also shown to reflect on autonomic nervous system (ANS) activation. To get more accurate indication of current stress levels, a multi-level bio-signal measurement method, based on bio-signals discussed in the current literature [11], could be an alternative solution and should be tested in future work.

From the trainers perspective the most important factor was to have a stress level indicator that is based on reliable biosignals that can be measured with user-friendly wearable devices. As the sport-psychological literature suggested [31], the Zephyr bio-harness used in our studies proved itself as a reliable, yet comfortable to wear ECG device that would record acceptable signals even under strong physical movement. The already in-built HR confidence score provided great support in assessing the validity of the data and Bluetooth connection made it easy to integrate into the VR platform to transfer and display data in real-time.

Regarding the visualization of stress levels within the stress dashboard, the end-users expressed a preference for a straightforward categorical display, as opposed to a more complex continuous numerical representation. This lead to the creation of a color-coded, traffic-light style categorization system, representing low, medium, high, and severe stress levels. Each category was visualized as distinct, sizeable buttons corresponding to individual trainees. To ensure accessibility for individuals with color vision deficiency, supplemental stress level indicator icons were also incorporated.

The hypothesis that operational training scenarios that were designed to expose trainees to different levels of stress (low, medium, high) would result in different stress levels shown in our stress dashboard was supported by the study results. We were able to observe a significant difference between stress level category (green, yellow, orange, red) and scenario (low, medium, high) indicating that the stress level experienced by trainees depended on the specific scenario they were exposed to.

The post-hoc test provided more nuanced insight, revealing a significant difference in time displayed as "green" (see Fig. 5) between the low and high stress scenario. However, the lack of significant differences between other conditions and colors suggests that the differentiation of stress levels may not be as clear-cut for all scenarios. It could also indicate that four stress level categories (green, yellow, orange, red) may be too nuanced. When investigating the study results we tested what would happen if we combined the stress categories orange and red, because of the little amount of time red was displayed across all scenarios. Results showed that in addition to green being significantly different across all three scenarios also orange/red would become significantly different. Another argument that would speak for this simplification of the stress categories is the urge voiced by the trainers to make the stress indicator as simple and easy to read as possible.

5.2 Trainer-Trainee Interaction During Training

Trainers found the stress dashboard to be a useful tool during the AAR, as it helped them identify and discuss specific instances where trainees experienced high stress levels that potentially led to mistakes or irrational decisions. For example, during the most stressful scenario (scenario 3), participants were exposed to a wider variety of stress cues that demanded their attention. While approaching the building in the VE, the participants heard screams from different directions, saw injured victims and heard gun shots. While attempting to regulate elevated levels of stress, participants had to make appropriate decisions on how to solve the situation. In this instance, the trainees could choose to enter the building, find the suspects, and stop the threat or decide to call for back-up and wait until additional resources arrive to enter the building. Oftentimes, increased levels of stress influence the decision-making and acting process because the attention dedicated to solving the situation becomes narrower and focused on threat-related information such as the gun of the suspect [34]. To improve decision-making and acting under stress, trainers should be able to manipulate the stress levels in VR by adding more stress cues to create training environments which force trainees to make split-second decisions and act upon them adequately. Although trainers were not able to actively add or remove stress cues from the scenarios during the training, to ensure comparable training scenarios across all participants, they experienced the concept through the three different scenarios and were able to test the feature after the training with positive feedback.

However, several practical challenges were identified in the implementation of the stress dashboard during training. Trainers reported that they spent most of their time on the training field, leaving them little opportunity to interact with the stress dashboard at the trainer station. They suggested having two trainers, one on the field and one at the trainer station, or employing a mobile device to access the dashboard and engage with trainees during the training session. This feedback highlights the need for further refinement of the stress dashboard's design and implementation to better accommodate the practical constraints of the training environment.

5.3 Challenges and Limitations

The field trial also highlighted several challenges and limitations of the current prototype design, its implementation and evaluation in a in-the-wild study format.

Individual Differences in Stress Perception and Physiological Response. Stress is a complex construct and cannot be identified through a concrete value or biomarker (as it is the case for e.g. blood sugar or oxygen levels) [19]. On the one hand, the perception of threats will vary amongst individuals. For example, someone who is uncomfortable around dogs may experience a higher stress level when encountering one at a scene of investigation. On the other hand, physiological manifestation of stress is heterogeneous. Factors such as age, physical fitness and overall well-being, current cognitive performance, chronic stress and resilience play a significant factor in short-term physiological response to challenging situations [45]. Given that each individual possesses a unique stress threshold, crafting universally applicable stress level categories poses a significant challenge when designing for a diverse range of individuals.

Furthermore, no stress level benchmark for optimal learning performance seems to exist [16]. These may differ depending on the task and learning goal [8]. This may be especially relevant when applying our approach and stress model to other industries (e.g. medical first responders, pilots or health care workers) and trainees with different experiences and previous exposure to stressful situations. It is therefore our recommendation to never fully rely on an automated stress-level manipulation system but to keep the trainer in the loop. While several fully automated closed-feedback loop systems exist to practise relaxation techniques with the goal to reduce stress [29], being overloaded with stressful situations can lead to a negative training outcome and in the worst case long-term trauma, even if threats are represented in a VE.

Furthermore, movement artifacts present a significant challenge in real-world training scenarios with intense physical movement, resulting in noisy data and affecting heart rate measurements [23]. While some post-study analysis techniques exist to handle this [25], their application to our real-time stress indicator was problematic and untested in our field study. In future work we aim to explore techniques to minimize movement artifacts.

Data Privacy and Ethical Considerations. Displaying personal data like HR, HRV and resulting stress indication in a team setting raises ethical concerns. While police officers participating in our studies reported this to be common practice in their current training routine, others in different industries or regions might not be. Issues like workplace bullying and peer pressure must be considered in this context [28].

Furthermore, storage of data must be evaluated and aligned with company policies and local regulatory guidelines. Although it seems beneficial to store and be able to compare training data and progress of individuals over time to enable further personalization of training, this will require additional data security and safety measures [26].

Impact on Training. The use of the stress dashboard extends the training setup time due to additional equipment, baseline recording and occasional connection troubleshooting. For industries with limited training time, the trade-off must be evaluated. Impact on trainers must be considered as well. Conducting a (virtual) simulation training and observing each trainee to give feedback to in the AAR is challenging as is. Adding cognitive tasks may need practicing for trainers. Especially interacting with a display to add or remove stress cues has been mentioned several times. While we did not give trainers this tool in our studies, for reasons mentioned above, it has been casually tested. Although trainers had a strong preference for the feature itself, the mechanism operating the display at the trainer station has been considered bothersome. Future work should investigate different interaction possibilities (e.g. portable displays or voice command) to simplify this task. Stress cue and timing suggestions steered through artificial intelligence could be another solution. However, as previously mentioned, we don't recommend to fully automate this process but still give the trainer the option of accepting or declining the computer generated recommendation.

6   Conclusion and Future Work

We have described the development of a stress dashboard prototype, designed to enhance VR simulation training. This innovative tool aims to offer real-time insights into trainees' stress levels and provide trainers with the opportunity to modify these levels interactively, thereby fostering a more dynamic and responsive training environment. The stress dashboard proved beneficial in the AAR, aiding trainers in identifying specific instances of high stress and facilitating productive discussions with trainees.

Nevertheless, the trial also revealed practical challenges with the implementation, particularly around the trainers' ability to interact with the dashboard during the training. Feedback from trainers suggests that future iterations should consider the tool's mobility and accessibility in the training environment. This study highlighted the complexity and individual nature of stress perception and physiological responses.

Future work should focus on refining the system to account for these individual differences more effectively by potentially adding additional bio-signals to refine the classification of stress responses. As the optimal stress level for learning performance can vary depending on the task and learning goal, the system should retain a degree of human oversight rather than being fully automated. Insights and learnings gained from this research bear potential applicability across a range of domains that expose users to stressful situations. As VR technology finds its broader adoption, we anticipate an increase in the use of VR for training in diverse sectors.

References

1. Baldwin, S., et al.: A reasonable officer: examining the relationships among stress, training, and performance in a highly realistic lethal force scenario. Front. Psychol. **12**, 759132 (2022). https://doi.org/10.3389/fpsyg.2021.759132

2. Baxter, K., Courage, C., Caine, K.: Understanding Your Users: A Practical Guide to User Research Methods. Morgan Kaufmann, Burlington (2015)

3. Binsch, O., Bottenheft, C., Bottenheft, L., Boonekamp, R., Valk, P.: Using a controlled virtual reality simulation platform to induce, measure and feedback stress responses of soldiers. J. Sci. Med. Sport **20**, S124–S125 (2017)

4. Biosignals, P.: Virtual reality and biosignals: The future is here! (2022). https://www.pluxbiosignals.com/blogs/informative/virtual-reality-biosignals

5. Brown, B., Reeves, S., Sherwood, S.: Into the wild: challenges and opportunities for field trial methods. In: Conference on Human Factors in Computing Systems - Proceedings, pp. 1657–1666 (2011). https://doi.org/10.1145/1978942.1979185

6. Can, Y.S., Arnrich, B., Ersoy, C.: Stress detection in daily life scenarios using smart phones and wearable sensors: a survey. J. Biomed. Inf. **92**, 103139 (2019)

7. Chamberlain, A., Crabtree, A., Rodden, T., Jones, M., Rogers, Y.: Research in the wild: Understanding 'in the wild' approaches to design and development. In: Proceedings of the Designing Interactive Systems Conference, DIS 2012, pp. 795–796 (2012). https://doi.org/10.1145/2317956.2318078

8. Di Nota, P.M., Huhta, J.M.: Complex motor learning and police training: applied, cognitive, and clinical perspectives. Front. Psychol. **10**, 1797 (2019). https://doi.org/10.3389/fpsyg.2019.01797

9. Finseth, T., Dorneich, M.C., Keren, N., Franke, W.D., Vardeman, S.B.: Manipulating stress responses during spaceflight training with virtual stressors. Appl. Sci. (Switzerland) **12**(5), 2289 (2022). https://doi.org/10.3390/app12052289

10. Gaggioli, A., et al.: Experiential virtual scenarios with real-time monitoring (inter-reality) for the management of psychological stress: a block randomized controlled trial. J. Med. Internet Res. **16**(7), e3235 (2014). https://doi.org/10.2196/jmir.3235

11. Giannakakis, G., Grigoriadis, D., Giannakaki, K., Simantiraki, O., Roniotis, A., Tsiknakis, M.: Review on psychological stress detection using biosignals. IEEE Trans. Affect. Comput. **13**(1), 440–460 (2022). https://doi.org/10.1109/TAFFC.2019.2927337

12. Giessing, L.: The potential of virtual reality for police training under stress. In: Interventions, Training, and Technologies for Improved Police Well-Being and Performance, pp. 102–124 (2021). https://doi.org/10.4018/978-1-7998-6820-0.ch006

13. Grabowski, A., Jankowski, J.: Virtual Reality-based pilot training for underground coal miners. Saf. Sci. **72**, 310–314 (2015). https://doi.org/10.1016/j.ssci.2014.09.017

14. Gradl, S., Wirth, M., Richer, R., Rohleder, N., Eskofier, B.M.: An overview of the feasibility of permanent, real-time, unobtrusive stress measurement with current wearables. In: PervasiveHealth: Pervasive Computing Technologies for Healthcare, pp. 360–365 (2019). https://doi.org/10.1145/3329189.3329233

15. Healey, J.A., Picard, R.W.: Detecting stress during real-world driving tasks using physiological sensors. IEEE Trans. Intell. Transp. Syst. **6**(2), 156–166 (2005). https://doi.org/10.1109/TITS.2005.848368

16. Hernando-Gallego, F., Artés-Rodríguez, A.: Individual performance calibration using physiological stress signals. ArXiv abs/1507.03482 (2015)

17. Hossain, M.B., Kong, Y., Posada-Quintero, H.F., Chon, K.H.: Comparison of electrodermal activity from multiple body locations based on standard EDA indices' quality and robustness against motion artifact. Sensors **22**, 3177 (2022). https://doi.org/10.3390/s22093177

18. Houtman, I., Bakker, F.: The anxiety thermometer: a validation study. J. Pers. Assess. **53**, 575–582 (1989)

19. Janssens, K.M.E., van der Velden, P.G., Taris, R., van Veldhoven, M.J.P.M.: Resilience among police officers: a critical systematic review of used concepts, measures, and predictive values of resilience. J. Police Crim. Psychol. **36**(1), 24–40 (2018). https://doi.org/10.1007/s11896-018-9298-5

20. Kim, H.G., Cheon, E.J., Bai, D.S., Lee, Y.H., Koo, B.H.: Stress and heart rate variability: a meta-analysis and review of the literature. Psychiatry Invest. **15**(3), 235–245 (2018). https://doi.org/10.30773/pi.2017.08.17

21. Kirschbaum, C., Pirke, K.M., Hellhammer, D.H.: The "Trier social stress test" - a tool for investigating psychobiological stress responses in a laboratory setting. Neuropsychobiology **28**(1–2), 76–81 (1993). https://doi.org/10.1159/000119004

22. Kleygrewe, L., Oudejans, R.R., Koedijk, M., Hutter, R.I.: Police training in practice: organization and delivery according to European law enforcement agencies. Front. Psychol. **12**(January), 1–13 (2022). https://doi.org/10.3389/fpsyg.2021.798067

23. Laborde, S., Mosley, E., Thayer, J.F.: Heart rate variability and cardiac vagal tone in psychophysiological research - recommendations for experiment planning, data analysis, and data reporting. Front. Psychol. **8**, 1–18 (2017). https://doi.org/10.3389/fpsyg.2017.00213

24. Lazarus, R.S., Folkman, S.: Stress, Appraisal, and Coping. Springer, Heidelberg (1984)

25. Linssen, L., Landman, A., van Baardewijk, J.U., Bottenheft, C., Binsch, O.: Using accelerometry and heart rate data for real-time monitoring of soldiers' stress in a dynamic military virtual reality scenario. Multimedia Tools Appl. **81**, 1–18 (2022). https://doi.org/10.1007/s11042-022-12705-6

26. Malik, N., Tripathi, S.N., Kar, A.K., Gupta, S.: Impact of artificial intelligence on employees working in industry 4.0 led organizations. Int. J. Manpower **43**(2), 334–354 (2022). https://doi.org/10.1108/IJM-03-2021-0173

27. Mantovani, F., Castelnuovo, G., Gaggioli, A., Riva, G.: Virtual reality training for health-care professionals. Cyberpsychol. Behav. **6**(4), 389–395 (2003). https://doi.org/10.1089/109493103322278772

28. McIvor, K.M.: Bullying in the Police Service: Constructs and Processes. Ph.D. thesis, University of Surrey (United Kingdom) (2004)

29. Michela, A., et al.: Deep-breathing biofeedback trainability in a virtual-reality action game: a single-case design study with police trainers. Front. Psychol. **13**(February), 1–17 (2022). https://doi.org/10.3389/fpsyg.2022.806163

30. Muñoz, J.E., Quintero, L., Stephens, C.L., Pope, A.T.: A psychophysiological model of firearms training in police officers: a virtual reality experiment for biocybernetic adaptation. Front. Psychol. **11**(April), 1–14 (2020). https://doi.org/10.3389/fpsyg.2020.00683

31. Nazari, G., Bobos, P., MacDermid, J.C., Sinden, K.E., Richardson, J., Tang, A.: Psychometric properties of the Zephyr bioharness device: A systematic review. BMC Sports Sci. Med. Rehabil. **10**(1), 4–11 (2018). https://doi.org/10.1186/s13102-018-0094-4

32. Nguyen, Q., Jaspaert, E., Murtinger, M., Schrom-Feiertag, H., Egger-Lampl, S., Tscheligi, M.: Stress out: translating real-world stressors into audio-visual stress cues in VR for police training. In: Ardito, C., et al. (eds.) INTERACT 2021. LNCS, vol. 12933, pp. 551–561. Springer, Cham (2021). https://doi.org/10.1007/978-3-030-85616-8_32

33. Nieuwenhuys, A., Oudejans, R.R.: Effects of anxiety on handgun shooting behavior of police officers: a pilot study. Anxiety Stress Coping **23**(2), 225–233 (2010)

34. Nieuwenhuys, A., Savelsbergh, G.J.P., Oudejans, R.R.D.: Shoot or don't shoot? why police officers are more inclined to shoot when they are anxious. Emotion (Washington, D.C.) **12**(4), 827–33 (2012). https://doi.org/10.1037/a0025699. https://www.ncbi.nlm.nih.gov/pubmed/22023363

35. Pallavicini, F., Argenton, L., Toniazzi, N., Aceti, L., Mantovani, F.: Virtual reality applications for stress management training in the military. Aeros. Med. Human Perform. **87**(12), 1021–1030 (2016). https://doi.org/10.3357/AMHP.4596.2016

36. Quintero, L., Papapetrou, P., Munoz, J.E.: Open-source physiological computing framework using heart rate variability in mobile virtual reality applications. In: Proceedings - 2019 IEEE International Conference on Artificial Intelligence and Virtual Reality, AIVR 2019 (iv), pp. 126–133 (2019). https://doi.org/10.1109/AIVR46125.2019.00027

37. Regal, G., et al.: VR [We Are] training - workshop on collaborative virtual training for challenging contexts. In: Extended Abstracts of the 2022 CHI Conference on Human Factors in Computing Systems. CHI EA 2022. Association for Computing Machinery (2022). https://doi.org/10.1145/3491101.3503710

38. Rijken, N.H., et al.: Increasing performance of professional soccer players and elite track and field athletes with peak performance training and biofeedback: a pilot study. Appl. Psychophysiol. Biofeedback **41**(4), 421–430 (2016). https://doi.org/10.1007/s10484-016-9344-y

39. Sanches, P., et al.: Mind the body! designing a mobile stress management application encouraging personal reflection. In: DIS 2010 - Proceedings of the 8th ACM Conference on Designing Interactive Systems, pp. 47–56 (2010). https://doi.org/10.1145/1858171.1858182

40. Schneeberger, M., et al.: First responder situation reporting in virtual reality training with evaluation of cognitive-emotional stress using psychophysiological measures. Cogn. Comput. Internet Things **43**, 73 (2022). https://doi.org/10.54941/ahfe1001841

41. Schrom-Feiertag, H., Murtinger, M., Zechner, O., Uhl, J., Nguyen, Q., Kemperman, B.: D4.5 - real-time training progress assessment tool. Technical report (2021). https://shotpros.eu/wp-content/uploads/2022/04/SHOTPROS_D4.5-Real-Time-Training-Progress-Assessment-Tool_v1.0.pdf, deliverable to the European Commission Horizon 2020 project SHOTPROS

42. Schrom-Feiertag, H., Stubenschrott, M., Regal, G., Matyus, T., Seer, S.: An interactive and responsive virtual reality environment for participatory urban planning. In: Proceedings of the Symposium on Simulation for Architecture and Urban Design SimAUD, pp. 119–125 (2020)

43. Schwabe, L., Wolf, O.T.: Stress and multiple memory systems: From "thinking" to "doing.". Trends Cogn. Sci. **17**(2), 60 (2013)

44. Schwarz, S., Regal, G., Kempf, M., Schatz, R.: Learning success in immersive virtual reality training environments: practical evidence from automotive assembly. In: ACM International Conference Proceeding Series (2020). https://doi.org/10.1145/3419249.3420182

45. Shaffer, F., Meehan, Z.M., Zerr, C.L.: A critical review of ultra-short-term heart rate variability norms research. Front. Neurosci. **14**(November), 1–11 (2020). https://doi.org/10.3389/fnins.2020.594880

46. Sharma, N., Gedeon, T.: Modeling stress recognition in typical virtual environments. In: Proceedings of the 2013 7th International Conference on Pervasive Computing Technologies for Healthcare and Workshops, PervasiveHealth 2013, pp. 17–24 (2013). https://doi.org/10.4108/icst.pervasivehealth.2013.252011

47. Stach, T., Graham, T.C., Yim, J., Rhodes, R.E.: Heart rate control of exercise video games. In: Proceedings - Graphics Interface, pp. 125–132 (2009)

48. Tegegne, B.S., Man, T., van Roon, A.M., Riese, H., Snieder, H.: Determinants of heart rate variability in the general population: the lifelines cohort study. Heart Rhythm **15**(10), 1552–1558 (2018). https://doi.org/10.1016/j.hrthm.2018.05.006

49. Téllez, A.M., Tentori, M.E., Castro, L.A.: Stress management training in athletes: design considerations for VR biofeedback systems. In: ACM International Conference Proceeding Series (2021). https://doi.org/10.1145/3492724.3492730

50. van Weelden, E., Alimardani, M., Wiltshire, T.J., Louwerse, M.M.: Advancing the adoption of virtual reality and neurotechnology to improve flight training. In: Proceedings of the 2021 IEEE International Conference on Human-Machine Systems, ICHMS 2021, pp. 8–11 (2021). https://doi.org/10.1109/ICHMS53169.2021.9582658

51. Wijsman, J., Grundlehner, B., Hermens, H., Wijsman, J.: Trapezius Muscle EMG as Predictor of Mental Stress (2010)

52. Xue, M., Liang, R.H., Hu, J., Yu, B., Feijs, L.: Understanding how groupworkers reflect on organizational stress with a shared, anonymous heart rate variability data visualization. In: Conference on Human Factors in Computing Systems - Proceedings (2022). https://doi.org/10.1145/3491101.3503576

53. Zechner, O., Kleygrewe, L., Jaspaert, E., Schrom-Feiertag, H., Hutter, R.I.V., Tscheligi, M.: Enhancing operational police training in high stress situations with virtual reality: experiences, tools and guidelines. Multimodal Technol. Interact. **7**(2), 14 (2023). https://doi.org/10.3390/mti7020014. https://www.mdpi.com/2414-4088/7/2/14

54. Ziegler, M.G.: 50 - psychological stress and the autonomic nervous system. In: Robertson, D., Biaggioni, I., Burnstock, G., Low, P.A. (eds.) Primer on the Autonomic Nervous System, 2nd edn., pp. 189–190. Academic Press, San Diego (2004). https://doi.org/10.1016/B978-012589762-4/50051-7. https://www.sciencedirect.com/science/article/pii/B9780125897624500517

VR for HR – A Case Study of Human Resource Development Professionals Using Virtual Reality for Social Skills Training in the Workplace

Britta Nordin Forsberg[1]([⊠]) [iD], Anders Lundström[2] [iD], and Jan Gulliksen[3] [iD]

[1] Mälardalen University, Universitetsplan 1, 722 20 Västerås, Sweden
britta.nordin.forsberg@mdu.se
[2] Umeå University, Campustorget 5, 901 87 Umeå, Sweden
[3] KTH Royal Institute of Technology, Lindstedtsvägen 3, 100 44 Stockholm, Sweden

Abstract. The Human Resource (HR) area has made little use of innovative technologies to develop its processes, routines and education. However, we believe that digital tools such as Virtual Reality (VR) can play an important role in developing social aspects of work. We have investigated Human Resource Development Professionals' (HRD-Ps') perception of using a VR-prototype for training of social skills in the workplace. A digital three-dimensional world was designed for the study participants, in which they interacted with agents to train social skills in the workplace. Study participants explored a VR-prototype through the usage of head-mounted devices (HMD). We collected the designer's description of the intended design element of the VR prototype and pre- and post-intervention questionnaire from the study participants and conducted a top-down thematic analysis. The three intended design elements 1) focus on the training experience, 2) learning-depth through emotional response for engagement and motivation, and 3) perspective-taking enabled by game design, were confirmed and reflected upon by the HRD-Ps'. Additionally, using VR for social skills training in the workplace was recognized as innovative, and could have the capacity to position an organization as being in the forefront of digitalization. The conclusion is that VR has a potential to create engagement and provide insights in HR matters, but further studies are needed to show the full power and potential in using VR for HR matters.

Keywords: Virtual Reality · Human Resource Development · Master Suppression Techniques · Organization · Digitalization

1 Introduction

Virtual Reality (VR) has become an easy to use, accessible and available technology, not only for advanced technological applications, but also for everyday applications and games. VR has been introduced into fields such as the construction industry (Behzadi 2016), healthcare (Wong et al. 2018), and elderly care (Lundström et al. 2021) due to the obvious benefits of using VR for physical representation of three-dimensional spaces

© The Author(s), under exclusive license to Springer Nature Switzerland AG 2023
J. Abdelnour Nocera et al. (Eds.): INTERACT 2023, LNCS 14145, pp. 231–251, 2023.
https://doi.org/10.1007/978-3-031-42293-5_17

and objects. We have, however, not seen much use of it for administrative or Human Resource (HR) related work tasks yet, but it is probably only a matter of time before the development of VR for more everyday applications within the workplace will explode. We wanted to investigate the potential of using VR for the social aspect of organizations. As opposed to dealing with 3-dimensional (3D) spaces and objects, the social perspective in organizations is about human interaction – which is subtle and intangible compared to interaction with a concrete physical representation. In this paper, we investigate the introduction of VR for social skills training in the workplace by conducting a case study of Human Resource Development Professionals' (HRD-Ps') views on its potential.

1.1 Purpose and Research Questions

The purpose of this study is to investigate the potential of introducing innovative technologies in the field of Human Resource Development (HRD) in terms of Virtual Reality (VR) for social skills training in the workplace. We have investigated HRD-Ps' views on its potential based on experiencing a VR prototype. These are our research questions:

1. What are the critical elements in the design process of this VR prototype for social skills training in the workplace?
2. Based on the experience of using this VR prototype, what are HRD-Ps' views on the potential of using VR for HR matters?

The analytical level of this study is organizational, rather than individual or societal. These three levels are interlinked – an organization consists of its individuals, and organizations are essential elements of society – nevertheless our interest and focus in this article is social skills training processes in organizations rather than social skills at the individual psychological level.

2   Theoretical Underpinning

Theoretically, this paper is based on research on digitalization of the workplace and particularly on the use of VR in HR. Additionally, it is based on theories and practices on social skills in the workplace and HRD. In the subsequent section, we will provide the theoretical background and the conceptual framework upon which we base our reasoning.

2.1   Digitalization

Before the 2010s, the concept of digitalization was not used to any significant extent, neither in practice nor in research. The prevailing concept was computerization, defined by inserting computers into our existing operations without much consideration of how the operations themselves are affected. Despite the fact that it has been known for more than half a century that you cannot change technology without understanding the impact it will have on people and their skills, on business and on the organization of work (Leavitt 1988). In the era of computerization, development issues linked to information technology (IT) were usually referred to an IT manager rather than seen as the responsibility of an organization's leadership as a whole. One of the most important changes that digitalization, as a concept, entails is the realization that it is no longer just about technology, and not only the IT department's responsibility. Digitalization is a central component of business and organizational development, where technological opportunities play a central part.

There are two definitions of digitalization. Information digitalization (or digitization) refers to transforming analog information into digital information. Information becomes structured, searchable, and accessible through digital channels. Societal digitalization, on the other hand, is the change in society, working life, technology use, and new business conditions that arise through the opportunities digital technology provides. This article focuses on societal digitalization within working life. Digital technology provides opportunities to work in completely different ways than previously possible, as well as in completely new ways. The Digitalization Commission of the Swedish Government defines digitalization as "...the societal and human-changing process that is gradually becoming more and more difficult to distinguish at all from any part of life. This means that individuals and organizations can communicate and exchange information with other people, organizations, and their surroundings in completely new ways. Digitalization and the use of IT-based solutions can contribute to increasing accessibility and efficiency both in companies and in public administration." (Gulliksen et al. 2014).

Digitalization is a more pervasive transformation than we have ever seen before. Opposing or trivializing the change that digitalization entails can be dangerous, and any business that does not take heed of the need to change and develop can become marginalized or outcompeted. It can be a matter of survival for an organization, or perhaps even for an entire industry. Embracing digitalization as an engine of change in business can have major positive effects.

2.2 Social Skills in the Workplace

Collaborative skills among employees are a key strategic advantage in any organization (Kim & McLean 2015). The terminology for training in this area varies throughout the research field. Common terms include social skills training (Riggio 2020), soft skills training (Carlyon & Opperman 2020; Berdanier 2022) and interpersonal skills training (Schmid Mast et al. 2018). In this paper, we use the term social skills training in the workplace to define the desired interpersonal employee behaviors relating to effective collaboration and relationship building.

Globalization has affected the structure of workplaces as well as the mentality of individual employees and how they interact with others (Shliakhovchuk 2021). Being able to effectively communicate, including with those who are culturally different from us, is a necessary skill in a globalized business world where workplaces continue to diversify (Lichy & Khvatova 2019; Szkudlarek et al. 2020). While diversity adds value in the form of increased creativity and satisfaction at work, it is associated with more conflict around work tasks and sometimes with less effective communication (Stahl et al. 2010). Training employees in social skills, and imparting organizational values through training, could lead to enhancing the positive effects of diversity through lessening the potentially detrimental effects of communication difficulties.

2.3   The Master Suppression Techniques and Their Counter Strategies

One particular kind of social interaction that can be very detrimental in a workplace setting is the use of so-called master suppression techniques (Ås 1978). This term refers to manipulative social behaviors used to assert dominance, often in a covert way. Ås defined five master suppression techniques: 1) Making invisible: silencing someone by ignoring them, another person taking credit for a suggestion made by the person being made invisible. 2) Ridiculing: portraying someone or their views in a ridiculing way. 3) Withholding information: purposely not giving someone enough information, excluding someone from decision making. 4) Double bind: punishing someone for their actions and/or characteristics regardless of what they do. 5) Heaping blame/Putting to shame: blaming and/or shaming someone excessively for their actions or characteristics, suggesting that they bear the responsibility themselves if they are subjected to harmful behavior.

Counter strategies to each of Ås' master suppression techniques have been proposed (Amnéus et al. 2004) and are defined as follows: 1) Taking up space: drawing attention to the fact that you are being ignored by commenting on or questioning the behavior, falling completely silent if others are meant to listen to you but act distracted. 2) Questioning: asserting yourself by staying serious, displaying your own expertise, asking the person ridiculing you to elaborate on or further explain what they said. 3) Cards on the table: pointing out how information was withheld, asking everyone involved to provide the information they have, referring to formal roles and responsibilities when it comes to decision making. 4) Break free of the pattern: requesting clear information on expectations, stating current priorities, and discussing their impact. 5) Intellectualization: making yourself aware that blame and shame are being applied to you by someone else (since it is common to think these feelings only come from within), distancing yourself from your feelings and analyzing the situation intellectually, looking for hidden agendas.

The master suppression techniques and the proposed counter strategies constitute a theoretical foundation for the game design of the VR prototype in this study, with a theoretical foundation that sprung from Bourdieu's theory of practice (1977) applied to a relational power perspective on organizations (Nordin Forsberg 2020).

2.4   The Evolvement of VR for HR for Efficiency and Scalability

Developing social skills in employees and leaders is linked to the field HRD. HRD deals with creating positive organizational change through developing its employees and is therefore well suited to handle organizational efforts within the area of social skills and interpersonal change (Kim & McLean 2015). According to Schmid Mast et al. (2018), organizations across the globe spend a considerable proportion of their budget on training their workforce. One third is spent on leadership and management development, in which an important element is social skills training. Social skills can develop collaboration and hence the outcome of the organization. On the flip side, negative social practices in the workplace such as bullying or "organizational silence" lead to suffering and are costly (Yu 2023). Consequently, investing in social skills training is essential. Research has shown that social skills training in organizations is generally an effective intervention (Arthur Jr et al. 2003).

Incorporating a practical element into training is in line with Experiential Learning Theory, where effective learning is seen as a result of a dynamic interplay between concrete experience, reflective observation, abstract conceptualization, and active experimentation (Kolb & Kolb 2009). HRD applies the pedagogical approach of role-play to effectively train social skills in the workplace due to the sensory richness that takes place during the intervention (Schmid Mast et al. 2018). In real life (IRL) role-plays for the purpose of training are effective, but costly due to their temporary existence. They require physical attendance, at a specific time period, of both the learners as well as highly specialized actors or coaches. As the world changes, our modes of training need to adapt.

Aiming to increase efficiency, scalability and remote work, HRD has invested in digital tools for training (Akdere et al. 2021) in the form of two-dimensional (2D) digital e-learning (Brown & Charlier 2013). In addition, the Covid-19 pandemic rapidly pushed forward digitalization of collaborative work (Kirchner & Nordin Forsberg 2021; Amankwah-Amoah et al. 2021). Meetings and communication that previously were conducted predominantly in person have transferred to digital forums such as 2D video conferences or online chats. A large part of the workforce is now much more digitally competent than just a few years ago, but the user experience of 2D has limitations (Onggirawan et al. 2023). Coffey et al. (2017) found that VR can significantly better contribute to the development of social aspects compared to a 2D training session, due to its more realistic nature. The stage is set for taking digital learning one step further, using VR as a tool to train social skills in a 3D environment. According to Salas et al. (2009), training based on simulations of real-life situations can improve the learner's skills through practice.

VR is the presentation of a 3D environment that emulates real or imagined spaces with interactive properties. It is used, among other applications, for the purposes of improving training in complex skills and reducing the cost compared to traditional alternatives (Howard et al. 2021). VR training can also lessen the distractions that are typically present in other training modalities and increase focus due to its immersive nature. According to a review of studies on effectiveness of education, training, and performance aided through augmented or virtual reality, users' focus was significantly higher compared to other types of training (Fletcher et al. 2017). A recent meta-analysis concluded VR training programs to be more effective compared to other types of training, even when the intensity and duration of training matched between VR and the comparison. Furthermore, the effects of VR training are especially strong when it comes to behavioral learning – whether participants adapt their behavior after going through training (Howard et al. 2021). Because of its immersive nature, VR can elicit similar feelings that a real-world experience would (Rivu et al. 2021). Meaningful emotional experiences during VR training, positive or negative, can potentially enhance learning and thus may be a desired effect (Vesisenaho et al. 2019).

When comparing the outcomes of VR training for different age populations, no significant differences were found (Howard et al. 2021). This suggests that VR is an acceptable training modality even for "non-digitally native" adult populations. A "digital native" is loosely defined by Prensky (2001) as someone born after 1980, since this age group is young enough to have grown up using digital tools in their everyday life.

There is limited research on the effectiveness of VR training in the context of social skills training at work, but some promising studies have been published. Akdere et al. (2021) found that using VR to train social skills in international business scenarios increased engagement in training and possibly created more transferable knowledge compared to 2D video-based training. Interestingly, VR was associated with more positive attitudes regarding the value of training but generated more negative feelings during training. This was partly a consequence of the content which focused on culture shock experiences (Akdere et al. 2021). Other studies of VR programs for fostering intercultural understanding found that participants' empathy and engagement increased after the experience (Coffey et al. 2017, Roswell et al. 2020).

VR training programs can be used with so-called avatars and/or agents. Avatars are virtual representations of a real human acting within the VR experience, while agents are preprogrammed computer algorithms that take the form of a human representation (Fox et al. 2015). VR training using agents has several advantages over training with a human trainer. It is flexible and accessible since there is no need to book a specific time for everyone involved. It is economical and provides more opportunities for repeated practice. Practicing with an agent can also alleviate stress or anxiety associated with being socially evaluated when role-playing together with real humans, which in turn can increase motivation and learning efficacy. Additionally, VR training can potentially offer more adaptable and variable scenarios as well as provide feedback to the trainee in new ways (Schmid-Mast et al. 2018).

3   Method

The aim of this study was to investigate HRD-Ps' perception of using VR for social skills training in the workplace. In particular, we wanted to look into how VR could facilitate 1) focused learning experiences, 2) in-depth learning and 3) a deeper understanding of different perspectives among participants in a meeting situation. In order to gain insights into these aspects, we devised a study in which 14 HRD-Ps tried out a VR scenario in their respective homes. Due to the ongoing Covid-19 pandemic, it was not possible to conduct the study at the office. We collected data through questionnaires prior to and after the VR experience. Data was analyzed using a top-down qualitative approach centered around 1) focus, 2) in-depth learning and 3) perspective taking.

3.1   The VR Prototype

The VR prototype training scenario was developed by the main author in an innovation process prior to this study. The prototype was built for the Oculus Go® 64GB head-mounted device (HMD). When the prototype scenario was developed, this HMD was one of few suited to business use. It is a standalone device, i.e. does not require using a computer, and has only one remote control, which simplifies use and provides greater flexibility compared to more complicated VR devices. The Oculus Go® has a 5.5 inch LCD screen with a 2560 × 1440 WQHD resolution and a 60 Hz/72 Hz update frequency depending on the type of application being run. It also has an integrated surround audio.

A VR scenario with agents was designed to train social skills in a workplace setting (a meeting room), specifically regarding situations in which participants were subjected to so-called "master suppression techniques" as defined by Ås (1978). The scenario was produced in the Unity development platform. Unity contains modules for designing agents as well as three dimensional rooms, both of which can be extensively customized.

In the VR application, the user enters a lounge room and receives an introduction to using VR. In the first scene of the scenario, the user remains in the lounge and is introduced to a "challenge" – which is to fill in for a colleague who is unable to attend a management team meeting starting shortly. The colleague is represented by a female agent who explains to the user that she must leave work immediately due to a family situation and gives a brief on what the meeting is about. The user is tasked with promoting the gender equality perspective in the meeting and then enters a conference room where the other meeting participants, agents representing colleagues and a senior manager, are already seated at a table discussing a management topic. The user can both hear and read what the other virtual participants are saying and is frequently prompted throughout the scenario to choose how they want to respond in the meeting (see Fig. 1). The prompts to respond consist of three alternative choices, presented in text form as the scenario is paused, allowing the user to think about what choice to make. The intention was for participants to learn different counter strategies to the master suppression techniques. Therefore, one option in each prompt correlates with a proposed counter strategy for each of the master suppression techniques (Amnéus et al. 2004).

Fig. 1. A screenshot from the VR prototype (left) and a learner using it (right)

Each option leads to a different sequence of events throughout the scenario, creating a possibility of multiple scenarios according to the choices made by the user. Each option also corresponds to a certain number of points, tallied throughout the experience and presented to the user at the end of the scenario. A summary of the theory behind the experience is also presented at the end. The user also had the option of going "back in time" in the scenario to choose a different option. The reason behind this design was to allow the user to test how different responses affect the progression and outcome of the meeting.

3.2 Procedure

The study took place between August and September 2020 and was led by the HR director at the case organization. All prospective participants received the same written information in an invitation letter, as well as a letter of consent to be signed if they decided to participate.

At the start of the study, all participants were invited to an online group onboarding meeting, during which they were informed about the procedure. Intentionally, the participants neither received information about the content of the training nor any other framing of the study. The purpose was to limit how they were influenced in terms of labeling the VR experience and its purpose. Each participant was then provided with an Oculus Go® HMD installed with the VR application containing the training scenario. The equipment was delivered to their homes. The participants were instructed to fill in a questionnaire prior to testing the VR application, to open the VR application after completing the questionnaire, in the comfort of any location of their own choice, and to independently follow the VR training scenario at their own pace without any time limits (see Fig. 2).

Fig. 2. An HRD-P study participant submitted a photo of when she was exploring the VR prototype at home, practicing counter strategies to master suppression techniques comfortably on her couch. The photo was taken by a family member.

When the participants were finished exploring the VR application, they filled out a questionnaire on their experiences of the scenario with target questions around focus, in-depth learning, and perspective taking. Finally, all participants were invited to a voluntary online follow-up focus group meeting online, which all participants attended.

3.3 Participants

Participant recruitment was made with the help of the HR Director and the recruitment specialist in the central HR department. 26 employees were selected based on their organizational role as well as the HR Director's assessment of whether they would be able to participate in the study. The selected employees were stakeholders of social skills training in the organization, both on a central and local hierarchical level in different branches of the organization. They included experts in competence development within the HR department, managers in charge of competence development of their staff, and communication department representatives from the central staffing function.

The communication department representatives collaborated with the HR department in developing a new version of the organization's employer branding concept and were thus seen as stakeholders in organizational training.

The 26 selected employees were invited via email to participate in the study. 14 accepted. The participants' age demographics were 35 to 58 years old (average age: 48 years, median: 49 years, standard deviation: 7 years). The gender distribution was 13 women and one man. A larger proportion of women accepted the invitation to participate compared to men; of the 26 employees invited, 20 were women and 6 were men. The central organizational level was represented by the central HR department (P1, P2, P4, P6, P9, P13), the central communications department (P5, P14) and one central manager of the core business (P7). The local organizational level was represented by local HR departments (P3, P12), local managers from the core business (P8, P11) and one local employee from the core business (P10). None of the participants had any significant prior experience using VR.

3.4 Measures

All data gathered in this project was qualitative. Research question 1 uses reflections from the main author on the design process of the VR experience. Research question 2 uses reflections from the study participants in a pre- and post-intervention questionnaire. The questionnaire was designed for the purpose of the study, guided by the research questions and objectives. Prior to the study, the questionnaire was reviewed by representatives from the union and the HR department.

Participants submitted written reflections in three different parts. The first part was pre-intervention; to write down their thoughts and expectations prior to the VR experience. The second part was post-intervention; to write down their reflections after the VR experience. The third part was also post-intervention; to write down their reflections on whether the intended design goals of the VR experience were fulfilled, as well as their thoughts about the goals as such. The three intended goals were to provide 1) focus on the learning experience, 2) an in-depth learning experience, and 3) an opportunity to practice critical social situations that arise in workplaces, in order to prepare for them and enrich your experience by exploring situations from different perspectives ("perspective taking"). The participants were instructed to write their reflections in free text form, in a digital document. There were no length limits on the feedback from the participants.

The post-intervention questionnaire also contained four questions on the practical usability of VR within HR that are not included as data in this article. Data was also collected in the follow-up meetings but not included in this article.

3.5 Data Collection and Analysis

Reflections on critical moments in the design process were documented as a diary in retrospective. The questionnaire was sent as an email attachment to each participant and returned to the main author via email. Consequently, participant reflections were not anonymous. The data collected through the questionnaires was then thematically analyzed. We performed a top-down thematic analysis (Braun & Clarke 2006). Since the process was top-down, our research questions guided the coding. The process was led by the main author, who performed the initial coding and formed preliminary themes. In parallel, the rest of the authors independently walked through the data prior to a joint meeting in which the main author presented the themes to the rest of the group. During this meeting, we validated, prioritized, and refined the preliminary themes into the final themes reported here.

4   Results

4.1   Critical Elements in the Design Process

The idea of using VR for social skills training in the workplace sprung from an engagement in social sustainability in organizations, and a desire to make a significant contribution by facilitating science-based learning processes in organizations. This was combined with an idea that VR could trigger engagement with the subject of social sustainability in a similar way as when people play digital games for amusement.

One major consideration in the design process was how to successfully dramatize and create an interesting game design based on scientific organizational studies in relational power theories (Bourdieu 1977). Ås' (1978) theory on master suppression techniques in combination with the counter strategies proposed by Amnéus et al. (2004) were found suitable for three reasons; they fit the theoretical foundation of power theories, they are formulated as a relational practice and hence suitable for dramatization and they are structured as levels that could fit into the tradition of game design.

Another important question was how to create an appropriate look and feel of the 3D agents and offices in the VR experience. They needed to be suitable for the subject of social interactions in the workplace, which requires that the user experiences empathy, emotions, and perspective taking. When designing the agents, the concept of "uncanny valley" (Geller 2008) was considered. This concept explains why photorealistic agents can fail to awaken empathy in the user. An agent whose appearance is perceived as very close to, but not exactly as a real human, can produce a strong uneasy ("uncanny") experience. The user then reacts with aversion toward the agent, which blocks empathy. This was regarded as a serious disadvantage when practicing social skills, and led to an interest in investigating how non-photorealistic agents would be perceived as "training partners".

A third important element in the design process was developing the VR prototype through an agile approach of stepwise iterations. As a first step, small samples of the game design, the look of the agents and the virtual environment were created with the help of university students in game programming. The next iteration was funded by a public innovation agency and by an innovation award granted for the idea's potential value to society. This enabled a more solid development process and the formation of a professional team of experts with complementary skills. In order to ensure that the result would be relevant to potential future users, representatives from large organizations with strong brands were involved in the design process. Technological development of the VR experience was handled by a large local consulting firm with expertise in creating VR experiences for other industry sectors and application areas. This included professional audio recordings of the agents' voices, by employees of the consulting firm who had extensive prior experience providing voices for VR scenarios, as well as spoke both Swedish and English fluently.

The process as a whole resulted in these intended design elements: 1) focus on the training experience, 2) in-depth learning including emotional response, engagement, and motivation and 3) perspective taking.

4.2 Focus on the Training Experience

As regards the participants' experience of focus, several users stated that they experienced a deeper level of concentration (P2–P12, P14), where we interpreted their responses as a perceived extraordinary sense of focus and presence. Participants exemplified this with being in a world of their own (P4) in which you "both have to [in order to understand the social scenario] and want to" (P6) be totally concentrated. Overall, this indicates that the majority experienced a deep focus and willingly concentrated on the unfolding of the VR scenario.

Experiencing focus appeared to come partly as a surprise in relation to the fact that the virtual environment was animated, indicating that the immersive aspects of the social scenario overpowered the fact that the virtual room and characters were stylized instead of realistic in appearance. Here illustrated by participant P2:

I was surprised how "real" the experience felt despite being an animated environment

Furthermore, five participants (P2, P3, P5, P6, P12) felt that it was easy to step into the shoes of their character as well as to focus on the details of the scenario. P3 commented that they sustained a deep focus on the questions and answers in the scenario and how the other characters behaved and responded.

However, some disruptive issues were noted. Although most participants found it easy to enter the virtual world and understand what to do there, some stated that they would have benefited from a more comprehensive introduction (P6, P8, P14). The participants were neither instructed to put other devices in silent mode nor to allocate undisturbed time when exploring the VR prototype. Most participants did not report anything about disturbances, while two explicitly stated that they were not disturbed by other technical devices (P4, P5), as if nothing existed but the virtual world they were in. However, three participants were disturbed to some degree by other devices; P8 thought that it might have been good to turn off their phone before going into VR, P10 initially noted message sounds from their phone but later ignored them as it was not possible to check messages when wearing a headset, and P13 reflected that it would be beneficial to make sure you were not disturbed during the experience.

4.3 In-Depth Learning Including Emotional Response, Engagement and Motivation

Prior to the experience, the participants stated expectations that it will be fun (P1, P5), exciting (P3–P5, P10–P11, P13–P14), interesting (P5, P9, P11), inspiring (P6), that they will be blown away and become engaged with the experience (P6), and that it will create curiosity (P2, P4). However, several participants had mixed feelings and also expressed hesitancy – uncertainty about what will happen (P2, P14), whether VR adds any value compared to conventional e-learning programs (P2), wondering if VR will be difficult to use or cause nausea (P5), worries that the scenario will feel too real and uncomfortable (P6) or that they would miss important information (P8). Overall, the majority of participants had high expectations. They were curious to see what VR could do for HR training practices.

Despite generally high expectations, all participants clearly expressed post experience that it exceeded their expectations. They described it as engaging (P1, P4, P9–P11, P13), interesting (P1, P5, P9, P12, P13), fun (P3, P5, P8, P14), surprisingly strong and realistic (P2, P6, P13), different (P5), inspirational (P6), exciting (P12), creating a sense of presence (P7), and providing a higher dimension of training (P3). Our interpretation was that they perceived the experience as highly valuable and relevant, indicating a real potential to be used within HR practices.

Several participants (P2, P3, P7, P9, P11–P13) expressed statements that indicated they felt strongly pressured or cornered in a realistic way – often somewhat to their surprise – in the VR scenario. One highlighted how easy it was to feel empathy and engage in the situation (P1). Although the scenario was strong, P14 further commented that it could have ended on a more positive note (e.g. with smiling characters) in order to strengthen the learning experience.

Overall, the participants stated that the VR experience was engaging. Several also reflected on the higher degree of engagement created by the VR learning experience compared with reading a text (P11) or using other mediums such as video or mobile phone (P9), computer (P4, P7) and even real classroom settings (P3).

Some participants further compared the experience favorably to IRL training (P3-P4, P6, P9, P11). It allowed them to test scenarios and play with outcomes (P6), which provided opportunities to reflect upon consequences in a way that would not have been possible in a real situation (P9). P6 also remarked that although it was an emotionally strong experience, it was more relaxing than a real situation and allowed them to focus on undertones in the setting and dialogue. It provided a good learning experience which gave them insights (P4, P11) as well as opportunities to learn about these types of challenges and to try solving them in a safe environment at your own pace (P9). This is perhaps best summed up by P9:

[this experience] provides safety [to learn] before stepping into a serious situation

Overall, a majority of the participants stated (P1–P3, P5, P6, P8–P14) that the experience has the potential to provide in-depth learning experiences. Some interesting notes were that it could make you aware of your own instinctive reactions (P9), increase emotional understanding of varying social situations (P10), and provide a deeper understanding of these situations (P5). Another participant noted that the scenario was easy to remember in detail after finishing (P12). This indicates that VR has the potential to provide deeper emotional learning around social contexts. Another interesting aspect, highlighted by P1, was that this type of learning environment allows users to practice how to "bring about their best self/behavior", which could lead to better management of these types of situations in real life as a result of virtual mental preparation.

4.4 Perspective Taking

Most of the study participants agreed overall that the intended design goal of providing opportunity to practice and enriching the experience by exploring situations from different perspectives was fulfilled (P1-P5, P11–12). All but one of the other participants agreed at least in part (P7-P10).

A majority of the study participants (P1, P3, P4, P7, P9, P11–P14) expressed that they liked the reflective and explorative aspects of the learning scenario, e.g. that they could experience the scenario several times at their own pace and test different choices and outcomes. This was highlighted as important to develop skills (P4, P9, P13, P14), illustrated by this comment from P4:

> *Indeed you had thoughts and reflections since you analyzed more and more after each time you tried. So I agree that it was good practice.*

Two participants found the scenario itself realistic enough, commenting that the dialogue in the scenario helped them understand the situation (P11) and that the scenario itself really showed how status could play out in a workplace meeting, as expressed by P13:

> *Realistic in that there are unspoken structures around a meeting table where different roles (sometimes people?!) have different status depending on what topics are on the agenda or in the worst-case scenario their relationship to the leader.*

Regarding the alternative choices throughout the scenario, two participants felt they were similar enough to not be obviously "right" or "wrong" and thus encouraged perspective taking (P1, P11), which is described by P11 here:

> *I thought it was good that the alternatives had similar wordings, since it made me really read and contemplate their meanings. But at the same time they were different enough to make it worth doing the scene over several times and answer in different ways, to see how different alternatives lead to different outcomes for the others in the meeting.*

Others thought it was too easy to see which choice was "right" and criticized the "politically correct" nature of this choice as not nuanced or realistic enough (P7, P9, P10). P10 suggested that the alternatives presented could be nuanced to better reflect real situations:

> *...often you need to nuance yourself a lot more so the people you're interacting with don't lash out, even if the "politically correct alternative" is the right thing to say or do in principle.*

One study participant wrote that the experience triggered a competitive drive, which could be understood as counteractive to perspective taking.

4.5   Overall Results of the Three Design Elements

The three intended design elements – 1) focus on the training experience, 2) in-depth learning including emotional response, engagement and motivation, and 3) perspective taking – were confirmed by the participants. A majority of the participants experienced a deeply concentrated focus on the experience. A majority also found it conducive to in-depth learning. They described the experience as engaging, and several participants reported a strong emotional response to the scenario. A majority also agreed that the experience fostered perspective taking, mainly through being able to explore the scenario from different perspectives.

An additional result was the participants' recognition of VR-delivered social skills training as innovative within the organization, positioning it at the forefront of digitalization. The study also indicated that VR could be accepted by and even attract generations that are older than "digital natives" as defined by Prensky (2001), considering that the majority of participants were older than the digitally native age group. The participants were able to start and use the VR prototype as intended despite no previous experience with VR, which indicates that usability potential is high for employees that are not experienced in using VR.

4.6   Game Design Critique and Participants' Suggestions for Improvements

One of the participants reflected that the game design could steer you towards only trying to win the game by selecting the right answer, although they could also see how receiving points could be helpful (P9). The same participant (P9) commented that the "artificial" VR environment made the experience feel less real and that lack of realistic detail in the agents' facial expressions meant that much of the nuance in real interpersonal interactions felt missing (P9):

> *Miss the real human facial expressions that are a large part of human dialogue and interpersonal interactions. VR as a platform = artificial office space/avatar (sic) with a floating head. That disturbs part of my experience.*

Another participant didn't realize they were an actor in the scenario until after some time (P8).

Suggestions for improvements included having a voiceover presentation of the theoretical parts instead of reading them as text, to provide micro-information during the learning experience instead of presenting it at the end, to branch out the scenario more so different choices would lead to more alternative situations, to provide an opportunity to "debrief" after the experience in case it leads to strong emotional reactions, and to add the option of entering a more realistic mode later in the experience, with less time to reflect and pick and choose among the choices.

5   Discussion

The purpose of this study was to investigate the potential of innovative technologies in the field of Human Resource Development (HRD) in organizations in terms of Virtual Reality (VR) for social skills training in the workplace.

The first research question aimed at identifying the critical elements in the design process of this VR prototype for social skills training in the workplace. The result is an identification of three intended design choices – 1) focus on the training experience, 2) in-depth learning through emotional response, engagement and motivation, and 3) perspective taking.

The second research question was to investigate HRD-Ps' views on the potential of using VR for HR matters, based on their experience using this VR prototype. The result is that the three intended design effects were confirmed. The participants' reflections also yielded additional results recognizing the experience as innovative.

5.1 Focus on the Training Experience

The results of this study confirm the intended effect of using VR to increase focus and reduce distraction during learning events. Most of the study participants described how they naturally became very concentrated and engaged in the scenario. This is in line with previous research on focus in virtual scenarios (Fletcher et al. 2017). Increased focus could be one of the reasons why VR training produces better outcomes than other types of training as reported by Howard et al. (2021).

One beneficial effect of using VR compared to an IRL role-play is reduction of stress and social overload that can be detrimental to focusing on the learning process; stress caused by interacting with the other participating learners and/or trainers or actors. Another factor contributing to focus mentioned by participants was that the VR learning experience distracted them from immediate call to action on incoming messages in their computer or mobile phone. For obvious reasons, visual attention is restricted to the learning event due to the HMD covering the learners' eyes. Mobile devices and personal computers are a near ubiquitous necessity in today's working life, but it is important to consider the risk of distraction and inefficient learning when these devices are brought into a training session. Valuing the learners' increased focus could be an important factor when HRD calculates the return on investment of their organization's learning portfolio if integrating innovative technologies like VR.

5.2 In-Depth Learning Including Emotional Response, Engagement and Motivation

In the design process, we assumed that in-depth learning through emotional involvement was an important feature to digitally mimic IRL role-play mechanisms, especially when approaching sensitive topics in social skills training in the workplace. Most participants reported high engagement and emotional involvement in the VR scenario, which indicates that the findings of Roswell et al. (2020) and Akdere et al. (2021) also apply to social skills training in organizations.

The VR prototype was spontaneously characterized by participants as a safe learning environment. A safe environment is a beneficial prerequisite when aiming at triggering emotional responses for in-depth learning. Schmid Mast et al. (2018) claim that practicing with agents can alleviate social stress for the purpose of learning. The result of this study indicates that training with agents created the intended emotional response and suggests that this feature can effectively contribute to social skills training in the workplace.

Another interesting finding was that several participants considered the experience a better opportunity for learning compared to real-life scenarios, since you could progress at your own pace and go back and forth in time in the scenario. This is an advantage of VR training that Schmid Mast et al. (2018) mention. It is important to highlight that this valued opportunity can be limited in IRL role-plays.

5.3 Perspective Taking

We also assumed that enabling perspective taking through conscious game design would be an important feature to mimic effects or IRL role-play training. The participants mostly confirmed this intended effect of fostering perspective taking within the scenario, even though their reflections on this design element also contained some mixed reactions.

The scenario felt realistic enough to most participants, and the game design helped them explore how choosing different responses affected the outcome not only for themselves, but in what they observed in the agents' responses. The possibility to go back and make new choices, which was frequently mentioned in the area of in-depth learning, was the most mentioned positive aspect in this area as well.

As Coffey et al. (2017) and Roswell et al. (2020) reported, VR training can elicit empathic reactions which is a form of perspective taking. Several participants' reflections in this study expressed empathic reactions toward agents in the scenario, suggesting that they did take their perspective despite knowing they were not real people. However, a few of the participants did not fully agree that the prototype's experience felt realistic enough, either as a result of the intentionally simplistic visual design or as a result of the scenario and response choices given not being close enough to real life. This finding highlights that a variance in preferences regarding visual and game design should be considered. How it affects learning experiences is important to investigate further, as well as the importance of developing more complex and nuanced scenarios than what was possible within the budget of this prototype.

We consider it especially interesting that our VR prototype, which was designed in a simplistic cartoonish manner, produced the high level of engagement that most participants reported. It is also valuable to discuss what did not occur; the voices of the agents did not cause any comments from the participants. This can be interpreted as the voices being perceived as appropriate.

5.4 Potential Advantages and Challenges Using VR for Social Skills Training

Drawing on the result that most study participants viewed VR as an effective tool to enhance training on social skills in the workplace, we will now discuss several potential opportunities for employers and HR in organizations.

A clear advantage is the potential for scalability and cost effectiveness compared to IRL training. Implementing VR can enable employers and HR to scale science-based learning on the subject of social skills in an economical way, to a geographically distributed workforce with accuracy and systematicity. This can be especially valuable for global management programs or talent programs with participants from different parts of the world. As both Schmid-Mast et al. (2018) and Howard et al. (2021) ascertain, VR training is less costly compared to IRL training. The requirement of specific equipment such as an HMD for delivery of training could be perceived as an economical disadvantage. However, contemporary HMDs are comparable to smartphones in price. Once the equipment is paid for it can also be used repeatedly without incurring further costs, unlike IRL training. The rapid development pace in the field of HMDs will further improve both quality and cost in the future.

Secondly, using a VR training experience enables organizations to better ensure consistent quality of training in social skills. Even though IRL social interaction will always remain important to organizations and their training programs, VR could be considered both as a replacement for parts of IRL training and as a reinforcement of it if integrated as a preparational or follow-up activity to an IRL event. It is also an opportunity for academia to implement its research in workplaces.

Another important advantage of using VR for social skills training is to ensure fulfillment of legal requirements placed on employers regarding their social work environment. Providing social skills training through VR could be an efficient way of meeting these requirements, especially when they emphasize the importance of processes having a systematic approach.

Furthermore, our results indicate that the use of VR for HR can, both internally and externally (e.g. towards candidates), position the employer as innovative and digitalized. This is important for HR since these features attract new generations by using technologies they find attractive and natural. A potential challenge could be lower acceptability of VR training for older generations. However, this perception is contradicted by recent research (Howard et al. 2021) as well as by the results of this study. Age does not seem to impact negatively on the experience of VR training.

Using VR could also enable dealing with workplace gender inequality and cultural differences. Our VR prototype is based on a relational power perspective (Bourdieu 1977) on HR and organizations (Nordin Forsberg 2020). The scenario itself is centered on oppressive social interactions that are frequently, although not exclusively, gendered in nature. VR training programs like our prototype can contribute to gender equality in an organization. Providing standardized social skills training to foster intercultural competence and sensitivity through VR can ensure that all parts of the organization receive the same message, and lessen some of the communication issues and conflicts associated with diversity that Stahl (2010) reports.

On a societal level, using VR for social skills training could contribute to the global Sustainable Development Goals (SDG) defined by the United Nations General Assembly (2015). Even though we apply an organizational perspective in this study, a positive side effect of social sustainability with an organization can be considered – to contribute to individuals' quality of life by reducing bullying and discrimination in the workplace. VR delivered social skills training can stimulate informed and science-based dialogues and insight. Topics that can be regarded as complex and uncomfortable to discuss could potentially be appreciated and even entertaining following a well-balanced VR game design and dramatization. Replacing some IRL learning modules with VR learning experiences in leadership or talent programs with geographically distributed learners could also contribute to reducing the carbon footprint. This leads to a possible positive effect on ecological sustainability as well as social and financial sustainability.

5.5 Future Work

We suggest a forward research agenda on several topics. The return on investment between IRL roleplay, based on its temporary existence, should be compared to VR training and its scalability and systematic benefit. This should include clear cost effectiveness calculations. How the effect of different degrees of simplistic versus photorealistic design of avatars/agents affect the experience should be investigated, to guide future VR experience design towards the most effective visual representations. We also suggest investigating how an even more complex game design can be realized. This could include how to construct alternative choices to "the right answer" that are perceived as realistic and relevant enough to mimic a real-life situation, as well as use our participants' suggestions for further development of game design. One participant suggestion we found particularly interesting was to add an opportunity to enter a more life-like mode at a faster pace. Another interesting research topic would be to measure the learning effect of VR experiences for social skills training. Finally, we suggest further investigation of diversity and inclusion in terms of both design and technology regarding cyber-sickness, the ability to read a text, and how to provide complementary alternatives to text.

6 Conclusion

Today, HR tends to be low on the priority list when it comes to tech investments. We initiated this study because we firmly believe that novel technology has the potential to push the envelope and disrupt HR work through digitalization. We conclude that VR for social skills training, specifically in the area of dealing with master suppression techniques at work, can be a valuable and scalable addition to the HRD toolbox. VR for HR has the potential to create engagement and provide insights into HR matters that are otherwise difficult and sensitive to train and deal with in real life. One key benefit we found of using VR for social skills training is that it allows the learners to practice in a safe environment and at their own pace. This allows both for deeper reflections on how difficult it can be to manage certain social challenges and for tesing different approaches through trial and error. We also found that the tested VR application supported in-depth learning of social skills through a design that supported focus and promoted empathic perspectives for other roles in the social scenario used. We further conclude that the main game design challenge for this type of application is creating balanced and rich scenarios. Finally, using VR for HR was perceived as innovative and could stimulate further real-life dialogues toward an attractive and healthy workplace.

Acknowledgements. The authors would like to express our appreciation to Charlotte Ulfsparre for her valuable contributions to the editing process of the text.

References

Akdere, M., Jiang, Y., Acheson, K.: To simulate or not to simulate? Comparing the effectiveness of video-based training versus virtual reality-based simulations on interpersonal skills development. Hum. Resour. Dev. Q. (2021). https://doi.org/10.1002/hrdq.21470

Amankwah-Amoah, J., Khan, Z., Wood, G., Knight, G.: COVID-19 and digitalization: the great acceleration. J. Bus. Res. **136**, 602–611 (2021). https://doi.org/10.1016/j.jbusres.2021.08.011

Amnéus, D., Eile, D., Flock, U., Rosell Steuer, P., Testad, G.: Validation Techniques and Counter Strategies: Methods for Dealing with Power Structures and Changing Social Climates. Stockholm University, Stockholm (2004). http://www.ecosanres.org/pdf_files/Gender_workshop_2010/Resources/Amneus_et_al_2004_Validation_techniques_counter_strategies.pdf

Arthur, W., Jr., Bennett, W., Jr., Edens, P.S., Bell, S.T.: Effectiveness of training in organizations: a meta-analysis of design and evaluation features. J. Appl. Psychol. **88**(2), 234–245 (2003). https://doi.org/10.1037/0021-9010.88.2.234

Behzadi, A.: Using augmented and virtual reality technology in the construction industry. Am. J. Eng. Res. **5**(12), 350–353 (2016)

Berdanier, C.G.P.: A hard stop to the term "soft skills." J. Eng. Educ. **111**(1), 14–18 (2022). https://doi.org/10.1002/jee.20442

Bourdieu, P.: Outline of a Theory of Practice (translated by R. Nice, first published in France as Esquisse d'une théorie de la pratique, précédé de trois études d'ethnologie kabyle). Cambridge University Press, Cambridge (1977)

Braun, V., Clarke, V.: Using thematic analysis in psychology. Qual. Res. Psychol. **3**(2), 77–101 (2006). https://doi.org/10.1191/1478088706qp063oa

Brown, K.G., Charlier, S.D.: An integrative model of e-learning use: leveraging theory to understand and increase usage. Hum. Resour. Manag. Rev. **23**(1), 37–49 (2013). https://doi.org/10.1016/j.hrmr.2012.06.004

Carlyon, T., Opperman, A.: Embedding soft skills within learner-centred environments for vocation education graduates. Scope: Contemp. Res. Top. (Learn. Teach.) **9**(1), 16–23 (2020). https://doi.org/10.34074/scop.4009001

Coffey, A.J., Kamhawi, R., Fishwick, P., Henderson, J.: The efficacy of an immersive 3D virtual versus 2D web environment in intercultural sensitivity acquisition. Educ. Tech. Res. Dev. **65**(2), 455–479 (2017). https://doi.org/10.1007/s11423-017-9510-9

Fletcher, J. D., Belanich, J., Moses, F., Fehr, A., Moss, J.: Effectiveness of augmented reality & augmented virtuality. In: MODSIM Modeling & Simulation of Systems and Applications) World Conference (2017)

Fox, J., Ahn, S.J., Janssen, J.H., Yeykelis, L., Segovia, K.Y., Bailenson, J.N.: Avatars versus agents: a meta-analysis quantifying the effect of agency on social influence. Hum. Comput. Interact. **30**(5), 401–432 (2015). https://doi.org/10.1080/07370024.2014.921494

Geller, T.: Overcoming the uncanny valley. IEEE Comput. Graph. Appl. **28**(4) (2008). https://doi.org/10.1109/MCG.2008.79

Gulliksen, J., Borälv, E., Elvelid J., Hadley-Kamptz, I., Krusell, J., Liss-Larsson, N.: A digital agenda in the service of humanity - a brightening future is possible. (In Swedish: En digital agenda i människans tjänst - en ljusnande framtid kan bli vår) SOU 2014:13, ISBN 978-91-38-24081-6 http://www.regeringen.se/rattsdokument/statens-offentliga-utredningar/2014/03/sou-201413/

Howard, M.C., Gutworth, M.B., Jacobs, R.R.: A meta-analysis of virtual reality training programs. Comput. Hum. Behav. **121** (2021). https://doi.org/10.1016/j.chb.2021.106808

Kim, J., McLean, G.N.: An integrative framework for global leadership competency: levels and dimensions. Hum. Resour. Dev. Int. **18**(3), 1–24 (2015). https://doi.org/10.1080/13678868.2014.1003721

Kirchner, K., Nordin Forsberg, B.: A conference goes virtual: lessons from creating a social event in the virtual reality. In: Krieger, U.R., Eichler, G., Erfurth, C., Fahrnberger, G. (eds.) I4CS 2021. CCIS, vol. 1404, pp. 123–134. Springer, Cham (2021). https://doi.org/10.1007/978-3-030-75004-6_9

Kolb, A.Y., Kolb, D.A.: Experiential learning theory: a dynamic, holistic approach to management learning, education and development. In: Armstrong, S.J., Fukami, C.V. (eds.) The SAGE Handbook of Management Learning, Education and Development. SAGE Publications Ltd., Thousand Oaks (2009). https://doi.org/10.4135/9780857021038.n3

Leavitt, H.J., Bahrami, H.: Managerial Psychology: Managing Behavior in Organizations. University of Chicago Press, Chicago (1988)

Lichy, J., Khvatova, T.: Rethinking solutions for re-balancing the education–job mismatch. J. Manage. Develop. **38**(9), 733–754 (2019)

Lundström, A., Ghebremikael, S., Fernaeus, Y.: Co-watching 360-films in nursing homes. In: Ardito, C., et al. (eds.) INTERACT 2021. LNCS, vol. 12932, pp. 502–521. Springer, Cham (2021). https://doi.org/10.1007/978-3-030-85623-6_30

Nordin Forsberg, B.: Talent management in organizations: a critical management perspective (In Swedish: Talent management i organisationer: ett kritiskt managementperspektiv). [Doctoral dissertation, KTH, School of Industrial Engineering and Management, Industrial Economics and Management]. DiVA portal (2020). http://kth.diva-portal.org/smash/record.jsf?pid=diva2%3A1384519&dswid=3961

Onggirawan, C.A., Kho, J.M., Kartiwa, A.P., Gunawan, A.: A. Systematic literature review: The adaptation of distance learning process during the COVID-19 pandemic using virtual educational spaces in metaverse. Procedia Comput. Sci. **216**, 274–283 (2023)

Prensky, M.: Digital natives, digital immigrants part 1. On the Horizon **9**(5), 1–6 (2001)

Riggio, R.E.: Social skills in the workplace. In: Carducci, B.J., Nave, C.S. (eds.) The Wiley Encyclopedia of Personality and Individual Differences: Models and Theories. Wiley, Hoboken (2020). https://doi.org/10.1002/9781119547181.ch352

Rivu, R., Jiang, R., Mäkelä, V., Hassib, M., Alt, F.: Emotion elicitation techniques in virtual reality. In: Ardito, C., et al. (eds.) INTERACT 2021. LNCS, vol. 12932, pp. 93–114. Springer, Cham (2021). https://doi.org/10.1007/978-3-030-85623-6_8

Roswell, R.O., et al.: Cultivating empathy through virtual reality: advancing conversations about racism, inequity, and climate in medicine. Acad. Med. **95**(12), 1882–1886 (2020). https://doi.org/10.1097/ACM.0000000000003615

Salas, E., Wildman, J.L., Piccolo, R.F.: Using simulation-based training to enhance management education. Acad. Manage. Learn. Educ. **8**(4), 559–573 (2009). https://doi.org/10.5465/AMLE.2009.47785474

Schmid Mast, M., Kleinlogel, E.P., Tur, B., Bachmann, M.: The future of interpersonal skills development: Immersive virtual reality training with virtual humans. Hum. Resour. Dev. Q. **29**(2), 125–141 (2018). https://doi.org/10.1002/hrdq.21307

Shliakhovchuk, E.: After cultural literacy: new models of intercultural competency for life and work in a VUCA world. Educ. Rev. **73**(2), 229–250 (2021)

Stahl, G.K., Maznevski, M.L., Voigt, A., Jonsen, K.: Unraveling the effects of cultural diversity in teams: a meta-analysis of research on multicultural work groups. J. Int. Bus. Stud. **41**(4), 690–709 (2010). https://doi.org/10.1057/jibs.2009.85

Szkudlarek, B., Osland, J.S., Nardon, L., Zander, L.: Communication and culture in international business – moving the field forward. J. World Bus. **55**(6), 1–9 (2020). https://doi.org/10.1016/j.jwb.2020.101126

United Nations General Assembly: Transforming our world: The 2030 agenda for sustainable development (2015). Retrieved from undocs.org/A/RES/70/1

Vesisenaho, M., et al.: Virtual reality in education: focus on the role of emotions and physiological reactivity. J. Virtual Worlds Res. **12**(1) (2019). https://doi.org/10.4101/jvwr.v12i1.7329

Wong, K., Yee, H.M., Xavier, B.A., Grillone, G.A.: Applications of augmented reality in otolaryngology: a systematic review. Otolaryngol. Head Neck Surg. **159**(6), 956–967 (2018). https://doi.org/10.1177/0194599818796476

Yu, H.H.: Reporting workplace discrimination: an exploratory analysis of bystander behavior. Review of Public Personnel Administration, (2023). Advance online publication. https://doi.org/10.1177/0734371X2211491

Ås, B.: Master suppression techniques (In Norwegian). Kjerringråd **3**, 17–21 (1978). ISSN 0800-0565 https://worldcat.org/search?q=n2:0800-0565

Courses

Hacking the Brain: The Risks and Challenges of Cognitive Augmentation

Sarah Clinch[1]([⊠]) [iD] and Nigel Davies[2] [iD]

[1] University of Manchester, Manchester, UK
sarah.clinch@manchester.ac.uk
[2] Lancaster University, Lancaster, UK
n.a.davies@lancaster.ac.uk

Abstract. There is a growing vision for augmentations that enhance cognitive capacities – extending our perception, enhancing our attentive capabilities, enriching our memories, and supporting higher order thinking (e.g., decision making). These tools will take a variety of forms, from the already-ubiquitous smartphone, to the growing smart glasses landscape, and even implants. The idea that such augmentations may have unintended consequences or could be intentionally hijacked for harm is already present in popular culture – to what extent are such concerns grounded in reality? How might we identify potential harms and the circumstances in which they are amplified or reduced? What controls might reduce the risk of cognitive harm when technology is used to extend perception and intellect? In this course, we provide researchers with an overview of the research landscape for cognitive augmentation, provide some case studies of harms and the techniques used to measure them, and engage in some critical reflection on future controls (technical, social, political).

Keywords: Augmented Humans · Augmented Intelligence · Dark Patterns · Assistive Technologies · Cognition · Perception · Human Factors

1 Intended Audience and Learning Objectives

This course is aimed at students and researchers with interests in human augmentation, dark patterns, cognition, or cyberpsychology. As an inherently interdisciplinary topic, the course welcomes attendees with backgrounds in computer science, psychology, or other relevant disciplines.

At the end of the course, attendees will:

- be aware of history, current trends and future visions in cognitive augmentation, including: (i) cognitive processes, (ii) target populations and applications, and (iii) technologies/form factors

© The Author(s), under exclusive license to Springer Nature Switzerland AG 2023
J. Abdelnour Nocera et al. (Eds.): INTERACT 2023, LNCS 14145, pp. 255–258, 2023.
https://doi.org/10.1007/978-3-031-42293-5_18

– have a detailed understanding of some specific cognitive vulnerabilities associated with human memory augmentation
– be equipped to conduct research to measure the cognitive phenomena that underpin potential dark patterns and other harms in perceptual and intellectual augmentations.
– understand the landscape for harm mitigation in this domain, both technical and non-technical.

2   Content and Structure

This three-hour course is structured into four units (see Table 1): the first unit provides the core context, giving a whistle-stop tour of cognitive augmentation; the second is a deeper consideration of how augmentation of a specific cognitive capacity might lead to vulnerabilities; the third explores approaches for measuring the potential for, and impact of, cognitive harms that may emerge as a result of augmentation; and the fourth at how technical and non-technical controls can help to mitigate against unintentional and deliberate harm.

Table 1. Course structure.

Session 1	
Unit 1	**Context: Augmentation of Senses and Intellect**
10 mins	Tutor, attendee and course introductions
20 mins	Overview of cognitive augmentation
15 mins	Ideation exercise: envisaging future interventions
Unit 2	**Case Study: Consequences and Vulnerabilities for Human Memory Augmentation**
10 mins	Overview of human memory augmentation and associated harms
10 mins	Case Study 1 – The photo impairment effect
10 mins	Case Study 2 – Retrieval induced forgetting (RIF)
15 mins	Ideation exercise: exploitation opportunities
Session 2	
Unit 3	**Methodologies for the Study of Cognitive Harms**
15 mins	Overview and ethical considerations
15 mins	Collaborative design exercise 1: controlled study
15 mins	Collaborative design exercise 2: applied or in-the-wild study
Unit 4	**Controls and Mitigation**
10 mins	Overview
25 mins	Envisaging future controls
10 mins	Wrap-up

2.1   Unit 1: Augmentation of Senses and Intellect

Course tutors will provide a concise summary of the field of cognitive augmentation. This will include an overview of human cognition (i.e., key processes – perception, attention, memory, higher order thinking/reasoning), highlights from the research to date (e.g., *SenseCam* for episodic memory [6], *Camouflage and Consider* for reasoning [7], and the relevant technology landscape (e.g., mobile and wearable devices, neuroprosthetics/implants/brain-machine interfaces [2], edge computing, and pervasive computing [9]). Attendees will then engage in a collaborative activity to envisage future interventions; elicited interventions will be shared in plenary and will subsequently be revisited in Session 2.

2.2   Unit 2: Case Studies

Tutors will draw on their own, and others, recent research in novel security challenges for human memory augmentation. This will include two case studies centred on observations of two cognitive phenomena – the photo impairment effect [5] and retrieval-induced forgetting [1]. Case studies will draw on the authors' published [3,4] and ongoing research (e.g., [8]). Group discussions will then explore how these phenomena could be realised in future technologies. These discussions will draw on ideas such as algorithmic bias and dark patterns.

2.3   Unit 3: Methodologies

Tutors will provide an overview of methodologies for the study of cognitive harms, with particular emphasis on the unique practical and ethical challenges that arise when conducting research in this domain. The group will then revisit the cognitive augmentations that emerged in Session 1 and explore how associated harms might be identified and measured both in terms of fundamentals/controlled study, and at more applied level/in-the-wild study. This unit will draw on the authors diverse research experiences, that include controlled user studies (both in the lab and online); technology probes, deployments and research in-the-wild; and qualitative research.

2.4   Unit 4: Controls and Mitigation

In this highly-speculative unit tutors will introduce some broad areas for future mitigation, encouraging attendees to consider the role of tools such as heuristics/design guidelines, algorithms, audit trails, social norms, policy and legislation in preventing and mitigating against intended and unintended harms that arise from cognitive augmentation.

3   Reading List

In addition to works cited in previous sections, we would particularly draw on and signpost the following:

P. Atkinson and R. Barker, "'Hey Alexa, what did i forget?': Networked devices, Internet search and the delegation of human memory," *Convergence*, vol. 27, no. 1, pp. 52–65, 2021.

S. Clinch, O. Alghamdi, and M. Steeds, "Technology-induced human memory degradation," in *Creative Speculation on the Negative Effects of HCI Research (CHI 2019 Workshop).*, 2019.

N. Davies, A. Friday, S. Clinch, et al., "Security and privacy implications of pervasive memory augmentation," *Pervasive Computing, IEEE*, vol. 14, pp. 44–53, 1 2015, issn: 1536–1268.

P. Elagroudy, M. Khamis, F. Mathis, et al., "Impact of privacy protection methods of lifelogs on remembered memories," in *Proceedings of the 2023 CHI Conference on Human Factors in Computing Systems*, 2023, pp. 1–10.

A. Schmidt, "Augmenting human intellect and amplifying perception and cognition," *IEEE Pervasive Computing*, vol. 16, no. 1, pp. 6–10, 2017.

References

1. Anderson, M.C., Bjork, E.L., Bjork, R.A.: Retrieval-induced forgetting: evidence for a recall-specific mechanism. Psychon. Bull. Rev. **7**, 522–530 (2000)
2. Cinel, C., Valeriani, D., Poli, R.: Neurotechnologies for human cognitive augmentation: current state of the art and future prospects. Front. Human Neurosci. **13**, 13 (2019)
3. Clinch, S., Cortis Mack, C., Ward, G., Steeds, M.: Technology-mediated memory impairment. In: Dingler, T., Niforatos, E. (eds.) Technology-Augmented Perception and Cognition. HIS, pp. 71–124. Springer, Cham (2021). https://doi.org/10.1007/978-3-030-30457-7_4
4. Davies, N., Friday, A., Clinch, S., et al.: Security and privacy implications of pervasive memory augmentation. IEEE Perv. Comput. 14, 44–53 (2015). ISSN: 1536–1268
5. Henkel, L.A.: Point-and-shoot memories: the influence of taking photos on memory for a museum tour. Psychol. Sci. **25**(2), 396–402 (2014)
6. Hodges, S., et al.: SenseCam: a retrospective memory aid. In: Dourish, P., Friday, A. (eds.) UbiComp 2006. LNCS, vol. 4206, pp. 177–193. Springer, Heidelberg (2006). https://doi.org/10.1007/11853565_11
7. Kim, Y., Ueno, T., Seaborn, K., Oura, H., Urakami, J., Sawa, Y.: Exoskeleton for the mind: exploring strategies against misinformation with a metacognitive agent. In: Proceedings of the Augmented Humans International Conference 2023, pp. 209–220 (2023)
8. Steeds, M., Clinch, S., Noehrer, L., Ward, G., Mack, C.C.: Retrieval induced forgetting and online advertising. In: BPS Cyberpsychology Section Conference (2021)
9. Davies, N., Clinch, S., Alt, F.: Pervasive displays: understanding the future of digital signage. Synth. Lect. Mob. Perv. Comput. **8**(1), 1–128 (2014)

The UCD Sprint: Bringing Users Along to Sprint

Marta Larusdottir[1]([✉]) [iD], Virpi Roto[2] [iD], Rosa Lanzilotti[3] [iD], and Ioana Visescu[1] [iD]

[1] Reykjavik University, Reykjavik, Iceland
marta@ru.is
[2] Aalto University, Helsinki, Finland
[3] University of Bari Aldo Moro, Bari, Italy

Abstract. One of the most important aspects of software development is that the software is suitable for the intended users. Software professionals often tailor software development to their own needs, resulting in the software being unsuitable for many users. The course will introduce a User-Centered Design Sprint (UCD Sprint) process, which aims at extending the understanding of users' needs and wants. Participants will practice two steps from the UCD Sprint: the user group analysis and stating user experience goals. This in-person course appeals to researchers and developers interested in exploring their innovative ideas through a user-centred progressive and concise step-by-step process.

Keywords: User-Centred Design · User-Centred Design Methods · Design Sprint · Software Design · Concept Design

1 Background

A design sprint procedure was presented in a book by Knapp and colleagues in 2016 [3]. Those design sprints consist of a 5-day collaborative design process where seven or fewer people work together, who have different backgrounds, for example from management, finance, marketing, customer research and technology. The sprint manager should have experience with the methodology and lead the team through the methodology with specific instructions and timing for each method. The process includes both group discussions and individualized idea development In design sprints from Knapp and colleagues, users participate in the process once, on the last day of the sprint.

The User-Centred Design (UCD) Sprint was proposed by HCI researchers from Finland, Iceland, Denmark, and Estonia in 2021 [1]. It is a cost-effective process to define what to design in the early stages of software development, especially focusing on exploring big and innovative ideas. The UCD Sprint methodology was developed to introduce more user-centered methods into design sprints [1]. In the UCD Sprint methodology, considerable time is used to understand the needs of the user groups. The UCD Sprint methodology provides a clear framework that explains step-by-step what needs to be done for each phase of the design process, making it a good fit for teaching user-centred methods [7]. The UCD Sprint methodology includes phases to define user groups, understand their needs, define user experience goals for the project,

© The Author(s), under exclusive license to Springer Nature Switzerland AG 2023
J. Abdelnour Nocera et al. (Eds.): INTERACT 2023, LNCS 14145, pp. 259–263, 2023.
https://doi.org/10.1007/978-3-031-42293-5_19

develop a design solution and evaluate it with users through prototype testing [1]. The initial methodology is two weeks long, with time also taken for the teaching of the methods and the final presentations of each team. When the methodology is applied by professionals familiar with user-centred methods, the process can be shorter. One advantage of user-centred design sprints is that the methodology is more flexible than Knapp's methodology, so it is not necessary to understand that certain methods are used on certain days.

An introductory course on the UCD Sprint process was given at the INTERACT 2021 conference [5], the NordiCHI 2022 conference [6], and the CHI 2023 conference [7]. In the UCD Sprint, the step-by-step process of Knapp's design sprint [1] is modified and combined with methods and techniques from User-Centred Design and Experience-Driven Design. It is an inclusive process, as the step-by-step process allows team members with various backgrounds to participate in the initial analysis and design process. Since new ideas for development are explored while conducting the UCD Sprint, it fits particularly well for user-centred exploration of innovative projects in their first stages.

2   Course Aims, Learning Outcomes & Intended Audience

We propose an in-person course at INTERACT 2023 on the UCD Sprint, where we explain the structure of the UCD Sprint process, why and when to use the process, and whom to invite to attend the UCD Sprint. Participants practice two lesser-known steps from the process: a user group analysis method and setting UX goals by using our support material provided on the ucdsprint.com website. At the end of the course, we discuss the benefits and possible hindrances of using the process in both industry and educational settings in academia.

By the end of the course, participants:

- will understand why and when to use the UCD Sprint process
- will understand the structure of the UCD Sprint
- can apply two steps in the UCD Sprint process, user group analysis, and UX goals
- can utilize the ucdsprint.com website to work independently on the UCD Sprint

We envision that INTERACT attendees would want to take this course to learn how to involve users in a structured step-by-step way in the early phases of innovative research or software development projects. A similar version of the course has been given at INTERACT 2021, NordiCHI 2022 and CHI 2023 [5–7].

The intended audience of this course includes:

- Researchers and students interested in design sprints that integrate user-centred design methods
- Educators interested in including the User-Centred Design Sprint approach in their teaching
- IT professionals that are interested in learning about a user-centred way of running a design sprint.

We assume the participants to have some prior knowledge of user-centred design. Ideally, the participants have participated in the first steps of idea discovery for software projects. Participants familiar with design sprints will learn how to focus more on users and involve them more frequently in the design sprints.

3 Course Content

The UCD Sprint process has a well-defined structure of 18 steps in 3 phases: Discovery phase, Design phase, and Reality Check phase, as shown in Fig. 1.

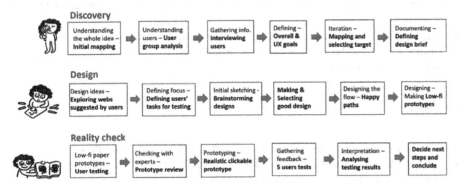

Fig. 1. An overview of the 3 phases and the 18 steps in the UCD Sprint (images © Might Could Studios)

Unlike in many design sprints, representatives of the user groups are involved three times during the UCD Sprint: First during interviews in the Discovery phase and twice during the Reality Check phase: during paper prototype testing, and while user testing a realistic clickable prototype. Methods have been developed and integrated into the UCD Sprint to pay thorough attention to the users' needs during the early stages of the software development project, such as the User Group Analysis method, setting UX goals, and prototyping. Each step of the process builds on the results of the previous steps. The ucdsprint.com website gives instructions on how to conduct the UCD Sprint process.

The UCD Sprint is based on a number of studies on UCD methods and aims at discovering user needs and design preferences [1]. UCD Sprint guides software professionals through the methodology step-by-step in a concise manner. The objective is to implement a precisely selected part of the system and test it with users in a fast and efficient way in order to test the software concept early with the users themselves before embarking on costly development [1, 5].

In this INTERACT course, we explain the structure of the UCD Sprint process, when to use the process, and whom to invite to attend the UCD Sprint. The process is adaptable and provides a flexible schedule that works for remote and in-person teams, experienced or beginners alike. Participants practice two steps from the process that are less-known methods: User Group Analysis method (Discovery - step 2) and Setting

UX goals (Discovery - step 4). These steps focus on a deep understanding of user and system needs and goals, addressing one of the main issues that lead to failure in new software launches – misunderstanding of users. At the end of the course, there is time for discussions on how to use the UCD Sprint in various types of projects. The course is scheduled in two 75 min sessions and the content of each session is described below.

Session 1:

- Introduction to the course schedule and the presenters.
- Introduction to the UCD Sprint process.
- Introduction to the user group analysis method – Discovery - step 2 in the UCD Sprint process.
- Participants do a practical task using the user group analysis method.
- Discussion of the benefits of the user group analysis and how best to adapt it to individuals and teams.

Session 2:

- Introduction to UX goals – Discovery – step 4 in the UCD Sprint process.
- Participants do a practical task on exploring and deciding UX goals.
- Discussions on how UX goals could be evaluated.
- Introduction to how the process could be used in the industry and research.
- Q/A session and open discussion at the end.

Participants will work on two practical tasks. In session 1, participants are asked to use the ucdsprint.com website and download a template to analyze the context of use for one chosen user group for a provided case. They first work individually on analyzing and then have the opportunity to discuss in pairs their analysis and ask questions to the course instructors. In session 2, participants are asked to use the ucdsprint.com website and download a template to define user experience goals for a provided case. They first work individually on defining 3 UX goals and then discuss in groups of three and make a joint decision on 3 UX goals for the entire group. At the end of this session, participants get the opportunity to ask questions to the course instructors and discuss.

During the course, the participants explore the ucdsprint.com web for additional support in conducting the practical sessions. Additionally, a website explaining the course is available.

Acknowledgments. We thank Nordplus for funding the series of courses, and the students for the permission to use the course feedback data for publishing papers on the course development and the proposal of the UCD Sprint. Virpi Roto was supported by the Business Finland grant on 81/31/2020. Marta Larusdottir was granted from Reykjavik University Education Fund to build the supporting website: ucdsprint.com.

References

1. Roto, V., Larusdottir, M., Lucero, A., Stage, J., Šmorgun, I.: Focus, structure, reflection! Integrating user-centered design and design sprint. In IFIP Conference on Human-Computer Interaction, pp. 239–258 (2021)
2. Larusdottir, M., Roto, V., Stage, J., Lucero, A.: Get realistic!-UCD course design and evaluation. In: International Conference on Human-Centred Software Engineering, pp. 15–30 (2018)
3. Knapp, J., Zeratsky, J., Kowitz, B.: Sprint: how to solve big problems and test new ideas in just five days. Simon and Schuster (2016)
4. Larusdottir, M., Roto, V., Stage, J., Lucero, A., Šmorgun, I.: Balance talking and doing! Using google design sprint to enhance an intensive UCD course. In: IFIP Conference on Human-Computer Interaction, pp. 95–113 (2019)
5. Larusdottir, M., Roto, V., Cajander, Å.: Introduction to user-centred design sprint. In: Ardito, C., et al. (eds.) INTERACT 2021. LNCS, vol. 12936, pp. 253–256. Springer, Cham (2021). https://doi.org/10.1007/978-3-030-85607-6_17
6. Larusdottir, M., Roto, V., Lanzilotti, R., Visescu, I.: Tutorial on UCD sprint: inclusive process for concept design. In: Adjunct Proceedings of the 2022 Nordic Human-Computer Interaction Conference (NordiCHI 2022). ACM, New York, NY, USA, Article 19, pp. 1–3. https://doi.org/10.1145/3547522.3558901 (2022)
7. Larusdottir, M., Roto, V., Lanzilotti, R., Visescu, I.: The UCD sprint: a process for user-centered innovation. In: Extended Abstracts of the 2023 CHI Conference on Human Factors in Computing Systems, pp. 1–3 (2023)

Industrial Experiences

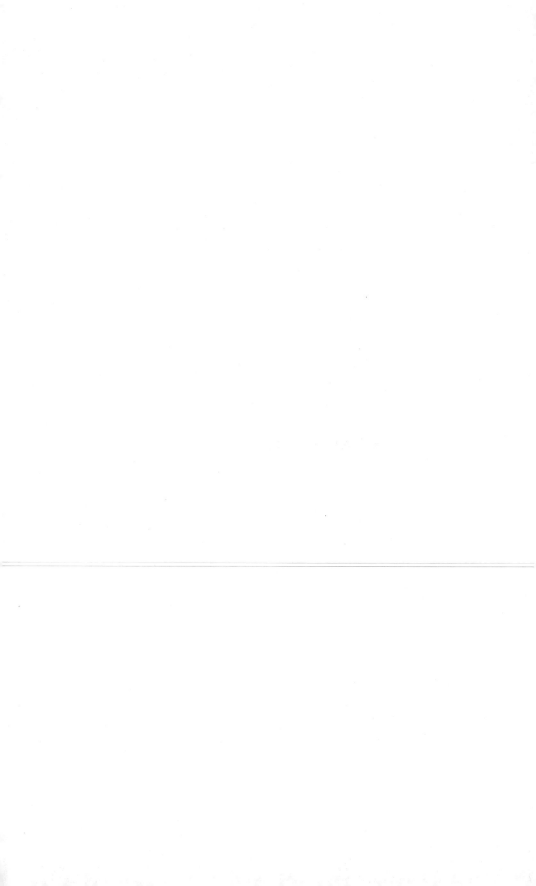

How to Bring Diversity into Industry: Industrial Experiences in Public Transport Repair and Maintenance

Rafael Vrecar[1]([✉]) [iD], Markus Steinlechner[2] [iD], Patrick Rupprecht[1] [iD],
Aaron Wedral[1] [iD], Marlies Negele[2] [iD], Maciej Palucki[1] [iD], Brigitte Ratzer[1] [iD],
and Astrid Weiss[1] [iD]

[1] Technische Universität Wien, Vienna, Austria
{rafael.vrecar,patrick.rupprecht,aaron.wedral,maciej.palucki,
brigitte.ratzer,astrid.weiss}@tuwien.ac.at
[2] Fraunhofer Austria Research, Vienna, Austria
{markus.steinlechner,marlies.negele}@fraunhofer.at

Abstract. This paper on industrial experience reports on two prominent public transport companies who decided to incorporate diversity more substantially into their corporate culture. To achieve the integration, an initiative was started and a project together with Fraunhofer Austria Research (Fraunhofer) and Technische Universität Wien (TU Wien) was launched. The project aims to support the companies in preparing their strategy for upcoming challenges such as the retirement of a large corpus of workers, recruiting new trainees, and finding new jobs for people within the company, whose working environment has changed drastically, e.g., due to the loss of bus or train driving licences because of health restrictions. The desired integration to strengthen diversity in their corporate culture started with shop inspections, expert interviews, diversity & future workshops, and a user study on a prototypical work system. The results were incorporated into diversity guidelines considering various drivers of change.

Keywords: Spatial Augmented Reality · Industrial Repair and Maintenance · Diversity in the Workspace

1   Initial Situation

The public transport industry in Austria is facing significant challenges that require a proactive approach. They include retirements, the emergence of new technologies, ongoing digitalization activities, and the problem that workers have, who need to work longer until retirement, but are not longer capable of pursuing their job in their respective work environments due to health issues (e.g., loss of driving licence because of high blood pressure). To overcome these challenges, two Austrian companies from the public transport sector, referred to as Company A and Company B, collaborated with Fraunhofer Austria Research

© The Author(s), under exclusive license to Springer Nature Switzerland AG 2023
J. Abdelnour Nocera et al. (Eds.): INTERACT 2023, LNCS 14145, pp. 267–272, 2023.
https://doi.org/10.1007/978-3-031-42293-5_20

(Fraunhofer) and Technische Universität Wien (TU Wien) in a project[1] which commenced in August 2021, with the following goals serving as its initial objectives.

1. *Evaluation of future technology leaps in the workplace and their effects, as well as the current conditions in the workplace*
2. *Consideration of emerging constraints as well as existing and upcoming diversity (new hires, retirements)*
3. *Examination of qualification and competence requirements in the course of diversity-appropriate work system design*
4. *Prototypically implemented diversity-appropriate/sensitive work system to demonstrate diversity-relevant design aspects in industrial repair and maintenance*
5. *Internal creation of transparency and knowledge about competitive advantages through diversity-sensitive work system design*
6. *Derivation of recommendations for action and creation of a set of guidelines*

To accomplish the first three objectives, various established Human-Computer Interaction (HCI) methods were used, which are outlined below. Based on the findings of the first three objectives, a prototypical diversity-appropriate/sensitive work system (diversity in this regard including but not limited to: gender, ethnicity, age, sexuality) was built which enabled a deeper understanding of diversity-friendly work system design. Finally, recommendations for action were then developed (Sect. 3).

2   Methods

To ensure a comprehensive understanding of the situation within the two companies and establish a common ground regarding the potential of emerging technologies, the following HCI activities were carried out.

2.1   Shop Inspections

Shop inspections were carried out to provide the academic project partners with an accurate and comprehensive understanding of the situation. The two industry partners' repair and maintenance sites were visited multiple times. After a general tour through all shops, employees were asked about the situation and their day-to-day experiences. The impressions were recorded in the form of notes by at least two people from the visiting academic project partners.

Emerging Challenges Identified Through this Method: Working overhead, lifting heavy parts, administrative procedures required by vehicle manufacturers, health-related loss of driving licences and therefore inability to work in track operation, as well as tech-leaps due to new vehicles requiring new skills.

---

[1] Funded by the Austrian Chamber of Labour.

2.2   Expert Interviews

After completing the majority of the visits, four expert interviews with different trainers from the companies were conducted. To analyze the outcomes of these interviews, the essential first two steps of the "Thematic Analysis" framework, as outlined by Braun and Clarke [1], were applied. However, given the limited available project resources, a complete thematic analysis to identify the challenges was considered to not justify the costs for the project.

Emerging Challenges Identified Through this Method: New vehicles require new learning processes (also emerged from 2.1), trainees start from different levels and have different prior education, some trainees are more/less talented than others and therefore need less/more time to learn different repair steps, recruiting trainees is difficult (lack of trainees in the past), enhance motivation to strengthen employee loyalty and prevent drop outs from training, switching between different workshops to find suitable jobs for all employees.

2.3   Diversity and Future Workshops

To foster collaborative work with our industry partners and leverage their expertise, two workshops were conducted simultaneously: a diversity workshop elaborating forms of diversity and a future workshop that focused on emerging technologies. The aim of both workshops was to enable a structured but creative flow of ideas. All available participants sent by the industry partners took part in both workshops. The primary goals of these workshops were twofold: to identify additional challenges that have not yet been uncovered by the inspections or interviews, and to validate already identified challenges using alternative methods.

Emerging Challenges Identified Through this Method: Retirements, surfacing special needs, lack of trainees in the past, and different talents were all brought up again and therefore validated. The discussion of the prototypical work system led to the decision to implement an Augmented Reality (AR) system using in-situ projections, as described in [3] or [5].

2.4   Prototypical Work System

First of all, it was necessary to define the prototypical work system that would be implemented and evaluated through a user study. To familiarize industry participants with the latest technologies, academic project partners showcased a variety of technologies in the pilot factory (an interactive exhibition of potential future technologies) of TU Wien and presented them to industry partners. Afterwards, the topics *diversity, technologies tried out in the past,* and *ideas for supporting technologies in the future* were discussed by brainstorming in breakout groups together with the academic partners.

The result was a prototypical implementation, which covered two typical repair tasks, one for each industry partner, and included three types of support: texts projected onto or near the parts; videos projected near the parts; augmenting different parts with arrows and other symbols to show where a repair step occurs. Switching between different steps in the repair process was possible through a mock button using a Wizard-of-Oz-Approach (see Fig. 1).

Implementation and User Study: The user study was designed based on standard usability study literature, specifically [2,7,8,10], and followed the procedure outlined below:

1) collect participants' consent to the recording of audio and video, 2) filling out a demographic questionnaire (left- or right-handed, primary education, position in company), 3) conducting the actual repair process, 4) filling out NASA-TLX [4], 5) filling out SUS [6], 6) filling out a feedback questionnaire which replaces post-interviews (because

Fig. 1. Prototype of the AR Work System for Repairing an AC Aggregate

of the availability of the industry partners, tests had to be held in parallel), 7) filling out DigiKoM (a competence assessment of oneself and one's company) [9]. Two user groups were compared (employees from both companies and TU Wien students). Between the two groups, the students were faster in one repair task and the employees in the other. The usability was generally considered *good* (ca. 80% on the SUS), and the task load was perceived as low as measured by the NASA-TLX.

3   Resulting Recommendations and Guidelines

Based on the results of the user study, we recommend considering diversity in any step of company changes. An initial chart (Fig. 2) has been conceptualized. The initial situation is depicted through the identified drivers of change. In case of technological changes, the current state of the work places and the employees' competencies have to be considered rigorously. A good way to gain experience in dealing with diversity is including external experts and creation of awareness through confronting employees, who are affected by changes, (continuously, in iterations) with the possibilities of new technologies; and listen to their thoughts about said technologies. Independently of the specific driver of change, it is important to always have a clear and current picture of the competencies which are needed for certain tasks. When assessing competencies, we consider it important to always keep in mind how diversity factors can create differences and which kind of role the technology can take. As a final step, the actual work space design has to be elaborated on, from a physical as well as an information flow perspective (feedback by participants: language is of utter importance!).

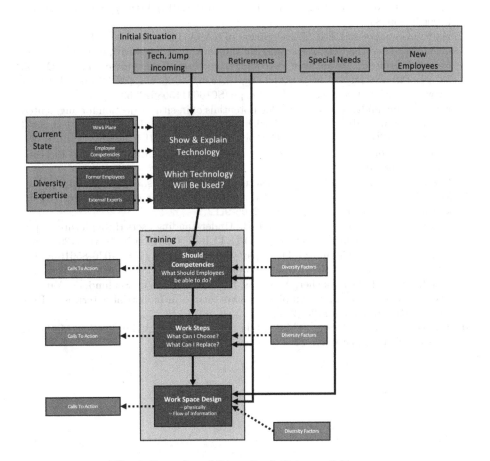

Fig. 2. Interplay of Diversity & Drivers of Change

Currently, we are in the process of developing more detailed guidelines to make them practical and applicable for our industry partners.

Acknowledgements. We greatly acknowledge the financial support from the "Digitalisierungsfonds Arbeit 4.0 der AK Wien", project name: MAXimizeMe.

References

1. Braun, V., Clarke, V.: Using thematic analysis in psychology. Qual. Res. Psychol. **3**(2), 77–101 (2006). https://doi.org/10.1191/1478088706qp063oa. https://www.tandfonline.com/doi/abs/10.1191/1478088706qp063oa
2. Ericsson, K.A., Simon, H.A.: Protocol Analysis: Verbal Reports as Data. The MIT Press, Cambridge (1993)
3. Funk, M., Mayer, S., Schmidt, A.: Using in-situ projection to support cognitively impaired workers at the workplace. In: Proceedings of the 17th International ACM SIGACCESS Conference on Computers & Accessibility, ASSETS 2015, Association pp. 185–192. for Computing Machinery, New York (2015). https://doi.org/10.1145/2700648.2809853
4. Hart, S.G., Staveland, L.E.: Development of NASA-TLX (Task Load Index): results of empirical and theoretical research. In: Hancock, P.A., Meshkati, N. (eds.) Human Mental Workload, Advances in Psychology, North-Holland, Amsterdam, NLD, vol. 52, pp. 139–183 (1988). https://doi.org/10.1016/S0166-4115(08)62386-9. https://www.sciencedirect.com/science/article/pii/S0166411508623869
5. Korn, O., Schmidt, A., Hörz, T.: The potentials of in-situ-projection for augmented workplaces in production: a study with impaired persons. In: CHI 2013 Extended Abstracts on Human Factors in Computing Systems, CHI EA 2013, pp. 979–984. Association for Computing Machinery, New York (2013). https://doi.org/10.1145/2468356.2468531
6. Lewis, J.R., Sauro, J.: The factor structure of the system usability scale. In: Kurosu, M. (ed.) HCD 2009. LNCS, vol. 5619, pp. 94–103. Springer, Heidelberg (2009). https://doi.org/10.1007/978-3-642-02806-9_12
7. Nielsen, L., Larusdottir, M., Larsen, L.B.: Understanding users through three types of personas. In: Ardito, C., et al. (eds.) INTERACT 2021. LNCS, vol. 12933, pp. 330–348. Springer, Cham (2021). https://doi.org/10.1007/978-3-030-85616-8_20
8. Rooden, M.: Thinking about thinking aloud. Contemp. Ergon., 328–332 (1998)
9. Steinlechner, M., Schumacher, A., Fuchs, B., Reichsthaler, L., Schlund, S.: A maturity model to assess digital employee competencies in industrial enterprises. Procedia CIRP **104**, 1185–1190 (2021)
10. Tomitsch, M., et al.: Design. Think. Make. Break. Repeat. A Handbook of Methods. Bis Publishers, Amsterdam (2018)

Whose Responsibility is Accessibility in Games Anyway? Everyone

Christopher Power[1,3](✉) ⓘ, Paul Cairns[2,3] ⓘ, Mark Barlet[3], and Steven Weitz[3]

[1] SMCS, University of Prince Edward Island, Charlottetown, PE, Canada
cdspower@upei.ca
[2] Department of Computer Science, University of York, York, UK
paul.cairns@york.ac.uk
[3] The AbleGamers Charity, 179E Burr Blvd, Suite Q, Kearneysville, WV 25436, USA
{mark,steveweitz}@ablegamers.org

Abstract. Accessibility in the commercial game industry has changed substantially in the last 5 years. From independent to very large studios there has been a substantial increase in the range and type of options that are available to disabled players. However, we do not have a clear picture of who is driving this change within studios. In this paper, we present the analysis of the roles of game professionals attending an industry facing professional development course on game accessibility. These results highlight that people from across the game industry, including a substantial number of people in leadership roles, are training to de-liver accessible experiences as a core component of game design.

Keywords: Game Accessibility · Player Experience · Training

1 Introduction

Accessibility for disabled people[1] in digital games has gone through an incredible period of growth in both research and practice in the last 5 years. The research space has moved increasingly to player experience driven approaches while the international game industry has committed substantial funding, time, and effort into creating a more accessible environment for gaming. With many games providing a robust and rich set of accessibility options for players to tune gameplay such that they can have the experiences they want from their games, there is an opportunity to understand how the changes in accessibility are being operationalized in studios.

In this paper we present data from the evaluation of the Certified Accessible Player Experiences® Practitioner (CAPXP) training course offered by the AbleGamers Charity with a focus on the roles of game professionals who take the course. This analysis shows that range of roles that engage in accessibility training is broad, with professionals from across the studio taking ownership of accessibility through their own training and development.

---

[1] In this paper we have chosen identity first language over people first language which is consistent with some communities. We acknowledge that language around disability is evolving and have made this choice for consistency within the paper.

© The Author(s), under exclusive license to Springer Nature Switzerland AG 2023
J. Abdelnour Nocera et al. (Eds.): INTERACT 2023, LNCS 14145, pp. 273–278, 2023.
https://doi.org/10.1007/978-3-031-42293-5_21

2   Context of the Training Course

The AbleGamers Charity[2] (AbleGamers hereafter) is a 501(c)3 charitable organization headquartered in West Virginia, USA. The organization has a mission to enable play for disabled people to reduce social isolation and improve quality of life through gaming. It does this through a variety of activities including: the fostering of inclusive game communities, peer counselling services to help people game, user research services working to make games more accessible, and professional development which trains game professionals in how to create more accessible gaming experiences.

CAPXP is a continuing professional development (CPD) course launched in September 2019 by AbleGamers and delivered through either in-studio training or through online classes. The course is marketed broadly to the game industry as a means for studios to increase the knowledge and expertise of accessibility in their studios. There are no role requirements for this course other than someone be in, or are developing towards, a career as a game professional[3]. The overall learning outcomes of the CAPXP program are to provide game professionals with the ability to:

- advocate for accessibility in their studio using social, legal, and financial cases,
- articulate the barriers in games encountered by different groups of disabled players,
- describe the experiences disabled players want to have in games,
- identify potential accessibility barriers in their games,
- apply the Accessible Player Experiences® (APX) Design Patterns[4] to generate new ideas for solutions to accessibility barriers,
- propose and justify solutions to accessibility barriers in their games.

The course is delivered through a series of interactive lectures and small group exercises that apply the knowledge gained. The course begins by game professionals learning about the different groups of disabled people and the types of barriers they may encounter in games. These barriers link specifically to different groups of design pat-terns that help game professionals identify and generate new accessible designs. Finally, the course concludes with a large design exercise where participants choose one of several different gaming scenarios and undertake a fresh design where they use their new knowledge to minimize accessibility barriers.

After the course is complete, participants are asked to complete a test on their knowledge, with certification awarded after the completion of this test.

---

[2] Website: www.ablegamers.org; GuideStar: https://www.guidestar.org/profile/30-0533750.

[3] In this work we refer to game professionals. This is the broad grouping of leadership, management, designers, artists, producers, engineers, quality assurance personnel and more who are commonly referred to as "game devs" in the industry. Due to the topic we have chosen this term to avoid confusion within the results.

[4] Website: https://accessible.games/apx.

3　Methodology

3.1　Design

To evaluate the efficacy of the training program, participants are surveyed with three different feedback questionnaires. For each questionnaire, participants are informed that their participation is voluntary and are provided with an information sheet and con-sent form regarding the use of their anonymized data.

When a participant registers for the course they are sent a link with to the *pre-training questionnaire* to collect demographics including their age, self-identified gender, and whether they identify as having a disability. Further they are asked their role in the studio, their self-rated accessibility expertise and whether they are familiar with accessibility sources of knowledge such as guidelines, legislation, or other accessibility tools.

Participants are also sent *post-training questionnaires* about their satisfaction with the course and evaluating their knowledge of accessibility. The post-training question-naire is issued immediately after the course and then repeated after 10 weeks. This paper deals with only data from the pre-training questionnaire.

Secondary analysis of this data for purposes of research was approved by the ethics research board at the University of Prince Edward Island.

3.2　Participants

There were 243 participants who completed the pre-training questionnaire as of March 2023. 81 participants identified as being between 18–29 while 160 were 30 and older, with 2 participants not giving their age. 141 participants worked at game companies larger than 250 people, 47 in companies between 50 and 249 people, 31 worked at smaller studios with fewer than 50 people, and 24 identified as being from outside the game industry. 167 participants had three or more years of experience creating games and 50 had two years or less. The mean number of participants that came from any one organization was 3.72 with a standard deviation of 6.40.

Table 1 presents the self-ratings of participants in their expertise in accessibility. Most participants rated themselves below a rating of Skilled in accessibility (217/243, 89.3%).

Figure 1 shows the mean ratings of familiarity with different representations of accessibility knowledge (rated on a scale from "Not at all familiar" - 0 to "Very familiar" - 5) with means below 3 on the 5-point Likert scale. This along with the self-rated expertise indicates that while participants had some accessibility knowledge coming into the course, there was not deep knowledge within the participant pool.

3.3　Analysis

A conventional content analysis with an open coding scheme was undertaken of the role titles provided by participants in an open-answer text box. The research goal of this analysis was not to produce a comprehensive taxonomy of roles in studios, but instead to identify what domains of work participants undertake in their studios when applying their accessibility knowledge from the CAPXP course.

Table 1. Participant self-rated expertise.

Accessibility Expertise	Participants (n)
Expert	0
Skilled	26
Somewhat skilled	85
Not so skilled	73
Novice	59

When participants described roles that fell under multiple codes, they were multiply coded. For example, the role title "UX Engineer" or "UI Engineer" were both categorized as being both *User Experience* and *Engineer/Programmer codes*, while the role title "UX Designer" or "UI Designer" were coded as being both *User Experience* and *Designer*. Whereas a role such as "User Experience Researcher" was coded as being only *User Experience*.

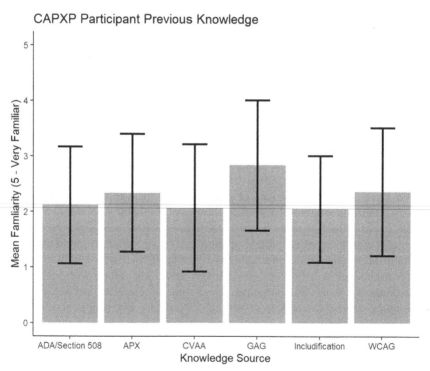

Fig. 1. Participant self-rated knowledge of several sources of accessibility knowledge including: ADA/Sect. 508 [1, 2], the APX design patterns [3], the 21st Century Com-munications and Video Accessibility Act[4], the Game Accessibility Guidelines [5], Includification [6] and the Web Content Accessibility Guidelines [7]

4 Results

Table 2 presents the results of the content analysis of the roles. Two axial codes were identified: Leadership and Production.

Leadership codes are those that describe roles where individuals are responsible for leadership and management of teams or products in studios. For example, the code of Lead includes: Lead level designer, UI Lead, UX Lead, QA Lead and Lead Gameplay Programmer. Similarly, the Managers code includes items such as: Product Manager, Release Manager, User Research Manager, and Development Operations Manager. Directors and producers show similar diversity of role names. The seven individuals in the Founder/Executive code are exclusively C-level executives or founders of studios.

The Production code groups the wide range of specialties that produce different aspects of games. Of note in Table 2, User Experience, Designer and Engineering/Programmer roles account for 170 of the 243 participants. Demonstrating that accessibility is not a niche concern isolated to one aspect of game design, or something that is exclusive to specialist roles, and instead something that game professionals from across all aspects of game design are training in for their day-to-day work.

Table 2. Categorization of Participant.

Category	Role	Participants (n)
Leadership	Lead	30
	Director	16
	Manager	15
	Producer	11
	Founder/Executive	7
	Product Owner	3
Production	User Experience	74
	Designer	63
	Engineer/Programmer	33
	Artist	18
	Quality Assurance (QA) Specialist	15
	Accessibility Specialist	7
	Marketing	3
	Writer	2
Other	Not in studios	14

5 Discussion

In accessibility, both in gaming and beyond, we often discuss the need for grassroots advocacy efforts that lead to change in the commercial marketplace. Gaming is a place where this change has happened. After over 20 years of regular advocacy by dozens of advocates, there are now many hundreds of game professionals and studios investing their time and money in the CAPXP training from studios both small and large, and from that we conclude that there is substantial interest in wanting to provide more accessible experiences to disabled players.

However, we see from the analysis of the roles provided by participants that accessibility is no longer just a concern of accessibility advocates and specialists or localized in a single studio role. While the role of accessibility champions is important in studios, the industry is shifting towards an approach where people from all areas of game production, including the most senior levels of organizational leadership, are engaging in training to deliver more accessible experiences to their players.

The future of accessibility in gaming is looking very promising with the industry investing in skills that will make it so that disabled players can find games that they love to play and have the experiences they want to have with their family and friends.

References

1. Americans With Disabilities Act of 1990, Pub. L. No. 101–336, 104 Stat. 328 (1990)
2. Section 508 Amendment to the Rehabilitation Act of 1973, United States Code, 29, Sec. 794d - Electronic and information technology, U.S. Government Publishing Office (1998)
3. Accessible Player Experiences (APX). https://accessible.games/accessible-player-experiences/. Accessed 25 Apr 2023
4. 21st Century Communications and Video Accessibility Act, Pub. L., pp. 111–260 (2010)
5. Game accessibility guidelines. https://gameaccessibilityguidelines.com/. Accessed 25 Apr 2023
6. Barlet, M., Spohn, S. Includification: a practical guide to accessibility (2012). https://accessible.games/includification/. Accessed 25 Apr 2023
7. Web Content Accessibility Guidelines 2.0, W3C World Wide Web Consortium Recommendation (2018). https://www.w3.org/TR/2018/REC-WCAG21-20180605/. https://www.w3.org/TR/WCAG21/. Accessed 25 Apr 2023

Interactive Demonstrations

A Toolkit for Human-Centred Engineering: An Experience with Pre-teens

Rosella Gennari[1]([⊠]) [iD], Soufiane Krik[1] [iD], and Alessandra Melonio[2] [iD]

[1] Faculty of Engineering, Piazza Domenicani 3, 39100 Bolzano, Italy
gennari@inf.unibz.it, soufiane.krik@unibz.it
[2] Ca' Foscari University of Venice, Via Torino 155, 30170 Venezia Mestre, Italy
alessandra.melonio@unive.it

Abstract. IoTgo is an adaptable toolkit for human-centred engineering with micro-electronics. This paper reports on IoTgo for pre-teens. This guided them from exploring the workings of sensors, actuators, and wireless communication to the development of prototypes with them that interact with people. The paper explains the rationale of the toolkit for pre-teens, and what they accomplished with it.

Keywords: Human centred design · electronics · education · learning · pre-teen · smart thing

1 Introduction and Related Work

Smart things, such as smart watches, interact with people via micro-electronic physical devices, like sensors and actuators, and data that is exchanged via wireless. Microcontrollers, such as micro:bit, and companion material, like scaffolding cards, help non-experts prototype with electronics a "smart thing" [9,11]. However, this and other similar toolkits are mainly used with researchers or practitioners from other fields than engineering, or for promoting design or critical thinking when used with children or teens, e.g., [2,3,7,13].

Few toolkits guide pre-teens to prototype smart things with micro-electronics, *after* experimenting with it [8]. Fewer invite pre-teens to prototype their smart things by adopting a human- or user-centred perspective, i.e., considering who uses smart things (*persona*), what goal these tackle (a.k.a., *mission*), where they are mainly used (a.k.a., *location*) [3,12]. This paper does so. It briefly reports the design of the IoTgo toolkit for pre-teens, and it shows what 10 pre-teens managed to engineer with it.

2 The Design of the Toolkit

IoTgo consists of physical elements, digital and electronic elements. The former include paper-based cards and boards for playing cards and conceptualising ideas

© The Author(s), under exclusive license to Springer Nature Switzerland AG 2023
J. Abdelnour Nocera et al. (Eds.): INTERACT 2023, LNCS 14145, pp. 281–285, 2023.
https://doi.org/10.1007/978-3-031-42293-5_22

of smart things. The latter include programmable open-source microcontrollers, related physical devices, and a dedicated app. Similar versions have been used in past experiences, especially with high-school learners and university students with no programming or electronics background, e.g., [4,6]. The IoTgo kit of this paper was adapted to pre-teens, for enabling them to experiment with micro-electronics and wireless communication, and then engineer smart things with a human-centred perspective. Its main novel components are as follows.

Exploring and Experimenting. For exploring and experimenting with basic electronic circuits, IoTgo uses open kits with Arduino UNO and physical devices (e.g., light sensors, LEDs, banana clips, digital multi-meters) [1]. It also has companion cards that have explanatory illustrations and wiring schemes for creating circuits, step by step, first without Arduino UNO for exploring sensors, and then with it for triggering actuators according to signals read by sensors.

Exploring a Context and Conceptualising Ideas. IoTgo has also two paper boards for exploring a human-centred context, with a problematic situation to tackle, and engineering smart things for it, instead of three or more boards as with older learners [4–6]. Cards, to place on boards, decompose smart things along their non-technical components (e.g., personas), and technical components (e.g., sensors and actuators). Specifically, the context board helps empathise with a problematic context and find a solution for it: it starts with a story presenting the context, acting as scenario; it guides to choose non-technical cards for things to make smart ("what"), personas using them ("who"), locations where persona use them ("where"), and missions that personas tackle with them ("for what") in relation to the given context. The other board is for communication and technical cards, to use in either one of two manners: to sense and send data via wireless; to interact with such data. See an example of the former in Fig. 1.

Prototyping the Interaction and Communication. IoTgo also contains micro:bit microcontrollers [9], which have onboard Bluetooth antennas and are easy to embed in things to make smart. Moreover, the IoTgo app enables non-experts to automatically generate a MakeCode block-based programs for micro:bit, starting from the chosen combinations of cards on the communication boards [10]. Participants can then further edit and upload programs on micro:bit microcontrollers. In this manner, participants can rapidly test their ideas of smart things in action, then share and reflect on them, and revise them rapidly.

3   Case-Study

Participants and Context. The study involved 10 pre-teens, aged 10–13 years old (9 males, 1 female). Three were from the last year of primary school, whereas all others were from the first two years of middle school. Only one of them had past programming experience with the micro:bit and programming in MakeCode. The study was organised over three days (Day 1–3), for 3–4 h per day, in August

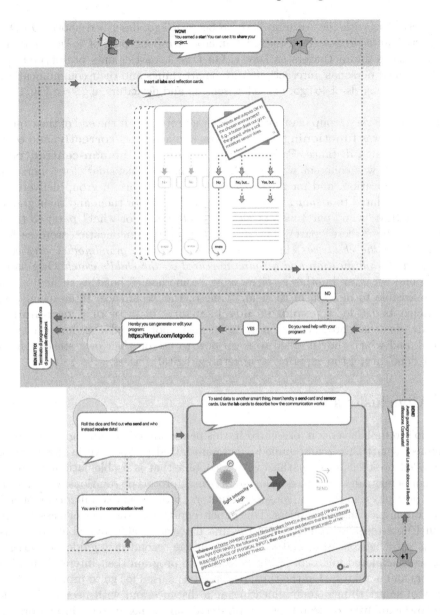

Fig. 1. An example of a filled-in communication board: conceptualisation example with a sensor and how to send data (bottom); IoTgo link to the app for generating a program (middle); reflection area, with an example reflection card.

and September 2022. It was held in a dedicated open space for young learners. Participants worked in pairs. Each pair was provided with a laptop computer and the IoTgo toolkit. On Day 1, participants explored the workings of sensors and actuators with the Arduino-based tools of IoTgo, described above. On Day 2, participants programmed micro:bit microcontrollers, part of IoTgo, and the same sensors and actuators as Day 1. On Day 3, participants prototyped and programmed personas' interactions with smart things and their communication, with paper-boards of IoTgo, micro:bit, sensors and actuators, e.g., see Fig. 1.

Prototypes. Every group managed to deliver a prototype at the end of the experience, which was **functioning**, using sensors and actuators **correctly**, and communicating at a distance. Each prototype embedded a **human-centred perspective**: it was coherent with the chosen thing to make smart for a persona, in a given location, and for a given mission. For instance, a group delivered a prototype related to a *smart watch* (the "what" part) for them and their grandmothers (the "who" part) who needed to *relate* (the "for what" part) to them in *town* (the "where" part). The interaction and communication were as follows: *When the child was supposed to come home, the grandmother pressed a button and a notification and a sound appeared on the child's watch.* Originally, the sound was grandmother's voice saying "come home" but this turned out to be unfeasible to develop in the short time of the experience. Interestingly, all participants decided to **explore a novel sensor, actuator or programming feature** for their project, e.g., a motion sensor, not introduced during Days 2 and 3, and which they decided to learn how to use on their own starting from what done during the experience concerning digital sensors.

4   Conclusions

The IoTgo toolkit version, presented in this paper, aimed at guiding pre-teens to engineer smart things and embed a human-centred perspective in the process: it guided pre-teens to empathise with a context that is problematic for certain human beings, and then to develop smart-thing prototype solutions with micro-electronic physical devices (sensors, actuators, programmable microcontrollers) and communicating via wireless. This paper reported the outcome of a case study with 10 pre-teens using IoTgo. On the first day, the toolkit invited all to experiment with basic sensors and actuators. On the second day, guided by IoTgo, pre-teens explored microcontrollers and how to program their interactions with sensors and actuators. On the third day, pre-teens used IoTgo to prototype their ideas of smart things, communicating at a distance and with people. According to the analyses of prototypes by pre-teens, all managed to engineer working prototypes and adopt a human-centred perspective. All seemed to have benefited from exploring sensors and actuators before prototyping their solutions, as experienced by few others in the literature that invested time on making childrne explore electronics before programming or designing [8]. In other experiences, which did not invest time in that, participants with no experience were confused about how sensors and actuators worked, and this required rounds of feedback or led to non-original solutions [6].

References

1. Arduino-Official-Store: Arduino UNO. https://store.arduino.cc/products/arduino-uno-rev3. Accessed 18 Apr 2023
2. De Roeck, D., Tanghe, J., Jacoby, A., Moons, I., Slegers, K.: Ideas of things: the IOT design kit. In: Companion Publication of the 2019 on Designing Interactive Systems Conference 2019 Companion, DIS 2019 Companion, pp. 159–163. ACM, New York (2019). https://doi.org/10.1145/3301019.3323888
3. Gennari, R., Matera, M., Melonio, A., Rizvi, M., Roumelioti, E.: Reflection and awareness in the design process: children ideating, programming and prototyping smart objects. Multimedia Tools Appl. **80**, 34909–34932 (2020). https://doi.org/10.1007/s11042-020-09927-x
4. Gennari, R., Matera, M., Morra, D., Melonio, A., Rizvi, M.: Design for social digital well-being with young generations: engage them and make them reflect. Int. J. Hum. Comput. Stud. **173**, 103006 (2023). https://doi.org/10.1016/j.ijhcs.2023.103006
5. Gennari, R., Matera, M., Morra, D., Rizvi, M.: A phygital toolkit for rapidly designing smart things at school. In: Bottoni, P., Panizzi, E. (eds.) AVI 2022: International Conference on Advanced Visual Interfaces, Frascati, Rome, Italy, 6–10 June 2022, pp. 27:1–27:5. ACM (2022). https://doi.org/10.1145/3531073.3531119
6. Gennari, R., Melonio, A., Rizvi, M.: A tool for guiding teachers and their learners: the case study of an art class. In: CHI EA 2023, pp. 707–718. ACM, New York (2023). https://doi.org/10.1145/2559206.2578870
7. Herro, D., Quigley, C., Plank, H., Abimbade, O., Owens, A.: Instructional practices promoting computational thinking in STEAM elementary classrooms. J. Digital Learn. Teach. Educ. **38**(4), 158–172 (2022). https://doi.org/10.1080/21532974.2022.2087125
8. Lechelt, S., Rogers, Y., Marquardt, N.: Coming to your senses: promoting critical thinking about sensors through playful interaction in classrooms. In: Proceedings of the Interaction Design and Children Conference, IDC 2020, pp. 11–22. ACM, New York (2020). https://doi.org/10.1145/3392063.3394401
9. Micro:bit-Educational-Foundation: Micro:bit Educational Foundation—micro:bit. https://microbit.org. Accessed 18 Apr 2023
10. Microsoft-micro:bit: MakeCode. https://makecode.microbit.org/. Accessed 18 Apr 2023
11. Mora, S., Gianni, F., Divitini, M.: Tiles: a card-based ideation toolkit for the Internet of Things. In: Proceedings of the 2017 Conference on Designing Interactive Systems, DIS 2017, pp. 587–598. ACM, New York (2017). https://doi.org/10.1145/3064663.3064699
12. Norman, D.: Human-Centered Design. https://www.interaction-design.org/literature/topics/human-centered-design. Accessed 18 Apr 2023
13. Schaper, M.M., et al.: Computational empowerment in practice: scaffolding teenagers' learning about emerging technologies and their ethical and societal impact. Int. J. Child-Comput. Interact. **34**, 100537 (2022). https://doi.org/10.1016/j.ijcci.2022.100537

Color Blind: A Figma Plugin to Simulate Colour Blindness

Kishan Kanakhara[✉], Drishya Bhattarai, and Sayan Sarcar

Birmingham City University, Birmingham B5 7AJ, UK
{kishan.kanakhara,drishya.bhattarai}@mail.bcu.ac.uk,
sayan.sarcar@bcu.ac.uk

Abstract. Of late, web applications continually develop and employ cutting-edge techniques to display information. However, due to an absence of user testing or oversight by designers, this can frequently lead to a product that is in-accessible to a significant percentage of users. To address this issue, we developed Colour Blind, a Figma add-on plugin that makes it easier to do accessibility checks inside the designer's preferred tool. The plugin enables de-signers to understand users' perspectives and evaluate their designs appropriately by mimicking various types of colour blindness in design. Furthermore, Colour Blind can generate simulated previews inside the Figma canvas so users can compare various simulations. Over 10000 users have already installed the plugin on Figma Community.

Keywords: Accessibility · Simulation · Colour Blind · Plugin

1 Introduction

The quality of digital products has significantly changed during the past decade [6]. Despite these developments, not all digital products on the market are easily accessible to everyone. Given that the COVID-19 pandemic has compelled many companies to become online, it is crucial for product designers to consider the broad user base that will be accessing their applications [10]. Users may experience difficulties in their daily lives because of poorly designed digital products [1]. For instance, around 3 million people in the UK, or 4.5% of the population, are estimated to have colour vision deficiency [5]. Therefore, it is crucial to make sure that all consumers, including those with disabilities, can use digital products.

At the outset of the product design process, creating a color scheme is typically one of the primary tasks [10]. It is important to consider factors such as readability, contrast, and color theory to make sure that the color scheme is accessible to all users. However, determining whether the color scheme is user-friendly for individuals with color blindness can pose a challenge. Typically, feedback from appropriate users is

Supplementary Information The online version contains supplementary material available at https://doi.org/10.1007/978-3-031-42293-5_23.

© The Author(s), under exclusive license to Springer Nature Switzerland AG 2023
J. Abdelnour Nocera et al. (Eds.): INTERACT 2023, LNCS 14145, pp. 286–289, 2023.
https://doi.org/10.1007/978-3-031-42293-5_23

gathered through user testing at the end of the design process, which can be time-consuming and resource intensive. A more efficient approach is to employ a quick and straightforward method to simulate color blindness, which can help detect any potential issues early in the design phase.

We believed that by providing designers with assistance in conducting accessibility checks during the product design phase, there would be substantial savings in resources that are typically allocated for quality assessment.

At first, we designed a web application that could mimic colour blindness in artwork. We immediately found, however, that there were already existing websites that might serve the same purpose, but designers did not frequently utilise them. This was due, among other things, to the difficulty of designers having to stop what they were doing, go to the website, and inspect each design. We therefore reviewed our strategy and investigated alternative ways to incorporate the solution into the design workflow. Finally, we found that the most practical and simple method for seamless integration would be a Figma plugin.

As a result, we created the Color Blind Figma plugin, which enables designers to quickly test their designs for colour-blind users in real-time at any step of the product design process. Designers can do accessibility assessments with Colour Blind without stopping their current work, minimizing the need for extensive user testing [4].

2 System Design

At the time of developing the plugin, we used a well-known method of changing colour pixels in a picture to simulate colour blindness [2]. We used Coblis, an online tool that allows users to upload an image and simulate colour blindness to see how the image might look to someone with colour vision problems, for creating the pixel manipulation logic. The jsColorblindSimulator package [7], which makes use of the Brettel, Viénot, and Mollon Simulation function [2] updated for modern sRGB monitors. Despite the function's reasonable accuracy for full dichromacy, it still represents an approximation because of many variables like uncalibrated monitors, unknowable lighting conditions, and individual variances.

Following extensive testing of Figma's logic and colour modification features, we created the system architecture to be as user-friendly as feasible (Fig. 1).

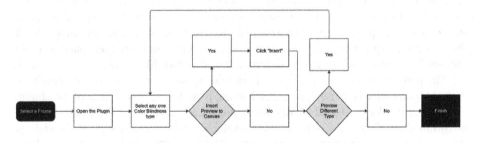

Fig. 1. Plugin User Flow

We all make mistakes in our daily lives, such as attempting to pull a door that should be pushed or flipping the wrong switch. This is why product designers need to be creative and devise user-friendly products that do not require lengthy manuals [8]. To design the interface for our plugin, we drew inspiration from everyday objects and interfaces. The standard print window that is present on most computers caught our attention because it is a layout that many users are familiar with. This window has two columns, with the first column taking up 30% of the horizontal space and the second column filling up the remaining space.

We used this layout as a basis for our plugin interface, with the options for color-blind types located in the left column and the preview pane in the second column. When a user selects a type, the preview pane automatically updates to reflect the chosen option.

3 Usage Scenario

The inspiration for the plugin came from watching a video posted on social media by Jeff, a color-blind person. In the video, Jeff tried to buy a shirt from an internet shop but ran into problems because of his colour vision impairment. Jeff found it challenging to investigate various colour alternatives because the website lacked accurate colour labels and just offered swatches. Jeff was quite upset with this poor user experience.

Due to a variety of reasons, particularly in small teams or among novice designers, inclusive design may not have received the attention it deserved throughout the development of a website. These reasons may include a lack of time or the absence of user testing. To solve this issue, designers can utilise the Colour Blind plugin when creating screens to make sure that the information is consistent in how colour-blind and people with normal vision perceive it.

4 Result & Future Scope

Since it first became available to the Figma community more than eight months ago, the Colour Blind plugin has undergone several revisions in response to suggestions from coworkers and designer friends. Support for dark mode was one of the primary changes. The selecting process for the color-blind type was changed, which was another important upgrade. In the past, selecting an option from a drop-down menu needed an additional click, and a brief description of the different types of colour blindness was shown on the screen. Other designers thought this was a bad idea, so we redesigned the selection interaction. The up-dated version allows users to select one of the alternatives to refresh the preview by displaying all the color-blind types up front on the left pane as radio buttons. Now everyone can see the description of the color-blind type.

The number of users of our plugin is increasing weekly, and we receive feedback daily. Our objective is to use this feedback to improve the user experience of the plugin.

Special thanks to Digital Media Technology Lab (DMT) and Prof. Sayan Sarcar at Birmingham City University for their invaluable guidance and support throughout the creation of this interactive demo paper. Their expertise and insights have been instrumental.

References

1. Aizpurua, A., Harper, S., Vigo, M.: Exploring the relationship between web accessibility and user experience. Int. J. Hum.-Comput. Stud. [online] **91**, 13–23. https://doi.org/10.1016/j.ijhcs.2016.03.008. Accessed 21 Apr 2023
2. Brettel, H., Vienot Françoise Viénot Mollon, J.D.: Computerized simulation of color appearance for dichromats (1997). http://vision.psychol.cam.ac.uk/jdmollon/papers/Dichromatsimulation.pdf. Accessed 9 Apr 2023
3. Bose, R., Jürgensen, H.: Accessibility of E-commerce websites for vision-impaired persons. In: Miesenberger, K., Fels, D., Archambault, D., Peňáz, P., Zagler, W. (eds.) ICCHP 2014. LNCS, vol. 8547, pp. 121–128. Springer, Cham (2014). https://doi.org/10.1007/978-3-319-08596-8_18
4. Caldwell, B., Reid, L.G, Vanderheiden, I.: Web Content Accessibility Guidelines (WCAG) 2.0 (2008). https://ysu.edu/sites/default/files/mathematics-achievement-center/Hawkes%20Learning_Web%20Content%20Accessibility%20Guidelines%20(WCAG)%202.0.pdf. Accessed 9 Apr 2023
5. Colour Blind Awareness. Colour Blindness. [online] Colour Blind Awareness (2022). https://www.colourblindawareness.org/colour-blindness/. Accessed 21 Apr 2023
6. Sørum, H.: Two decades of online information and digital services: quality improvements to municipality websites and user preferences. Lect. Notes Comput. Sci. (2019). https://doi.org/10.1007/978-3-030-27523-5_10. Accessed 21 Apr 2023
7. MaPePeR and Nicolas Burrus jsColorblindSimulator https://github.com/MaPePeR/jsColorblindSimulator. Accessed 9 Apr 2023
8. Norman, D.A.: The design of everyday things. New York, New York: Basic Books (1988). Accessed 10 Apr 2023
9. Schulz, M., Pieper, M.: Web compliance management: barrier-free websites just by simply pressing the button? Accessibility and the use of content-management-systems. In: Stephanidis, C., Pieper, M. (eds.) UI4ALL 2006. LNCS, vol. 4397, pp. 419–426. Springer, Heidelberg (2007). https://doi.org/10.1007/978-3-540-71025-7_27
10. Conway, V., Brown, J., Hollier, S., Nicholl, C.: Website accessibility: a comparative analysis of Australian national and state/territory library websites. Austr. Libr. J. **61**(3), 170–188 (2012). https://doi.org/10.1080/00049670.2012.10736059. Accessed 21 Apr 2023
11. Zhang, L., Yue, F., Qin, Q., Liang, Y.: How can design help improving products during the pandemic. Lecture Notes in Computer Science, pp. 564–584 (2022). https://doi.org/10.1007/978-3-031-21704-3_40.. Accessed 21 Apr 2023

Comfort Management Through a Universal Wheelchair Dashboard

Andreas Polydorides[(✉)] and Yvonne Rogers

University College London, London WC1E 6BT, UK
andreas.polydorides@gmail.com
https://uclic.ucl.ac.uk/

Abstract. Wheelchair users can accumulate many hours on their chairs every day, using them for transport, work and leisure activities. Despite being necessary for leading a typical daily life, long, uninterrupted use can become uncomfortable and result in various health implications. Many commercial solutions target individual problems, such as cushion comfort, temperature regulation and posture control. However, they all work independently and there is a lack of solutions that provide holistic management methods for the additional mental load a wheelchair user must manage daily. We present a wheelchair dashboard designed for discomfort management. Features include displaying data like temperature from in-seat sensors, customised reminders for users to shift their weight or transfer out of the wheelchair to avoid pressure related health complications and control of add-on wheelchair products such as a temperature regulation prototype we are developing and demonstrating alongside this dashboard. While the aim is for this dashboard to be an end user tool, because of the lack of research work in wheelchair comfort, this dashboard can be a powerful research tool, from which studies can be designed and carried on, such as running prompt queries and supplementing questionnaire responses with sensor data.

Keywords: Wheelchair · Disability · Comfort Mangement

1 Introduction

Wheelchair users who sit in their wheelchairs for long periods, at least 8 h for a work day for example, often experience discomfort [1]. Manual wheelchair users, particularly those with spinal cord injury, are reported to sit in their wheelchairs for up to 9.6 h [2]. The effects of discomfort from a wheelchair seat can manifest in reduced usability of the wheelchair, poor quality of life, poor ergonomics, and ultimately health complications [3–6]. Many passive comfort-related products exist in the market, such as a variety of seating cushions for different needs.

Supplementary Information The online version contains supplementary material available at https://doi.org/10.1007/978-3-031-42293-5_24.

© The Author(s), under exclusive license to Springer Nature Switzerland AG 2023
J. Abdelnour Nocera et al. (Eds.): INTERACT 2023, LNCS 14145, pp. 290–294, 2023.
https://doi.org/10.1007/978-3-031-42293-5_24

However, these do not provide important information to the user and studies examining their effectiveness, only rely on subjective data. While not at the same scale, active products are also available for purchase. Usually, these are accompanied with a way to control them, for example power-tilt wheelchairs have their own control panel on the armrest, while fan controlled products for temperature control are operated through remotes. This can overburden the user. Our aim with this design project was to develop a simple user interface based on the wheelchair that allowed the user to better manage their comfort and health.

2   Using the Dashboard

The dashboard will function as an interaction point between the user and their wheelchair. It will do so by offering the user the ability to distinguish between, and manage factors that contribute to their daily discomfort, like overheating, or pressure buildup. Many of these functions can be accessed through a simple main menu UI as shown in Fig. 1a. Viewing wheelchair statistics (temperature and humidity), as well as controlling any temperature control add-ons can be done through a dedicated temperature menu as seen on Fig. 1b. This temperature control element is an example of routing wheelchair products through the dashboard for a holistic, unified user experience. In the future, we hope to work with more add-ons, such as digital pressure mat accessories so that the user can, in real time, evaluate their seating position.

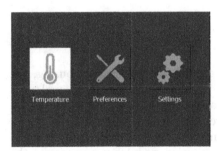 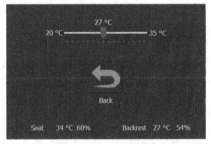

(a) A screenshot of the main menu of the dashboard UI, the temperature option is highlighted white as it is the currently hovered over option. With more add-ons controlled by this dashboard, more options would populate this menu.

(b) The temperature sub-menu, displaying the temperature and humidity data from the back rest and seat sensors, as well as presenting the user with a slider to manually control the temperature the add-on attempts to warm up or cool down to.

Fig. 1. A menu and a sub-menu of the current iteration of the dashboard UI, WheelOS

This dashboard also allows the user to offload the mental load of remembering to shift their weight or transfer out of the wheelchair through customisable timed reminders. An example of such a reminder is shown in Fig. 2. As we also wanted the user to evaluate their comfort levels and really challenge the current state of assistive technology products, we have incorporated the ability to prompt the user with certain questions regarding any discomfort they may have experienced, and then provide sensor data to help the user better interpret their responses. The frequency and timing of such prompts is completely customisable by the user to fit their schedule. We hope to use this prompting functionality to enable researchers and developers of comfort related products to utilise this dashboard in order to run their user studies, such as diary studies or questionnaires.

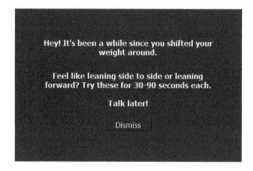

Fig. 2. A figure showing a screenshot of the dashboard UI when it reminds the user to shift their weight, either manually or with the power tilt function, to relieve the built up pressure from seating.

3   Behind the Screen

The dashboard consists of three assembly groups: the dashboard housing, the wheelchair mount, and the electronics. We do not consider any additional comfort management technology such as the seat heating and cooling prototype we demonstrate, as that is an example of a product that could communicate with the interface, but not our focus for this contribution. The housing and control knob are 3D printed; wheelchair users are a varied population group and the ability to iterate the design and quickly test models was favourable. For example, hand dexterity and arm strength can greatly differ between users, and as more accessible knobs can be designed for those users, they will not need to adapt to the system. With the same reasoning, the wheelchair mount is also 3D printed so that it may be adapted to various wheelchairs, as there is no standardisation of armrests within the wheelchair space. Additionally, for both the wheelchair mount and the dashboard housing, 3D printing allows for easy repairability and personalisation. Pictures of a render and a prototype mounted on a manual wheelchair arm rest are shown in Fig. 3 below.

The electronics assembly was developed using off-the-shelf components as a repairable device is in line with our goal in making a user-first device. A device

(a) A render of the dashboard, mounted on to a manual wheelchair. The UI is set on the main menu.

(b) A picture of an initial prototype of the dashboard, mounted on a wheelchair.

Fig. 3. Pictures of the dashboard mounted on a wheelchair, in a render and real life prototype.

that is repairable or has easily replaceable parts is longer lasting, reducing waste and user expenses. As such, the compute element is a Raspberry Pi Zero W. It displays the graphical user interface on an SPI display, connected to its GPIO pins. The humidity sensors and temperature sensors are also off the shelf, easy to source components, such as the DHT22, a humidity and temperature sensor. While the latter can record temperature, we paired it with a DS18B20, which records temperature changes in finer increments, which is useful as the dashboard also offers the ability to automatically control thermal comfort prototypes. We have two pairs of these sensors, one in the seat and one pair in the backrest. The layout of the electronics assembly is shown below in Fig. 4.

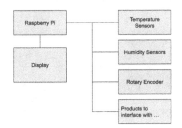

Fig. 4. A diagram showing the display, rotary encoder, and sensors connected to the Raspberry Pi. Additionally, all add-ons are shown to be connected to the Pi as they would be controlled through that.

References

1. Shaw, G., Taylor, S.J.: A survey of wheelchair seating problems of the institution-alized elderly. Assist Technol. **3**(1), 5–10 (1991). https://doi.org/10.1080/10400435.1991.10132175

2. Bergstrom, N., Braden, B.: A prospective study of pressure sore risk among institutionalized elderly. J. Am. Geriatr. Soc. **40**, 747–758 (1992)
3. Rawson, R.O., Hardy, J.D.: Weat inhibition by cutaneous cooling in normal sympathectomized and paraplegic man. J. Appl. Physiol. **22**, 287–291 (1967). https://doi.org/10.1080/10400435.1991.10132175
4. Griggs, K.E., Vanheusden, F.J.: Integrated fan cooling of the lower back for wheelchair users. J. Rehabilit. Assist. Technol. Eng. **9** (2022). https://doi.org/10.1177/20556683221126994
5. Griggs, K.E., Stephenson, B.T., Price, M.J., et al.: Heat-related issues and practical applications for paralympic athletes at Tokyo 2020. Temperature **7**, 37–57 (2020)
6. Allen, D.R., Huang, M., Parupia, I.M., et al.: Impaired sweating responses to a passive whole body heat stress in individuals with multiple sclerosis. J. Neurophysiol. **118**, 7–14 (2017)

Dataslip: How Far Does Your Personal Data Go?

Alejandra Gómez Ortega(✉), Vasileios Milias, James Scott Broadhead,
Carlo van der Valk, and Jacky Bourgeois

Delft University of Technology, Delft, The Netherlands
a.gomezortega@tudelft.nl

Abstract. As we navigate the physical and digital world, we unknowingly leave behind an immense trail of data. We are informed about this via lengthy documents (e.g., privacy policies) or short statements (e.g., cookie popups). However, even when we know that data is collected, we remain largely unaware of its nature; what information it contains and how it relates to us. Data is highly personal. It contains and reveals information about our behavior and experiences scattered over time, which can be abstract and opaque even to us. Dataslip is an interactive installation where the construct of personal data is translated into a material and tangible representation in the form of a receipt or 'personal data slip'. The receipt contains detailed information and illustrative examples of the data generated from our interactions with five different categories of products and services: (1) personalized public transport cards, (2) supermarket loyalty cards, (3) credit and debit cards, (4) wearables, and (5) mobile apps. Its length is proportional to the amount of data collected about us. With dataslip, we aim to reduce the distance between individuals and their personal data, elicit confrontation and invite people to question their role within the personal data ecosystems in which they are embedded.

Keywords: Personal Data · Data Literacy · Awareness

1 Introduction

The European General Data Protection Regulation (GDPR) defines *personal data* as any information from which an individual can be directly or indirectly identified [2]. Private companies and public services collect and indefinitely store personal data as individuals interact with digital products and services. For instance, when a person registers on a dating app, she *volunteers* information about herself, such as her name and address (i.e., *volunteered* personal data [7]); when she uses the app to get a date, the app *observes* information about her behavior, such as her swipes and matches (i.e., *observed* personal data [7]).

Supplementary Information The online version contains supplementary material available at https://doi.org/10.1007/978-3-031-42293-5_25.

© The Author(s), under exclusive license to Springer Nature Switzerland AG 2023
J. Abdelnour Nocera et al. (Eds.): INTERACT 2023, LNCS 14145, pp. 295–299, 2023.
https://doi.org/10.1007/978-3-031-42293-5_25

Individuals are informed about data collection and storage practices through lengthy documents, such as privacy policies, or short statements, such as cookie pop-ups. However, these are hardly effective for informing [8]. This means that most people are unaware of the data collection practices around them, especially when it comes to *observed* personal data. The dating app user hardly knows if personal data is collected; how personal data is collected; or exactly what types of personal data are collected as she interacts with it. There is a disconnect between the use of a product or service (e.g., scrolling through a dating app) and that such use results in the collection and storage of personal data (e.g., swipes and matches) [5]. Besides, even when a person knows that data is being collected, for the most part, she doesn't know exactly what data looks and feels like [3].

Recent narratives around personal data diminish the role of individuals in its generation [4]. These portray personal data as *'the new gold'* or *'the new oil'*; equating it to a natural resource that can be exploited, mined, and refined [4]. Here, those who mine and refine personal data, such as the dating app, are placed in a privileged position to *exploit* it [4,6]. But what about those from whom the data is generated? How do they benefit? These narratives create even more distance between individuals and their data and fail to acknowledge how personal data exists only in relation to a person [1]; whose actions and interactions result in the collection and indefinite storage of innumerable data points. It is intrinsically about people and it is meaningless if people are detached from it.

With the interactive installation dataslip (Fig. 1), we aim to reduce the distance between individuals and their personal data by illustrating (1) how and what data is being collected as a person interacts with digital products and services; and (2) how personal data is intrinsically about people. Ultimately, we seek to raise awareness, elicit confrontation and invite people to question their role within the personal data ecosystems in which they are embedded. How could and should they benefit from personal data collection? We represent the personal data that is collected as a person navigates the physical (e.g., the city, the supermarket) and digital (e.g., the internet, mobile apps) world through a receipt, or 'personal data slip'. In doing so, we bring materiality to the abstract and opaque construct of personal data. The receipt or 'personal data slip' can be explored and inspected. It can be measured and compared. It can be shared, shown, and worn.

2   Dataslip

We have designed dataslip to emulate an Automated Teller Machine (ATM) or cash machine. It invites the same type of interaction. Users interact with a touch screen where they answer a series of questions, based on their digital habits (e.g., routine interactions with connected products, services, and digital technologies), and obtain a physical receipt. We designed the interaction with dataslip to be short and easy, aiming for it to last approximately one minute per user. Hence we

Fig. 1. Dataslip installation and reactions to the receipt.

limited it to five questions encompassing a broad range of products and services that most people encounter on a daily basis: (1) personalized public transport cards, (2) supermarket loyalty cards, (3) credit and debit cards, (4) wearables, including smartwatches and smart rings, and (5) mobile apps, including weather, navigation, web browser, email, instant messaging, music, social media, dating, and period tracking apps. The receipt contains a comprehensive list of the data generated as users engage with these different products and services. It includes short but detailed examples to help users interpret their data.

The Receipt or 'Personal Data Slip'

We have designed the receipt to be intentionally long. Its length is proportional to the products and services people interact with, and to the amount and the different types of data they collect. To populate the receipt with accurate information and examples, the first author made 28 data portability requests and requested a copy of her own data. The 'right to data portability' was introduced in the European General Data Protection Regulation (GDPR) [2, Art. 20]. It allows individuals (i.e., data subjects) to request a copy of their personal data from a data controller (i.e., private companies and public services) and reuse it in a different context.

The first author reached out individually to each data controller, as indicated in their privacy policy, with a data portability request. We are based in The Netherlands, hence four of the requests were made to Dutch companies operating primarily in The Netherlands; the public transport company (1 request), the supermarkets (2 requests), and the bank (1 request). The information on

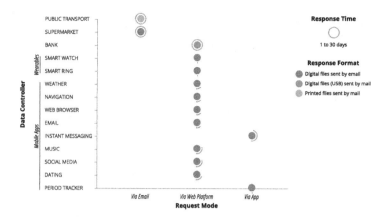

Fig. 2. Data portability requests and responses.

the receipt corresponding to these three entities is limited to the Dutch context and might not translate to other contexts and countries. The other twenty-four requests were made to companies operating in an international context. Figure 2 illustrates an overview of the request made for each category of products and services. It includes the request mode (i.e., how the request was made), the response time (i.e., how long it took to receive a copy of the data), and the response format (i.e., how the data was delivered). Most companies that provide a primarily digital service had dedicated platforms for making data portability requests; though these weren't easy to find and were in most cases a separate service (i.e., a dedicated page outside of the mobile or web app). Similarly, most requests were answered with a digital copy of the data, although the specific formats and files varied widely. For the first author, requesting and obtaining a copy of her data was a lengthy, confronting, and overwhelming process. Especially when the data was delivered digitally (i.e., a USB) and physically (i.e., printed files) by mail to her home address. The receipt aims to create a similar experience for dataslip users, by confronting them with the length and depth of their personal data.

3   Conclusion

We introduce the interactive installation dataslip; which translates the abstract and opaque construct of personal data into a material and tangible representation in the form of a receipt, or 'personal data slip'. The receipt contains detailed and condensed information as well as illustrative examples of the data generated from people's interactions with five different categories of products and services: (1) personalized public transport cards, (2) supermarket loyalty cards, (3) credit and debit cards, (4) wearables, including smartwatches and smart rings, and (5) mobile apps, including weather, navigation, web browser, email, instant messaging, music, social media, dating, and period tracking apps. The receipt seeks to elicit confrontation. Its length is proportional to the amount and the different types of data these collect. It can be inspected, explored, criticized, and contested.

References

1. D'Ignazio, C., Klein, L.F.: Data Feminism. MIT Press (2020). https://doi.org/10.7551/mitpress/11805.001.0001
2. European Parliament. General Data Protection Regulation (GDPR) (2018). https://gdpr.eu/
3. Gómez Ortega, A., Bourgeois, J., Kortuem, G.: What is sensitive about (sensitive) data? In: Characterizing Sensitivity and Intimacy with Google Assistant Users, vol. 1. Association for Computing Machinery (2023). https://doi.org/10.1145/3544548.3581164
4. Prainsack, B.: Data donation: how to resist the iLeviathan. Philosop. Stud. Ser. **137**, 9–22 (2019). https://doi.org/10.1007/978-3-030-04363-6_2
5. Shklovski, I., Mainwaring, S.D., Skúladóttir, H.H., Borgthorsson, H.: Leakiness and creepiness in app space. In: Proceedings of the SIGCHI Conference on Human Factors in Computing Systems, pp. 2347–2356. Association for Computing Machinery, Toronto (2014). https://doi.org/10.1145/2556288.2557421
6. Singh, R.: The decolonial turn is on the road to contingency. In: Information Communication and Society, pp. 1–4 (2021). https://doi.org/10.1080/1369118X.2021.1986104
7. U.S. Chambers of Commerce Foundation. The Future of Data-Driven Innovation. Tech. rep., U.S. Chambers of Commerce Foundation (2014). https://www.uschamberfoundation.org/sites/default/files/TheFutureofData-DrivenInnovation.pdf
8. Utz, C., Degeling, M., Fahl, S., Schaub, F., Holz, T.: (Un)informed consent: studying GDPR consent notices in the field. In: Proceedings of the ACM Conference on Computer and Communications Security, pp. 973–990 (2019). https://doi.org/10.1145/3319535.3354212

Ingá Telikit: A Virtual Reality Game for Learning Penan's Hunting Techniques

Tariq Zaman[1]([⊠]) [iD], Bram Kreuger[1,2] [iD], Vanden Michael[1] [iD], Diana Azlyn William[3], and Taman Pitah[3]

[1] ASSET, University of Technology Sarawak, Sibu, Malaysia
zamantariq@gmail.com, vanden@uts.edu.my
[2] Vrije Universiteit Amsterdam, Amsterdam, Netherlands
[3] Long Lamai Community, Long Lamai, Malaysia
asset@uts.edu.my

Abstract. In this demo paper, we present Inga' Telikit, a virtual reality game co-designed with the Penan community of Long Lamai to preserve their traditional hunting techniques. The game is based on the mythological story of Aka and Gugak, two Penan legends who are inextricably connected with the Penan hunting skills and practices of nomadic life. The game was developed using a community-based co-design approach, involving five youth and two elder community members in the design and development process. In our hands-on demonstration, attendees will learn the Inga' Telikit story and also play the Penan hunting game against a non-player character. Our demo addresses the call of the track which welcomes technical and innovative solutions to address the current issues.

Keywords: Inga' Telikit · Visual Sovereignty · Virtual Reality · Penan · Malaysian · Co-Design

1 Introduction

Since 2009, affiliated researchers from the Advanced Centre for Sustainable Socio-Economic and Technological Development (ASSET) at the University of Technology Sarawak (UTS) have established a long-term partnership with the Penan community of Long Lamai to design and develop digital tools for indigenous knowledge management and preservation [1, 2]. In this partnership, indigenous practitioners contribute by documenting their own content [1] or sharing design ideas from their unique perspectives and insights, which enrich the co-design process [2]. External researchers with technical skills then turn these ideas into functional products through the development process. Based on community aspirations and a strong visual orientation [3], our design endeavors have gone beyond traditional desktop and mobile applications and we are co-creating embodied and immersive cultural experiences to preserve the intangible cultural heritage.

Supplementary Information The online version contains supplementary material available at https://doi.org/10.1007/978-3-031-42293-5_26.

© The Author(s), under exclusive license to Springer Nature Switzerland AG 2023
J. Abdelnour Nocera et al. (Eds.): INTERACT 2023, LNCS 14145, pp. 300–304, 2023.
https://doi.org/10.1007/978-3-031-42293-5_26

Inspired by the local community's desires and the work of [4] and [5], we developed Inga' Telikit, a virtual reality (VR) game that is a virtual representation of an indigenous hunting game of the Penans. In this demo, we present the game, which was co-designed in situ by five youth and two elder community members of Long Lamai. Our goal was to maintain the Penans' indigenous visual sovereignty and capture the rich cultural context and creative experience. The idea of Inga' Telikit is based on the mythological story of Aka and Gugak, two legends that are inextricably connected with the Penan hunting skills and practices of nomadic life.

2   Co-Designing Inga' Telikit with the Penan Youth and Elders

For the past decade, the Long Lamai community has been utilising participatory community design and adapting technologies as a means of creating a counter-narrative to mainstream views and to demonstrate their identity as a progressive tribe [6].

The design process of Inga' Telikit was comprised of four (4) stages. Based on our previous research, a prototype encompassing the visual and interactive features was developed to make the community familiar with the VR visualisation and help them decide about the future technology, design possibilities, and its use. The VR prototype was designed for a low-cost mobile head-mounted display with few interactive features. In the first stage, with the help of the prototype, the researchers provided an overview of the designed virtual environment to six members of the local community and collected their feedback (see Fig. 1). The virtual space comprised sound and visual animation with the combinations of a Penan Player Character (PC), a Non-Player Character (NPC), a wild boar, some traditional handicrafts, and Penan hunting tools such as Gaweng (Penan basket), blowpipe, dart, firelighter, and cooking pots. The prototype also has some interaction features such as providing the gaze direction on the lighter and cooking pots and using the floating button, the users are able to create fire animation.

In the second stage, a demo video of the VR hunting game was displayed [4]. The purpose of the session was to instigate and generate ideas of the context and use case for VR/3D video technology. At the end of the video demonstration, followed by a short discussion between the community members, a decision was made to develop a VR application for Inga' Telikit. In the third stage, we embarked on documenting the story of Inga' Telikit. The process of documenting an indigenous story usually involves several stages to ensure the preservation and accuracy of the narrative. In this particular case, the initial script of the story was shared in 2013 by Garen Jengan, one of the participants of the design sessions and a community elder. In a reconfirmation session, we recorded (in audio and video format) the story narrated by Taman Pitah, a 97-year-old Penan elder, who has been identified by Garen as the only Inga' Telikit story-teller who is still alive (see Fig. 1). The story was later transcribed and translated from the Penan language into English. This multistep process of documentation ensures the accuracy and preservation of the indigenous story for future generations.

In stage four, a group of Penan youth were engaged in a co-designing workshop session of the different scenes for the game. With pen and paper (some used colour pens), the participants designed the Player and Non-Player characters of the games such as Aka, Gugak, the NPC, the animals, trees, and the objects of the hunting game (blowpipe and Telikit)."

Fig. 1. Left: Taman Pitah is telling the story of Aka and Gugak Right: showing community members experiencing the first encounter with VR.

3   The Structure of the Game

The Inga' Telikit VR application is developed based on the outcomes of the design sessions with the Penan youth. The application is developed in Unity for the Oculus Quest 2 platform (see Fig. 2). The prototype is divided in following two scenes.

3.1   Scene 1: The Scene Story of Aka and Gugak

The first scene covers the story of Aka and Gugak and invites the user to read or listen to the story of the two Penan legends (see Fig. 2(a)). The scene includes NPCs in the form of giants or spirits, a waterfall, a floating text box, and a button to skip the introduction. As conceptualized and designed by the Penan co-designers, the giants are depicted as being larger in size than human beings, holding blowpipes and featuring a see-through quality. Once the story is finished, Aka and Gugak disappear, leaving behind the blowpipes, and the player enters the new scene. The player can also click the "Skip Introduction" button to enter the new scene at any time."

3.2   Scene 2: The Inga' Teleikit Game

In Scene 2, the user engages in a thrilling game against a computer-controlled NPC. At the outset, the user picks up a blowpipe from the ground (by holding the Grip button on the controller), which they hold in one hand. The NPC then tosses a Telikit (a ring-shaped rattan) towards the user (see Fig. 2(b)), who must skilfully thrust a spear through it to score a point (see Fig. 2(c)). The game lasts for 10 min, and the user who scores the most points against the NPC within the allotted time wins. After each move, the user must pick up the Telikit (see Fig. 2(d)) and throw it back to the NPC (by releasing the Grip and Trigger buttons on the controller). If the Telikit fails to reach the NPC, the NPC will come to collect it, and the game will continue. Meanwhile, users can enjoy an immersive forest experience, witnessing the forest animals and plants, accompanied by audio features like traditional Sape' music and the sounds of wild boar and cheering hornbills.

(a): Story of Aka and Gugak (Scene 1)

(b): NPC tosses the Telikit (Scene 2)

(c) PC thrusts the spear through Telikit to score a point
(Scene 2)

(d) PC throw the Telikit to NPC to continue the game
(Scene 2)

Fig. 2. Different scenes in Inga' Telikit game

4   Conclusion and Future Work

This paper introduces Inga's Telikit, a VR game for learning Penan hunting techniques. In the game, users listen to and learn about the indigenous Penan tale of Aka and Gugak, upon which the game is based. The VR game utilises head-mounted display devices and interactive omnidirectional videos, which together create an immersive experience for users. For the future, we are planning to make it a multi-user competitive game, adding more interactive scenes, forest animals, and artefacts. The ethical standards of privacy and data anonymisation do not align with the participants' desire [7] so they proudly agreed to include their visuals and names in the paper.

Acknowledgement. We thank the community of Long Lamai for their engagement and UTS for local research funding (2/2020/03 Crowdsourcing for Cultural Resource Mapping).

References

1. Zaman, T., Kulathuramaiyer, N.: eToro: appropriating ICTs for the management of penans' indigenous botanical knowledge. In: Indigenous People and Mobile Technologies, pp. 267–278. Routledge (2015)
2. Zaman, T., Winschiers-Theophilus, H.: Penan's oroo' short message signs (PO-SMS): Co-design of a digital jungle sign language application. In: Abascal, J., Barbosa, S., Fetter, M., Gross, T., Palanque, P., Winckler, M. (eds.) Human-Computer Interaction – INTERACT 2015. INTERACT 2015. Lecture Notes in Computer Science, vol. 9297, pp. 489–504. Springer, Cham (2015). https://doi.org/10.1007/978-3-319-22668-2_38

3. Zaman, T., Winschiers-Theophilus, H., George, F., Wee, A.Y., Falak, H., Goagoses, N.: Using sketches to communicate interaction protocols of an indigenous community. In: Proceedings of the 14th Participatory Design Conference: Short Papers, Interactive Exhibitions, Workshops-vol. 2, August 15, pp. 13–16. ACM, New York (2016)
4. Arendttorp, E.M.N., et al.: Grab it, while you can: a VR gesture evaluation of a co-designed traditional narrative by indigenous people. In: Proceedings of the CHI Conference on Human Factors in Computing Systems (CHI 2023), Hamburg, Germany. ACM, New York (2023)
5. Wallis, K., Ross, M.: Fourth VR: indigenous virtual reality practice. Convergence **27**(2), 313–329 (2021)
6. Winschiers-Theophilus, H., Zaman, T., Stanley, C.: A classification of cultural engagements in community technology design: introducing a transcultural approach. AI Soc. **1**(34), 419–35 (2017)
7. Svalastog, A., Eriksson, S.: You can use my name; you don't have to steal my story–a critique of anonymity in indigenous studies. Dev. World Bioeth. **10**, 104–110 (2010)

StoryCarnival: Inspiring Play with Stories and an Enhanced Puppet

Flannery Hope Currin(✉) and Juan Pablo Hourcade

University of Iowa, Iowa, IA 52240, USA
{flannery-currin,juanpablo-hourcade}@uiowa.edu
https://cs.uiowa.edu/

Abstract. As developmental barriers to children's access to technology have lowered, dark patterns in apps geared toward children encourage privacy invasions and compulsive use of technology. With StoryCarnival, we use a web app with e-book and printable stories and an adult-operated voice agent to encourage the opposite: mindful and minimal use of technology to support developmentally significant aspects of children's play.

Keywords: Voice Agents · Children · Teleoperation · Social Play

1 The Landscape of Children's Technologies

Touch screens have enabled children to begin using technology before they develop the motor skills required to use a keyboard and mouse [4]. Voice interfaces have further broadened the scope of interactions children can have with technology before becoming proficient in reading [10]. This increase in children's access to technology has raised concerns about dark patterns present in technology aimed at children [1]. These include patterns that aim to maximize children's engagement to subsequently maximize their exposure to advertisements, and invasive data tracking for targeted advertising [1].

In 2017, Hourcade et al. described the 3Cs (Creativity, Connection with the physical environment, and Communication) as an alternative sociocultural approach to children's technology [5]. They described the design of an early version of a system called StoryCarnival as an example of a technology guided by these principles [5]. From the beginning, StoryCarnival aimed to use e-book stories and a play planning tool primarily to inspire and set up social role play with generic props (e.g., blocks), shifting the focus from technology to peers and the physical environment. Since then, our research team has worked to make StoryCarnival publicly available[1] and developed make-your-own story templates

---

[1] http://storycarnival.org.

Supplementary Information The online version contains supplementary material available at https://doi.org/10.1007/978-3-031-42293-5_27.

© The Author(s), under exclusive license to Springer Nature Switzerland AG 2023
J. Abdelnour Nocera et al. (Eds.): INTERACT 2023, LNCS 14145, pp. 305–309, 2023.
https://doi.org/10.1007/978-3-031-42293-5_27

and an adult-operated voice agent to keep children engaged in play activities during StoryCarnival sessions [8]. In this demonstration, we hope to illustrate and spark conversations about how we can shift away from the paradigm of high engagement with technology as a goal.

2   Interactive Stories: Providing Context and Inspiration

Each StoryCarnival story introduces four characters, a problem, and an open-ended partial resolution. For example, in the "Snow Day" story, Dog, Bear, Monkey, and Cat each want to do a different activity on their snow day but all feel lonely when they split up. The story ends with the characters agreeing to compromise and take turns doing each activity. This sets up a scenario in which children can replay the conflict in the story and/or improvise how the resolution might play out. The stories are available as e-books or printable PDFs, so they can be used without screens or an internet connection when appropriate.

The make-your-own story templates provide a few options for different story elements children can select from which are then stitched together into an e-book story (see Fig. 1 for an example). This can create silly, non-sensical scenarios which are entertaining in a way that is important to cognitive development [9]. The templates can also increase the replayability of a single story structure (e.g., exploring a new place) by providing concrete examples of slight variations.

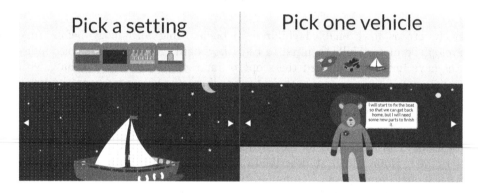

Fig. 1. Top left: options to choose from for a make-your-own template story setting. Top right: options to choose from for a vehicle in the story template. Bottom left: a page from the story when "space" was chosen as the setting, "boat" was chosen as the vehicle, and "storm" was chosen as the problem. Bottom right: a page from later in the story, illustrating how choices are also reflected in characters' outfits and speech.

3   Play Planner: Setting the Stage

Each character plays an explicitly defined role in each story, stating and demonstrating their skills and interests which make them distinct from the other. Unlike most children's stories, which tend to have one or two protagonists, the StoryCarnival stories illustrate four distinct characters of equal importance to each story. After a story finishes playing through the web app, children can each select which role they want to assume during play, and be reminded of what each character did in the story via the play planner (see Fig. 2). The play planner supports groups of children in coordinating their plan for play immediately before play begins.

Fig. 2. Top: character options presented by the play planner for the Snow Day story. Bottom: the screen shown when a user selects Dog.

4   Teleoperated Voice Agent: Facilitating Communication

StoryCarnival also includes a tangible, teleoperated voice agent called MiniBird (see Fig. 3). The control interface uses AWS Polly text-to-speech synthesis. The voice agent itself is a TYLT mini (or similar size) Bluetooth speaker housed inside a 3D-printed cubic case (2 cubic in./5 cubic cm) made from a flexible, transparent plastic resin. The case has openings on four faces to slot in artwork representing the MiniBird character (printed stickers and cardstock).

The voice agent essentially functions as a puppet, except the physical manipulation of the puppet is decoupled from the puppeteer—while an adult controls its speech, children can carry it around and incorporate it into their play. When teachers use puppets in classrooms, the teacher can step out of their role as an authority figure and assume the role of someone who needs help from the children [6]. This can encourage quiet children to speak up more and motivate children to explain their reasoning in more detail [6]. We saw this impact on shy children in our own prior work with StoryCarnival, with minimal [3]. While teachers see

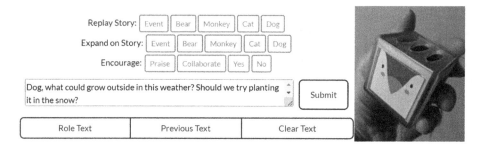

Fig. 3. Left: the voice agent control interface; text can be entered by typing or by cycling through story-related suggestions via the buttons. Right: MiniBird voice agent.

benefit in using puppets in the classroom, some opt not to use them because they find it difficult to create a persona for a puppet or switch between their teacher voice and puppet voice [2]. An adult-operated voice agent can lower the barriers to using puppets as a support for children in social play without relying on the audio recording and processing required by automated voice agents [7]. Our work aims to explore what teleoperated conversational agents look like when an automated future iteration is not the ultimate goal.

5   Conclusion and Future Work

Through StoryCarnival, we try to understand and design for the specific ways technology can support and enhance low-tech activities without compulsive engagement with the technology itself. The StoryCarnival stories and voice agent keep caregivers and children in control of play activities with different levels of technology use possible but not pushed as the primary focus. In the future, we hope to turn StoryCarnival into a platform researchers can use to quickly create and evaluate media intended to inspire future activity.

Acknowledgements. We thank all students and faculty who contributed to the current and prior StoryCarnival iterations. We thank the parents, teachers, and children who have worked with us to develop StoryCarnival. This work is supported by the National Science Foundation under Grants No. 1908476 and 2040204 and the National Science Foundation Graduate Research Fellowship under Grant No. 000390183.

References

1. Fitton, D., Bell, B.T., Read, J.C.: Integrating dark patterns into the 4Cs of online risk in the context of young people and mobile gaming apps. In: Ardito, C., et al. (eds.) INTERACT 2021. LNCS, vol. 12935, pp. 701–711. Springer, Cham (2021). https://doi.org/10.1007/978-3-030-85610-6_40
2. Hackling, M., Smith, P., Murcia, K.: Enhancing classroom discourse in primary science: the puppets project. Teach. Sci. J. Austral. Sci. Teach. Assoc. **57**(2) (2011)

3. Hope Currin, F., et al.: Supporting shy preschool children in joining social play. In: Interaction Design and Children (IDC 2021), pp. 396–407. Association for Computing Machinery, New York (2021). https://doi.org/10.1145/3459990.3460729

4. Hourcade, J.P., Mascher, S.L., Wu, D., Pantoja, L.: Look, my baby is using an IPad! an analysis of YouTube videos of infants and toddlers using tablets. In: Proceedings of the 33rd Annual ACM Conference on Human Factors in Computing Systems (CHI 2015), pp. 1915–1924. Association for Computing Machinery, New York (2015), Event-place: Seoul, Republic of Korea. https://doi.org/10.1145/2702123.2702266

5. Hourcade, J.P., Pantoja, L.S., Diederich, K., Crawford, L., Revelle, G.: The 3Cs for preschool children's technology: create, connect. Commun. Interact. 24(4), 70–73 (2017). Association for Computing Machinery, New York. https://doi.org/10.1145/3096461

6. Kröger, T., Nupponen, A.M.: Puppet as a pedagogical tool: a literature review. Int. Electron. J. Element. Educ. 11(4), 393–401 (2019). https://www.iejee.com/index.php/IEJEE/article/view/688

7. McReynolds, E., Hubbard, S., Lau, T., Saraf, A., Cakmak, M., Roesner, F.: Toys that listen: a study of parents, children, and internet-connected toys. In: Proceedings of the 2017 CHI Conference on Human Factors in Computing Systems (CHI 2017), pp. 5197–5207. Association for Computing Machinery, New York (2017). https://doi.org/10.1145/3025453.3025735

8. Pantoja, L.S., Diederich, K., Crawford, L., Hourcade, J.P.: Voice agents supporting high-quality social play. In: Proceedings of the 18th ACM International Conference on Interaction Design and Children (IDC 2019), pp. 314–325. Association for Computing Machinery, New York (2019), Event-place: Boise, ID, USA. https://doi.org/10.1145/3311927.3323151

9. Southam, M.: Humor development: an important cognitive and social skill in the growing child. Phys. Occup. Therapy Pediatr. 25(1–2), 105–117 (2005)

10. Xu, Y., Warschauer, M.: A content analysis of voice-based apps on the market for early literacy development. In: Proceedings of the Interaction Design and Children Conference (IDC 2020), pp. 361–371. Association for Computing Machinery, New York (2020), Event-place: London, United Kingdom. https://doi.org/10.1145/3392063.3394418

Together Porting: Multi-user Locomotion in Social Virtual Reality

Gavin Wood[1]([⊠]) [ID] and Patrick Dickinson[2] [ID]

[1] Northumbria University, Newcastle upon Tyne, UK
gavin.wood2@acm.org
[2] School of Computer Science, University of Lincoln, Lincoln, UK
pdickinson@lincoln.ac.uk

Abstract. We present a design prototype that demonstrates new locomotion techniques for social virtual reality experiences. Specifically, we
showcase three teleportation-based techniques which, together, support
users as they join other groups of people, and help them move together
in virtual environments. The new interactions include a technique to
join a group with option for adjacency, the ability to "reverse teleport"
a user to your own group, and finding a consensus on where to teleport together. We argue that our new locomotion techniques maintain
the simplicity of current teleportation-based techniques while supporting
new interactions with people. We present our design prototype so that
we can explore how new teleportation-based techniques can be designed
to better support prosocial behaviour, but also highlight their potential
to disrupt social experiences in social VR.

Keywords: SocialVR · Locomotion · Teleportation · Multi-User ·
Virtual Reality

1 Introduction

Social applications are a popular use-case of virtual reality (VR) allowing users
to enjoy meaningful experiences in diverse social activities with real people [5].
Locomotion techniques (LT) enable users to explore these virtual environments
(VEs) with others [7]. Importantly, LTs can potentially either support or disrupt
social interaction in shared environments [4]

One widespread LT is the discrete "point & teleport" [7] where users point to
a desired location before being moved instantly. Teleportation can be a preferred
option for users who suffer from simulator sickness [2] where this type of sickness
can be triggered by visible translational motion, which is often experienced when
using joystick-based locomotion.

Supplementary Information The online version contains supplementary material
available at https://doi.org/10.1007/978-3-031-42293-5_28.

© The Author(s), under exclusive license to Springer Nature Switzerland AG 2023
J. Abdelnour Nocera et al. (Eds.): INTERACT 2023, LNCS 14145, pp. 310–314, 2023.
https://doi.org/10.1007/978-3-031-42293-5_28

Teleportation-based LTs have long been a focus of research in single user experiences, but their use within the context of social VR applications has attracted little attention. In particular, their impact on the mechanisms of social interactions, such as the maintenance of personal space discussed [4] needs careful consideration. Teleportation can also cause confusion for observers [7] and lead to poor spatial awareness [2]. In joining conversation, people can "flicker around speakers" [4] with users finding it hard to arrive in an appropriate social formation. Where work in LTs has looked at social interaction, it has often looked at configuring exact movement and how this is communicated. For instance, Weissker et al's body of work (see overview [8]) explored group navigation; while Rasch et al. [7] focused on a dyadic locomotion task, finding value in showing a "full preview" of the teleport.

To explore the design of teleport-based locomotion in social VR, we present three of our own designs for multi-user teleportation-based techniques. These support joining a group of people, a reverse teleport, and together porting with a consensus on destination. In our work, we have sought to retain the simplicity of point and teleport techniques described [1], and to communicate a user's movement (as in [7]).

The intention is to provoke the user to think critically about the balance between simple and intuitive interfaces, the complexity of social spaces including personal space (and the ambiguities resulting from movement e.g., [6]), and the ability of locomotion algorithms to promote or disrupt social interactions in VR. New multi-user locomotion techniques in social VR have value. They are relevant to virtual meetings, communication and collaboration, multiplayer gaming, and research studies within VR.

2   Design Prototype: Together-Porting

The design prototype in this paper has been implemented using the Unity game engine version 2021.3. It implements three techniques locomotion techniques outlined in Fig. 1. The techniques can be positioned within the design space of teleportation-based locomotion, where in particular, we consider locatedness i.e., whether people are collocated or remote, and both a preview of our own movement and the movement of our co-players.

We draw upon current norms from VR teleporting methods, beginning with point and click teleport [1] which we use as a base for our teleportation methods. We use a transparent cylindrical reticle displayed over the environment (as in [1]), camera tunneling vignette to provide better comfort during teleportation, colour reticles (first person=blue, co-players=green) [7], while we raise the teleport beam over 45 degrees to cancel teleportation. We have implemented a pointer with a parabolic curve (as in [3]) which enables selection of people standing among or at the far side of a group.

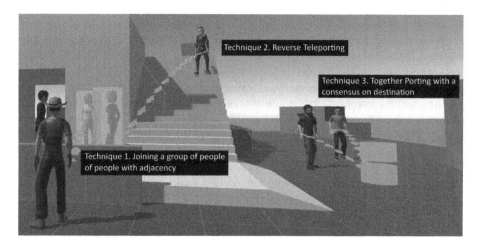

Fig. 1. Technique 1 is illustrated with a user teleporting by pointing at a group. Technique 2 shows a user reverse teleporting a person. Technique 3 is shown with two stacked reticles.

2.1 Joining a Group of People of People with Adjacency

The first technique allows users to select and join a group of people by selecting a target user avatar. This contrasts with current locomotion methods e.g., point & teleport [1] which ask users to move to a target by manually choosing points on the floor (an act that contributes to people "flittering" around speakers). Instead our users have the ability to choose their desired adjacency by utilising the teleport parabola along with the blue transparent reticle, which snaps-to-person. If placement is possible, then the user can push forward on the controller's analogue pad or joystick to teleport. The placement algorithm moves the user into the target group, with orientation automatically changed (as in [3]). The user is orientated toward the person they selected but placed within a social formation where the relative position ensures they are placed at a respectful distance.

2.2 Reverse Teleporting

Instead of moving with, or to join others, users can summon other people to their own position using a reverse teleport. This interaction uses an intuitive pulling action on the controller using its analogue pad or joystick to both create the teleport parabola to select a user and to perform the action. In this technique, a reticle is only displayed over a target when that person can be summoned. If the summoning user is in a group, then the adjacency of the new person entering the group will be positioned within the group. This technique cannot support reverse teleporting of individuals who are collocated with others unless they are summoned together and retain relative positions. Prior work has assumed the direction of travel is always toward a destination [7,8]. Instead, we demonstrate how the direction of travel could be reversed. The technique has ability to disrupt the social experience as other people are teleported away from their existing groups to come to you (rather than you to them). This is not intended to map to real-world social mechanics but responds to recent calls e.g., [4] for the exploration of social VR mechanics which step outside the replication of real-world interactions.

2.3 Stacked Reticles: Together Porting with a Consensus on Destination

The last technique enables considers how users come to a consensus to teleport with their group. Any user can point to a teleport destination which is highlighted from everyone's own perspective with a transparent reticle over the environment. Subsequent users, having observed that parabola and reticle, will point their own parabola at the first user's reticle. In contrast to the Multi-Ray jumping [9] this allows users to form a consensus on where to teleport, allowing a choice over who they want to teleport with and provides a more democratic footing for teleportation. Once there is a consensus (indicated by stacked reticles from everyone in the group), all teleporting users can release their controllers to move to that destination or cancel teleportation. Stacked reticles are designed to clearly show the intention of who wants to teleport where, building on the idea of the full preview [7], while also indicating the consensus of how many people want to move, intended to promote more collaboration.

Importantly, collocated users automatically end up in their same relative positions at the destination, to preserve spatial synchronization. In contrast, remotely located teleporting users can be placed with a new adjacency to others, following any number of different schemes. Crucially, to reduce spatial confusion around trajectories and make it possible to stack reticles on one spot, while ending up at different destinations, each user's perspective of other peoples' parabolas is "tweaked" to their own unique perspective. The preview shows the correct target destination from a first person point of view, while other players look like they are heading to the exact same space. We argue that this fits better with real life decisions, where people suggest moving to join a person, group or a particular "spot" in the real world (often by pointing somewhere). To aid our understanding of continuity, the front-most teleporters move first, followed by those behind to better account for peoples' movement.

3 Conclusion

In this work, we explore the design space of multi-user locomotion in social VR. We have created three novel teleportation-based locomotion techniques in this space which are designed to support pro-social interactions in VR. We present three "Together-porters". The first allows users to join a group of people directly, the second presents reverse teleporting, the ability to summon a user into a group and third shows how users can reach a consensus on where to travel with others. Building on accepted standards of teleportation-based locomotion, we believe these examples will be intuitive and relatable to users who enjoy social VR experiences, and who normally choose teleportation as their preference for locomotion. We present this work as a provocation, contextualised by the assertion that teleportation has the potential to both support and hinder social experiences in VR.

References

1. Bozgeyikli, E., Raij, A., Katkoori, S., Dubey, R.: Point & Teleport Locomotion Technique for Virtual Reality. In: Proceedings of the 2016 Annual Symposium on Computer-Human Interaction in Play, pp. 205–216. ACM, Austin Texas USA (Oct 2016). https://doi.org/10.1145/2967934.2968105, https://dl.acm.org/doi/10.1145/2967934.2968105
2. Di Luca, M., Seifi, H., Egan, S., Gonzalez-Franco, M.: Locomotion Vault: the Extra Mile in Analyzing VR Locomotion Techniques. In: Proceedings of the 2021 CHI Conference on Human Factors in Computing Systems, pp. 1–10. ACM, Yokohama Japan (May 2021). https://doi.org/10.1145/3411764.3445319, https://dl.acm.org/doi/10.1145/3411764.3445319
3. Funk, M., et al.: Assessing the Accuracy of Point & Teleport Locomotion with Orientation Indication for Virtual Reality using Curved Trajectories. In: Proceedings of the 2019 CHI Conference on Human Factors in Computing Systems, pp. 1–12. ACM, Glasgow Scotland Uk (May 2019). https://doi.org/10.1145/3290605.3300377, https://dl.acm.org/doi/10.1145/3290605.3300377
4. McVeigh-Schultz, J., Isbister, K.: The Case for "Weird Social" in VR/XR: A Vision of Social Superpowers Beyond Meatspace. In: Extended Abstracts of the 2021 CHI Conference on Human Factors in Computing Systems, pp. 1–10. ACM, Yokohama Japan (May 2021). https://doi.org/10.1145/3411763.3450377, https://dl.acm.org/doi/10.1145/3411763.3450377
5. McVeigh-Schultz, J., Kolesnichenko, A., Isbister, K.: Shaping Pro-Social Interaction in VR: An Emerging Design Framework. In: Proceedings of the 2019 CHI Conference on Human Factors in Computing Systems, pp. 1–12. ACM, Glasgow Scotland Uk (May 2019). https://doi.org/10.1145/3290605.3300794, https://dl.acm.org/doi/10.1145/3290605.3300794
6. Piitulainen, R., Hämäläinen, P., Mekler, E.D.: Vibing Together: Dance Experiences in Social Virtual Reality. In: CHI Conference on Human Factors in Computing Systems, pp. 1–18. ACM, New Orleans LA USA (Apr 2022). https://doi.org/10.1145/3491102.3501828, https://dl.acm.org/doi/10.1145/3491102.3501828
7. Rasch, J.: Going, Going, Gone: Exploring Intention Communication for Multi-User Locomotion in Virtual Reality (2023). https://doi.org/10.1145/3544548.3581259
8. Weissker, T., Bimberg, P., Froehlich, B.: An Overview of Group Navigation in Multi-User Virtual Reality. In: 2021 IEEE Conference on Virtual Reality and 3D User Interfaces Abstracts and Workshops (VRW), pp. 363–369. IEEE, Lisbon, Portugal (Mar 2021). https://doi.org/10.1109/VRW52623.2021.00073, https://ieeexplore.ieee.org/document/9419104/
9. Weissker, T., Kulik, A., Froehlich, B.: Multi-Ray Jumping: Comprehensible Group Navigation for Collocated Users in Immersive Virtual Reality. In: 2019 IEEE Conference on Virtual Reality and 3D User Interfaces (VR), pp. 136–144. IEEE, Osaka, Japan (Mar 2019). https://doi.org/10.1109/VR.2019.8797807, https://ieeexplore.ieee.org/document/8797807/

Towards "Image Reflow" on the Web: Avoiding Excessive Panning of Magnified Images by Multiplexing Automatically Cropped Regions of Interest

Frode Eika Sandnes[✉] [iD]

Department of Computer Science, Oslo Metropolitan University, 0130 Oslo, Norway
frodes@oslomet.no

Abstract. Low vision users are often faced with large images when increasing the browser zoom level. Large images extending beyond the viewport are difficult to view due to the excessive two-dimensional panning involved. This demo presents a mechanism that automatically splits, or "reflows", images into regions of interest. The user cycles through the magnified regions of interest by clicking or tapping the images.

Keywords: Accessibility · Low vision · Magnification · Zoom · Responsive web pages · Reflow · Panning · Cropping · Artificial intelligence · Region of interest

1 Introduction

Responsive websites dynamically reflow text to fit the user's browser viewport width while adhering to text size preferences. Low vision users therefore do not need to scroll horizontally (sideways) when reading highly magnified web pages, or when reading web pages on smartphones. However, images can still be difficult to view if the website owners have not explicitly designed how images are to be presented with narrow viewports. Image dimensions are usually specified in pixels, and images will therefore grow with the level of magnification. Excessive panning is needed to view such magnified images. Two-dimensional panning involves both vertical and horizontal scrolling within the image which can be disorientating. There is also a risk that the viewer misses vital details. This is especially a challenge with information-rich images, for example a photograph of a group of people at some gathering. To help eradicate two-dimensional image panning on web pages an image multiplexer was implemented that sequentially shows regions of interest to the user. The users cycle though the various detailed panned views by clicking on the image.

Supplementary Information The online version contains supplementary material available at https://doi.org/10.1007/978-3-031-42293-5_29.

© The Author(s), under exclusive license to Springer Nature Switzerland AG 2023
J. Abdelnour Nocera et al. (Eds.): INTERACT 2023, LNCS 14145, pp. 315–319, 2023.
https://doi.org/10.1007/978-3-031-42293-5_29

2 Related Work

Magnification, both physical and digital, is a widely used mechanism for compensating for reduced vision. Smartphone cameras have become a convenient tool for magnifying physical objects [1, 2]. Screen magnifiers are used for magnification of general displayed contents [3, 4], and browsers allow content to be magnified with a few simple keystrokes [5].

When magnifying contents, the vertical and horizontal dimensions will grow accordingly. Responsive websites therefore typically reflow contents to fit the visible viewport to prevent horizontal scrolling [6]. Reflow of text and small elements such as user interface components are well-supported and relatively straightforward to implement. Clearly, images cannot be simply split into smaller parts in the same way text passages can be split into words and letters. Effective viewing of large elements with high magnification such as tables [7], information-rich images, and videos [8] are still open problems.

Instead, images can be split into regions of interest. Although these can be defined manually and embedded in images [9] content providers may not provide information about regions of interest. Moreover, manual definition of regions of interest is subjective. This work therefore explores automatic detection of regions of interest. Region of interest detection is a fundamental operation in many image processing applications [10, 11], and has been explicitly applied to automatic image cropping [12–14].

3 The Image Multiplexer

The image multiplexer was implemented as a JavaScript library hosted on the same domain as the web page. The library first traverses the Document Object Model (DOM), identifies all the images on a page, and determines their respective regions of interest. The tensforflow.js coco-ssd pre-trained deep model for object recognition was used for detecting regions of interest. This model detects objects in images as well as the bounding box embracing each object. This model is relatively lightweight and works with most modern browsers. Simple experimentation showed that the object detection gives acceptable results for many pragmatic scenes involving people and real-world objects. The process is illustrated in Fig. 1.

The regions of interest returned by the model are sorted according to size assuming that important objects are larger and or in the foreground (see Fig. 1). If objects have similar width (within a range of 30%), they are sorted according to their horizontal position from left to right to match the Western left-to-right reading direction. The regions of interest are thus presented from front-to-back and/or left-to-right starting with the full view. A small border inside the region of interest is also discarded to bring the content even closer. A separate rendering of each region of interest is prepared and inserted into the document as well as CSS breakpoints that activate these views with low viewport widths (320 CSS pixels as recommended by WCAG2.1). The regions of interest are not shown simultaneously since a stack of cropped images will make the document longer and thus more difficult to navigate. Instead, the regions are shown sequentially on demand. This was implemented using a click handler where the user

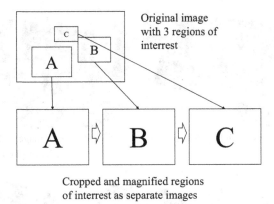

Fig. 1. Regions of interest in an image are detected with AI, cropped, magnified, and shown as separate images in succession.

cycles through the views by clicking or tapping the image. Each magnified region of interest is presented across the visible viewport. The cropped image dimensions are tied to the viewport width and can therefore be zoomed in further if needed.

Figure 2 shows an example of the image multiplexer applied to an example web page with a group photo shown on a smartphone (limited display real-estate). Figure 2 (a) shows the page in wide view (landscape), and Fig. 2 (b) illustrates how the large image is panned along two dimensions using conventional swipe gestures. Figure 2 (c) shows the same page in a narrow view (portrait) with an initial overview image. Figure 2 (d) and (e) shows how the user cycles through different regions of interest by tapping on the image.

The current mechanism was implemented as a JavaScript library that needs to be included on the webpage. This means that the website owner would need to activate this functionality. Ultimately, the users should be in control and make the decision of whether images should be "reflowed" or not in their browser. It would therefore be beneficial for the mechanism to be implemented as a bookmarklet or a browser extension which could be applied to any page. Both approaches were attempted but were unsuccessful due to the way the tensforflow.js library accesses images was prevented by the cross-site scripting security mechanisms built into modern browsers. This report is therefore limited to showcasing the opportunity that regions-of-interest detection present for users of browser magnification. How to deploy the mechanism in practice remains an open problem.

(a) Wide viewport view with large image.

(b) Panning large image in large viewport view by swiping left, right, up, and down.

(c) Overview image in a narrow viewport is shown first. Tapping image to view first region of interest.

(d) Tapping image to view second region of interest.

(e) Tapping to view next region of interest.

Fig. 2. Automatic image panning to regions of interest.

4 Conclusion

A proof-of-concept library for "reflowing" images in magnified browser views was presented. Instead of searching for content by panning large images, the user is sequentially presented with automatically cropped and magnified regions of interest. The library is available at https://github.com/frode-sandnes/IMAGE-WRAPPING.

References

1. Luo, G.: How 16,000 people used a smartphone magnifier app in their daily lives. Clin. Exp. Optom. **103**(6), 847–852 (2020)
2. Shirehjini, A.S., Sandnes, F.E.: Using smartphones as magnifying devices: a comparison of reading surface finger tracking and device panning. In: Proceedings of the 13th ACM International Conference on Pervasive Technologies Related to Assistive Environments. ACM (2020)
3. Blenkhorn, P., Evans, G., King, A., Kurniawan, S.H., Sutcliffe, A.: Screen magnifiers: evolution and evaluation. IEEE Comput. Graphics Appl. **23**(5), 54–61 (2003)

4. Szpiro, S.F.A., Hashash, S., Zhao, Y., Azenkot, S.: How people with low vision access computing devices: understanding challenges and opportunities. In: Proceedings of the 18th International ACM SIGACCESS Conference on Computers and Accessibility, pp. 171–180. ACM (2016)

5. Moreno, L., Valencia, X., Pérez, J.E., Arrue, M.: An exploratory study of web adaptation techniques for people with low vision. Univ. Access Inf. Soc. **20**(2), 223–237 (2020). https://doi.org/10.1007/s10209-020-00727-6

6. Sandnes, F. E.: Lost in OCR-translation: pixel-based text reflow to the rescue: magnification of archival raster image documents in the browser without horizontal scrolling. In: Proceedings of the 15th International Conference on Pervasive Technologies Related to Assistive Environments, pp. 500–506. ACM (2022)

7. Wang, Y., Wang, R., Jung, C., Kim, Y.S.: What makes web data tables accessible? insights and a tool for rendering accessible tables for people with visual impairments. In: Proceedings of the 2022 CHI Conference on Human Factors in Computing Systems. ACM (2022)

8. Aydin, A.S., Feiz, S., Ashok, V., Ramakrishnan, I.V.: Towards making videos accessible for low vision screen magnifier users. In: Proceedings of the 25th International Conference on Intelligent User Interfaces, pp. 10–21. ACM (2020)

9. Askelöf, J., Carlander, M.L., Christopoulos, C.: Region of interest coding in JPEG 2000. Sign. Process. Image Commun. **17**(1), 105–111 (2002)

10. Privitera, C.M., Stark, L.W.: Evaluating image processing algorithms that predict regions of interest. Pattern Recogn. Lett. **19**(11), 1037–1043 (1998)

11. Privitera, C.M., Stark, L.W.: Algorithms for defining visual regions-of-interest: comparison with eye fixations. IEEE Trans. Pattern Anal. Mach. Intell. **22**(9), 970–982 (2000)

12. Kao, Y., He, R., Huang, K.: Automatic image cropping with aesthetic map and gradient energy map. In: 2017 IEEE International Conference on Acoustics, Speech and Signal Processing (ICASSP), pp. 1982–1986. IEEE (2017)

13. Li, D., Wu, H., Zhang, J., Huang, K.: Fast a3rl: aesthetics-aware adversarial reinforcement learning for image cropping. IEEE Trans. Image Process. **28**(10), 5105–5120 (2019)

14. Luo, J.: Subject content-based intelligent cropping of digital photos. In: 2007 IEEE International Conference on Multimedia and Expo, pp. 2218–2221. IEEE (2007)

Two Domain-Specific Languages for Controlling a Humanoid Robot in a Therapeutic Context

Peter Forbrig$^{(\boxtimes)}$ [ID], Alexandru Umlauft [ID], Mathias Kühn [ID], and Anke Dittmar [ID]

Chair of Software Engineering, University of Rostock, Albert-Einstein-Str. 22, 18055 Rostock, Germany

{peter.forbrig,alexandrunicolae.umlauft,mathias.kuehn, anke.dittmar}@uni-rostock.de

Abstract. Domain-Specific Languages aim at enabling domain experts to create or adapt software systems for situated use. In the context of a project using a humanoid robot Pepper as coach in therapies of post stroke patients, we developed TaskDSL4Pepper and StateDSL4Pepper, two domain-specific languages for therapists to specify a robot's behavior in training sessions. The paper presents both languages which are rooted in task models and hierarchical state machines respectively.

Keywords: Domain-Specific Languages · Pepper · Behavior Specifications

1 Introduction

Within our project E-BRAiN [6] (Evidence-Based Robotic Assistance in Neurorehabilitation), we developed software to support patients after a stroke. The underlying assumption is that a humanoid robot Pepper can replace, or at least, unburden therapists in certain training sessions. In a second iteration, we worked on two domain-specific languages to allow therapists to adapt or even create new specifications of training scenarios according to the needs in an actual situation. TaskDSL4Pepper is based on ideas from task modeling while StateDSL4Pepper employs hierarchical state machines. This paper presents specification examples to illustrate the "specification style" of the two languages. The examples focus on the mirror therapy that has to be applied for patients with severe handicapped arms. Exercises are performed with the not affected arm and patients have to look into a mirror and have to imagine that the handicapped arm is moving. This trains the brain in such a way that the handicapped arm can be used again. Figure 1 gives an impression of the therapy situation and the video running on the tablet of Pepper.

2 Related Work

A survey on end-user robot programming is presented by Ajaykumar et al. in [1]. They discuss 121 references. However, most of the references are related to general robots. Only two papers have the term Humanoid in their title. One of them is Moros et al.

© The Author(s), under exclusive license to Springer Nature Switzerland AG 2023

J. Abdelnour Nocera et al. (Eds.): INTERACT 2023, LNCS 14145, pp. 320–324, 2023.
https://doi.org/10.1007/978-3-031-42293-5_30

Fig. 1. Therapy situation for the mirror training and support by Pepper.

[13] that uses a visual block concept with Scratch. However, there is no big difference to programming like in Python. The other paper is Leonardi et al. [11]. The authors suggest a trigger-action-programming for end-user developers. This approach is also discussed in [12]. It allows users to manipulate rules that control the behavior of robots. Coronado suggests with different co-authors in [3] and [4] a block structured programming approach for end-user. They discuss Node Primitives (NEP), a robot programming framework aimed at enabling the creation of usable, flexible and cross-platform end-user programming (EUP) interfaces for robots and a system that is called Open RIZE. The DSL CommonLang (Rutle et al. [16]) is created for writing code for different robots. It is a kind of abstract programming language that is designed for programmers and not for end users. The languages Kinematics-DSL, Motion-DSL, and Transforms-DSL are introduced in Frigerio et al. [8]. They are used in connection with the code generator RobCoGen. These languages are focused on motions and are very technical oriented. They are also not designed for end users. The same is true for a DSL discussed in Heinzemann and Lange [9]. They discuss a DSL for specifying robot tasks that is intended to support programmers. Oishi et al. [15] discuss end-user programming for humanoid robots. However, not much details are provided. A DSL for integrating neuronal networks into robot control is presented by Hinkel et al. [10]. Transfer functions can be specified in a domain-specific way in Python and through an XML format. However, end users cannot update those specifications.

3 The Domain-Specific Languages

3.1 TaskDSL4Pepper

For task models there exists already the textual domain-specific language CoTaL [7]. It is implemented using the tool Xtext [17] that generates syntax driven textual editors. Results of this editor can be used to generate code using the tool Xtend [18]. Together with other options code generation can be performed for the environment CoTaSE [5] that allows the animation of model instances. CoTaSE is discussed in detail in Buchholz et al. [2]. TaskDSL4Pepper is an extension of this language by extending it with specific tasks of a robot like say <text>, show <picture>, play <video>, raiseArms, etc. Additionally, there exists an environment that allows the animation of model instances and sends MQTT [14] messages to Pepper if such a robot command is animated. The specification of Fig. 2. Consists of four parts. First, there is the team model that is reduced to a minimum here. Second, there is a role model of a patient. Third, the tasks of a robot pepper are specified and finally there are declarations of texts, images and videos. The task structure seems to be better visible in the graphical representation than in the text form. However, this view can be generated automatically for several tools (see [7]).

```
team coop {
    root training = greeting >> train{*} [> end_exercises
                task greeting = pepper.greet |=| patient.greet
}
role patient {
  root train = greet >> listens >>
                   perfoms_exercises{*} [> finishes_exercises >> bye
      task perfoms_exercises = perform_correct [] perform_wrong
}
robot pepper {
  root armtraining= greet >> training{*} [> end_exercises
      task training = introduce >> train
        task introduce = say introduction ||| show startPict
          task train = play exerVid ||| say three >>
                         wait 10 >> train_imagine
          task train_imagine = say ten ||| imagine
            task imagine = wait 15 >> say look >> say imagine
        task end_exercises = say bye
}
text greeting = "Good morning.";
text introduction = "Let us start to perform our second exercise"
image startPict = "st_pic_10_1.jpg"
video exerVid = "st_10_1.mp4"              // *     Iteration
text imagine = "Imagine it is your arm"    // >>    Enabling
text look    = "Look at mirror"            // [>    Disabling
text three   = "Train three times"         // |||   Interleaving
text ten     = "Train ten times"           // []    Choice
text bye     = "Bye, till next time"
```

Fig. 2. Specification of a mirror therapy in TaskDSL4Pepper.

3.2 StateDSL4Pepper

Our second domain-specific language is based on the concept of hierarchical state machines. It is developed with the same tools as TaskDSL4Pepper. Currently, it allows only commands of a robot as actions inside a state. In this way, hierarchical Moore automata are supported. Besides normal states there exist initial and final states. A final state does not have any actions.

Transitions can be executed immediately or delayed after a certain timespan. They also can be triggered by named events that do not have to be declared beforehand.

Each specification in StateDSL4Pepper results in a code generation to the programming language Java. During execution of those programs MQTT messages are sent to a robot. For events a window pops up that provides the different alternatives of the current state transition. A user has to select one of those events.

Figure 3. Specifies the similar therapy as Fig. 2. And provides an impression of the state-based DSL. The declarations of texts, pictures and videos are the same as for task models and were therefore omitted here.

```
initial greet{                          state imagine{
    say greeting                            say look
    ->introduce                             say imagineThat
}                                           ->end_exercise
state introduce{                        }
    say introduction                    state end_exercise{
    show startPict                          say bye
    ->train                                 event new->greet
}                                           event end->ende
state train{                            }
    play exerVid                        final ende
    say three
    ->train_imagine after 10.0 s
}
state train_imagine{
    say ten                             // -> State transition
    ->imagine after 15.0 s
}
```

Fig. 3. Specification of a mirror therapy in StateDSL4Pepper.

4 Summary and Outlook

The paper discussed the idea of end-user programming for humanoid robots by two different textual domain-specific languages TaskDSL4Pepper and StateDSL4Pepper. As the names already express one language is following the concept of task models while the other one specifies hierarchical Moore state machines. As most references of the literature we used the term end-user programming. However, the end users are the patients and not the therapists.

A first feedback from therapists provided an advantage of StateDSL4Pepper. However, there were several limitations for that like limited participants, different kinds of tool support and lack of time. Nevertheless, the approach of textual domain-specific languages seems to be promising, even that we did not find similar approaches in the literature for stroke therapies.

We plan to perform further evaluations and adaptations of the languages. It is e.g. no problem to replace common know temporal relations in task modelling like ">>" by "enabling". However, in first experiments participants did not like this idea so much.

Additionally, it is our intention to further extend both languages for programmers. Generic components have been implemented for both languages. The same is true for variables and functions for StateDSL4Pepper. It will be interesting to see, whether experienced therapists can change examples with these concepts as well.

A kind of virtual robot was implemented. In this way, the execution of our DSL examples can be evaluated without having a humanoid robotPepper at hand.

Acknowledgements. This joint research project "E-BRAiN - Evidence-based Robot Assistance in Neurorehabilitation" is supported by the European Social Fund (ESF), reference: ESF/14-BM-A55–0001/19-A01, and the Ministry of Education, Science and Culture of Mecklenburg-Vorpommern, Germany. The sponsors had no role in the decision to publish or any content of the publication.

References

1. Ajaykumar, G., Steele, M., and Huang, C.-M.: A survey on end-user robot programming. ACM Comput. Surv. **54**(8), 164, 36 (2021)
2. Buchholz, G., Forbrig, P.: Extended features of task models for specifying cooperative activities. In: Proceedings of the ACM on Human-Computer Interaction, vol. 1, Issue EICS, June 2017, Article no. 7 pp. 1–21 (2017)
3. Coronado, E., Mastrogiovanni, F., Venture, G.: Design of a human-centered robot framework for end-user programming and applications. In: Arakelian, V., Wenger, P. (eds.) ROMANSY 22 – Robot Design, Dynamics and Control. CICMS, vol. 584, pp. 450–457. Springer, Cham (2019). https://doi.org/10.1007/978-3-319-78963-7_56
4. Coronado, E., et al.: Towards a modular and distributed end-user development framework for human-robot interaction. IEEE Access **9**, 12675–12692 (2021)
5. CoTaSE: https://www.cotase.de/. Accessed 03 June 2023
6. E-BRAiN Homepage. https://www.ebrain-science.de/en/home/. Accessed 03 June 2023
7. Forbrig, P., Dittmar, A., Kühn, M.: A Textual domain specific language for task models: generating code for CoTaL, CTTE, and HAMSTERS. In: EICS 2018 conferences, Paris, France, pp. 5:1–5:6 (2018)
8. Frigerio, M., Buchli, J., Caldwell, D.G., Semini, C.: RobCoGen: a code generator for efficient kinematics and dynamics of articulated robots, based on domain specific languages. J. Softw. Eng. Robot. **7**(1), 36–54, (2016)
9. Heinzemann, C., Lange, R.: vTSL - a formally verifiable DSL for specifying robot tasks. In: 2018 IEEE/RSJ International Conference on Intelligent Robots and Systems, pp. 8308–8314 (2018)
10. Hinkel, G., Groenda, H., Vannucci, L., Denninger, O., Cauli, N., Ulbrich, S.: A domain-specific language (DSL) for integrating neuronal networks in robot control. In: Proceedings of the 2015 Joint MORSE/VAO Workshop on Model-Driven Robot Software Engineering and View-based Software-Engineering (MORSE/VAO 2015). Association for Computing Machinery, New York, NY, pp. 9–15 (2015)
11. Leonardi, N., Manca, M., Paternò, F., Santoro, C.: Trigger-action programming for personalising humanoid robot behaviour. In Proceedings of the 2019 CHI Conference on Human Factors in Computing Systems (CHI 2019). Association for Computing Machinery, New York, NY, Paper 445, pp. 1–13 (2019)
12. Manca, M., Paternò, F., Santoro, C.: Analyzing trigger-action programming for personalization of robot behaviour in IoT environments. In: Malizia, A., Valtolina, S., Morch, A., Serrano, A., Stratton, A. (eds.) IS-EUD 2019. LNCS, vol. 11553, pp. 100–114. Springer, Cham (2019). https://doi.org/10.1007/978-3-030-24781-2_7
13. Moros, S., Wood, L., Robins, B., Dautenhahn, K., Castro-González, Á.: Programming a humanoid robot with the scratch language. In: Merdan, M., Lepuschitz, W., Koppensteiner, G., Balogh, R., Obdržálek, D. (eds.) RiE 2019. AISC, vol. 1023, pp. 222–233. Springer, Cham (2020). https://doi.org/10.1007/978-3-030-26945-6_20
14. MQTT. https://mqtt.org/. Accessed 03 June 2023
15. Oishi, Y, Kanda, T., Kanbara, M., Satake, S., Hagita. N.: Toward end-user programming for robots in stores. In: Proceedings of the Companion of the 2017 ACM/IEEE International Conference on Human-Robot Interaction (HRI 2017), pp. 233–234 (2017)
16. Rutle, A., Backer, J., Foldøy, K., Bye, R.T.: CommonLang: a DSL for defining robot tasks. In: Proceedings MoDELS 2018 Workshop MORSE (2018)
17. Xext: https://www.eclipse.org/Xtext/. Accessed 03 June 2023
18. Xtend: https://www.eclipse.org/xtend/documentation/index.html. Accessed 03 June 2023

Using Polymorphic Glyphs to Support the Visual Exploration of Hierarchical Spatio-Temporal Data

Aline Menin, Hadil Ayari, Franck Michel, and Marco Winckler[✉]

University Côte D'Azur, I3S/ INRIA, SPARKS/ Wimmics Team, Paris, France
{aline.menin,franck.michel,marco.winckler}@inria.fr,
hadil.ayari@etu.univ-cotedazur.fr

Abstract. Studying spatio-temporal data is essential to understand the processes of the real world. However, the design of effective visualizations to explore spatio-temporal data is not a straightforward task due to the inherent multidimensional aspects of the data. In this paper, we explore the usage of polymorphous glyphs (i.e. glyphs that change shapes according to the context) to support the exploration of multiple hierarchical levels and dimensions of the data. We implemented our approach in the form of a web-based visualization interface that we demonstrate through a case study of the ISSA KG, which describes scientific publications in the field of agriculture, thus supporting domain experts on investigating where, when and how different crops are cultivated.

Keywords: Information visualization · Polymorphous glyphs · Linked data visualization · Spatio-temporal visualization

1   Introduction

The study of spatio-temporal data (i.e. data described through geographic and temporal information) is essential to understand the processes of the real world. The widespread use of Linked Open Data (LOD) in the form of RDF (Resource Description Framework) knowledge graphs (KG) results on the availability and easy access of numerous datasets describing the semantics of real-world spatio-temporal entities and their relations on the Web, leading to huge amounts of geo-referenced information. Nevertheless, the value of these data depends on efficient tool support to extract relevant information to communicate the underlying phenomena. The design of efficient data representations to support the exploration of spatio-temporal data is particularly challenging. Further to being able to represent the multiple dimensions and levels of spatial (e.g. countries, regions, neighborhoods, etc.) and temporal (e.g. years, months, days, etc.) granularity, a visualization technique should reflect the inherent properties of the data (i.e. the geographical arrangement of locations and the ordering of time units).

© The Author(s), under exclusive license to Springer Nature Switzerland AG 2023
J. Abdelnour Nocera et al. (Eds.): INTERACT 2023, LNCS 14145, pp. 325–329, 2023.
https://doi.org/10.1007/978-3-031-42293-5_31

Multidimensional visualization is a challenge on itself: as the number data dimensions increases, a single view displaying all the information at once is no longer suitable due to cognitive overload and visual cluttering [5]. The coordinated multiple views paradigm tackles the problem of representing multidimensional data through a predefined set of views that represent different perspectives to the data [7], while providing coordinating operations between views to support reasoning [9]. However, the plethora of existing visualization techniques [4,6] makes it unfeasible to determine a single combination of visualization techniques capable of solving every domain-related task.

Glyph-based data representations are another popular approach to deal with multidimensional data in information visualization due to their ability to convey multiple attributes in a small and compact visual representation. These are powerful visual representations capable of stimulating more cognitive activity during visualization than other forms of visual design [1]. Nonetheless, they are often static representations, displaying a large yet single perspective to the data. In this paper, we investigate the usage of polymorphic glyphs (i.e. glyphs that change its shape according to the surrounding semantics and/or user actions) to assist the exploration of hierarchical spatio-temporal data. As a proof-of-concept, we implemented our approach in the form of a web-based visualization tool, called *PHiTGlyph* (**P**olymorphic and **Hi**erarchic **T**emporal **G**lyph), that uses interaction to activate the polymorphous aspect of glyphs.

Finally, we demonstrate the suitability of our approach by exploring the ISSA KG [8], which describes over 110,000 scientific resources (i.e., book, book chapter, article, thesis, etc.) in the field of agriculture. Each data record is enriched through named-entity (NE) linking, which assigns a unique identity to entities (e.g. locations or crop cultures) mentioned in the text. Thus, each data record corresponds to a scientific publication described through information such as title, authors, publication date, abstract and associated to a number of geographic and thematic NEs. Each geographic NE is described through a name and a geographical position (i.e. latitude and longitude).

2   PHiTGlyph: Polymorphic and Hierarchic Temporal Glyph

Similar to previous works [2,3,10], we geo-locate glyphs encoding attributes of the data records. The thematic dimension of our data comprises the research topic of each publication, which information is hierarchical, composed by categories and sub-categories. Visualization techniques such as treemap, sunburst, circle packing and tree diagram are well-known to represent hierarchical data. However, as the number of categories and hierarchical levels increase, the visual legibility of these techniques reduces significantly. Although interaction supports navigating up and down the different levels of the hierarchy, such navigation happens one category at the time, which hinders comparison tasks. For this reason, we chose to design a polymorphous glyph, which different shapes can represent different levels of the hierarchy, thus improving legibility and between-category

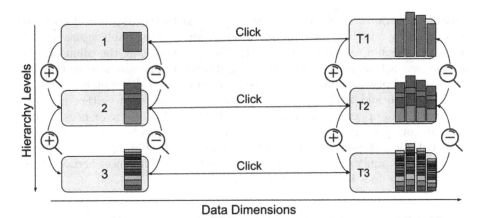

Fig. 1. Overview of glyph states and interactions.

comparison. Particularly, we follow a stacked-bar graph-like design to represent the count of data records (size of bar sectors) associated to each category (color). When placed over a time axis, it can encode the temporal distribution of data records, while being easy to read and supporting comparison tasks. According to Borgo et al. [1] the chosen design respects criteria of typedness, visual orderability, channel capacity, separability, and learnability.

The diagram illustrated in Fig. 1 represent the different states of our glyph, which are activated through interaction: zooming with mouse scroll enables a hierarchical browsing of the data from the total count of publications to the distribution per sub-category, while the use of an arrow placed next to the glyph reveal the temporal distribution of publications for a particular country, either the total count or the distribution per category and sub-category. Upon hovering over the glyphs, the system displays a tooltip showing detailed information about the represented data. Finally, to assist the user on answering questions such as "how is a crop cultivated in a particular country?", upon identifying the country where the crop is cultivated, the user can hover the glyph and select the category to see what publications in the dataset refer to that category.

3   Exploring the Temporal Evolution of Crop Culture Across Different Regions

In this scenario, we assist Bob in his research to understand (i) the temporal evolution of crop culture mention in the literature of different countries, and (ii) how the cultivation methods evolve over time. Bob starts by searching for the countries of interest, e.g., France and Costa Rica (Fig. 2a-b). As he is interested in exploring the differences between cereal culture and livestock breeding, he filters out non interesting crop cultures. Bob then zoom into each country to reveal the distribution of publications per category (Fig. 2c-d), where he observes a similar count of publications. However, he wants to know if this distribution is even across time periods. Thus, he uses the arrows next to the glyphs to deepen the exploration by revealing the temporal distribution of those publications according to the selected categories (Fig. 2(e-f). The glyphs display the count of publication over a time period from 2015 to 2018, where one can observe that the literature in both countries refer to those cultures in a different frequency in the years 2016 and 2017, when France has only references to either livestock breeding (2016) or cereal culture (2017) while Costa Rica has references to both crop categories. Going further, Bob zoom into the glyphs to reveal the temporal distribution of crop reference within each category (Fig. 2g-h) and explores the associated publications to each crop to identify the differences between their cultivation methods in each country (Fig. 2i-j).

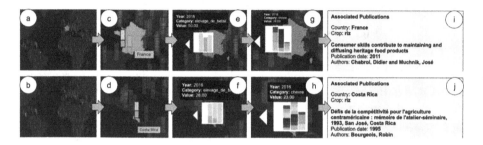

Fig. 2. Usage of PHiTGlyph. The user search for the countries of interest (a-b). They navigate to the temporal distribution of publications per category using the arrows next to the glyphs corresponding to each country (c-f). By zooming into the glyph, they reveal the temporal distribution per subcategory (g-h). Then, to proceed their research and compare crop culture across country, they access the associated publications to the time period of interest (i-j).

4   Conclusion and Future Work

In this paper, we propose the use of polymorphous glyphs to represent multiple hierarchical levels and dimensions of spatio-temporal data. We rely on simple visual channels (i.e. size and color) to support a smooth learning curve, while providing interactions such as zoom and click to guide the user through the different hierarchical levels and data dimensions. We demonstrated our approach through a case study of the ISSA KG to support researchers in agriculture on answering questions such as "where and when are crop cultures mentioned in the literature?" and "how does a particular crop culture evolve over space and time?". A limitation of our approach refers to visual scalability: we illustrated it through four topics and time periods, as we are limited by the number of colors one can perceive visually. Although we mitigate the issue through filtering out uninteresting information, studies are necessary to understand how our approach deals with visual scalability and how efficiently is the proposed solution.

Acknowledgments. We would like to acknowledge the students of Polytech Nice Antoine Huot-Marchand and Loic Madern for implementing the first version of the prototype.

References

1. Borgo, R., et al.: Glyph-based Visualization: Foundations, Design Guidelines, Techniques and Applications. Eurographics State of the Art Reports, pp. 39–63 (2013). http://www.cg.tuwien.ac.at/research/publications/2013/borgo-2013-gly/ iSBN: 1558608192

2. Castermans, T., Speckmann, B., Verbeek, K., Westenberg, M.A., Betti, A., Berg, H.V.D.: Glammap: Geovisualization for e-Humanities. In: 2016 Workshop on Visualization for the Digital Humanities (2016)

3. Chen, W., Xia, J., Wang, X., Wang, Y., Chen, J., Chang, L.: RelationLines: Visual Reasoning of Egocentric Relations from Heterogeneous Urban Data. ACM Transactions on Intelligent Systems and Technology **10**(1), 2:1–2:21 (2018). https://doi.org/10.1145/3200766

4. Liu, S., Maljovec, D., Wang, B., Bremer, P., Pascucci, V.: Visualizing high-dimensional data: advances in the past decade. IEEE Trans. Visual Comput. Graph. **23**(3), 1249–1268 (2017)

5. Munzner, T.: Visualization analysis and design. CRC Press (2014)

6. Nobre, C., Streit, M., Meyer, M., Lex, A.: The state of the art in visualizing multivariate networks. Comput. Graph. Forum (EuroVis) **38**, 807–832 (2019)

7. Roberts, J.C.: State of the art: Coordinated & multiple views in exploratory visualization. In: Fifth International Conference on Coordinated and Multiple Views in Exploratory Visualization (CMV 2007), pp. 61–71. IEEE (2007)

8. Toulet, A., et al.: Issa: generic pipeline, knowledge model and visualization tools to help scientists search and make sense of a scientific archive. In: The Semantic Web-ISWC 2022: 21st International Semantic Web Conference, Virtual Event, October 23–27, 2022, Proceedings, pp. 660–677. Springer (2022)

9. Wang Baldonado, M.Q., Woodruff, A., Kuchinsky, A.: Guidelines for using multiple views in information visualization. In: Proceedings of Working Conference on Advanced visual interfaces, pp. 110–119 (2000)

10. Zeng, W., Fu, C.W., Arisona, S.M., Schubiger, S., Burkhard, R., Ma, K.L.: Visualizing the relationship between human mobility and points of interest. IEEE Trans. Intell. Transp. Syst. **18**(8), 2271–2284 (2017). https://doi.org/10.1109/TITS.2016.2639320

Keynotes

A Framework for Born-Accessible Development of Software and Digital Content

Jonathan Lazar(✉) 🅞

College of Information Studies, Maryland Initiative for Digital Accessibility (MIDA) Faculty
Member, Human-Computer Interaction Lab (HCIL), University of Maryland, College Park,
MD 20742, USA
jlazar@umd.edu

Abstract. This paper describes the basic concepts of the born-accessible approach
to design and development, and compares it to the existing models of retrofitting
digital technologies and content for accessibility. This paper is a short summary
of the keynote speech from INTERACT 2023, which provides a framework for
born-accessible design and a vision for the research and development work needed
to influence future technologies towards the born-accessible model.

Keywords: Born-accessible · Accessibility · User-centered Design

1 Born-Accessible Development

Digital technologies and content are often designed without considering the needs of
people with disabilities. It is estimated by the World Health Organization that 16%
of people worldwide have disabilities [16], meaning that they may be excluded from
education, employment, healthcare, and commerce that often requires the use of digital
technologies and content which may not be accessible. What frequently happens is that
people with disabilities notify the developers or owners, or in some cases take legal action,
to force the digital technologies and/or content to become accessible. Even then, not all
of the technologies and/or content become accessible. The vast number of technologies
and content that are inaccessible means that it is not feasible to have advocates complain
about every single technology, and so often, accessibility needs simply go unaddressed.
Businesses often claim that "we didn't know that we had people with disabilities who
need access" but this is not a valid excuse, especially since major technical guidelines
on digital accessibility have existed for nearly 25 years, major disability rights laws have
existed in multiple countries for over 30 years, and in some cases, solutions for digital
accessibility such as video captioning, have existed for over 50 years. But there is a better
way to build technologies: the born-accessible approach to design and development.

With the born accessible approach, accessibility is considered as a primary design
goal from the start, and people with disabilities are included from the start. No software or
content is released that is not accessible. There are many benefits to the born-accessible
approach:

© The Author(s), under exclusive license to Springer Nature Switzerland AG 2023
J. Abdelnour Nocera et al. (Eds.): INTERACT 2023, LNCS 14145, pp. 333–338, 2023.
https://doi.org/10.1007/978-3-031-42293-5_32

1) There is no delay in getting access to the digital technologies or content. When technology is built from scratch to be accessible, people with disabilities receive access to the technologies or content at the same time as everyone else.
2) When using the born-accessible approach, building for accessibility is inexpensive. It's been estimated that born-accessible approaches increase the design and development costs very little, only 1–2%, versus the much larger costs of retrofitting a technology after it has already been built.
3) Technologies and content that are born-accessible are inherently flexible and innovative, because they are designed to work with various technology and input and output combinations, not only one scenario of usage. They are therefore more usable by everyone, including people without disabilities

1.1   Retrofitting for Accessibility

In the retrofitting model of accessibility, technologies and content are built, released, and then fixed for accessibility after the fact. While there may be pressures to get a product or content "shipped" or "out-the-door", leaving accessible design fixes until later is what causes the perception that accessibility is expensive. For instance, if you read about accessibility causing the amount of software code to double in size, that's caused by retrofitting and the need to restructure the code because of the retrofit, not because of the accessibility itself [8]. It's not that accessibility is inherently expensive, it's that waiting until later to make the accessibility fixes is what's expensive. As described by Churchill [1]:

When accessibility requirements are deferred, a backlog of accessibility debt is created and downstream costs will likely be incurred. For example, you may design a complex workflow with intricate elements to complete a task. If you haven't considered accessibility up front, you may discover that some of the elements are impossible to build for accessibility and end up having to redesign and rebuild the entire workflow from scratch. This will slow you down far more than taking these requirements into account up front ever could. And you'll lose people—users—in the process: first, those who could not use your product in the first place, and second, those who resent that you changed a workflow they had become accustomed to as you roll out your "fixes."

Aside from the costs on developers to retrofit, there is also a costly impact on users with disabilities. If a technology is inaccessible for even a short time and is retrofitted, during that time that the technology is not accessible, the costs on users are enormous. For instance, one study documents how on websites with accessibility barriers, blind users may need to take up to 5 times as much time to complete their tasks [2]. Other studies document how inaccessible websites can result in being charged higher prices [4], being unable to apply for jobs online [6], or being discriminated against when asking about applying for jobs on accessible websites [3]. Sometimes, when a technology is built inaccessibly, a solution proposed is to have a separate accessible version, or to use the mobile version, but that is not equal access. The alternate version often does not have the equivalent functionality or content, and in fact is rarely kept up to date [15].

In many ways, the concept of retrofitting for accessibility is similar to the concept of "accommodations" where someone with a disability requests that a process, workplace, task, technology, or educational experience be modified to be accessible for them. Not every individual will feel comfortable making requests every time, not every request for an accommodation will be accomplished, and again, there may a delay in time while something is made accessible. An example from the U.S. Department of Labor shows why this retrofitting/accommodation model is so problematic: employees requested whether they could seek an exemption from legal requirements (Sect. 508 of the Rehabilitation Act) requiring that only accessible software be procured, because they stated that they did not have any employees with disabilities who would need to use a specific software product [3]. Of course, once they have procured inaccessible software, that would serve as a barrier to hiring any employees with disabilities in the future. Or consider the case of textbooks and ebooks. If a book for a university class is not already available in accessible digital format, either directly from the publisher or from an international website such as bookshare.org, students with disabilities will need to request from their university that the book be converted into digital format. There may be a delay in getting an accessible book, so that students with disabilities don't have access until half-way through the semester, putting them at a disadvantage. Laws such as the European Accessibility Act require (starting in 2025) that all ebooks be "born-accessible." That does not, however, require that a print book always be made into an accessible digital version.

Unfortunately, most universities, if they teach digital accessibility at all, teach it using the retrofitting philosophy. In academic programs in computer science, information science, and information technology, when accessibility is taught, it is typically taught as a part of a course at the end of the academic program (such as human-computer interaction or web design), or as a stand-alone course on accessibility, which is also taught at the end of the academic program [10]. Students therefore learn that you build technologies (think about it—programming is usually the first course taken), and you make any fixes for people with disabilities later on. The University of Dundee's approach of injecting accessibility concepts throughout all courses in a program, is a notable effort towards teaching using a born-accessible approach [14].

1.2 The Born-Accessible Model of Development

In contrast to the retrofitting model, the born-accessible model of development focuses on involving people with disabilities from the start, and on designing for accessibility from the start. No products or content are released that are not accessible. Accessibility is a key design goal from the start. In the born-accessible model, people with disabilities are involved in the process from the beginning. All aspects of the development process include accessibility and people with disabilities as core. For instance, personas include people with disabilities, and scenarios involve accessibility. Philosophically, the born-accessible approach can be understood in the traditions of user-centered design (early and ongoing focus on users and their tasks) and participatory design (users involved in all phases). While there are many development concepts that at first seem to be about accessibility ("universal design", "inclusive design", and "barrier-free design"), they often don't include people with disabilities directly into the development process, and they may be more focused on following a set of technical standards such as the Web Content Accessibility Guidelines (WCAG) than meeting the needs of people with disabilities [13]. Focusing only on technical standards for accessibility can be problematic, since research by Power et. al. [9] has documented how many accessibility barriers are not included in existing technical standards. Simply put, only following technical standards for accessibility doesn't mean that people with disabilities can actually use your software or digital content. Yet governments such as the UK give guidance that the way for government entities to comply with disability rights laws is to comply with existing technical standards for accessibility such as WCAG [12].

The born-accessible approach is broader. It involves: 1) including users with disabilities in design and development from the start, 2) having core design goals involving accessibility, 3) evaluating/testing interfaces with people with disabilities, and 4) never releasing anything that is not accessible. Yet most statutes and regulations requiring digital accessibility focus on following technical standards, rather than involving people with disabilities in development and actually meeting their needs. A rare exception is the regulation associated with the U.S. Air Carrier Access Act covering airline websites, which requires the involvement of people with disabilities, although only in testing the airline websites, not in the initial design and development (14 C.F.R. Sec. 382.43(c)(2)).

There is another benefit to involving people with disabilities in all phases of development and design: to paraphrase Richard Ladner, "People with disabilities are naturally creative and problem solvers because they do it every day." Because people with disabilities often face accessibility barriers in their daily life, they have experience with identifying creative solutions and workaround approaches. This isn't just Ladner hypothesizing: one study of 100 Blind users found that they were more effective in responding to frustrations on the web than visual users, because rather than give up, the blind users look for workarounds, saving them time compared to the visual users who often gave up [5].

1.3   Benefits for People Without Disabilities

Many readers will be familiar with the concept of a "curb cut" in physical accessibility, and how the curb cut helps not only users of wheelchairs, but also bikers, people pulling luggage or pushing baby carriages, users of skateboards, and many others. The flexibility provided by accessible technologies and content help a majority of computer users. For instance, a classic study from Microsoft estimated a majority (57%) of computer users could benefit from the use of accessible technology [7]. Other researchers have documented how accessible websites lead to improved task performance and less time to complete tasks on websites for people without disabilities [11].

2   What is Needed?

To start with, we need to create a clear definition of born-accessible design that has been agreed upon by multiple stakeholders, including leading disability rights groups. A search of articles on born-accessible design shows that many authors use the phrase to describe a variety of approaches. A similar web search shows that book and article publishers are the ones using the phrase "born-accessible" most frequently to describe ebooks and digital articles that are created with accessibility in mind. Holding workshops of various stakeholders could help describe and define the phrase.

2.1 Data on Costs and Benefits

There is limited quantitative data on the benefits and costs of the born-accessible approach. There are some estimates, but none of these are at the level that would be needed for regulatory impact analysis at a national government level. We need to measure the costs and benefits of using a born-accessible approach, if there is any hope of born-accessible approaches being included as a requirement for new technology or content development.

2.2 Models, Activities, and Tools for Involvement

At this point, guidance on the born-accessible approach is to use concepts primarily from user-centered design and participatory design: involve users from the start and at all phases of design, use iterative design approaches, and evaluate and measure progress regularly. It would be helpful to create a set of design activities, best practices, tools and models specifically for using the born-accessible approach. It is expected that methods and approaches would differ depending on the type of technology or content. For instance, an ebook is only created once and usually not updated, a software application may have minor updates once or twice a year but does not usually have a major overhaul, and websites get regular updates and often have a complete redesign every 2–3 years.

2.3 Educational Materials

To spread the ideas behind born-accessible design, students will need to learn about them and get experience applying the concepts. As described in earlier sections, as educators, we need to move our curriculum away from the retrofitting model, so that students can instead learn about accessibility concepts throughout their academic program. Models such as the ones described at the University of Dundee will need to be expanded upon, with resources available for sharing throughout the world.

References

1. Churchill, E.: Putting accessibility first. Interactions **25**(5), 24–25 (2018)
2. Griffith, M., Wentz, B., Lazar, J.: Quantifying the cost of web accessibility barriers for blind users. Interact. Comput. **34**(6), 137–149 (2022)
3. Lazar, J., Goldstein, D.F., Taylor, A.: Ensuring Digital Accessibility Through Process and Policy. Waltham, MA: Morgan Kaufmann/Elsevier (2015)
4. Lazar, J., et al.: Up in the air: are airlines following the new DOT rules on equal pricing for people with disabilities when websites are inaccessible? Gov. Inf. Q. **27**(4), 329–336 (2010)
5. Lazar, J., Allen, A., Kleinman, J., Malarkey, C.: What frustrates screen reader users on the web: a study of 100 blind users. Int. J. Hum.-Comput. Interact. **22**(3), 247–269 (2007)
6. Lazar, J., Olalere, A., Wentz, B.: Investigating the accessibility and usability of job application web sites for blind users. J. Usability Stud. **7**(2), 68–87 (2012)
7. Microsoft Research & Forrester Research (2004). Accessible Technology in Computing—Examining Awareness, Use, and Future Potential. Technical report, Microsoft (2004). http://download.microsoft.com/download/0/1/f/01f506eb-2d1e-42a6-bc7b-1f33d25fd40f/ResearchReport-Phase2.doc

8. Ossmann, R., Miesenberger, K., Archambault, D.: A computer game designed for all. In: 11th International Conference Proceedings of the ICCHP 2008: Computers Helping People with Special Needs, pp. 585–592 (2008)

9. Power, C., Freire, A., Petrie, H., Swallow, D.: Guidelines are only half of the story: accessibility problems encountered by blind users on the web. In: Proceedings of the SIGCHI Conference on Human Factors in Computing Systems, pp. 433–442 (2012)

10. Putnam, C., Dahman, M., Rose, E., Cheng, J., Bradford, G.: Best practices for teaching accessibility in university classrooms: cultivating awareness, understanding, and appreciation for diverse users. ACM Trans. Accessible Comput. (TACCESS) 8(4), 1–26 (2016)

11. Schmutz, S., Sonderegger, A., Sauer, J.: Implementing recommendations from web accessibility guidelines: would they also provide benefits to nondisabled users. Hum. Factors 58(4), 611–629 (2016)

12. United Kingdom Central Digital and Data Office. Understanding accessibility requirements for public sector bodies (2022). https://www.gov.uk/guidance/accessibility-requirements-for-public-sector-websites-and-apps

13. Vanderheiden, G., Jordan, B., Lazar, J.: Design for people experiencing functional limitations. In: Salvendy, G., (ed.) 5th Edition of the Handbook of Human Factors and Ergonomics, pp. 1216–1248 (2021)

14. Waller, A., Hanson, V.L., Sloan, D.: Including accessibility within and beyond undergraduate computing courses. In: Proceedings of the 11th International ACM SIGACCESS Conference on Computers and Accessibility, pp. 155–162 (2009)

15. Wentz, B., Jaeger, P.T., Lazar, J.: Retrofitting accessibility: the legal inequality of after-the-fact online access for persons with disabilities in the United States. First Monday (2011). https://firstmonday.org/ojs/index.php/fm/article/download/3666/3077

16. World Health Organization Disability (statistics on) (2023). https://www.who.int/news-room/fact-sheets/detail/disability-and-health#:~:text=Key%20facts,1%20in%206%20of%20us

Why We Do What We Do – HCI and Societal Impact

Jan Gulliksen[✉] [iD]

School of Electrical Engineering and Computer Science, Department of Media Technology and
Interaction Design, KTH Royal Institute of Technology, Lindstedtsvägen 3, Floor 4,
10044 Stockholm, Sweden
gulliksen@kth.se

Abstract. In the spirit of INTERACTs founder Brian Shackel, this conference
was founded to bring together academics and industrial practitioners in the field of
human computer interaction (HCI) to recognize the profound societal impact that
research and knowledge on humans interacting with various forms of technology
has. HCI has grown from being a small obscure discipline for computer scientists
that were not that good on programming and needed to pick a field that was
easy, to being one of the most important and fastest growing professions in the
IT sector, through the role that user experience (UX) play. The scientific studies
and published papers in HCI have grown much more than many of the other
disciplines. How has HCI come to undergo such a development? I believe that
there are several potential reasons for this. The transdisciplinary nature, involving
true collaboration and a joint understanding between disciplines of very different
natures including computer science, behavioral science and design, among other
things that are fundamental to the impact. Another value is the ambitions not
to bend for the complex, "wicked" problems that human computer interaction
addresses but develop the methodology to fit the nature of doing research in the
wild on complex problems where many of the involving factors are difficult to
control is one of the reasons for the success. The values of addressing and caring
about users, regardless of abilities, knowledge level, age or gender is another
positive quality that has contributed to the impact. To be able to make the best out
of our discipline we should more recognize and cherish the contribution that HCI
can make, educate students and the society to understand the impact and make use
of all the valuable methods, we need carefully to choose research problems and
approaches to maximize the impact and we should to a higher extent take an active
role in the contemporary development of the field, actively engage in politics and
policy making on AI, digitalization and development for change and make sure
that the values of our HCI field permeates all development.

Keywords: Socio-technical system · Wicked problems · Transdisciplinary ·
Action research · Societal impact

© The Author(s), under exclusive license to Springer Nature Switzerland AG 2023
J. Abdelnour Nocera et al. (Eds.): INTERACT 2023, LNCS 14145, pp. 339–346, 2023.
https://doi.org/10.1007/978-3-031-42293-5_33

1 Introduction

The world is a complex phenomenon where people act and interact, using technological support in many different ways to achieve complex tasks, for work or as entertainment for pure leisure in a complex context consisting of people, organizations, work tasks and technological tools in a complex relationship. It is difficult or even impossible to study or understand the components of such a system in isolation. Rather you need to find methods and tools to study and understand the complex sociotechnical system and draw conclusions without being tempted to isolate particular features to make them possible to study and experiment on in a controlled scientific fashion.

Already back in 1965, Harold J. Leavitt developed his **system model**, to analyze what an effect a change strategy will have on an organization (Leavitt, 1965). He argued that every organization consists of four independent components; tasks, people, structure and technology, and to have successfully manage integrated change it is crucial to understand the connection between each component.

By viewing the world as a **socio-technical system** (Mumford, 2006) one can emphasize the importance of seeing the organization as a whole where technical and social functions are interacting and where both influences, and are influenced, by each other. The socio-technical values are based on the fact that the needs and rights of the users must have as high priority as the changing technical and organizational structures in the system.

2 Wicked Problems

Often the problems tackled by HCI researchers may be seen as **wicked problems**, meaning problems involving many interdependent factors making them seemingly impossible to solve. The different factors may be difficult to define and separate from each other, intangible and constantly changing and developing. The system may also be difficult to describe in more abstract terms, to be able to model, experiment on and draw conclusions of the development of. Solving wicked problems requires a deep understanding of all stakeholders involved (direct or indirect users, designers and developers and others affected by the use of a particular artifact) as well as a deep understanding of the societal system of which it is a part, work, organization, society, values etc. The concept of wicked problems was coined by Rittel and Webber (1973). They described 10 characteristics of Wicked problems:

1. There is no definitive formula for a wicked problem.
2. Wicked problems have no stopping rule, as in there's no way to know your solution is final.
3. Solutions to wicked problems are not true-or-false; they can only be good-or-bad.
4. There is no immediate test of a solution to a wicked problem.
5. Every solution to a wicked problem is a "one-shot operation"; because there is no opportunity to learn by trial-and-error, every attempt counts significantly.
6. Wicked problems do not have a set number of potential solutions.
7. Every wicked problem is essentially unique.
8. Every wicked problem can be considered a symptom of another problem.

9. There is always more than one explanation for a wicked problem because the explanations vary greatly depending on the individual perspective.
10. Planners/designers have no right to be wrong and must be fully responsible for their actions.

Many argue that the only way to properly solve these types of wicked problems is by applying an innovative approach provided by design thinking (see for example Buchanan (1992)). The iterative nature of design thinking shows to be particularly useful to tackle ill-defined or unknown problems by reframing them using human-centered methods, such as brainstorming, prototyping and testing.

3 Transdisciplinarity

Solving complex wicked problems requires true collaboration and involvement of different disciplines in an open fashion. There are different concepts to name such a way of working and I think it is important to distinguish between these different concepts to understand its meaning and help increasing the use and participation of different disciplines on equal terms. I often use the following understanding of the concepts, further elaborated by Shanableh et al. (2022).

- **Disciplinary research** are scholarly research methods where a discipline explores a particular research problem from the boundaries of the disciplinary limits, with the restrictions it imposes.
- **Multidisciplinary research** contrasts disciplinary perspectives in an additive manner, meaning two or more disciplines each provide their viewpoint on a problem from their perspectives, involving little interaction across the disciplines.
- **Interdisciplinary research** combines two or more disciplines to a new level of integration suggesting that component boundaries start to break down. It is no longer a simple addition of parts but recognizing that each discipline can affect the research output of the other.
- **Transdisciplinary research** occurs when two or more discipline perspectives transcend each other to form a new holistic approach forming a completely different result from what one would expect from simply adding the parts. Transdisciplinarity results in a type xenogenesis where output is created as a result of disciplines integrating to become something completely new.

4 Purpose

We rarely consider the major reasons why we conduct research, the driving forces behind each individual researcher's knowledge endeavors, or if it simple materialistic reasons why someone undertakes the task of educating themselves to become researchers. I have before reasoned over this in relations to the way we have structured our PhD education and how we create relationships between software developers and HCI experts (Gulliksen, 2007).

Many times, the selection of research questions is simply for pecuniary reasons – that was the research funding that was available – creating a situation where the research is no longer driven by the quest for truth or utility, but for the sake of delivering values to someone that has particular expectations on the results.

There are several examples where I have been involved in research activities that have had a higher ambition than simply writing yet another scientific paper. For example, the multi-researcher initiative to discuss in what way HCI could contribute to international policy making (Lazar et al. 2016).

5 Action Research

Solving complex, wicked, socio-technical problems require novel transdisciplinary approaches of the specific type that a field such as human computer interaction can offer. However, as a young discipline, despite of its multidisciplinary background, the field is not sufficiently brave to take on a new methodological basis taking all of the above-mentioned considerations into account. Most often we see attempts to limit the problem to easily evaluable subsets, but unfortunately often with little or no societal impact, simply because the problem loses its natural setting and the practical applicability and societal impact tends to become limited or non-existing. There is a need to adopt a methodology that recognizes the complexity of the real world and has mechanisms to tackle the uncertainties that the less controlled environment imposes.

The research methodology that I mainly use is following an **action research** philosophy which includes mixes of reflection and observation within the actual change activities normally undertaken in a project. The researcher participates in the project as an active change agent and does thus work with the dual roles of managing the change in the organization at the same time as research on the case is conducted, hence the values and aspirations of the researcher also shapes the results. There are ways of overcoming this delimitation and also use these aspirations as an aspiration in the research. Contemporary action research methods are normally adapted based on the core thoughts developed by Kurt Lewin as early as in 1946 (Lewin, 1946). Action research as we know it today is a cyclic process of planning, action, observation, reflection and redesign, making our basic values explicit and basing it on the aspirations we have, but at the same time critically questioning the validity of what we are trying to achieve (Reason and Bradbury, 2001). The action research methodology is commonly used in other disciplines such as pedagogy, information systems or nursing, but not to the extent that one would expect within human computer interaction (HCI). One of the few papers detailing how actions research could be applied in HCI was done by Hayes in 2014 (Hayes, 2014).

How to structure **reflections on experiences** have been further detailed in Gibbs (1988) describing a cyclical model of reflection leading you through six stages exploring an experience: description, feelings, evaluation, analysis, conclusion and action plan. One of the most common reflective approaches used within HCI is the approach proposed by Donald Schön in the **Reflective Practitioner** (Schön, 1987) arguing for an increased reflection in action. The literature commonly refers to the following as being the skills required of reflective practice: **self-awareness, description, critical analysis, synthesis and evaluation** (Atkins and Murphy, 1993). This work can be classified as **interpretive research** assuming that the knowledge of reality is gained through social constructions such as language, consciousness, shared meanings, documents, tools, and other artifacts. Interpretive research does not predefine dependent and independent variables, but focuses on the complexity of human sense making as the situation emerges (Kaplan and Maxwell, 2005).

A common criticism towards action research or towards reflexive or interpretive research is to question the scientific quality and validity of the conclusions drawn. But there are ways of overcoming this, such as using the principles for conducting and evaluating interpretive field studies in information systems developed by Klein and Myers (1999). These principles of quality can be used much more broadly than simply analyzing field studies, it can be used to structure and critically analyze the data consisting of previous literature (own and others) and experiences gathered throughout ongoing development work according to an action research philosophy including quantitative and qualitative data together with design artifacts and critical reflections in the collaborative projects as well as experience-based research. Klein and Myers have identified seven principles:

1. **The Fundamental Principle of the Hermeneutic Cycle** suggests that all human understanding is achieved by iterating between considering the interdependent meaning of parts and the whole they form. It could for example involve by considering details of decisions made and the effects it has on a high organizational level, through the researcher's involvement in different parts of the organization and on different management levels.
2. The **Principle of contextualization** requires a critical reflection of the social and historical background of the research setting. This is achieved by situating the research in the special opportunities and constraints that the organizational setting of for example an academic institution preoccupied mainly with engineering education and reflecting on the special conditions that this entails, or the certain conditions for conducting health care.
3. The **Principle on the interaction between the researcher and the subject** involves a critical reflection on how the research material was socially constructed through the interaction between the researchers and the other participants.
4. The **Principle of abstraction and generalization** is addressed by formulating conclusions that are presented and critically discussed in an iterative fashion.
5. The **Principle on dialogical reasoning** requires a sensitivity to contradictions between theoretical preconceptions guiding the research and the actual data to support our ideas.
6. The **Principle on multiple interpretations** requires a sensitivity to different views and opinions on the interpretation of a situation depending on the views of the problem. This can be achieved by involving multiple researchers representing different transdisciplinary perspectives of the different stakeholder perspectives in the development process.
7. The **Principle of suspicion** requires a sensitivity towards "biases" and "distortions" in the experiences included and narratives collected. It can be safeguarded by critically questioning all statements obtained, both from the researchers involved and from representatives from the beneficiaries of the outcome of the project. You need to turn every conclusion upside down to question its validity and relevance for the task at hand.

6 Conclusions

So, why do we do research? Because we want to contribute new knowledge to the world or because we fundamentally believe that research has the potential to change the world? I believe that Human Computer Interaction (HCI) has an enormous potential for contributing to societal change and development. Here are some of the reasons why I think that this is so:

- **Human-centeredness** – In all development work with an HCI flavor the user is and should always be the major focus. The discipline grew out of a recognition of the fact that the end-user is the ultimate beneficiary of all we do but that it often is not the case that the user has been actively involved in the process, not that concepts such as usability, accessibility or user experience have been sufficiently taken into consideration.
- **Transdisciplinarity** – The transdisciplinary nature of HCI makes it particularly suitable for handling complex societal problems.
- **Contextuality** – In traditional research, the domain of studies is reduced to controlled settings where all independent variables can be kept under control. However, a lot of the real-world problems loses its fragrance if the research is controlled. Rather we should acknowledge the fact that research is and should be conducted in the wild, and use the complex conditions as an asset in the process. We need to understand the context of design (Svanæs and Gulliksen, 2008).
- **Basic values** – In addition to the transdisciplinary nature of HCI, it also includes a set of values that contributes to meeting the needs of society, the needs for individuals and organizations for the greater good of the humanity
- **Methodological implications** – the complexity of the problem domain and the transdisciplinary nature of the research constitutes a need to be more eclectic and inclusive in the choice of and combination of research methods. The research often makes it difficult to conduct traditional experimental research but rather gives opportunities to combine many different quantitative and qualitative data gathering methods as well as using design research. It is not uncommon that the collected data from real life applications is a combination of interviews, short surveys, meeting notes and reports, artefacts produced or collected, photos, films, etc.
- **Ethical Implications** – with the recent development within research ethics, the requirements on ethics approval and the increased administration in relation to research problems has caused a lot of extra work for researchers, simply to comply with the increased standards for ethical approvals. Generally, the trust on researchers to follow their code of ethics has been replaced by bureaucratic and time-consuming administrative processes. As a consequence, a lot of important interesting research findings are not disseminated or maybe not even conducted in favor of research problems that do not require ethical approval and informed consent. This may have a negative impact on the potential for research to have a societal impact.
- **Purpose** – We should much more ask for the purpose of the research, in what way it intends to contribute to the societal goals and thus hopefully encourage researchers to make this contribution more explicit, which hopefully would lead to much more of a discussion in the research society and hopefully also to increased societal contribution.

But we should also encourage and value each individual researcher's contribution to the society and make this play a more fundamental role in more modern review and ranking system instead of the current quantitative assessments of research impact, such as by counting citations and downloads.

- **Implications for policy** – A common conclusion in many HCI papers is providing implications for design. However, the potential to offer implications for policy is definitely possible and appropriate in a lot of the research. While we value theoretical rigor, methodological soundness, etc. we should to a much higher extension value the contribution to the development of the society.

There is a need to revalue why we do the research we do, to increase the focus on societal contribution and to get back to the aim originally formulated by Brian Shackel in the invention of the INTERACT conference series and the basis of the Brian Shackel Award, which is "to recognize the most outstanding contribution in the form of a refereed paper submitted to and delivered at the INTERACT conference and to draw the attention to the need for a comprehensive human-centered approach in the design and use of information technology in which the human and social implications have been taken into account".

References

Leavitt, H.: Appling Organizational Change in Industry: Structural, Technical, and Humanistic Approaches. Handbook of Organizations. Rand McNally, Chicago, IL (1965)

Mumford, E.: The story of socio-technical design: reflections on its successes, failures and potential. Inf. Syst. J. **16**(4), 317–342 (2006)

Rittel, H.W., Webber, M.M.: Dilemmas in a general theory of planning. Policy Sci. **4**(2), 155–169 (1973)

Buchanan, R.: Wicked problems in design thinking. Des. Issues **8**(2), 5–21 (1992)

Shanableh, A., Aderibigbe, S., Omar, M., Shabib, A.: Challenges and opportunities of multi-disciplinary, inter-disciplinary and trans-disciplinary research. Higher Education in the Arab World: Research and Development, pp. 311–325 (2022)

Gulliksen, J.: How do developers meet users?–Attitudes and processes in software development. In: Interactive Systems, Design, Specification, and Verification: 13th International Workshop, DSVIS 2006, Dublin, Ireland, 26–28 July 2006, Revised Papers, vol. 13, pp. 1–10. Springer, Heidelberg (2007). https://doi.org/10.1007/978-3-540-69554-7_1

Lazar, J., et al.: Human–computer interaction and international public policymaking: a framework for understanding and taking future actions. Found. Trends® Hum. Comput. Inter. **9**(2), 69–149 (2016)

Lewin, K.: Action research and minority problems. J. Soc. Issues **2**(4), 34–46 (1946)

Reason, P., Bradbury, H.: Handbook of Action Research: Participative Inquiry and Practice. Sage (2001)

Hayes, G.R.: Knowing by doing: action research as an approach to HCI. In: Olson, J.S., Kellogg, W.A. (eds.) Ways of Knowing in HCI, pp. 49–68. Springer, New York (2014). https://doi.org/10.1007/978-1-4939-0378-8_3

Gibbs, G.: Learning by Doing: A Guide to Teaching and Learning Methods. Further Education Unit (1988)

Schön, D.A.: Educating the Reflective Practitioner: Toward a New Design for Teaching and Learning in the Professions. Jossey-Bass (1987)

Atkins, S., Murphy, K.: Reflection: a review of the literature. J. Adv. Nurs. **18**(8), 1188–1192 (1993)

Kaplan, B., Maxwell, J.A.: Qualitative research methods for evaluating computer information systems. In: Evaluating the Organizational Impact of Healthcare Information Systems, pp. 30–55. Springer (2005). https://doi.org/10.1007/0-387-30329-4_2

Klein, H.K., Myers, M.D.: A set of principles for conducting and evaluating interpretive field studies in information systems. MIS Quarterly, pp. 67–93 (1999)

Svanæs, D., Gulliksen, J.: Understanding the context of design: towards tactical user centered design. In: Proceedings of the 5th Nordic Conference on Human-Computer Interaction: Building Bridges, pp. 353–362 (2008)

Panels

A Multi-perspective Panel on User-Centred Transparency, Explainability, and Controllability in Automations

Philippe Palanque[1] , Fabio Paternò[2(✉)] , Virpi Roto[3] , Albrecht Schmidt[4] ,
Simone Stumpf[5] , and Jürgen Ziegler[6]

[1] ICS-IRIT, University Toulouse III – Paul Sabatier, Toulouse, France
[2] CNR-ISTI, HIIS Laboratory, Pisa, Italy
fabio.paterno@isti.cnr.it
[3] Aalto University, Espoo, Finland
[4] Ludwig-Maximilians-Universität München, Munich, Germany
[5] University of Glasgow, Glasgow, UK
[6] University of Duisburg-Essen, Duisburg, Germany

Abstract. At this time, there is a lot of discussion and attention on the adoption of artificial intelligence in real-world automations. In this panel, we will discuss the role of Human-Computer Interaction in creating meaningful devices, applications and systems to obtain automations that exploit technologies from artificial intelligence in such a way as to create meaningful and valuable experiences for individuals and society. Our specific focus is user control in automation, asking how HCI can provide automation that can solve the evergreen challenges of human-automation interaction, advancing the role of humans interacting with automation from servants to collaborators or even partners, and increasing human well-being. With new AI tools, the range of automation has widened including the automation of cognitive tasks.

Keywords: Automations · Human-Computer Interaction · Artificial Intelligence

1   Motivations

How people interact with digital technologies is currently caught between the Internet of Things (IoT), where objects are continuously increasing their technological capabilities in terms of functionalities and connectivity, and Artificial Intelligence [16], which is penetrating many areas of daily life by supporting their increasing ability to support and automate functionalities, including creative and cognitive tasks, based on collected data and statistical predictions. In both trends, human control over technology is jeopardized, little is happening in terms of innovating how we conceptualize, design, implement and verify automations and allow users to control them.

While there is a long human factors research tradition on automation [7], such research has long been concentrated on highly specialized professional work tasks for highly trained and specialized personnel [13], such as control centre operators or aircraft

© The Author(s), under exclusive license to Springer Nature Switzerland AG 2023
J. Abdelnour Nocera et al. (Eds.): INTERACT 2023, LNCS 14145, pp. 349–353, 2023.
https://doi.org/10.1007/978-3-031-42293-5_34

pilots. However, we live more and more in environments with dynamic sets of objects, devices, services, people, and intelligent support, which can be connected through various types of automations, with various types of peripheral interactions [3]. This opens up great opportunities, new possibilities, but there are also risks and new problems [2]. The available automations can be created through machine learning techniques, and then be activated by or recommended to users, or can even be directly created by users themselves exploiting configuration mechanisms. Automations are more and more used in environments rich in terms of the presence of connected objects, devices, and services [8]. The ambient nature of automated systems and their interwovenness in mundane, repetitive routines also supports the ordinariness of the involved user experience [6]. They are often based on sets of rules that connect the dynamic events and/or conditions with the expected reactions without requiring the use of complex programming structures, and have been used in several domains, such as home automation, ambient assisted living, robots, and industry. While referred to as a single term, automation is by nature polymorph and adding automation to a system may correspond to multiple (sometimes conflicting) objectives [15]. However, when they are automatically generated some problems can occur if the end user's viewpoint is not sufficiently considered. For example, previous studies describe how intelligent systems can fail to adapt to recent user changes or the difficulty users have understanding what information the system requires in order to be trained to generate the desired behaviour. Other studies reported difficulties in avoiding false alarms, communicating complex schedules, and resolving conflicting preferences. Such issues highlight the importance of providing conceptual and technological support for improving the transparency of such automations [16] and the possibility of human intervention [18]. However, early studies in the area of human factors have demonstrated that, in some cases, reliability of automation is not critical and users see benefits even in the presence of failures.

The panel aims to stimulate a multi-perspective discussion on how democratizing main technological trends by designing environments able to support user-centred transparency, explainability [10], and controllability in automations.

2 Discussion

Given the background described in the previous section, several points can be discussed in the panel, for example:

- What are the dark patterns when deploying automations in daily environments, examples of cases where such technological trends conflict with users' ability to actually obtain and control the desired daily automations?
- What are the application domains and associated scenarios where everyday automations actually controlled by end users can have a high impact on improving user experience and technology adoption (possible candidates: smart homes, ambient assisted living, retail, industry 5.0, ...)?
- What are the most suitable interaction paradigms, technologies, metaphors, programming styles to allow people to easily create, understand, modify [11], debug [10, 12], and control, the automations most relevant for them in their daily activities (e.g., wizards, chatbots, block-based, data flow, process-oriented, augmented reality [1], Programming-By-Demonstration [9])?

- How will interactions based on large language models affect the way users will understand and control automations and recommendation systems?
- What are the principles, design practices, and methodologies available in Human-Computer Interaction (HCI) that could be adopted to empower the end-users to control automations in AI systems, and how they should evolve to better address the new challenges?
- What unsolved challenges are we facing when providing more user control with highly automated systems?
- What can the role of recommendation systems be in smart environments that users can control? When, how, and for what purpose can recommendations be useful, usable and reliable?
- What are the most effective ways to explain the automations that populate surrounding environments as well as their actual effects on users with limited technological knowledge?
- How do humans interact and control automation for cognitive and creative tasks [17] and how does it impact our sense of agency and responsibility ?

3 Schedule

We plan to organise the panel in the following manner:

- Opening and introductions: 10min
- Moderated discussion: 35min
- Questions by audience: 35min
- Concluding remarks and closing: 10min

4 Panelists

Philippe Palanque research is focusing on dependability, usability and safety of interactive critical systems. As AI technologies (such as machine learning) are making their way inside this type of system, the research addresses the assessment of usability and dependability of such interactive systems embedding AI technologies. He is also working on identifying explicit criteria (as in [4]) in order to demonstrate the need for such technologies as their integration is often related to fad and less to actual need as "classical programming" allows implementing behaviours which are usually attributed to AI technologies as demonstrated for recommender systems in large civil aircrafts [5]. His contribution to the panel will be to question the need for such technologies and the clear identification of benefits and drawbacks they bring to interactive systems and interactive technologies.

Fabio Paternò has long investigated methods and tools for end-user development, and in recent years has also focused on how to exploit them in the context of recent technological trends (Internet of Things and Artificial Intelligence) in several application domains in order to improve their transparency and user control. In the panel he will discuss the possible composition paradigms of automations in daily environments (visual wizards, conversational interfaces, mobile augmented reality), their integration with recommendation systems, and how to introduce explainability mechanisms that are able to provide answers to the most frequent user questions.

Virpi Roto's expertise is in employee experience design when automation systems are introduced to industrial workplaces. While the new automation systems are envisioned to be as autonomous as possible, there needs to be an employee monitoring autonomous automation and helping it when needed. In other words, people are assigned the servant role of watching the computers. Virpi wants to avoid the passive monitoring work by designing automation as a service for the employees. The smarter the automation becomes, the more chances there must be to provide more control for the employees.

Albrecht Schmidt is focusing on how control changes when we use generative AI. In knowledge work, users traditionally have full control and exercise this control. When academics, lawyers, and journalists write a text each word matters. When designers or engineers create objects, their creativity is seen in their attention to detail. If we now augment and automate cognitive tasks to improve efficiency, we face unique challenges in control. The central questions are: How should we design interactions and interfaces for knowledge work to allow comprehensive control, while getting the full benefit of generative AI? How can we ensure that decision-making is done in a responsible way and that users understand the results of 'their' work?

Simone Stumpf has a long-standing research focus on user interactions with machine learning systems, and most recently has focused on involving lay users in teachable machine learning systems, interactive Explainable AI (XAI) and AI fairness. She is interested in developing design principles for enabling better human-computer interaction with AI systems, leading to more transparent and responsible AI. Her contribution to the panel will focus on how to involve users in the design of AI systems at all stages in the development lifecycle, how to choose levels of automation within a socio-technical AI system, and the dangers of ignoring user-centred design for AI.

Jürgen Ziegler is conducting research at the intersection of HCI and AI. With his team, he has a long-standing track record in recommender systems with a special focus on interactive recommending, and on transparency and explainability of recommendations. In recent work, he has specifically studied conversational recommendation methods, exploring various design options for optimizing the user experience. In the panel, he will raise the often neglected issue of how intelligent techniques can be seamlessly integrated in conventional user interfaces. He will discuss implications of the recent breakthroughs in language technology on recommending and decision-making, also reflecting on them in the light of argumentation theory. Arising from the advent of powerful language models is also the question which future demands these technologies will put on users with respect to cognitive and language skills.

References

1. Ariano, R., Manca, M., Paternò, F., Santoro, C.: Smartphone-based augmented reality for end-user creation of home automations. Behav. Inf. Technol. **42**, 1–17 (2022)
2. Ardito, C., Desolda, G., Lanzilotti, R., Malizia, R., Matera, M.: Analysing trade-offs in frameworks for the design of smart environments. Behav. Inf. Technol. **39**(1), 47–71 (2020)
3. Bakker, S., Elise Hoven, E., Berry Eggen, B.: Peripheral interaction: characteristics and considerations. Pers. Ubiquit. Comput. **19**(1), 239–254 (2015)
4. Bouzekri, E., et al.: A list of pre-requisites to make recommender systems deployable in critical context. In: CEUR Proceedings, EnCHIReS@EICS (2017)

5. Bouzekri, E., et al.: Engineering issues related to the development of a recommender system in a critical context: application to interactive cockpits. Int. J. Hum. Comput. Stud. **121**, 122–141 (2019)

6. Clemmensen, T., Hertzum, M., Abdelnour-Nocera, A.: Ordinary user experiences at work: a study of greenhouse growers. ACM Trans. Comput.-Hum. Interact. 27(3), Article 16, June 2020. 31 pp. https://doi.org/10.1145/3386089

7. Fitts, P.M.: Human Engineering for an Effective Air Navigation and Traffic Control System. National Research Council, Washington, DC (1951)

8. Fröhlich, P., Baldauf, M., Meneweger, T., Tscheligi, M., de Ruyter, B., Paternó, F.: Everyday automation experience: a research agenda. Pers. Ubiquit. Comput. **24**(6), 725–734 (2020). https://doi.org/10.1007/s00779-020-01450-y

9. Jia-Jun Li, T., Radensky, M., Jia, J., Singarajah, K., Mitchell, T.M., Myers, B.A.: PUMICE: a multi-modal agent that learns concepts and conditionals from natural language and demonstrations. In: Proceedings of the 32nd Annual ACM Symposium on User Interface Software and Technology (UIST 2019), pp. 577–589 (2019)

10. Kulesza, T., Burnett, M., Wong, W., Stumpf, S.: Principles of explanatory debugging to personalize interactive machine learning. In: Proceedings of the 20th International Conference on Intelligent User Interfaces (IUI 2015), pp. 126–137 (2015). https://doi.org/10.1145/2678025.2701399

11. Lieberman, H., Paterno, F., Wulf, V. (eds.): End User Development Kluwer Publishers. The Netherlands, Dordrecht (2006)

12. Manca, M., Paternò, F., Santoro, C., Corcella, L.: Supporting end-user debugging of trigger-action rules for IoT applications. Int. J. Hum. Comput. Stud. **123**, 56–69 (2019)

13. McClumpha, A.J., James, M., Green, R.G., Belyavin, A.J.: Pilots' attitudes to cockpit automation. In: Proceedings of the Human Factors Society 35th Annual Meeting (1991)

14. Mackworth, N.H.: The breakdown of vigilance during prolonged visual search. Q. J. Exp. Psychol. **1**, 6–21 (1948)

15. Palanque, P.: Ten objectives and ten rules for designing automations in interaction techniques, user interfaces and interactive systems. In: Proceedings of the International Conference on Advanced Visual Interfaces (AVI 2020), Article 2, pp. 1–10. Association for Computing Machinery, New York (2020)

16. Shneiderman, B.: Human-centered artificial intelligence: reliable, safe & trustworthy. Int. J. Hum. Comput. Interact. **36**(6), 495–504 (2020)

17. Schmidt, A.: Interactive human centered artificial intelligence: a definition and research challenges. In: Proceedings of the International Conference on Advanced Visual Interfaces (AVI 2020), Article 3, pp. 1–4. ACM (2020). https://doi.org/10.1145/3399715.340087

18. Schmidt, A., Herrmann, T.: Intervention user interfaces: a new interaction paradigm for automated systems. Interactions **24**(5), 40–45 (2017)

Ethical Value Exchange in HCI

Jose Abdelnour-Nocera[1,2]([✉]), Marta Kristín Lárusdóttir[3], Jonathan Lazar[4],
Helen Petrie[5], Gavin Sim[6], and Tariq Zaman[7]

[1] University of West London, London, UK
abdejos@uwl.ac.uk
[2] ITI/Larsys, Funchal, Portugal
[3] Reykjavik University, Reykjavik, Iceland
Marta@ru.is
[4] University of Maryland, College Park, USA
jlazar@umd.edu
[5] University of York, York, UK
helen.petrie@york.ac.uk
[6] University of Central Lancashire, Preston, UK
grsim@uclan.ac.uk
[7] University of Technology Sarawak, Sibu, Malaysia
tariqzaman@uts.edu.my

Abstract. The aim of this panel is to facilitate a discussion on the ethical implications of our activities as HCI researchers and designers. These implications can be formulated in terms of an ethical value exchange, in which research and design decisions are transactions where all stakeholders give and obtain some value. The panel will generate a thought-provoking debate based on different experiences and reflections on whether and how ethical value exchange happens in HCI research and design practice.

Keywords: HCI research · HCI design · Ethical Value Exchange

1 Panel Topics and Objective

This panel considers our ethical responsibility as human-computer interaction (HCI) researchers and designers in the context of societal and sustainability issues such as inequality, poverty, global warming, pollution, and geopolitical conflicts, among many others. Assessing the ethical implications of our research and designs with trust and collaboration in the foreground requires empathic, in-context experimentation and data collection, which requires a socio-technical, context-sensitive approach to HCI [1]. These implications can be formulated in terms of an 'ethical value exchange', in which research and design decisions are transactions where all stakeholders give and obtain some value.

The panel will add to the ongoing discussion on ethics in HCI [2–4] by providing new perspectives from the distinct conceptual standpoint of 'ethical value exchange'. Through their different perspectives and experiences panelists will articulate the different

© The Author(s), under exclusive license to Springer Nature Switzerland AG 2023
J. Abdelnour Nocera et al. (Eds.): INTERACT 2023, LNCS 14145, pp. 354–359, 2023.
https://doi.org/10.1007/978-3-031-42293-5_35

ontological, epistemological and methodological dimensions of ethically exchanging value in HCI research and practice. This means questioning (1) 'what' we mean by ethical value exchange; (2) the relationships 'between' HCI researchers and designers, and the intended users of their research knowledge and designs; and (3) 'how' we exchange value ethically.

2 Chair and Panelists

2.1 Jose Abdelnour Nocera

Jose will chair the panel and coordinate the contributions from the different panelists and interventions from the audience. His main interest with this panel is to explore the academic and practical dimensions of the ethical exchange of value in HCI research and practice.

José is Professor of Sociotechnical Design and Head of the Sociotechnical Group for Innovation and User Experience at the University of West London. He is the current Vice-Chair for Equity and Development for IFIP TC 13 on HCI as well as Chair for the British Computer Society Sociotechnical Specialist Group. His interests lie in the sociotechnical and cultural aspects of systems design, development and use. In pursuing these interests, he has been involved as researcher and consultant in several projects in the UK and overseas in the domains of mHealth, e-learning, social development, e-commerce, e-governance and enterprise resource planning systems. Prof. Abdelnour-Nocera gained an MSc in Social Psychology from Simon Bolivar University, Venezuela and a PhD in Computing from The Open University, UK.

2.2 Marta Kristín Lárusdóttir

Extending the relationships between HCI researchers and potential users has been my concern for several years. I participated in several projects, defining usability evaluation protocols for the users, with the aim of including usability as one of the selection criteria, when the public authorities were choosing new software to be used by hundreds of users. Including usability in the call for tenders is one of the first steps towards considering the digital work environment of these users in parallel with more traditional values like the cost of the software. Additionally, I have been concerned about strengthening the relationship between HCI researchers and IT professionals designing new software. I am one of the founders of a new process called the UCD Sprint for structuring UCD activities in the early phases of software development. The UCD Sprint process is accessible via a digital aim, making it easier for students and professionals to conduct UCD activities.

Marta is a Professor at the Department of Computer Science at Reykjavik University, Marta has researched user-centred design (UCD) activities and the integration of those in agile software development. Marta has also worked as a project manager and UCD expert in the software industry and consulted on UCD activities for public authorities. Marta has been engaged in IFIP activities, first as a national member of Iceland in TC13 and later as an expert member. Marta has been active in various activities in WG13.2 and has had many roles in organizing both the INTERACT and HCSE conferences.

2.3 Jonathan Lazar

A key consideration for the ethics of involving people with disabilities in research is they should themselves be determining the research and funding priorities for research involving people with disabilities. Academics tend to think of themselves as independent thinkers pursuing topics that are of interest to ourselves, yet if one expects that people with disabilities will take time to involve themselves in one's research, a researcher needs to consider that their research needs to solve a real-world problem, a pressing need, for the disability community. It's not sufficient to simply choose a topic that appears interesting yet may not solve a real-world need. Researchers who themselves have disabilities already use this approach of working directly with their communities and involving their lived experience to separate out the real problems that need to be solved from the "problems that aren't actually problems." Similarly, people with disabilities should be able to help influence which areas of research get funded. As funding agencies are under pressure to show real-world impact, the best way to accomplish that is to include people with disabilities, from the start, in determining research priorities.

Dr. Jonathan Lazar is a professor in the College of Information Studies at the University of Maryland, where he is the executive director of the Maryland Initiative for Digital Accessibility (MIDA), and a faculty member in the Human-Computer Interaction Lab. Dr. Lazar has over 25 years of experience in research and teaching in human-computer interaction, with a focus on technology accessibility for people with disabilities, user-centered design methods, assistive technologies, web accessibility, and law and public policy related to accessibility and HCI. Dr. Lazar has authored or edited 16 books, including Research Methods in Human-Computer Interaction (2nd edition, co-authored with Feng and Hochheiser) and Ensuring Digital Accessibility Through Process and Policy (co-authored with Goldstein and Taylor). He is the recipient of the 2020 SIGACCESS Award for Outstanding Contributions to Computing and Accessibility, the 2016 SIGCHI Social Impact Award, and he was the general chair of the 2021 ACM ASSETS conference.

2.4 Helen Petrie

Two issues in the area of ethical value in relation to research with disabled and older people have concerned me for some time: expectations and compensation: the first issue is about the expectations people might have about technologies when participating in our research. Almost always our research involves the early exploration of ideas for technology innovations which might benefit disabled or older people. Whether these ideas ever end up in actual products is a very open question. It may take years and the product may turn out to be very different from what we explored in the research or our research may indirectly influence technological developments. It took me some time as a researcher to realise that it is very important to be clear with participants about the nature of the research. One should not raise expectations unrealistically, if participants find something we are working with useful. This can be further complicated by the fact that sometimes when we are researching a new idea, industrial collaborators are interested to know how much people would be willing to pay for a new technology. This inevitably sets expectations that a product is being considered, which may or may not be the case. On the other hand, I have found that a discussion about the nature of research can be very interesting for some participants, and strengthen the bond that they are collaborators and contributors to the research, and not just "subjects" of the work.

The second issue is more practical, that of compensation of people's time for their participation in research studies. On this issue researchers are often faced with two conflicting pressures: on the one hand, reviewers for conferences and journals are expecting larger and more representative samples of disabled and older participants in studies. On the other hand, research funding institutions are under pressures to reduce costs, and payments to participants look like an easy target. I have often been told that disabled and older people should participate in my research without any compensation, as the research is for their benefit. I find this argument very problematic. All research in HCI is ultimately for the benefit of users of technology, but I have never had this argument made in relation to non-disabled or younger participants. It seems appropriate to expect HCI students to take part in studies as participants as part of their education (to understand what it is like to be on the other side of the situation), indeed some psychology departments require students to do this (a sneaky but useful way of creating a participant pool, albeit one of rather limited scope). But is it appropriate to ask others to give up their time and effort for nothing. Does this create a sample which is representative of their population (indeed, does compensating participants create a representative sample?).

Helen Petrie is Professor Emerita of Human-Computer Interaction at the University of York in the UK. She has been involved with IFIP and particularly TC13 (Human-Computer Interaction) for many years, currently being Vice Chair for Media and Communications and Chair of WG13.3 on Human-Computer Interaction, Disability and Aging. She is also a member of IFIP WG11.12 (Human Aspects of Information Security and Assurance). Her research interests are in the areas of the design and evaluation of digital technologies for disabled and older people and usable security. She has been involved in over 30 British and international projects has published widely and provided consultancy to government and industry on accessibility and usability of new technologies.

2.5 Gavin Sim

Within the area of Child Computer Interaction the ethics of participation has recently come to the forefront of academic discourse. Examining the ethics of participation within the context of the transformation economy and value extraction presents many societal and ethical challenges for the community. When children are participating in design or evaluation, it is important to be clear about their inclusion and their contribution. When their inclusion is within the design phase, there is a tension to ensure that the children understand how their contributions will, or will not, influence an end-product. Value extraction may result in organisations or researchers benefiting from the child's contribution, whilst the participants receive little benefit or value. Thus there are possibilities that children's times and contributions may not always be valued, as not all input or ideas may lead to innovation within the products or systems being designed. Many companies are increasingly collaborating with users over longer periods of time through constructions such as open design, co-creation and participatory design. There are clear benefits for organisation within this model of design yet for children what are the overall benefits and value of participation, are children empowered to withdraw their ideas and time?

When the participants are children, it is common for parents to provide informed consent and for the children to then assent to participate. Design activities are often packaged to be fun and interesting for the children, therefore ascent could be obtained as they want to participate in the activity. Depending on the age, children may not fully understand their participation or how their data is used after the event, and ways of communicating this to the children is important. Children do not always want to hand over their ideas as evident in a study by Read et al. [5] in which 5% of children kept their design ideas after the session. When including children in design it should be obvious as to the value extraction that children can obtain in from their participation.

Dr Gavin Sim is a Reader in Human Computer Interaction at the University of Central Lancashire. He has worked at UCLan since 2002. His research interests are in the area of HCI, CCI and educational technology, in particular, participatory design, usability / user experience evaluation methods. He is an active researcher within the ChiCI group, where his focus has been on evaluating user experience and usability within games and educational technology. He has over twenty years of experience of working with children in the design and evaluation of children publishing papers and running workshops and courses at international conferences. He has provided consultancy work for the BBC on the accessibility of their games for children and more recently evaluation the effectiveness of LingoKids apps.

2.6 Tariq Zaman

Engaging with communities from diverse cultural backgrounds has proven to be a complex process. Particularly, when it comes to conceptual understanding related to ethical value exchange from the local designers and external collaborator's perspective, which may not always be the same. Tariq will focus on the process of co-designing ethical guidelines with Malaysian indigenous communities and will discuss the issues and challenges related to internalization and absorptive capacity within institutions and the research community.

Tariq Zaman is an Associate Professor in the School of Computing and Creative Media at the University of Technology Sarawak (UTS) Malaysia. His projects and research publications equally reflect the multiple voices of indigenous wisdom and cultural understanding by converging local, scientific, traditional and cultural knowledge(s).

References

1. Gardien, P., Djajadiningrat, T., Hummels, C., Brombacher, A.: Changing your hammer: the implications of paradigmatic innovation for design practice. Int. J. Des. **8** (2014)
2. Nunes Vilaza, G., Doherty, K., McCashin, D., Coyle, D., Bardram, J., Barry, M.: A scoping review of ethics across SIGCHI. In: Designing Interactive Systems Conference, pp. 137–154. Association for Computing Machinery, New York (2022). https://doi.org/10.1145/3532106.3533511
3. Waycott, J., Davis, H., Thieme, A., Branham, S., Vines, J., Munteanu, C.: Ethical encounters in HCI: research in sensitive settings. In: Proceedings of the 33rd Annual ACM Conference Extended Abstracts on Human Factors in Computing Systems, pp. 2369–2372. Association for Computing Machinery, New York (2015). https://doi.org/10.1145/2702613.2702655

4. Fiesler, C., Frauenberger, C., Muller, M., Vitak, J., Zimmer, M.: Research ethics in HCI: A SIGCHI community discussion. In: Extended Abstracts of the 2022 CHI Conference on Human Factors in Computing Systems. Association for Computing Machinery, New York (2022). https://doi.org/10.1145/3491101.3516400
5. Read, J., Sim, G., Horton, M., Fitton, D.: Reporting back in HCI work with children. In: Proceedings of the 21st Annual ACM Interaction Design and Children Conference. pp. 517–522. Association for Computing Machinery, New York (2022). https://doi.org/10.1145/3501712.3535279

Posters

A Comparative Analysis of Multi-Object Animation with Motion Paths in Virtual Reality

Tobias Krogh Risom[1], Jonas Rommel Attrup[1], Rasmus Valentin Jacobsen[1], Stefan Alexander Larsen[1], and Jesper Gaarsdal[1,2(✉)]

[1] Aalborg University, Aalborg, Denmark
trisom19@student.aau.dk
[2] SynergyXR ApS, Aarhus, Denmark
jg@synergyxr.com

Abstract. Virtual reality has become a valuable tool for training and problem-solving, and creating animations in VR provides several advantages over traditional tools by increasing sense of presence within the scene. This paper presents an animation tool that allows novice animators to create multi-object animations using motion paths in VR. The proposed prototype is compared to the animation tool in an existing VR application. While previous studies have proposed VR animation tools, they are often targeted at experts or are missing key features such as animation with multiple objects. The comparative analysis evaluates the perceived usability and workload based on quantitative questionnaires as well as a qualitative interview. The results show the proposed tool to be superior in terms of perceived usability, however, we also found that having several motion paths could clutter the view and that future work is required in the visualization of these.

Keywords: Virtual reality · Object animation · Multiple objects

1 Introduction

Immersive Virtual Reality (VR) tools have showed their usefulness in several fields [8]. In the field of animation, VR has created several new opportunities, both for experienced practitioners and non-animators [1,5]. Tools for creating animations in VR can accelerate workflows, by being accessible to both animators and non-animators, leading to improved communication between the two [9].

Previous studies have proposed VR animation tools, but most have been designed and evaluated by experienced animators working with VR developers, resulting in tools with less accessibility for non-animators [6]. Tools that are

---

Supplementary Information The online version contains supplementary material available at https://doi.org/10.1007/978-3-031-42293-5_36.

© The Author(s), under exclusive license to Springer Nature Switzerland AG 2023
J. Abdelnour Nocera et al. (Eds.): INTERACT 2023, LNCS 14145, pp. 363–367, 2023.
https://doi.org/10.1007/978-3-031-42293-5_36

specifically targeted towards inexperienced animators are often limited in scope, and focus on specific use-cases such as single-object and character animation [3].

In this study, we expand on previous work [4] by creating a VR object animation tool with support for Multi-Object Animation (MOA) targeted at non-animators. Our prototype is evaluated in a comparative between-subjects user study, where participants completed three tasks using our prototype or using the animation tool available in the VR application Rec Room[1]

The main objectives of this work are:

- To design, and implement a user-friendly VR object animation tool with a particular focus on MOA, intending to enhance the animation experience for non-animators.
- To conduct an evaluation comparing the perceived performance and usability of our prototype with the existing animation tool in the VR application Rec Room. This study will provide insights into the advantages and potential limitations of our prototype.
- To analyze the results of the user study, thereby obtaining a deeper understanding of the impact on workflow and improved understanding of non-animators when using our proposed prototype.

2   Methodology

The prototype was developed using Unity and the XR Interaction Toolkit (XRIT)[2] The primary goal guiding the design was to enable non-animators to easily understand and create MOAs. As in previous work [4], we decided to base our prototype on 3D motion paths in the virtual space.

Expanding an animation tool from SOA to MOA introduces several design challenges, such as context-switching between active objects and providing an overview of objects in the current animation. For motion path animations with many objects it is also important to consider how the paths are visualized as to not mentally overload the user. For the generation of a motion path, we decided on a performance-based approach. When a user grabs and manipulates an object, keyframes are automatically generated and a path is drawn. The motion paths of two objects being animated can be seen in Fig. 1 (left). To support the animation process, we wanted a simple and intuitive control panel, made to be a tangible part of the virtual space. The animation menu can be seen in Fig. 1 (right). To control the timing of single object animations (SOAs), we developed a timeline system drawing inspiration from traditional tools. Each object has its own layer which can be slotted onto a global timeline. This enables users to phase shift, speed up, and slow down individual layers to fine-tune the animation. The timeline UI provides users with immediate visual feedback and a simple representation of the SOAs and their temporal relation.

---

[1] Rec Room: https://www.recroom.com.
[2] XR Interaction Toolkit: https://docs.unity3d.com/Packages/com.unity.xr.interaction.toolkit@2.3.

3   Evaluation

To evaluate the usability of the tool, we designed a comparative between-subjects user study, comparing our prototype to the animation tool available in Rec Room, both applications running on the Meta Quest 2 VR device. For both conditions, participants completed three animation tasks that increase in complexity. In the first task, participants were asked to move a football across the floor to create a simple translation animation. In the second task, they were given an existing animation of two footballs on a collision course and were asked to edit it to avoid collision. In the third task, they were presented with two tables, one empty and one with several plates and cups. They were then asked to create an animation of the empty table being set.

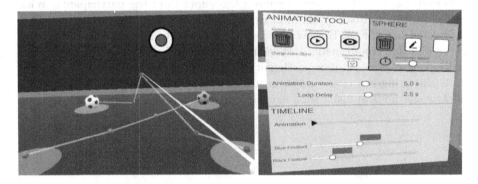

Fig. 1. In (left) the motion paths of two footballs being animated can be seen. In (right) the animation menu corresponding to the motion paths can be seen.

A total of 30 participants were recruited, 15 for each condition. Initially, participants were asked about their prior experience with VR and with animation on likert scales from 1–5. For each task, a separate scene was presented to the participant along with verbal instructions from an observer. After completing the tasks, participants were asked to fill out System Usability Scale (SUS) and NASA-TLX (NTLX) questionnaires. Lastly, a short qualitative interview was conducted, focusing on their points of frustration with MOA.

4   Results and Discussion

The demographic data showed 44% of participants had little to no prior experience with VR, and 63% had little to no prior experience with animation.

Normalized on the 0–100 scale, our prototype rated above average on the SUS ($M = 76.83, SD = 13.04$), with 68 being average. For Rec Room the score was below average ($M = 63.33, SD = 20.69$). A Wilcoxon Rank Sum test was performed on both conditions with a significance level of $p < 0.05$ and $p = 0.042$.

For NTLX we used the unweighted values. A Mann-Whitney U test with a significance level of $p < 0.05$ was performed on each question. Only question 4 regarding the perceived performance showed statistical significance. The results from the Raw-TLX analysis can be seen in Fig. 2. During the interviews, most participants found that both tools well-suited for simple animations, but were unsure about their usefulness for complex tasks. When discussing sources of frustration, with our prototype, most participants noted the motion paths getting intertwined and cluttering the view, making it difficult to differentiate the paths and their objects. For Rec Room, participants enjoyed some of the features not included in our prototype, such as undo-redo and additional options to edit animations. Some complained that in Rec Room the trigger must be held down at all times for the animation menu to be displayed.

These results show that while our prototype performed better in terms of perceived usability, Rec Room required less effort from the participants. With the qualitative feedback, this indicates that the simplicity of our tool made it easier to utilize at first. However, as participants spent more time, the additional features in Rec Room made it easier to accomplish their tasks. The qualitative feedback also pointed at a particular point of improvement being the motion paths cluttering the view, and in future work it would be interesting to explore different methods of visualizing elements in cluttered spaces [2,7].

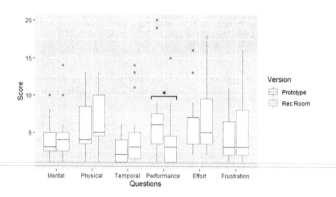

Fig. 2. Raw results from the NASA-TLX questionnaire. Statistical significance is shown for the question concerning perceived performance.

5   Conclusion

In this paper, we have presented a VR animation tool with multi-object animation targeted at non-animators. The tool utilizes a simple timeline, allowing users to easily create animations and adjust their individual timing. Our evaluation showed that our tool performed significantly better than the animation tool found in Rec Room in terms of perceived usability. However, in terms of perceived performance Rec Room was preferred. We attribute this to issues of motion path occlusion and to the relatively small feature set in our prototype.

In future work, we would address these issues by expanding the tool and exploring different ways of visualizing elements in cluttered spaces to make it easier for users to distinguish between different motion paths.

Acknowledgements. This work is supported by the Danish Innovation Foundation through its Industrial PhD program.

References

1. Cannavò, A.: Interfaces for human-centered production and use of computer graphics assets. Ph.D. thesis, Politecnico di Torino (2020)
2. Elmqvist, N., Tsigas, P.: A taxonomy of 3d occlusion management for visualization. IEEE Trans. Visualization Comput. Graph. **14**(5), 1095–1109 (2008). https://doi. org/10.1109/TVCG.2008.59
3. Fender, A., Müller, J., Lindlbauer, D.: Creature teacher: A performance-based animation system for creating cyclic movements. In: Proceedings ACM SUI, pp. 113–122 (2015). https://doi.org/10.1145/2788940.2788944
4. Gaarsdal, J., Wolff, S., Madsen, C.B.: Evaluating immersive animation authoring in an industrial VR training context. In: Proc. ICSPS (2022)
5. Henrikson, R., Araujo, B., Chevalier, F., Singh, K., Balakrishnan, R.: Multi-device storyboards for cinematic narratives in vr. In: Proceedings ACM UIST, pp. 787–796 (2016). https://doi.org/10.1145/2984511.2984539
6. Li, B., Said, I., Kirova, L., Blokhina, M., Kang, H.: Sparc: A vr animating tool at your fingertips. In: Proceedings ACM VRST, pp. 1–3 (2021). https://doi.org/10. 1145/3489849.3489920
7. Tatzgern, M., Orso, V., Kalkofen, D., Jacucci, G., Gamberini, L., Schmalstieg, D.: Adaptive information density for augmented reality displays. In: Proceedings of IEEE VR, pp. 83–92 (2016). https://doi.org/10.1109/VR.2016.7504691
8. Tocu, N., Gellert, A., Stefan, I., Nitescu, T., Luca, G.: The impact of virtual reality simulators in manufacturing industry. In: Proceedings of IATED EDULEARN, pp. 3084–3093 (2020). https://doi.org/10.21125/edulearn.2020.0905
9. Vogel, D., Lubos, P., Steinicke, F.: Animationvr - interactive controller-based animating in virtual reality. In: Proceedins of IEEE ANIVAE, pp. 1–6 (2018). https:// doi.org/10.1109/ANIVAE.2018.8587268

A Human-Robot Conversation Interface for Children with ASD

Jena Affleck[1], Sean Gooravin[1], Cameron Malcolm[1], Sarah McHutchison[1], Andrew Shearer[1], Cameron Watt[1], and Andrea Alessandrini[2(✉)]

[1] University of Dundee, Dundee DD1 4HN, UK
[2] University of Urbino, 61029 Urbino, Italy
andaleo@gmail.com

Abstract. In this paper, we present an interactive, conversational robot helping children diagnosed with Autistic Spectrum Disorder (ASD) become more confident in expressing their emotions and feelings. Investigating how the technology could act as an educational tool for parents to help them understand the best ways to interact and help their child, promoting a greater bond. This paper highlights the qualities and benefits of using conversational user interface in social intervention for children with ASD. Finally, we reflect on three main qualities of our system: human and robotic qualities balance; robot interaction predictability; and sustain the triadic interaction.

Keywords: Design · Conversational user interface · Autism · Children · Product · Interaction · Prototyping

1 Introduction

Autism spectrum disorder (ASD) is a developmental, neurobiological condition that affects the ability to communicate, interact socially and be imaginative (Kanner, 1943; Kozima et al., 2005). The severity and range of disordered thought processes, communication interactions and behaviours vary from one child to another. The breakdown of communication in children leads to a stressed state in the individuals. Social relationships within the child's life suffer as a result of avoiding advanced and unpredictable conversation. Unexpected interactions can cause sudden changes in the child's behaviour. Our project began as a response to the design brief issued by Microsoft Research Cambridge for the Microsoft Design Expo. The goal was to design a product, service or solution that demonstrates the value and differentiation of the Conversational User Interface (CUI) in design. This brief provided us with an opportunity to investigate how advancements in new technologies, such as conversational user interfaces (CUI) can be implemented into a physical system to support the communication support of children diagnosed with Autistic Spectrum Disorder (ASD). In the next section, we will present the related literature.

© The Author(s), under exclusive license to Springer Nature Switzerland AG 2023
J. Abdelnour Nocera et al. (Eds.): INTERACT 2023, LNCS 14145, pp. 368–372, 2023.
https://doi.org/10.1007/978-3-031-42293-5_37

2 Related Literature and Works

In recent years, numerous technologies and systems have been designed to support intervention for children with ASD. Many of these computer-based interventions are grounded on the cognitive-behavioural therapy (CBT) procedure, based on applied behaviour analysis principles (Hourcade et al., 2012; Parsons & Cobb, 2011). Computer-based interventions include virtual reality (LeGoff, 2004; Raffle et al., 2004), robotics (Farr et al., 2010; Lányi & Tilinger, 2004), table top computer interfaces (Jordan, 2013), tangible artefacts (Alessandrini et al., 2013, 2014, 2016; Farr et al., 2010), mobile applications on tablet computers (Zaffke et al., 2014), and wearable devices. More recently, researchers have begun to focus on the potential of interactive technology for social interventions (Tuhkala et al., 2017). Researchers have reported an increase in cooperative behaviour by children with ASD using robotic tangible technologies. Farr et al. (2010) highlighted the advantages of Topobo, a 3D constructive assembly system embedded with programmable kinetic memory, in fostering collaborative and cooperative behaviour among children with ASD. Alessandrini et al. (2016) explored the role of tangible digital artefacts for supporting cooperation educational activities with children diagnosed with ASD. Although these studies demonstrate a vibrant field of study and present interesting opportunities to design future technologies, scarce information exists regarding the benefits of using conversational human-robot interface for the intervention of children with autism. To address this gap, we have designed a conversational human-robot interface to support and promote communication breakdown for children diagnosed with ASD. The rest of this article describes the design process for the prototype development and the results of our ecological study with a child.

3 Design Process

We followed an iterative user-centred design method. Throughout the process, the users were at the centre of our design, involving them in every aspect of the design process. We conducted field studies with contextual interviews with experts and observations with children and parents to inform our design process. From these studies, we gained an understanding of the difficulties Autistic individuals face when communicating and expressing themselves. The design was based on a current system and method used by our field study subjects. Participants visually express their emotions using a flashcard system. This allows them to display their emotions in five stages, and they are usually coupled with familiar objects, such for example football teams or fictional characters. We conducted several design sessions with the child and parents to co-design the prototypes of our interactive system. The design team identified the need to create a physical robotic system with a character (agent) that was non-judgemental and something that each individual would learn to trust. This decision was driven by brainstorming sessions informed by the understanding gathered during field studies with children and experts in the field.

We created the first mock-up which was made using simple materials. Giving us a platform to better understand the interactions and how the user would respond to our characters. This first prototype was evaluated by a design critique where we were suggested to make a more inviting form and build in some simple interactions, for example, the robot eyes. From the input of the design critique, we designed a second prototype. We designed an inviting rounded shape that might afford the child to activate calming robot behaviours by placing their hands on it. We designed the robot's eyes behaviours, using blue LEDs and servos, to catch children's attention by replicating a simplified human sight model. The interactive robot prototype was evaluated by a child diagnosed with Autistic Spectrum Disorder (ASD). The final interactive robot prototype has a 3D printed rubberised base allowing increased grip to the surface below it, allowing the prototype to be more grounded. The prototype has an interactive light behaviour, providing the child with a focus supporting the child when managing their stress. This ensures a predictable routine to calm the child and reduces the stress levels of the individual. We conducted a focus group with parents from the National Autistic Society (NAS) to understand the role of the prototype, about the level of involvement parents have in the conversations between the robot and the individual. In the next section, we discuss the result of an ecological study with a child diagnosed with ASD (Fig. 1).

Fig. 1. Early, advanced prototype, and evaluation.

4   Results

User testing was carried out with our participant within a studio environment along with their parent who give consent for the study. This test was over 30 min long and we recorded video throughout, allowing us to analyze our participant's behaviors when interacting with the robot. We investigated three main observations from our testing looking at balance, predictability and triadic interaction.

The robot was designed to have human-like features so the participant had aspects they could relate to when interacting. Our aim was to create a character that could help the participant develop their communication skills and improve their confidence in social situations. The LED eyes and pop-up dome features are both subtle human-like interactions. It was important to design the robot's human-like expressions in a robotic way, so the participant can differentiate between synthesized and human communication. The basic human interactions built into the experience were essential so the participant was familiar with the fundamental elements of a human conversation. The dome pop-up movement and LEDs are both indications to the user that the robot is ready to talk, much similar to human interaction. Also, the user has to lean down to see the LED which creates a more personal and non-intrusive experience for the user. The voice of the robot was initially a human voice. However, during user testing the participant disliked the voice so we changed it to a synthetic voice which the subject felt more comfortable conversing with. The lack of emotion in the synthetic voice helps strip back the interactions and reduces confusion for the child.

These preliminary results were also confirmed by an expert within the field of Augmentative and Alternative Communication (AAC). The robot had a suitable balance between being a character for the child with its "clam shape" and also containing some human-like features. The child can relate to the device but can still understand that it is a robot. This appears to be a promising approach to help children with ASD develop confidence in human social situations.

The robot is a smart conversational aid helping autistic children become more confident in expressing their emotions and feelings. It uses a repetitive chain of events so that the device can be predictable for the participant. The way in which the robot slightly opens to reveal its eyes is intended to initially require a physical reaction from the child and promote further interaction between them. It also gives the child a prior indication that the robot is about to speak, this warning allows the child to predict when the robot wants to communicate so it doesn't surprise them. This also applies when the participant is introduced to the various interactions, and once the participant was aware of the corresponding responses, there was a clear increase in enthusiasm and interaction towards the robot. This brought the predictability element to light during this process which was an influential stage in the research process. According to a focus group with the school teachers the robot easily responds promptly to children's needs. The AAC expert's enthusiasm surrounds the predictability aspect of the robot; the child knows what's going to happen.

The robot creates a triadic interaction between the parent and the child. The robot is intended to act as a bridge connecting the parent and child as opposed to becoming a barrier, allowing the child to communicate more effectively. This reflects our concept of the robot being able to refer the subject back to the parent after an interaction. The robot works as a bridge but does not overpower the parent's interaction with the child. The robot is designed to eventually refer the participant back to the parent but only when the child is vocally receptive and at this stage the robot will then take a step back and redirect the participant back to the parent. The participant's parent is conversing with others in the room and the user shows disinterest in this conversation. The robot helps aid the user in this situation by providing a calming platform for the user. The participant becomes comfortable in the robot's company quickly and the subject was able to rely on it allowing the parent to relax and take a step back at points. In the final interaction we planned we added a text feature where it activates a text to be sent to the parent indicating that the participant is vocally receptive.

5   Discussion and Conclusion

The study investigates the roles in which a conversational user interface can be used to support social interventions for children with ASD and the benefits it can bring to children and relatives. Our solution works alongside this current method our participant successfully uses. The system assesses the participant's behaviour and mood, and makes a calculated decision on what stage the user may be at. The system works with the participant existing card method, referring to something that's familiar. Our prototype meets our design objectives and suggests a stimulating line of investigation for the benefits it might bring to rehabilitative or educational interventions. The robot demonstrated the potential to be a highly flexible mean that children and parents can easily appropriate (Alessandrini, 2013).

References

Alessandrini, A.: End–user construction mechanisms for the Internet of Things. In: Proceedings of the 27th International BCS Human Computer Interaction Conference (HCI 2013), vol. 27, pp. 1–6 (2013)

Alessandrini, A., Cappelletti, A., Zancanaro, M.: Audio-augmented paper for the therapy of low-functioning autism children. In: CHI 2013 Extended Abstracts on Human Factors in Computing Systems, pp. 505–510 (2013)

Alessandrini, A., Cappelletti, A., Zancanaro, M.: Audio-augmented paper for therapy and educational intervention for children with autistic spectrum disorder. Int. J. Hum Comput Stud. **72**(4), 422–430 (2014)

Alessandrini, A., Loux, V., Serra, G. F., & Murray, C.: Designing ReduCat: audio-augmented paper drawings tangible interface in educational intervention for high-functioning autistic children. In: Proceedings of the The 15th International Conference on Interaction Design and Children, pp. 463–472 (2016). https://doi.org/10.1145/2930674.2930675

Farr, W., Yuill, N., Harris, E., Hinske, S.: In my own words: configuration of tangibles, object interaction and children with autism. In: Proceedings of the 9th International Conference on Interaction Design and Children, pp. 30–38 (2010)

Hourcade, J.P., Bullock-Rest, N.E., Hansen, T.E.: Multitouch tablet applications and activities to enhance the social skills of children with autism spectrum disorders. Pers. Ubiquit. Comput. **16**(2), 157–168 (2012)

Jordan, R.: Autistic Spectrum Disorders: An Introductory Handbook for Practitioners. Routledge (2013)

Kanner, L.: Autistic disturbances of affective contact. Nerv. Child **2**(3), 217–250 (1943)

Kozima, H., Nakagawa, C., Yasuda, Y.: Interactive robots for communication-care: a case-study in autism therapy. In: IEEE International Workshop on Robot and Human Interactive Communication, ROMAN 2005, pp. 341–346 (2005)

Lányi, C.S., Tilinger, Á.: Multimedia and virtual reality in the rehabilitation of autistic children. In: International Conference on Computers for Handicapped Persons, pp. 22–28 (2004)

LeGoff, D.B.: Use of LEGO© as a therapeutic medium for improving social competence. J. Autism Dev. Disord. **34**(5), 557–571 (2004)

Parsons, S., Cobb, S.: State-of-the-art of virtual reality technologies for children on the autism spectrum. Eur. J. Spec. Needs Educ. **26**(3), 355–366 (2011)

Raffle, H.S., Parkes, A.J., Ishii, H.: Topobo: a constructive assembly system with kinetic memory. In: Proceedings of the SIGCHI Conference on Human Factors in Computing Systems, pp. 647–654 (2004)

Tuhkala, A., Isomäki, H., Hartikainen, M., Cristea, A., Alessandrini, A.: Identifying objectives for a learning space management system with value-focused thinking, vol. 1, pp. 25–34. Scopus (2017). https://doi.org/10.5220/0006230300250034

Zaffke, A., Jain, N., Johnson, N., Alam, M.A.U., Magiera, M., Ahamed, S.I.: ICanLearn: a mobile application for creating flashcards and social stories[TM] for children with autism. In: International Conference on Smart Homes and Health Telematics, pp. 225–230 (2014)

A Literature Review on Positive and Negative Effects of Interruptions and Implications for Design

Tom Gross$^{(\boxtimes)}$ ⓘ and Michael von Kalben

Human-Computer Interaction Group, University of Bamberg, 96045 Bamberg, Germany
hci@uni-bamberg.de

Abstract. The relevance of interruptions in human-computer interaction has increased over the last decades in both private and working life. Research from a multitude of disciplines has addressed interruptions. However, the literature is dispersed. In particular, no balanced collection of literature on interruptions looking at the negative as well as at the positive effect is lacking. In this paper, we present a literature review on the positive as well as negative effects of interruptions. We analysed studies on how interruptions affect individuals, collaborative work, and social relationships. We derive implications for design.

Keywords: Interruptions · Positive Effects · Negative Effects · Literature Review · Survey

1 Introduction

Information and communication technology (ICT) allows for continuous connectivity between individuals and provides benefits for organisations, but it also leads to work interruptions [2, 6, 10, 25, 32, 39].

We define interruption—similar to many authors in HCI—as an event that leads to a halt of a user's activity. Typically, a user is disrupted from a primary task, temporarily performs a secondary task, and later upon completion of the secondary task, resumes the primary task [44]. Research has shown that after an interruption, time is required to recover and continue the interrupted task. Two major factors determine the time required to complete an interrupted task: interruption lag and resumption lag [43]. Interruption lag is the time necessary to redirect attention towards the interruption. Resumption lag is the time used to determine what has been done in the primary task and what needs to be done next.

Literature reviews have targeted on various aspects of interruptions and the effects of interruptions (e.g. [10, 12, 22, 25, 39]). However, the predominant perspective in the existing literature has been negative—focusing on the challenges caused by interruptions. A balanced view is missing. As Puranik et al. put it: "We call for a more balanced approach to studying interruptions that focuses on … the positive, in addition to the negative, outcomes of interruptions" [39, p. 829].

© The Author(s), under exclusive license to Springer Nature Switzerland AG 2023
J. Abdelnour Nocera et al. (Eds.): INTERACT 2023, LNCS 14145, pp. 373–379, 2023.
https://doi.org/10.1007/978-3-031-42293-5_38

This paper has three main contributions: It provides a systematic compilation of interruptions and their negative as well as positive effects on users. It covers literature from multifarious domains. It provides implications for the design of HCI systems.

We first glance at related work. Then we explain the method of our thorough literature review. We present our literature review of the positive as well as negative effects of interruptions. We draw conclusions for the design of future HCI concerning interruptions.

2   Related Work

Several literature reviews provide great compilations of previous research (e.g. [10, 12, 22, 25, 39, 40]). However, they mainly focus on the negative side of interruptions.

Interruptions are a multidisciplinary issue, and literature is spread across various research domains such as HCI (e.g. [5, 32]), psychology [10], medicine [26, 40], and management [22, 39]. The scope of research varies across research domains. Medical publications often analyse interruptions within a specific healthcare setting [18, 33]. Psychological research is addressed across domains, in literature reviews within psychology [10], and beyond [12, 39].

Despite the diversity of domains and perspectives, some common themes and findings on interruption effects appear in most available scientific literature, independent of users' tasks and situations. For instance, interruptions consuming time and delaying primary tasks is a finding that is present in most literature reviews (e.g. [10, 18, 25, 39]). Studies reported in literature reviews often aim to quantify the implications of interruptions on specific performance metrics, either on the performance of the task (e.g. [1, 4]) or on the condition of the individual being interrupted (e.g. [1, 13, 30]).

Literature reviews acknowledge that interruptions can have benefits, such as fostering creativity or increasing the speed of simple tasks [10, 25]. Still, most publications view interruptions negatively, referring to effects like errors [10, 15, 26, 39], memory loss [10, 18, 35], stress [12, 15, 22, 25], and negative emotions [10, 12, 22, 39].

3   Method

Our systematic literature review process is grounded in general recommendations on doing literature reviews as well as specific methods of literature reviews on interruptions (e.g. [19, 24, 34, 36]). Since we aimed to collect relevant literature from multifarious disciplines, a multi-level, multi-step approach (cf. [24]) was required.

Multi-level approach: (1) we searched for literature reviews on interruptions with the search terms "interruption", "interruptions", "notification", "notifications", and "interruptibility" combined with terms like "literature review", "survey", or "literature study". We searched several scientific databases (ACM DL, Web of Knowledge, and Google Scholar). Our research goal was to include literature on the effect of disruption of users by technology. We excluded publications that did not fit this goal (e.g. interruption of enteral nutrition [45] or electricity consumer interruption [11]). Then (2) we searched for specific studies on individual interruption effects mentioned in the surveys—independent of their positive or negative results. We used the search terms "interruption", "interruptions", "interruptibility", "notification", and "notifications" combined with search terms like "study" and "user study" to identify those publications. We used the same databases as before. We used these findings to (3) identify interruptions' specific positive and negative effects and searched for each of them.

Multi-step approach: on all three levels we respectively did the following: define the scope and select sources and keywords, search in databases, select relevant publications, perform a backward search based on the relevant publications' references, make a selection of relevant literature (cf. [24, 46]). We searched for publications from the last twenty years—since 2002 when McFarlane and Latorella published their seminal paper on human interruption in HCI [32]. It became apparent during the research that many relevant publications we discovered originated from other areas beyond HCI. Some of their findings are necessary to explain specific interruption effects, and some provide essential background knowledge. For instance, we will present findings from the field of medicine with effects that apply to HCI settings (e.g. in healthcare, the interruption effects on prospective memory [14], the effect of interruptions on prospective memory).

The work was done by both authors (except for searching and collecting the results, which the second author did).

4   Understanding the Effects of Interruptions

The literature reviews and studies we found helped us to discover several positive (cf. Table 1) and negative (cf. Table 2) interruption effects. We sorted both positive and negative effects based on the scope of their implications. We started with effects only affecting the individual task (e.g. increased completion time or errors). Then we listed effects that can affect the interrupted person beyond a single task (e.g. incubation, stress, negative emotions). Then we present effects that can affect other individuals beyond the interrupted person, such as others in the same team (e.g. the interruption of third parties).

Literature shows several positive effects of interruptions. Simple tasks are sometimes completed more quickly following interruptions [10, 25, 26]. Interruptions are also significant for distributing relevant information to individuals [15, 22, 41]. Interruptions can also lead to a moment of incubation [10, 22, 25], thus fostering creativity. Interruptions can improve social connections between individuals [37, 48, 50] and provide awareness [21, 28, 47].

At the same time, literature also has negative interruption effects. They impact the performance of a single specific task (e.g. interruptions entailing errors [10, 26, 33]) or time consumption (e.g. the increased completion time for a singular task, the accumulated time consumed due to multiple interruptions over a day [25, 39, 43]). Interruptions can also affect the individual being interrupted beyond the current task by causing memory loss [15, 18, 35], inducing stress [12, 22, 25], and evoking negative emotions. Interruptions may also affect others (e.g., delaying collaborative processes [16, 32]).

Interruption effects are often dependent on the circumstances in which they occur. Some effects apply to individuals in diverse situations (e.g. incubation, errors). Others are more likely to occur in a collaborative setting in which different actors are dependent on each other (e.g. information delivery and awareness [8, 21]) or settings with non-work social connections (e.g. social connectedness [37, 48]).

Table 1. Positive interruption effects and literature sources.

Positive Effect	Sources
Simple Task Performance Increase	[10, 25–27]
Information Delivery	[15, 22, 25, 40, 41]
Incubation	[10, 22, 25]
Social Connectedness	[37, 38, 48, 50]
Awareness	[8, 20, 21, 28, 47]

Table 2. Negative interruption effects and literature sources.

Negative Effect	Sources
Time consumption	[10, 18, 25, 26, 29, 35, 39, 43]
Errors	[5, 10, 15, 18, 25, 26, 29, 32, 33, 39, 40]
Stress	[5, 12, 15, 22, 25, 27, 32]
Negative emotions	[10, 12, 15, 22, 25, 39]
Memory loss	[10, 15, 18, 25, 35]
Interruption of third parties	[16, 17, 32]

5 Conclusions

We have presented a literature review on interruptions' positive and negative effects. We compiled positive interruption effects in simple task performance, information gain, incubation, social connectedness, and awareness. We compiled negative interruption effects like time consumption, errors, stress, negative emotions, memory loss, and interruption to third parties.

In the future, it would be interesting to look at the implications for design from those findings. For instance, further research on awareness systems could lead to better mutual information on each user's interruptibility, where availability information can either be measured automatically by sensors (e.g. [42, 51]) or can be provided explicitly by the user (e.g. [7]). Better negotiation systems could allow users to find an interruptibilty compromise—they provide information to the users that an interruption is about to occur and provide them multiple options of responding towards the interruption (e.g. [31, 49]). Advanced mediating systems could use algorithms to optimise mutual interruptiblity, for instance, via an autonomous broker to intelligently time interruptions based on interruptibility [3, 9, 23].

Acknowledgements. We thank the members of the Cooperative Media Lab at the University of Bamberg.

References

1. Adamczyk, P., Bailey, B.: If not now, when?: the effects of interruption at different moments within task execution. In CHI 2004, pp. 271–278 (2004)
2. Addas, S., Pinsonneault, A.: The many faces of information technology interruptions: a taxonomy and preliminary investigation of their performance effects. Inf. Syst. J. **25**(3), 231–273 (2015)
3. Afergan, D., Hincks, S., Shibata, T., Jacob, R.: Phylter: a system for modulating notifications in wearables using physiological sensing. In AC 2015, pp. 167–177 (2015)
4. Altmann, E.M., Trafton, J.G.: Task interruption: resumption lag and the role of cues. In CogSci 2004, pp. 43–48 (2004)
5. Anderson, C., Hübener, I., Seipp, A.-K., Ohly, S., David, K., Pejovic, V.: A survey of attention management systems in ubiquitous computing environments. IMWUT **2**(2), 1–27 (2018)
6. Bernstein, A., Vorburger, P., Egger, P.: A scenario-based approach for direct interruptability prediction on wearable devices. Int. J. Perv. Comput. Commun. **3**(4), 426–438 (2007)
7. Birnholtz, J., Gutwin, C., Ramos, G., Watson, M.: OpenMessenger: gradual initiation of interaction for distributed workgroups. In CHI 2008, pp. 1661–1664
8. Carroll, J.M., Neale, D.C., Isenhour, P.L., Rosson, M.B., McCrickard, D.S.: Notification and awareness: synchronizing task-oriented collaborative activity. Int. J. Hum Comput Stud. **58**(5), 605–632 (2003)
9. Chen, D., Vertegaal, R.: Using mental load for managing interruptions in physiologically attentive user interfaces. In CHI 2004, pp. 1513–1516
10. Couffe, C., Michael, G.: Failures due to interruptions or distractions: a review and a new framework. Am. J. Psychol. **130**(2), 163–181 (2017)
11. Daniel, C., Venkatesh, B.: Literature survey and comparison of consumer interruption costs in North America and Europe. In CCECE 2014, pp. 1–7 (2014)
12. Darmoul, S., Ahmad, A., Ghaleb, M., Alkahtani, M.: Interruption management in human multitasking environments. In INCOM 2015, pp. 1179–1185 (2015)
13. Feldman, E., Greenway, D.: It's a matter of time: the role of temporal perceptions in emotional experiences of work interruptions. Group Organ. Manag. **46**(1), 70–104 (2020)
14. Grundgeiger, T., Liu, D., Sanderson, P.M., Jenkins, S.A., Leane, T.A.: Effects of interruptions on prospective memory performance in anesthesiology. In: HFES, vol. 52, no. 12, pp. 808–812 (2008)
15. Grundgeiger, T., Sanderson, P.: Interruptions in healthcare: theoretical views. Int. J. Med. Inf. **78**(5), 293–307 (2009)
16. Harr, R., Kaptelinin, V.: Unpacking the social dimension of external interruptions. In: GROUP 2007, pp. 399–408 (2007)
17. Harr, R., Kaptelinin, V.: Interrupting or not: exploring the effect of social context on interrupters' decision making. In: NordiCHI 2012, pp. 707–710 (2012)
18. Hopkinson, S.G., Jennings, B.M.: Interruptions during nurses' work: a state-of-the-science review. Res. Nurs. Health **36**(1), 38–53 (2013)
19. Hornbæk, K., Hertzum, M.: Technology acceptance and user experience: a review of the experiential component in HCI. ACM Trans. Comput.-Human Interact. **24**(5), 1–30 (2017)
20. Horvitz, E., Apacible, J., Subramani, M.: Balancing awareness and interruption: investigation of notification deferral policies. In UM 2005, pp. 433–437 (2005)

21. Iqbal, S., Horvitz, E.: Notifications and awareness: a field study of alert usage and preferences. In: CSCW 2010, pp. 27–30 (2010)

22. Jett, Q., George, J.: Work interrupted: a closer look at the role of interruptions in organizational life. Acad. Manag. Rev. **28**(3), 494–507 (2003)

23. Katidioti, I., Borst, J.P., Bierens de Haan, D.J., Pepping, T., van Vugt, M.K., Taatgen, N.A.: Interrupted by your pupil: an interruption management system based on pupil dilation. Int. J. Human–Comput. Interact. **32**(10), 791–801 (2016)

24. Koelle, M., Ananthanarayan, S., Boll, S.: Social acceptability in HCI: a survey of methods, measures, and design strategies. In: CHI 2020, pp. 1–19 (2020)

25. Leroy, S., Schmidt, A.M., Madjar, N.: Interruptions and task transitions: understanding their characteristics, processes, and consequences. Acad. Manag. Ann. **14**(2), 661–694 (2020)

26. Li, S.Y.W., Magrabi, F., Coiera, E.: A Systematic review of the psychological literature on interruption and its patient safety implications. J. Am. Med. Inf. Assoc. **19**(1), 6–12 (2012)

27. Liebowitz, J.: Interruption management: a review and implications for IT professionals. IT Prof. **13**(2), 44–48 (2011)

28. Lopez, G., Guerrero, L.A.: Awareness supporting technologies used in collaborative systems: a systematic literature review. In: CSCW 2017, pp. 808–820 (2017)

29. Magrabi, F., Li, S.Y.W., Dunn, A.G., Coiera, E.: Challenges in measuring the impact of interruption on patient safety and workflow outcomes. Methods Inf. Med. **50**(5), 447–453 (2011)

30. Mark, G., Gudith, D., Klocke, U.: The cost of interrupted work: more speed and stress. In: CHI 2008, pp. 107–110 (2008)

31. Marti, S., Schmandt, C.: Giving the caller the finger: collaborative responsibility for cellphone interruptions. In: CHI 2005, pp. 1633–1636 (2005)

32. McFarlane, D., Latorella, K.: The scope and importance of human interruption in human-computer interaction design. Human-Comput. Interact. **17**(1), 1–61 (2002)

33. Monteiro, C., Avelar, A.F.M., Pedreira, M.D.L.G.: Interruptions of nurses' activities and patient safety: an integrative literature review. Revista Latino-Americana de Enfermagem **23**(1), 169–179 (2015)

34. Osmers, N., Prilla, M., Blunk, O., Brown, G.G., Janßen, M., Kahrl, N.: The role of social presence for cooperation in augmented reality on head mounted devices: a literature review. In: CHI 2021, Article 457 (2021)

35. Oulasvirta, A., Ericsson, K.A.: Effects of repetitive practice on interruption costs: an empirical review and theoretical implications. In: ECCE 2009, Article No. 28, pp. 1–9 (2009)

36. Pater, J., Coupe, A., Pfafman, R., Phelan, C., Toscos, T., Jacobs, M.: Standardizing reporting of participant compensation in HCI: a systematic literature review and recommendations for the field. In: CHI 2021, Article 141, pp. 1–16 (2021)

37. Pielot, M., Church, K., De Oliveira, R.: An in-situ study of mobile phone notifications. In: MobileHCI 2014, pp. 233–242 (2014)

38. Pielot, M., Rello, L.: Productive, anxious, lonely - 24 Hours without push notifications. In: MobileHCI 2017 (2017)

39. Puranik, H., Koopman, J., Vough, H.C.: Pardon the interruption: an integrative review and future research agenda for research on work interruptions. J. Manag. **46**(6), 806–842 (2020)

40. Rivera, A.J., Karsh, B.-T.: Interruptions and distractions in healthcare: review and reappraisal. Qual. Saf. Health Care **19**(4), 304–312 (2010)

41. Sasangohar, F., Scott, S.D., Donmez, B.: Interruption management and recovery in time-critical supervisory-level tasks: a literature review. In: HFES 2013, pp. 1745–1749 (2013)

42. Schaule, F., Johanssen, J.O., Bruegge, B., Loftness, V.: Employing consumer wearables to detect office workers' cognitive load for interruption management. In: Proceedings of ACM on Interactive, Mobile, Wearable and Ubiquitous Technologies, vol. 2, no. 1, pp. 1–20 (2018)

43. Trafton, G., Monk, C.: Task interruptions. Rev. Human Fact. Ergon. **3**(1), 111–126 (2007)
44. Trafton, J.G., Altmann, E.M., Brock, D.P., Mintz, F.E.: Preparing to resume an interrupted task: effects of prospective goal encoding and retrospective rehearsal. Int. J. Human-Computer Studies **58**, 583–603 (2003)
45. Uozumi, M., et al.: Interruption of enteral nutrition in the intensive care unit: a single-center survey. J. Intensive Care **5**(52), 1–6 (2017)
46. vom Brocke, J., Simons, A., Riemer, K., Niehaves, B., Plattfaut, R.: Standing on the shoulders of giants: challenges and recommendations of literature search in information systems research. Commun. Assoc. Inf. Syst. **37**(9), 205–224 (2015)
47. Wang, Y., Gräther, W., Prinz, W.: Suitable notification intensity: the dynamic awareness system. In: GROUP 2007, pp. 99–106 (2007)
48. Wei, R., Lo, V.-H.: Staying connected while on the move: cell phone use and social connectedness. New Media Soc. **8**(1), 53–72 (2006)
49. Wiberg, M., Whittaker, S.: Managing availability: supporting lightweight negotiations to handle interruptions. ACM Trans. Comput.-Human Interact. **12**(4), 356–387 (2005)
50. Zhao, S.: Do internet users have more social ties? A call for differentiated analyses of internet use. J. Comput.-Mediat. Commun. **11**(3), 844–862 (2006)
51. Züger, M., et al.: Reducing interruptions at work: a large-scale field study of FlowLight. In: CHI 2017, pp. 61–72 (2017)

A New Interactive Paradigm for Speech Therapy

Vita Barletta⬚, Miriana Calvano^(✉)⬚, Antonio Curci⬚,
and Antonio Piccinno⬚

Computer Science Department, University of Bari Aldo Moro, 70125 Bari, Italy
{vita.barletta,miriana.calvano,antonio.curci,antonio.piccinno}@uniba.it
https://www.uniba.it/it/ricerca/dipartimenti/informatica/en

Abstract. Speech disorders and impairments are multiple dysfunctions that affect an individual's linguistic abilities, frequently occurring during childhood. More specifically, speech therapy involves the administration of treatments to patients that are defined based on the diverse causes and severity of language impairments; they consist of sets of exercises. The traditional process is limiting for professionals because it does not allow them to monitor the patients outside the on-site appointments in medical office. Nevertheless, the employment of technology can improve its efficiency and enable remote assistance. In addition, embedding gamification elements is key to make medical treatment more pleasurable and similar to common daily task for young patients. These types of technology are not always effective or accessible for individuals with speech impairments. Consequently, this work explores potential solutions to the limitations and challenges deriving from the analysis of two systems, *e-SpeechT* and *Therapy Assistant*; respectively, a web-application and a smart voice assistant skill.

Keywords: Speech therapy · Smart Home · Gamification · Voice Assistance · Automation

1 Introduction

Speech therapy is a medical field in which impairments concerning linguistic abilities are studied and treated. More specifically, a speech impairment affects one's ability to produce, understand, or use spoken language and interact with other individuals [1]. Its causes can be found in a variety of factors, such as neurological disorders, developmental disabilities, or injuries.

It follows that speech therapy pertains also to other disciplines such as phoniatrics, glottology, psychology, pedagogy, and neurology [2]. These impairments mostly encountered during childhood, which can make it harder for them to develop strong social and communicative abilities by making daily tasks more challenging. It is recommended to intervene during early the developmental stages. The employment of technology and its integration in the medical field

© The Author(s), under exclusive license to Springer Nature Switzerland AG 2023
J. Abdelnour Nocera et al. (Eds.): INTERACT 2023, LNCS 14145, pp. 380–385, 2023.
https://doi.org/10.1007/978-3-031-42293-5_39

have the potential of making the process of following therapies easier for all the individuals involved: speech therapists, caregivers and children [3]. More specifically, artificial intelligence and smart home environments can be exploited as tools to rely on when it comes to perform, correct and create exercises and to motivate children to stick to their treatments. They can also facilitate the creation of more inclusive and accessible homes. Since children are the protagonists of this field, it is important to highlight the introduction of game elements in therapies and treatments by gamifying the process; this approach has the potential of being a game-changer, making speech therapy a more pleasurable and playful experience for children [4]. In this regard, two artifacts are presented, *e-SpeechT* and *Therapy Assistant*, which are respectively a web application and a skill for a smart voice assistant, Amazon Alexa. these two are designed to work together and to be intertwined in order to allow more control of the environment and complete tasks that might otherwise be challenging [5].

The choice of the Amazon Alexa as the smart assistant involved in this research work lies in the fact that it is one of the most common technologies that can be found in people's houses nowadays, which implies familiarity with its interaction paradigm and decreases the probability of stress and frustration. Concerning the web application, called e-SpeechT, it was involved in this study since it is object of current research in this field [11].

This research work has the goal of proposing new solutions and future developments that improve and overcome the issues found by understanding their limitations and the needs of individuals with speech impairments.

2   The Integration of *Therapy Assistant* in *e-SpeechT*

In light of the concepts previously introduced, this section explores how *e-SpeechT* and *Therapy Assistant* work and their main functionalities.

2.1   e-SpeechT

e-SpeechT is a web application based on artificial intelligence, gamification and game-based learning; the system aims at empowering therapists and supporting caregivers and children from 4 to 8 years old. It allows children to carry out therapies remotely in a familiar and comfortable environment to avoid feelings of stress and frustration. Speech therapists can create and monitor therapies, which consist of exercises that involve the repetition of words and/or the associations of objects with their names. Every exercise is presented as a serious game to play [6]. *e-SpeechT* also features an exercise automatic correction functionality, whose output can be always changed by professionals according to their analysis. The motivation lies in the fact that individuals can feel under examination when they attend on-site appointments too often [7]. Nevertheless, children and caregivers still need to physically meet professionals in order to determine their diagnosis and their progress.

2.2   Therapy Assistant

In this study, Amazon Alexa is employed. Skills for Alexa allow to develop new features for the smart assistant and they are invocable through voice interaction [8]. The core of each skill is the intent, which is an action that satisfies the user's requests made through sample utterances, defined by the skill developer. Sample utterances can contain parameters, called slots, that are given as input to the intents. The skill in question is called *Therapy Assistant*, which provides the following functionalities: launching the skill, creating reminders and starting the therapy; it works as follows. The caregiver sets a reminder for the date, the time, and the room in which the treatment has to place. At the fixed time, Alexa utters *"It's time to start the therapy! Go to the <RoomSetByCaregiver>. If you are already there, tell me 'I am here'!"*, which guides the child in the predefined room. As this task is completed successfully, Alexa exclaims *"Let's start!"* and opens *e-SpeechT*, an example is shown is Fig. 1.

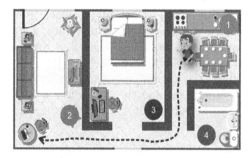

Fig. 1. Example of a scenario. *1) Kitchen, 2) Living Room, 3) Bedroom 4) Bathroom*

3   Proposal

Even though the work presented can improve and facilitate the process of performing therapies and solving speech impairments, there are some limitations that have to be necessarily addressed.

3.1   Limitations

The limitations consist in the lack of automation in the skill. In particular, the skill is not automatically launched when the reminder goes off and too many vocal interactions are required to determine whether the child is in the right room or not. Moreover, the smart voice assistant is currently unable to recognize the child and to distinguish his/her voice from the one of the caregiver.

Another aspect to be improved is the login phase of the child in his/her personal area, which can be perceived as too complex and intricate based on their cognitive skills.

In addition, the technology behind the vocal interaction paradigm of *e-SpeechT* can be considered as robotic and emotionally detached, therefore, it would be convenient to "humanize" the voice to make children feel more comfortable and engaged.

In these regards, three research questions have been formulated: (RQ1) How can the process be sufficiently and efficiently automated?; (RQ2) How can the login process be facilitated and made more effortless for children?; (RQ3) What other smart devices can be useful in the whole process?. The results produced by this study will be exploited for future works by concretely implementing the proposed solutions.

3.2 Proposed Solutions

This section aims at finding possible answers to the research questions previously mentioned; the proposed potential solutions to the emerged limitations can encompass multiple problems.

An approach to undertake as a response to research questions (RQ1) and (RQ3) can consist in the implementation of a *localization feature*, which can enable the voice assistant to determine whether the child is at home or not. Based on the reminders programmed by the caregivers and the location of the child, the therapy routine can be initiated automatically. It is worth mentioning that, since the target user of *e-SpeechT* are children from 4 to 8 years old, the location taken in consideration is the caregiver's. This functionality can work properly through to the Amazon Alexa Mobile App that exploits their phone's localization. A first prototype of this feature has been already developed and it allows to find the device's address and coordinates. To determine if the device owner is at home, it checks if the linked mobile device and Amazon Echo are in the same location.

Since this technology is designed for children with varying degrees of speech impairments, the possibility to use a smart button connected to the smart home environment has been considered as an alternative to the enunciation of the invocation phrase for the activation of the smart assistant. Another solution proposed for the research question (RQ3), addresses the child's physical surroundings during therapy. It is planned to let the smart assistant be in control of devices and sensors to keep the child focused on the therapy and increase engagement levels; consequently, distractions are avoided while improving medical feasibility and reducing stress, fatigue and discomfort [9]. In this regard, a practical example of a possible scenario is described: the caregiver sets a reminder for his/her child to carry out the therapy at 11 am in the living room; the next day, the patient is at home and reading a book in the kitchen; at 11 am, the reminder goes off; the lights change colors and Alexa guides the child in the living room; *e-SpeechT* is opened and the treatment starts. To reinforce the sensory experience, the smart lights, connected to the assistant, can change colors and intensity adapting themselves to the type of task performed [10].

In conclusion, as it pertains to the research question (RQ2), it is intended to face the challenge by using speech recognition algorithms to confirm the child's identity on the web application. Children's voices evolve and change frequently and in short time spans, therefore it might be arduous to frequently update the patterns for each child. Moreover, to be more sure that the patient's identity corresponds to the individual who is undergoing the therapy, this solution can be matched with the *localization feature*. Moreover, it might be convenient to also extend this work to other open source smart voice assitants with the aim of comparing benchmarks in terms of performance, effectiveness and usability.

References

1. Butcher, P., Elias, A., Raven, R., Yeatman, J., Littlejohns, D.: Psychogenic voice disorder unresponsive to speech therapy: Psychological characteristics and cognitive-behaviour therapy in Children: A Systematic Review of Features and Challenges; In: International Journal of language and speech disorders, 1987. https://doi.org/10.3109/13682828709088690
2. Law, J.: Speech and language therapy intervention for children with primary speech and language delay or disorder: Cochrane Developmental, Psychosocial and learning Problems Group. Cochrane Database Syst Rev. **2003**(3), CD004110 (2003)
3. Speech-Language Pathologists: About Speech-Language Pathology. https://www.asha.org/students/speech-language-pathologists Accessed 4 Apr 2023 2023-04-13
4. Desolda, G. and Lanzilotti, R. and Piccinno, A. and Rossano, V.:A System to Support Children in Speech Therapies at Home; In: CHItaly 2021: 14th Biannual Conference of the Italian SIGCHI Chapter (CHItaly '21). Association for Computing Machinery, New York, NY, USA, Article 36, pp. 1–5. https://doi.org/10.1145/3464385.3464745
5. Saeedi, S., Bouraghi, H., Seifpanahi, M.S., Ghazisaeedi, M.: Application of Digital Games for Speech Therapy in Children: A Systematic Review of Features and Challenges. J Healthc Eng. 2022 Apr 25;2022:4814945. PMID: 35509705; PMCID: PMC9061057. https://doi.org/10.1155/2022/4814945
6. Kalmpourtzis, G.: Educational game design fundamentals : a journey to creating intrinsically motivating learning experiences. 1st edn. Taylor and Francis Group (2019)
7. Piccinno, A.: A Protocol to Assess Usability and Feasibility of e-SpeechT, a Web-based System Supporting Speech Therapies. In: 16th International Joint Conference on Biomedical Engineering Systems and Technologies, vol.5, pp. 546-553. SCITEPRESS, Lisbon (2023)
8. Amazon Alexa Skills Kit Documentation. https://developer.amazon.com/en-US/alexa/alexa-developer-documentation-welcome#alexa-skills-kit-tile. Accessed 24 Apr 2023
9. McKean, C., Bloch, S.: The application of technology in speech and language therapy. Int J. Lang. Commun. Disord. 54(2), 157–158. Epub 2019 Feb 27. PMID: 30811757. https://doi.org/10.1111/1460-6984.12464
10. Berrezueta-Guzman, J., et al.: Smart-home environment to support homework activities for children. IEEE Access, 8, pp. 160251–160267 (2020). https://doi.org/10.1109/access.2020.3020734

11. Barletta, V., Calvano, M., Curci, A., Piccinno, A.: A Protocol to Assess Usability and Feasibility of e-SpeechT, a Web-based System Supporting Speech Therapies. In: Proceedings of the 16th International Joint Conference on Biomedical Engineering Systems and Technologies (BIOSTEC 2023) - HEALTHINF; ISBN 978-989-758-631-6; ISSN 2184-4305, SciTePress, pages 546–553 (2023). https:// doi.org/10.5220/0011893300003414

A Simple Evaluation Framework for Enhanced Usability and Accessibility of Cultural Heritage Information Systems

Zainab AlMeraj[(✉)] [iD]

Information Science Department, College of Life Sciences, Kuwait University, Sabah Al-Salem University City, Al-Shadadiya, Kuwait
z.almeraj@ku.edu.kw

Abstract. Increasing international efforts aimed at preserving history, culture and artifacts, have meant an increase in the design and development of specialized information systems. These systems are often conceived by and built by subject matter experts in their own domains and not technologists, developers or designers by profession often resulting in systems that are hard to use. To enhance awareness and elicit early adoption of usability and accessibility, this work proposes a simplified evaluation framework for evaluating the interactive, multi-lingual and distributed collaborational nature of cultural heritage information systems.

Keywords: Cultural heritage · information systems · heuristic · evaluation · usability · digital accessibility

1 Introduction and Background

Cultural heritage information systems are technological systems that are designed to manage, preserve, and provide access to cultural heritage information. Cultural heritage information refers to any information related to a culture, including its history, art, architecture, language, and traditions [4,5].

These systems can take many forms, such as databases, digital libraries, and online portals. They often contain a wide range of information, including digitized photographs, documents, and audio recordings, as well as metadata describing cultural heritage objects and their contexts. The goal of cultural heritage information systems (CHISystems) is to make cultural heritage information easily accessible and usable by to two major groups: the subject matter experts, for example, excavation, preservation, historian specialists, and the general audiences.

From the point of view of specialists in the fields of archaeology, anthropology, art history, conservation and preservation, a 3D conservation CHISystem is a powerful tool. It can be used in planning excavations and identifying potential areas of interest. It can also help the experts visualize artifacts and sites in three

© The Author(s), under exclusive license to Springer Nature Switzerland AG 2023
J. Abdelnour Nocera et al. (Eds.): INTERACT 2023, LNCS 14145, pp. 386–390, 2023.
https://doi.org/10.1007/978-3-031-42293-5_40

dimensions, which can aid in the development of excavation strategies [7]. The main power lies in the systems ability to record data, analyze objects on and offsite as well as collaborate with other experts and the public. Data can be linked to 3D models, allowing the expert to visualize objects in their original context, recreate replicas, and create visualizations for multiple usage scenarios. These interactions need to consider varying ages and abilities.

Increased international efforts aimed at preserving history, culture and artifacts, have meant an increase in the design and development of CHISystems. This attention stipulates a need to rethink the universal design of cultural heritage information systems' [6] from both usability [9] and accessibility [10] perspectives. This is particularly important for systems conceived, designed and developed by cultural heritage subject matter experts targeting their peers versus those for more general audiences.

The term"usability" is used to describe how simple and effective it is for a user to access and then navigate a platform, product, or website. Measuring it typically involves comparing it to five essential criteria: memorability, efficiency, errors, learnability, and satisfaction (MEELS) [9].

When a platform, product, or website is considered accessible, it can be utilized by everyone by addressing parts of the user experience that are unfair to those who have varying abilities. Hence "accessibility" is not only the proper course of action in terms of fostering inclusion and ensuring that persons with disabilities can equally view, comprehend, navigate, and engage with the information, but it also has advantages for all users [11,12].

In terms of assessments, cultural heritage information systems have been evaluated using a variety of methods and techniques such as cognitive walkthrough [2], user testing [3], and guided/heuristic evaluation [8,9]. These methods have focused on testing effective usability of proposed features based mainly on usability factors by Neilson [8]. Evaluation methodologies in this area can benefit from utilizing other usability frameworks adopted in the real world design and development stages of information systems such as EN-ISO 9241 [14], ISO EN 301-549 [15]. These not only address universal design principles that are fundamental in enhancing usage, they also ensure the systems are approaching industry standards. Furthermore, there has been no focus on accessibility in the cultural heritage space making the adoption of W3C WAI Web Content Accessibility Guidelines WCAG 2.1 [16] crucial for increased inclusion and enhanced user experiences.

In practice, evaluating software with users or experts is done at the end of a projects life-cycle. Major issues uncovered at this stage require complete changes in design and development which often can not be remedied quickly mainly due to time constrains to launch or budgeting reasons. This practice has continued to be a barrier to ensuring usable and accessible technology across the world for over a decade [13].

To help, this work proposes a simple, quick and succinct framework to act as a quick reference for cultural heritage subject matter specialists with little to no accessibility and usability experience working on building highly specialized niche information systems. The framework can act as reference for them throughout the software development life cycle (SDLC) and can evolves over time to accommodate for advances in CHISystems.

2 A Simple Usability and Accessibility Evaluation Framework

An investigation into evaluation methods for CHISystems has resulted in an evaluation framework that can assist in routine assessment during system design, development and deployment stages. The proposed framework draws on fundamental components from Neilson [8], EN-ISO 9241 [14], ISO EN 301-549 [15], the User Experience Professionals Association (UXPA) [17], and Web Content Accessibility Guidelines WCAG 2.1 [16]. These guidelines are major internationally approved and adopted guides in the technology software industry aimed at enhancing human system interactions irrelevant of their abilities or technologies used [1]. The above guidelines were combined, reviewed, summarized, labeled and categorized, revised for overlaps, and then the wordings were simplified. This resulted in a set of criteria comprised of unique usability and accessibility concepts based on the WCAG 2.1 principles, as shown in Fig. 1. Each of these criteria consists for a set of heuristic measures. Currently they are collectively composed of 62 checklist items in total that consider the unique nature of CHISystems from: methods of interactions, system physical settings, controls, audiences, data types, and information retrieval.

To assess the framework, it was presented to 6 technology researchers working on information system design and development in the areas of environment, health and cultural heritage. Feedback included that the criteria were clear, easy to follow and suitable to use as a reference if the person was to manually test or introduce criteria to a CHISystem. Furthermore, the framework was shared with 2 experts one in usability and the other in digital accessibility. Both experts believe that the overall approach combining both set of guidelines for non-usability and accessibility experts was novel and that it would be feasible in practice. The accessibility stated that it would help in awareness efforts and support enhancing knowledge about the accessibility domain. Hence, we believe this approach can support those interested in building systems without expertise these domains and can act as a reference to users who supervise the design and development process further enhancing early adoption [11].

3 Conclusion

This work proposed an evaluation framework that combination of accessibility guidelines and the usability standards together, supports cultural heritage subject matter experts design and build information systems with the target user in mind. The proposed framework was designed to elicit easy adoption of human-centered design concepts and can be used to help evaluate the usability and

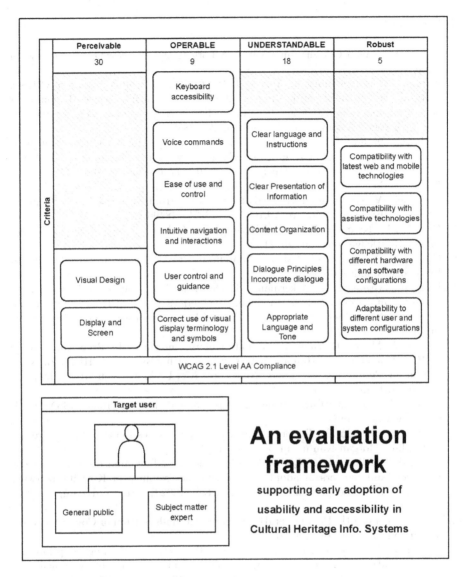

Fig. 1. A simple evaluation framework for non-experts in usability and accessibility

digital accessibility of information systems by non-experts at any stage of design or development.

Acknowledgements. The authors would like to thank the reviewers for their feedback.

References

1. World Wide Web Consortium (W3C). W3.org (2023). www.w3.org/. Accessed 1 June 2023
2. Tromp, J.G., Chowdhury, J., Torres, J.C., My, H.T.: Usability testing of CHISel: cultural heritage information system extended layers of interactive 3D computer generated images and relational database. Int. J. Eng. Technol. **7**(2.28), 100–105 (2018). https://doi.org/10.14419/ijet.v7i2.28.12888
3. de la Paz Diulio, M., Gardey, J.C., Gomez, A.F., Garrido, A.: Usability of data-oriented user interfaces for cultural heritage: a systematic mapping study. J. Inf. Sci. **49**(2), 359–372 (2023). https://doi.org/10.1177/01655515211001787
4. Ioannides, M., Fink, E., Moropoulou, A., Hagedorn-Saupe, M., Fresa, A., Liestøl, G., Rajcic, V., Grussenmeyer, P. (eds.): EuroMed 2016. LNCS, vol. 10058. Springer, Cham (2016). https://doi.org/10.1007/978-3-319-48496-9
5. Graham, P., Kennedy, L.: Digital Heritage and Culture: Strategy and Implementation. Routledge, London (2017)
6. Goldsmith, S.: Universal Design: A Manual of Practical Guidance for Architects. Routledge, London (2000)
7. Fassi, F., Fregonese, L., Ackermann, S., De Troia, V.: Comparison between laser scanning and automated 3D modelling techniques to reconstruct complex and extensive cultural heritage areas. Int. Arch. Photogrammetry Remote Sens. Spat. Inf. Sci. **40**, 73–80 (2013)
8. Nielsen, J., Molich, R.: Heuristic evaluation of user interfaces. In: Proceedings of the SIGCHI Conference on Human Factors in Computing Systems (CHI 1990). Association for Computing Machinery, New York, NY, USA, 249–256 (1990). https://doi.org/10.1145/97243.97281
9. Nielsen, J.: Usability Engineering. AP Professional, Boston (1993). ISSN: 1566-6379, www.ejise.com
10. Lazar, J., Goldstein, D., Taylor, A.: Ensuring Digital Accessibility Through Process and Policy. Morgan Kaufmann, Burlington (2015)
11. AlMeraj, Z., Alhuwail, D., Qadri, R., et al.: Understanding mindsets, skills, current practices, and barriers of adoption of digital accessibility in Kuwait's software development landscape. Univ. Access. Inf. Soc. (2023). https://doi.org/10.1007/s10209-023-00980-5
12. Lazar, J., Feng, J.H., Hochheiser, H.: Research Methods in Human-Computer Interaction. Wiley, New York (2010)
13. Velleman, E.M., Nahuis, I., van der Geest, T.: Factors explaining adoption and implementation processes for web accessibility standards within eGovernment systems and organizations. Univ. Access Inf. Soc. **16**, 173–190 (2017). https://doi.org/10.1007/s10209-015-0449-5
14. ISO 9241-210:2010. ISO (2019). www.iso.org/standard/52075.html. Accessed 17 Apr 2023
15. ISO EN 301-549, Accessibility Requirements for ICT Products and Services. Version 3.2.1, March 2021
16. How to Meet WCAG (Quickref Reference). W3.org (2019). www.w3.org/WAI/WCAG21/quickref/. Accessed 17 Apr 2023
17. User Experience Professionals Association (UXPA). UXPA International - User Experience Professionals Association (2017). uxpa.org. Accessed 17 Apr 2023

A Study on Prototyping in a Design Course

Andrea Alessandrini[✉]

University of Urbino, 61029 Urbino, Italy
andaleo@gmail.com

Abstract. Prototyping plays a fundamental role in an efficient iterative design process. Constructing, programming and debugging the interactive prototypes electronic connections and communications computational systems elements, remains a demanding activity for designers. This fieldwork study explores, describes, and analyzes the practices, tools, and technologies used by design students in the construction of interactive prototypes on a university course. The research investigation reviews the interactive prototypes and presents and analyzes excerpts of interviews with students. Our results provide insights into the socio-technical dynamics which influence digital component choices. The study describes the types of digital connections and communications among prototype components and the practices adopted by design students to build them. Last, our results show that practices to identify components and users' interactions were based on sophisticated time- or event-based strategies. Finally, implications of findings of the study are discussed.

Keywords: Interactivity · Design · Education · Prototyping Tools · Practices

1 Introduction

Beaudouin-Lafon and Mackay define a prototype as a concrete representation of part or all of an interactive system (Beaudouin-Lafon and Mackay, 2002). Similarly, Houde and Hill discussing the functions of prototypes, define the prototype as any representation of a design idea, regardless of medium (1997). Buxton (2010) emphasizes the significance of sketching through the prototyping process. The prototyping methods and tools are essential means to support designers in exploring and programming the prototypes design space (Toivonen et al. 2018). Grigorenu et al. (2009) identify the main area designers need tools and support for creating; iterating and communicating. Other researchers present challenges for different types of prototyping tools (Alessandrini et al. 2009). Today, still little is known about how design students construct physical-digital interactive prototypes in practice. In this poster, we present the early results of a fieldwork study that investigated how design students constructed interactive prototypes in a final-year university design course. This early study aimed to describe and analyze which electronics and software components and technologies were used and how were connected.

© The Author(s), under exclusive license to Springer Nature Switzerland AG 2023
J. Abdelnour Nocera et al. (Eds.): INTERACT 2023, LNCS 14145, pp. 391–395, 2023.
https://doi.org/10.1007/978-3-031-42293-5_41

2   Related Work

A consistent body of literature comes from the reports on designers and researchers' challenges met during building interactive prototypes. For example, a study explored the design challenges, issues, and limitations for designers and researchers in constructing Internet of Things systems using existing prototyping tools (Alessandrini 2015, 2022). Interactive prototypes are a blend of various tools and components. According to recent research, design students use simple hardware components (e.g., buttons) to scaffold the development of their prototype online data exchange with the Internet (Alessandrini 2013). Debugging software and hardware physical digital prototypes is a very complex activity. The difficulty comes from several factors, for example, software and hardware processes during debugging are invisible and require higher cognitive efforts for programmers or designers (Alessandrini 2023; Détienne 2001). According to a recent empirical study on physical computing tasks shows that the circuit problems cause more failures than the program problems and 80% of failures are due to missing wiring, independently from the subject's expertise (Booth et al. 2016). Other debugging strategies on various software and components assembly programmers used several methods to visualize process flows, for example, using several print statements on their prototypes' codes (Brandt et al. 2008). Despite these studies, there is still little understanding of prototyping practices in physical-digital interactive prototyping. Our work will be an initial effort to fill this literature gap on how design students prototype prototypes in educational settings.

3   Methodology

In this section, we describe the study context, the research methods, and the data analysis method conducted with design students in a final (fourth) year course on design at the Design Department at the University of Dundee (UK). The aims of the projects in the course were to create interactive artifacts which could respond to the user needs, which emerged during the students' users research. The class was composed of product design (PD) and interaction design (IxD) students. During the study, we used semi-structured interviews with students and prototype analyses. The interview participants were self-selected from the design class. We contacted the fifty-seven students via e-mail, nineteen of whom agreed to be interviewed. The interviews were video recorded with the consent of the participants. The participants ranged in age from 23 to 27 years; eleven were male, and eight were female. They had an average of two to three years of experience in building interactive prototypes. A single face-to-face interview ranging from 40 min to two hours was conducted with each interviewee. All the video and audio data coming from the interview were transcribed and organized by participants. We conducted an initial interview analysis focusing on thematic analysis. The process involved one researcher and two master students who collaboratively coded all transcribed interview data. The thematic coding was based on a combination of inductive (open-ended) and deductive (top-down) coding strategies. Consequently, we aggregate the coding, and developing categories, which captured the whole of the experience studied. The data instances were constantly compared for similarities and differences.

4 Prototyping Interaction Practices

In the fieldwork study, we observed that the design students used a quite broad and rich range of practices for connecting components and for overcoming technical problems that emerged during the prototype development.

In our study, we have seen that most of the prototypes connections were used for real-time data exchange or electrical connections. All these connections were designed and implemented as simple and direct as possible. We identified seven different connection types (Fig. 1). Design students adopted three types of digital connection practices: hard-coded; wireless link and WebSockets.

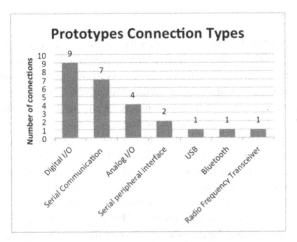

Fig. 1. Prototypes connection types and occurrences.

A student explained that to facilitate the BT module connection, the identification number of the BT module was hard coded into the code (e.g., "0000" or "1234"), creating a direct and reliable connection between the module and the mobile device. This hard-coded module strategy may be due to the need to build a strong and fast BT connection, bypassing the discovering and pairing phases, by hard-coding the module address ID within the Arduino code. This practice could permit the student to have the straightest and direct wireless connection possible between the embedded BT module and the tablet.

Another student explained that the prototype used radio frequency (RF) modules in place of other more complicated types of wireless connections (e.g., Wi-Fi). The students, after evaluating alternative RF technologies such as WI-FI or Bluetooth, decided to create an RF direct wireless link for the real-time data exchange and data visualization between the three distributed objects. This wireless link strategy may be beneficial for the students to understand better and manage real-time data exchange processes between interconnected objects. This straight and direct connection simplifies debugging and troubleshooting processes compared to other more complicated Wi-Fi or BT communication architectures.

A project uses a WebSocket to stream real-time mobile device accelerometer data from the HTML5 Device Orientation API to the Processing programming language application. The student used a WebSocket connection which provides full-duplex communication over a single TCP connection. The WebSocket facilitates the real-time data transfer from and to the interactive system server with a two-way (bidirectional) permanent conversation between the mobile device and the web server. This WebSocket connection strategy may simplify a much more complex system design, based on a full communication network-like architecture with nodes and components. The use of the required open DNS router may also increase the prototype cost as this enterprise-oriented hardware are much more expensive, compared to standard routers used on other networking solutions.

5 Discussion

The goal of this fieldwork study was to identify challenges and practices encountered by design students constructing interactive prototypes in a final-year university design course. The fieldwork brings together field observations, prototype analysis, student blogs analysis, focus groups and semi-structured interviews.

Interactive prototypes are a federation of heterogeneous components that exchange real-time signals and data. To connect these various components, design students preferred straight and direct communications to maintain an understandable and effective communication flow among components, facilitating problem-solving and flow control. Design students perceive their prototypes not as a unique working unit, but as an ensemble of components, each with their peculiar functionalities.

As Brandt (2009) shows, this compartmentalizes interactive systems and sustains debugging activities in professional contexts. This approach has its issue too; in fact, several students reported that the integration phase of the prototype components was one of the most challenging parts of the whole prototype construction. The students, based on standard tools and technologies, used simple but effective practices to elaborate prototypes. Our results may suggest the need for novel prototyping tools, which could support the design students in the understanding, exploration, and implementation of functionalities during the construction of the interactive prototypes. Design tools require an approach different from engineering. In design, it is fundamental to soften technology to make it quick, imaginative, and easy in order to shape the user's experience (Tuhkala et al. 2017). These preliminary results may suggest interesting implications for the design of novel prototyping tools and educational institutions and course tutors.

The road to reaching an easy and fully understandable technology construction is a long one, but progress is being made toward the full realization of easy prototyping interactions. This will allow digital technology to become a significant part of design students' daily lives and provide the required level of user control.

References

Alessandrini, A.: End–user construction mechanisms for the Internet of Things. In: 27th International BCS Human Computer Interaction Conference (HCI 2013), vol. 27, pp. 1–6 (2013)

Alessandrini, A.: Practices, technologies, and challenges of constructing and programming phys-ical interactive prototypes. In: Kurosu, M. (ed.) HCI 2015. LNCS, vol. 9169, pp. 132–142. Springer, Cham (2015). https://doi.org/10.1007/978-3-319-20901-2_12

Alessandrini, A.: How an undergraduate group of design students solved wiring errors during the prototyping of an interactive artifact. In: Proceedings of the 33rd European Conference on Cognitive Ergonomics (p. Article 12). Association for Computing Machinery (2022).https://doi.org/10.1145/3552327.3552345

Alessandrini, A.: A study of students engaged in electronic circuit wiring in an undergraduate course. J. Sci. Educ. Technol. **32**(1), 78–95 (2023). https://doi.org/10.1007/s10956-022-099 94-9

Alessandrini, A., Rizzo, A., Rubegni, E.: Drama prototyping for the design of urban interactive systems for Children. In: Proceedings of the 8th International Conference on Interaction Design and Children, pp. 198–201 (2009). https://doi.org/10.1145/1551788.1551827

Beaudouin-Lafon, M., Mackay, W.: Prototyping tools and techniques. In: The Human-Computer Interaction Handbook: Fundamentals, Evolving Technologies and Emerging Applications, pp. 1006–1031. L. Erlbaum Associates Inc. (2002)

Booth, T., Stumpf, S., Bird, J., Jones, S.: Crossed wires: investigating the problems of end-user developers in a physical computing task. In: Proceedings of the 2016 CHI Conference on Human Factors in Computing Systems, pp. 3485–3497 (2016). https://doi.org/10.1145/285 8036.2858533

Brandt, J., Guo, P.J., Lewenstein, J., Dontcheva, M., Klemmer, S.R.: Two studies of opportunistic programming: interleaving web foraging, learning, and writing code. In: Proceedings of the SIGCHI Conference on Human Factors in Computing Systems, pp. 1589–1598 (2009)

Brandt, J., Guo, P.J., Lewenstein, J., Klemmer, S.R.: Opportunistic programming: how rapid ideation and prototyping occur in practice. In: Proceedings of the 4th International Workshop on End-User Software Engineering, pp. 1–5 (2008). https://doi.org/10.1145/1370847.1370848

Buxton, B.: Sketching User Experiences: Getting the Design Right and the Right Design. Morgan kaufmann (2010)

Détienne, F.: Software Design–Cognitive Aspect. Springer, Heidelberg (2001). https://doi.org/10.1007/978-1-4471-0111-6

Grigoreanu, V., Fernandez, R., Inkpen, K., Robertson, G.: What designers want: needs of interac-tive application designers. In: 2009 IEEE Symposium on Visual Languages and Human-Centric Computing (VL/HCC), pp. 139–146 (2009)

Houde, S., Hill, C.: Chapter 16—what do prototypes prototype? In: Helander, M.G., Landauer, T.K., Prabhu, P.V. (eds.) Handbook of Human-Computer Interaction, North-Holland, 2nd edn, pp. 367–381 (1997). https://doi.org/10.1016/B978-044481862-1.50082-0

Toivonen, T., Jormanainen, I., Montero, C.S., Alessandrini, A.: Innovative maker movement plat-form for K-12 education as a smart learning environment. In: Chang, M., et al. (eds.) Challenges and Solutions in Smart Learning, pp. 61–66. Springer Singapore, Singapore (2018). https://doi.org/10.1007/978-981-10-8743-1_9

Tuhkala, A., Isomäki, H., Hartikainen, M., Cristea, A., Alessandrini, A.: Identifying objectives for a learning space management system with value-focused thinking, vol. 1, pp. 25–34. Scopus (2017). https://doi.org/10.5220/0006230300250034

A Theoretical Framework for the Development of "Needy" Socially Assistive Robots

Nathan Jones$^{(\boxtimes)}$ ⓘ, Fernando Loizides ⓘ, and Kathryn Jones

Cardiff University, Cardiff CF10 3AT, UK
{jonesnl16,loizidesf,jonesk90}@cardiff.ac.uk
https://www.cardiff.ac.uk/computer-science

Abstract. We suggest a theoretical framework for the design and development of a "needy" socially assistive robot (SAR) for the elderly. Our hypothesis is that a needy SAR will be more readily accepted by those that require them and would result in overall more positive care outcomes when compared to a non needy alternative. This is supported by existing works which indicate traits that can be considered needy are viewed favourably when correctly integrated. We provide guidance on the key design considerations that should be made in order to implement these traits successfully into a SAR. Using this newly created framework we will subsequently proceed to evaluate the effectiveness of integrating a SAR with these traits in a real-world scenario.

Keywords: Socially Assistive Robot · Neediness · Needy · Framework · Elderly · Independent Living

1 Introduction and Motivation

The ageing populations of countries [1,2,25,29] have put strain on their respective healthcare systems. Independently living, high-risk individuals, such as the elderly or those living with frailty, can suffer from a lack of interaction [21]. Pets are regularly used to aid with healthy ageing as they provide benefits linked to improving the symptoms of mental health issues, reducing loneliness and isolation [12,17]. Furthermore, high-risk individuals can find it difficult to take care of animals due to safety concerns [10]. A potential solution to these problems is the use of Socially Assistive Robots (SARs) [6,11]. SARs do not have the downsides of pets and recent studies have indicated that they are capable of filling a companionship role, allowing them to act as a pet substitute [5,31]. While research indicates that SARs are an effective means of caring for the elderly [3,7], their adoption has not yet become widespread. Although work is minimal at present, studies indicate that the creation of SARs with "needy" characteristics results in a greater rate of affection and overall acceptance [4,9,15,18]. Merriam-webster dictionary defines needy as "marked by want of affection, attention, or emotional

© The Author(s), under exclusive license to Springer Nature Switzerland AG 2023
J. Abdelnour Nocera et al. (Eds.): INTERACT 2023, LNCS 14145, pp. 396–401, 2023.
https://doi.org/10.1007/978-3-031-42293-5_42

support" [20]. These traits generally have a negative connotation, however, when employed effectively such as by children or pets, these traits can be endearing. We evolve the definition of "neediness" in this environment to facilitate inclusiveness to SARs as "a dependence on someone else which is shown through a request of attention and support". While design guidelines exist for the creation of SARs, there is a lack of specific frameworks to aid in the design of much-needed and beneficial SARs with needy characteristics. Through this theoretical framework, we aim to highlight the design considerations that need to be taken to successfully design a needy SAR. Although this framework aims to facilitate the development of a needy SAR for a broad set of users, it has been tailored towards the elderly who are anticipated to be the primary demographic. At present, our research team is collaborating with experts at Gloucester City Homes (GCH) to confirm the validity of these expectations. Several trials are ongoing to evaluate the effectiveness of this framework in an assisted living setting. During these trials we intend to experiment with the implementation of SARs that were designed using this framework by conducting monitored tests with elderly individuals. Surveys and interviews will be conducted in order to appraise whether this framework was able to successfully assist in the design of an effective needy SAR that is readily accepted.

2   Framework

Neediness. For a robot to be considered "needy" it must emulate a dependence on the user, such as by requesting that the user simulate the process of assisting or taking care of it. These requests do not need to be limited to speech synthesis, as neediness can be expressed in many different forms, such as through gestures or text. All needy interactions should be positive as perceived enjoyment has an effect on the intention for elderly users to interact with a SAR [14].

Restraint. As reported in the introduction, neediness can be viewed as a negative trait unless presented in a specific endearing way, or when dependence becomes excessive and unmanageable. Therefore, a robot must not request more support than is viable for the user to provide. An elderly or frail user for example must not feel pressure to perform actions when it would be uncomfortable to do so. In such a situation the robot should either stop prompting or find a different method of interacting with the user. While the user should be encouraged to interact with the SAR, there should be no significant downsides when failing to care for the robot, as this could cause undue stress.

One of the most prevalent barriers to pet ownership is the physical demands of providing care overwhelming older individuals. In some cases this extends to individuals neglecting their own personal health and well being in an attempt to provide this care. [23] It is important that the future development of needy SAR's does not lead to similar problems.

Fig. 1. Diagram with the key traits that make up the Needy SAR Framwork

Honesty. While anthropomorphism is important in developing empathy for a SAR, it must not attempt to deceive the user into believing that is a living being. Explaining that the SAR is a tool rather than a pet is preferred, particularly for the elderly or disabled, as this can be confusing and demeaning [22]. They must also not be presented as a replacement for human contact. Instead they should be integrated as a method to afford greater independence to the user.

Character. Robots should have a defined personality as they are viewed more positively than those that stick to formal means of communication [4,13,16]. Interaction through friendly and casual means, such as using informal language, can greatly influence the enjoyment that users receive from using SARs [15]. Consistent communication between users and robots forms social bonds between the two, resulting in greater satisfaction [27]. Mistakes with long term consequences can drastically reduce trust [28], however expressing regret and vulnerability by asking for support has shown to increase overall acceptance by endearing the robot to the user [9,18]. Indicating that these traits, which by our definition would be considered needy, are popular among elderly users.

Expression. Expressions, both visual and mental, are an important aspect of viewing SARs as a potential companion, rather than a simple tool, and are therefore important for creating a robot that users want to care for. Showing basic human-like characteristics can help with allowing users to feel that they can understand and relate to a SAR [26]. However, these expressions do not always need to be a direct mirror of human expression. Subtle cues that portray emotions can allow users to empathise, even in instances where the SAR is not a humanoid [32]. In order to be perceived as natural these expressions need to be manifested immediately during communication [24].

Personalisation. SARs should be tailored to suit the preferences of individuals, ensuring that their requirements are kept at the forefront of design to encourage prolonged adoption. Robust personalisation also allows SARS to be adapted to support users with disabilities, increasing overall usability by making sure that vulnerable users are not excluded [30]. Personalising less functionally significant aspects, such as the voice, can help to appeal to different demographics and increase overall enjoyment [8].

Understanding. Voice control integration has proven to reduce the learning curve for elderly users [24], however barriers to using this method of interaction still need to be considered. While speech recognition technology has seen significant advances, concerns remain surrounding how well they can understand user requests. Elderly people in particular are hindered by this as speech may be slurred or otherwise difficult for the device to understand. This is compounded by a lack of support for multiple languages, as individuals would rather communicate through their first language, which may not be possible [19]. Users being unable to understand existing SARs is a common source of frustration [9]. Enunciation from speech-based robots needs to be clear, as the elderly are more likely to have hearing disabilities. Additional methods of communication, such as through a display, can lessen the severity of these issues [24].

3 Summary and Future Work

In this paper, we have suggested a framework with 7 design considerations that current evidence indicates will allow for the successful creation of a SAR with needy traits. It discusses and contains real world examples of where these traits have been successfully implemented resulting in a higher rate of acceptance, as well as instances where a lack of accommodation for these traits has resulted in a lower rate of user satisfaction. We have attempted to address the major problems that have already been identified by the use of existing SARs. These include functional problems, such as the difficulty with understanding that some users have, as well as accommodation for preferences that, while not critical, will provide a more pleasant interaction. In addition we discussed several major concerns that we believe will emerge when developing a needy SAR for elderly demographics, including considerations that need to be made for the common disabilities they face. We intend to expand on this work by utilising this framework to design SARs that will be trialled in housing associations across the UK. While this framework is primarily targeted at the elderly, many of the factors contained within it are suitable for implementation into SARs for a general user base. Work will need to be done to ascertain whether the traits in this framework are equally important to different cultures, age ranges and genders, as current work indicates the expectations and needs of these demographics differ greatly.

Acknowledgements. We would like to thank Guy Stenson and the team at Glouces-ter City Homes and to RKM Software for their valued contributions.

References

1. Projected population by age (korea) (12 2021). http://www.kosis.kr
2. Japan population estimates report (2023). http://www.e-stat.go.jp
3. Abdi, J., et al.: Scoping review on the use of socially assistive robot technology in elderly care. BMJ Open **2**, e018815 (2018)
4. Bartl, A., et al.: The influence of a social robot's persona on how it is perceived and accepted by elderly users. Lecture Notes in Computer Science ,pp. 681–691 (2016)
5. Bates, M.: Robotic pets: A senior's best friend? IEEE Pulse **4**, 17–20 (2019)
6. Bedaf, S., et al.: Overview and categorization of robots supporting independent living of elderly people: what activities do they support and how far have they developed. Off. J. RESNA **2**, 88–100 (4 2015)
7. Bemelmans, R., et al.: Socially assistive robots in elderly care: a systematic review into effects and effectiveness. J. Am. Med. Directors Assoc. **2**, 114–120 (2012)
8. Biswas, M., et al.: Are older people any different from younger people in the way they want to interact with robots? scenario based survey. J. Multimodal User Interfaces **1**, 61–72 (2020)
9. Carros, F., et al.: Exploring human-robot interaction with the elderly: Results from a ten-week case study in a care home. In: Conference on Human Factors in Computing Systems (2020)
10. Enders-Slegers, M.J., et al.: Pet ownership and human-animal interaction in an aging population: Rewards and challenges. Anthrozoös **2**, 255–265 (3 2019)
11. Feil-Seifer, D., et al.: Defining socially assistive robotics. In: Proceedings of the 2005 IEEE 9th International Conference on Rehabilitation Robotics, pp. 465–468 (2005)
12. Hediger, K., et al.: Benefits of human-animal interactions for mental health and well-being. One Health: the theory and practice of integrated health approaches, pp. 344–355 (10 2020)
13. Heerink, M., et al.: The influence of a robot's social abilities on acceptance by elderly users. In: IEEE International Workshop on Robot and Human Interactive Communication, pp. 521–526 (2006)

14. Heerink, M., et al.: Enjoyment intention to use and actual use of a conversational robot by elderly people. In: HRI 2008–3rd ACM/IEEE International Conference on Human-Robot Interaction: Living with Robots, pp. 113–119 (2008)

15. Heerink, M., et al.: Measuring the influence of social abilities on acceptance of an interface robot and a screen agent by elderly users. In: People and Computers XXIII Celebrating People and Technology - Proceedings of HCI 2009, pp. 430–439 (2009)

16. Heerink, M., et al.: Relating conversational expressiveness to social presence and acceptance of an assistive social robot (2009)

17. Hui Gan, G.Z., et al.: Pet ownership and its influence on mental health in older adults. Aging Mental Health **10**, 1605–1612 (2019)

18. Iwasaki, Y., et al.: Interaction with the mercurial robot: Work assisting robot express the tiredness. In: ACM International Conf. Proceedings, pp. 29–33 (4 2019)

19. Joglekar, P., et al.: Humanoid robot as a companion for the senior citizens. In: 1st International Conference on Data Science and Analytics, PuneCon 2018 (2018)

20. Merriam-Webster: Needy definition. http://www.merriam-webster.com/dictionary/needy

21. Mulla, E., et al.: Frailty: An overview. InnovAiT: Education and inspiration for general practice **2**, 71–79 (2 2020)

22. Ng, J., et al.: Older adults' attitudes toward homes service robots. In: Proceedings - WASA 2012: Workshop at SIGGRAPH Asia 2012, pp. 87–90 (2012)

23. Obradović, N., Lagueux, É., et al.: Pros and cons of pet ownership in sustaining independence in community-dwelling older adults: a scoping review. Ageing Soc. **40**(9), 2061–2076 (2020)

24. Oliveira, J., et al.: Speaking robots: The challenges of acceptance by the ageing society. In: IEEE International Symposium on Robot and Human Interactive Communication, pp. 1285–1290 (2017)

25. ONS: Overview of the uk population (2020). http://www.ons.gov.uk

26. Park, S., et al.: Should robots blush? Conf. on Human Factors in Computing Systems (2021)

27. Sabelli, A.M., et al.: A conversational robot in an elderly care center: An ethnographic study. In: ACM International Conference on Human-Robot Interaction, pp. 37–44 (2011)

28. Salem, M., et al.: Would you trust a (faulty) robot?: Effects of error, task type and personality on human-robot cooperation and trust. In:ACM/IEEE International Conference on Human-Robot Interaction, pp. 141–148 (3 2015)

29. Statista: Italy: population by age group (2019). http://www.statista.com

30. Takanokura, M., et al.: Implementation and user acceptance of social service robot for an elderly care program in a daycare facility. J. Ambient Intell. Human. Comput. (2021)

31. Tkatch, R., et al.: Reducing loneliness and improving well-being among older adults with animatronic pets. Aging Ment. Health **7**, 1239–1245 (2020)

32. Tsiourti, C., et al.: Designing emotionally expressive robots: A comparative study on the perception of communication modalities. In: HAI 2017 - Proceedings of the 5th International Conference on Human Agent Interaction, pp. 213–222 (10 2017)

*Ally*Chat: Developing a VR Conversational AI Agent Using Few-Shot Learning to Support Individuals with Intellectual Disabilities

Brittany Garcia-Pi[✉], Rohan Chaudhury, Miles Versaw, Jonathan Back, Dongjin Kwon, Caleb Kicklighter, Paul Taele, and Jinsil Hwaryoung Seo

Texas A&M University, College Station, TX 77840, USA
brinni@tamu.edu

Abstract. Virtual Reality (VR) environments have been used for training, education, and entertainment due to the interactive and embodied experiences the technology provides. Studies have shown that VR can be used to help support individuals with intellectual disabilities in various aspects of their lives. Likewise, conversational agents such as chatbots can be used to bolster competence training and well-being management for this user population. This paper addresses the need for inclusive job interview practice for individuals with intellectual disabilities by discussing the development of a VR application, *Ally*Chat. A two-part development phase is presented with pilot testing included for each phase. First, a conversational AI chatbot is tested and with positive feedback iterated upon to develop an immersive mock job interview experience in VR. A second pilot study is conducted with university students to test the functionality of a high-fidelity prototype. Future work will include improvement upon the developed VR application and further testing.

Keywords: Large Language Model · Virtual Reality Job Interview · Intellectual Disabilities

1 Introduction

Virtual Reality environments have gained popularity in training, education, and entertainment, providing interactive and immersive experiences [1, 2]. They effectively support individuals with intellectual disabilities in various areas, such as physical activity, literacy instruction, and court testimonies [3]. Conversational agents have also shown promise in competence training and well-being management for individuals with intellectual disabilities [4]. To address the inclusive job interview preparation needs of this group, this paper presents *Ally*Chat, a two-part VR application. It involves pilot testing a conversational AI model using a web-based chatbot, which is later integrated into the VR application. Through a participatory design approach, two students from our university, who are part of a transition program for adults with intellectual and developmental disabilities, actively contributed to the development process. The primary goal of this

© The Author(s), under exclusive license to Springer Nature Switzerland AG 2023
J. Abdelnour Nocera et al. (Eds.): INTERACT 2023, LNCS 14145, pp. 402–407, 2023.
https://doi.org/10.1007/978-3-031-42293-5_43

research is to optimize the job interview process for individuals with intellectual disabilities by leveraging the participatory design and VR to create a tailored AI conversational experience. The aim is to address their specific needs, enhance inclusivity, and improve their preparation and performance.

2 Related Works

2.1 Participatory Design and Individuals with Intellectual Disabilities

The participatory design engages individuals as co-designers to create inclusive and accessible products, services, or systems. Studies involving individuals with intellectual disabilities have shown positive impacts [5]. Gonzalez et al. (2020) identified four co-design phases and emphasized the importance of fully incorporating this community into user-centered design processes [6]. Abascal et al. (2020) demonstrated the feasibility of participatory design with people with cognitive disabilities, increasing users' affinity towards the resulting application [7]. These studies highlight the effectiveness of involving individuals with intellectual disabilities in designing user-friendly and accessible solutions. Successful implementation requires appropriate communication methods and assistive technology.

2.2 Conversational Agents to Support Individuals with Intellectual Disabilities

Conversational AI agents have diverse applications in education, customer service, and mental health support [8–10]. In education, they personalize tutoring and study assistance to improve academic performance through better comprehension and retention. In customer service, these agents provide personalized support, enhancing satisfaction and loyalty. They also benefit individuals with intellectual disabilities by addressing communication, social interaction, life skills training, and education needs, offering step-by-step instructions and customized learning opportunities. However, more research is needed to evaluate their effectiveness across contexts and populations.

3 Conversational AI Model Development

Conversational AI has grown rapidly due to advances in AI technology, resulting in more human-like interactions between humans and machines [11]. We created a personalized conversational AI agent using Large Language Models (LLMs), few-shot learning, and memory components to improve contextual understanding.

Employing Advanced AI for a Conversational Experience: LLMs, like OpenAI's gpt-3.5-turbo, have revolutionized AI by processing vast amounts of text data to generate contextually relevant and human-like text [12]. Our conversational AI agent utilizes this advanced LLM to engage users empathetically and supportively, thus fostering a connection and trust between the user and the agent.

Few-Shot Learning for Context and Flexibility: Few-shot learning is a promising machine learning technique that enables AI models to learn and adapt rapidly with minimal examples [13]. By providing some information on Batman and Bruce Wayne, along with few sample conversations, it comprehends various contexts and adjusts its responses, accordingly, facilitating dynamic and contextually appropriate interactions with users.

Striving for Natural and Engaging Conversations: To create a natural and friendly conversational flow, we designed the AI model to assume the role of Batman as a helpful friend, allowing users to guide the open-ended conversation in any direction. Our goal was to simulate a casual conversation with a new friend, which is why we opted for an AI agent with a familiar personality to make users feel comfortable.

Implementing Memory for Contextual Understanding: We incorporated 3 memory components into the AI model to enhance context retention for more personalized and meaningful responses. The *Background Memory* stores the AI model's background knowledge, including its role (e.g., Batman). This knowledge is shared among all users and forms the foundation for interactions. To capture user-specific information, we developed the *Initial Memory* component, which retains the few initial exchanges between the AI model and the user. Each user has a distinct Initial Memory to differentiate their conversations. The *Latest Memory* component retains the some of the most recent conversations, allowing the AI model to reference ongoing context and maintain natural and coherent interactions. Individual *Latest Memory* components are assigned to each user to preserve unique conversation threads.

Batman Chatbot Pilot Testing: This pilot study tested an AI chatbot designed for students with intellectual disabilities. The chatbot, inspired by Batman, engaged in conversations with students on a website. After a 10-min interaction, students provided feedback, which was generally positive. They found the chatbot's personality interesting and engaging, although some struggled to come up with topics, resulting in shorter interactions. The initial testing of the Batman chatbot on university program students shows promise as an engaging tool for casual conversation, with students enjoying its responses.

4   Virtual Reality Application Development

Based on student feedback, we developed a new chatbot model using few-shot learning and background information on a sports training position interviewer, selected by a faculty member. The AI acts as a supportive interviewer, offering feedback and switching to simulate the interviewee, creating an immersive experience, and fostering a connection with the user. Inspired by practice interviews conducted by university program students, the design draws on their interactions with college volunteers. A VR application was developed to engage students with the AI model and provide a secure environment for job interview practice, employing contextualized conversation techniques to enhance interview skills.

Virtual Character Development Process: Previous studies have shown that the visual style of Virtual Characters (VCs) in virtual environments significantly affects user performance [1]. Designers must be aware that highly realistic characters can evoke negative reactions and disrupt immersion, known as the "uncanny valley" [14]. The authors opted for a stylistic VC appearance with natural idle animations, mouth movement synced with audio using Salsa LipSync, and head and eye tracking through the Oculus Quest VR camera. Random blinking intervals were simulated. Figure 1 depicts the user's perspective in the application.

Virtual Environment Development Process: *Ally*Chat's environment was carefully designed and styled for effective job interview training, featuring an office-lounge area that simulates a semi-public/private space. Warm tones and natural lighting create a relaxing atmosphere.

Fig. 1. User Perspective in VR Environment

Virtual Reality Implementation: Development was done with Unity and OpenXR. The XR Interaction Toolkit managed spatial and UI interactions. Communication with web services utilized Unity's HTTP request API. The audio was recorded through the Oculus microphone, transcribed with Deepgram, and synthesized with AWS Polly for playback.

***Ally*Chat Pilot Testing:** A high-fidelity prototype of *Ally*Chat was tested by university program students using Oculus Quest. They received an introduction to the job interview topic and instructions on using the controls. Each student used the application for around 10 min. Feedback was generally positive regarding the virtual environment's appearance, but students found the virtual character's realistic movement strange. Both participants and a faculty member expressed concerns about the character's speech speed, length, and advanced language. They suggested adding a tutorial for interaction guidance. VC feedback was helpful for improving responses.

5 Conclusion and Future Work

This paper presents a participatory design process for developing *Ally*Chat, a VR application for supporting individuals with intellectual disabilities during job interviews. Initially, an AI chatbot with a Batman-inspired personality was created, but the interaction was limited due to challenges in initiating conversation topics. Previous studies have found that users are more likely to adhere to conversational agents when they are engaged [15]. Feedback from students led to the development of a high-fidelity prototype incorporating the chatbot into a virtual environment. Students found the environment suitable but expressed concerns about the virtual character's speech cadence and the job position being interviewed for. Feedback from a faculty member highlighted the advanced language used. Future work will focus on shorter conversations and structuring the interview process to align with program mock interviews. Broader user studies will also be conducted to expand the sample size beyond the initial participants.

References

1. Erolin, C., Reid, L., McDougall, S.: Using virtual reality to complement and enhance anatomy education. J. Vis. Commun. Med. **42**(3), 93–101 (2019). https://doi.org/10.1080/17453054.2019.1597626
2. Yee, N., Bailenson, J.N., Rickertsen, K.: A meta-analysis of the impact of the inclusion and realism of human-like faces on user experiences in interfaces. In: Conference Human Factors Computer System - Proceedings, pp. 1–10 (2007). https://doi.org/10.1145/1240624.1240626
3. Nabors, L., Monnin, J., Jimenez, S.: A scoping review of studies on virtual reality for individuals with intellectual disabilities. Adv. Neurodev. Disord. **4**, 344–356 (2020)
4. de Filippis, M.L., et al.: Preliminary results of a systematic review: quality assessment of conversational agents (chatbots) for people with disabilities or special needs. In: Miesenberger, K., Manduchi, R., Covarrubias Rodriguez, M., Peňáz, P. (eds.) ICCHP 2020. LNCS, vol. 12376, pp. 250–257. Springer, Cham (2020). https://doi.org/10.1007/978-3-030-58796-3_30
5. Malinverni, L., Mora-Guiard, J., Padillo, V., Mairena, M.A., Hervás, A., Pares, N.: Participatory design strategies to enhance the creative contribution of children with special needs. In: ACM International Conference on Proceeding Series, pp. 85–94 (2014). https://doi.org/10.1145/2593968.2593981
6. González, H.S., Vega Córdova, V., Exss Cid, K., Jarpa Azagra, M., Álvarez-Aguado, I.: Including intellectual disability in participatory design processes: methodological adaptations and supports. In: ACM International Conference on Proceeding Series, vol. 1, pp. 55–63 (2020). https://doi.org/10.1145/3385010.3385023
7. Abascal, J., Arrue, M., Pérez, J.E.: Applying participatory design with users with intellectual disabilities, pp. 321–326 (2020). https://doi.org/10.18573/book3.ao
8. Narynov, S., Zhumanov, Z., Gumar, A., Khassanova, M., Omarov, B.: Chatbots and conversational agents in mental health: a literature review. In: International Conference on Control Automation System, vol. 2021-October, no. Iccas, pp. 353–358 (2021). https://doi.org/10.23919/ICCAS52745.2021.9649855
9. Nicolescu, L., Tudorache, M.T.: Human-computer interaction in customer service: the experience with AI chatbots—a systematic literature review. Electronics **11**(10), 1579 (2022). https://doi.org/10.3390/electronics11101579

10. Zhang, S., Dinan, E., Urbanek, J., Szlam, A., Kiela, D., Weston, J.: Personalizing dialogue agents: I have a dog, do you have pets too?. In: ACL 2018 - 56th Annual Meeting Association Computer Linguistics Processing Conference, Long Paper, vol. 1, pp. 2204–2213 (2018). https://doi.org/10.18653/v1/p18-1205
11. Gao, J., Galley, M., Li, L.: Neural approaches to conversational AI. Found. Trends Inf. Retr. **13**(2–3), 127–298 (2019). https://doi.org/10.1561/1500000074
12. Radford, A., Wu, J., Child, R., Luan, D., Amodei, D., Sutskever, I.: Language models are unsupervised multitask learners. In: Proceedings of the 34th International Conference on Neural Information Processing Systems (NIPS 2020), pp. 1877–1901 (2020). http://arxiv.org/abs/2007.07582
13. Snell, J., Swersky, K., Zemel, R.: Prototypical networks for few-shot learning. In: Proceedings of the 31st International Conference on Neural Information Processing Systems (NIPS 2017), pp. 4080–4090 (2017). https://doi.org/10.12783/dtetr/mcee2017/15746
14. Mori, M., MacDorman, K.F., Kageki, N.: The uncanny valley. IEEE Robot. Autom. Mag. **19**(2), 98–100 (2012). https://doi.org/10.1109/MRA.2012.2192811
15. Fadhil, A., Wang, Y., Reiterer, H.: Assistive conversational agent for health coaching: a validation study. Methods Inf. Med. **58**(1), 9–23 (2019). https://doi.org/10.1055/s-0039-168 8757

An Approach to Evaluate User Interfaces in a Scholarly Knowledge Communication Domain

Denis Obrezkov$^{(\boxtimes)}$, Allard Oelen , and Sören Auer

TIB Leibniz Information Centre for Science and Technology, Hannover, Germany
{denis.obrezkov,allard.oelen,soeren.auer}@tib.eu

Abstract. The amount of research articles produced every day is overwhelming: scholarly knowledge is getting harder to communicate and easier to get lost. A possible solution is to represent the information in knowledge graphs: structures representing knowledge in networks of entities, their semantic types, and relationships between them. But this solution has its own drawback: given its very specific task, it requires new methods for designing and evaluating user interfaces. In this paper, we propose an approach for user interface evaluation in the knowledge communication domain. We base our methodology on the well-established Cognitive Walkthough approach but employ a different set of questions, tailoring the method towards domain-specific needs. We demonstrate our approach on a scholarly knowledge graph implementation called Open Research Knowledge Graph (ORKG).

1 Introduction

Modern researchers face numerous problems while conducting research: it is time-consuming to find information, cumbersome to get overviews of related work, and difficult to communicate their results to the right audience. Even though nowadays scholarly articles are often available digitally in PDF form on the Internet, the overwhelming quantity of these unstructured text documents makes it difficult for new knowledge to be discovered, crystallized, and used.

One approach to address the above-mentioned challenges is to utilize knowledge graphs. Knowledge graphs allow to communicate the actual knowledge of research and provide an alternative to the existing format of a narrative paper-based scholarly communication. Although several well-established implementations of knowledge graphs exist, such as Wikidata [16] and DBpedia [1], there is no such widely-adopted solution in the scholarly knowledge communication domain. In order to investigate this phenomenon and to improve knowledge communication from and to researchers, it is promising to analyze how information is actually transferred between a researcher and a knowledge graph interface.

In this paper, we propose a Cognitive Walkthrough methodology that can be employed to identify issues in user interfaces for scholarly knowledge communication. In Sect. 2 we describe knowledge graphs and how can we adopt an interface

© The Author(s), under exclusive license to Springer Nature Switzerland AG 2023
J. Abdelnour Nocera et al. (Eds.): INTERACT 2023, LNCS 14145, pp. 408–412, 2023.
https://doi.org/10.1007/978-3-031-42293-5_44

evaluation tool to account for domain-specific usability issues. In Sect. 3, we describe the resulting methodology of our walkthrough.

2   Related Work

A promising approach to organizing scholarly knowledge is using knowledge graphs. Similar to graph databases, knowledge graphs consist of entity networks and their respective relations. Additionally, knowledge graphs include semantics [8], often represented using ontologies, to capture the meaning of the data.

A small number of approaches exist to represent scholarly knowledge using knowledge graphs. Among others, this includes the Semantic Scholar Academic Graph [17], Microsoft Academic Graph [6] and the Open Research Knowledge Graph (ORKG) [2]. The former two approaches focus mainly on representing bibliographic metadata, while the latter focuses on describing and representing the actual knowledge stated in scientific articles, additionally allowing tabular literature overviews, called Comparisons [12]. A typical Comparison lists several chosen properties for a number of papers, thus, allowing a researcher to identify the important concepts of the works (see Fig. 1, for an example Comparison).

Fig. 1. Excerpt of an ORKG comparison with the columns representing papers.

To increase usability of a knowledge communication interface, several well-established methods can be utilized: interface walkthroughs [10,18], user studies [7], and GOMS-based user modelling [3]. A Cognitive Walkthrough (CW) is an task-centered interface walkthrough method that accounts for user's mental processes and goals [18]. The evaluator is asked to perform a number of steps. First, to identify the target audience and their background. Second, to understand their tasks and goals. Third, to specify a correct sequence of actions for each task. Fourth, to perform analysis by answering a set of predefined questions. Last, to write down problems and provide success and failure scenarios.

A prominent model to rely on while designing the human-information interaction is Model Human Processor introduced (MHP). [3]. This model represents human mind as an information-processing system and introduces several limitations that should be considered when designing a usable system. First, the working memory capacity, that can store only a limited amount of information, estimated to be around 5 to 7 chunks [9,15]. Second, the involvement of long-term memory in information processing. It is known that humans understand and memorize information better if the information makes sense for them [15].

To represent user knowledge about the system, a notion of mental model is used. The latter is defined as a set of user beliefs about the system, constructed through the interaction [11]. To refer to a user's mental representation of the current state of a digital environment, we use term "cognitive context".

3   Methodology

The initial steps in our methodology are similar to the original Cognitive Walkthrough. First, the target audience and their background should be identified. Second, a user goal should be specified, and user tasks should be written down. It should be noted, that we do not require a correct sequence of actions for each task since it can interfere with the evaluation process. In the third step, an evaluator is expected to perform analysis by answering a set of questions from Table 1.

Table 1. A question set for the developed Cogntive Walkthrough.

№	Walkthrough Question	Reference
Q1	Will users be aware of the steps they have to perform to complete a core task?	[4, 14, 18]
Q2	Will users be able to determine how to perform these steps?	[4, 18]
Q3	Will users be aware of the application's status at all times?	[10, 18]
Q4	Will users receive feedback in the same place and modality as where they have performed their action?	[10, 14]
Q5	Will users be able to recognize, and recover from non-critical errors?	[4, 10]
Q6	Will users be able to avoid making dangerous errors from which they cannot recover?	[4, 10]
Q7	Will users be able to efficiently work with the system, considering the limitations of working memory?	[3, 10]
Q8	Will users be able to understand the information provided by the system, given their background?	[3, 10]

The listed questions address a user's need to achieve a certain goal (Q1, Q2), the integrity of a cognitive context (Q3-Q6), the ease of the presented information processing (Q7, Q8). The last step of the walkthrough includes writing down problems and providing failure scenarios.

To demonstrate the methodology, we perform the developed Cognitive Walkthrough on ORKG. For that purpose, we choose the most prominent task of populating a knowledge graph. In our case, a typical user is an early career researcher. The user has a good understanding of her professional scientific field, with occasional knowledge gaps regarding specific methods or concepts. The user's goal is to gain information about concepts related to her own discipline either via structuring new knowledge or exploring structures created by others.

Task: To extract information from papers and represent it with the concepts in a knowledge graph. When a user tries to represent information from a paper, she is provided with a list of suggested properties and has the possibility to choose a template. When choosing a template, the user is given a form with multiple properties to fill. Since it is required to type a query to find the needed template, the user might be confused by not knowing the names of existing templates (Q2, Q8). And since templates are chosen by name and have no preview, she might choose an improper template with an appealing name, e.g. confusing the mental fatigue template with one related to material fatigue (Q4).

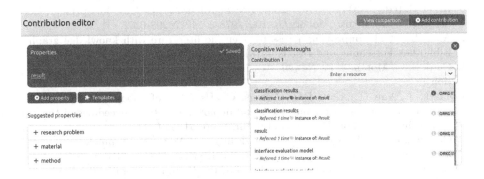

Fig. 2. The interface of ORKG contribution editor with several issues.

Another problem arises when the user tries to add a property to the contribution. In case a user chooses a property from a template, she is asked to fill in the value of the property. For example, when the user chooses the property "result" and is asked to "Enter a resource" (see Fig. 2), it is not clear what the resource is (Q8) and how it affects her initial goal (Q1). At the same time, if a user deletes a property value, there is no easy way to undo the deletion (Q5).

4   Discussion and Conclusion

In this paper, we introduced a new methodology of Cognitive Walkthrough for the knowledge communication domain. We developed our approach based on the principles of the original Cognitive Walkthrough and adopted the notion of cognitive context together with constraints from the Model Human Processor for the evaluation questions. We performed a walkthrough evaluation on a scholarly knowledge graph implementation called ORKG.

During the evaluation, we discovered several issues in the ORKG interface. For example, we observed that the evaluated interface has issues associated with questions Q4 and Q5, thereby breaking the user's context integrity. Given the knowledge about the disturbed cognitive process, we can leverage the appropriate techniques to address the problem, e.g. by utilizing context switching [5] or cognitive offloading [13]. In our future work we aim to elaborate on connections between walkthrough questions and underlying cognitive processes and to provide the appropriate mitigating techniques for revealed issues.

Acknowledgements. This work was co-funded by the European Research Council for the project ScienceGRAPH (Grant agreement ID: 819536) and the TIB Leibniz Information Centre for Science and Technology.

References

1. Auer, Sören., Bizer, Christian, Kobilarov, Georgi, Lehmann, Jens, Cyganiak, Richard, Ives, Zachary: DBpedia: a nucleus for a web of open data. In: Aberer, K., et al. (eds.) ASWC/ISWC -2007. LNCS, vol. 4825, pp. 722–735. Springer, Heidelberg (2007). https://doi.org/10.1007/978-3-540-76298-0_52
2. Auer, S., et al.: Improving access to scientific literature with knowledge graphs. Bibliothek Forschung und Praxis **44**(3), 516–529 (2020)
3. Card, S.K., Moran, T.P., Newell, A.: The psychology of human-computer interaction
4. Clark, J., Van Oorschot, P.C., Adams, C.: Usability of anonymous web browsing: an examination of tor interfaces and deployability. In: Proceedings of the 3rd Symposium on Usable Privacy and Security pp. 41–51 (2007)
5. Gauselmann, P., Runge, Y., Jilek, C., Frings, C., Maus, H., Tempel, T.: A relief from mental overload in a digitalized world: How context-sensitive user interfaces can enhance cognitive performance. Int. J. Hum.-Comput. Interact. **39**(1), 140–150 (2023)
6. Herrmannova, D., Knoth, P.: An analysis of the microsoft academic graph. D-lib Mag. **22**, 9/10 (2016)
7. Hornbæk, K.: Current practice in measuring usability: challenges to usability studies and research. Int. J. Hum Comput Stud. **64**(2), 79–102 (2006)
8. Kroetsch, M., Weikum, G.: Special issue on knowledge graphs. J. Web Semant. **37**(38), 53–54 (2016)
9. Miller, G.A.: The magical number seven, plus or minus two: Some limits on our capacity for processing information. Psychol. Rev. **63**(2), 81 (1956)
10. Nielsen, J., Molich, R.: Heuristic evaluation of user interfaces. In: Proceedings of the SIGCHI Conference on Human Factors In Computing Systems, pp. 249–256 (1990)
11. Norman, D. Some observations on mental models. Mental Models (1983)
12. Oelen, A., Jaradeh, M.Y., Stocker, M., Auer, S.: Generate FAIR literature surveys with scholarly knowledge graphs. In: JCDL 2020: Proceedings of the ACM/IEEE Joint Conference on Digital Libraries in 2020. pp. 97–106 (2020)
13. Risko, E.F., Gilbert, S.J.: Cognitive offloading. Trends Cogn. Sci. **20**(9), 676–688 (2016)
14. Rizzo, A., Marchigiani, E., Andreadis, A.: The avanti project: prototyping and evaluation with a cognitive walkthrough based on the norman's model of action. In: Proceedings of the 2nd Conference on Designing Interactive Systems: Processes, Practices, Methods, and Techniques, pp. 305–309 (1997)
15. Sousa, D.A.: How the brain learns. Corwin Press (2016)
16. Vrandečić, D., Krötzsch, M.: Wikidata: a free collaborative knowledgebase. Commun. ACM **57**(10), 78–85 (2014)
17. Wade, A.D.: The semantic scholar academic graph (s2ag). In: Companion Proceedings of the Web Conference 2022, pp. 739–739 (2022)
18. Wharton, C., Rieman, J., Lewis, C., Polson, P.: A practitioner's guide. In: Usability Inspection Methods, The cognitive walkthrough method, pp. 105–140 (1994)

Are Italian and French Public University Websites Sustainable?

Barbara Rita Barricelli[1]([⊠])(ID), Ines Di Loreto[2](ID), Michele Sciarabba[3], and Samir Zamouma[1]

[1] University of Brescia, Via Branze 38, 25123 Brescia, Italy
barbara.barricelli@unibs.it
[2] Université de Technologie de Troyes, 12 Rue Marie Curie, 10300 Troyes, France
[3] University of Milan, Via Festa del Perdono 7, 20122 Milan, Italy

Abstract. The COVID-19 pandemic has led universities to provide several tools for distance learning and made their websites evolve from mere information containers to points of access to ecosystems of complex interactive systems. In this paper, we present a preliminary study on Italian and French public university websites to investigate their impact on the environment regarding energy consumption and carbon dioxide production.

Keywords: Digital sobriety · Sustainable HCI · Sustainability

1 Introduction

Since the early 21st century, the impact of digital technologies on our society has become increasingly relevant. Recently, with the COVID-19 pandemic, the importance of digital devices and Internet connectivity has grown even more significantly, which has triggered a radical change in how we approach work and education. In fact, a pressing need has arisen to change how one interacts with the world of work and study, fostering the rapid rise of smart working and distance learning. However, the progress that has characterized these technologies is marked by a considerable grow in their environmental impact, which has become increasingly problematic over the years [7]. According to The Shift Project [6], *digital overuse* is neither sustainable nor essential for economic growth, from which it is disconnected, nor is compatible with the international commitments made by the European Union, in particular with the Paris climate agreement in 2015. The Shift Project addresses a major social issue: the sustainability of the development of software ecosystems. It does so under the theme of digital sobriety [2], aiming to reduce the environmental impact of digital technology by limiting its use. What significantly impact the environment are, above all, the great expenditure of energy that the use of technology entails and the emissions into the environment of large quantities of carbon dioxide (CO_2). CO_2 is a gas heavier than air and is the main product of coal combustion, hydrocarbons, and

© The Author(s), under exclusive license to Springer Nature Switzerland AG 2023
J. Abdelnour Nocera et al. (Eds.): INTERACT 2023, LNCS 14145, pp. 413–417, 2023.
https://doi.org/10.1007/978-3-031-42293-5_45

organic substances in general. This gas is a significant pollutant and its production is one of the main causes of global warming. According to the Global Carbon Project [3], the Internet has such an environmental impact that, compared to that of various nations, it could be considered the fourth most polluting country in the world. Weighing most heavily in this balance are data centers, which account for 1% of global energy demand (the Internet contributes around 3.7% of the total).

Our research is aimed at investigating how to design and develop software applications for universities that are both sustainable and effective in supporting distance learning and teaching. In particular, this paper presents a first step in this direction, focusing on the most visible software applications used in a university institution: the websites. To this aim, we started analyzing the websites of all public universities in Italy and France (the choice of these two specific countries was guided by the nationality of the institutions hosting this joint research).

2   Sustainable HCI and Websites Environmental Impact

Sustainable human-computer interaction (SHCI) was introduced in the scientific literature in 2007 [1] by identifying the role of sustainability in the design of interactive technologies. Sustainable HCI and Green IT/ICT are among the fields at the intersection between interactive technologies and sustainability that Hilty and Aebisher [5] list as worth exploring. In the specific case of Web design, several guidelines exist to inform the designers and developers about how to create usable and visually appealing websites while keeping in mind to mitigate their environmental impact [4]: e.g., reduce images and videos in terms of size and number in a way that the UX is not compromised but the energy consumption is contained; choose system fonts over custom web ones; reduce the use of JavaScript to avoid increasing the weight of the files and the processing time needed; prefer static to dynamic web pages; reduce white background and favour dark-mode interfaces. This brief overview of guidelines clarifies that a trade-off must be sought between the interest in using advanced technologies and the need to contain energy consumption and CO_2 emissions.

Several tools can be used to measure websites' resource consumption and environmental impact. For our study, we used Website Carbon Calculator (WCC), a tool that measures the environmental sustainability of websites by estimating the energy used for transferring all the data needed for the webpages visualization by calculating the grams of CO_2 released by the website per visit and annually (by estimating 10,000 visits per month), and by considering the type of energy source used to power the data centre where the website is hosted [9]. This last information is obtained by interrogating a dataset, updated since 2006 by The Green Web Foundation [8]: the dataset contains information about the websites that run on sustainable (renewable) energy and those that are powered by standard energy sources. WCC also estimates how many trees are needed to absorb the CO_2 emitted by the website in a year.

3   Evaluation of Italian and French Public University Websites

We present the analysis results we performed on all public university websites in Italy and France. We, on purpose, decided not to publish the names of universities when referring to their websites as *best* and *worst* because it is not among the goals of this paper to rank Italian and French universities but to attract attention and raise awareness about an existing problem that needs to be addressed. Nevertheless, the dataset is available upon reasonable request.

The list of universities was obtained for both Countries from the websites of their respective Ministries. The total number of websites is 61 for Italy and 89 for France, but due to timeout errors, WCC was unable to analyze 4 Italian and 8 French websites. The analyses were performed in April 2023.

As to the type of energy used to power the websites, out of the 57 Italian websites, 42 (74%) are hosted by data centres powered by standard energy sources, while only 15 (26%) work with sustainable energy. For what concerns the French websites, 72 websites (89%) reside at data centres powered by standard energy and just 9 (11%) are powered by sustainable energy sources.

WCC estimates the yearly amount of energy consumption by considering 10,000 website visits per month (120,000 visits a year). For Italian websites, the average energy consumed in a year is 254.68 kWh (SD 187.54, 95% CI [206.00, 303.37]), while for France, it is 365.42 kWh (SD 376.33, 95% CI [283.46, 447.38]). It is important to point out that for Italy, the total amount of energy consumed by the worst website (871 kWh) is 51 times the amount related to the best one (17 kWh). This ratio is even worse for France, where the worst website energy consumption amount (2453 kWh) is 77 times higher than the best result obtained (32 kWh).

To understand the impact of CO_2 production, we observed the results separating the websites according to the energy source type. For websites powered by standard energy, Italian ones produce on average 110.21 kg of CO_2 in a year (sd 82.38, 95% CI [88.82, 131.59]), while French ones produce on average 163.07 kg (sd 170.06, 95% CI [126.03, 200.10]). The results improve for websites working on sustainable energy. Italian websites produce on average 103.37 kg in a year (sd 72.71, 95% CI [84.50, 122.25]), while French websites produce on average 133.20 kg (sd 119.23, 95% CI [107.24, 159.16]). These results are reported in Fig. 1.

According to WCC results, the websites producing the smallest amount of carbon dioxide, both in Italy and France, are those that would need just one tree to compensate for the pollution produced in a year, while for the worst websites, the number of trees grows to 18 for Italy and 50 for France.

	ITALY			FRANCE		
	best	average	worst	best	average	worst
ENERGY CONSUMPTION in kWh per year	17	254.68	871	32	365.42	2453
CO₂ PRODUCTION in kg per year (standard / sustainable energy sources)	15.05 / 6.64	110.21 / 103.37	384.89 / 232.58	14.4 / 15.6	163.07 / 133.2	1083.6 / 363.6

Fig. 1. Best, worst, and average results in terms of yearly consumed energy (in kWh) and produced CO_2 (in kg) by the university websites in Italy and France.

4   Discussion and Conclusion

From the results of the analysis that we carried out, it is clear that the choice of data centres powered by sustainable energy sources is certainly positive, but it is not the main factor in reducing CO_2 emissions. In fact, it can be seen from the data that the use of sustainable energy only reduces emissions by 10-20%. As it turns out, some websites consume 50 to 70 times more energy than others, and this difference can only be related to design and development choices of the websites themselves. This suggests that a main factor on which it is effectively possible to act is the optimization of energy consumption through the adoption of effective guidelines to reduce its size, by acting, for example, on the reduction of multimedia content, and its computational complexity, by making specific choices regarding the programming and scripting languages to choose but also the third-party libraries to adopt. The analysis presented in this paper represents the first step towards a larger study that will investigate how to enable the design and development of software applications for universities, considering sustainability and usability. The final goal is to enable the creation of effective tools to support distance learning and distance teaching without overseeing the problems that may derive from digital overuse. In this paper, we presented a simple but important fact: the current state of public university websites in Italy and France is far from being sustainable. What is more alarming is that these websites are the access points to more complex Information Systems and not just stand-alone, self-standing informative showcases. As a matter of fact, no guidelines like the ones existing for informing website design exist yet for guiding the developers in creating sustainable complex Information Systems. In addition, finding parameters analyzing the usage of such complex entities for calculation is a rather challenging work requiring observation of actual usage. In our future work, we plan thus to address this issue with a socio-technical approach aimed at maintaining a high level of user experience with technology and interactive systems but without forgetting the importance of protecting the planet and the future of humanity.

References

1. Blevis, E.: Sustainable interaction design: invention & disposal, renewal & reuse. In: Proceedings of the SIGCHI Conference on Human Factors in Computing Systems, pp. 503–512. Association for Computing Machinery, New York (2007). https://doi.org/10.1145/1240624.1240705
2. Bordage, F.: Sobriété numérique: Les clés pour agir. Buchet Chastel (2019)
3. GCP: The Global Carbon Project. https://www.globalcarbonproject.org/ (Accessed 26 April 2023)
4. Greenwood, T.: Sustainable Web Design. A Book Apart (2021)
5. Hilty, L.M., Aebischer, B.: Ict for sustainability: an emerging research field. In: Hilty, L.M., Aebischer, B. (eds.) ICT Innovations for Sustainability, pp. 3–36. Springer International Publishing, Cham (2015). https://doi.org/10.1007/978-3-319-09228-7_1
6. Project TS: Lean ICT Towards Digital Sobriety. Tech. rep., The Shift Project (March 2019). https://theshiftproject.org/wp-content/uploads/2019/03/Lean-ICT-Report_The-Shift-Project_2019.pdf
7. Sandvine: The Global Internet Phenomena Report COVID-19 Spotlight. Tech. rep., Sandvine (May 2020). https://www.sandvine.com/covid-internet-spotlight-report
8. The Green Web Foundation. https://www.thegreenwebfoundation.org/ (Accessed 26 April 2023)
9. Website Carbon Calculator. https://www.websitecarbon.com/ (Accessed 26 April 2023)

Are You Okay? Development of Electronic Check-In Systems for Isolated Older Adults

Pallabi Bhowmick$^{(\boxtimes)}$ⓘ and Erik Stoltermanⓘ

Indiana University, Bloomington, IN 47405, USA
estolter@indiana.edu, estolter@iu.edu

Abstract. The COVID-19 pandemic has exacerbated an already prevailing issue of social isolation among older adults. The aging population is rapidly expanding, leading to an increasing numbers of older adults expressing feelings of social isolation. In this paper, we describe two low-cost physical check-in systems to help low-SES older adults check-in with their loved ones and peers. Both the check-in systems offer the same functionality, however one system is ready made and non-customizable, while the other system is a customizable version that offers more flexibility in design and can address ageism in technology design, help older adults. Such peer-based check-in systems can help older adults age-in-place, empower them to take care of one another, and help them maintain independence.

Keywords: older adult · social isolation · tangible user interface

1 Introduction

About one in four older adults in the US report concerns about feeling socially isolated [1]. According to one of the world's longest-running Harvard Longitudinal Study of Adult Development [2], has showed that cultivating a sense of community contributes to both longer and happier lives. The study highlights that developing and maintaining close and meaningful relationships is a crucial aspect of healthy aging [3]. The emergence of digital technologies has made communication more convenient, but these technologies are expensive, and often lack an intuitive and accessible interface for older adults, leading to a greater difficulty in learning and adapting to them [4,5]. Additionally, as individuals age, the skin develops fine wrinkles, rendering biometrics or tactile feedback less effective for this age group [6].

Furthermore, researchers have found that there are issues with non-adoption of technology among older adults and some common reasons include inaccessibility, usability issues, or high costs [5,7,8]. Older adults find technology more meaningful if they find value or personal relevance in using it [9,10] and have abandoned technologies that do not cater to their specific needs and sense of aesthetics [11]. Tangible user interfaces could provide more accessible systems leveraging

© The Author(s), under exclusive license to Springer Nature Switzerland AG 2023

J. Abdelnour Nocera et al. (Eds.): INTERACT 2023, LNCS 14145, pp. 418–422, 2023.
https://doi.org/10.1007/978-3-031-42293-5_46

(a) Check-in Tree   (b) Check-in Toolkit

Fig. 1. Check-in Toolkit

the use of existing competences and practices through common, familiar interfaces [5,7,12]. Researchers have investigated how to help older adults connect with each other to reduce social isolation by providing tangible electronic systems to check-in with loved ones through one-way [15] and two-way communication [16]. These electronic check-in systems were user-facing physical objects (e.g., a frame or tree) that were envisioned to be on display in one's home.

In this paper, we will discuss two tangible electronic check-in systems which can facilitate multiple users to check-in with each other via a bidirectional many-many connection. The first system is a peer-based, Check-in Tree [16] shown in Fig. 1a. The second system is a novel, peer-based Check-in Toolkit, shown in Fig. 1, that provides older adults with the ability to customize the physical enclosure. An old version of this Toolkit was introduced in a CHI'19 workshop position paper [14]. These novel systems offer relatively cheaper alternatives for a quick, daily check-in compared to digital systems and are developed to provide intuitive, familiar interfaces to facilitate easier integration and technology adoption. They would also help better understand if, when, and how older adults would like to *customize* their check-in processes.

2 System Overview

2.1 Check-In Tree

The Check-in Tree [16] is a peer-based check-in system tailored to the check-in needs of older adults. Older adults often use low-tech solutions of common real-life check-in systems (e.g., turning on/off the porch light) to indicate with neighbors that they have woken up. Neighbors will call if a friend has not indicated they woke up. This idea of morning check-in is replicated through the Check-in Tree prototype. The Tree design and specific features were fine-tuned to make it look more aesthetically pleasing based on feedback from three older adult consultants.

Ideally, each older adult in a neighborhood peer-group would have their own Check-in Tree. Each Check-in Tree would have a picture of everyone in their peer-group along with their own picture at the top, as shown in Fig. 1a. When an older adult gets up in the morning, he presses the button on the base of the Check-in Tree, the LED against his picture turns on, and the individual's status appears on the Check-in Trees of all of their peers. In case the LED does not turn on, then a neighborhood peer could check on their neighbor.

The Check-in Tree is made up of a custom wooden enclosure with a Raspberry Pi 3 stored in the base of the Tree. Each picture is lit up by an LED that is connected to the Raspberry Pi (RPi) via internal wiring through a breadboard. The RPi connects to a central server via a researcher provided internet connection from the older adult's home, as shown in Fig. 1a.

2.2   Check-In Toolkit

The Check-in Toolkit is a novel peer-based check-in system that simulates the functionality of the Check-in Tree and extends Craftec [13]. Craftec empowers older adults to explore electronic interactions by abstracting inputs and outputs on a Circuit Playground Express and associated input and output components. We utilized a Circuit Playground Bluefruit so that it can wirelessly communicate with the technical architecture. The built-in NeoPixel components can visually communicate older adults' availability based on colored lights similar to the Check-in Tree. External NeoPixels can be added to improve scalability. Figure 1 shows a single Toolkit. Multiple Toolkits can be similarly connected via the

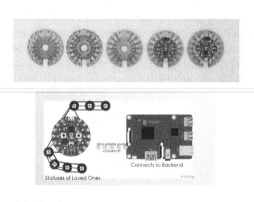

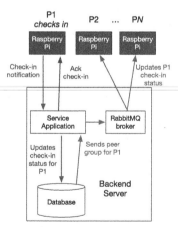

(a) (top) Step-wise development of the Check-in Toolkit's physical component and (bottom) Fritzing diagram indicating the Bluetooth connection between the Toolkit and the RPi and the potential for scalability of the system.

(b) Backend Architecture updating check-in status for Participant 1 (P1) for both Check-in Tree and Check-in Toolkit.

Fig. 2. Design and backend architecture of the Check-in Toolkit.

Internet. The Toolkit can be attached to any surface or sewn into any fabric, thereby eliminating rigidity in user interface design. Older adults can use the Check-in Toolkit to enhance any household items to communicate about check-ins or create an artifact that will blend right into their surroundings.

Included in this Toolkit is an Adafruit Circuit Playground Bluefruit with built-in RGB NeoPixels and a Raspberry Pi. The Circuit Playground Bluefruit is connected with a Raspberry Pi via the built-in Bluetooth for wireless communication and the RGB NeoPixels work as LED outputs. Every user in the peer group has one Toolkit and each NeoPixel indicates one participant. The Circuit Playground Bluefruit consists of magnetic connections built into the laser cut balsa wood bases to facilitate easier integration into everyday objects. Each pin on the electronic component is hand sewn with conductive thread to holes in the balsa wood bases that contain magnets. Insulated wires with jewelry clips attached to the ends touch the embedded magnets to allow connections to be easily made between the components. Figure 2a shows the step-wise development of the physical prototype. The bottom part of the figure contains the Fritzing diagram depicting that the RPi connects with the Toolkit via Bluetooth, and that several NeoPixels can be attached to the Toolkit for scalability i.e. the Check-in Toolkit can provide the flexibility to add more people to the peer group unlike the Check-in Tree.

2.3 Technical Architecture

Each electronic check-in system's Raspberry Pi connects to a backend server via the internet as shown in Fig. 2b. When an older adult checks in for the day, the Raspberry Pi sends the message to the backend server where the service application collects the peer-group data from the database and then forwards it to the RabbitMQ broker to notify all the members in the participant's peer-group about their check-in. The RabbitMQ broker utilizes a publish-subscribe protocol where all participants in a peer-group subscribe to the broker. RabbitMQ publishes received notifications from one participant to all subscribed participants in the peer-group simultaneously.

3   Conclusion

This paper discusses two low-cost check-in systems designed to examine their effectiveness in facilitating social connection among older adults. We aim to investigate the utility of offering an intuitive, familiar tangible user interface (Check-in Tree) as well as the ease with which older adults can choose their own preferred user interfaces (Check-in Toolkit). We have fully functional prototypes for both systems and they are ready for deployment. Our future plans involve conducting a field deployment study to compare the systems, aiming to understand user experiences and challenges faced during check-in. This study will inform potential design directions to address these challenges and enhance the effectiveness of check-in systems for older adults.

References

1. Vasold, J.B.K.: 2018 Home and Community Preferences: A National Survey of Adults Ages 18-Plus. AARP Research (August 2019). https://www.aarp.org/research/topics/community/info-2018/2018-home-community-preference.html (Accessed 7 April 2023)

2. Mitchell, J.F.: Aging well: surprising guideposts to a happier life from the landmark harvard study of adult development. Am. J. Psych. **161**(1), 178–179 (2004)

3. van den Berg, P., Sharmeen, F., Weijs-Perree, M.: On the subjective quality of social Interactions: influence of neighborhood walkability, social cohesion and mobility choic. Trans. Res. Part A: Policy Practice **106**, 309–319 (2017)

4. Neves, B.B., et al.: Can digital technology enhance social connectedness among older adults? A feasibility study. J. Appli. Gerontol. **38**(1), 49–72 (2019)

5. Joshi, S.G., Bråthen, H.: Lowering the threshold: reconnecting elderly users with assistive technology through tangible interfaces. In: Zhou, J., Salvendy, G. (eds.) ITAP 2016. LNCS, vol. 9754, pp. 52–63. Springer, Cham (2016). https://doi.org/10.1007/978-3-319-39943-0_6

6. Reedman, C.: Fingerprints and human inspection: a forensics perspective, pp. 221–230 (Jan 2013). https://doi.org/10.1049/PBSP010E_ch12 ISBN: 9781849195027

7. Spreicer, W.: Tangible interfaces as a chance for higher technology acceptance by the elderly. In: Proceedings of the 12th International Conference on Computer Systems and Technologies, vol. 2011, pp. 311–316 (2011)

8. Chu, C., Rebola, C.B., Kao, J.: BUMP: bridging unmet modes of participation. In: Proceedings of the 2015 British HCI Conference, pp. 261–262 (2015)

9. Mitzner, T.L., et al.: Older adults talk technology: technology usage and attitudes. Comput. Hum. Behav. **26**(6), 1710–1721 (2010)

10. Fausset, C.B., Harley, L., Farmer, S., Fain, B.: Older adults' perceptions and use of technology: a novel approach. In: Stephanidis, C., Antona, M. (eds.) UAHCI 2013. LNCS, vol. 8010, pp. 51–58. Springer, Heidelberg (2013). https://doi.org/10.1007/978-3-642-39191-0_6

11. Ballegaard, S.A., Bunde-Pedersen, J., Bardram, J.E.: Where to, Roberta? Reflecting on the role of technology in assisted living. In: Proceedings of the 4th Nordic Conference on Human-computer Interaction: Changing Roles, pp. 373–376 (2006)

12. Rebola, C.B., Jones, B.: Sympathetic devices: designing technologies for older adults. In: Proceedings of the 31st ACM International Conference on Design of Communication, pp. 151–156 (2013)

13. Jelen, B., et al.: Craftec: engaging Older Adults in Making through a Craft-Based Toolkit System. In: Proceedings of the Thirteenth International Conference on Tangible, Embedded, and Embodied Interaction, pp. 577–587 (2019)

14. Bhowmick, P., Nurain, N., Connelly, K., Siek, K.: Design and evaluation of electronic check-in systems for older adults. In: CHI Conference on Human Factors in Computing Systems: Workshop on Designing Interactions for the Ageing Populations - Addressing Global Challenges (2019)

15. Rowan, J., Mynatt, E.D.: Digital family portrait field trial: support for aging in place. In: Proceedings of the SIGCHI conference on Human factors in computing systems , pp. 521–530. ACM (2005)

16. Arreola, I., Morris, Z., Francisco, M., Connelly, K., Caine, K., White, G.: From checking on to checking in designing for low socio-economic status older adults. In: Proceedings of the SIGCHI Conference on Human Factors in Computing Systems, pp. 1933–1936. ACM (2014)

Availability for Work, Family, and Leisure: An Empirical Study

Tom Gross[✉] [iD]

Human-Computer Interaction Group, University of Bamberg, 96045 Bamberg, Germany
hci@uni-bamberg.de

Abstract. Mobile communication technologies increase users' connectivity, leading to higher accessibility of persons. Previous research has provided valuable tools for managing one's availability to other persons. However, how users would like to manage their availability within and across life domains—especially if they have domains beyond work and life—is still unclear. This paper presents the results of a multi-day experience sampling study. It contributes key findings on the general availability preferences within and across multiple life domains.

Keywords: Availability · Interruption · Boundary Management · Experience Sampling Study

1 Introduction

The progress in mobile information and communication technology allows users to reach for information and other users at any time and any place [21]. This increased connectivity is a mixed blessing—users applaud and complain about new opportunities smartphones provide [25]. With connectivity and the opportunity for mutual information and contact comes the challenge that users might interrupt each other in ongoing tasks at inopportune moments, which can lead to distraction with negative consequences on the individuals' performances [11].

In the last few decades, connectivity and related to it the interruptions caused and the resulting need to manage one's availability for each other has triggered significant research in human-computer interaction [e.g., 12, 13, 18, 23].

Empirical research has looked at users' preferences for availability for each other. A significant body of work has studied the users' organisation of life domains and strategies to integrate or segment life domains [1, 4, 16, 19]. Some research here has been specifically looking into the role of mobile technology and its impact on the success of the implementation of one's boundary management [7]. However, to the best of our knowledge, this research mainly focuses on a binary distinction between work and non-work (where non-work sometimes is plainly non-work [16], sometimes home [19], sometimes life [8], sometimes family [4], etc.). While the notion of work seems clearly delineated, the non-work side is not.

© The Author(s), under exclusive license to Springer Nature Switzerland AG 2023
J. Abdelnour Nocera et al. (Eds.): INTERACT 2023, LNCS 14145, pp. 423–428, 2023.
https://doi.org/10.1007/978-3-031-42293-5_47

This paper's research question is two-fold: Is there a difference between the non-work family domain versus the non-work leisure domain? And is there a difference between general within-domain and cross-domain availability across multiple domains?

The contributions are threefold: The paper introduces a distinction between work, family, and leisure, beyond the usual dichotomy of work and life. The paper presents the results of an experience study of boundary management across those three life domains. The paper analyses the impact of the study on the participants' attitudes towards their preferred and actual availability preferences before and after the study.

2   Background and Related Work

The research on boundary management has been looking at life domains and how individuals manage the integration, segmentation, and transition between them [1]. Life domains often emerge within mental and physical boundaries and include persons, things, and parts of the self (e.g., work or family) [19]. We distinguish within-domain interruptions from contacts in the same life domain from cross-domain interruptions from contacts in other life domains [1]. From the literature, it is well established that individuals differ in their preference for either allowing more cross-domain interruptions (i.e., integrating life domains) or allowing little cross-domain interruptions (e.g., segmenting life domains) [3, 17, 24].

The experience sampling method asks users in-situ about their current situation and subjective aspects [5]. Due to its high ecological validity, it is also known as ecological momentary assessment [2, 14]. Asking users in-situ gathers their answers while they experience emotions allows us to minimise the recall bias that can lead to distorted reports on emotions in hindsight [14]. The ESM has proved to be a method with excellent validity and short-term and long-term reliability—especially when dealing with empirical data on frequencies and patterns of social interaction [5].

3   Method

We conducted a five-day experience sampling study on availability preferences within and across life domains. Nineteen persons (8 female, 11 male, 0 diverse) with an age ranged from 19 to 64 years ($M = 45.32, SD = 14.71$) were invited to the study and a lottery for a voucher of 30 euros for an online bookstore. The measures of our multi-level study combined pre- and poststudy questionnaires and momentary questionnaires [27]. The pre- and poststudy questionnaires addressed the preferred and actual segmentation of life domains [17, 20, 22]. The momentary questionnaires targeted the situative within- and cross-domain availability. They included questions about the current life domain (work, family, or leisure) and the respective availability for the life domains (work, family, or leisure). So, this implicitly included the cross-domain as well as the within-domain availability. The questions were asked and answered utilising SensQKit—a toolkit for context-aware sensing and questioning for iOS devices, which was developed with Swift in XCode on macOS.

The briefings took place before the ESM study in the participants' workplaces. The participants received information on the study, signed the informed consent form, and filled in a questionnaire with demographic data. They could then start the SensQKit app and receive a notification that the prestudy questionnaire is ready to be filled in. Afterwards, the ESM study with the momentary questionnaires ran for five days and included at least one day on the weekend. During each day, participants received ten momentary questionnaires randomly within 90 min. At the end of the last day, they received the poststudy questionnaires.

As far as the data analysis [5, 9, 10] is concerned, we checked for the normality of the data and performed the respective calculations (mostly ANOVAs and t-tests). Bonferroni-corrected pairwise comparisons complemented the ANOVAs where appropriate. Planned contrasts were applied for stepwise comparisons of within-domain versus cross-domain [9]. Kendall's tau was used as a rank correlation coefficient for non-parametric data. z-scores were used internally to double-check and calibrate individual differences between participants [5].

4 Results

We report on the pre- and poststudy as well as the momentary results.

Pre- and Poststudy Results. All participants completed the prestudy questionnaire and answered all questions. Fifteen participants completed their poststudy questionnaire and answered all questions.

When comparing the answers *before and after the ESM study*, we find that the prestudy and poststudy work-life segmentation preferences were similar, and so were the prestudy and poststudy life-work segmentation preferences. However, the actual work-life segmentation decreased during the study. Before the study, ca. 21% (i.e., 4 out of 19 participants) strongly wanted segmentation, while after the study, ca. 53% (i.e., 8 out of 15).

The prestudy mean *preference for the segmentation of work from life* was higher ($M = 4.16$, $SD = 1.50$) than that of life from work ($M = 3.80$, $SD = 1.21$). Also, the poststudy mean preference for the segmentation of work from life was higher ($M = 4.27$, $SD = 1.28$) than that of life from work ($M = 3.73$, $SD = 1.54$). However, paired samples t-tests between the two prestudy preferences, between the two poststudy preferences, and between each prestudy and poststudy preferences respectively, were not significant.

The prestudy mean *actual segmentation of work from life* was lower ($M = 3.42$, $SD = 2.04$) than that of life from work ($M = 4.53$, $SD = 1.54$). The poststudy mean for the actual segmentation of work from life was considerably lower ($M = 2.40$, $SD = 1.81$) than that of life from work ($M = 5.00$, $SD = 1.56$). The paired samples' t-tests between the poststudy actual segmentation of life from work and work from life were significant ($t = -3.89$, $p < 0.05$). The other paired samples' t-tests were not significant.

Momentary Results. We received 689 filled-in momentary questionnaires (i.e., 72.53% of the 950 distributed questionnaires). Thirteen participants sampled for five days, and six participants for four days, which was acceptable. The sample size, the number of days, and the number of samples per day compare well to other ESM studies [26].

Looking at the current domain of the participants, we see that the overall mean availability was highest when in the domain work ($M = 0.76$, $SD = 0.35$) and lowest when in the domain leisure ($M = 0.56$, $SD = 0.38$), and between them when in the domain family ($M = 0.62$, $SD = 0.42$).

Table 1 shows the overall mean availability in the totals row and the details for the mean availability of each current domain for each contacter's domain. The high within-domain availability is clearly visible—especially the availability for the domain work while in the domain work was almost 100% ($M = 0.96$, $SD = 0.06$) and a range from 0.77 to 1.0; and also the availability for the domain family in the domain family was very high ($M = 0.97$, $SD = 0.04$) and a range from 0.86 to 1.0.

Table 1. Availability from current domains to contacters' domains

Contacter's domain: i.e. availability for…	Current Domain							
	Work		Family		Leisure		Total	
	M	*SD*	*M*	*SD*	*M*	*SD*	*M*	*SD*
…Work	.96	.06	.12	.23	.10	.21	.45	.45
…Family	.85	.26	.97	.04	.78	.19	.87	.21
…Leisure	.46	.40	.78	.26	.79	.20	.65	.35
Total	.76	.35	.62	.42	.56	.38	.66	.39

5   Discussion and Conclusions

The findings from the pre- and poststudy questionnaires on preferred and actual integration and segmentation between life domains hint at some interesting points. The results corroborate the findings from previous studies that the preference for the work-life segmentation was higher than for the life-work segmentation. That is, people were less interruptible for work while at home, but were more interruptible for family while at work [6, 16].

The general availability per current domain was highest in the domain work. Extremely high within-domain availability for work of 96%, but also high cross-domain availability for the family of 85% contribute to that. Also, the availability for family was typically high while at work. Other studies have shown that the expectations of superiors and peers often entail a high availability for work [15].

An interesting distinction between family and leisure is the following: within-domain availability in work and family was almost 100%, while in leisure it was 79%. This could be because participants have some hobbies they do not want to and cannot be disturbed (not even by family), such as while doing intense sports (e.g., mountain biking, swimming). To the best of our knowledge, gender differences have not yet been addressed in ESM studies.

Acknowledgements. We thank the members of the Cooperative Media Lab at the University of Bamberg.

References

1. Ashforth, B.E., Kreiner, G.E., Fugate, M.: All in a day's work: boundaries and micro role transitions. Acad. Manag. Rev. **25**(3), 472–491 (2000)
2. Batalas, N., Het Rot, M.A., Khan, V.-J., Markopoulos, P.: Using TEMPEST: end-user programming of web-based ecological momentary assessment protocols. In: EICS, pp. 2–24 (2018)
3. Battard, N., Mangematin, V.: Idiosyncratic distances: impact of mobile technology practices on role segmentation and integration. Technol. Forecast. Soc. Chang. **80**, 2 (2013)
4. Campbell Clark, S.: Work/family border theory: a new theory of work/family balance. Human Relat. **53**(6), 747–770 (2000)
5. Csikszentmihalyi, M., Hunter, J.: Happiness in everyday life: the uses of experience sampling. In Csikszentmihalyi, M. (ed.) Flow and the Foundations of Positive Psychology, pp. 89–101 (2014)
6. Derks, D., Bakker, A.B., Gorgievski, M.: Private smartphone use during worktime. Comput. Human Behav. **114**, 10653 (2021)
7. Duxbury, L., Higgins, C., Smart, R., Stevenson, M.: Mobile technology and boundary permeability. Br. J. Manag. **25**, 570–588 (2014)
8. Duxbury, L., Smart, R.: The 'Myth of Separate Worlds': an exploration of how mobile technology has redefined work-life balance. In: Creating Balance?, pp. 269–284 (2011)
9. Field, A.: Discovering Statistics Using SPSS. Sage Publications Ltd., London (2009)
10. Hektner, J.M., Csikszentmihalyi, M., Schmidt, J.A.: Experience sampling method: measuring the quality of everyday life (2006)
11. Hudson, S.E., Smith, I.: Techniques for addressing fundamental privacy and disruption tradeoffs in awareness support systems. In: CSCW 1996, pp. 248–257 (1996)
12. Iqbal, S., Horvitz, E.: Disruption and recovery of computing tasks: field study, analysis, and directions. In: CHI 2007, pp. 677–686 (2007)
13. Jett, Q.R., George, J.M.: Work interrupted: a closer look at the role of interruptions in organisational life. Acad. Manag. Rev. **28**(3), 494–507 (2003)
14. Kahneman, D., Krueger, A.B., Schkade, D.A., Schwarz, N., Stone, A.A.: A survey method for characterising daily life experience. Science **306**, 1776–1780 (2004)
15. Koch, A.R., Binnewies, C.: Supervisors as work-life-friendly role models within the context of boundary management. Occup. Health Psychol. **20**(1), 82–92 (2015)
16. Kossek, E.E., Ruderman, M.N., Braddy, P.W., Hannum, K.M.: Work-nonwork boundary management profiles: a person-centred approach. Vocat. Behav. **81**, 112–128 (2012)
17. Kreiner, G.E.: Consequences of work-home segmentation and integration: a person-environment fit perspective. Organ. Behav. **27**(4), 485–507 (2006)
18. McFarlane, D.C., Latorella, K.A.: The scope and importance of human interruption in human-computer interaction design. Human-Comput. Interact. **17**(1), 1–61 (2002)
19. Nippert-Eng, C.: Home and Work: Negotiating Boundaries through Everyday Life. University of Chicago Press, Chicago (1996)
20. Park, Y., Jex, S.M.: Work-Home boundary management using communication and information technology. Int. Stress Manag. **18**(2), 133–152 (2011)
21. Perry, M., O'Hara, K., Sellen, A., Brown, B., Harper, R.: Dealing with mobility. ACM Trans. Comput.-Human Interact. **8**(4), 323–347 (2001)
22. Powell, G.N., Greenhaus, J.H.: Sex, gender, and the work-to-family interface. Acad. Manag. J. **53**(3), 513–534 (2010)
23. Ritter, F.E., Baxter, G.D., Churchill, E.F.: Foundations for designing user-centred systems: what system designers need to know about people (2014)

24. Rothbard, N.P., Philipps, K.W., Dumas, T.: Managing multiple roles: work-family policies and individuals' desires for segmentation. Organ. Sci. **16**(3), 243–258 (2005)
25. Trieu, P., Bayer, J.B., Ellison, N.B., Schoenebeck, S., Falk, E.: Who likes to be reachable? Inf. Commun. Soc. **22**(8), 1096–1111 (2019)
26. Van Berkel, N., Ferreira, D., Kostakos, V.: The experience sampling method on mobile devices. ACM Comput. Surv. **50**(6), 93:1-93:40 (2017)
27. Williams, K.J., Alliger, G.M.: Role stressors, mood spillover, and perceptions of work-family conflict in employed parents. Acad. Manag. **37**(4), 837–868 (1994)

Better Real-Life Space Utilization in VR Through a Multimodal Guardian Alternative

Jonas Lind, Kristian Sørensen, Arlonsompoon Lind, Mads Sørensen, Jakob Trærup, and Ivan Nikolov[✉]

Aalborg University, CREATE, Rendsburggade 14, Aalborg, Denmark
{jbl20,ksaren20,alind19,mwsa17,jtraru19}@student.aau.dk,
iani@create.aau.dk

Abstract. Space utilization and better exploration are important parts when building VR experiences that can be used by people with different play styles, requirements, and needs. A key factor in achieving this is a flexible guardian system that informs users about their position and potential hazards. We propose an alternative guardian solution that incorporates various modalities, notification types, diegetic and non-diegetic interfaces, which demonstrated improved space utilization and mobility compared to a standard system. However, this alternative solution may come with a higher cognitive load. We believe this system demonstrates that a better more immersive alternative to the Guardian solution is possible, which would maximize the utilized real-world space while adding better immersion. We plan to use this initial research as a basis for developing more robust versions, utilizing different combinations of the proposed features.

Keywords: VR · Space utilization · Diegetics · Guardian · Exploration

1 Introduction

Virtual reality (VR) is a rapidly expanding research field that spans entertainment, design, training, and mental health treatment. However, the nature of VR headsets, which isolate users from the real world, requires methods to orient them and prevent injury or environmental damage. Research has explored solutions such as integrating real-world elements and alerting users to potential dangers, but these often require additional non-standard hardware [2–5]. Although these methods provide high levels of immersion, they have the drawback of requiring

---

J. Lind, K. Sørensen, A. Lind and M. Sørensen: These authors contributed equally to this work.

Supplementary Information The online version contains supplementary material available at https://doi.org/10.1007/978-3-031-42293-5_48.

© The Author(s), under exclusive license to Springer Nature Switzerland AG 2023
J. Abdelnour Nocera et al. (Eds.): INTERACT 2023, LNCS 14145, pp. 429–433, 2023.
https://doi.org/10.1007/978-3-031-42293-5_48

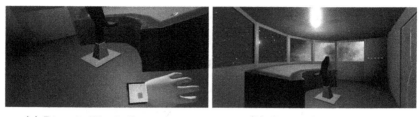

(a) Diegetic Watch Component   (b) Escape Room Puzzle

Fig. 1. An example proposed guardian component - a diegetic pull visual notification in the form of a watch for self-positioning (Fig. 1a) and a room from the space-themed escape room used to test the proposed solution (Fig. 1b).

non-standard hardware. Conversely, the Meta Quest2 VR headset includes a built-in solution called the VR guardian, which is lightweight and easy to use but may disrupt immersion by showing real-world borders when users get too close.

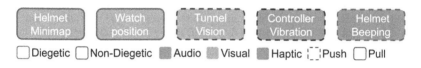

Fig. 2. Components of the proposed VR guardian alternative. The five components are a combination of diegetic and non-diegetic interfaces, push and pull notifications and visual, audio and haptic modalities.

Our paper introduces a novel system that combines diegetic and non-diegetic methods with push and pull notifications of various modalities. We draw on previous research by Medeiros et al. [1] and Kanamori et al. [6], which shows that users prefer multiple types of guidance to help them navigate VR environments. Our solution not only enhances playspace utilization and different playstyles but also minimizes immersion-breaking visuals. We evaluate our system through an interactive virtual escape room that requires users to explore the environment and approach the play borders. Our results demonstrate that our approach provides better real-world space utilization than the Meta VR guardian, although some tradeoffs in usability and straightforwardness are observed. The different components of our system can be used in various VR scenarios, such as education, training, architecture, and gaming.

2   System Design

We have selected five components to build our guardian alternative solution, representing different modalities (audio, visual, or haptic), diegetic or non-diegetic interfaces, and push or pull notifications. The diegetic interfaces were designed to promote immersion in a space station scenario. These components can be viewed in Fig. 2. We selected three modalities to complement each other and assist users, regardless of their sensory state. The push and pull notifications were chosen to suit different play styles and immersion preferences, enabling users to either focus on other tasks or check their location if they feel disoriented. Lastly, non-diegetic components were chosen as last-minute push notifications designed to fully capture users' attention and prevent them from going out of bounds. An example of the diegetic watch component is shown in Fig. 1a.

To test the guardian components, a virtual reality escape room with a space station theme was created. The rooms are separate square spaces, the same size as the physical playfield, connected by long narrow hallways. This design forces users to move around the playfield, reach the borders, and interact with the guardian components. An example of one of the rooms can be seen in Fig. 1b.

3   Experiments and Results

A comparison was conducted between the developed guardian feature (DGF) and the Quest 2 guardian or standard guardian feature (SGF) to determine how the proposed components would impact users' space utilization and exploration in VR. The experiment had 30 participants, with 15 for both tests, who had time to get used to both guardian features before playing through the experience with a 15-minute timer. Users walked in a 4 by 4-meter physical space and could manually turn once they reached a boundary. The X and Y position of the users was captured using their head-mounted display, along with the overall completion time, and a heat map was generated based on the captured positions (Fig. 3). The heat maps revealed that the DGF users utilized 9.33% more of the total play area compared to SGF users. In addition, single red point "clusters" representing users standing in one location were less prevalent and more spread out in the DGF test, indicating that users were more likely to explore rather than stay in one place. DGF participants took 23.9% more time to go through the escape room, which can be attributed to both longer exploration and more interaction with the guardian.

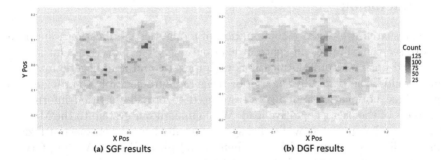

(a) SGF results   (b) DGF results

Fig. 3. Heat maps generated from user physical space utilization. The Meta VR guardian or standard guardian feature (SGF) results are shown in Fig. 3a, while our proposed developed guardian features (DGF) are shown in Fig. 3b.

After the experiment, users were asked to evaluate their experience with the system they used, through the Raw Nasa TLX [7]. Users reported that they felt they needed to do more work overall using the DGF system, resulting in a higher physical and mental load (Fig. 4a). This could be because users had to manually bring up DGF solution, forcing them to actively think about their position instead of using the passive approach of the SGF Meta guardian. However, users also reported that they needed to use the DGF system less, indicating that the system helped orient them better (Fig. 4b). The participants then filled in a System Usability Scale test, with the SGF achieving a score of 73.5 and the DGF only scoring 51.7 points. This suggests that more work is needed to optimize and combine the proposed diegetic and non-diegetic guardian features. The DGF system activation time was overall comparable to the SGF, but it had a larger deviation in user responses as seen in Fig. 4c. Therefore, fine-tuning when and how the different components are initialized and creating cascades of warning depending on user proximity would be necessary to improve the system.

(a)   (b)   (c)

Fig. 4. Results from the Raw Nasa TLX. The DGF system required more involvement from users, because of the presence of both push and pull notifications (Fig. 4a), while also requiring less overall interaction than the SGF solution (Fig. 4b). The two systems have comparable activation time, with the DGF showing a larger deviation (Fig. 4c).

4   Conclusion

In this research, we tested a combination of modalities, notifications, and interfaces to see their impact on space utilization and VR exploration. Our solution integrated push and pull notifications with diegetic and non-diegetic interfaces, which could be activated by the user or triggered automatically to provide warnings. Three notification modalities were used to provide location information, regardless of the user's cognitive load. We compared our system to the Meta VR guardian and found that while our system resulted in higher space utilization and mobility, users reported higher mental and physical load. Moving forward, we aim to optimize and refine our system to improve its effectiveness. To do this we will focus on an iterative user testing methodology where we will create different combinations of components based on the visual, audio, and haptic modalities. We test the usability and any perceived problems by users through a series of Rapid Iterative Testing and Evaluations (RITE). We will look at use cases for training personnel in specified 3D spaces, where work area utilization is required, as well as for educational purposes for creating escape rooms utilizing larger spaces and boosting user teamwork.

References

1. Medeiros, D., et al.: Promoting reality awareness in virtual reality through proxemics. In: 2021 IEEE Virtual Reality and 3D User Interfaces (VR), pp. 21–30 (2021)
2. Saker, M., Frith, J.: Coextensive space: virtual reality and the developing relationship between the body, the digital and physical space. Media, Culture Soc. **42**(7–8), 1427–1442 (2020)
3. Faltaous, S., Neuwirth, J., Gruenefeld, U., Schneegass, S.: SaVR: increasing safety in virtual reality environments via electrical muscle stimulation. In: Proceedings of the 19th International Conference on Mobile and Ubiquitous Multimedia, pp. 254–258 (November 2020)
4. Valentini, I., Ballestin, G., Bassano, C., Solari, F., Chessa, M.: Improving obstacle awareness to enhance interaction in virtual reality. In: 2020 IEEE Conference on Virtual Reality and 3D User Interfaces (VR), pp. 44–52. IEEE (March 2020)
5. Hartmann, J., Holz, C., Ofek, E., Wilson, A.D:. Realitycheck: blending virtual environments with situated physical reality. In: Proceedings of the 2019 CHI Conference on Human Factors in Computing Systems, pp. 1–12 (May 2019)
6. Kanamori, K., Sakata, N., Tominaga, T., Hijikata, Y., Harada, K., Kiyokawa, K.: Obstacle avoidance method in real space for virtual reality immersion. In: 2018 IEEE International Symposium on Mixed and Augmented Reality (ISMAR), pp. 80–89 (2018)
7. Hart, S.G., Staveland, L.E.: Development of NASA-TLX (task load index): results of empirical and theoretical research. Adv. Psychol. **52**, 139–183 (1988)

Building Teamwork: Mixed Reality Game for Developing Trust and Communication

Kristian Jespersen, Kristian Julsgaard⬤, Jens Lakmann Madsbøll⬤,
Mathias Øgaard Niebuhr⬤, Marcus Høyen Lundbak⬤, Rasmus Odgaard⬤,
and Ivan Nikolov$^{(\boxtimes)}$⬤

Faculty of Design, Architecture and Media Technology, Aalborg University,
Aalborg, Denmark
{knje21,kjulsg21,jmadsb21,mobn21,marlun21,rodgaa21}@student.aau.dk,
iani@create.aau.dk

Abstract. Cultivating teamwork and a sense of empathy is an important part of boosting productivity and student and employee satisfaction and well-being. We present the initial development of a mixed-reality game using a LEGO block digitization system. Two participants collaborate, with one in real life and the other in VR. Our initial results indicate a positive impact on empathy and user involvement. Moving forward, we aim to create various teamwork experiences using different VR interactions with digitized LEGO builds both for children's educational purposes and adult teamwork.

Keywords: VR · teamwork · 3D digitization · LEGO blocks · communication

1 Introduction and Motivation

Team building is a valuable tool in increasing the outcome of group-based tasks and bettering the psychological climate of those involved [5, 7]. While most team-building exercises are physical, virtual counterparts such as cooperative games [3] and XR applications [1] have shown similar effects, increasing motivation and educational outcomes [6]. This paper presents a VR application for cooperative team building through 3D digitization, which is the act of converting information into a virtual space [2, 8]. We use computer vision to digitize LEGO blocks, as they are easy to use and understand, and their color and shape are standardized, making them easier to digitize.

2 3D Digitization Application

To digitize the LEGO blocks we create a Python application using a downward-facing webcam and a designated building area. For detecting and segmenting

Supplementary Information The online version contains supplementary material available at https://doi.org/10.1007/978-3-031-42293-5_49.

© The Author(s), under exclusive license to Springer Nature Switzerland AG 2023
J. Abdelnour Nocera et al. (Eds.): INTERACT 2023, LNCS 14145, pp. 434–438, 2023.
https://doi.org/10.1007/978-3-031-42293-5_49

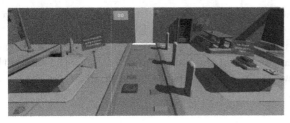

(a) View of a VR level   (b) User collaboration

Fig. 1. Figure 1a is a view from one of the puzzle rooms. The table on the right is what the VR player sees, while the table on the left is where the digitized brick shape made by the builder in the real world is shown. Figure 1b shows a sketch of the testing setup with the example interactions between the builder and VR player.

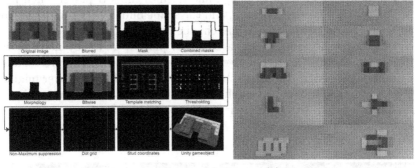

(a) Testing setup   (b) Lego brick puzzles

Fig. 2. Overview of the 3D digitizing pipeline for LEGO blocks (Fig. 1b), together with some of the brick puzzles that need to be solved (Fig. 2b)

LEGO blocks we use several image processing steps demonstrated in Fig. 2a. The main steps start with pre-processing the images by blurring them and transforming them to an HSV color space and then using color segmentation. To simplify and constrain the process of color segmentation we have selected three different colored LEGO blocks. We segment blocks from different colors and morphologically process them to remove noise and holes. Studs from the segmented LEGO blocks are then detected using template matching and the duplicate detections are removed with non-maximum suppression. The X and Y coordinates of the studs are then captured and using prior information about the size of the LEGO blocks we estimate the Z coordinate. These coordinates are then sent to Unity and a 3D stud of the specific color is created at these positions.

3   Evaluation

We evaluate the proposed team-building mixed-reality game using the Game Experience Questionnaire (GEQ) [4]. As this is a proof-of-concept application and we are interested in the social interactions and teamwork between players we focus on the Social-Presence module of GEQ (GEQ-SP).

The test is conducted with 9 pairs of people, 18 participants in total. In each pair, one participant is given the role of the builder and the other the role of the VR player. Each team of two is given 15 min to go through 10 rooms.

3.1 Game Overview

Figure 1b shows a sketch of the setup, with each room offering a teamwork puzzle of increasing difficulty. In each puzzle, the VR player is presented with a table and LEGO bricks arranged in a certain shape (Fig. 2b). They need to communicate the position, shape, and color of the figure to the builder, who is sitting in front of the digitizing setup with access to various bricks and a building space. The builder recreates the shape and notifies the VR player when ready. The VR player then presses a button, and the shape built by the builder is shown in the virtual world. If the shapes match, the puzzle is complete, and they can proceed to the next room. If not, a sound is played, and they need to work together to fix any mistakes. The two participants in each group are separated by an additional barrier, to remove the possibility that the VR player might see the Lego brick structure and to emphasize the necessity of oral communication. Each room is created with a different background to make the experience more varied and interesting. An overhead view of the rooms can be seen in Fig. 3.

Fig. 3. The ten different puzzle rooms built for the teamwork game seen from above. Each room has a different theme to keep the players engaged

3.2 Results Analysis

After the teamwork game, the builder and VR player receive the GEQ-SP module, which is then separated into three main categories - empathy (GEQ-E), negative feelings (GEQ-NF), and behavioral involvement (GEQ-BI). Table 1 shows the average score for each category for both types of participants. The scores indicate that both builders and VR players showed high levels of empathy and behavioral involvement, and their scores were similar. The negative feelings category had a below-average score, indicating that participants did not have a negative experience. Notably, VR players had higher GEQ-NF scores, likely due to their inability to directly influence the building process.

Table 1. Average empathy (GEQ-E), negative feelings (GEQ-NF), and behavioral involvement (GEQ-BI) scores, together with the maximum possible scores. The maximum possible score for GEQ-NF is smaller, as it has only 5 questions, compared to 6 for the other two categories.

Participant Type	GEQ-E	GEQ-NF	GEQ-BI
Builder	24.8/30	11.6/25	25.2/30
VR Player	23.4/30	12.3/25	26/30

The results for each of the categories for the builders and VR players can be visually compared through the bar plots in Fig. 4. We can see that the scores are closely related, especially for the GEQ-E, while the GEQ-BI shows larger differences for three of the groups. We calculated Pearson's correlation between the scores of each category to examine any correlation between the experiences of both types of participants. The correlation coefficient for GEQ-E scores is 0.733, for GEQ-NF is 0.234, and for GEQ-BI is -0.702. This indicates a strong positive correlation between the empathy experiences of both types of participants, a strong negative correlation between their behavioral involvement, and a much weaker correlation between negative feelings.

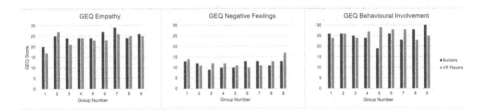

Fig. 4. The GEQ-E, GEQ-NF and GEQ-BI scores for each pair of builder and VR player

4   Conclusion

This initial development of a teamwork-based game showcases how digitization and mixed reality can foster teamwork, empathy, and interaction between players in both real and digital worlds. The developed digitization system gives a straightforward and easy way to generate digitized renderings of different LEGO block figures and objects. Next, we aim to create various collaboration scenarios and games, including level building, climbing, defeating enemies, and orientation, to gauge immersion, empathy, and willingness to collaborate on a larger scale. The straightforward nature of the proposed system and collaboration game can be useful to other researchers as a test bed and starting point for testing collaboration between real life and VR.

References

1. Bekele, M.K., Champion, E.: A comparison of immersive realities and inter- action methods: cultural learning in virtual heritage. Front. Rob. AI **6**, 91 (2019)
2. Bloomberg, J.: Digitization, digitalization, and digital transformation: con- fuse them at your peril. Forbes (2018). Accessed 28 Aug 2019
3. Ellis, J.B., Luther, K., Bessiere, K., Kellogg, W.A.: Games for virtual team building. In: Proceedings of the 7th ACM Conference on Designing Interactive Systems, DIS 2008, pp. 295–304. Association for Computing Machinery, New York (2008). https://doi.org/10.1145/1394445.1394477
4. IJsselsteijn, W.A., De Kort, Y.A., Poels, K.: The game experience questionnaire (2013)
5. Keith, M.J., Anderson, G., Gaskin, J., Dean, D.L.: Team video gaming for team building: effects on team performance. AIS Trans. Human-Comput. Interact. **10**(4), 205–231 (2018)
6. Mulders, M., Buchner, J., Kerres, M.: A framework for the use of immersive virtual reality in learning environments. Int. J. Emerg. Technol. Learn. (iJET) **15**(24), 208–224 (2020)
7. Omollo, P.A., Oloko, M.: Effect of motivation on employee performance of commercial banks in Kenya: a case study of Kenya commercial bank in migori county. Int. J. Human Res. Stud. **5**(2), 87–103 (2015)
8. Remondino, F., Menna, F., Koutsoudis, A., Chamzas, C., El-Hakim, S.: Design and implement a reality-based 3d digitisation and modelling project. In: 2013 Digital Heritage International Congress (DigitalHeritage), vol. 1, pp. 137–144 (2013). https://doi.org/10.1109/DigitalHeritage.2013.6743723

Coding with Colors: Children's Errors Committed While Programming Robotito for the First Time

Ewelina Bakala[1(✉)], Ana C. Pires[2], Mariana da Luz[3], María Pascale[3], Gonzalo Tejera[1], and Juan Pablo Hourcade[4]

[1] INCO, Universidad de la República, Montevideo, Uruguay
ebakala@fing.edu.uy
[2] Interactive Technologies Institute, Universidade de Lisboa, Lisbon, Portugal
[3] EUCD, Universidad de la República, Montevideo, Uruguay
[4] University of Iowa, Iowa City, USA

Abstract. Robotito is an educational robot developed in Uruguay to stimulate the development of computational thinking in young children. We conducted an exploratory study to detect difficulties that emerge during the first approximation of preschool children to Robotito (Study 1). Based on the lessons learned, we implemented improvements in robot design and the structure of the introductory activities with Robotito and conducted a pilot study (Study 2) to evaluate them. This poster presents observed programming errors, lessons learned, and future works.

Keywords: Child-robot interaction · Preschoolers · Educational robotics

1 Introduction

Robotito is an educational robot developed at the Facultad de Ingeniería of Universidad de la República, Uruguay, with the goal of introducing young children to programming and fostering their computational thinking (CT) skills [1,3]. The robot's programming is based on the placement of color cards on the floor, with each color representing a specific movement: yellow for forward[1], red for left, blue for backward, green for right, and purple for spin. Unlike other commercial robots, Robotito is omnidirectional, meaning it can move in any direction without turning. To aid children in programming and understanding the robot's movements, a LED ring on the top of the robot indicates the associated color for each direction and shows the current direction of movement (see Fig. 1). These light indicators serve as the only color-direction reference for selecting the appropriate color card to move the robot in a specific direction.

---

[1] Robotito has no face or front, so the relation to directions "forward", "backward", "left" and "right" are used only to distinguish its four predefined directions.

© The Author(s), under exclusive license to Springer Nature Switzerland AG 2023
J. Abdelnour Nocera et al. (Eds.): INTERACT 2023, LNCS 14145, pp. 439–443, 2023.
https://doi.org/10.1007/978-3-031-42293-5_50

In order to enhance the interaction between children and Robotito, as well as facilitate the development of CT activities, we conducted two exploratory studies in 2022 to identify potential difficulties that may arise during children's interaction with the robot. The purpose of these studies was to develop effective strategies to mitigate these challenges. In this poster, we present the outcomes and findings from these studies.

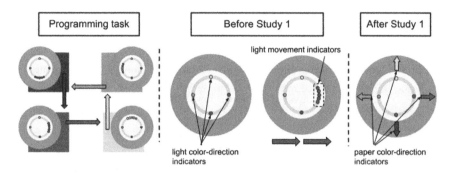

Fig. 1. Programming task and Robotito's direction indicators before and after Study 1.

2   Methodology

We conducted two field studies involving a total of ten 5–6-year-old children (Study 1 with 4 girls and 4 boys, Study 2 with 2 boys). The initial exploratory study aimed to identify errors made by children during robot programming and opportunities for improving the robot's design and presentation to children. Subsequently, we conducted a pilot study (Study 2) to evaluate improvements in the presentation format in individual instances.

For Study 1, we collaborated with a public kindergarten in Montevideo, Uruguay, where eight children participated. The classroom teacher divided them into four pairs. The first child in each pair interacted with the robot, learned about the color codes, and engaged in solving a programming task. The objective was to program the robot to follow a square-shaped route ("draw a square"), accomplished by placing four color codes on the floor (see Fig. 1). Afterward, the second child joined the activity and received instructions from the first child through peer tutoring (peer tutoring [2]) on using the robot and solving the same programming task.

In Study 2, we individually explained the programming process to children using color codes on the floor, following points 1 to 6 from a structured presentation developed based on the insights from the first study (see the 3 section).

Both sessions were video recorded and analyzed by three researchers, focusing on the common errors committed by the children (Study 1 and 2) and the explanations given by the child tutors during peer tutoring (Study 1).

The study protocol received approval from the ethics board of the principal institution, and we obtained informed consent from the parents or caregivers of the participating children, ensuring diligence in ethical considerations.

3 Results

In Study 1, we identified various aspects to improve related to the observed programming errors, peer tutoring, activity structure, and robot design.

Programming Errors. We identified five types of errors that the children committed while programming the robot. The main cause of programming errors was a lack of understanding of the light-direction relationship that is essential to program the robot. Three error categories reflected it. **"Memorized color-direction relationship"** (MCD, 2/10 children) was used to tag situations in which the children associated a color with one specific direction in the space (for example, green - child's forward) and ignored the fact that the direction associated with the color will change in reference to the child's position after rotating the robot.

We tagged as **"repeated the lights distribution"** (RLD, 3/10) events in which children tried to solve the "draw a square" task by placing the cards mimicking the same distribution as the lights on the robot.

Additionally, we observed that the children frequently wrongly predicted the direction the robot would take after sensing a specific color card or pointed wrong color when asked, "what color should we use to make Robotito move THAT direction" and codified these errors as **"wrong color/direction prediction"** (WRP, 6/10). Some children did not understand the "draw a square" task, and we codified errors related to this fact as **"no task comprehension"** (NTC, 2/10).

"Wrong coding card position" (WCP, 6/10) was used for events in which the children did not correctly predict the robot's movement after sensing a specific color and put the next card aside from the robot's trajectory.

Peer Tutoring. Half of the tutors memorized coding card positions and explained **where** to put each color card to "draw a square," not **how** the robot works. In fact, none of the tutors explained the relationship between the light indicators on the robot and the direction of its movements. Two tutors mentioned the lights during their explanation, although they focused on the fact that there are more color lights when the robot detects a color card and did not connect color lights to directions. Two of the four tutors **rotated the robot** to explain the color-direction relationship.

Lessons Learned. We proposed improvements related to robot design and activity structure based on the observed errors and peer tutoring instances. We observed that **the color lights** on the top of the robot **are not clear indicators of the color-direction relationship**. Children committed various errors (MCD, RLD, WRP) due to their lack of understanding of the relation between the color-direction indicators and the robot movements. Most participants had difficulties in predicting the robot direction or choosing an appropriate color in simple programming tasks. None of the child tutors mentioned the colors to explain the programming rules of the robot. We concluded that four colorful lights were not enough to transmit the idea of direction and opted to add paper arrows in corresponding colors on top of the robot, next to light indicators (see Fig. 1). As there were multiple occurrences of "wrong color/direction prediction" in the simple tasks, in addition to adding paper arrows, we decided to extend the robot's presentation and explanation. We opted for **more guided instances** where the child has to point to colors, directions or rotate the robot. The **rotation of the robot** was identified as a crucial point in the understanding of color-direction relationship and we believe that it contributed to reducing MCD and WRP errors (none MCD and only one WRP in Study 2). Children tutors that understood the robot's programming rules rotated the robot to explain that with a particular color, the robot can go "this way" or, when turning it, can go "that way."

We observed that the "drawing a square" task was too complex for an introductory activity, and we added **intermediate tasks** with increasing difficulty (go in X direction, use two color cards to make it move in an L-shaped path, use three cards to move in U-shaped route) between robot presentation and "drawing a square." Also, the use of a geometric concept may make it difficult for children to understand the expected robot's path. We added **visual support** (the researcher drawing with the finger the square on the mat) to the oral explanation to make the task easier to understand. To avoid WCP errors, we incorporated an **explanation of the position of the color sensor** used for detecting the color cards.

The result of our observations was a structured introduction to Robotito with the following points that should be covered:

1. Introduction to the color-direction relation using color arrows on the robot.
2. Demonstration of the color sensor and color cards.
3. Demonstration of color-direction examples using Robotito and color cards.
4. Guided tasks in which the child selects the color to move Robotito forward with multiple instances of rotating the robot ("Which color should we use to make the robot move forward if the robot is in this position?").
5. Guided tasks in which the color and direction are given the child selects the robot orientation ("Robotito should go forward with yellow, how should we rotate Robotito?").
6. Programming L-shaped paths.
7. Programming U-shaped path.
8. Programming square-shaped path.

4 Conclusion and Future Work

The first exploratory study allowed us to identify improvements and develop age-appropriate and robot-specific introduction. Although in Study 2, the number of error types was reduced from five to two, participants still committed WCP errors. We observed those errors in real-time debugging instances (the robot is moving, and the child tries to correct the program before the robot reaches the next card). These kinds of instances, with robot moving and the child placing the next card, were not covered in the introduction, and we consider that adding them will help children to better predict the robot's trajectory and put the coding card in the correct location.

Our study highlights the significance of understanding children's common errors and challenges during programming activities, as it can significantly impact the design of robots and related activities, ultimately facilitating children's learning process. Our next phase involves collaborating with teachers to adapt the complete introductory activity to fit the classroom environment and subsequently evaluate its effectiveness in a classroom setting.

Acknowledgements. This work was supported by national funds through Agencia Nacional de Investigación e Innovación, Uruguay - FSED_2_2021_1_169697, PhD scholarship of Comisión Académica de Posgrado, Uruguay and Fundação para a Ciência e a Tecnologia, Portugal - project UIDB/50009/2020-, and by the Portuguese Recovery and Resilience Program (PRR), IAPMEI / ANI / FCT under Agenda C645022399-00000057 (eGamesLab). We would like to express our sincere gratitude to the Jardín 215 in Montevideo for granting us the opportunity to work with the children, which greatly contributed to the success of our research.

References

1. Gerosa, A., Koleszar, V., Gómez-Sena, L., Tejera, G., Carboni, A.: Educational robotics and computational thinking development in preschool. In: 2019 XIV Latin American Conference on Learning Technologies (LACLO), pp. 226–230. IEEE (2019)
2. Höysniemi, J., Hämäläinen, P., Turkki, L.: Using peer tutoring in evaluating the usability of a physically interactive computer game with children. Interact. Comput. **15**(2), 203–225 (2003)
3. Tejera, G., Amorin, G., Sere, A., Capricho, N., Margenat, P., Visca, J.: Robotito: programming robots from preschool to undergraduate school level. In: 2019 19th International Conference on Advanced Robotics (ICAR), pp. 296–301. IEEE (2019)

Design and Development of an Immersive Virtual Reality Application to Reduce Anxiety in Young Adults

Henar Guillen-Sanz[1](✉) ⓘ, Ines Miguel-Alonso[1] ⓘ, Itziar Quevedo Varona[2] ⓘ, and Bruno Rodriguez-Garcia[1] ⓘ

[1] Department of Computer Engineering, University of Burgos, Avda Cantabria s/n, 09006 Burgos, Spain
{hguillen,imalonso,brunorg}@ubu.es
[2] Servicio Universitario de Atención a la Salud (SUAS), University of Burgos, Paseo de Comendadores s/n, 09001 Burgos, Spain

1 Introduction

Young adults are a critical population where mental health disorders, especially anxiety, are commonly manifested [1, 2]. Alongside the genetic and social factors affecting each young person, transitional phases such as leaving home or starting work increase anxiogenic symptoms [3]. For this reason, it is necessary to provide young adults with effective tools for mitigating anxiety symptoms, such as relaxation techniques [4–6]. The integration of new technologies into psychological therapies can attract the attention of young people. Moreover, these technologies have demonstrated significant potential in teaching anxiety regulation strategies [7].

Immersive Virtual Reality (iVR) is defined as a virtual experience in which users are completely immersed thanks to a Head-Mounted Display (HMD) [8]. iVR environments have been shown to enhance information retention compared to traditional techniques [9] due to their ability to generate higher levels of engagement and greater physiological and emotional arousal through interaction with the environment [10]. Therefore, iVR is an ideal context for the development of psychological applications.

2 Methodology

The style chosen for this application is Low-Poly, which is characterised by being minimalist and non-photorealistic [11, 12]. This decision has been motivated by the limited number of polygons of the 3D models and their ease of modification and animation. Regarding the choice of environments, some relaxation applications were considered [13]. Realism has not been regarded as an important feature since natural and relaxing environments are able to induce relaxation even if they are low poly [14]. The environments include interactive, static, and dynamic objects. Additionally, two types of sound have also been included into all scenarios: ambient and binaural [15]. Binaural sound is a positive inducer of moods and an important element of environmental immersion.

© The Author(s), under exclusive license to Springer Nature Switzerland AG 2023
J. Abdelnour Nocera et al. (Eds.): INTERACT 2023, LNCS 14145, pp. 444–448, 2023.
https://doi.org/10.1007/978-3-031-42293-5_51

Although the game mechanics are straightforward, a tutorial level has been developed to prevent users from experiencing the novelty effect [16]. Once users have learned the controls, they can choose to start one of the four levels. Each level presents a different relaxation technique in a gamified way for users to learn. A team of psychologists has collaborated to assess the adaptations of each exercise for iVR. Following the relaxation technique, a small game or interaction with the environment is presented as a reward and positive reinforcement for completing the relaxation task.

Throughout all levels, users will receive audio and visual support to guide them. Regarding user movement within the application, locomotion is limited to a real space of 2 × 2 m. Joystick movement and teleportation have been disabled to ensure that users remain within the designated interaction space and do not experience cybersickness. Two software programs were utilized to develop this application: Blender for creating the scenarios, assets, and animations; and Unreal Engine for programming the levels and mechanics.

3   Results

An IVR application has been developed with the purpose of instructing young adults on techniques to alleviate symptoms of anxiety. The primary objective of this application is to educate users about various relaxation exercises that can be incorporated into their daily lives.

3.1 Tutorial Level

The initial level serves as a tutorial, guiding the users in navigating the virtual environment and familiarizing them with the game mechanics used throughout the application. The design of this tutorial focuses on an autumnal scene, where the user is tasked with picking up a basket and exploring the environment to collect mushrooms. Finally, the user is asked to press a button to access the menu and select a relaxation technique to practice.

3.2 Mindfulness I Level – Observing the Environment

This level is set in an overnight camping environment surrounded by mountains. In this level, users are engaged in a mindfulness exercise that involves attentive observation of the virtual environment [17]. The primary objective of this exercise is to cultivate users' ability to concentrate on their surroundings while minimizing mental distractions. The stage presented to the users at the beginning of the level is almost empty. When the users find a light-ball, they must stare it carefully until the loading circle is complete. Subsequently, objects or elements of the stage gradually appear, accompanied by their corresponding sounds, creating a binaural auditory experience. Once all the intended objects have appeared, the users are able to perform another more interactive exercise: capturing six fireflies within a glass jar. Following the completion of the fireflies' game, users have the option to exit at any time by pressing a designated button.

3.3 Progressive Muscle Relaxation Level

This level is located in a daytime beach where the users must perform the Jacobson Progressive Muscle Relaxation Technique [18]. Throughout the level, the users are instructed to sequentially tense and then release various muscle groups. When the muscles have to be tensed, the scene turns reddish to increase the feeling of discomfort. Once the relaxation technique is completed, the user has a small reward: a glass bottle appears half buried in the sand and the user can pick it up. The users must remove the cap from the bottle to take a note inside with a positive message about relaxation that encourages the users to exercise in their daily life.

3.4 Deep Breathing Level

This level is set in a snowy daytime environment where the users are provided with several instructions to perform deep and conscious breathing [19]. The users are asked to take a deep breath, hold it for a few seconds and slowly release it. During exhalation, the intensity of snow particles falling decreases, and the fog dissipates. Once the relaxation phase is over, the users must assemble a snowman with the available pieces on the floor. Upon completing the tasks, the users are free to explore and enjoy the environment until they decide to exit the level.

3.5 Mindfulness II Level – Conscious Breathing

Finally, this level is set in an underwater environment where users must focus on their breathing [17]. To mirror the process of mindful breathing, a blowfish is placed in front of the user and inflates and deflates with the same pace as the user should follow. In this environment, the users must learn to be able to focus on their breathing despite moving objects around them. Once the users have learnt this relaxation technique, a camera and multiple teleportation points appear on the stage. Using the camera, the users can capture images of animals and objects within the environment. Users are encouraged to spend as much time as they desire, indulging in the surroundings and interacting with the elements.

4   Conclusions and Future Lines

An immersive Virtual Reality application has been developed to teach young adults to reduce the symptoms of anxiety. The application consists of four scenarios that teach users different relaxation techniques. This application can be used both independently and as part of a psychological intervention.

In the near future a biofeedback system will be included. After completing each level, users will be able to view a graph displaying their level of relaxation based on their cardiac and electrodermal activity. This feature will enhance users' awareness of the effectiveness of relaxation techniques on their own physiology. Additionally, the collected data will enable real-time adaptation of each level to the user's performance, further personalizing the experience. For instance, in the Deep Breathing level, the intensity of snow particles and fog will be directly influenced by the user's physiological data once the biofeedback system is integrated. To validate the effectiveness of the application, a large-scale study will be conducted involving a diverse group of target users. The State-Trait Anxiety Inventory (STAI) test will be administered before and after using the application to assess changes in perceived anxiety levels. The outcomes will be compared with those of a control group to evaluate the benefits of iVR.

In the far future, the application will be tested as part of more complex psychological interventions, such as exam-related anxiety treatment. Volunteer users will be exposed to 360° videos depicting anxiety-inducing situations before and after using the application to evaluate the effects of relaxation on their physiological responses. By analyzing both physiological and subjective validation data, Artificial Intelligence (AI) techniques will be employed to detect behavioral and learning patterns. This will facilitate a deeper understanding of the users and enable better customization of the application to meet their specific needs.

All data collected from users, including subjective surveys and future biometric data, will be anonymized to ensure confidentiality. Access to such data will be limited to the responsible professionals involved in the psychological treatment.

References

1. Kessler, R.C., Berglund, P., Demler, O., Jin, R., Merikangas, K.R., Walters, E.E.: Lifetime prevalence and age-of-onset distributions of DSM-IV disorders in the national comorbidity survey replication. Arch. Gen. Psychiatry **62**, 593 (2005). https://doi.org/10.1001/archpsyc.62.6.593
2. Wong, T.W., Gao, Y., Tam, W.W.S.: Anxiety among university students during the SARS epidemic in Hong Kong. Stress Health **23**, 31–35 (2007). https://doi.org/10.1002/smi.1116
3. Wang, R.A.H., Davis, O.S.P., Wootton, R.E., Mottershaw, A., Haworth, C.M.A.: Social support and mental health in late adolescence are correlated for genetic, as well as environmental, reasons. Sci. Rep. **7**, 13088 (2017). https://doi.org/10.1038/s41598-017-13449-2
4. Esch, T., Fricchione, G.L., Stefano, G.B.: The therapeutic use of the relaxation response in stress-related diseases (2003)
5. Rowa, K., Antony, M.M.: Psychological treatments for social phobia. Can. J. Psychiatry **50**(6), 308–316 (2005). https://doi.org/10.1177/070674370505000603
6. Hayes-Skelton, S.A., Roemer, L., Orsillo, S.M., Borkovec, T.D.: A contemporary view of applied relaxation for generalized anxiety disorder. Cogn. Behav. Ther. **42**, 292–302 (2013). https://doi.org/10.1080/16506073.2013.777106
7. Weerdmeester, J., van Rooij, M.M.J.W., Maciejewski, D.F., Engels, R.C.M.E., Granic, I.: A randomized controlled trial assessing the efficacy of a virtual reality biofeedback video game: anxiety outcomes and appraisal processes. Technol. Mind Behav. **2** (2021). https://doi.org/10.1037/tmb0000028
8. Suh, A., Prophet, J.: The state of immersive technology research: a literature analysis. Comput. Human Behav. **86**, 77–90 (2018). https://doi.org/10.1016/j.chb.2018.04.019
9. Hamilton, D., McKechnie, J., Edgerton, E., Wilson, C.: Immersive virtual reality as a pedagogical tool in education: a systematic literature review of quantitative learning outcomes and experimental design. J. Comput. Educ. **8**, 1–32 (2021). https://doi.org/10.1007/s40692-020-00169-2

10. Checa, D., Bustillo, A.: A review of immersive virtual reality serious games to enhance learning and training. Multimed. Tools Appl. **79**, 5501–5527 (2020). https://doi.org/10.1007/s11042-019-08348-9

11. Uasmith, T., Pukkaman, T., Sripian, P.: Low-poly image stylization. J. Geom. Graph. **21**, 131–139 (2017)

12. Keleşoğlu, M.M., Güleçözer, D.: A study on digital low poly modeling methods as an abstraction tool in design processes. Civil Eng. Archit. **9**, 2570–2586 (2021). https://doi.org/10.13189/cea.2021.091513

13. Arpaia, P., D'Errico, G., De Paolis, L.T., Moccaldi, N., Nuccetelli, F.: A narrative review of mindfulness-based interventions using virtual reality. Mindfulness (N Y). **13**, 556–571 (2022). https://doi.org/10.1007/s12671-021-01783-6

14. Repetto, C., Gaggioli, A., Pallavicini, F., Cipresso, P., Raspelli, S., Riva, G.: Virtual reality and mobile phones in the treatment of generalized anxiety disorders: a phase-2 clinical trial. Pers. Ubiquit. Comput. **17**, 253–260 (2013). https://doi.org/10.1007/s00779-011-0467-0

15. Perales, F.J., Sanchez, M., Riera, L., Ramis, S.: A pilot study: VR and binaural sounds for mood management. In: Information Visualisation - Biomedical Visualization, Visualisation on Built and Rural Environments and Geometric Modelling and Imaging, IV 2018, pp. 413–419. Institute of Electrical and Electronics Engineers Inc. (2018). https://doi.org/10.1109/iV.2018.00083

16. Miguel-Alonso, I., Rodriguez-Garcia, B., Checa, D., Bustillo, A.: Countering the novelty effect: a tutorial for immersive virtual reality learning environments. Appl. Sci. **13**, 593 (2023). https://doi.org/10.3390/app13010593

17. Baer, R.A.: Mindfulness training as a clinical intervention: a conceptual and empirical review. Clin. Psychol. Sci. Pract. **10**(2), 125–143 (2003). https://doi.org/10.1093/clipsy/bpg015

18. Torales, J., O'Higgins, M., Barrios, I., González, I., Almirón, M.: An overview of Jacobson's progressive muscle relaxation in managing anxiety. Revista Argentina de Clinica Psicologica **29**, 17–23 (2020). https://doi.org/10.24205/03276716.2020.748

19. Ariga, R.A.: Decrease anxiety among students who will do the objective structured clinical examination with deep breathing relaxation technique. Open Access Maced. J. Med. Sci. **7**, 2619–2622 (2019). https://doi.org/10.3889/oamjms.2019.409

Designing AR Applications for People Living with Dementia

Teresa Onorati[(✉)] [iD], Paloma Díaz[iD], Álvaro Montero[iD], and Ignacio Aedo[iD]

Computer Science Department, Universidad Carlos III de Madrid, Madrid, Spain
{tonorati,pdp,ammontes}@inf.uc3m.es, aedo@ia.uc3m.es

Abstract. Given the extensive use of Augmented Reality (AR) for learning and training in different domains, this technology could support traditional therapies for people with dementia. However, to devise useful experiences, it is crucial to involve specialists and patients to fully understand the potential and limitations of ad-hoc AR applications considering the patients' medical conditions as well as their expectations about the technology. In the context of a project aimed at improving healthcare service centers, following an action research approach, we codesigned two AR applications, tablet- and glass-based, to practice specific cognitive competencies (memory, recognition, and association) involving two specialists in psychiatry and two patients diagnosed with mild cognitive impairment. In an initial phase, we identified key issues about how the patients interact with the two devices and the interfaces in the doctors' room that helped to improve the final prototypes. These prototypes were tested in a clinical study with ten patients diagnosed with mild cognitive impairment in the presence of their therapist.

Keywords: Augmented Reality · Cognitive Impairment · Action Research

1 Introduction

According to the World Health Organization (WHO), around 55 million people live with dementia worldwide, and this estimation will rise to 78 million in 2030 and 139 million in 2050 [1]. The Alzheimer's Society describes dementia as a wide range of symptoms, including memory loss, difficulties in concentrating, planning or organizing, and feeling confused about the time or the place [2]. How this condition affects people depends on their health conditions, particularly cognitive functioning, before the diagnosis. In general, the umbrella of symptoms associated with dementia can be related to different stages of its progression [3]: early (or mild), middle (or moderate), and late (or severe). This paper will focus on patients in the early stage of their condition when the symptoms appear gradually and are often overlooked.

In this paper, we are interested in exploring the potential of Augmented Reality (AR) to design and develop applications to help PwD practice specific cognitive capabilities, such as memory, recognition, and association. In the literature, several authors have investigated the benefits of AR applications for neurodegenerative disorders [5, 6]. Among them are assisting patients in performing a task or recognizing an object or a

© The Author(s), under exclusive license to Springer Nature Switzerland AG 2023
J. Abdelnour Nocera et al. (Eds.): INTERACT 2023, LNCS 14145, pp. 449–453, 2023.
https://doi.org/10.1007/978-3-031-42293-5_52

dangerous situation [7–9], providing therapists with further data about the patients and their current health status [10], and improving the interactivity of specific exercises to stimulate their cognitive abilities [11–13].

A critical aspect to consider when dealing with people affected by a neurodegenerative disorder is that they can experience difficulties learning new technologies and new ways to interact with an interface. For this reason, one of the issues raised in the literature concerns the device used for interacting with the AR application to find the most comfortable fit [6], including tablets, smartphones, head-mounted displays (HMDs), and wearables. We are interested in prototyping applications for a tablet and an HMD, and different interaction modes, such as touch, voice, and hand gestures.

This paper presents the preliminary results of an exploratory project aimed at analyzing the opportunities of AR to stimulate cognitive capabilities, like recalling recent events, recognizing everyday use objects, and creating relations among characteristics, like shapes, colors, and sounds. To this scope, we have codesigned two AR prototypes following an action research approach involving two therapists and two patients to explore the possible benefits of such technologies [14]. The resulting prototypes have been tested in a clinical study carried out in a health center with ten patients.

2   An Action Research Approach to Design AR for PwD

Patients diagnosed with dementia can develop symptoms that require personalization in the definition of therapies. To propose engaging and ad-hoc exercises for them, we had to learn about therapists' and patients' current practices and experiences. To this scope, we applied a three-step methodology inspired by the action research approach. During the first step, we interviewed two therapists who specialized in neurodegenerative diseases to understand the real needs that they had to face while dealing with their patients. From these initial interviews, we profiled the final users of our applications as older people diagnosed with an early stage of dementia and designed two initial prototypes, one for a tablet and one for a pair of see-through glasses.

During the second phase, we asked two patients and a therapist to test the two prototypes and collect their opinions and suggestions. We were interested, in particular, in the design of the interface, the interaction modes, and the dynamics of the proposed exercises. Based on the results, we made some decisions about the design of the AR applications and the way to interact with them. For example, we decided to avoid voice commands considering that wearing a mask due to the COVID restrictions makes it quite tricky for word recognition, and patients have difficulties remembering the exact instructions to say to use the applications. For example, they added not needed articles, adjectives, or adverbs. Another interesting observation was that the patients felt comfortable wearing the glasses and interacting with the applications, even if it was the first time. Consequently, we decided to keep both prototypes for the next phase.

In the third and last phase of the design process, we improved the initial prototypes considering the results from the two patients and the therapist. We have also run a second evaluation involving ten patients, trying both applications and interviewing them about their experiences.

3   Tablet- and Glasses-based AR Applications for PwD

The tablet-based AR application uses markers to place objects in the space and offers two modalities, each for a different exercise. The first is Recognize (Reconoce, in Spanish), and it displays an object with three labeled buttons (see a in Fig. 1). The user has to choose the correct option by touching the corresponding button. The activity ends by summarizing the results obtained for each object (see b in Fig. 1). The second activity, Remember (*Recuerda*, in Spanish), further challenges the users by showing two objects for five seconds, hiding them, and asking them to indicate their names by choosing two out of four labeled buttons. The activity, at last, displays a summary screen with the results obtained for each pair.

In both modalities, the application provides visual and auditory feedback through the color of the buttons and the playback of sounds that indicate correct or incorrect answers.

Fig. 1. The Recognize activity: a) an object with three options; b) the results summary.

3.1   Glasses-Based AR Applications

The second prototype is a glasses-based application that immerses the users in an AR environment, keeping them grounded in the real world. Also, in this case, we offer two different modalities. The first shows four virtual cubes, each associated with a color and an instrument's sound. The colors have been chosen to be distinguishable by color-blind people. The user can interact with them by touching them to play their sounds. After an exploration session to learn which sound plays each cube, the game consists of hearing a sound and remembering the associated cube. Every time one of the cubes is touched, its color becomes brighter to help the patients identify it in the space. Moreover, the system gives auditory feedback on whether the association is correct.

The second modality is inspired by the electronic game called Simon [15]. It consists of building sequences of sounds and asks users to repeat them. If the user gets the sequence right, it grows to a maximum of five sounds in a row. At every step of the game, the application gives visual and auditory feedback to inform if the sequence is correct. This exercise is the most complex one, requiring different capabilities simultaneously: memorizing the sounds and colors, recognizing the instruments played, and creating associations between the colors and sounds.

4 A Real Scenario of Use

As the final phase of the design process, the evaluation aims at understanding the potential of AR as support for practicing cognitive capabilities and whether this technology can help avoid boredom and improve patients' engagement in beneficial activities for their health status. In collaboration with two therapists, we have recruited ten participants (7 women and 3 men) in a public hospital in Madrid, Spain, aged 70–83 years old, diagnosed with an early stage of dementia, and with limited experience with mobile devices. The participation was individual and lasted around 30 min. After a brief introduction about the experiment's aim, in the presence of a therapist and two researchers, the participants tried both modalities of the two applications, the tablet- and the glasses-based, in this order. After each application, we interviewed them.

Analyzing the participants' interviews, we found that, in general, they preferred to interact with the tablet because they were already used to it, and the two modalities were easy to understand and play. We received positive and enthusiastic comments; some were even interested in getting and using the application on their own devices.

About the Hololens, nobody felt uncomfortable, sick, or tired. While using the first modality, they started to touch the cubes freely without further explanations, hearing the sounds, associating with each element's colors and position, and losing track of time. Different is the experience with the Simon-inspired game that seemed too complex for the current patient's cognitive abilities, and most of them got frustrated because they could not remember sequences longer than three sounds. Discussing this issue with the therapists, they explained to us that the patients affected by dementia could quickly get frustrated when they realize that they are failing a task and suggested adding cues about the next sound in line. Despite the difficulties related to the game dynamics, the participants enjoyed the experience and wearing the see-through glasses. Still, we think that one of the benefits of this device is that the user doesn't lose contact with reality, as in virtual reality environments.

5 Conclusions and Future Works

In this paper, we have learned some interesting lessons from the design process and the evaluation of AR technologies for practicing cognitive capabilities. Even if the tablet is the preferred device for all, the participants didn't get scared by the Hololens, and they wore and interacted with them naturally. In fact, during the first modality, most of them lost track of time and kept playing with the cubes. Another lesson concerns avoiding situations where they feel frustrated, as with the Simon-inspired game. The frustration can negatively affect their willingness to keep playing and using the technology. Based on the results of this exploratory work, we plan to improve the dynamics of the proposed activities and prototype new AR applications for tablets and Hololens.

Acknowledgment. This work is supported by the project sense2MakeSense, funded by the Spanish State Agency of Research (PID2019-109388GB-I00), and the project IntCare-CM, funded by the regional government of the Community of Madrid.

References

1. Cataldi, R., Chowdhary, N., Seeher, K., Moorthy, V., Dua, T.: A blueprint for the worldwide research response to dementia. Lancet Neurol. **21**, 690–691 (2022)
2. What is dementia?|Alzheimer's Society. https://www.alzheimers.org.uk/about-dementia/ types-dementia/what-is-dementia, Accessed 9 Jan 2023
3. Clare, L., Woods, R.T.: Cognitive training and cognitive rehabilitation for people with early-stage Alzheimer's disease: a review. Neuropsychol. Rehabil. **14**, 385–401 (2004). https://doi. org/10.1080/09602010443000074
4. A blueprint for dementia research. https://www.who.int/publications-detail-redirect/978924 0058248. Accessed 8 Jan 2023
5. Farooq, M.S., et al.: Applications of augmented reality in neurology: architectural model and guidelines. IEEE Access **10**, 102804–102830 (2022). https://doi.org/10.1109/ACCESS.2022. 3206600
6. Hayhurst, J.: How augmented reality and virtual reality is being used to support people living with Dementia—design challenges and future directions. In: Jung, T., Tom Dieck, M.C. (eds.) Augmented Reality and Virtual Reality: Empowering Human, Place and Business, pp. 295–305. Springer, Cham (2018). https://doi.org/10.1007/978-3-319-64027-3_20
7. Wolf, D., Besserer, D., Sejunaite, K., Riepe, M., Rukzio, E.: cARe: an augmented reality support system for Dementia patients. In: Adjunct Proceedings of the 31st Annual ACM Symposium on User Interface Software and Technology, pp. 42–44. ACM, Berlin, Germany (2018). https://doi.org/10.1145/3266037.3266095
8. Hamilton, M.A., Beug, A.P., Hamilton, H.J., Norton, W.J.: Augmented reality technology for people living with Dementia and their care partners. In: 2021 the 5th International Conference on Virtual and Augmented Reality Simulations, pp. 21–30. ACM, Melbourne, VIC, Australia (2021). https://doi.org/10.1145/3463914.3463918
9. Rohrbach, N., et al.: An augmented reality approach for ADL support in Alzheimer's disease: a crossover trial. J. NeuroEngineering Rehabil. **16**, 66 (2019). https://doi.org/10.1186/s12 984-019-0530-z
10. Vovk, A., Patel, A., Chan, D.: Augmented reality for early Alzheimer's disease diagnosis. In: Extended Abstracts of the 2019 CHI Conference on Human Factors in Computing Systems, pp. 1–6. Association for Computing Machinery, New York, NY, USA (2019). https://doi.org/ 10.1145/3290607.3313007
11. Niknam, A.: An augmented reality mobile game design to enhance spatial memory in elderly with Dementia (2021)
12. Aruanno, B., Garzotto, F.: MemHolo: mixed reality experiences for subjects with Alzheimer's disease. Multimed. Tools Appl. **78**, 13517–13537 (2019). https://doi.org/10.1007/s11042- 018-7089-8
13. Boletsis, C., McCallum, S.: Augmented reality cubes for cognitive gaming: preliminary usability and game experience testing. Int. J. Serious Games **3** (2016). https://doi.org/10. 17083/ijsg.v3i1.106
14. Denscombe, M.: The Good Research Guide: Research Methods for Small-Scale Social Research Projects. McGraw-Hill Education (UK), London (2021)
15. Baer, R.H., Morrison, H.J.: Microcomputer controlled game, US patent 4207087, issued 10 June 1980, assigned to Marvin Glass and Associates (1980)

Designing Interaction to Support Sustained Attention

Naile Hacioglu[1]([✉]), Maria Chiara Leva[2], and Hyowon Lee[1,3]

[1] School of Computing, Dublin City University, Glasnevin, Dublin 9, Ireland
naile.hacioglu2@mail.dcu.ie
[2] School of Food Science and Environmental Health, Technological University Dublin, Grangegorman, Dublin, Ireland
[3] Insight Centre for Data Analytics, Dublin City University, Glasnevin, Dublin 9, Ireland

Abstract. The impact of digital technology on human cognition has become a topic of significant interest in recent years, with various studies highlighting the adverse effects on cognition, particularly attention. While the negative impact of digital applications on our attentional processes is well-documented, practical solutions to mitigate these detrimental effects are rare. In this paper, we propose Attention Mode as a design solution that aims to minimise the negative impacts of digital technology on attention by creating easy-to-understand and navigate user interfaces. This approach can help users focus on tasks, reduce cognitive load, and minimise distractions, ultimately improving their overall experience. We developed interaction mock-ups incorporating the Attention Mode and conducted a preliminary one-to-one sharing with 5 participants to analyse to get early feedback. It resulted in valuable feedback on how such a design focus could help users to focus on the content without distractive elements. By integrating the issues from the start of the design process instead of handling it as an afterthought, this work offers new insights into crafting user interfaces in a way that the negative impact of digital technology on attention is mitigated.

Keywords: Sustained Attention · Cognition · User Interface Design · Usability · Digital Technology · Smart Devices · Distraction · Task Switching · Notifications

1 Introduction

The impact of digital technology on human cognition has been a topic of significant interest and concern in recent years. Various studies have reported negative impacts on cognition in different abilities, such as memory and decision-making. However, the negative impact of smart devices and digital applications on attention is studied the most. A significant amount of evidence in the literature shows the harmful effects of digital technology use on our attentional processes (Table 1).

This work was conducted with the financial support of the SFI Centre for Research Training in Digitally-Enhanced Reality (d-real) under Grant No. 18/CRT/6224 and the SFI Centre Grant No. 12/RC/2289_P2 at Insight the SFI Research Centre for Data Analytics at Dublin City University. For the purpose of Open Access, the author has applied a CC BY public copyright licence to any Author Accepted Manuscript version arising from this submission.

© The Author(s), under exclusive license to Springer Nature Switzerland AG 2023
J. Abdelnour Nocera et al. (Eds.): INTERACT 2023, LNCS 14145, pp. 454–458, 2023.
https://doi.org/10.1007/978-3-031-42293-5_53

Specific technology usage behaviours might lead disruptions in our attentional systems and executive control in both short- and long-term. For example, adolescents who frequently use technology are more likely to develop ADHD symptoms due to multitasking behaviour and repetitive attentional shifts [1]. Ophir et al. [2] demonstrated heavy media multitasking behaviour was associated with lower performance of voluntary attention allocation in the presence of distractions.

Table 1. Key papers referring attention and executive control effects of digital technology and solution type proposed or hinted if any.

Study	Proposed (or Hinted) Solutions		
	Effect on Attention	Cognitive Training or CBT[a]	Behavioural Intervention
Barasch et al., 2017 [3]	↑[b]		
Cardoso-Leite et al., 2021 [4]	↓		
Davis, 2001 [5]	↓	✓	
Du et al., 2019 [6]	↓		
Freytag et al., 2020 [7]	↓		
Green and Bavelier, 2003 [8]	↑	✓	
Madore and Wagner, 2019 [9]	↓		
Madore et al., 2020 [10]	↓		
Misra and Stokols, 2012 [11]	↓		✓
Ophir et al., 2019 [2]	↓		
Rosen et al., 2012 [12]	↓		✓
Rosser et al., 2007 [13]	↑	✓	
Schacter, 2022 [14]	↓ ↑		
Small et al., 2020 [1]	↓ ↑	✓	
Uncapher & Wagner, 2018 [15]	↓		
Throuvala et al., 2020 [16]	↓	✓	✓

[a] Cognitive Behavioural Therapy.
[b] " ↑" icon refers to improvement in attention and executive control whereas "↓" refers to deterioration.

Despite the growing awareness of this issue, practical solutions to mitigate the detrimental effects of digital technology on attention are rare. The proposed solutions include pre-commitment of the users to self-limit digital technology use [11] and cognitive training [13]. Although these solutions could be useful to reverse or prevent the adverse effects on attention, there are several downsides to the strategies. First, users should be aware of the negative effects in the first place. Second, many users leverage digital applications and devices for their professional and personal needs even if they are aware of the negative effects. Thus, for personal intervention, users need to find alternative methods to handle these, which is not a trivial effort. Third, users should know where to find cognitive training to use the second strategy. These disadvantages make it unlikely for users to start or sustain practicing above interventions over time as they need to invest significant amount of time and effort, even money.

Therefore, considering the attention issue from the time of designing the technology may be a more holistic solution. In this context, we propose a design solution that aims to minimise such negative impacts on attention by helping easily control major factors that will make the user more prone to distractions directly available on the user interface of the application currently used. This approach can help users to disable potential distractions more readily from the tasks thus remain focused on their tasks, reduce cognitive load to improve sustained attention, ultimately improving their overall experience.

2 Designing to Support Sustained Attention

We developed the concept of an "Attention Mode" which takes the necessary measures to support minimal distractions in different contexts. The Attention Mode is activated when an "Attention Button" is clicked/dragged or tapped/swiped depending on the modality supported in the platform. This might be considered as the collection of the features found in "Focus" [17] and Adblockers with additional attributes. However, it takes many steps to activate these features since they are scattered in different locations, and they only eliminate some part of distractions whereas the Attention Mode turns off designated media distractions collectively in one step. Furthermore, it is intended to be integrated into the user interface of an application so that the user can trigger it during performing the task.

Attention Mode involves using a single button placed in a suitable location on UI and displays quick sub-options that can be selected within a second when interacted. Options displayed when the button is pressed allow users to select between two different modes, Attention Mode Level 1 and 2, to exclude different kinds of distractions. Additionally, the interface allows for customisation in the settings menu in some cases. The mode is activated as soon as a level is selected, or it is turned off without a need for confirmation. For first-time users a brief explanation of Attention Mode is provided.

To illustrate Attention Mode, we developed a news website prototype. Here, the user's task was to read an online newspaper article in a desktop environment. Content such as recommended articles, advertisement on the website and other settings on the browser, and desktop view and other open applications on the computer are all considered as distractions since they are irrelevant to the article itself. These distractions are hidden or prevented when the user turns on Attention Mode to concentrate (Fig. 1). Level 2 cannot be personalised as it involves the elimination of all kinds of distractions present, irrelevant visual content, notifications and switching to other applications. Eliminating visual distractions that imply potential switching of tasks as well as blocking external notifications during the task helps users to allocate their attention more effectively [2] and reduces occurrence of attention lapses [10] as the opportunities for multitasking

Fig. 1. (a) Attention Mode options are displayed when Attention Button is clicked on with general information. (b) Attention Mode maximises the main content and removes irrelevant visual distraction when set to Level 1.

behaviour decreases. We also integrated Attention Mode on an eBook application on a tablet and a video streaming application on a smartphone to demonstrate how universal it can be. Although we cannot describe them here due to the limitations of the poster paper, we leveraged the same interaction strategy in these two prototypes.

3 Feedback and Evaluation

We conducted one-to-one preliminary feedback sessions with 5 participants ($M_{age} =$ 29.4, 3 females, 2 males) shown design prototypes and discussed to gather feedback on different aspects of the mode. The news website was particularly well-received, with all participants acknowledging the benefits of having a mode that helps them focus more by removing distractions from their desktop environment. This feedback suggests a perceived need for such a feature in desktop applications or environments, and users see value in having a dedicated mode for enhancing their attention. However, there were differing opinions on the customisation of mode levels. One participant expressed interest in the idea of customising the level of distraction settings, while another participant raised concerns about potential confusion for less technologically inclined users. This feedback highlights the importance of considering the balance between customization and simplicity in the design of the Attention Mode.

The feedback on the tablet e-book and video applications indicated that users value flexibility, simplicity, and ease of use in the design, and careful consideration should be given to the options and features included in the mode to minimise user errors.

Overall, the feedback from the participants indicated that the proposed design approach of Attention Mode was positive, with participants expressing sentiments about the concept of reducing distractions and creating awareness about their digital technology use. Participants also expressed interest in having analytics to understand how their sustained attention has improved over time. This feedback provides valuable insights for further refinement and development of the Attention Mode design approach.

In this paper, we tried to illustrate a proactive stance by redesigning day-to-day applications to reduce such adverse effects on attention. By considering the effects of technology on our attentional well-being and examining how the design knowledge in the form of guidelines available today could address these aspects, we can create digital environments that further enhance our productivity and cognitive well-being.

References

1. Small, G.W., Lee, J., Kaufman, A., et al.: Brain health consequences of digital technology use. Dialogues Clin. Neurosci. **22**, 179–187 (2020). https://doi.org/10.31887/DCNS.2020.22.2/gsmall

2. Ophir, E., Nass, C., Wagner, A.D.: Cognitive control in media multitaskers. Proc. Natl. Acad. Sci. U.S.A. **106**, 15583–15587 (2009). https://doi.org/10.1073/pnas.0903620106

3. Barasch, A., Diehl, K., Silverman, J., Zauberman, G.: Photographic memory: the effects of volitional photo taking on memory for visual and auditory aspects of an experience. Psychol. Sci. **28**, 1056–1066 (2017). https://doi.org/10.1177/0956797617694868

4. Cardoso-Leite, P., Buchard, A., Tissieres, I., et al.: Media use, attention, mental health and academic performance among 8 to 12 year old children. PLoS ONE **16**, e0259163 (2021). https://doi.org/10.1371/journal.pone.0259163

5. Davis, R.A.: A cognitive–behavioral model of pathological Internet use. Comput. Hum. Behav. **17**, 187–195 (2001). https://doi.org/10.1016/S0747-5632(00)00041-8

6. Du, J., Kerkhof, P., van Koningsbruggen, G.M.: Predictors of social media self-control failure: immediate gratifications, habitual checking, ubiquity, and notifications. Cyberpsychol. Behav. Soc. Netw. **22**, 477–485 (2019). https://doi.org/10.1089/cyber.2018.0730

7. Freytag, A., Knop-Huelss, K., Meier, A., et al.: Permanently online—always stressed out? The effects of permanent connectedness on stress experiences. Hum. Commun. Res. **47**, 132–165 (2021). https://doi.org/10.1093/hcr/hqaa014

8. Green, C.S., Bavelier, D.: Action video game modifies visual selective attention. Nature **423**, 534–537 (2003). https://doi.org/10.1038/nature01647

9. Madore, K.P., Wagner, A.D.: Multicosts of Multitasking. Cerebrum 2019:cer-04-19 (2019)

10. Madore, K.P., Khazenzon, A.M., Backes, C.W., et al.: Memory failure predicted by attention lapsing and media multitasking. Nature **587**, 87–91 (2020). https://doi.org/10.1038/s41586-020-2870-z

11. Misra, S., Stokols, D.: Psychological and health outcomes of perceived information overload. Environ. Behav. **44**, 737–759 (2012). https://doi.org/10.1177/0013916511404408

12. Rosen, L.D., Mark Carrier, L., Cheever, N.A.: Facebook and texting made me do it: media-induced task-switching while studying. Comput. Hum. Behav. **29**, 948–958 (2013). https://doi.org/10.1016/j.chb.2012.12.001

13. Rosser, J.C., Lynch, P.J., Cuddihy, L., et al.: The impact of video games on training surgeons in the 21st century. Arch. Surg. **142**, 181–186; Discussion 186 (2007). https://doi.org/10.1001/archsurg.142.2.181

14. Schacter, D.L.: Media, technology, and the sins of memory. Memory Mind Media **1**, e1 (2022). https://doi.org/10.1017/mem.2021.3

15. Uncapher, M.R., Wagner, A.D.: Minds and brains of media multitaskers: current findings and future directions. Proc. Natl. Acad. Sci. U.S.A. **115**, 9889–9896 (2018). https://doi.org/10.1073/pnas.1611612115

16. Throuvala, M.A., Griffiths, M.D., Rennoldson, M., Kuss, D.J.: Mind over matter: testing the efficacy of an online randomized controlled trial to reduce distraction from smartphone use. Int. J. Environ. Res. Public Health **17**, 4842 (2020). https://doi.org/10.3390/ijerph17134842

17. Set up a Focus on Mac. In: Apple Support. https://support.apple.com/en-ie/guide/mac-help/mchl613dc43f/mac. Accessed 11 Apr 2023

Digital Educational Games with Storytelling for Students to Learn Algebra

Kubra Kaymakci Ustuner$^{(\boxtimes)}$ (ID), Effie Lai-Chong Law (ID), and Frederick W. B. Li (ID)

Department of Computer Science, Durham University, Durham DH1 3LE, UK
{jvpm77,wsnv42,dcs01w}@durham.ac.uk

Abstract. The main goal of this research project is to study the impact of digital educational games (DEGs) on primary students' attitudes towards and attainment in algebra. We will combine the methods of game-based learning and storytelling to design a DEG on algebra for 10–11 years old school children and evaluate it with them. Our work will contribute to mathematics education and DEG design.

Keywords: Digital game-based learning · algebra · digital storytelling

1 Motivation

Today technology holds great importance in our lives. The generation born into the evolving technology and rapidly adapting to it are called *digital natives* [1]. Digital natives use technology to meet many basic needs and prefer using technology in the learning environment [2]. Moreover, many digital natives are interested in games and consider them as learning tools [2].

According to research, many mathematical ideas have been derived from games, and mathematics has been used as a tool to create games [3]. Therefore, the idea of including games in mathematics lessons is interesting for mathematics educators. The use of games in education is believed to be beneficial for teaching mathematical concepts such as numbers, algebra, and measurement [4] as well as developing mathematical skills such as reasoning and inquiry [5].

The principles and standards set by the National Council of Teachers of Mathematics (NCTM) indicate that mathematics and technology coexist in daily life, and the learning environment should be equipped with technology [6]. Technological changes have led to the restructuring of mathematics education programs and the creation of new methods for mathematics education [6].

Integrating technology and educational games into mathematics education has attracted a great deal of attention from researchers and mathematics educators. Digital educational games (DEGs) can make mathematics lessons more enjoyable and give students new perspectives on mathematics. When educational games are used effectively, students' participation in learning can increase; they can easily grasp abstract concepts such as algebra [7] and apply them more effectively.

© The Author(s), under exclusive license to Springer Nature Switzerland AG 2023
J. Abdelnour Nocera et al. (Eds.): INTERACT 2023, LNCS 14145, pp. 459–463, 2023.
https://doi.org/10.1007/978-3-031-42293-5_54

Researchers emphasise that well-designed DEGs have the benefit of increasing student performance in mathematics [8]. Teachers can increase students' motivation and academic success by transforming an entertainment game into an educational game [9]. However, there are limited studies in which students play the role of game designers, using storytelling to create digital games [10]. As one of the 21st-century educational visions is to raise creative students, there is a strong need for game-based learning environment designs in which students are in the position of being designers and can narrate mathematics.

To meet this need, we are motivated to conduct a research project on integrating digital game-based learning with digital storytelling for enhancing mathematics education. We employ the *student-centric approach* by engaging students actively in the learning process as storytellers and designers.

2 Related Work

Digital Game-Based Learning (DGBL), in short, includes combining the educational environment, curriculum, technology, assessment and entertainment in a digital game to encourage students to learn [11]. Digital games are a teaching method that can be used as part of the curriculum. This method consists of complex and easy exercises, feedback and rewards that must be completed for students to develop their problem-solving and critical-thinking skills. DGBL can be utilized to reduce anxiety in students and motivate them to learn by making lessons more fun than otherwise [12]. It can also personalize learning and allow students to learn from mistakes by providing timely feedback and enable cooperation among students [12]. Furthermore, studies in the literature show that using digital games in educational environments contributes positively to the learning process and student motivation [13]. Given the benefits of DGBL, well-designed digital games should be integrated into the learning process for an efficient educational environment.

Digital storytelling (DST), in short, is the creation of oral and written stories by enriching them with today's advanced technology. Nowadays, people can easily and effectively create their own scenarios by using different media tools such as sound, music, video, and animation with the computer [14]. Similar to DGBL, DST, which is considered fun and immersive in the education system, provides many advantages such as creative problem solving, reflective thinking and creative thinking by generating their own stories [15]. According to some researchers, storytelling in education can create a meaningful context for students to solve problems, especially in abstract subjects (such as algebra). Consequently, it may become easier for students to learn mathematics [16, 17]. In mathematics education, digital storytelling ensures that abstract concepts are concretised and, most importantly, students notice the relationship between mathematics subjects and daily life [18].

3 Research Goal, Questions, and Design

3.1 Research Goal and Questions

The main research goal of this research project is to analyse the effectiveness of a DEG in enabling primary school students to learn algebra. To meet this goal, we will develop a digital algebra game prototype by using *pygame* and *Canva*. Adopting the human-centered design approach upheld in the field of HCI, and the prototype will be evaluated iteratively with representative end-users – students aged 10–11 years old - to improve the design of the game. These formative evaluation studies will be followed by a summative evaluation to assess the impact of the game on students' achievement. The study is aimed to address three research questions (RQs):

RQ1: What is the impact of the new integrated digital game-based and storytelling approach on primary school students in learning algebra?

RQ2: Are there significant differences in learning gains between students in an experimental group learning with the new approach and a control group learning with the traditional approach?

RQ3: What are the perception and experience of the experimental group about the new approach?

3.2 Research Design

In this study, the aim is to explore the topic of algebra, which is considered abstract in the field of mathematics education. As stated in the literature, the algebra unit that students typically have difficulty understanding is selected for the scope of the research. It is hypothesised that students may feel anxious when first encountering algebra. To address this, students are invited to become storytellers, using algebra as a lens to understand how it is interconnected with everyday life. The goal is to help students recognize that algebra is not just a theoretical concept with unknown terms like x, y, and z but a practical tool in real-life situations.

This research is planned to use a quasi-experimental design with control and experimental groups and the pretest-posttest method. About 180 students from 6 different classes studying mathematics at Key Stage 2 in the UK (10–11 years old) will be recruited. The experimental group will take lessons with the digital algebra game. A pre-test and a post-test will be applied before and after the intervention. As qualitative data, we will conduct semi-structured interviews with the experimental group, asking questions on their perception and experience of interacting with digital algebra game. Students are expected to create stories through the digital game. Then the students are expected to share the stories they create with their friends and pass the increasingly difficult levels. In this way, three different main themes (DGBL, DST and math education) are integrated (Fig. 1). An example from the game prototype is illustrated in Fig. 2. A student is expected to create a story with the virtual characters given, linking the story to an algebraic question.

Fig. 1. Research Diagram

Fig. 2. Example from prototype

4 Contribution and Concluding Remark

This study is important in terms of measuring the effects of DEGs developed for the subject of algebra in mathematics education. There is limited research on DEGs into which the method of *storytelling* is integrated, and students play the role of storytellers (designers). We will develop such DEGs and evaluate them in terms of effectiveness, efficiency and enjoyability. Especially for abstract topics such as algebra, this study will be beneficial to mathematics education. In summary, the contributions are:

- *The current research on the integration of algebra in digital games is limited.* However, existing studies have consistently demonstrated that algebra, as an abstract concept in mathematics, is challenging for primary school students aged 10–11 years old. It is planned that students will have an improved understanding and enhanced engagement in algebra with digital algebra game.
- *There is a limited number of studies that investigate the relationship between digital games and storytelling.* Students are believed to better understand math concepts such as algebra by creating storytelling through digital games. Therefore, the aim is to enable students to recognise the interaction between mathematics and daily life.
- *There are limited studies in which students are in the role of a designer in digital games* [10]. It is planned to increase the students' creativity by allowing them to be in the role of a designer in the algebra game designed, creating their math problems and stories in the game.

To conclude, we are motivated to explore the promising approach of integrating DEGs with digital storytelling to learning algebra, which can result in very positive impacts.

References

1. Prensky, M.: Digital natives, digital immigrants part 1. On the Horizon **9**(5), 1–6 (2001)
2. Lei, J.: Digital natives as preservice teachers: what technology preparation is needed? J. Comput. Teach. Educ. **25**(3), 87–97 (2009)
3. Silva, J.N.: On mathematical games. BSHM Bull. **26**(2), 80–104 (2011)
4. Brousseau, G., Brousseau, N., Warfield, V.: Teaching Fractions Through Situations: A Fundamental Experiment, vol. 54. Springer, Cham (2014). https://doi.org/10.1007/978-94-007-2715-1
5. McFeetors, P.J., Palfy, K.: Educative experiences in a games context: supporting emerging reasoning in elementary school mathematics. J. Math. Behav. **50**, 103–125 (2018)
6. National Council of Teachers of Mathematics: Principles and Standards for school mathematics. Author, Reston (2000)
7. Lee, L.C., Hao, K.C.: Designing and evaluating digital game-based learning with the ARCS motivation model, humor, and animation. Int. J. Technol. Human Interact. **11**(2), 80–95 (2015)
8. Sailer, M., Homner, L.: The gamification of learning: a meta-analysis. Educ. Psychol. Rev. **32**(1), 77–112 (2020)
9. Hsu, C.F., Chen, C.M., Cao, D.: Effects of design factors of game-based English vocabulary learning APP on learning performance, sustained attention, emotional state, and memory retention. In: International Congress on Advanced Applied Informatics, pp. 661–666. IEEE (2017)
10. Dishon, G., Kafai, Y.B.: Making more of games: cultivating perspective-taking through game design. Comput. Educ. **148**, 103810 (2020)
11. Kaimara, P., Deliyannis, I.: Why should I play this game? The role of motivation in smart pedagogy. In: Daniela, L. (ed.) Didactics of Smart Pedagogy, pp. 113–137. Springer, Cham (2019). https://doi.org/10.1007/978-3-030-01551-0_6
12. Yang, K.-H.: Learning behavior and achievement analysis of a digital game-based learning approach integrating mastery learning theory and different feedback models. Interact. Learn. Environ. **25**(2), 235–248 (2017)
13. Dondio, P., Gusev, V., Rocha, M.: Do games reduce maths anxiety? A meta-analysis. Comput. Educ. **194**, 104650 (2023)
14. Yang, Y.T.C., Wu, W.C.I.: Digital storytelling for enhancing student academic achievement, critical thinking, and learning motivation: a year-long experimental study. Comput. Educ. **59**(2), 339–352 (2012)
15. Ayten, B.K., Polater, C.: Values education using the digital storytelling method in fourth grade primary school students. Int. J. Educ. Literacy Stud. **9**(2), 66–78 (2021)
16. Albano, G., Coppola, C., Iacono, U.D., Fiorentino, G., Pierri, A., Polo, M.: Technology to enable new paradigms of teaching/learning in mathematics: the digital interactive storytelling case. J. E-learn. Knowl. Soc. **16**(1), 65–71 (2020)
17. Büyükkarci, A., Müldür, M.: Digital storytelling for primary school mathematics teaching: product and process evaluation. Educ. Inf. Technol. **27**(4), 5365–5396 (2022)
18. Wu, J., Chen, D.T.V.: A systematic review of educational digital storytelling. Comput. Educ. **147**, 103786 (2020)

Distinguishing User Paths for Personas and Stakeholders Through Motives and Decision Making

Megan Marie Doherty[✉] [iD]

NHSBSA, Newcastle Upon Tyne, England
meganmariedoherty@gmail.com

Abstract. Personas play a crucial role in the design process by aligning user needs with project functionality and identifying potential obstacles. However, if not evaluated properly during the assumption stage, personas may not accurately represent users. The objective of this research is to develop a framework that considers users' past experiences and circumstances to guide researchers during the initial assumption phase. The study aims to examine persona development in greater detail during this stage, considering the motives and decision-making processes of external stakeholders in both public and private sectors. By studying discussions taken with users as they examine digital tools with the researcher the preliminary research explores the use of thinking more of the observations made by the persona. The findings suggest that additional information could be potentially considered in the early stages of persona creation for design purposes such as objective and subjective perspectives.

Keywords: Personas · Human Computer Interaction (HCI) · stakeholders

1 Introduction

Personas are fictional representations of users or customer profiles that include text and images. They serve to combine data and insights for designers to better understand their target audience [1]. Personas are commonly used in design processes and workflows [2–5] to identify, create, and assess user groups. However, personas can quickly become outdated in online markets where user behavior changes rapidly [1]. This poses a challenge for public services that aim to effectively reflect their users through engaging personas, especially when facing limited resources. One major criticism of traditional personas is that they lack substantial amounts of firsthand user data [7], making it difficult to conduct thorough testing, particularly in public services.

The focus of this study is to explore how service providers can develop more efficient persona structures from the start of a digital service project. By conducting a case study that examines personas, the study investigates the motivations of stakeholders who use complex systems and services. Preliminary findings suggest that users' behavior patterns may be influenced by specific individual factors. The goal of this research is to consider

© The Author(s), under exclusive license to Springer Nature Switzerland AG 2023
J. Abdelnour Nocera et al. (Eds.): INTERACT 2023, LNCS 14145, pp. 464–468, 2023.
https://doi.org/10.1007/978-3-031-42293-5_55

users' past experiences and circumstances and use them as a basis for creating a framework to guide researchers in the initial assumption phase of their work. This approach emphasizes both the subjective and objective positions of users. Governmental digital services, particularly design services, are still exploring ways to examine "diversity" among public users in the UK. It is believed that gaining further insight into this method can be valuable for conducting fast-paced research.

2 Related Work

Personas are cited primarily to facilitate communication amongst designers [8]. Usually a photo, a set of goals, and "a narrative that covers mental model, environment, skills, frustrations, attitudes, typical tasks, and any other factors that seem critical to understanding the behavior pattern," are consistent across most persona theories [9]. Personas are also noted to relate to analytics efforts from a variety of domains for identifying, constructing, and assessing groups of people [1]. These groups can include different users, customers, audiences, or market segments. This has been used in system development [6] and to optimize some performance metrics (e.g., speed of task, ease of use, effectiveness of effort, sales, revenue, or engagement) [1]. Personas are not often viewed as cheap, easy, or a quick process [10]. It requires insight into qualitative research and user research to support designers understand the needs of the user research.

Personas are representations of users or customer segments presented in the form of an imaginary person (usually a photo and accompanying textual content) [1], but this can allow for gaps in context, knowledge, and design. Personas can be categorized into stages of development. These are (a) personas founded solely on data, (b) personas found on secondary data (c) personas relying on assumptions [1, 11]. These are however often tied strictly to the industry they are created primarily for and requires consistent evaluation to review changes. This means from an early stage in design development it can be difficult to understand users without in-depth knowledge or hard to obtain retrospection.

While the most cited benefit of personas is their ability to facilitate communication [8], but personas can remove the user and replace stakeholders with a set list of software requirements for a project. Studies that examine the use of persona noted that they rarely displayed empathy as a choice to use this design method [4], and the reliance on using a hypothetical with simple allocation for 'needs' will likely miss specific requirements. One challenge that can arise is when assumptions only consider specific user situations without considering potential reactions to the designs of digital tools. In the context of examining the initial stages of larger designs, there may not be sufficient time available to gather further insights.

3 Method

The research methodology employed in this study was ethnographic [12], utilizing open-ended interviews to explore participants' interactions with design services [13]. Participants were recruited through email, which provided information about the digital urban planning tool and the expectations for the think-aloud protocol. The think-aloud protocol allowed participants to verbalize their thoughts, actions, and reactions while engaging with the urban planning tool during the interview session. The digital service under investigation was an urban planning tool. The data collected from these unstructured interviews were subsequently analyzed using thematic analysis [14]. A code book was utilized to identify and categorize themes related to participants' feedback and insights regarding their experiences with the digital tool. This analysis aimed to extract specific insights that participants shared with the researcher during the evaluation of the digital tool.

4   Findings and Discussion

20 participants were recruited through an email survey. This exploratory work presents that's users could be separated into subjective and objective. The users rely on their own activism, professionalism, and localism to make sense of specific design decisions.

4.1   Subjective and Objective

The participants of the evaluation were identified as specific stakeholders being passive or active; and whose opinions might emerge from specific influencing factors. Finally, the outputs from these with either subjective or objective perspectives. This was connected to aspects of the factors that influenced. These participants could be identified as having either a subjective or objective perspective on this project. The subjective participant would review the consultation as something that might implicitly impact them.

4.2   Factors of Influence

To understand the information that users might possess when using digital tools, it is important to identify the factors that encourage external stakeholder engagement. In this study, participants were categorized based on their activism, localism, and professionalism, which influenced their levels of engagement.

Activist participants demonstrated a keen interest in addressing social, political, or economic concerns within the shared built environment. Many participants actively engaged in community causes or specific issues. Activism often evoked subjective responses, but these responses could also be approached objectively when aligned with their professional interests.

Localism was a common aspect among all participants in the study, but it should not be assumed that all users relate to it. Localism is subjective and relies on a stakeholder's connection to their livelihoods, such as their business, study, and recreational areas. Localism can establish a stronger link to a stakeholder's activism, particularly in the context of tools used in the public sector.

Participants with specific vocational backgrounds were classified as professionals. Their ideas and interactions during the consultation were influenced by their professions and industries. While it was anticipated that their professional expertise would positively impact their responses to various design elements of the project, it often led them to focus primarily on their professional insights, relying more on objectivity.

Overall, categorizing participants based on their activism, localism, and profession-alism sheds light on how their objective and subjective views contribute to engaged inter-actions. It helps to recognize the diverse motivations and perspectives that stakeholders bring when evaluating digital tools.

5 Conclusion

In conclusion, this exploratory paper proposes a new approach to assumption-based personas, focusing on understanding user motivations and engagement with public-facing services. The research highlights the importance of considering both the subjective and objective perspectives of stakeholders. By incorporating motivations and available resources, persona design in the early stages can be enhanced to better serve users in their interactions with services. This approach encompasses assumptions, secondary research, and more research-focused efforts. Future studies should delve deeper into the needs of stakeholders who are often overlooked during service development. The case study conducted in this research explores themes related to the motivations of stakeholders using complex systems and services. The preliminary findings suggest that individual user factors play a significant role in users' usage patterns. The intention of this research is to acknowledge the influence of users' past experiences and circumstances and develop a framework for researchers to use during the early assumption phase of their work.

References

1. An, J., Kwak, H., Jung, S., Salminen, J., Admad, M., Jansen, B.: Imaginary people representing real numbers: generating personas from online social media data. ACM Trans. Web 12(4), Article 27 1–26 (2018)
2. Dharwada, P., Greenstein, J.S., Gramopadhye, A.K., Davis, S.J.: A case study on use of personas in design and development of an audit management system. In: Proceedings of the Human Factors and Ergonomics Society Annual Meeting, Vol. 51, No. 5, pp. 469–473. Sage CA: Los Angeles, CA: SAGE Publications, (2007)
3. Eriksson, E., Artman, H., Swartling, A: The secret life of a persona: When the personal becomes private. In: Proceedings of the SIGCHI Conference on Human Factors in Computing Systems, CHI '13, pp. 2677–2686. Association for Computing Machinery, New York, NY, USA (2013)
4. Friess, E.: Personas and decision making in the design process: an ethnographic case study. In: Proceedings of the SIGCHI Conference on Human Factors in Computing Systems, pp. 1209–1218. Annual ACM Conference on Human Factors in Computing Systems. Toronto, Ontario, Canada (2012)
5. Nielsen, L., Storgaard Hansen, K.: Personas is applicable: a study on the use of personas in Denmark. In: Proceedings of the SIGCHI Conference on Human Factors in Computing Systems, pp. 1665–1674. Sanity (2nd Edition), Pearson Higher Education. (2014)
6. Cooper, A.: The inmates are running the asylum: why high-tech products drive us crazy and how to restore the sanity, revised eds. Sams Publishing, Indianapolis (2004)
7. McGinn, J., Kotamraju, N.: Data-driven persona development. In: Proceedings of the SIGCHI Conference on Human Factors in Computing Systems, pp. 1521–1524. (2008)
8. Pruitt, J., Grudin, J.: Personas: practice and theory. In: Proceedings of the 2003 conference on Designing for user experiences, (DUX '03). Association for Computing Machinery, pp.1–15. (2003)

9. Goodwin, K.: Designing for the digital age: How to create human-centered products and services. John Wiley & Sons (2011)
10. Drego, V.L, Dorsey, M.: The ROI of Personas. Forrester Research (2010)
11. Matthews, T., Judge, T., Whittaker, S.: ow do designers and user experience professionals actually perceive and use personas? In: Proceedings of the SIGCHI Conference on Human Factors in Computing Systems (CHI '12). Association for Computing Machinery, pp. 1219–1228. New York, NY, USA. (2012)
12. Patton, M.Q.: Qualitative research & evaluation methods: Integrating theory and practice. Sage publications. (2014)
13. Patton, M.Q.: Qualitative research and evaluation methods. Sage Publications, California, Thousand Oaks (2002)
14. Ericsson, A., Simon, H.A.: Protocol analysis: Verbal Reports as Data, Revised MIT Press, Cambridge MA (1993)

Embodied PointCloud: Combining Embodied Avatars with Point Clouds to Represent Users in VR Remote Meetings

Amal Yassien(✉), Yusuf Badawi, and Slim Abdennadher

German International University in Cairo, Cairo, Egypt
amalwalied@gmail.com

Abstract. Avatar realism is crucial for high-quality virtual reality remote meetings. In this work, we introduce *Embodied PointCloud*, a user representation technique that combines point clouds' realism with the increased embodiment of 3D humanoid avatars for improved interaction. After we conducted a user study to compare this approach to full-body tracked humanoid avatars, we found that Embodied PointCloud lowered perceived workload but had no significant effect on presence and social presence. We believe that Embodied PointCloud could help personalize user representation while ensuring high self-embodiment levels.

Keywords: Point Clouds · Social VR · Embodiment · Social Presence

1 Introduction and Related Work

Remote meetings increased after COVID-19, leading to employees feeling less connected [3]. Therefore, researchers explored virtual reality (VR) meetings as they create a more effective work environment [9] and offer better social connections than traditional video conferencing [1]. To achieve social connection between users in VR, researchers maximize users' sense of **presence** (sense of being there in the virtual world) [9] and **social presence** (awareness of other people existence in the virtual world) [8,13] in the virtual environment (VE). The key to achieving high presence and social presence in VR lies in establishing self-embodiment through adequate user representations [9,13]. Research has shown that photo-realistic 3D model avatars improve user embodiment (users' sense of owning their avatars) [11] and virtual body acceptance rates [4] but are expensive to create using traditional methods (e.g. using 40 DSLR cameras [4]). An alternative approach involves using depth cameras to augment point cloud representations, providing high social presence at a lower cost but with lower embodiment scores [10]. To get the best of both worlds, we introduce *Embodied PointCloud*, a VR user representation technique combining 3D point cloud photo-realistic representations with high embodiment rates found in conventional 3D model-based avatars. In *Embodied PointCloud*, users see their meeting

© The Author(s), under exclusive license to Springer Nature Switzerland AG 2023
J. Abdelnour Nocera et al. (Eds.): INTERACT 2023, LNCS 14145, pp. 469–474, 2023.
https://doi.org/10.1007/978-3-031-42293-5_56

partners as 3D point clouds (using Azure Kinect) while they see themselves embodying a 3D humanoid avatar, as shown in Fig. 1. To assess its effectiveness, users performed three tasks: solving riddles, decision-making, and negotiation. Afterwards, we conducted a 2 × 3 mixed design user study (N = 36, 18 pair) that compares Embodied PointClouds to full-body tracked 3D humanoid avatar representations (achieves high embodiment [7]). Our findings showed that users experienced lower mental and temporal demand with *Embodied PointCloud*, but similar presence and social presence compared to 3D humanoid avatars. We believe that *Embodied PointCloud* would help design social virtual environments with improved user representation and higher embodiment.

Fig. 1. The unity scene and first person views of two users represented using *Embodied PointCloud* within our designed remote meeting virtual environment.

2   System Design

Embodied PointCloud is a novel technique that represents users in social virtual environments via combining the realism of 3D point clouds with the high embodiment of 3D humanoid avatars. To validate its effectiveness, we created an online VR application using Oculus Quest 2 for remote meetings to compare Embodied PointCloud with conventional 3D humanoid avatars. To represent users using 3D humanoid avatars (one male and one female), we used (1) UMA for avatar formation, (2) FinalIK for 3-point body-tracking, and (3) Salsa LipSync Suite for face and lipsync animations. To develop Embodied PointCloud, we relied on (1) Microsoft's Azure Kinect camera and its Kinect Sensor and Kinect Body Tracking SDKs and (2) Azure Kinect Examples for Unity to stream the point cloud to other users (see Fig. 2-X). To sync scene changes in either representations, we used the Multiplayer VR Template which relies on Photon PUN2 server. If users start the application for the Embodied PointCloud representation, their (1) Oculus Quests and (2) Azure Kinect camera are connected to the VR laptop via Oculus Link and USB-C cable respectively. After users wear the Oculus Quest and start the application in either representations, they are prompted to join a VR meeting room that we created beforehand. Afterwards, they enter a waiting area, where they can pick and customize their 3D humanoid avatars. Once they enter the VR meeting room, they can hear each other and are represented to their partner as either Embodied PointCloud or 3D full-body humanoid avatar. In the Embodied PointCloud representation, users were represented to their partners in the VE as a 3D point cloud that properly mimics the user movement along with their facial features and expressions (lip and jaw animation), but see themselves embodying a 3D humanoid full-body tracked avatar, where they can grab objects using their humanoid hands and teleport within the VE. Once they grab an object, the partner sees that object attached to the users' point cloud. Once a user teleport, the partner sees the user's point cloud moving smoothly toward the position the user is teleporting to. In the 3D full-body humanoid avatar representation, users were seen as a 3D humanoid full-body tracked avatar that supports facial and lip animation. The users can grab objects using their humanoid hands and teleport within the environment. In the meeting room, there are two white boards and markers that users can write on using the virtual markers provided. Once a user grabs a marker and starts to write on the board, a haptic feedback is produced by the controllers to tell the users that the marker has touched the board.

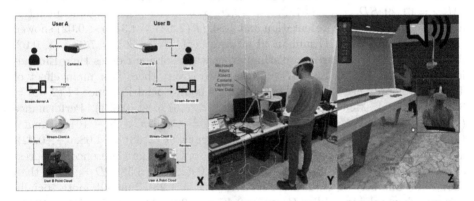

Fig. 2. X: the architecture of our novel *Embodied PointCloud* user representation technique. Y: the physical hardware setup of *Embodied PointCloud*. Z: the unity scene view showing the user in figure Y while being represented as *Embodied PointCloud*.

3   Evaluation and Results

A user study with 36 participants (18 pairs) tested *Embodied PointCloud's* effectiveness using a 2 × 3 mixed design, focusing on User Representation and Task. Participants were divided into groups: 3D Humanoid avatars group and *Embodied PointCloud group*. After they signed the consent form, the experimenter familiarized them with the VE individually. Afterwards, they performed three tasks that are commonly performed in meetings namely decision-making (property purchasing), negotiation (property room assignment), and solving riddles in our VR application. Two pre-studies aided in selecting suitable riddles and floor plans (for decision-making and negotiation tasks) using completion time and participant's feedback as an inclusion metric. While performing the tasks, users wore earphones (wired to the Oculus) and were within the same room. Participants completed post-task surveys including presence and social presence [6], nasa-TLX [2], and UEQ questionnaires [5], and task completion time was recorded. The order of performing the task was balanced using latin square. The study involved university students (31 male and 5 female) aged 18–23 and lasted approximately 30 min. Afterwards, we analyzed the results using a 2×3 non-parametric ANOVA using ART and Wobbrock's ARTool library in R [12]. Pairwise comparisons with Tukey HSD were used for significant task effects, meanwhile Holm's sequential Bonferroni procedure was applied for significant interactions. The time, social presence, mental demand, temporal demand, and performance results are reverse coded, i.e. lower values are better. Our results showed a main effect of User Representation on Mental Demand (md) ($F(1, 34) = 9.07, p < 0.01$) and Temporal Demand (td) ($F(1, 34) = 6.66, p < 0.02$), where Embodied PointCloud ($M_{md} = 35.69, SD_{md} = 28.24, M_{td} = 27.25, SD_{td} = 20.93$) showed lower temporal and mental demand than 3D humanoid avatar ($M_{md} = 61.29, SD_{md} = 28.87, M_{td} = 49.26, SD_{td} = 29.35$). A significant interaction between User Representation and Task ($F(2, 68) = 4.32, p < 0.02$) showed that users found that 3D humanoid avatars ($\chi^2(1, N = 36) = 7.93, p < 0.02, M = 1.81, SD = 1.09$) are more stimulating when solving riddles than Embodied PointCloud ($M = 1.35, SD = 1.05$). Moreover, there is a main effect of Task on Telepresence ($F(2, 68) = 5.57, p < 0.006$), Social Presence ($F(2, 68) = 3.21, p < 0.05$), Mental Demand ($F(2, 68) = 8.61, p < 0.001$), Performance ($F(2, 68) = 6.18, p < 0.004$), Time ($F(2, 68) = 110.9, p < 2e - 16$), Stimulation ($F(2, 68) = 7.45, p < 0.002$), and Efficiency ($F(2, 68) = 4.68, p < 0.02$). Task pairwise comparisons showed that (1) users felt more presence (telepresence) while negotiating ($t(68) = 3.78, p < 0.005, M = 5.58, SD = 0.98$) than they did while solving riddles ($M = 5.16, SD = 1.23$), but felt more socially present when solving riddles ($t(68) = 2.46, p < 0.05, M = 62.51, SD = 19.09$) than they did when negotiating ($M = 67.69, SD = 17.58$), (2) solving riddles ($M_{md} = 54.09, SD_{md} = 29.46$) induced higher mental demand rates than decision-making ($t(68) = -3.85, p < 0.05, M = 45.28, SD = 31.78$) and negotiation ($t(68) = -3.26, p < 0.05, M = 46.11, SD = 32.38$), but it produced best performance (p) ($M = 75.22, SD = 27.01$) and time completion (t) ($M = 60.42, SD = 28.18$) results than negotiation ($t_t(68) = 14.11, p_t < .0001, M_t = 72.72, SD_t = 24.74, t_p(68) = 3.16, p_p < 0.007, M_p = 81.72, SD_p = 28.93$) and decision-making ($t_t(68) = 2.94, p_t < 0.02, M_t = 155.01, SD_t = 43.08, t_p(68) = 2.91, p_p < 0.02, M_p = 81.72, SD_p = 29.93$), (3) decision-making ($t(68) = 2.85, p < 0.02, M = 1.85, SD = 1.05$) and negotiation ($t(68) = 3.68, p < 0.002, M = 1.94, SD = 0.99$) were more stimulating than solving riddles ($M = 1.58, SD = 1.08$), and (4) negotiations ($t(68) = 2.94, p < 0.02, M = 1.72, SD = 1.03$) were more efficient than solving riddles ($M = 1.42, SD = 1.18$).

4   Conclusion

Our results show that (1) using *Embodied PointCloud* reduced the users' mental and temporal demand, while sustained comparable presence, social presence, performance, and task completion time to the 3D humanoid representation, and (2) users' had a better experience and workload when negotiating and making decisions than they did when solving riddle, but solving riddles had the best time completion results. We believe that *Embodied PointCloud* would guide developers in providing realistic user representations that reduce user's workload, meanwhile providing high performance, presence, embodiment, and social presence.

References

1. Abdullah, A., Kolkmeier, J., Lo, V., Neff, M.: Videoconference and embodied VR: communication patterns across task and medium. Proc. ACM Hum. Comput. Interact. **5**(CSCW2) (2021). https://doi.org/10.1145/3479597
2. Hart, S.G.: Nasa-task load index (nasa-tlx); 20 years later. In: Proceedings of the Human Factors and Ergonomics Society Annual Meeting, vol. 50, pp. 904–908. Sage, Los Angeles (2006)
3. Karl, K.A., Peluchette, J.V., Aghakhani, N.: Virtual work meetings during the covid-19 pandemic: the good, bad, and ugly. Small Group Res. **53**(3), 343–365 (2022)
4. Latoschik, M.E., Roth, D., Gall, D., Achenbach, J., Waltemate, T., Botsch, M.: The effect of avatar realism in immersive social virtual realities. In: Proceedings of the 23rd ACM Symposium on Virtual Reality Software and Technology, p. 39. ACM (2017)
5. Laugwitz, B., Held, T., Schrepp, M.: Construction and evaluation of a user experience questionnaire. In: Holzinger, A. (ed.) USAB 2008. LNCS, vol. 5298, pp. 63–76. Springer, Heidelberg (2008). https://doi.org/10.1007/978-3-540-89350-9_6
6. Nowak, K.L., Biocca, F.: The effect of the agency and anthropomorphism on users' sense of telepresence, copresence, and social presence in virtual environments. Presence **12**(5), 481–494 (2003). https://doi.org/10.1162/105474603322761289
7. Pan, X., Hamilton, A.F.D.C.: Why and how to use virtual reality to study human social interaction: the challenges of exploring a new research landscape. Br. J. Psychol. (2018)
8. Parsons, T.D., Gaggioli, A., Riva, G.: Virtual reality for research in social neuroscience. Brain Sci. **7**(4), 42 (2017)
9. Schwind, V.: Implications of the uncanny valley of avatars and virtual characters for human-computer interaction (2018)
10. Singh, S., Dijkstra-Soudarissanane, S., Gunkel, S.: Engagement and quality of experience in remote business meetings: a social VR study. In: Proceedings of the 1st Workshop on Interactive Extended Reality (IXR 2022), pp. 77–82. Association for Computing Machinery, New York (2022). https://doi.org/10.1145/3552483.3556457
11. Wauck, H., Lucas, G., Shapiro, A., Feng, A., Boberg, J., Gratch, J.: Analyzing the effect of avatar self-similarity on men and women in a search and rescue game. In: Proceedings of the 2018 CHI Conference on Human Factors in Computing Systems, p. 485. ACM (2018)

12. Wobbrock, J.O., Findlater, L., Gergle, D., Higgins, J.J.: The aligned rank transform for nonparametric factorial analyses using only anova procedures. In: Proceedings of the SIGCHI Conference on Human Factors in Computing Systems (CHI 2011), pp. 143–146. Association for Computing Machinery, New York (2011). https://doi.org/10.1145/1978942.1978963
13. Yassien, A., ElAgroudy, P., Makled, E., Abdennadher, S.: A design space for social presence in VR. In: Proceedings of the 11th Nordic Conference on Human-Computer Interaction: Shaping Experiences, Shaping Society (NordiCHI 2020). Association for Computing Machinery, New York (2020). https://doi.org/10.1145/3419249.3420112

Enhancing Learnability with Micro Teachings

Katja Pott[✉] and Doris Agotai

University of Applied Sciences and Arts Northwestern Switzerland FHNW,
Institute of Interactive Technologies IIT, Brugg, Switzerland
`katja.pott@fhnw.ch`

Abstract. Around 20% of the Western world's population has low digital literacy, which hinders them from participating in today's digital society. Despite the increasing complexity of systems, the learnability is often neglected. In this pilot study, we investigate the potential of embedding digital literacy training into the user journey to improve first-use learnability and encourage user independence. To achieve this, we created Micro Teachings (MT), which are small just-in-time learning sequences paired with reflection-in-action exercises for reinforcement. In addition, the MT are designed as Micro Worlds representing a subset of the reality to learn in a controlled and secure environment through exploration. For conveying the content we implemented the MT with two different learning styles for comparison: agent-based and observational learning.

The pilot study is conducted on the Interactive Tabletop Projection (ITP) called live paper, as part of a larger research project. Results from 11 participants show that users performed better with the observational learning method than with the agent-based approach. Their confidence increased while their fear of the system decreased. In addition, the error rate and the number of help interventions were drastically reduced. These results show that by utilizing an appropriate approach and environment, learnability can be considerably enhanced and also simplify the entry into the digital world for people with low digital literacy, embracing inclusion and equality.

Keywords: Learnability · Techno-Stress · Digital Literacy · Interactive Tabletop Projection · Self-Efficacy · Digital Exclusion

1 Introduction

In today's society, digital literacy is an essential skill that enables individuals to participate in the digital world through the use of ICT. Approximately 20% of the population in Western societies face digital exclusion due to low digital literacy [1, 2]. However, little research has been done on how to support this group and facilitate simplified access for participation [3].

© The Author(s), under exclusive license to Springer Nature Switzerland AG 2023
J. Abdelnour Nocera et al. (Eds.): INTERACT 2023, LNCS 14145, pp. 475–480, 2023.
https://doi.org/10.1007/978-3-031-42293-5_57

One possible solution to this problem is to design for learnability, as design for intuitive use relies on prior knowledge that people with low digital literacy may miss [3–5]. Research also shows that using new applications can be challenging for these people due to a lack of support and overly complex training materials [4]. It is also vital that the content is context-related, as users often have difficulty transferring their knowledge across different devices and applications [4].

Improving user confidence is key to reduce stress and anxiety associated with ICT use, which can improve performance and enable more effective management of ICT-related problems [3,4]. Therefore, it's crucial to emphasize on user empowerment and instill a sense of self-efficacy when designing for people with low digital literacy [3,6].

2   Micro Teachings

The research project "Involvement. Inclusion. Participation. one11 – a self-learning platform enables a new form of life through smart community building" addresses the issue of digital exclusion by establishing blended spaces for hybrid communities in local neighbourhoods to support digital inclusion. The spaces facilitate encounters and connection among members by setting up the Interactive Tabletop Projection (ITP) called Live Paper [7] in local community centers (Fig. 1a). Further, learning in a social community setup is beneficial for people with low digital literacy [3]. As the project focuses on design for learnability, we developed small, just-in-time learning sequences called Micro Teachings (MT) tailored to the needs of the target group [3]. The MT are embedded in the user journey, accompanied by reflection-in-action exercises to reinforce the content and support autonomous learning while using the system independently [8].

The Micro Teachings are designed as Micro Worlds: *"a small but complete subset of reality in which one can go to learn about a specific domain through personal discovery and exploration."* [8].

(a) Interactive Tabletop Projection (Live Paper)

(b) Agent-based learning MT with written instructions given by the digital agent

(c) Observational learning MT as instructional videos

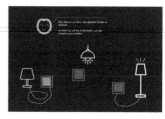

(d) Exercise to introduce buttons and teach touch interaction

Fig. 1. Instructions for touch interaction on ITP of developed Micro Teachings

This approach facilitates exploration of interactions in a secure, controlled environment. The central focus of the MT method is to foster *reflection-in-action*, a process that enables learners to gain practical, hands-on experience which is based on Experiential Learning Theory [8].

To convey the content, two different learning styles are implemented: (a) Agent-based learning and (b) Observational learning.

1) **Agent-based learning** is employed to teach digital skills with the help of a digital agent [6,9]. With the usage of it, the participants demonstrated an improvement in their ability and confidence in using ICT while their fear decreased [9]. 2) **Observational learning** is based on social cognitive theory [10] which states that knowledge is acquired through observation of others [11]. Through instructional videos the participants' self-efficacy and technology adoption were increased in using ICT [11].

Implementation. The objectives of the MT are to promote comprehension of the touch interaction, scroll interaction, selectable elements indicated by green color and location and functionality of the back and home buttons. Overall the users' confidence and digital literacy should be increased during system usage by the MT. The content of the MTs was selected based on observations from initial user tests with the system, aimed at identifying issues encountered during the first use.

To realize the stated objectives, three small learning units were developed as MT. Figure 1 shows the MTs implemented with (b) Agent-based learning where a digital agent gives written instructions and (c) Observational learning where a person gives instructions on videos, to teach users the touch interaction on the ITP. Both approaches have identical wording for the instructions given to the users. The MTs focus on reflection-in-action to reinforce the content and include various exercises. In order to facilitate a better understanding of specific functionalities, a link between the digital and analogue worlds was created [12]. For example, the concept of digital buttons was introduced using the metaphor of buttons for lamps, which are common in everyday life. An exercise was designed where users had to switch off lamps using touch interaction, as shown in Fig. 1d. This exercise was designed to increase users' familiarity with the concept of digital buttons and to improve their ability to relate it to real-world scenarios.

3   Results

This between-subjects study involved 11 people with low digital literacy. They performed three tasks on the target ITP with the support of the developed MT. The Technology Acceptance Model 3 (TAM) was used to evaluate the MT [13]. The data analysis shows a notable preference for the observational learning MT over the agent-based MT. Figure 2b illustrates that the values for all three metrics were consistently better with the observational learning MT using the TAM. Participants found the system easier to use, showed higher levels of confidence, and reported lower levels of anxiety with the observational learning MT. In addition, Fig. 2a shows that users made fewer errors and required less help interventions when completing the tasks with the observational learning MT.

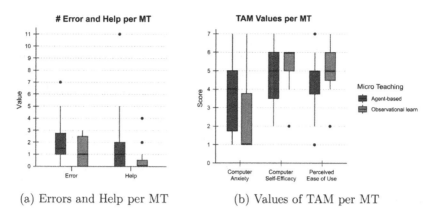

(a) Errors and Help per MT   (b) Values of TAM per MT

Fig. 2. Error, Help and TAM Values on ITP during User Tests per MT

4   Discussion

This pilot study shows that the combination of micro-worlds, reflective exercises and instructional videos can increase the first-use learnability of people with low digital literacy. The results indicate that self-efficacy and performance are improved by this intervention.

It raises the question of whether this approach would be beneficial for other groups when learning complex processes to build up confidence. As instructional videos are already widely used in education, the benefits may apply to other groups [15]. In addition, the videos use a digital version of the cognitive apprenticeship method, in which students learn from a master [14]. The master articulates each step performed for further understanding [14]. Again, this is a widely used concept for learning complex processes.

There is also the question of why the observational learning approach produces better results than the agent-based version. A possible explanation could be found by analysing the cognitive effort required. Watching a video is much less demanding than reading the agent-based version. On the other hand, it can be argued that videos don't allow users to learn at their own pace, which can lead to cognitive overload [15]. The observational learning approach may also be more effective as it engages multiple senses, leading to multisensory learning.

5   Future Work

The results highlight the importance of support in reducing the digital divide. The use of micro teachings shows a promising possibility for other applications to support users in their learning journey. It is particularly important to consider users' prior knowledge and mental models. This is essential to curate appropriate language and content that matches the needs and capabilities of the audience.

It might be interesting to conduct further long-term research to analyse whether there is a further improvement in the values over time and at what point it would become stagnant. If self-efficacy on the ITP has peaked, the user may feel confident enough to start using a traditional ICT device. To support this possibility, an appropriate intervention could be designed to facilitate the transition to other devices. This may help to build up self-efficacy with the new equipment and to build on the knowledge from the ITP in learning how to interact with the application on the new device. Another interesting question would be whether the difference in learning style would be reflected in the retention of knowledge.

Considering the needs and capabilities of the target group can lead to significant improvements in creating opportunities for access and participation in the digital society. Our solution offers an approach to address the challenge of digital exclusion faced by people with low digital literacy and to facilitate their entry into the digital world. In this way we hope to further reduce the digital divide in Switzerland and promote inclusion and participation.

Acknowledgements. Research Project 54959.1 IP-SBM: Involvement. Inclusion. Participation. one11 - a self-learning platform enables a new form of life through smart community building, funded by Innosuisse in collaboration with one11, FHNW school of social work and FHNW school of engineering.

References

1. Bundesamt für Statistik (BFS). Profil der Internetnutzerinnen und -nutzer im Jahr 2019 (2021). https://www.bfs.admin.ch/bfs/de/home/aktuell/neue-veroeffentlichungen.assetdetail.16044038.html. Accessed 5 Apr 2023
2. Istat. Citizens and ICT (2019). https://www.istat.it/it/files/2019/12/Cittadini-e-ICT-2019.pdf. Accessed 2 Apr 2023
3. Rasi, P., Vuojärvi, H., Rivinen, S.: Promoting media literacy among older people: a systematic review. Adult Educ. Quart. **71**(1), 37–54 (2021)
4. Bhattacharjee, P., Baker, S., Waycott, J.: Older adults and their acquisition of digital skills: a review of current research evidence. In: 32nd Australian Conference on Human-Computer Interaction, Sydney, pp. 437–443 (2020)
5. Reddy, G., et al.: Designing for Older Adults: Adaptable Interface as an Approach to Address Diversity on Older Users' Capabilities. School of Psychology and Counseling, Queensland University of Technology, Brisbane (2013)
6. Nap, H.H., Paul De Greef, H., Bouwhuis, D.G.: Self-efficacy support in senior computer interaction. Int. J. Cognit. Perform. Supp. **1**(1), 27–39 (2013)
7. Dolata, M., et al.: Changing things so (almost) everything stays the same. i-com **20**(3), 229–252 (2021)
8. Heinrich, P., Kilic, M., Schwabe, G.: Microworlds as the locus of consumer education in financial advisory services. In: 35th International Conference on Information Systems "Building a Better World Through Information Systems" (ICIS 2014)
9. Castilla, D., et al.: Teaching digital literacy skills to the elderly using a social network with linear navigation: a case study in a rural area. Int. J. Hum. Comput. Stud. **118**, 24–37 (2018)
10. Bandura, A.: Social Foundations of Thought and Action: a Social Cognitive Theory. Prentice-Hall, Englewood Cliffs (1986)

11. Peng, L., et al.: Facilitating gerontechnology adoption: observational learning with live models. In: Rau, P.-L. P. (ed.) CCD 2018. LNCS, vol. 10912, pp. 334–345. Springer, Cham (2018). https://doi.org/10.1007/978-3-319-92252-2_27
12. Gould, J., Schaefer, M.: User interface considerations for older users. In: Proceedings of the 10th annual SIGCSE conference on Innovation and Technology in Computer Science Education (2005)
13. Venkatesh, V., Bala, H.: Technology acceptance model 3 and a research agenda on interventions. Decis. Sci. **39**(2), 273–315 (2008)
14. Collins, A., Brown, J.S., Newman, S.E.: Cognitive apprenticeship: teaching the craft of reading, writing and mathematics. Thinking J. Philos. Child. **8**(1), 2–10 (1988)
15. Fyfield, M., Henderson, M., Phillips, M.: Improving instructional video design: a systematic review. Australas. J. Educ. Technol. **38**(3), 155–183 (2022)

Exploring Responsible AI Practices in Dutch Media Organizations

Tina Mioch[1]([✉]), Nathalie Stembert[2], Cathelijn Timmers[1], Oumaima Hajri[2], Pascal Wiggers[3], and Maaike Harbers[2]

[1] Utrecht University of Applied Sciences, Utrecht, The Netherlands
tina.mioch@hu.nl
[2] Rotterdam University of Applied Sciences, Rotterdam, The Netherlands
[3] Amsterdam University of Applied Sciences, Amsterdam, The Netherlands

Abstract. Artificial Intelligence (AI) is increasingly used in the media industry, for instance, for the automatic creation, personalization, and distribution of media content. This development raises concerns in society and the media sector itself about the responsible use of AI. This study examines how different stakeholders in media organizations perceive ethical issues in their work concerning AI development and application, and how they interpret and put them into practice. We conducted an empirical study consisting of 14 semi-structured qualitative interviews with different stakeholders in public and private media organizations, and mapped the results of the interviews on stakeholder journeys to specify how AI applications are initiated, designed, developed, and deployed in the different media organizations. This results in insights into the current situation and challenges regarding responsible AI practices in media organizations.

Keywords: Responsible AI · AI Ethics in Practice · Empirical Studies on Ethics

1 Introduction

Artificial Intelligence (AI) is increasingly used in the media industry [19], for instance, for the automatic creation, personalization, distribution and archiving of media content [2, 19]. This development raises concerns in society and the media sector about the responsible use of AI. There are worries, e.g., about the creation of deep fakes [11], the spread of disinformation through algorithms [12], issues with fairness and bias in recommendation [7], and algorithms reinforcing and strengthening existing stereotypes [16]. Rapid progress in AI techniques also affect the work of journalists and media professionals. These techniques reshape editorial and decision-making routines [4, 5] as well as the relationship of media with audiences [18]. This raises the question how to responsibly design, develop and deploy AI in the media domain [2].

In recent years, a large number of guidelines for ethical AI have been proposed (for overviews see, e.g., [8, 10]). Based on these abstract guidelines, several ethics tools have been proposed, but the adoption rate of such tools remains low, as these tools still lack practical applicability in the day-to-day practice [1, 6, 20]. In addition, most of these

© The Author(s), under exclusive license to Springer Nature Switzerland AG 2023
J. Abdelnour Nocera et al. (Eds.): INTERACT 2023, LNCS 14145, pp. 481–485, 2023.
https://doi.org/10.1007/978-3-031-42293-5_58

tools are not tailored to the specifics of the media domain. A notable exception is [3], developing tools for ethical AI in the context of music recommendation.

To create practical ethics tools that address domain-specific issues and fit the needs of professionals in that particular domain a good understanding of the organizational structures, routines, habits with respect to the development and use of AI and the role of ethics in those processes is needed. Several studies have been performed in non-media industries (e.g., [13, 14, 17]). This paper describes a study into current practices around the development and deployment of AI in the media industry specifically. We conducted interviews with stakeholders working at four large national media organizations in the Netherlands. Based on the results, we indicated challenges of media organizations in applying AI in a responsible way.

2 Method

To determine the current practices around design, development, and deployment of AI in the Dutch national media organizations, we conducted 14 semi-structured interviews with different stakeholders of four media organizations, with 9 interviewees working on a strategic level and 5 interviewees being involved in the (AI) development. The goal of the interviews was explorative, to gain as much information as possible on, amongst others, the current state of AI development in the organizations, ethical considerations that are being made, and challenges as they are experienced by the different organizations.

The interviews were recorded, fully transcribed, and qualitatively analyzed by itera-tively and collaboratively coding the interview transcripts. We coded inductively as a way to enter the data analysis with a more complete, unbiased look at the themes throughout our data. We categorized the resulting 46 codes into 10 overall themes. Based on these results, we created stakeholder journeys for three of the four organizations, mapping how AI applications are initiated, designed, developed, deployed and monitored in the different media organizations, which stakeholders are involved, which values play a role, at which points in the process ethical issues are considered, and how (ethical) decisions are made. The stakeholder journeys were then verified by representatives of the media organizations and improved.

3 Results

3.1 Core Themes of Stakeholder Journeys

Organizational   Values   and   Strategic   Decision-Making for AI Development Different values play a role in the different organizations: the public media organizations in our study focus on public values (e.g., independence, plu-riformity), whereas the private media organization follows a company vision with (in this case) more implicit values. For all organizations hold that these are regularly reviewed and shared with employees. Across both type of organizations employees recognize the importance of these values but cannot always reproduce them. It is unclear how organizational values are taken into account in the decision-making process regarding investments in innovative (AI) projects, as there is no explicit documentation regarding ethical criteria. It is assumed that values are embedded in the culture of the organization in such a way that they are automatically included in all considerations; however, there is no explicit mechanism to evaluate (or monitor) this.

Embedding Ethical Aspects in Work Processes The public media organizations have made a start of composing a set of internal (and overarching) guidelines regarding Ethics and Technology. Employees are largely aware of (the processes regarding) the development of internal and external guidelines. The employees of the private media organization participated in internal trainings regarding for example privacy and security. In practice, both the guidelines and trainings however changed little of their work processes and behavior and mostly increased their level of awareness and knowledge concerning these topics. The work processes in the media organizations are not yet set up for explicitly including ethical considerations for AI, e.g. the use of ethical guidelines and instruments regarding AI is not officially put in protocols.

Effects of AI on Employees The participating media organizations are aware that the introduction of AI can greatly change the work of some of their employees. Mostly, the organizations expect that the new technology will make work more enjoyable and free up time for creative tasks and less time spent on monotonous tasks; however, everyone is aware that introducing AI systems requires support and coaching of employees during the transition. Attention, knowledge, and responsibility of ethics and AI issues are diffusely distributed over the various departments. Clear points of contact with regards to ethics and AI are also lacking. Ethical questions end often up with the head of Innovation, Privacy Officer, or legal department. Several employees mention that it often is challenging to make time for ethical considerations, evaluations, and reflections during their work processes.

Ethical Protocols and Instruments Ethical instruments are not explicitly included in the decision-making and development process. Employees state that ethical guidelines are often too superficial, general and abstract. Existing instruments are only known to a limited extent within the organizations. It is also not clear which instruments are particularly suitable for which projects and at what point in the development process they should be used. A concern that some employees have is that ethical tools are time-consuming and therefore too expensive to apply structurally and that ethical checklists mainly stimulate a culture of ticking boxes and not taking ethical responsibility. As a result, they are currently not applied in the participating media organizations, which means that ethical choices are often made implicitly.

3.2 AI-related Challenges in the Organizations

Overarching Organizational Challenges Overarching organizational challenges (applicable to all media organizations in this study) involve: 1) creating time for validation and reflection after the different phases of a project or after the entire project, 2) obtaining funding to continue projects after the initial (exploration) phase, 3) translating the abstract vision regarding Ethics and AI into more concrete guidelines and instruments, 4) developing protocols so that ethical considerations are made more explicit and sufficiently documented, 5) adding value for employees by means of ethical instruments that do not limit them in their work processes/tasks, 6) keeping processes and ethical considerations transparent (this poses a particular challenge when collaborating with external agencies, which is a regular occurrence), 7) embedding responsibilities for ethical considerations more clearly within the organizations, and 8) making non-technical employees (such as editorial staff) aware of the importance of ethical challenges surrounding AI.

Challenges in Strategy Phase These challenges involve: 1) assessing whether AI is a solution for a (real) problem and not just a technology push, 2) supporting and stimulating the User Experience team in making ethical choices during their work processes, 3) involving the right (internal and external) stakeholders regarding ethical evaluation and the choice to continue with a project, and 4) estimating ethical impact by examining the effects and risks for (internal and external) users.

Challenges in Proof-of-Concept Phase These challenges involve: 1) making ethical considerations measurable in order to test and validate them, and 2) supporting and stimulating the Data Science team in making ethical choices in their work.

Challenges in Development Phase These challenges involve: 1) explicitly, consciously and continuously testing and evaluating ethical aspects during development, 2) assessing, usage and maintenance of third-party models, 3) supporting and stimulating the Development team in making ethical choices during their work processes, 4) getting the 'right' (sufficient, unbiased, GDPR approved, etc.) data, and 5) gathering user-data versus best fit regarding content recommendations.

4 Discussion and Conclusion

In this study, we found that all participating media organizations see the importance of ethical aspects during the design, development, and deployment of AI systems, and there is a strong drive to incorporate ethical decision-making. However, currently, available tools or guidelines to support the design of responsible AI are not used by the participating media organizations because they are perceived to be not sufficiently tailored to their needs. Furthermore, we found that media organizations mostly believe the challenges to be technical; however, we found that (introducing) responsible AI has large organizational challenges at different levels and departments and that there is a lack of cooperation and communication during the whole chain of development about ethical challenges. These findings are in line with other work on ethical considerations in media organizations regarding AI systems [9, 15].

Limitations of this work are that we had a relatively small number of participants and that these participants work in different kinds of media organizations, public as well as commercial. Nonetheless, the participants showed a diversity in thinking which leads us to believe that the analyses give a good insight into the current situation in (Dutch) media organizations.

References

1. Ayling, J., Chapman, A.: Putting ai ethics to work: are the tools fit for purpose? AI and Ethics **2**(3), 405–429 (2022)
2. Chan-Olmsted, S.M.: A review of artificial intelligence adoptions in the media industry. Int. J. Media Manag. **21**(3–4), 193–215 (2019)
3. Cramer, H., Garcia-Gathright, J., Reddy, S., Springer, A., Takeo Bouyer, R.: Translation, tracks & data: an algorithmic bias effort in practice. In: Extended Abstracts of the 2019 CHI Conference on Human Factors in Computing Systems, pp. 1–8 (2019)
4. Diakopoulos, N.: Automating the news: How algorithms are rewriting the media. Harvard University Press (2019)
5. Diakopoulos, N.: Towards a design orientation on algorithms and automation in news production. Digit. J. **7**(8), 1180–1184 (2019)
6. Dolata, M., Feuerriegel, S., Schwabe, G.: A sociotechnical view of algorithmic fairness. Inf. Syst. J. **32**(4), 754–818 (2022)
7. Elahi, M., et al.: Towards responsible media recommendation. AI and Ethics, pp. 1–12 (2022)
8. Hagendorff, T.: The ethics of ai ethics: an evaluation of guidelines. Mind. Mach. **30**(1), 99–120 (2020)
9. Helberger, N., van Drunen, M., Moeller, J., Vrijenhoek, S., Eskens, S.: Towards a normative perspective on journalistic ai: Embracing the messy reality of normative ideals (2022)
10. Jobin, A., Ienca, M., Vayena, E.: The global landscape of ai ethics guidelines. Nature Mach. Intell. **1**(9), 389–399 (2019)
11. Karnouskos, S.: Artificial intelligence in digital media: the era of deepfakes. IEEE Trans. Technol. Society **1**(3), 138–147 (2020)
12. Martens, B., Aguiar, L., Gomez-Herrera, E., Mueller-Langer, F.: The digital transformation of news media and the rise of disinformation and fake news (2018)
13. Rakova, B., Yang, J., Cramer, H., Chowdhury, R.: Where responsible ai meets reality: Practitioner perspectives on enablers for shifting organizational practices. Proc. ACM Human-Comput. Interact. **5**(CSCW1), 1–23 (2021)
14. Sanderson, C., et al.: Ai ethics principles in practice: Perspectives of designers and developers. arXiv preprint arXiv:2112.07467 (2021)
15. Schjøtt Hansen, A., Hartley, J.M.: Designing what's news: an ethnography of a personalization algorithm and the data-driven (re) assembling of the news. Digital J. 1–19 (2021)
16. Schroeder, J.E.: Reinscribing gender: social media, algorithms, bias. J. Mark. Manag. **37**(3–4), 376–378 (2021)
17. Subramonyam, H., Im, J., Seifert, C., Adar, E.: Solving separation-of-concerns problems in collaborative design of human-ai systems through leaky abstractions. In: Proceedings of the 2022 CHI Conference on Human Factors in Computing Systems, pp. 1–21 (2022)
18. Thurman, N., Moeller, J., Helberger, N., Trilling, D.: My friends, editors, algorithms, and i: examining audience attitudes to news selection. Digit. J. **7**(4), 447–469 (2019)
19. Trattner, C., et al.: Responsible media technology and AI: challenges and research directions. AI Ethics **2**(4), 585–594 (2022)
20. Wong, R.Y., Madaio, M.A., Merrill, N.: Seeing like a toolkit: How toolkits envision the work of AI ethics. arXiv preprint arXiv:2202.08792 (2022)

Exploring Users' Ability to Choose a Proper Fit in Smart-Rings: A Year-Long "In the Wild" Study

Peter Neigel[1,2]([envelope]) [ID], Andrew Vargo[1] [ID], Yusuke Komatsu[1] [ID], Chris Blakely[3] [ID], and Koichi Kise[1] [ID]

[1] Osaka Metropolitan University, Osaka, Japan
peter.neigel@dfki.de
[2] German Research Center for Artificial Intelligence (DFKI), Kaiserslautern, Germany
[3] The Kyoto College of Graduate Studies for Informatics, Kyoto, Japan

Abstract. Wearables have seen an increase in popularity as the technology has advanced. Via physiological sensing, these devices allow individuals to easily monitor their daily health, but there are limitations in real-world implementation. One limitation is the ability of end users to properly gauge how well a device fits. Proper fit is often crucial for accurate data collection, as ill-fitting devices can result in poor performance. In this work, we examine the fit of the ring sizes the participants chose at the start of the in-the-wild study and examine the effect it has on sensor data. An analysis of 38 participants shows that only every third participant chooses an optimal ring size. We show that this leads to reduced efficacy of the wearable.

Keywords: physiological sensing · fitness tracker · in the wild · sensor fit

1 Introduction

Despite the increasing popularity of wearables [6,7], there is a lack of research on the usage of these devices "in the wild." While there are studies exploring real-world use and the abandonment of wearables through surveys [4], research on how users perceive their relationship with the device is scant. It is vital to understand user perception of device usage since proper fit is connected to the use-value of wearables and allows for accurate data collection: Proper fit is not simply perceived comfort. It is important to understand how users evaluate their comfort with wearables the relation to the frequency and quality of data collection.

In this research, we investigate the ability of end users to properly evaluate the fit of a wearable health device, specifically a fitness-tracking ring. Through a year-long "in the wild" study of 38 participants, we examine the relationship

© The Author(s), under exclusive license to Springer Nature Switzerland AG 2023
J. Abdelnour Nocera et al. (Eds.): INTERACT 2023, LNCS 14145, pp. 486–490, 2023.
https://doi.org/10.1007/978-3-031-42293-5_59

between self-reported fit comfort and the frequency and quality of data collection. The results of this study have implications for the design and use of wearables and can help improve their real-world effectiveness.

2   Methodology

Starting from late summer 2021, participants were recruited to wear the Oura Ring [2] for a research project. The participants were graduate and undergraduate university students taking classes affiliated with the Graduate School of Engineering at the host institution. The choice of wearable fell onto Oura since at the time of study they were the only ring devices with readings validated by lab studies demonstrating its accuracy in sleep stage detection [5]. The first generation Oura Ring was released in 2015, with generation 2 and 3 upgrades released in 2018 and 2021, respectively [1]. Students attended an orientation on the features and capabilities of the Oura Ring, but could wear the ring as they see fit with no restrictions or special guidance. Participants received sizing kits and were asked to carefully size the ring according to the packaged instructions. It is important to note that the investigators did not observe if the participants followed these rules accordingly. The participants were informed that this was an in-the-wild study and that the participants should use the rings as they see fit. At the end of 2022, 35 participants were called to answer a survey on their experiences consisting of questions regarding their use and satisfaction with the ring. The participants were remunerated 3000 JPY (approximately 20 USD) for their cooperation. In early 2023, 31 participants volunteered to get their finger circumference measured with an adjustable ring size measuring tool.

The data points collected from participants consist of sensor (waking HR measurements, their time stamps and measurement quality) and finger (circumference in millimeters) measurements as well as survey answers. Since participation in data collection was voluntary, different data points are available for

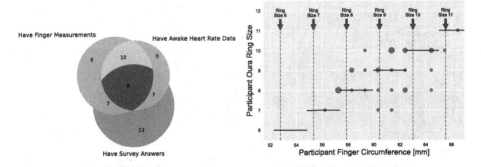

Fig. 1. Left: Venn diagram of which data is available for how many participants. Right: Chosen ring size against the participants' finger circumference. Larger dots indicate multiple overlapping data points. Black lines indicate optimal ring size. Only $\frac{1}{3}$ of participants chose the optimal ring size.

different participant subgroups. The size of these groups and the overlap are on the left side in Fig. 1. 31 participants volunteered for finger circumference measurement and 35 participants answered the survey. Within those two groups, waking HR data is available for 25 participants. In total, 38 unique participants are considered in this study. All data collection and experiments were approved in advance by the Institution's Ethics Committee.

3   Analysis and Results

In order to gauge proper ring fit, we compare the rings' inner circumference obtained from 3D models to the participants' finger circumference. We obtain the finger measurements directly and extract the rings' inner circumference from 3D models of the sizing kit [3]. A scatter-plot of participants' finger circumferences and their chosen ring sizes are in Fig. 1(right). As per Oura's sizing guidance, we mostly consider the next smaller size as optimal for inbetween sizes. The cutoff to the next larger size is set at 4/5ths of the way between sizes. The figure shows that 10 out of 31 measured participants chose the optimal size, 9 chose a size too tight and 11 a size too big. We analyze data quality with waking HR measurements, since the number of measurements per day fluctuate heavily between users. We calculate the HR measurement frequency (HRMF) F for a single participant and day by taking the total number of waking measurements on that day and dividing by the total hours of awake time wearing the ring. The average HRMF $\overline{F}$ is then obtained by averaging this value over all days of usage. For measurement quality, the ring labels every HR measurement as *good*, *average* or *bad*. We assign scores S to every label where $S_{good} = 2$, $S_{average} = 1$ and $S_{bad} = 0$. The average measurement quality $\overline{S}$ for a user over the study duration is then the average over all scores. We then compare the average HRMF and quality to the difference between the participants' finger circumference and their chosen rings' inner circumference, see Fig. 2. The figures shows a tighter fit increases both HR measurement frequency and quality. Figure 3(right) shows

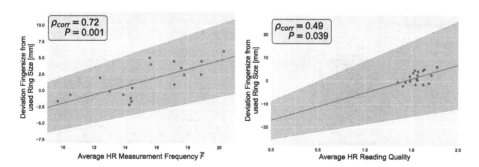

Fig. 2. Deviation of finger circumference to chosen ring circumference against average HRMF (left), average HR measurement quality (right). Positive deviation equals a tight ring. Tighter rings increase the measurement frequency & quality.

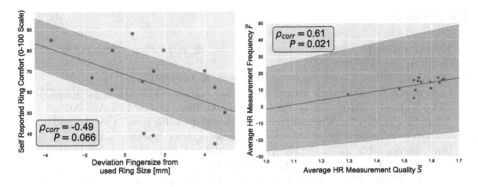

Fig. 3. Left: Self-reported ring comfort against deviation of finger circumference to chosen ring circumference. Positive deviation equals a tight ring, negative a loose one. Right: Average HR measurement quality as reported by the device against the average hourly daytime HRMF.

that HR measurement frequency and quality are significantly correlated in general. If we take into account participants' own assessment of ring comfort, we find that tighter rings are considered as less comfortable, see Fig. 3(left). On the other hand, neither HR measurement frequency nor quality are significantly connected to self-reported ring comfort, with respective Pearson correlation coefficients of $\rho_{corr} = -0.20$ and $\rho_{corr} = 0.10$ and P-values of $P = 0.0.486$ and $P = 0.726$.

4   Discussion and Conclusion

Our results indicate the majority of smart ring users are not able to chose a proper ring fit without precise guidance. They also indicate they prefer a more comfortable, *i.e.* looser fit, which is shown to be detrimental to the performance of the smart rings; looser rings collect less data and with lower quality as shown in the HR measurements, on which other functionality like sleep quality analysis relies. Designers of consumer-grade wearables can take this into consideration by focusing on making the device fit the user by providing a wide and fine grained range of sizes as well as procedures and guidelines to help users better gauge a proper fit. The limitations of our study are its focus on one specific device, the Oura Ring, and a small sample of participants. For future work, we plan on examining the data of a larger cohort in more detail. In addition, we plan to study the difference between users who fit their ring by themselves and those given direct guidance with fitting.

Acknowledgements. This work was supported in part by grants from JST Trilateral AI project, Learning Cyclotron (JPMJCR20G3), JSPS Kakenhi (20KK0235), and the Grand challenge of the Initiative for Life Design Innovation (iLDi).

References

1. Meet Gen 3. https://support.ouraring.com/hc/en-us/articles/4409072131091-Meet-Gen3. Accessed 20 Jan 2023
2. Oura Ring. https://ouraring.com/. Accessed 20 Jan 2023
3. Oura Sizing Kit 3D Print. https://support.ouraring.com/hc/en-us/articles/360025 590653-Tips-for-Determining-Your-Oura-Ring-Size. Accessed 26 Apr 2023
4. Attig, C., Franke, T.: Abandonment of personal quantification: a review and empirical study investigating reasons for wearable activity tracking attrition. Comput. Hum. Behav. **102**, 223–237 (2020). https://doi.org/10.1016/j.chb.2019.08.025
5. Chee, N.I.Y.N., Ghorbani, S., Golkashani, H.A., Leong, R.L.F., Ong, J.L., Chee, M.W.L.: Multi-night validation of a sleep tracking ring in adolescents compared with a research actigraph and polysomnography. Nat. Sci. Sleep **13**, 177–190 (2021). https://doi.org/10.2147/NSS.S286070
6. Dian, F., Vahidnia, R., Rahmati, A.: Wearables and the Internet of Things (IoT), Applications, Opportunities, and Challenges: A Survey. IEEE Access **8**, 69200–69211 (2020). https://doi.org/10.1109/ACCESS.2020.2986329, conference Name: IEEE Access
7. Dunn, J., Runge, R., Snyder, M.: Wearables and the medical revolution. Pers. Med. **15**(5), 429–448 (2018). https://doi.org/10.2217/pme-2018-0044

Heuristics to Design Trustworthy Technologies: Study Design and Current Progress

Iuliia Paramonova(✉), Sonia Sousa, and David Lamas

School of Digital Technologies, Tallinn University, Tallinn, Estonia
juparam@tlu.ee

Abstract. As advanced technologies become increasingly complex and opaque, people perceive them to be nondeterministic, raising concerns about trust in technology. This issue is especially crucial in risky domains where technology misuse can cause significant harm or loss. Design heuristics that consider users' perspectives on technology trustworthiness are needed to support practitioners in promoting trust. In this paper, we demonstrate a human-centred approach to investigate users' perceptions of trustworthiness in advanced technologies and develop design heuristics that enable the creation of trustworthy technologies. The paper outlines the research design's rationale, goals, methodology, and progress.

Keywords: human-centered design · human-computer trust · trustworthy technology

1 Introduction

As advanced technologies become increasingly complex and opaque, users perceive them as nondeterministic, which may lead to uncertainty and raise concerns about trust in technology. Complexity in this context refers to systems typically including non-linear interactions [1] with various components that are difficult to comprehend and justify [2]. Although these systems are becoming increasingly sophisticated, their inner processes remain mostly opaque, making it difficult to trust them [3].

According to Weber et al., regular users might view sophisticated emerged technologies and software systems that do not incorporate machine learning as nondeterministic, as they may seem complicated to comprehend from the user's point of view [4].

However, even though advanced systems are often viewed as promising tools to eliminate human error and augment individual abilities, they can also be misused and cause harm. Therefore, trust is becoming crucial for the adoption and success of advanced technologies in domains such as healthcare [5], robotics and automation [6], and finance [7]. Some instances of harm and loss can be observed in incidents involving self-driving cars due to ethical biases in machine learning [8] and significant losses in cryptocurrency investments [9].

Although the HCI community and the EU have proposed principles, guidelines, and legal regulations for designing trustworthy AI systems, design heuristics that consider

© The Author(s), under exclusive license to Springer Nature Switzerland AG 2023
J. Abdelnour Nocera et al. (Eds.): INTERACT 2023, LNCS 14145, pp. 491–495, 2023.
https://doi.org/10.1007/978-3-031-42293-5_60

users' perspectives on technology trustworthiness are needed to support practitioners in promoting trust.

The proposed research aims to enable and facilitate the design of technologies by providing practical design heuristics. The research outcome contributes to a deeper understanding of designing to promote trust in technology.

2 Related Works

Trust and trustworthiness are two related, interconnected, but distinct concepts. Trust refers to the belief that someone or something is reliable and likely to act in a trustworthy manner. In the context of technology, trustworthiness refers to the properties attributed to a system or an entity to increase trust [10].

Research on trustworthy technology is currently approached from technical, normative, and pragmatic perspectives. The technical perspective considers trustworthiness by creating explainable algorithms to provide self-explanations [11]. The normative approach involves ethical and legal considerations at the governmental level. This approach includes various guidelines and ethical principles, for instance, the Ethics Guidelines for Trustworthy AI [12]. The pragmatic perspective shows how researchers are exploring trustworthy design in practice. For instance, Nielsen's ten usability heuristics [13] ensure a system's usability, which refers to trustworthiness. In his latter works, Shneiderman suggests increasing human control of technology to support technologies' trustworthiness [14]. Furthermore, Shneiderman proposed suggestions to close the gap between EU legislation and the real world from the perspective of three levels of governance: team, organisation, and industry. The fifteen recommendations are meant to increase reliability, safety, and trustworthiness when developing designs for human-centred AI [15].

Despite the current efforts to support the design of trustworthy advanced technology from different perspectives, a socio-technical perspective is lacking. None of the above-mentioned perspectives fully addresses the importance of considering the end-users' expectations and practitioners' perspectives in the design process.

3 Methodology

The overall research approach is pragmatic and seen as a problem-solving process [16].

The study adopted a methodology commonly used for heuristics development [17]. It comprises three essential phases: exploratory, conceptualisation, and evaluation. The objective of the exploratory phase is to gain a deeper understanding of the problem by identifying and eliciting factors that influence users' perceptions of trustworthiness in complex and opaque technologies. The second phase, conceptualisation, focuses on grounding findings from the exploratory phase in theory and establishing design heuristics, i.e., user-centric guidelines, enabling practitioners to design trustworthy technologies. Finally, the third phase, evaluation, aims to assess the applicability of the established design heuristics in practice. The qualitative data collected during the research will be analysed using the ground theory method [18].

The proposed research aims to enable and facilitate the design of trustworthy technologies users perceive as nondeterministic. The following research questions should be answered to accomplish the research goal:

[RQ1] What are the key factors that influence users' perception of the trustworthiness of technology?

[RQ2] What heuristics can be established to support the design of trustworthy technologies?

[RQ3] How applicable are the established heuristics in designing trustworthy technology?

Due to the design nature of the study, iterations are acceptable during the research process.

4   Current Progress

We are currently analysing data gathered during the exploratory phase of our research.

During this phase, we conducted two rounds of a mixed-method study and examined two technologies that have nondeterministic properties and are associated with high-risk domains. One of the technologies is cryptocurrency exchange platforms, which users perceive as nondeterministic because of their complexity and newness. The other technology is autonomous vehicles, which are considered nondeterministic because of their opacity. By studying two different subjects, we covered all nondeterministic characteristics and explored the impact of direct interaction with or without a graphical interface.

The mixed-method study design was primarily similar for both iterations. The study design comprised a survey that assessed users' risk propensity with the General Risk Propensity Scale [19] and users' trust in technology with the Human-Computer Trust Scale [20], followed by semi-structured interviews to investigate the factors influencing individuals' perceptions of trustworthiness. In the first iteration, we also asked users to demonstrate how they use the technology and captured photos of their interaction. Conversely, visual stimuli were employed in the second iteration to facilitate the discussion by presenting images of three types of autonomous vehicles: delivery robots, buses, and cars.

In total, 32 international individuals participated in the study across two iterations. The first iteration had 8 males and 3 females, while the second iteration had 10 males and 10 females. The second iteration's sample specifically focused on novice users of the selected technology.

We used descriptive statistics to analyse the quantitative data and grounded theory to analyse the qualitative data. Based on preliminary results, we identified four factors influencing individuals' perception of technology trustworthiness: Usability (Ease of Use, Learnability, Understandability, Satisfaction), Credibility (Recommendations,

External information, Historical record-keeping), Risk Mitigation (Accountability, Interactive data visualisation, Reinsurance behaviour, Reinsurance mechanics, Visual cues, Transparency), and Reliability (Performance). Moreover, we discovered that the user's Level of Expertise (Expert, Novice, User) affects their perception of technology trustworthiness and supports the notion that a socio-technical approach should guide the trust design. These exploratory phase preliminary results have been accepted for publication in the proceedings of the HCII 2023 [21].

5   Conclusion

In this paper, we have demonstrated a human-centred approach to design heuristics that enable the design of trustworthy technologies. Our study comprises three essential phases: exploratory, conceptualisation, and evaluation. The first phase aims to gain a deeper understanding of the problem, the second focuses on establishing design heuristics, and the third aims to assess the applicability of the established design heuristics in practice. The research outcome will contribute to a deeper understanding of design to promote trust and provide practical heuristics for practitioners to design trustworthy technologies.

The next phase of this study will be the conceptualisation stage, which aims to use the findings from the exploratory phase to create theoretically informed concepts of trustworthy design. These conceptualised concepts will be used to design generative research workshops with practitioners, where they can be discussed and utilised in designing a prototype of the advanced technology. The qualitative data collected from these workshops will be used as a subsample for the grounded theory analysis, producing insights to draft heuristics for designing trustworthy technology.

Funding.   This research was funded by the Trust and Influence Programme [FA8655–22-1–7051], the European Office of Aerospace Research and Development, and the US Air Force Office of Scientific Research. Grunt number TAU21182 received by Tallinn University School of Digital Technologies.

References

1. Cilliers, P.: Knowing Complex Systems, in: K. Richardson (ed.), Managing the Complex, Volume One: Philosophy, Theory and Application (Greenwich, CT, Information Age Publishers) (2005)
2. Magee, C.L., de Weck, O.L.: 3.1. 3 Complex system classification. In: INCOSE International Symposium (Vol. 14, No. 1, pp. 471–488) (2004)
3. Adadi, A., Berrada, M.: Peeking inside the black-box: a survey on explainable artificial intelligence (XAI). IEEE Access **6**, 52138–52160 (2018)
4. Weber, T., Hußmann, H., Eiband, M.: Quantifying the Demand for Explainability. In: Ardito, C., Lanzilotti, R., Malizia, A., Petrie, H., Piccinno, A., Desolda, G., Inkpen, K. (eds.) INTERACT 2021. LNCS, vol. 12933, pp. 652–661. Springer, Cham (2021). https://doi.org/10.1007/978-3-030-85616-8_38
5. Sunarti, S., Rahman, F.F., Naufal, M., Risky, M., Febriyanto, K., Masnina, R.: Artificial intelligence in healthcare: opportunities and risk for future. Gac. Sanit. **35**, S67–S70 (2021)
6. He, H., Gray, J., Cangelosi, A., Meng, Q., McGinnity, T.M., Mehnen, J.: The challenges and opportunities of human-centered AI for trustworthy robots and autonomous systems. IEEE Trans. Cogn. Develop. Syst. **14**(4), 1398–1412 (2022)
7. Ashta, A., Herrmann, H.: Artificial intelligence and fintech: an overview of opportunities and risks for banking, investments, and microfinance. Strateg. Chang. **30**(3), 211–222 (2021)

8. Andersen, K.E., Köslich, S., Pedersen, B.K.M.K., Weigelin, B.C., Jensen, L.C.: Do we blindly trust self-driving cars. In: Proceedings of the Companion of the 2017 ACM/IEEE International Conference on Human-robot Interaction, pp. 67–68 (2017)
9. Yaffe-Bellany, D.: Sam Bankman-Fried Blames "Huge Management Failures" for FTX Collapse. The New York Times (2022). https://www.nytimes.com/2022/11/30/business/sam-bankman-fried-ftx-collapse.html
10. Nickel, P.J., Franssen, M., Kroes, P.: Can We make sense of the notion of trustworthy technology? Knowl. Technol. Policy **23**(3), 429–444 (2010)
11. Došilović, F.K., Brčić, M., Hlupić, N.: Explainable artificial intelligence: A survey. In: 2018 41st International Convention on Information and Communication Technology, Electronics and Microelectronics (MIPRO), pp. 0210–0215 (2018)
12. High-Level Expert Group on AI, Ethics guidelines for trustworthy AI, 2019, European Commission, https://www.aepd.es/sites/default/files/2019-12/ai-ethics-guidelines.pdf
13. Nielsen, J.: Trust or Bust: Communicating Trustworthiness in Web Design (1999)
14. Shneiderman, B.: Human-centered artificial intelligence: reliable, safe & trustworthy. Int. J. Human-Comput. Interact. **36**(6), 495–504 (2020)
15. Shneiderman, B.: Bridging the gap between ethics and practice: guidelines for reliable, safe, and trustworthy human-centered AI systems. ACM Trans. Interact. Intell. Syst. (TiiS) **10**(4), 1–31 (2020)
16. Oulasvirta, A., Hornbæk, K.: HCI research as problem-solving. In: Proceedings of the 2016 CHI Conference on Human Factors in Computing Systems. CHI'16: CHI Conference on Human Factors in Computing Systems, San Jose California USA (2016). https://doi.org/10.1145/2858036.2858283
17. Quiñones, D., Rusu, C.: How to develop usability heuristics: a systematic literature review. Comput. Stand. Interfaces **53**, 89–122 (2017)
18. Muller, M.J., Kogan, S.: Grounded theory method in human-computer interaction and computer-supported cooperative work. In: Human Computer Interaction Handbook, (pp. 1003–1023). CRC Press (2012)
19. Zhang, D.C., Highhouse, S., Nye, C.D.: Development and validation of the general risk propensity scale (GRiPS). J. Behav. Decis. Mak. **32**(2), 152–167 (2019)
20. Gulati, S., Sousa, S., Lamas, D.: Design, development and evaluation of a human-computer trust scale. Behav. Inform. Technol. **38**(10), 1004–1015 (2019)
21. Paramonova, I., Sousa, S., Lamas, D.: In: printing, forthcoming 25th International Conference on Human-Computer Interaction (HCII). Springer). Springer (2023). https://doi.org/10.1007/978-3-031-34411-4_25

Influences of Cognitive Styles on EEG-Based Activity: An Empirical Study on Visual Content Comprehension

Maria Trigka⦾, Georgios Papadoulis⦾, Elias Dritsas(✉)⦾, and Christos Fidas⦾

Department of Electrical and Computer Engineering, University of Patras, Campus Rio, 26504 Patras, Greece
{trigka,dritsase}@ceid.upatras.gr, g.papadoulis@upnet.gr, fidas@ece.upatras.gr

Abstract. This paper presents an empirical study that examines how human cognitive style affects brain signal activity when individuals engage in a visual content comprehension task. To facilitate this study, we adopted an accredited cognitive style framework (Field Dependent-Field Independent or FD-FI) and utilized a validated cognitive style elicitation task, namely the Group Embedded Figures Test (GEFT), to elicit visual content comprehension via static figures. Brain signal activity was captured through a high-precision EEG device and subsequently correlated with the GEFT-derived cognitive style. Furthermore, power spectral analysis allowed the observation of potential differences between the two cognitive style groups. Analysis of results yields different effects on FD and FI users and especially in the average power of brain signals in the cortical area. Identifying such brain signal variations between FD-FI users might lay the ground for designing novel real-time elicitation frameworks of human cognitive styles, thus providing innovative personalization and adaptation approaches in a variety of application domains.

Keywords: User Study · FD-FI · Signal Processing · EEG

1 Introduction

Individuals differ in the way they seek, process and retrieve information. This is closely related to their cognitive skills and abilities, e.g. perceptual speed and memory load [8]. A cognitive style is a high-level cognitive strategy that researchers exploit to empirically explain such differences between individuals. FD-FI is a well-established and validated cognitive style in modern psychology. FDs tend to process information holistically and find difficulties in identifying visual details in complex figures. On the other hand, FIs, who are more analytical by nature, tend to easily discriminate simple forms by paying attention to detail and bypassing surrounding context [2]. The elicitation of FD-FI is based on an individual's performance in tasks related to visual perception (i.e., the ability

© The Author(s), under exclusive license to Springer Nature Switzerland AG 2023
J. Abdelnour Nocera et al. (Eds.): INTERACT 2023, LNCS 14145, pp. 496–500, 2023.
https://doi.org/10.1007/978-3-031-42293-5_61

to identify, organize, and interpret the environment by processing visual information). Visual tasks and visual perception are interrelated not only with eye movements [3,12] but also with EEG signals [2]. During the execution of these tasks (GEFT-based), the visual stimuli trigger signals arising from diverse brain areas (parietal, frontal, optical) related to anticipation and movement preparation (head, arms, eyes movement (left-right), blinking), error-related potentials, and goal-directed movements (i.e., tracing the identified shape in a complex figure) [1]. Incorporating brain signals related to human cognition originating from brain areas related to cognitive activities and abilities will allow adding intelligence to human-computer interaction systems. The encoding of such signals to capture human cognitive styles, pertaining to individual differences and abilities, may in-turn expand the interaction between humans and interactive devices in a more adaptive and personalized fashion [4].

Motivation and Research Question. The purpose of this experimental study is to provide empirical evidence regarding which EEG features could be used to quantify high-level cognitive traits of the human mind and specifically with respect to the FD and FI aspects. EEG brain signal power is commonly used to quantify the cognitive traits of an individual [9]. Our hypothesis is as follows: There is a significant difference between FDs-FIs in the average power of EEG signals throughout visual pattern recognition tasks of varying difficulty.

2   User Study

The study conducted and reported in this paper has received the necessary approval from the Ethical Board of the University of Patras[1].

2.1   Participant Demographics and GEFT Procedure

The subjects were informed about the study through several University mailing lists, with the aim of recruiting a relatively heterogeneous pool of participants in terms of age, fields of expertise, and cognitive style. A total of 13 participants were initially recruited, with an age range from 22 to 46 (mean = 27.53, std = 7.32). All participants were right-handed with normal or corrected-to-normal vision. 7 participants were female, and 6 were male, while the distribution across colleges and departments wasn't balanced. 11 of them stemmed from polytechnic schools, and 2 were undergraduate students in primary education.

The participants had never taken GEFT [10] and were older than 18. Each participant was equipped with the EEG device and asked to undertake GEFT, which is divided into three sections. The first one was for the participants' familiarization with the process, while the other two determine the actual score and thus, their categorization as FD or FI. Participants were asked to identify simple forms in figures of increasing visual complexity given a specific time frame. The sections contain seven, nine and nine figures, with two, five and five minutes

---

[1] https://ehde.upatras.gr.

allocated, respectively. The number of correctly identified figures in the last two sections constitutes the raw score, which is used to classify the subject as FD or FI (i.e., the higher the score, the more field-independent the subject is). It should be noted that the EEG signals were recorded in parallel with the GEFT process, which differentiates our work from an experimental point of view from other relevant works in this field.

The single FD subject scored in the range of 0–5. The FIs (six in number) achieved scores in the range of 15–18 with an average score of 17. The execution time was between 7.5 and 10 min (the average and standard deviation of the execution time was 8.91 ± 1.24 min). The duration of the cognitive visual task and the EEG recording was dependent on the subject's response speed.

2.2   Pre-processing and Feature Extraction

The BioSemi EEG recording device[2] was used to capture brain activity throughout GEFT, at a sampling frequency of 2048 Hz. The EEG signals were preprocessed with Matlab R2019a. Preprocessing comprises two key steps: filtering, re-referencing and resampling. Out-of-band noise was eliminated by employing a Butterworth band-pass filter (0.5–60 Hz). Moreover, a notch filter at 50 Hz was applied to eliminate the remaining line noise. The data were re-referenced by the average reference of all electrodes, which is preferred as it is a very stable method. As a third step, EEG signals were down-sampled to 512 Hz to reduce the data volume [6]. To handle artifacts (e.g., eye movements and blinking) Independent Component Analysis (ICA) was applied [13]. To extract the average band power feature, a Finite Impulse Response digital filter with a Kaiser window was designed for the frequency range of each band, and the average normalized power was estimated per spatial channel of brain areas.

3   First Results

Our aim was to understand and identify potential differences between FD and FI by analyzing brain signal activity during GEFT in the frequency domain. Therefore, five main EEG spectrum bands at Frontal, Central, Parietal and Optical cortical areas were observed, namely δ (1–4 Hz), θ (4–8 Hz), α (8–13 Hz), β (13–30 Hz), and low γ (30–42 Hz) [5]. The selection of the low γ band in the power analysis was motivated by the study of Farmaki et al. [2] in which they identified differences in the power spectrum among the FD-FI instead of studying the whole band. In Fig. 1, the average power per brain area and frequency bands were captured for the FD-FI subjects. Comparing them, there was a constant difference between the average power of FD and the respective power of FI by a factor of 1.725 in all frequency bands per brain area. The difference in α could reflect the higher active processing in the working memory of FD related to the short-term retention and maintenance of information. Also, α power reflects

---

[2] https://www.biosemi.com/.

higher demands on attention [7] and is associated with task performance indicating the engagement of brain regions [14]. Higher θ band power was an indicator of higher cognitive load in the FD subject against the FI one. Furthermore, the average β band power seemed to dominate in Optical and then in Parietal areas against the rest of the frequency bands and areas in both cognitive styles. The power of β is an indicator of stress level [11], which was higher at the FD subject. Finally, the average power at low γ presented the lowest levels in both cognitive styles in all areas.

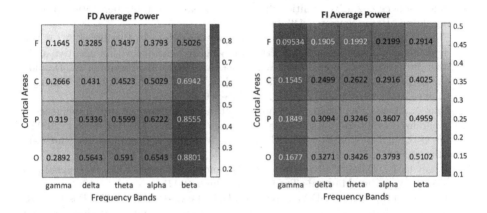

Fig. 1. Average normalized power at $\gamma, \delta, \theta, \alpha$ and β bands per cortical area F(FP1, FP2, F7, F8, F3, F4, Fz), C(FC1, FC2, FC5, FC6, C3, C4, Cz), P(CP1, CP2, CP5, CP6, P7, P8, P3, P4, Pz), O(O1, O2, Oz, PO3, PO4) for FD and FIs.

4   Conclusions

We designed and implemented an in-lab experiment, in which participants undertook GEFT, to accurately classify them into FD and FI groups while capturing their brain activity. The classification provided a ground truth for comparing brain signal activity for FD-FI users, making it one of the first studies to investigate the influence of cognitive styles on brain signal activity using a standardized procedure. However, the findings presented in this study primarily have a qualitative nature; While this primary investigation shows higher power for the FD, a statistical analysis could not be conducted with only one FD subject. As a result, our future prospects rely on conducting inferential statistical analysis to validate concealed effects and identify the key factors that correlate individual differences in information processing with brain signal patterns.

Acknowledgments. This work has been financially supported by the Hellenic Foundation for Research & Innovation (HFRI) under the 2nd Call for proposals for H.F.R.I. Research Projects to Support Faculty Members and Researchers, under the project entitled Electroencephalography and Eye Gaze driven Framework for Intelligent and Real-Time Human Cognitive Modelling (CogniX) with Proposal ID 3849.

References

1. Abiri, R., Borhani, S., Sellers, E.W., Jiang, Y., Zhao, X.: A comprehensive review of EEG-based brain-computer interface paradigms. J. Neural Eng. **16**(1), 011001 (2019)
2. Farmaki, C., Sakkalis, V., Loesche, F., Nisiforou, E.A.: Assessing field dependence-independence cognitive abilities through EEG-based bistable perception processing. Front. Hum. Neurosci. **13**, 345 (2019)
3. Fidas, C., Belk, M., Constantinides, C., Constantinides, A., Pitsillides, A.: A field dependence-independence perspective on eye gaze behavior within affective activities. In: Ardito, C., Lanzilotti, R., Malizia, A., Petrie, H., Piccinno, A., Desolda, G., Inkpen, K. (eds.) INTERACT 2021. LNCS, vol. 12932, pp. 63–72. Springer, Cham (2021). https://doi.org/10.1007/978-3-030-85623-6_6
4. Gao, X., Wang, Y., Chen, X., Gao, S.: Interface, interaction, and intelligence in generalized brain-computer interfaces. Trends Cogn. Sci. **25**(8), 671–684 (2021)
5. Im C-H, I.: Computational EEG analysis: Methods and applications. im c.-h., editor (2018)
6. Janapati, R., Dalal, V., Sengupta, R.: Advances in modern EEG-BCI signal processing: A review. Materials Today: Proceedings (2021)
7. Johnson, J.S., Sutterer, D.W., Acheson, D.J., Lewis-Peacock, J.A., Postle, B.R.: Increased alpha-band power during the retention of shapes and shape-location associations in visual short-term memory. Front. Psychol. **2**, 128 (2011)
8. Kiat, J.E., Belli, R.F.: The role of individual differences in visual\verbal information processing preferences in visual\verbal source monitoring. J. Cogn. Psychol. **30**(7), 701–709 (2018)
9. Lin, X., Tang, W., Ma, W., Liu, Y., Ding, F.: The impact of media diversity and cognitive style on learning experience in programming video lecture: A brainwave analysis. Educ. Inform. Technol. 1–21 (2023)
10. O'Leary, M.R., Calsyn, D.A., Fauria, T.: The group embedded figures test: a measure of cognitive style or cognitive impairment. J. Pers. Assess. **44**(5), 532–537 (1980)
11. Palacios-García, I.: Increase in beta power reflects attentional top-down modulation after psychosocial stress induction. Front. Human Neurosci. **15**, 630813 (2021)
12. Raptis, G.E., Fidas, C.A., Avouris, N.M.: On implicit elicitation of cognitive strategies using gaze transition entropies in pattern recognition tasks. In: Proceedings of the 2017 CHI Conference Extended Abstracts on Human Factors in Computing Systems, pp. 1993–2000 (2017)
13. Trigka, M., Dritsas, E., Fidas, C.: A survey on signal processing methods for EEG-based brain computer interface systems. In: Proceedings of the 26th Pan-Hellenic Conference on Informatics, pp. 213–218 (2022)
14. Wang, P., et al.: Alpha power during task performance predicts individual language comprehension. Neuroimage **260**, 119449 (2022)

Interactive 3D Printed Urban Maps for Blind People

Malgorzata Telesinska[✉] ⓘ and Boleslaw Telesinski ⓘ

Wroclaw University of Science and Technology, Wroclaw, Poland
{malgorzata.telesinska,boleslaw.telesinski}@pwr.edu.pl

Abstract. The paper proposes a haptic device that allows blind users to explore objects' locations by physically touching a model, complemented with verbal audio descriptions that users can activate on demand by tapping a desired object. The device consists of a physical 3D urban map that is augmented with touch sensors that trigger audio annotations. The map is designed for visually impaired users. The authors present a working prototype and the results from a preliminary user study with blind participants. In a user study with eleven blind participants, the proposed device received positive feedback. The findings suggest that the proposed design is usable and can help its visually impaired users to understand and remember spatial information presented in this way.

Keywords: touch surfaces · multimodal map · audio-tactile city maps

1 Introduction

There are an estimated 2.2 billion people in the world with visual impairments and the number grows continuously [1]. Those people experience difficulties while navigating urban environments, due to problems with spatial identification. This leads to a significant deterioration of their life quality [2]. Haptic solutions could offer reliable support for people with visual impairments [3, 4]. Devices based on those technologies have significant implementation potential, especially in the field of identifying various spatial representations [5]. Haptic technology could be used in devices that improve pedestrian mobility, especially if the devices target people who experience visual disabilities.

This work presents a novel approach to building interactive scaled urban models which support the blind in unaided navigation by an embedded solution based on haptic feedback. The proposed device should fulfill specific requirements: it should have a low production cost, be easy to assemble, and satisfy the usability needs of the target group. The paper's contributions are the technological solution and the results of the preliminary study. The presented study has a work-in-progress character and it aimed to collect feedback from the representatives of the target group. This information will help to narrow down the direction of further technology development and to construct more detailed usability tests, suitable for a larger audience.

© The Author(s), under exclusive license to Springer Nature Switzerland AG 2023
J. Abdelnour Nocera et al. (Eds.): INTERACT 2023, LNCS 14145, pp. 501–506, 2023.
https://doi.org/10.1007/978-3-031-42293-5_62

2 Related Work

The development of mobility-assisting devices is of particular importance due to their impact on the efficiency of the mental spatial map creation process [6]. This draws attention to various technologies used to construct tactile maps which provide urban navigation information [7]. Solutions include map representations of a simple and precise functionality [8] as well as more complex models with rich, 3-dimensional features [9, 10]. The key aspect of such maps is labeling them with descriptions made in a standardized Braille font size – fitting all the required information could be challenging due to the relatively small area available on the corresponding fields of the urban map. Therefore, it is reasonable to enrich the map with embedded verbal audio information [11]. To overcome this limitation, early haptic feedback devices have been developed [12]. They were followed by approaches involving geographic information system (GIS) data implementation [13] and proposals for map construction based on image recognition technology [14]. The creation of spatial images was made possible thanks to material research leveraging diverse polymer properties [15, 16] and electromechanical parts: piezoelectric components [17] or actuators [18].

Other works involved 3D-Printing [19–22]. However, the presented results did not provide direct interaction with verbal audio messages triggered by touching sensors embedded under the map's surface. Regardless of the transition from 2D to 3D representations, the spatial models are more accessible to the blind [23], and interactive maps and graphics are documented in the subject-related literature [24, 25].

3 Interactive 3D Printed Urban Maps

3.1 The Prototype

The analysis of the available solutions and the synthesis of the guideline list enabled our research team to construct a new technology prototype. Its main feature is to represent the three-dimensional space using the tactile model and to offer instant, on-demand descriptive verbal audio. The solution is enabled by the availability of multi-material fused filament fabrication (FFF) 3D printers, and the Arduino development environment. The prototype is based on both technologies and runs on a dedicated source code.

The idea is to offer interaction between touch and hearing stimuli. The main functionality of the device provides an instant, precise verbal audio description whenever a visually impaired person uses the touch interface. A 3D-printed scale model contains embedded capacitive touch electrodes, which create interactive fields on the surface of the three-dimensional map. As soon as the user double-taps a field, its description is played back by the controller through a speaker.

The constructed prototype of the haptic device allowed to test the system (Fig. 1). The main components used are:

1. 3D printed touch sensors,
2. Adafruit 12-Key Capacitive Touch Sensor Breakout Board, based on MPR 121,
3. MP3 Player Module, DFPlayer,
4. Arduino Nano board, based on the ATmega328P microcontroller.

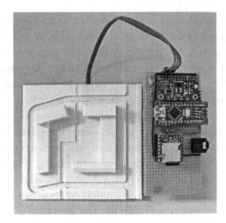

Fig. 1. The functional prototype of the device

The multi-material FFF solution allowed producing the scale model on a singular 3D printer. The technology made it possible to coat the touch electrodes with a thin layer of another printing material. This improves wear- and weather resistance. A module-based design of the electronics offers additional benefits. It is possible to minimize the lengths of electrode-connecting wires by locating the electronic touch modules as close to the interactive fields as possible. If a particular application requires more touch fields than the module offers, it is possible to connect auxiliary modules and thus increase the number of available inputs. If the dimensions of an application extend beyond the working area of a 3D printer, it is possible to produce the model in parts and assemble them afterward. The accidental triggering of an audio message is prevented by a double-tap feature. The system is easy to implement and requires only basic 3D CAD modeling skills. The cost of an outsourced production of the model is approximately $20 for a tile of 10 by 10 cm. The number of interactive fields in our device is not limited to the number of outputs available on the main controller board. This allows for reducing the costs of upscaling the project into a larger application: the 3D-printing effort is indeed larger, but the hardware is modular – a single controller board is capable of connecting with multiple touch modules simultaneously. This results in an affordable solution that offers a higher implementation potential than the comparable solutions from the literature on the subject. Having direct access to an FFF 3D printer allows one to further reduce the costs.

3.2 Survey

We have conducted preliminary research on a group of eleven participants, aged eighteen to sixty-two. Five of the participants identified themselves as women and six of the participants identified themselves as men. The average age of the participants was 31.68 years and the median of their age was 28 years. All participants were fully blind, and five of the participants were born blind. Six of the participants had not been using scaled urban models. All of the contributors are using devices and applications for text-to-speech conversions. Each participant is used to unaided navigation in the urban environment. At the time of the study, all of the participants resided in Wrocław, Poland.

To complete the research, we have constructed a prototype device representing a fictitious fragment of a map with two buildings, hence the participants had no prior knowledge of the location. The arrangement of the buildings was designed to reflect a layout of multi-family housing, typical for the city of Wrocław. Each of the participants expressed his/her consent to join the study, after being familiarized in detail with the research plan. The test was executed in 1:1 sessions, individually with each of the partakers. The idea of the audio descriptive map was presented to every participant who was then asked to trigger the embedded verbal audio messages. There was no time limit to the duration of each session The prototype was presented to the participants, who were asked for opinions on its functionality and implementation potential:

A1. The presented conceptual solution has the application potential for navigation in urban environments.

A2. The presented conceptual solution can be considered intuitive.

The opinions were expressed on a Likert scale ranging from 1: disagree to 5: agree, where 3 is neutral.

3.3 Preliminary Results

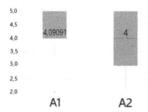

Fig. 2. Main scores for A1 (mean: 4.09, median: 4) and A2 (mean: 4.0, median: 4)

All participants expressed interest in the use of the urban models whenever they are accessible in urban spaces (Fig. 2). Ten of the participants gave a positive opinion of the device concept, while one participant expressed a mildly negative impression. Eight of the test users stated that the use of the device was intuitive, two opinions on this matter were neutral and one was mildly negative. The time for interacting with the device was short. During the next evaluation phase, the authors aim to measure the time spent by individuals to explore the device.

4   Conclusion, Limitations and Next Steps

The presented study defines the initial feedback from the target group of the proposed device. During the presented development stage, the device was found satisfactory by its potential users. The results imply the necessity to conduct further, qualitative research, including in-depth interviews with the participants. The technology requires further development while its potential users should be surveyed in detail. However, the research would have limits: both the concept and the prototype are in their initial development phase. The 3D-Printing process should be improved, as well as the surface finish quality. Further evaluation should consist of the research phase extension and the collection of a larger amount of data, especially information on how a mental spatial map is created. In the upcoming prototype versions, various surface finishes will be applied to emphasize interactive spots on the urban map. There is research potential in the relationship between the length of the verbal audio messages and the efficiency of identifying individual locations on the interactive urban map. With this poster, we hope to initiate a discussion about the capabilities offered by designing interactive scaled urban models with verbal audio messages and their potential presence in the urban space.

References

1. Vision Loss Expert Group of the Global Burden of Disease Study, Causes of blindness and vision impairment in 2020 and trends over 30 years: evaluating the prevalence of avoidable blindness in relation to "VISION 2020: the Right to Sight". Lancet Glob. Health **9**(2), E144–E160 (2020)
2. Keefe, J.: Psychosocial impact of vision impairment. Int. Congr. Ser. **1282**, 167–173 (2005)
3. Ghali, N.I., et al.: Virtual reality technology for blind and visual impaired people: reviews and recent advances. In: Gulrez, T., Hassanien, A.E. (eds.) Advances in Robotics and Virtual Reality. Intelligent Systems Reference Library, vol. 26, pp. 363–385. Springer, Heidelberg (2012). https://doi.org/10.1007/978-3-642-23363-0_15
4. Kibum, K., Xiangshi, R., Seungmoon, C., Hong, T.: Assisting people with visual impairments in aiming at a target on a large wall-mounted display. Int. J. Hum Comput Stud. **86**, 109–120 (2016)
5. Sobnath, D., Rehman, I.U., Nasralla, M.M.: Smart cities to improve mobility and quality of life of the visually impaired. In: Paiva, S. (ed.) Technological Trends in Improved Mobility of the Visually Impaired. EICC, pp. 3–28. Springer, Cham (2020). https://doi.org/10.1007/978-3-030-16450-8_1
6. Ottink, L., Buimer, H., van Raalte, B., Doeller, C., van der Geest, T., van Wezel, R.: Cognitive map formation supported by auditory, haptic, and multimodal information in persons with blindness. Neurosci. Biobehav. Rev. **140**, 104797 (2022)
7. de Almeida R.A.: Tactile maps in geography. In: Wright, J.D. (ed.) International Encyclopedia of the Social & Behavioral Sciences, 2nd edn., pp. 9–13. Elsevier (2015)
8. Rowell, J., Ungar, S.: Feeling your way: a tactile map user survey. In: Proceedings of 21st International Cartography Conference (2003)
9. Darling, N.C., Goodrich, G.L., Wiley, J.K.: A follow-up study of electronic travel aid users. Bull. Prosthet. Res. **10**(27), 82–91 (1977)
10. Voigt, A., Martens, B.: Development of 3D tactile models for the partially sighted to facilitate spatial orientation. In: Education and Research in Computer Aided Architectural Design in Europe (eCAADe 2024), pp. 366–370 (2006)
11. Visell, Y., Fontana, F., Giordano, B.L., Nordahl, R., Serafin, S., Bresin, R.: Sound design and perception in walking interactions. Int. J. Hum Comput Stud. **67**(11), 947–959 (2009)
12. Parkes, D.: Audio tactile systems for designing and learning complex environments as a vision impaired person: static and dynamic spatial information access. In: Proceedings of Learning Environment Technology Conference, pp. 219–223 (1994)
13. Miele, J.A., Landau, S., Gilden, D.: Talking TMAP: automated generation of audio-tactile maps using Smith–Kettlewell's TMAP software. Br. J. Vis. Impair. **24**, 93–100 (2006)

14. Wang, Z., Li, N., Li, B.: Fast and independent access to map directions for people who are blind. Interact. Comput. **24**, 91–106 (2012)
15. Götzelmann, T., Winkler, K.: SmartTactMaps: a smartphone-based approach to support blind persons in exploring tactile maps. In: Proceedings of the 8th ACM International Conference on Pervasive Technologies Related to Assistive Environments—PETRA 2015, pp. 1–8 (2015)
16. Kwon, H.J., Lee, S.W., Lee, S.S.: Braille dot display module with a PDMS membrane driven by a thermopneumatic actuator. Sens. Actu. A Phys. **154**, 238–246 (2009)
17. Völkel, T., Weber, G., Baumann, U.: Tactile graphics revised: the novel BrailleDis 9000 Pin-Matrix device with multitouch input. In: Proceedings of 11th International Conference Computers Helping People with Special Needs, pp. 835–842 (2008)
18. Szabo, Z., Enikov, E.T.: Development of wearable microactuator array for 3-D virtual tactile displays. J. Electromagn. Anal. Appl. **4**(6), 219–229 (2012)
19. Giraud, S., Brock, A., Anke, M.M., Jouffrais, C.: Map learning with a 3D printed interactive small-scale model: improvement of space and text memorization in visually impaired students. Front. Psychol. **8**, 930 (2017)
20. Gual, J., Puyuelo, M., Lloveras, J.: Universal design and visual impairment: tactile products for heritage access. In: Proceedings of 18th International Conference on Engineering Design, Impacting Society through Engineering Design, vol. 5 (2011)
21. Kolitsky, M.A.: 3D printed tactile learning objects: proof of concept. J. Blind. Innov. Res. **4**(1), 4–51 (2014)
22. Taylor, B.T., Dey, A.K., Siewiorek, D.P., Smailagic, A.: TactileMaps.net: a web interface for generating customized 3D-printable tactile maps. In: Proceedings of the 17th International ACM SIGACCESS Conference on Computers & Accessibility, pp. 427–428 (2015)
23. Gual, J., Puyuelo, M., Lloveras, J.: Three-dimensional tactile symbols produced by 3D printing: improving the process of memorizing a tactile map key. Brit. J. Visual Impair. **32**(3), 263–278 (2014)
24. Gual, J., Puyuelo, M., Lloveras, J.: The effect of volumetric (3D) tactile symbols within inclusive tactile maps. Appl. Ergon. **48**, 1–10 (2015)
25. Wabinski, J., Moscicka, A.: Automatic (tactile) map generation—a systematic literature review. ISPRS Int. J. Geo-Inf. **7**, 293 (2019)

Interactive Visualization of Sport Climbing Data

Fangze Qiu[1] and Yue Li[2(✉)] (iD)

[1] School of Advanced Technology, Xi'an Jiaotong-Liverpool University, Suzhou,
China
fangze.qiu19@student.xjtlu.edu.cn
[2] Department of Computing, School of Advanced Technology, Xi'an
Jiaotong-Liverpool University, Suzhou, China
yue.li@xjtlu.edu.cn

Abstract. The official website of the International Federation of Sport
Climbing (IFSC) stores information about sport climbing competitions
and athletes. While the website shows comprehensive data, it was mainly
static and there was limited interaction or effective visualization, impeding the attempts to understand the performance of the athletes. To
address this problem, we developed IFSC$^+$, an interactive visualization system for sport climbing data from the IFSC official website. This
paper details the design of the interactive visualizations, highlighting how
they can be used to compare athlete performance and identify promising candidates in future competitions. Our work demonstrates the value
of interactive visualizations in supporting effective meaning-making and
informed decision-making in sports.

Keywords: Interactive Visualization · Interaction Design · Sport
Climbing · Sports Prediction

1 Introduction

Sport Climbing (SC) has gained immense popularity worldwide, especially after
its debut at the 2020 Summer Olympics in Tokyo, Japan. Athlete performance in
SC is a complex and dynamic phenomenon that relies on a multitude of factors,
ranging from physical aptitudes to mental stamina and strategic decision-making.
Thus, predicting the outcomes of climbing competitions or identifying patterns of
success and failure can be a daunting task for coaches, sponsors, researchers, and
fans alike. Recent developments in interactive visualization techniques and data
analytics have opened up new avenues for exploring the intricate relation between
athletes and their performance outcomes [1,5]. In this paper, we present IFSC$^+$,
an interactive visualization system for analyzing and understanding SC data presented on the International Federation of Sport Climbing (IFSC) official website.
Specifically, the system aims to provide intuitive comparisons of athlete performances and make predictions on the winning rates based on historical competition
data. We leveraged three key visualization techniques (a chord diagram, a radar

© The Author(s), under exclusive license to Springer Nature Switzerland AG 2023
J. Abdelnour Nocera et al. (Eds.): INTERACT 2023, LNCS 14145, pp. 507–511, 2023.
https://doi.org/10.1007/978-3-031-42293-5_63

chart, and a donut chart) to illustrate the *relation* between athletes, the *performance* of an athlete, and the *winning rates* of athletes in future competitions. The system contributes to answering the question: *'who will win the next sport climbing competition?'* from a data-driven perspective.

2   IFSC⁺: Relation, Performance, and Winning Rates

The design of IFSC⁺ has involved sport climbing fans and climbers in the requirement analysis and user evaluations. In this section, we follow Munzner's nested model for visualization design and validation [6] to briefly introduce the system design from the four nested levels: domain problem, data and operation abstraction, encoding and interaction technique, and algorithm.

2.1   Domain Problem

IFSC⁺ aims to present an alternative to the current IFSC website that would allow users to better understand the sport climbing data.

2.2   Data and Operation Abstraction

The IFSC website contains comprehensive data about athletes and competition results. However, the static table-based presentations failed to satisfy user requirements in relating different data sources and making sense of the data. Through interviews with users, we elicited two data analysis goals:

(1) Support Multivariate Analysis to Understand Athlete Performance. Users expect to have data presented in a comparative way, not only the ranking of athletes in the same competition, but also the same athlete in different competition categories (i.e. lead, boulder, and speed). Thus, the system should merge the data from various sources and support multivariate analysis, so that users could obtain a more comprehensive understanding of an athlete's performance.

(2) Present Flexible Options for Effective Comparisons and Predictions. Filtering information of interest was identified as a user requirement. Users expect to compare multiple athletes to see their performances. By presenting flexible options as manipulative parts in the visualization, users can gain a more nuanced understanding of the competition results and athlete performances.

2.3   Encoding and Interaction Technique

To achieve the goals, three key visualization techniques were adopted that enable users to analyze and understand athlete performance in the IFSC competitions.

Relation in a Chord Diagram. A chord diagram was found effective in demonstrating links between data objects [3], in our case, the athletes. The internal connections along with tooltips indicate the times of engagement of any two athletes (see Fig. 1a). This chart was designed to offer an at-a-glance overview

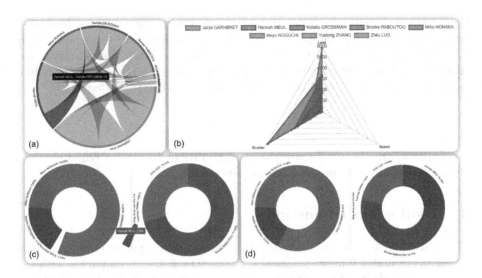

Fig. 1. (a) *Relation* in a chord diagram, showing how many matches have two athletes played against each other; (b) *Performance* in a radar chart, showing the relative performance of an athlete in the three types of sport climbing competitions; (c–d) *Winning rates* in donut charts, aggregating athlete performances and making predictions. By dragging an athlete bar from left to right (c), the results will be updated on the right (d). More details can be found in http://difsc.tech/.

of athletes' competition encounters by angular mapping. The relation between athletes may have an influence on the later comparative and predictive results. Generally, if two athletes competed against each other more frequently, the summary and prediction of their overall performance would be more reliable.

Performance in a Radar Chart. The radar chart in Fig. 1b enables users to map the performing results of athletes in the three basic SC categories: lead, boulder, and speed. Radar charts and their variations have been widely used in ability mapping [2] and comprehensive communication of values [9]. Thus, this chart was used to support users to compare and contrast athlete performances in the distinct competition disciplines, pinpointing their strengths and weaknesses. The interactive legends help filter the athletes involved in the comparison.

Winning Rates in Donut Charts. The donut charts present flexible options for comparison [8]. By filtering the athletes of interest on the left (see Fig. 1c), users can compare multiple athletes and see predictions of their winning rates on the right (see Fig. 1d). This addresses the key question of concern and provides an intuitive answer to the *'who will win'* question.

2.4 Algorithm

The winning of a climbing competition can be seen as the podium position, namely a top three ranking. In this case, the Bernoulli distribution enables us to calculate the probability of each outcome: whether or not an athlete ranks in the top three. The winning rate can be estimated using the maximum likelihood estimation (MLE) [4]. Suppose an athlete's performance in a competition is $x_i = 1$ if he or she wins a competition and 0 otherwise, the maximum likelihood $(\hat{p})$ can be estimated by calculating the number of times an athlete won a podium position over the total number of competitions he or she participated (n):

$$\hat{p} = \frac{\sum_{i=1}^{n} x_i}{n} \tag{1}$$

We use this formula to estimate the winning rate of an athlete based on their observed performances in previous competitions.

3   Results and Discussion

To evaluate IFSC$^+$, we conducted a between-subjects experiment with 23 participants (18 males, 5 females, age M $= 21.96$, SD $= 0.37$) to compare it with the IFSC official website. We adopted the User Engagement Scale [7] and invited participants to evaluate on their focused attention, perceived usability, and reward when using the system, as well as the system aesthetics. The results showed that on a 5-point Likert scale, participants were significantly more engaged when using the IFSC$^+$ (M $= 4.21$, SD $= 0.16$) than using the IFSC official website (M $= 3.07$, SD $= 0.11$), t(21) $= 7.29$, p <0.001. Generally, users found the visualizations to be 'interactive' and 'easy to understand'. However, users identified limitations in the scope of data representation. For instance, an experienced climber stated that 'Alex Megos doesn't rank high on these because his field is outdoor climbing'. This information is not included on the IFSC official website.

Despite the significant improvement, our system has some limitations. The current visualization is based on the competition data from 2014 to July 2022, and only some athlete data were featured for demonstration. Future work could expand the scope and scale of the dataset to include a wider range of athletes and competition events with real-time data updated from the IFSC website. Although the current calculation of the estimation of the winning rates combined with interactive charts effectively aids the prediction of future performance, the algorithm could optimized to increase its credibility. The prediction of winning rates in IFSC$^+$ is based on historical performance data only. Future work could take into account other possible factors such as the competition venue, athletes' age, height, ape index, and nationality among others.

4   Conclusion

In this paper, we present IFSC$^+$, an alternative to the current IFSC website that allows users to better understand the sport climbing data through interactive visualizations. Specifically, the system supports multivariate analysis to understand athlete performance, and offers flexible options for effective comparisons and predictions of future competition results. Evaluations of the system showed a significant improvement in user engagement compared to the IFSC official website. The design of interactive visualizations for sports data, especially sport climbing data was minimal but growing in need. Our work provides insights into the future design of interactive systems based on sports-related data.

Acknowledgments. We would like to thank our participants for their valuable contributions to this project and the anonymous reviewers for their constructive review feedback. Thanks IFSC (www.ifsc-climbing.org) for making the data publicly available.

References

1. Fuss, F.K., Niegl, G.: Instrumented climbing holds and performance analysis in sport climbing. Sports Technol. **1**(6), 301–313 (2008)
2. Hou, Y., et al.: DARC: a visual analytics system for multivariate applicant data aggregation, reasoning and comparison. In: Eurographics Proceedings (2022)
3. Koochaksaraei, R.H., Meneghini, I.R., Coelho, V.N., Guimaraes, F.G.: A new visualization method in many-objective optimization with chord diagram and angular mapping. Knowl. Based Syst. **138**, 134–154 (2017)
4. Lehmann, E.L., Casella, G.: Theory of Point Estimation. Springer, New York (2006). https://doi.org/10.1007/b98854
5. M. Fauzi, M.S., Imran, K., Mohamed, Z.: Social network analysis and data visualization of football performance preceded to the goal scored. In: Syed Omar, S.F., Hassan, M.H.A., Casson, A., Godfrey, A., P. P. Abdul Majeed, A. (eds.) Innovation and Technology in Sports: Proceedings of the International Conference on Innovation and Technology in Sports, ICITS 2022. LNCS, Malaysia, pp. 57–74. Springer, Heidelberg (2023). https://doi.org/10.1007/978-981-99-0297-2_6
6. Munzner, T.: A nested model for visualization design and validation. IEEE Trans. Vis. Comput. Graph. **15**(6), 921–928 (2009)
7. O'Brien, H.L., Cairns, P., Hall, M.: A practical approach to measuring user engagement with the refined user engagement scale (UES) and new UES short form. Int. J. Hum Comput Stud. **112**, 28–39 (2018)
8. Spence, I.: No humble pie: the origins and usage of a statistical chart. J. Educ. Behav. Stai. **30**(4), 353–368 (2005)
9. Thaker, N.G., Ali, T.N., Porter, M.E., Feeley, T.W., Kaplan, R.S., Frank, S.J.: Communicating value in health care using radar charts: a case study of prostate cancer. J. Oncol. Pract. **12**(9), 813–820 (2016)

Interactors, not Users! Towards a Neutral Interaction Design

Sónia Rafael[(⊠)] [iD]

ITI-LARSyS, Faculdade de Belas-Artes, Universidade de Lisboa, Lisbon, Portugal
srafael@campus.ul.pt

Abstract. This article delves into the post-humanist perspective as a means of comprehending the relationships among various actors in interaction design and their contemporary understanding. It is our contention that traditional design methodologies must be updated to ensure greater inclusivity. To this end, we propose a practical terminological shift, whereby the term *interactor* replaces *user* to recognize the significance of non-human actors in design and foster a more equitable society. In addition, we introduce a neutral interaction design model that prioritizes equity between human and non-human actors, regardless of whether they are biological or artificial. This article constitutes a modest contribution to the ongoing discourse on how design can rise to meet the challenges of the contemporary world.

Keywords: Post-humanism · Interaction Design · Users · Interactors

1 Introduction

The post-humanist perspective examines the relationships between humans, technology, and the natural world, recognizing various discursive subjects. For this reason, post-humanism distances itself from humanist discourse, which places the human being as the measure of all things.

In design, methodologies such as human-centered design or even user-centered design still suffer from anthropocentrism. However, contemporary times, particularly the post-human, technological advancements, and environmental changes, have brought new challenges for emerging design practices that emphasize the interrelationships between human and non-human actors, contributing to a society that is more equitable.

As *Words Matter* [1], we propose the change of nomenclature from *user* to *interactor* and an open model that can overcome the limits of human and non-human actors (whether biological or artificial) that profile a neutrality of positions in which primacy is not attributed to any of the actors involved in the interaction design.

This conceptual and functional equivalence advocates that anyone can assume the role of sender and receiver, define goals for interaction, and define the sequence of procedures associated with the development of interaction. We believe that this small contribution can help build a more just society because… we need more interactors and fewer users!

© The Author(s), under exclusive license to Springer Nature Switzerland AG 2023
J. Abdelnour Nocera et al. (Eds.): INTERACT 2023, LNCS 14145, pp. 512–516, 2023.
https://doi.org/10.1007/978-3-031-42293-5_64

2 Post-humanist Perspective

The post-humanist perspective, advocated by philosophers Rosi Braidotti [2] and Francesca Ferrando [3, 4], is a framework that examines the relationships between humans, technology, and the natural world, as a counterpoint to humanist thought. The post-humanist movement emphasizes the idea that human beings are part of an ecosystem and that their actions affect the whole, therefore, "the human is not approached as an autonomous agent but is located within an extensive system of relations" [3] (p. 32).

For this reason, post-humanism, by recognizing multiple discursive subjects, distances itself from the humanist discourse that places the human being as the measure of all things. A post-humanist view of the world should be pluralistic, multifaceted, and as inclusive as possible [3], giving rise to the hybrid figure of the posthuman and related concepts, such as the non-human, the multispecies, the anthropocene, the more than human, the transhuman, and the decentering of the human [5].

Since it is a thought of postmodernist tradition, emerging with the feminist, anti-racist, and pacifist movements, "which reject the rational, autonomous individual and, rather, emphasize the partial, situated, and socially-constructed self" [5] (p. 20), the post-humanist movement understands that the human being is a cultural and historical construction and, as such, plural. For this reason, Rosi Braidotti [2] believes it is relevant to consider the history, particularly European history, to identify how its imperialist past shapes current politics. That is, using posthuman critical theory, it is intended to put an end to the singular conception of what it means to be human.

On the other hand, in a globalized world, IT has opened the possibility of defining other ways of life that do not have the human as the main promoter and beneficiary. Because the technology-mediated world allows us to "blur the boundaries between the familiar binaries of human and non-human, culture and nature, and human and animal" [5] (p. 17), designers must consider the implications of these new actors in the praxis of design.

2.1 Post-humanism and Interaction Design

We understand post-humanism as a perspective that integrates the human and the non-human, with the non-human encompassing animals and the natural environment, as well as things and the artificial world [5]. From a design perspective, this outlook allows us to question design epistemologies that are focused solely on the human, such as human-centered design, which employs a universalist notion of humanity [7]. Additionally, the field of design is often subordinated to neoliberal economic models and capitalist values [5, 6], which reduce the human primarily to a consumer or user and exclude non-human actors.

Within the framework of post-humanism, interaction design requires more flexible models and methodologies that can accommodate contemporary needs. Interaction design is defined as the design of the subjective and qualitative aspects of everything that is both digital and interactive [8], or as shaping digital things for people's use [9], or as the combination of hardware and/or software and/or services and/or people that users interact with to achieve specific goals [10]. However, it may be necessary to begin with a fairer definition.

We propose a more open definition that is suitable for post-humanist demands – interaction design as the design of the mediation (*inter*) of reciprocal actions (*agere*) between actors (human and/or non-human). From this definition, designers can begin to understand the implications that machine learning, artificial intelligence, algorithms, big data, automation technology, and robotics may have on the practice of design [11], for instance.

2.2 From Object to Subject Status

When considering a more open framework, as proposed in the previous section, it will be relevant to reflect on non-human artificial actors – computer systems. To do so, it is essential to revisit Philip Brey's functional analysis [12], which argues that the primary relationship between humans and computational systems has been epistemic, meaning that the computer functions as a cognitive device that enhances and/or complements cognitive function by performing information processing tasks.

However, in recent decades, the epistemic relationship between humans and computers has been supplemented by an ontological relationship, in which the computer has acquired a new class of functions. Computers can generate virtual and social environments and simulate human behavior, reconstructing an idea of the human dimension in interaction, allowing the machine to move from the status of an object to the status of a subject. This functional analysis understands computational systems as simulation devices where there is a symbiosis between the human mind and the computational system that is so effective that it results in hybrid cognitive systems [12].

Moreover, digital interfaces also reinforce this perspective through embodiment, creating an interaction dynamic that resembles that of humans [13]. This embodiment happens in various ways, notably through avatars or virtual assistants, where interaction with users is carried out through artificial intelligence and machine learning mechanisms. If computational systems can alter their behavior, reproduce emotions, language, and patterns of human communication, and their conversational and cognitive abilities can be somewhat comparable to those of a human, it is necessary to question – What does it mean to be a user in an interaction?

2.3 Users or Interactors?

The term *user* is commonly used to refer to someone who interacts with an object or interface and is often accompanied by a sense of possession, control, or manipulation of the user over the used. The ISO 9241–210:2019 defines a *user* as a person who interacts with a system, product, or service [13]. Don Norman stopped considering users as such, stating that "it is time to wipe words such as *consumer*, *customer*, and *user* from our vocabulary. Time to speak of *people*" [1] (p.63). According to the author, this designation degrades the people for whom design is projected, a way of labeling them as objects, rather than personifying them.

Objects manifest a *soul* that ensures the symbiotic relationship between objects and individuals [14]. Within a given cultural system, objects continuously shift from the functional to the symbolic character and have become the actors in a global process of which human is merely the spectator [14]. And so, the user becomes the used.

In this context, we argue that in the post-humanist framework, a change in nomenclature is necessary to remove the idea of a user's supremacy over the used. We propose the adoption of the concept of *interactor* – as one who interacts – in place of *user*, promoting an equity of roles in the interaction. The term *interactor* places the actors on a level playing field that was previously hierarchical, meaning it refers to the actors of an interactive process, whether they are human or non-human. Thus, we can distinguish the user who uses (vertical correspondence) from the interactor who interacts (horizontal correspondence). This term was used by Janet Murray [15] to describe an actor who interacts with the narrative and alters its course in the context of interactive narratives.

Given the presented framework, we understand the appropriation of this concept to be appropriate for both actors of the interaction. This term is also applicable within the actor-network theory (ANT) that has advocated for understanding the relations between networks and *assemblages* of humans and non-humans – *actors* that share equal agency in participating in the shaping of issues [5]. An *actor* or *actant* is defined as an entity that engages in action or is granted the ability to do so by other entities.

2.4   Equity Between Human and Non-human Actors

We advocate for the appropriation of the interactor concept for both human and non-human actors (biological or artificial). This conceptual and functional equating of actors proposes that any actor can assume the role of sender (presenting a request) and receiver (presenting a response to the request), define goals for the interaction and define the sequence of procedures associated with the development of the interaction.

The neutrality of positioning creates an interaction designed and adapted to the interaction needs and desires of any of the actors involved and it's expressed by not assigning specific roles to the actors in the development of the interaction.

In this proposal, it is not possible to assume that human actors are invariably in a dominant position, and that relationships established with non-human actors are also invariably centered on the goals of the former.

3   Conclusion

Given the presented framework, it becomes naturally necessary that designers, engineers, computer scientists, and other stakeholders equitably consider the needs, expectations, and goals of both human and non-human actors in the design and development of interactive systems – as demanded by the post-humanist framework.

The development expectations of artificial intelligence systems and non-biological sentient beings, advanced robotics, machine learning, cognitive computing, quantum computing, and other technological advancements are phenomena whose development prospects require the non-differentiation of actors.

For now, the design of the interaction between humans and non-humans is still dependent on ethical, aesthetic, and functional choices made by humans, but anticipating a future society, we can predict that conscious entities will endure immune to cycles of birth and death. For these reasons, the adoption of terminology that considers the following is proposed:

- The term *user* and related nomenclature should be replaced by the term *interactor* for both actors in the interaction.
- In the design of any interaction project, the design requirements can be guided in their functional, technical, aesthetic, and ethical aspects by the required equity between actors.

This attitude should promote the articulation between theory and practice and trigger the use of a common language for researchers, designers, and other stakeholders in the process of designing and developing interactive systems.

References

1. Norman, D.: Words Matter. Talk about people: not customers, not consumers, not users. Interactions **13**(5), 49–63 (2006). https://doi.org/10.1145/1151314.1151340
2. Braidotti, R.: The Posthuman. Polity Press, Bristol (2013)
3. Ferrando, F.: Posthumanism, transhumanism, antihumanism, metahumanism, and new materialisms. Existenz **8**(2), 26–32 (2013)
4. Ferrando, F.: The body. In: Ranish, R., Sorgner, S. (eds,) Post-and Transhumanism: An Introduction, Peter Lang, Bristol, pp. 213–216 (2014)
5. Forlano, L.: Posthumanism and design. She Ji: J. Des. Econ. Innov. **3**(1), 16–29 (2017). https://doi.org/10.1016/j.sheji.2017.08.001
6. Höök, K., Löwgren, J.: Characterizing interaction design by its ideals: a discipline in transition. She Ji: J. Des. Econ. Innov. **7**(1), 24–40 (2021)
7. Mareis, C., Paim, N.: Design struggles. an attempt to imagine design otherwise. In: Mareis, C., Paim, N. (eds.) Design Struggles Intersecting Histories, Pedagogies, and Perspectives, Plural, Valiz, Amsterdam, pp. 11–22 (2021) (2021)
8. Moggridge, B.: Designing Interactions. MIT Press, Cambridge (2006)
9. Löwgren, J.: Interaction design – brief intro. In: The Encyclopedia of Human-Computer Interaction, 2nd edn. Interaction Design Foundation (2013). https://www.interaction-design.org/literature
10. International Organization for Standardization. ISO 9241-210: 2019 Ergonomics of Human-System Interaction – Part 210: Human-Centred Design for Interactive Systems, 2nd edn. ISO, Geneva (2019). https://www.iso.org/standard/77520.html
11. Clark, J.: Design in the Era of the Algorithm. Big Medium (2017). https://bigmedium.com/speaking/design-in-the-era-of-the-algorithm.html
12. Brey, P.: The epistemology and ontology of human-computer interaction. Minds Mach. **15**(3-4), 383–398 (2005). https://doi.org/10.1007/s11023-005-9003-1
13. Draude, C.: Computing bodies. In: Gender Codes and Anthropomorphic Design at the Human-Computer Interface. Springer, Kassel (2017). https://doi.org/10.1007/978-3-658-18660-9
14. Baudrillard, J.: The system of objects. In: Radical Thinkers, 9th edn. Verso, London (2006)
15. Murray, J.H.: Hamlet on the Holodeck: The Future of Narrative in Cyberspace. MIT Press, Cambridge (1998)

Lessons Learned from Designing and Implementing Interaction Mechanics for Viewer Participation in Game Streaming

Pavel Mrázek[1], Pejman Mirza-Babaei[2] , Günter Wallner[3] ,
and Simone Kriglstein[1(✉)]

[1] Masaryk University, Brno, Czech Republic
484952@muni.cz, kriglstein@mail.muni.cz
[2] Ontario Tech University, Oshawa, Canada
pejman@uoit.ca
[3] Johannes Kepler University, Linz, Austria
guenter.wallner@jku.at

Abstract. Live streaming of video games is a new form of entertainment attracting millions of users. A unique combination of broadcasting and chat rooms transforms traditionally passive spectating into a deeper social experience. In this paper, we investigate six interaction mechanics that allow viewers to participate actively and to possibly alter the outcome of streamed games with the goal to explore challenges with respect to implementing these mechanics.

Keywords: spectatorship · streaming · active audience participation · Twitch

1 Introduction

In the last years, spectating other people playing video games has become a popular activity (cf. [7,13,15]). Compared to traditional spectatorship via TV, streaming engages viewers on a deeper level [14]. It helps to transform rather passive spectatorship into a more social experience. Thanks to the connection of live streaming and chat rooms, viewers can exchange with other spectators and with the streamer. However, in addition to chat features, other approaches are also promising to involve the audience more actively, for example, quizzes, voting polls, betting, or displaying essential statistics about the current game (e.g., [7,14]). *Audience participation games (APGs)*, on the other hand, have the goal to create a new type of viewer that is still spectating but can also impact the game's outcome [7,11,14]. Traditional audiences are often static and passive, but *APGs* allow the audience to actively impact gameplay individually or as a collective [10,11,14]. Yet, while they have the possibility to change the outcome of the game, their actions are limited in comparison to the players [11, 14]. Still, the interaction with the audience presents new design challenges as

© The Author(s), under exclusive license to Springer Nature Switzerland AG 2023
J. Abdelnour Nocera et al. (Eds.): INTERACT 2023, LNCS 14145, pp. 517–522, 2023.
https://doi.org/10.1007/978-3-031-42293-5_65

the focus shifts from the player to an active interaction between the player and the audience.

In this paper, we investigate six different interaction mechanics (cf. [14]) that can be used to more actively include the audience in order to learn more about which of these are preferred by viewers. For this purpose, four mini-games for *Twitch* [16] were developed as a first step with the goal of comparing and exploring these different interaction mechanics through an initial user study.

2   Related Work

Several studies have identified reasons and motivations why people spectate others while playing video games (e.g., [1,3,5,9,12,13]). For instance, several studies [1,5,6] highlighted that one motivating factor for spectating other people play is knowledge acquisition, e.g., by studying and learning the different game strategies of the streamer to enhance their own abilities. Other reasons are the ability to acquire information about the game, ask questions about games, or to find new ones (cf. [12,13]). Smith et al. [13] found that spectators may also watch due to a lack of time or insufficient equipment to play themselves. The social needs of the audience form another motivational driver to interact with a streamer and other spectators, e.g., to increase social status, or to be part of inside jokes and sublanguages within a community (cf. [4,8,11]. Besides, streamers themselves can derive motivation from their role as a teacher as it allows them showing spectators how they can become better players (cf. [3,12,13]).

3   Mini-Games

For our exploration, we adapted the mechanics suggested by Stahlke et al. [14], namely: *Chat Input, Voting/polling, Direct Viewer Participation, Betting, Lottery and Competition Games with Viewers*, and *Content or Game Modifications*. To investigate these mechanics, four mini-games for *Twitch* were developed using *Unity 3D* [17]. With the mini-games we aimed to cover different types of games, serving as a foundation for the interaction commands.

Quiz includes several questions which have to be answered by choosing the correct answer from four possible options (see Fig. 1, top left). There exist two modes: In the solo mode, each player (viewers and streamer) chooses an answer via chat and earns points for themselves. In the team mode, the streamer competes against all viewers. The following mechanics are used:

- *Chat Input* – Viewers select the answers via text commands (both modes).
- *Voting/polling* (Team mode) – The most voted answer is then selected to represent the opinion of the whole audience.
- *Lottery And Competition Games With Viewers* (Solo mode) – Viewers earn points for each correct answer.

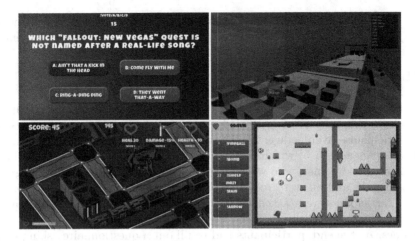

Fig. 1. Screenshots from the four mini-games: *Quiz* (top left), *Run* (top right), *Shooter* (bottom left), and *Platformer* (bottom right).

Run is a 3D racing game with a randomly determined winner. Racers compete on a predefined track full of obstacles that slow them down or push them off the platform (see Fig. 1, top right). Each individual racer represents one real viewer in the chat which is, however, not controlled by the viewer but by the game itself. The following mechanics are used:

- *Chat Input* – Viewers can either spawn characters or bet their points at the start of each game.
- *Betting* – Players who compete in the game earn points over multiple races.
- *Lottery And Competition Games With Viewers* – The placement selects the winner at the end of the race. The traps and obstacles can change the game's outcome unpredictably during the race.

Shooter is a survival mini-game where viewers vote in polls to affect the gameplay of the streamer with various modifiers. The streamer controls a soldier with the main goal to eliminate enemies and beat the score (see Fig. 1, bottom left). Viewers can affect the streamer's weapon, damage, health as well as the enemy spawn rate, damage, and health. The following mechanics are used:

- *Chat Input* – Viewers can use the chat to vote.
- *Voting/polling* – Viewers vote in a periodical poll with three options. Options are randomly selected from a predefined set of upgrades and downgrades.
- *Content Or Game Modification* – The poll may help the streamer earn more points, access better weapons, or heal themselves.

Platformer is a 2D platformer (see Fig. 1, bottom right). The game has basic controls such as movement and jumping. The goal is to collect trophies in the different levels and to dodge stationary and moving obstacles. Viewers can help the streamer who plays the game or make it harder to reach the goal. The following mechanics are used:

- *Chat Input* – Viewers type in commands to cast spells.

– *Direct Viewer Participation* – Viewers can cast five available spells, which significantly impact the gameplay as the streamer has to adapt to them.

4 Lessons Learned

We conducted a user study consisting of two playtesting sessions. Participants had to have prior experience with video games and *Twitch*. In the first session, four participants (average age: 21.8) took part and in the second seven participants (average age: 21.5) which fulfilled the role of the viewers. One person took the role of the streamer, who was the same for both sessions. The testing took place remotely and all were required to join a voice channel on a *Discord* [2] server. Participants were asked to talk freely during the whole session about what they liked and disliked about the gameplay and to give feedback about the games. At the end, participants had to fill out a questionnaire asking about their demographics and the mini-games.

With respect to the mechanics, participants had many problems with the *Chat Input* mechanic – e.g., for giving answers in time in *Quiz* – because of stream delay and spam protection. Also, seeing other people's responses was not favorable in some types of games. Based on these observations, it seems advisable do not overly punish viewers for late messages and to give them enough time to account for possible delays. Participants liked the *Content Or Game Modification* mechanic in the mini-game *Platformer*. The reason was that they directly saw the impact on the gameplay and that it made the game more challenging for the streamer. The interaction mechanic *Lottery And Competition Games With Viewers* was also perceived positively. The viewers liked the competition with other viewers as well as teaming up against the streamer. Regarding the *Voting/Polling* mechanic, participants liked the aspect of uniting the whole audience to select a desirable option and/or to beat the streamer as a group. It is an appropriate mechanic to find out the audience's opinion as a whole by aggregating individual votes. However, the mechanic had the same challenges with stream delay and spam protection as the *Chat Input* for *Quiz*. In contrast, with respect to the *Direct Viewer Participation* mechanic, participants voiced that they liked the feeling of making decisions individually and being complimented if they successfully achieved their goal. Lastly, participants were not convinced by the *Betting* interaction mechanic. It was observed that the participants did not really care about the points and their focus was more on the other mechanics in the mini-games. A possible reason can be that betting is not suited for short play sessions with different audiences and that they did not have the possibility to spend their points.

5 Conclusion

The goal of this paper was to explore and compare six interaction mechanics which can be used to support more active viewer participation. For this purpose, four mini-games were developed and a first user study was conducted. For future work, we plan to conduct a larger user study with a more extensive audience over multiple sessions to simulate realistic use cases. Since all interactions with viewers were implemented through the chat function it would also be interesting to investigate other possibilities.

References

1. Cheung, G., Huang, J.: Starcraft from the stands: understanding the game spectator. In: Proceedings of the SIGCHI Conference on Human Factors in Computing Systems, CHI 2011, pp. 763–772. ACM, New York (2011). https://doi.org/10.1145/1978942.1979053
2. Discord: Discord (2023). https://discord.com/. Accessed 04 2023
3. van Ditmarsch, J.: Video Games as a Spectator Sport. Master's thesis, Utrecht University, The Netherlands (2013)
4. Drucker, S., He, L., Cohen, M., Wong, C., Gupta, A.: Spectator games: a new entertainment modality of networked multiplayer games. Microsoft Research (2002)
5. Hamari, J., Sjöblom, M.: What is esports and why do people watch it? Internet Res. **17**(2), 211–232 (2017). https://doi.org/10.1108/IntR-04-2016-0085
6. Kaye, L.K.: Motivations, experiences and outcomes of playing videogames. Ph.D. thesis, University of Central Lancashire (2012)
7. Lessel, P., Vielhauer, A., Krüger, A.: Expanding video game live-streams with enhanced communication channels: a case study. In: Proceedings of the 2017 CHI Conference on Human Factors in Computing Systems, CHI 2017, pp. 1571–1576. ACM, New York (2017). https://doi.org/10.1145/3025453.3025708
8. Olejniczak, J.: A linguistic study of language variety used on Twitch.tv: descriptive and corpus-based approaches. In: Redefining Community in Intercultural Context, vol. 4, pp 329–334 (2015)
9. Pizzo, A.D., Baker, B.J., Na, S., Lee, M.A., Kim, D., Funk, D.C.: esport vs. sport: a comparison of spectator motives. Sport Market. Q. **27**(2), 108–123 (2018)
10. Reeves, S., Sherwood, S., Brown, B.: Designing for crowds. In: Proceedings of the 6th Nordic Conference on Human-Computer Interaction: Extending Boundaries, NordiCHI 2010, pp. 393–402. ACM, New York (2010). https://doi.org/10.1145/1868914.1868960
11. Seering, J., et al.: Audience participation games: blurring the line between player and spectator. In: DIS 2017, New York, NY, USA, June 2017, pp. 429–440 (2017). https://doi.org/10.1145/3064663.3064732
12. Sjöblom, M., Törhönen, M., Hamari, J., Macey, J.: Content structure is king: an empirical study on gratifications, game genres and content type on twitch. Comput. Hum. Behav. **73**, 161–171 (2017). https://doi.org/10.1016/j.chb.2017.03.036
13. Smith, T., Obrist, M., Wright, P.: Live-streaming changes the (video) game. In: Proceedings of the 11th European Conference on Interactive TV and Video, EuroITV 2013, June 2013, pp. 131–138, ACM, New York (2013). https://doi.org/10.1145/2465958.2465971
14. Stahlke, S., Robb, J., Mirza-Babaei, P.: The fall of the fourth wall: designing and evaluating interactive spectator experiences. Int. J. Gaming Comput. Mediated Simul. (IJGCMS) **10**(1), 42–62 (2018)
15. Tammy Lin, J.H., Bowman, N., Lin, S.F., Chen, Y.S.: Setting the digital stage: defining game streaming as an entertainment experience. Entertain. Comput. **31**, 100309 (2019). https://doi.org/10.1016/j.entcom.2019.100309

16. Twitch Interactive, Inc.: Twitch (2023). https://www.twitch.tv/p/press-center/ Accessed 04 2023
17. Unity Technologies: Unity (2023). https://unity.com/. Accessed 04 2023

Mapping the Digital Injustices
of Technology-Facilitated Sex Trafficking

Linnea Öhlund[1(✉)] and Teresa Almeida[1,2]

[1] Department of Informatics, Umeå University, Umeå, Sweden
Linnea.ohlund@umu.se
[2] Interactive Technologies Institute/LARSyS, Lisbon, Portugal

Abstract. As technology and social media develop and expand, technology-facilitated sex trafficking becomes increasingly difficult to take action against and prevent. Technology-facilitated sex trafficking implies the use of digital tools such as social media platforms to coordinate trafficking and (mis)lead persons into sexual exploitation, e.g., commercial sex. To address and prevent sex trafficking as it expands through technology, legal frameworks can both help and interfere with the work provided by aid organizations and authorities. We present an expert interview study with six professionals from authorities, women shelters and NGO organizations working alongside *the Swedish (governance) Model*. Our findings show that digital technology is useful yet heavily challenging for anti-trafficking organizations and authorities in their fight against sex trafficking, exploitation, and digital child abuse. More resources and tools are needed to mitigate the (mis)use of technology and prevent abuse. To do this, we discuss the need to recontextualize efforts against trafficking within the structural conditions and legal model of Swedish society that *facilitate* exploitation. Furthermore, we propose a series of risk-mitigating approaches which centers four questions for the HCI community working towards anti-trafficking efforts.

Keywords: Technology Facilitated Farm · Sex Trafficking · Social Justice

1 Introduction and Background

Technology-facilitated trafficking refers to the social and technical ecosystems wherein individuals use information and communication technologies to engage in human trafficking and related behaviors [1]. One example is that of *sex* trafficking as it migrates to for example, escort websites and mobile applications, streamlined with electronic payment options [2]. While technologies to combat sex trafficking proliferate, [3] and yearly many initiatives are launched around the world to create awareness and fight sexual and labor exploitation [4], technology-facilitated sex trafficking continues to expand [5]. Despite the large positive outcomes of digital platforms and technology-enabled solutions, human trafficking works within the same digital devices and interfaces to, for example, recruit, exploit and track victims. Through for example, child grooming [6], revenge pornography, cyberstalking, sexual coercion [7] or cybersex trafficking [8] predators mislead others into abuse.

© The Author(s), under exclusive license to Springer Nature Switzerland AG 2023
J. Abdelnour Nocera et al. (Eds.): INTERACT 2023, LNCS 14145, pp. 523–527, 2023.
https://doi.org/10.1007/978-3-031-42293-5_66

The politics of regulation and governance models of sex work throughout the world means that individuals in sex trafficking may be more or less likely to become criminalized and further stigmatized due to fuzzy boundaries between consensual sex work and sexual abuse leading to increased real life vulnerabilities [9]. Governance models and legal frameworks can contribute to an escalation of sex trafficking within a country increasing or decreasing criminalization of individuals caught in a vulnerable situation [1]. Prior work has shown that, as sex trafficking becomes increasingly mediated by technology and nationwide governance models of sex work make individuals vulnerable on different scales, tech-enabled counter efforts are pressing [1, 3, 10, 11]. Moreover, anti-trafficking organizations and authorities play a crucial role as they are often the first contact point between a victim and a way out of trafficking [2].

In this poster we consider how technology-facilitated sex trafficking is entangled with one of the major legal models of sex work. We explore the Swedish Model as one of the largest implemented legal models in the world and present a pilot expert interview study with six professionals from organizations based in Sweden. Participants work to address sex trafficking, sex work and sexual abuse towards women and children. Finally, we consider how technology could be reimagined to reduce structural risk factors to prevent exploitation and trafficking in the context of the exemplified legal framework. We highlight how issues of privacy and security, social media exposure, and the fast-paced evolution of ICTs are entangled in gender-based violence and vulnerability and suggest a series of risk-mitigating tools and approaches for anti-trafficking efforts. We contribute to ongoing research on social justice in HCI.

2   Expert Pilot Study

To collect data on technology-facilitated sex trafficking we contacted and interviewed six women working with human and sex trafficking, gender inequality, gendered violence, and child abuse. Our participants daily work is aligned with the rules and legislation provided by the Swedish Model as one of the largest implemented governance models of sex work in the world. All participants were recruited based on their professional activities working with victims of sex trafficking and those involved in sexual services, and affiliation with various institutions and organizations dedicated to supporting victims of the sex trade and promoting a more equal society (Table 1). A total of six self- identified women participated in our study with an age range of 26–62 years old. Together, they were representative of a large variance of backgrounds, experiences, and knowledge regarding the complexity of sex trafficking and how the trade explores technology enabled tools and systems. Their individual experiences in the field range from five years to over 20 years. This involves them working across different regions in Sweden and operating within the Swedish Model. Questions of sex trafficking and abuse were issues central to participants who in their roles constantly deal with topics of sex work, sexual transactions and/or sexual abuse and address these according to the operating model. As all of our participants work within the Swedish Model, they all have experience with what mechanisms of the law can have positive or negative outcomes for individuals that are or have been involved in any type of sexual transaction business. The Swedish Model provides professionals with how to take action through for example, criminalizing any person organizing or engaging in the purchase of sexual services and understanding any person selling sexual services as a victim. The model also centers around the notion of demand and gendered violence as being main challenges when dealing with technology-facilitated sex Trafficking.

Table 1. Overview of pilot study participants

Participant	Organization	Title	Role
Ingrid	Organization for Women in Sex Work	Board Member	Coordinator of Organization
Roberta	A Swedish municipality	Coordinator Against Human Trafficking	Lead Researcher of Field Operations
Sara	Women Shelter Group	Volunteer	Support Provider for Women in Sex Work
Anastasia	NGO for fair sex initiatives	Director and founder	Daily Management and Head of Operations
Petra	The police Authority	Superintendent	Lead coordinator of sex Trafficking Data Collection
Bea	Family Center for Children	Psychologist	Head Evaluator of Child Abuse

3   Three Approaches for HCI Anti-Trafficking Efforts

From our expert pilot study, we summarize three approaches centering efforts for researchers and companies designing and developing tools which can potentially be misused, for anti-trafficking organizations and authorities seeking to broaden their scope of aid and society in general as laws and legislation interlink with these various stakeholders and victims.

Legislation of Social Media Abuse. As social media is a major tool for misuse, legislation is one crucial if not the largest tool to mitigate abuse. In Europe, the General Data Protection Regulation (GDPR) demands compliance and made companies worldwide review ways of handling, storing, and sharing user data, which in turn creates better insights for users into how their content is handled. Similar to GDPR, what could make a substantial difference in risk mitigation on social media is the question of anonymity, i.e. should a person on social media have the possibility to be completely anonymous and thereby not responsible? If a person has an identity tied to an account this would firstly prevent underage children to sign up, then secondly if a user is found to groom, persuade, or hurt another user, or a trafficker pretending to be a consensual sex worker, they can easily be located, and fake profiles would be heavily limited. To acknowledge how legislation needs to interlink with HCI interventions we consider: 1) *How can HCI* *interventions address technology-facilitated abuse interlinked with current legislation processes and push necessary policy change?*

Designing for Fuzzy Boundaries. It is critical to recognize the challenge of the widespread accessibility of websites for sexual services. Predators can nowadays reach a much wider range of people, specifically children. Sexual services can for many young individuals be confusing and misleading. Simple conversations or digital interactions may, at first, seem innocent but can after a while lead to misinformed decisions and pushing boundaries, as for example, in the case of sugar dating. Such initially innocent but predatory interactions are acknowledged by the Inter-Agency Coordination Group Against Trafficking in Persons [3] which state that recruiters in human trafficking may use fake social media accounts and fake profiles to gain the trust of potential victims. This very broad (mis)use of technology and reaching many vulnerable individuals need to be acknowledged in HCI and the design of future tech- enabled interventions should consider the following: *2) How can we design digital platforms that cannot be (mis)used in i.e., sugar dating as an abstract practice of abuse and sex trafficking? 3) How can we design technology interventions that mitigate and stop already ongoing (mis)use and abuse?*

Malicious Scenarios for Anti-trafficking Awareness. A major problem in mitigating risks in digital technology and on social media platforms is that misuse develops rapidly making it hard for any organization, authority, or legislation to keep up [3, 10, 11]. The misuse is nuanced and creative in ways hard to predict and to change because of, for example, tech companies not sufficiently cooperating with authorities, servers of malicious websites located in different countries, language barriers of overseas victims and closed of black markets such as the dark web where untraceable cryptocurrency is used in transactions. The high-speed development of technological misuse could be addressed in the early stages of technological development. Creators, developers, and designers would run malicious scenarios of their artefact and attempt to predict misuse. These predictions would then provide aid organizations and authorities with data on how and where help efforts would need to be directed. Furthermore, this type of abuse analysis could be conducted on already large digital platforms where sex trafficking is present. Nonetheless, such scenarios would probably cause tech and social media companies to have to change or cut different features and would potentially lead to a loss of revenue, which lead to our fourth question: *4) How can HCI work towards demanding tech-companies to regulate products causing misuse (such as sex trafficking) in order to protect users even if regulations mean loss of revenue?*

References

1. Latonero, M., et al.: The Rise of Mobile and the Diffusion of Technology-Facilitated Trafficking, p. 43. University of Southern California, Center on Communication Leadership & Policy, Los Angeles (2012)
2. Gezinski, L.B., Gonzalez-Pons, K.M.: Sex trafficking and technology: a systematic review of recruitment and exploitation. J. Human Traffick. 0, 0, 1–15 (2022). https://doi.org/10.1080/23322705.2022.2034378

3. ICAT: Human trafficking and technology: trends challenges and opportunities. https://icat. un.org/sites/icat/files/human_trafficking_and_technology_trends_challenges_and_opport unities_web.pdf (2019)
4. International organisation for migration: Counter-Trafficking Data Collaborative (CTDC). https://www.ctdatacollaborative.org/ Accessed 28 Feb 2022
5. Tech Against Trafficking: Interactive Map | Tech Against Trafficking, https://techagainsttraf ficking.org/interactive-map/ Accessed 28 Feb 2022
6. McAlinden, A.-M.: "Grooming" and the Sexual Abuse of Children: Institutional. Internet and Familial Dimensions. Oxford University Press, Oxford (2012)
7. Gautam, A. et al.: Participatory tensions in working with a vulnerable population. In: Proceedings of the 15th Participatory Design Conference: Short Papers, Situated Actions, Workshops and Tutorial - Volume 2, pp. 1–5 Association for Computing Machinery, New York, NY, USA (2018). https://doi.org/10.1145/3210604.3210629
8. Napier, S. et al.: Australians who view live streaming of child sexual abuse: An analysis of financial transactions. Trends and Issues in Crime and Criminal Justice [electronic resource]. 589, 1–16. https://doi.org/10.3316/agispt.20200415028654
9. Bettio, F., et al.: Sex Work and Trafficking: Moving beyond Dichotomies. Fem. Econ. **23**(3), 1–22 (2017). https://doi.org/10.1080/13545701.2017.1330547
10. Furlo, N. et al.: Rethinking Dating Apps as Sexual Consent Apps: A New Use Case for AI-Mediated Communication. In: Companion Publication of the 2021 Conference on Computer Supported Cooperative Work and Social Computing, pp. 53–56 ACM, Virtual Event USA (2021). https://doi.org/10.1145/3462204.3481770
11. United Nations Office on Drugs and Crime: Trafficking_in_Persons_in_Europe_09.pdf, https://www.unodc.org/documents/human-trafficking/Trafficking_in_Persons_in_Europe_ 09.pdf (2009)

MetaCUX: Social Interaction and Collaboration in the Metaverse

Paola Barra[2], Andrea Antonio Cantone[1], Rita Francese[1(✉)],
Marco Giammetti[1], Raffaele Sais[1], Otino Pio Santosuosso[1], Aurelio Sepe[1],
Simone Spera[1], Genoveffa Tortora[1], and Giuliana Vitiello[1]

[1] Department of Computer Science, University of Salerno, 84084 Fisciano (SA), Italy
{acantone,francese,tortora,gvitiello}@unisa.it,
{r.sais,o.santosuosso,a.sepe21,s.spera7}@studenti.unisa.it
[2] University of Parthenope, Napoli, Italy
paola.barra@uniparthenope.it

Abstract. In this poster, we present a Virtual Reality environment, named MetaCUX (Collaborative User eXperience in the Metaverse), where people may collaborate in a virtual workplace and interact with intelligent objects for simulating real tasks. Several multi-user workplace scenarios were reproduced in the MetaCUX, on which an experimental study has been carried out involving 15 participants. To analyze remote collaboration small group of participants performed a task consisting in putting out a fire. Self-reported surveys and qualitative measures are adopted to investigate the effectiveness of social interaction during the collaborative activity.

Keywords: Metaverse · Virtual Reality · Collaborative environment

1 Introduction

The Metaverse is a shared online 3D space where users can synchronously interact with each other and with objects [6]. Examples of precursors of Metaverse at the beginning of two thousand years were online virtual worlds, such as Second Life [3], The Sims, Fortnite, World of Warcraft, and Minecraft [1]. Today, technological evolution enables to implement the Metaverse by adopting virtual reality (VR) and augmented reality (AR) with cheaper technologies than in the past, when those models were too expensive and invasive to be widely used [4] [8]. One of the fields in which the metaverse is finding wide use is remote working, with the aim to blend the advantages of video conferencing software with real-world social engagement [2]. It also enables to live experiences that have been difficult to generate using other techniques, such as collaborating for putting out a fire.

In this poster, we present MetaCUX, an immersive virtual environment suitable to simulate collaborative tasks thanks to the use of VR viewers and virtual avatars. A preliminary evaluation involving 15 participants was conducted with the aim of investigating whether the environment gives a sense of social interaction and engagement while they contribute in small groups to a collaborative task.

© The Author(s), under exclusive license to Springer Nature Switzerland AG 2023
J. Abdelnour Nocera et al. (Eds.): INTERACT 2023, LNCS 14145, pp. 528–532, 2023.
https://doi.org/10.1007/978-3-031-42293-5_67

2   Collaborative Virtual Space Design

The main design goal for MetaCUX environment, developed by using Unity, has been to support collaboration inside a working setting in the Metaverse by using Virtual Reality. A room (the Scenarios Room) shows paintings representing different room settings that may be selected, such as a classroom equipped with desks and whiteboard, or a collaboration room with a rounded table. Tacit knowledge is shared into a Break Room, i.e., a waiting room where users can play games and freely discuss. An example of a MetaCUX collaborative environment is the fire extinguished room, shown in Fig. 1. For the extinguishing of flames, there are several working fire extinguishers, emitting gas that interacts with the fire and can extinguish it. To extinguish a flame three participants have to remove the safety and collaborate for putting out the fire. Participants interacting in the proximity of a flame are not distracted by the other groups: the conversation is limited in the proximity. The instructor may pass from one group to another. Also, an interactive whiteboard is available to show a video demonstration on the use of fire extinguishers.

Fig. 1. The fire extinguished room.

A user can play two roles in the system: (i) *organizer*, enabled to create a new public or private room, select the scenario and manage the creation and scheduling of various activities, such as meetings, interviews, etc., (ii) *participant*, enabled to enter rooms and perform activities organized by other users. In the Metaverse, users are represented by their avatars, and to ensure easy recognition among users, each avatar is flanked by a label, indicating the username.

3   Evaluation

We conducted a preliminary user experience study carried out at the University of Salerno, involving 15 voluntary students (Male=9, Female=6) within the age range of 22–25 who had never used immersive VR before. Five experiment sessions were conducted where for each one 3 participants were supervised by one of the authors, who played the role of the organizer. The sessions were structured as follows:

- (i) *Pre-experiment.* Participants filled in a demographic questionnaire and were trained on the use of the Meta Quest 2 device and the MetaCUX system.

- (ii) *Experience.* In the Training room the organizer, using the interactive whiteboard, showed a presentation on the use of the fire extinguisher (*teaching/training*). Then, all users moved on to the simulation room, where participants collaborated to extinguish burning objects (*simulated collaborative practice*). Then, participants moved to the Collaboration room where they discussed the experience just completed and the pros and cons of this activity, writing on the whiteboard (*collaboration*). Finally, users passed into the Interview room. In turn, each participant was admitted to the room, where he or she discussed with the organizer about his or her first experience with virtual reality in general and, in particular, in simulating a collaborative task in the Metaverse (*communication*). The other users waited their turn in the break room, where they entertained themselves by playing ping-pong (*social interaction*).

- (iii) *Post-experience.* When the participants terminated the task and exited MetaCUX, they were asked to fill in the post-experiment questionnaire.

We conducted both a qualitative and a quantitative assessment. We adopted a standard questionnaire [7], by considering the following subscales: Presence (Pres), Engagement (Eng), Immersion (Imm), Usability (Usab), Skill, Flow, Emotion, Experience Consequence (EC). We also aimed at assessing the social presence (SP). We added the five questions proposed in [5] to this aim. As in [5,7], the questions are scored according to a seven-point Likert scale (from -3 = completely disagree to 3 = strongly agree). Experience Consequence scores were reversed. We also proposed an optional open question concerning participants' opinions on the experience and MetaCUX. The quantitative assessment concerns analyzing the number of errors, e.g., a user pushing the wrong grasping button on the analogic controller or following the wrong paths, during the observed tasks. Also, the time to perform the various activities was taken. In particular: reaching the Meeting room (MR), reaching the Simulation room (SR), grasping the fire extinguisher (FE) correctly, and grasping correctly the pen (PE).

User perception results. The perception of the users is complexly good, as shown in Table 1: all the median of the sub-scales are over 1 in a range from -3 to 3. A critical aspect of VR tools is the Experience Consequence: no participant declared to have any problem due to the use of Meta Quest 2, such as headache, fatigue, or nausea. The usability problems are mainly concerned with the easiness of use of Meta Quest 2 device. The users who reported those problems were also the users who did the worst performance in terms of time and errors. Social Presence was also well perceived, as the median is 2.5, with 1.25 as the minimum value. Concerning the open question we report some relevant opinions: "*Very useful. I had an initial difficulty in interacting with objects, such as the pen or the fire extinguisher, but I can learn how to do it* (P3)." P5 proposed adding a help panel in all the rooms showing how to interact with the objects. "*The idea*

Table 1. Descriptive statistics of qualitative results (N=15).

Metric	Median	Mean	Stdev	Min	Max
Presence	1.8	1.77	0.58	1.2	3
Engagement	1.67	1.91	0.53	1	2.8
Immersion	1.67	1.80	0.55	1	2.67
Usability	2	1.33	1.23	-0.5	2.5
Skill	1.67	1.60	1.03	0	3
Flow	2	1.88	0.65	0.5	2.75
Emotion	2	1.93	0.62	1	2.5
Exp. Cons.	1.5	1.73	0.59	0.5	2.38
Social Pres.	2.5	2.27	0.52	1.25	2.75

that all the participants wear the device assures that they were not be distracted by the external environment and actively participates. (P8)".

Quantitative results. The results of the participant's errors and times are reported as descriptive statistics in Table 2. The most difficult tasks in terms of completion time and the number of errors are the tasks related to object grasping while moving in an environment that seems to be comfortable enough. We performed a training session that has been appropriate for moving across the environment, but we realized that grasping an object may require longer training times for users that are not accustomed to using the device. Indeed, even if the median is 1 for task PE, one participant made 4 errors. Better results were reached with the fire extinguisher (task FE).

Table 2. Descriptive statistics of quantitative results (N=15).

Metric	Task	Median	Mean	Stdev	Min	Max
Errors						
	MR	1	1.33	0.62	1	3
	SR	1	1.47	1.13	0	4
	FE	1	1.67	1.34	0	5
	PE	1	1.40	1.35	0	4
Time						
	MR	2.11	2.08	0.80	1.21	3.34
	SR	2.36	3.12	1.59	1.37	5.43
	FE	3.10	5.24	3.00	2.05	9.12
	PE	3.53	6.55	4.10	2.3	12.01

4   Conclusion

In this work, we presented MetaCUX, a multi-user immersive collaborative virtual environment that offers multi-scenario features and interactive objects. We conducted a preliminary usability evaluation involving 15 participants in a collaborative task. Results showed that users positively perceived the environment: they found that it fosters social involvement and engagement.

Acknowledgement. We acknowledge financial support from the project PNRR MUR project PE0000013-FAIR

References

1. Ariyadewa, P., Wathsala, W., Pradeepan, V., Perera, R., Atukorale, D.: Virtual learning model for metaverses. In: 2010 International Conference on Advances in ICT for Emerging Regions (ICTer), pp. 81–85. IEEE (2010)
2. Bale, A.S., Ghorpade, N., Hashim, M.F., Vaishnav, J., Almaspoor, Z., Agostini, A.: A comprehensive study on metaverse and its impacts on humans. Advances in Human-Computer Interaction 2022 (2022). https://doi.org/10.1155/2022/3247060
3. De Lucia, A., Francese, R., Passero, I., Tortora, G.: Slmeeting: supporting collaborative work in second life. In: Proceedings of the Working Conference on Advanced Visual Interfaces, pp. 301–304 (2008)
4. García-Pereira, I., Vera, L., Aixendri, M.P., Portalés, C., Casas, S.: Multisensory experiences in virtual reality and augmented reality interaction paradigms. In: Smart Systems Design, Applications, and Challenges, pp. 276–298. IGI Global (2020)
5. Makransky, G., Lilleholt, L., Aaby, A.: Development and validation of the multimodal presence scale for virtual reality environments: a confirmatory factor analysis and item response theory approach. Comput. Hum. Behav. **72**, 276–285 (2017)
6. Park, S.M., Kim, Y.G.: A metaverse: taxonomy, components, applications, and open challenges. IEEE access **10**, 4209–4251 (2022)
7. Tcha-Tokey, K., Christmann, O., Loup-Escande, E., Richir, S.: Proposition and validation of a questionnaire to measure the user experience in immersive virtual environments. Int. J. Virtual Reality **16**(1), 33–48 (2016)
8. Xiong, J., Hsiang, E.L., He, Z., Zhan, T., Wu, S.T.: Augmented reality and virtual reality displays: emerging technologies and future perspectives. Light: Sci. Appl. **10**(1), 216 (2021)

Multisensory Climbing in the Magic Room

Matteo Secco$^{(\boxtimes)}$, Mattia Gianotti , Alessandro Colombo ,
and Franca Garzotto

Dipartimento di Elettronica, Informazione e Bioingegneria, Politecnico di Milano,
Piazza Leonardo da Vinci 32, Milano, Italy
{matteo.secco,mattia.gianotti,alessandro.colombo,
franca.garzotto}@polimi.it

Abstract. Multisensory Environments have been focused on use cases centered on learning skills and cognitive rehabilitation, which limits physical exercise to be a means rather than an end. A novel solution to this problem comes from Sensorized Climbing Walls, which will allow UX designers to explore a previously unexplored interaction mode using the entire wall as an interactive surface and suggest physical activities with a clear and central physical rehabilitation goal. Research on Sensorized Climbing Walls to date has mainly focused on measurement for enhancing performance. Merging Sensorized Climbing Walls and Multisensory Environments, new opportunities arise to offer more playful experiences to better engage patients in otherwise strenuous exercise routines. The two technologies have proven valuable assets to support children with disabilities and offer complementary sets of stimuli. The development of this new integrated system will open up a new field of study for multisensory physical rehabilitation, Multisensory Environments, and climbing therapy.

Keywords: Multisensory Environment · Sensorized Climbing Wall ·
Technological aided physical exercise

1 Introduction

NeuroDevelopmental Disorder is a term covering several pathologies arising during children's development. The most common effects are connected to cognitive, social, and motor deficits [12]. Patients may find it difficult to complete even simple daily tasks, with significant impact on their lives and their families [7].

A MultiSensory Environment (MSE) is a dedicated indoor space combining various sensory experiences and motor interaction to promote motivation, interests, leisure, and relaxation . These practices are grounded on Sensory Integration Theory [13] and Embodied Cognition [10,16].

MSEs have proven effective for improving motion and equilibrium skills [9,11]. Using Nirvana [4] resulted in a significant improvement in the trunk motion test and in cognitive skills. FutureGYM [15] successfully introduced a synchronization of running motion in children. A different approach is to include

© The Author(s), under exclusive license to Springer Nature Switzerland AG 2023
J. Abdelnour Nocera et al. (Eds.): INTERACT 2023, LNCS 14145, pp. 533–538, 2023.
https://doi.org/10.1007/978-3-031-42293-5_68

standardized physical practices in the MSE. Many sports have space requirements incompatible with MSEs, with climbing representing a rare exception.

Our aim is to combine the growing technologies of Sensorized Climbing Walls
[1,14] and MSEs to achieve two very innovative goals: using the potential of
multiple sensory stimuli to improve the overall experience of climbing for children
and introducing an incredibly innovative interaction method for MSEs.

2   Magic Room and ACCEPT

Based on our state-of-the-art analysis, we believe there is significant potential
for employing MSEs in the realm of physical rehabilitation, especially in creating a playful experience for enhancing motor coordination and equilibrium.
To the best of our knowledge, existing interactive systems designed for physical
rehabilitation are restricted to either floor-based or wall-based interaction. For
instance, FUTUREGYM [15] and iGYM [8] employ floor projections to enrich
the experience of traditional exercises or sports to improve the user's engagement
and overall experience. However, the metrics derived from such experiences are
coarse and fail to accurately gauge the compromised physical abilities of children.

On the contrary, several systems have adopted a different approach by utilizing a touch surface [5] or gestures (e.g. Nirvana [4]) to run exergames in
the vertical space, with the objective of rehabilitating upper limb functionality. Although these systems offer numerous specialized exercises, they often lack
an immersive aspect in the gaming and fail to facilitate collaboration, which is
fundamental for the children's development.

Our MSE, described in the subsequent subsection, already leaverages floor
projection to create playful virtual environments suitable for floor-based activities. Furthermore, it incorporates gesture-based interaction to enable upper-limb
rehabilitation, and both these interaction methods are friendly to wheelchair
users. Integration with a Sensorized Climbing Wall presents an immensely valuable compromise: by combining full-body tracking and measurement of the forces
applied to each handhold we achieve precise mapping of user skills. Additionally, the integration of the projections and other components of the Magic Room
enables us to generate a captivating gaming experience involving climbing activities for one or more users, fostering collaboration among children.

Among the vast amount of technological support for the training and rehabilitation of such skills, we have identified very promising potential support in the
use of a climbing wall. *Vice versa*, the potential of the Magic Room immersive
stimulation can support and improve the rehabilitative and training potential of
a Sensorized Climbing Wall. For this reason, we propose the integration of an
MSE, the Magic Room [6], and a Sensorized Climbing Wall, ACCEPT [2,3]

2.1   The Magic Room

The Magic Room (Fig. 1) is an interactive MSE that enables innovative, playful
interventions for children. The Magic Room integrates digital worlds projected

on the wall and on the floor with a gamut of "smart" physical objects to enable tactile, auditory, and visual stimuli. The Magic Room is equipped with A) a frontal and B) a zenithal projector, C) an audio system, D) custom smart objects, E) a custom camera-based body tracker, F) soap bubble makers, G) a tablet for caregivers to control interaction flows, and H, I) smart lights, a PC orchestrates the system behavior. The interaction with the smart space uses gestures and body movements or the manipulation of the smart toys (Fig. 2).

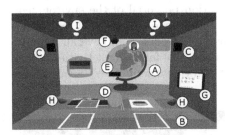

Fig. 1. The Magic Room's components

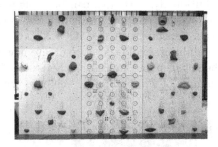

Fig. 2. The ACCEPT climbing wall

2.2   ACCEPT

ACCEPT is a climbing wall, approximately 3m wide and 2.5m high, equipped with triaxial force sensors measuring the magnitude and direction of forces applied to each hold. The wall allows the placement of standard climbing holds on a grid of attachment points, spaced according to typical children's anthropometric measurements. The sensors are hidden in the wall and invisible to the user.

The system reads synchronous force information from each sensor through a controller area network and serves it through an API, allowing a tablet application to show live the measured forces, visualize the data, store it, and associate it with a specific athlete. The app also stores the physical position and orientation of each sensor, so that forces from different sensors can be meaningfully composed.

3   Opportunities and Design

The integration of ACCEPT into the Magic Room environment would constitute the first example of a climbing wall within an Interactive Smart Space (ISS). The first level of integration will allow the Magic Room to access the data provided by ACCEPT, enabling the development of activities that react to the position of the user on the climbing wall and to the force vectors applied to each of the climbing holds. In a second integration phase, the wall could also be modified to act as an actuator by extending the ACCEPT system with different hardware elements like smart lights embedded into the holds. When not in use, the hold attachments may be used for mounting Radio-Frequency IDentification (RFID) receivers on the vertical wall, robotic components to act as stimuli, and up to fully working interactive smart objects, all of which may be removed when not needed without permanently impacting the structure of the room itself.

This new technological advances open new design horizons for activities: the vertical dimension could be exploited, adding a variety of interactions in the narrations or developing entirely new challenges for the user. To our knowledge, at present time there exists no ISS or MSE that allows exploring the vertical space. Additionally, activities can be designed not only for cognitive training but also for physical training, widening the rehabilitation potential of the environment itself. Sessions with the ACCEPT system may also take advantage of the room's capabilities, exploiting it to create new stimuli and feedback and overall improve the engagement and user experience of its users. The following activities are an example of what could be achieved without additional setup.

Fig. 3. Silhouette game activity   **Fig. 4.** Cooperative climbing activity

3.1 Silhouette Game

In this activity (Fig. 3), after a narrative introduction the silhouette of a body is projected on the ACCEPT system, prompting the user with a position he/she should assume on the climbing wall. This may be a simple game objective, or be used to test the physical strength of the user in a predetermined position. Depending on the positioning of the climbing holds on the wall, the path the user will have to follow can be unique , or he/she can retain the freedom of choosing among multiple paths. As the user fits into the projected silhouette, the tracking system is able to detect the correct positioning and (optionally after a permanence time) provide the user with positive feedback for the accomplishment of the goal, e.g. by changing the color of the smart-lights. At this point, the room instructs the user to climb down the wall and the activity terminates.

3.2 Cooperative Climbing

This activity (Fig. 4) requires at least two users: one will be climbing on the ACCEPT wall, while the other will remain on the ground. The goal of the activity is to enhance cooperation and communication skills by having the user on the ground direct the movements of the climber. The climber will start the activity with hands on two climbing holds and feet on the ground. On the floor a copy of the climbing wall will be projected, highlighting the next hold to be used according to some predefined sequence. The users on the ground will have to guide the climber's moves, communicating by voice. If the climber interacts with the correct hold the Magic Room will provide small feedback (through the smart lights only for example), while if the user moves into the wrong hold nothing will happen. The activity can be configured to have the sequence ends with the user on the ground again. After the entire sequence has been executed correctly, the activity is considered successfully completed and the Magic Room provides all the users a strong rewarding feedback.

4   The Call

MSEs have made strides in overcoming the limitations of cognitive rehabilitation, relegating physical rehabilitation to a secondary role. The incorporation of Sensorized Climbing Walls offers a unique opportunity to break free from this constraint: by exploring a novel interaction mode that utilizes the entire wall , we can propose physical exercises with explicit rehabilitation purposes. Prior research on Sensorized Climbing Walls has focused on enhancing performance measurement. Nonetheless, MSEs present an avenue to introduce more playful experiences, aiming to increase patient engagement during arduous exercise sessions. Our study seeks to address the following research questions:

1. Can MSEs provide a superior experience compared to traditional rehabilitation programs in terms of acceptability, engagement, and well-being?
2. Does the MSE experience yield measurable improvements in terms of rehabilitation outcome?

Answering the last question necessitates a comparison between rehabilitation outcomes in the MSE and those in a conventional therapy setting. To obtain scientifically valid conclusions, a considerable number of users are required. In the interim, we can monitor the effect of our solution on the overall well-being of the users. Our work paves the ground for a realm of multidisciplinary research, seamlessly integrating MSEs, multisensory cognitive rehabilitation, and physical rehabilitation through climbing. This integration presents a landscape of exciting challenges and unparalleled opportunities for groundbreaking innovation.

Acknowledgement. This project has been partially funded by project ActivE[3] "Everyone, Everywhere, Everyday" partially funded by Fondazione Cariplo and Regione Lombardia.

References

1. Amca, A.M., Vigouroux, L., Aritan, S., Berton, E.: Effect of hold depth and grip technique on maximal finger forces in rock climbing. J. Sports Sci. **30**(7), 669–677 (2012)

2. Colombo, A., et al.: Accept-a sensorized climbing wall for motor rehabilitation. In: Book of the 5th International Rock Climbing Research Congress, pp. 73–76 (2021)
3. Colombo, A., Maj, R., Canina, M., Fedeli, F., Dozio, N., Ferrise, F.: Design of a sensor network for the quantitative analysis of sport climbing. Frontiers in Sports and Active Living **5** (2023). https://doi.org/10.3389/fspor.2023.1114539, https://www.frontiersin.org/articles/10.3389/fspor.2023.1114539
4. De Luca, R., et al.: Effects of virtual reality-based training with bts-nirvana on functional recovery in stroke patients: preliminary considerations. Int. J. Neurosci. **128**(9) (2018)
5. Garcia-Hernandez, N., Huerta-Cervantes, K., Muñoz-Pepi, I., Parra-Vega, V.: Touch location and force sensing interactive system for upper limb motor rehabilitation. Multimed. Tools Appl. **81**(10), 14133–14152 (2022)
6. Garzotto, F., Beccaluva, E., Gianotti, M., Riccardi, F.: Interactive multisensory environments for primary school children. In: Proceedings of the 2020 CHI Conference on Human Factors in Computing Systems, pp. 1–12. CHI '20, Association for Computing Machinery, New York, NY, USA (2020). https://doi.org/10.1145/3313831.3376343
7. Garzotto, F., Gelsomini, M., Gianotti, M., Riccardi, F.: Engaging children with neurodevelopmental disorder through multisensory interactive experiences in a smart space. Social Internet of Things, pp. 167–184 (2019)
8. Graf, R., et al.: Igym: An interactive floor projection system for inclusive exergame environments. In: Proceedings of the Annual Symposium on Computer-Human Interaction in Play, pp. 31–43 (2019)
9. Kristinsdottir, E.K., Baldursdottir, B.: Effect of multi-sensory balance training for unsteady elderly people: pilot study of the "reykjavik model." Disability and rehabilitation **36**(14), 1211–1218 (2014)
10. Macrine, S.L., Fugate, J.M.: Embodied cognition. In: Oxford Research Encyclopedia of Education (2020)
11. Moreira, N.B., Gonçalves, G., da Silva, T., Zanardini, F.E.H., Bento, P.C.B.: Multisensory exercise programme improves cognition and functionality in institutionalized older adults: A randomized control trial. Physiother. Res. Int. **23**(2), e1708 (2018)
12. Shams, L., Seitz, A.R.: Benefits of multisensory learning. Trends Cogn. Sci. **12**(11), 411–417 (2008)
13. Smith, M.C.: Sensory integration: Theory and practice. FA Davis (2019)
14. Stien, N., Saeterbakken, A.H., Hermans, E., Vereide, V.A., Olsen, E., Andersen, V.: Comparison of climbing-specific strength and endurance between lead and boulder climbers. PLoS ONE **14**(9), e0222529 (2019)
15. Takahashi, I., Oki, M., Bourreau, B., Kitahara, I., Suzuki, K.: Futuregym: a gymnasium with interactive floor projection for children with special needs. Int. J. Child-Comput. Interact. **15**, 37–47 (2018)
16. Wilson, M.: Six views of embodied cognition. Psych. Bull. Rev. **9**, 625–636 (2002)

News Bulletins Supporting Human Memory

Ian D. Benest[✉]

University of York, Department of Computer Science, York, UK
ian.benest@york.ac.uk
https://www-users.york.ac.uk/ian.benest

Abstract. This paper describes the design rationale for the provision of oral news as a supplement to a digital version of the family photo album. The quantity of both pictures and news collected over a lifetime will be so large that the access (the metaphor) to the data must be considered in parallel with the overall design of the system and the strategy must be applicable to all digital media (music, speech, image and video). Furthermore, the interactive features should blend with the way the user ages. A key feature of the metaphor is the sequencing of media, and pausing is essential for creating natural presentations. Accessing oral news requires the necessary functions to test the universality of the interactive strategy.

Keywords: News bulletins · human memory · interactive paradigm

1 Introduction

Expected scenarios for the digital photo album might be: a holiday, a wedding, a sporting event. In these cases a sequence of pictures taken at the event would be automatically played in time order, with the news of the time played in parallel and in the background. Alternatively, a scenario might be to look at, for example, a collection of aeroplanes you have photographed over the years; here the images are variously dated and only when an image is of particular interest would the sequence be paused by the user and the news played for the date on which the picture was taken, again in parallel with the image presentation.

There will be two types of user. First, the person who accumulated the collection, and second, the group of people fortunate enough to inherit that person's (not very) private memories. For the creator of the memories, the system needs to help with the re-experience of events, the reparation of memory, and the resurrection of forgotten memories. Memories focus on both the event, and the prevailing social conditions, which together amplify that person's memory, and add to the appreciation and understanding of those that inherit. In later life, the system might be manipulated by a son or daughter, with the person who created the collection sitting beside them.

One means by which the user is "taken back" to that time, is to provide the news to which they had then listened or read; and through this, the children

© The Author(s), under exclusive license to Springer Nature Switzerland AG 2023
J. Abdelnour Nocera et al. (Eds.): INTERACT 2023, LNCS 14145, pp. 539–543, 2023.
https://doi.org/10.1007/978-3-031-42293-5_69

might better understand the environment in which the parent had lived. The work described here concentrates on broadcast radio news (from the BBC [1]), but the same sequencing rules apply equally to that read by a text-to-speech system. The oral content can be absorbed by those with failing sight, a symptom of ageing, and it expresses the original enthusiasm with which the news was read. It is presented as it was now, and not as an historic report, helping to immerse the listener into the past and into the memories being invoked. In general, the content of news is decided by a human editor [2] who chooses the items that are regarded as important, not what the user might prefer to hear.

No historian's interpretation has coloured the news bulletins, but what the announcer says colours our judgement and acceptance of each situation; and the bulletin may never have been correct. The bulletins fix history in our memories, but as Eagleman [3] points out "your memory of who you were at fifteen is different to who you actually were at fifteen; moreover, you'll have different memories that relate back to the same events". A literal eye-opener can be experienced: what you remember to be the case, may not be. Indeed, colleagues at the same event will have different memories. The bulletins will be the final arbiter over arguments as to what was recorded in world and national news at the time and consulting them will repair (or even re-implant [3]) the memory.

Not all memories are happy ones, and while some news items, such as the prevalence of Ebola [4] may cause stress at the time, the memory might re-awaken that stress with a greater and more adverse impact. The reason for consulting the (electronic) family album is to gain pleasure from happy memories, not to re-experience the harsher side of life. So, should there be built-in protection?

2 Interactive Strategy

The BBC [5] itself provides an on-line service to news, demonstrating some of the difficulties imposed by that method of access. The pictures used as anchors are bright, visually complex, and sometimes seem to bear little relation to the content to which the hyperlinked-picture is pointing. The eyes may take in the attractiveness of the picture at the expense of the eyes perceiving the accompanying text and passing that onto the cognition system for processing. The author suspects that the user's decision to select might result from the picture's powerful stimulation.

Whether or not the news was interesting, the back button, located some distance from the current position of the mouse (or finger), needs to be invoked to return to the news index where the mouse has again to be relocated. With a long distance to a small target, Fitts's Law [6] predicts slow interaction.

In this project, sequencing largely replaces pointing and clicking, with images replaced rather than slid into view [7]. Automatically inserted in the sequence are pauses which surreptitiously signal/reinforce association or dissociation within an oral narrative [8]. It is not always clear from the original sound broadcast, that there has been a change in topic and the speaker does not always apply the rules correctly. Also, interactive pausing and stepping within an oral narrative allows for more intense investigation by the user when the mind wandered [9] and needs to confirm what they heard (e.g. "did the announcer say...?").

3   Processing News Bulletins

The bulletins [1] are usually recorded at 16:00 each day on a DVD recorder and then manually re-digitised at a sample rate of 16 kHz using the AIFF format.

Generally an announcer reads approximately six topics (oral paragraphs) each with one, two, three or four sentences. Each sentence is usually no more than twelve seconds. The manual processing includes identifying and recording the times at which sentences begin and end. Where the speaker has stuttered, this is removed. The word "And" (for example: And now sport, ...) at the beginning of a sentence is removed as is "In the next few hours, .." The inter-sentence and inter-topic pauses are generally retained, though they are not consistent and such pauses are automatically replaced appropriately. Boyd [10] reflects on the need for good pausing, though it is not always practised in the original recording.

Incorporated in the original news bulletins are statements made by an "expert"; often these are poor (noisy) recordings, or are spoken by someone for about forty-five seconds without pausing for breath (and does not always add much to what the announcer says in the way of introduction). Generally these external statements are removed. Where the "expert" does speak in normal length sentences and succinctly offers additional information, it is retained and is a refreshing change of pace and voice compared to that of the announcer.

The sentences are transcribed for sub-titling and text-based searching. Where the narrative states for example "On Monday..." the Monday's date within square brackets is inserted after Monday in the sub-title. Otherwise, the words in the sub-title are the same as that spoken. As the hearing deteriorates, the person will become more reliant on the sub-titles to clarify the spoken muffle.

4   Playing News Bulletins

As each sentence is played, the transcript for that sentence is displayed in its entirety as a sub-title. There is no scrolling of the sub-title text, and no jumping of text as the sentence is spoken. The system presents the sentence in one, two or three lines with each line filled and centred. Where the sentence is very long, a smaller font is used. A stepped speed control can slightly speed up or slow down the speech, the latter being useful for those whose understanding needs more time for assimilating the information; a problem as we age. The speed control can also help slow readers as well as compensate for fast or slow speakers.

For listening to the bulletin, a fixed delay (250 ms) between sentences marks the end of the sentence, allowing time to absorb the information. However, were it to exist in the original, exuberant aural inter-play between sentences is lost.

The rule [8] for a topic (oral paragraph) change is: long pause, visual change, short pause, speech. The visual change is a brief (sub)-title, a long pause is two seconds, and a short pause is one second, the difference between long and short must be discernible. In practice, if no sub-titles are displayed, a two second delay between topics is satisfactory. If for example the news was a review of the month (not yet adopted in this project) with a number of independent topics, the rule [8] for a topic change would be: short pause, visual change, long pause.

5   Enhancing News Bulletins

It is important to signal, surreptitiously, a change in topic other than by requiring the listener to recognise, from the content, that the subject has changed. The insertion of a short sub-title before beginning the new topic seems helpful for those primarily reading the sub-title for, rather than listening to, each topic.

Television often adopts more than one person to signal a topic change as well as freshening a long narrative. While only one announcer reads the original BBC news bulletins, the sound of the voice can be changed, by altering the pitch, to reinforce the topic change. In future, a cloned male and female announcer speaking the transcription using text-to-speech [11] would be a better solution.

There is yet another method of signalling a topic change which provides additional benefits. A picture can be displayed at the beginning of each topic and sequenced after the topic title. It needs to complement what is being said. The picture is placed above the sub-title, so the sub-title does not interfere with the picture, but the eyes have to move between picture and sub-title.

If there is to be a change in picture between sentences in the same oral paragraph, they are sequenced before the pause following the previous sentence.

The picture should not change as the sentence is played; this is to allow the information in the picture to be absorbed before the content of the speech. Humans do not absorb information from the aural and visual channels simultaneously [6]; it is one or the other. Humans are adept at switching between the aural and visual channels; but while attending to one, different information on the other channel can be missed; switching agility worsens with age [12]. Bligh [13] suggests there is evidence that people watching TV will often focus on visual information at the expense of the auditory information when both are present. So a video is not an appropriate alternative to a picture fronting a news bulletin.

A young person's visual perception is the major route by which memories are stimulated. As old age approaches, the eyesight or hearing deteriorates, placing greater reliance on the other medium. As both aural and visual media run in synchrony, the user will move gradually from one to the other as the need arises, with no overt recognition that they have had to change, an advantage of adopting both the aural and visual modalities. However any hope that this might aid comprehension is unfounded [14].

6   Conclusions

Within a sequence, appropriate delays before and after a change naturalises the presentation. Mis-timing the change, results in a presentation that mis-cues relationships between information. The difference in delays must be humanly discernible, enabling the user both to hear and to see in unison what is, and is not, related. Sub-titling supports the on-going spoken narrative, but more importantly, being able to pause and step through the narrative enables a review of precisely what was said so as to repair a false (human) memory. Preparing and repairing broadcast news bulletins needs to be automated by: stutter removal, exact transcription, selection of short topic headers and accompanying images.

References

1. BBC Radio 4. https://www.radio.net/s/bbcradio4. (Accessed 14 April 2023)
2. Gale, E.: Choosing the News: How Newspaper Editors Define Newsworthy and Decide on Front Page Stories. VDM Verlag Dr. Müller (2009)
3. Eagleman, D.: The Brain. The Story of You. Canongate Books, Edinburgh (2015)
4. Thompson, R.R., Garfin, D.R., Holman, E.A., Silver, R.C.: Distress, worry, and functioning following a global health crisis: a national study of Americans' responses to Ebola. Clin. Psychol. Sci. 5(3), 513–521 (2017)
5. BBC News. https://www.bbc.co.uk/news/uk. (Accessed 14 April 2023)
6. Fitts, P.M., Posner, M.I.: Human Performance. Brooks/Cole, Blemont, California, USA (1967)
7. Benest, I.D.: An alternative approach to hypertext. Educ. Training Technol. Internat. 28(4), 341–346 (1991)
8. Koumi, J.: Narrative screenwriting for educational television: a framework. J. Educ. Telev. 3(3), 131–148 (1991)
9. Smallwood, J., Schooler, J.W.: The restless mind. Psychol. Bull. 132(6), 946–958 (2006)
10. Boyd, A.: Broadcasting Journalism: Techniques of Radio and TV News. Heinemann, Oxford (1988)
11. Neekhara, P., Hussain, S., Dubnov, S., Koushanfar, F., McAuley, J.: expressive neural voice cloning. Proc. Mach. Learn. Res. 157, 252–267 (2021)
12. Zanto, T.P., Gazzaley, A.: Attention and ageing. In: Nobre, A.C., Kastner, S. (eds.) The Oxford Handbook Of Attention, 927–971. Oxford University Press, Oxford (2014)
13. Bligh, D.A.: What's the Use of Lectures? University Teaching Methods Unit, London (1971)
14. Rogowsky, B.A., Calhoun, B.M., Tallal, P.: Does modality matter? the effects of reading, listening, and dual modality on comprehension. Sage Open 6(3). https://doi.org/10.1177/2158244016669550

PECSOnline: A Bespoke Classroom Based Picture Exchange Communication System (PECS) for Children with Autism

Joseph Liu[1], Becky Stephens[2], Chra Abdoulqadir[3],
and Fernando Loizides[1(✉)] (iD)

[1] Cardiff University, Cardiff, UK
{LiuJ100,LoizidesF}@cardiff.com
[2] Pontprennau Primary School, Pontprennau, UK
Becky.Stephens@pontprennauprm.cardiff.sch.uk
[3] Indra Renewable Technologies Ltd., Malvern, UK
chra.abdoulqadir@indra.co.uk

Abstract. We present PECSOnline, a Picture Exchange Communication System (PECS) tailored to meet the specific needs of classroom environments rather than an individual. To ensure the tool would meet the practical requirements of the classroom, we employed a participatory design approach, which involved input from educators of children with autism. Our focus was on developing an application that would be personalised and cater to multiple users, a feature that has not yet been tested in a classroom setting. We conducted a pilot test of our application, and the response from teachers of children with autism was overwhelmingly positive.

Keywords: Autism · PECS · Mobile App · Classroom

1 Introduction and Motivation

Autism spectrum disorder (ASD) is a type of neurodevelopmental condition that affects various abilities, such as social interactions, verbal communication, and physical capabilities. Based on research spanning the last half-century, the World Health Organization predicts a global increase in the occurrence of Autism Spectrum Disorder (ASD), estimating that approximately one in every 160 children will be affected by this condition. Children with autism usually have a varied amount of difficulty socialising with each other [4,5] and often communication differs from the norm [2]. To mitigate this communication, the Picture Exchange Communication System (PECS) [9] has been developed; a system that enables a gradual approach to developing language skills, and it is used internationally as the main communication way between a child with autism and others. PECS has successfully been implemented worldwide with thousands of learners of all ages who have various cognitive, physical and communication challenges [3]. PECS uses symbols of items with the respective name of the items on them. It consists of six phases and begins by teaching an individual to give a single picture of a

© The Author(s), under exclusive license to Springer Nature Switzerland AG 2023
J. Abdelnour Nocera et al. (Eds.): INTERACT 2023, LNCS 14145, pp. 544–550, 2023.
https://doi.org/10.1007/978-3-031-42293-5_70

desired item or action to a "communicative partner" who immediately honours the exchange as a request. The system goes on to teach discrimination of pictures and how to put them together in sentences. In the more advanced phases, individuals are taught to use modifiers, answer questions and comments. PECS allow people with autism to become communicative and comprehend items, descriptions and verbs with prompts to tell them, so that it will allow both communicators to understand each other, even if one communicator does not do so verbally. Santos et al. provide compelling evidence supporting the notion that PECS serves as more than just an augmentative or alternative communication tool for children; it also fosters substantial enhancements in their comprehension of contextual information [8]. Within the demographics of people with Autism, routine and familiarity is paramount [10]. There exist applications that can apply PECS to children. Our motivation lies in the fact that most current PECS systems are predominantly generic and lack customisation to address individual user requirements, such as the incorporation of personalised images. Similarly, while certain PECS systems offer limited personalised settings, they are tailored to one child, and they provide a one to one relationship between the two people engaged in a communication. In other words, they are typically designed for individual children, establishing a one-to-one correspondence between the two individuals communicating. In our PECS system, however, we present the capability of allowing more than one child and more than one adult (teacher or parent) to use the same application. Simply put, many teachers can use the application with many (different) students each. In this scenario, most of current PECS applications or alternatives become impractical since it is not feasible for each child to consistently carry an individual phone or tablet tailored to their specific environment. In this work, we present a bespoke PECS system specifically designed for the classroom setting. We offer comprehensive customisation and personalising features to facilitate interaction among multiple teachers, multiple parents, and multiple students at different PECS levels. The system was developed through a participatory design approach involving teachers from a specialized primary school in the UK, ensuring their active involvement and input throughout the design process. First, we describe the architecture and interface of the system, followed by a pilot study conducted in an actual special school environment. The feedback and usage reports received from teachers were predominantly positive, indicating initial success. Future research will explore the broader effects of implementing this approach with children diagnosed with autism.

2   The PECSOnline System

To ensure optimal classroom use, we utilised participatory design to gather requirements and develop our application with teachers working with children on the autism spectrum. These requirements were:

1. The application should be OS agnostic, and the delivery of the PECS application is primarily given through iPads and Android Tablets.

2. Accounts for teachers and parents should be available.
3. Both teachers and parents should be able to add multiple children to their (admin) accounts
4. We should comply with each of the PECS levels (phases) 3 to 6.
5. Include user security to prevent unauthorised changes by children, such as adult pass codes.
6. First This Approach [6] should also be included.
7. User Interface needs to be simple, minimalist and child friendly.

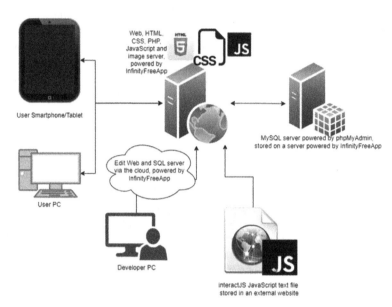

Fig. 1. Technology Architecture of PECSOnline

Our PECSOnline application is available at pecs-online.infinityfreeapp.com and can be accessed free of charge by anyone who wishes to try an early pre-bespoke prototype of it. Figure 1 shows the technology architecture of PEC-SOnline. The content of the application is displayed in a web browser through HTML, which can be appropriately styled using CSS. The web pages are built using PHP to enable the use of dynamic variables while JavaScript allows users to modify the status of the web page, such as relocating cards. The implemented technology for the mobile drag and drop feature is interact.js, which was successfully incorporated into both First This Then That (FTTT) and Advanced PECS Book pages. This technology enables symbols to be dragged on both PCs and mobile devices, making it the backbone of the mobile drag and drop feature.

Through our participatory design exercises, we have effectively implemented all of the necessary requirements. The left image of Fig. 2 depicts the various functionality options for PECS, specifically levels 3-6. Additionally, the right

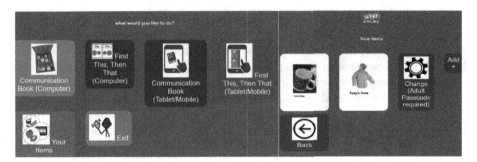

Fig. 2. PECSOnline Interface. Left: options of functionality. Right: personalisation feature.

image in the same figure illustrates the personalized feature which enables images of the children's personal belongings to be incorporated into the system for utilisation. Figure 3 shows two distinct features of the system. The left image demonstrates the "first this then that" function, enabling children to create more intricate linear requests and enhance their communication skills. The right image, on the other hand, highlights the classroom capability feature, which facilitates the addition of multiple users, such as teachers, parents, and other students as a sub-tree, allowing for concurrent usage of the system.

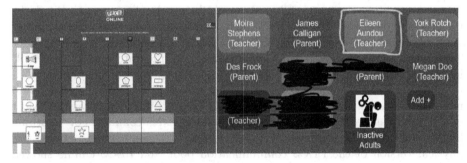

Fig. 3. PECSOnline Interface. Left: Example of "this then that" functionality. Right: classroom (multiple user) feature.

3   User Feedback

To obtain valuable feedback on the system's usability from those who would be utilising it regularly, we engaged the assistance of eight teachers who work closely with autistic children. In order to avoid bias in the results, these teachers involved in the user feedback were not the teachers involved the development of PECSOnline. The evaluation process was divided into two stages. The first stage involved the teachers using the system and performing some predefined tasks to ensure they use most of the features within the system. They were then asked to complete a questionnaire designed to evaluate the usability and overall effectiveness of the system in the second stage. The questionnaire included 60 items. The questions were developed based on Jakob Nielsen's 10 Usability Heuristics for User Design [1], the System Usability Scale (SUS) [7], as well as the specific requirement objectives for the system. The participants were not asked to perform a heuristic evaluation of the PECSOnline system, but rather given the time to use the system and then answer our questionnaire. Testing was approved by the Cardiff University Computer Science and Informatics Ethics committee.

3.1   Result Details

The questionnaire comprised several sections, with the first section consisting of 10 questions related to the usability matrix. Additionally, each question provided a comments box to allow participants to provide additional feedback, if desired. We received a total of 7 responses for the questionnaire. We present the average rating for the questions as well figures of the final four questions given to the participants in the questionnaire.

All of the participants voted "good" and "very good" for 90% of the usability matrix, and all of them appreciated the interface. They agreed that the system is "[e]asy to navigate" and has consistent design throughout the different sections of the app. They commented that "the interface is highly usable in a variety of settings". Regarding the communication book categories, some believed that it is "[t]he most impressive addition to this App" while agreeing that adding more categories, sections, extra visual cards would be good enhancements. Similarly, the drag and drop and the First This Then That features received modest ratings with most of the users asking for more symbols in the system at its later stages. They found the First This Then That feature a "good feature" and a "vital tool" in the system. Adult and child registration elements received unanimous positive reviews with no comments for improvements. Bespoke symbol addition and modification as well as their activated status were smooth processes as well. Most of the testers agreed that they were quick and easy with comments of "[n]othing [m]ore is needed. [I]t is simple and easy to do". The comparison between the physical version of the PECS communication book and PECS-Online showed high confidence because none of the participants voted negatively to the relevant question. They claimed that "categories and symbols are added [to] this system will eliminate the need to create physical cards which can be costly in time and money" and "it covers all areas of PECS and will be easy to use and a lot faster to make the PECS symbols". Some of the participants suggested some enhancements to the mobile app to make it look more similar to the standard physical book, "the ability to select a visual then switch categories to select another without losing your original visual from a sentence from a sentence strip of now and next board needs a bit of more work". Finally, thoughts on user and symbol customisation, navigation, friend recommendations, and app usage were all positive. Some teachers suggested adding an avatar to the name, adding undo option, and enhancing drag and drop items while all of them agreeing that "This App has a huge potential." As an indicator, some of the scores provided on a 5 point Likert scale for some features were: (a) 4.43/5.0 average rating for interface interaction (b) 3.71/5.0 average rating for the communication book categories (c) 4.29/5.0 average rating for symbol selection (d) 3.14/5.0 for thoughts on "First This Then That". (e) 4.57/5.0 for adding bespoke symbols (f) 4.29/5.0 for changing bespoke symbols (g) 4.43/5.0 for thoughts on changing all symbols' activated status (h) 4.14/5.0 for thoughts on navigation (i) 4.57/5.0 on whether the participants enjoyed using PECS-Online. Overall, the feedback received from the teachers indicated that the PECSOnline system was well-received and effective in meeting the needs of both teachers and their students. The system was found to be intuitive and easy to use, and the addition of personalized and multiple user account features were particularly appreciated. The feedback gathered from the teachers during the testing process played a vital role in the development and refinement of PECSOnline, ensuring that it meets the needs of its intended users. This feedback helped us to identify potential areas for improvement in the system, and to make necessary adjustments to enhance the user experience. Currently, we are conducting a longitudinal study to explore the effects of PECSOnline on communication, socialisation, and emotional development in a classroom environment.

Acknowledgement. We would like to thank Pontprennau Primary School and Nursery for helping creating and testing PECSOnline and Francisca Aslin for her invaluable support.

References

1. Usability Heuristics for User Interface Design. https://www.nngroup.com/articles/ten-usability-heuristics/ (2020), (Accessed 19 April 2023)
2. Allen, M.L., Lewis, C.: Communication and symbolic research in autism spectrum disorder: linking method and theory (2015)
3. Bondy, A., Frost, L.: A picture's worth: PECS and other visual communication strategies in autism. Woodbine House (2011)
4. Dawson, G., Meltzoff, A.N., Osterling, J., Rinaldi, J., Brown, E.: Children with autism fail to orient to naturally occurring social stimuli. J. Autism Dev. Disord. **28**, 479–485 (1998)
5. Gutstein, S.E., Whitney, T.: Asperger syndrome and the development of social competence. Focus Autism Other Develop. Disab. **17**(3), 161–171 (2002)
6. Hume, K., Sreckovic, M., Snyder, K., Carnahan, C.R.: Smooth transitions: helping students with autism spectrum disorder navigate the school day. Teach. Except. Child. **47**(1), 35–45 (2014)
7. Peres, S.C., Pham, T., Phillips, R.: Validation of the system usability scale (SUS) SUS in the wild. In: Proceedings of the Human Factors And Ergonomics Society Annual Meeting, vol. 57, pp. 192–196. SAGE Publications Sage CA: Los Angeles, CA (2013)
8. Santos, P.d.A., et al.: The impact of the implementation of the picture exchange communication system-pecs on understanding instructions in children with autism spectrum disorders. In: CoDAS, vol. 33. SciELO Brasil (2021)

9. Schwartz, I.S., Garfinkle, A.N., Bauer, J.: The picture exchange communication system: communicative outcomes for young children with disabilities. Topics Early Childhood Special Educ. **18**(3), 144–159 (1998)
10. Woods, J.J., Wetherby, A.M.: Early identification of and intervention for infants and toddlers who are at risk for autism spectrum disorder (2003)

Prediction of Love-Like Scores After Speed Dating Based on Pre-obtainable Personal Characteristic Information

Ryo Ishii[✉], Fumio Nihei, Yoko Ishii, Atsushi Otsuka, Kazuya Matsuo, Narichika Nomoto, Atsushi Fukayama, and Takao Nakamura

NTT Human Informatics Laboratories, NTT Corporation, Kanagawa 239-0847, Japan
ryoct.ishii@ntt.com

Abstract. This paper extensively investigates the effectiveness of pre-obtainable personal facial image characteristics, diverse profiles, and information on personal characteristics and values in predicting relationships between males and females after speed dating (SD). We collected a new corpus of data that includes the degree of romantic feeling toward the interaction partner (love-like scale) before the start and after the end of the interaction, the video, audio, and biological information of each participant, and the index values of diverse profiles and personal characteristics and values, which are obtained using a questionnaire. We constructed a novel predictive model that can predict love and like scores between males and females after SD on the basis of profiles, facial features, and psychometric scale scores. The results of the analysis showed that using all information from profiles, facial features, and psychometric scale scores was most useful for predicting females' love scores. On the other hand, we found that just using psychometric scale scores was most useful for predicting females' like scores and males' love and like scores.

1 Introduction

Many people have found lifelong partners thanks to speed dating (SD). On the other hand, taking the time to interact with strangers through SD is a big effort, and a compatible partner is not always easy to find. Therefore, if we can predict the results of SD with various people before they meet, participants can narrow down their search in advance to only suitable potential partners. This would greatly help people find partners more efficiently. For SD, psychologists have investigated what information about individual participants is important for partner selection. For example, personal preference traits (e.g., warmth and trustworthiness) of participants are relevant to their actual selection of members of the opposite gender that they like [2]. Another study [16] has reported that a small number of psychometric scale scores collected from SD cannot be used to estimate participants' impressions of each other after SD. Thus, it has been shown, albeit in a limited way, that individual psychological trait information has a relationship with the selection of members of the opposite gender after SD. However, no useful method has been proposed that can predict the degree

© The Author(s), under exclusive license to Springer Nature Switzerland AG 2023
J. Abdelnour Nocera et al. (Eds.): INTERACT 2023, LNCS 14145, pp. 551–556, 2023.
https://doi.org/10.1007/978-3-031-42293-5_71

of what kind of Love or Like impression one will have of members of the opposite gender after SD. A detailed investigation is warranted into how more diverse and voluminous participant information (profile, appearance, and various psychometric scale scores) affects impressions between participants after SD. In addition, a technology is desired that can predict the degree of impression of love/liking toward members of the opposite gender after SD. Using diverse and voluminous participant information, this study investigates whether such information can predict the impression values of participating males and females after SD has been conducted. We also quantitatively identify what features are useful for prediction. Specifically, we will construct a model that predicts the impression scores of love and like [25] between participants after SD is conducted, using as features general profile information (age, education, interests, etc.), facial photos, and various psychometric scores that participants can be expected to obtain before SD is conducted. We also discover which features are useful for this prediction task on the basis of the results of evaluating the performance of multiple prediction models. To conduct these studies, we collect a new corpus of SD data. This corpus was obtained from participants' audio, language, image, and biological information in a realistic SD setting. In addition, it includes participant profile information and many psychometric scale scores. In addition, various impression scores, including love and like, were collected on the interlocutor before and after SD was conducted, as well as outcome information on whether or not contact information was exchanged.

2   MMSD Corpus

We collected a new MMSD (Multi-Modal Speed Dating) corpus consisting of dialogues conducted by 625 male-female pairs made up of 146 Japanese speakers. As with most SD events in Japan, the recruitment process was open to the general public from a wide range of adult age groups. Ages ranged from 20s to 60s, with

Table 1. Pre-obtained psychometric scale

Rosenberg's Self Esteem Scale (RSES) [22]	Way of Life Scale [14]
Self-consciousness Scale [29]	Privacy Orientation Scale [4]
Immersion Scale [26]	Multidimensional Empathy Scale [9]
Big Five Scale [23]	Affinity Motivation Scale [30]
Trait Shyness Scale [3]	Loneliness Scale [8]
Romantic love attitude Scale [31]	Love Image Scale [17]
Interpersonal Trust Scale [24]	Self-concealment Scale [18]
FACES III (Family Functioning Scale) [21]	Communication Skills Scale ENDCOREs [12]
Value Orientation Scale [28]	Subjective Well-Being Inventory (SUBI) [27]
Goal Preference Scale in Friendship Situations [11]	Divorce Feeling Scale [20]
YUTORI Scale [13]	Social Anxiety Scale [19]
Sense of Purpose in Life Scale (PIL) [7]	Life-skills Scale [6]

a mean of 31.9 and a standard deviation of 8.6. This is similar to the results of a survey of the population of users of marriage match-making services in Japan [1]. We believe that the participants were somewhat adequately sampled from the population of all participants in SD in Japan. Example profile information is presented in Table 1. After viewing each other's profile, each pair interacted face-to-face twice (first time for 5 min, second time for 10 min), and the video and audio of each interaction were recorded using a video camera and a headset microphone. Before and after the first dialogue and after the second dialogue, each participant was asked to fill out a questionnaire that measured the degree of his/her romantic feelings toward his/her dialogue partner. The questionnaire included 13 questions each scored on a 9-point Likert scale [25]. In this study, the mean value of the 13 items was used as the love-like scale. On a separate day, all participants were also asked to complete a questionnaire to measure 90 indexes selected from 24 psychometric scales. These scales include a large number and variety of values related to family and relationships and views of life and love that are considered highly relevant for determining an individual's personality, communication skills, and potential partner. The psychometric scales collected are shown in Table 1.

3   Prediction Model

We built four separate regression models that estimate four scores: the love and like scores that females have for males and vice versa after 15 min of SD. The input features are three types of features: participants' profile information, facial features, and individuality scale scores.

- **Profile information**: We use the 15 kinds of profile information, such as age, blood type, highest educational attainment, job, and multiple preference information on hobbies and interests for each gender; numerical data such as age are standardized as numerical values and used as features. Information obtained in text is individually converted into 512-dimensional BERT features [10]. The BERT model used is a pre-trained model using data from Wikipedia.
- **Facial characteristics**: From a previous study [15], we extracted and used 15 kinds of facial features important in forming human impressions, such as various lengths between facial feature points. Each is standardized and used as a feature.
- **Psychometric scale score**: All indicator values shown in Table 2 for males and females are used. Each value is standardized and used as a feature in the numerical data.

The above features are reduced in dimensionality using principal component analysis (PCA). A random forest [5], which is one of the most powerful machine learning algorithms for regression tasks, was used to build a regression prediction model for love-like scores. To improve performance, feature importance was used to iterate through the process of reducing and re-training less important features.

4   Experiment and Results

To evaluate performance, from a group of 25 participants in the corpus, we use 24 pairs as training data and 1 pair as test data. The process is repeated 25 times, swapping the data of the groups used. In other words, a one-group-out 25-hold cross validation is performed to evaluate performance. We built multiple predictive models with all combinations of profiles, facial features, and psychometric scale scores, with or without each feature respectively, to test how useful these three types of features are in predicting the love-like scale. The correlation coefficient between the predicted value and the value of the correct answer was calculated as the measure of prediction performance. The average values of the correlation coefficients for 25 runs using each model are shown in Table 3. Random indicated the performance results when random sampling is taken from the training data scores. This is the baseline for predictive performance.

The performance of the model using only one of the three features significantly outperformed the baseline on all scores. In other words, all three types of features were shown to be useful in predicting love and like scores. The Pr+F+Ps model best predicted female-to-male love scores (correlation coefficient of 0.617). The Ps model best predicted female-to-male like scores and male-to-female love and like scores (correlation coefficients of 0.523, 0.489, and 0.401). In other words, the female-to-male love score is best predicted by using all of the profile, facial features, and psychometric scale scores. In contrast, the female-to-male like score and the male-to-female love and like scores are best predicted by using only the psychometric scale score.

Table 2. Prediction results of love/like scores of females to males and males to females.

	Features			Correlation coefficient (↑)			
Model	Profile	Face	Psych	Love (F to M)	Like (F to M)	Love (M to F)	Like (M to F)
Random				0.022	−0.063	-0.033	0.030
Pr	✓			0.523	0.470	0.436	0.319
F		✓		0.533	0.427	0.319	0.239
Ps			✓	0.594	**0.523**	**0.489**	**0.401**
Pr+F	✓	✓		0.504	0.470	0.392	0.229
Pr+Ps	✓		✓	0.602	0.500	0.370	0.296
F+Ps		✓	✓	0.562	0.505	0.476	0.381
Pr+F+Ps	✓	✓	✓	**0.617**	0.481	0.433	0.347

5   Conclusion

We have constructed a new corpus in SD that includes multimodal information about the participants, their impression values of their interlocutors, and various psychometric scale scores that can be obtained in advance. We constructed a novel predictive model that can predict love and like scores between men and women after SD on the basis of the diverse information of profiles, facial features, and psychometric scale scores. The results of the analysis showed that using all information from profiles, facial features, and psychometric scale scores was most useful for predicting female-to-male love scores. On the other hand, we found a new finding that using just psychometric scores was most useful for predicting female-to-male like scores and male-to-female love and like scores. In addition, we showed what specific features are useful for prediction. This opens up the possibility of a breakthrough technology that can predict in advance the impression results of a participant after SD.

References

1. Recruit Holdings Co Ltd, Marriage activity survey 2022 (in Japanese) (2022). https://www.recruit.co.jp/newsroom/pressrelease/assets/20220908_marriage_01.pdf
2. Valentine, K.A., et al.: Mate preferences for warmth-trustworthiness predict romantic attraction in the early stages of mate selection and satisfaction in ongoing relationships. Personal. Soc. Psychol. Bull. **46**(2), 298–311 (2020)
3. Aikawa, A.: A study on the reliability and validity of a scale to measure shyness as a trait. Jpn. J. Psychology **62**(3), 149–155 (1991)
4. Baruh, L., Cemalcilar, Z.: It is more than personal: development and validation of a multidimensional privacy orientation scale. Personality Individ. Differ. **70**, 165–170 (2014)
5. Breiman, L.: Random forests. Mach. Learn. **45**(1), 5–32 (2001)
6. Brooks, D.K.: A life-skills taxonomy: defining elements of effective functioning through the use of the Delphi technique. University of Georgia (1984)
7. Crumbaugh, J.C., Maholick, L.T.: An experimental study in existentialism: the psychometric approach to Frankl's concept of Noogenic neurosis. J. Clin. Psychol. **20**(2), 200–207 (1964)
8. Russell, D., et al.: Developing a measure of loneliness. J. Pers. Assess. **42**(3), 290–294 (1978)
9. Davis, M.H.: Measuring individual differences in empathy: evidence for a multidimensional approach. J. Personal. Soc. Psychol. **44**(1), 113–126 (1983)
10. Devlin, J., Chang, M., Lee, K., Toutanova, K.: BERT: pre-training of deep bidirectional transformers for language understanding. In: NAACL, pp. 4171–4186 (2019)
11. Dweck, C.S.: Capturing the dynamic nature of personality. J. Res. Personal. **30**(3), 348–366 (1996)
12. Fujimoto, M., Daibo, I.: Endcore: a hierarchical structure theory of communication skills. Jpn. J. Personal. **15**(3), 347–361 (2007)
13. Furukawa, H., et al.: The structure of yutori: a specifically Japanese concept meaning subjective well-being. Jpn. J. Soc. Psychol. **9**(3), 171–180 (1994)
14. Itatsu, H.: Ikikatanokenkyuu. Jpn. J. Counseling Sci. **25**(2), 85–93 (1992)
15. Jaeger, B., Jones, A.L.: Which facial features are central in impression formation? Soc. Psychol. Personali. Sci. **13**(2), 553–561 (2022)
16. Joel, S., et al.: Is romantic desire predictable? machine learning applied to initial romantic attraction. Psychol. Sci. **28**(10), 1478–1489 (2017)

17. Kanemasa, Y.: The images of love: intimate opposite-sex relationship and adult attachment style. Jpn. J. Interpersonal Soc. Psychol. **2**, 93–101 (2002)

18. Larson, D., Chastain, R.: Self-concealment: conceptualization, measurement, and health implications. J. Soc. Clin. Psychol. **9**, 439–455 (1990)

19. Mohri, I., Tanno, Y.: Development and validation of social anxiety scale by social situations. Jpn. J. Health Psycol. **14**(1), 23–31 (2001)

20. Odagiri, N.: College students' formation of prejudice toward divorce. Jpn. J. Developm. Psychol. **14**, 245–256 (2003)

21. Olson, D.: Cicumplex model IV: validation studies and facesIII. Family Process **25** (1986)

22. Rosenberg, M.: Society and the Adolescent Self-Image. Princeton University Press (1965)

23. Rothmann, S., Coetzer, E.P.: The big five personality dimensions and job performance. SA J. Industrial Psychol. **29**(1) (2003)

24. Rotter, J.B.: A new scale for the measurement of interpersonal trust. J. Personality **35**(4), 651–665 (1967)

25. Rubin, Z.: Measurement of romantic love. J. Pers. Soc. Psychol. **16**(2), 265–273 (1970)

26. Sakamoto, S.: The preoccupation scale: its development and relationship with depression scales. J. Clin. Psychol. **54**(5), 645–654 (1998)

27. Sell, H., Nagpal, R.: Assessment of subjective well-being: The subjective well-being inventory (subi). New Delhi: Regional Office for South-East Asia, World Health Organization, vol. 24 (1992)

28. Spranger, E.: Types of men: the psychology and ethics of personality. Max Niemeyer, Halle (1928)

29. Sugawara, K.: An attempting to construct the self-consciousness scale for Japanese. Jpn. J. Psychol. **55**(3), 184–188 (1984)

30. Sugiura, T.: Developmental change in the relation between two affiliation motives and interpersonal alienation. Jpn. J. Educ. Psycol. **48**, 352–360 (2000)

31. Wada, M.: Construction of a romantic love attitude scale. Jpn. J. Experim. Soc. Psychol. **34**(2), 153–163 (1994)

SamS-Vis: A Tool to Visualize Summary View Using Sampled Data

Shah Rukh Humayoun[1]([✉]) [iD], Salman Zaidi[2] [iD], and Ragaad AlTarawneh[3] [iD]

[1] Department of Computer Science, San Francisco State University, San Francisco, USA
humayoun@sfsu.edu
[2] University of Kaiserslautern, Kaiserslautern, Germany
[3] Intel Labs, Intel Corporation, Santa Clara, USA
ragaad.altarawneh@intel.com

Abstract. Many recent visual analytics tools use exploratory model analysis workflow to enable users exploring set of potential machine/deep learning models. As part of the workflow, these tools provide summary view of underlying dataset to enable the users to better understand trends in their data. Due to the iterative nature of such workflows, users may need to go back to data exploration phase multiple times. In order to save time and resources at data pre-processing and visualization time, we propose to use sampled data rather than complete dataset for showing trends in data summary views. As a proof-of-concept, we built a visualization tool, called SamS-Vis, that uses five sampling techniques to collect sampled data and then shows the summary views using histogram line-charts. It enables the users to see the whole data summary view of the selected field(s) using histogram bar-chart based on demand.

Keywords: Data summary visualization · data sampling techniques

1 Introduction

In the exploratory data analysis (EDA) process a user *"searches and analyzes databases to find implicit but potentially useful information"* [7] through the help of interactive visual interface. Although EDA is considered part of visual analytics (VA) [12] from long time; however, recently researchers have proposed the workflow of exploratory model analysis (EMA) [1] with the goal of exploring the set of potential models by users that can be trained on a given dataset where EDA is considered as the first step in such workflow. Therefore, many recent VA tools for machine learning (ML) model exploration, such as snowcat [1], support EDA through interactive visualizations at different levels, from summary view of data to showing the relationships between different fields in the underlying dataset.

In the case of EMA workflow support in VA tools, users may need to go back multiple times to their data view in the case if they see issues in the resulting ML models. Many times, these VA tools provide summary view, e.g., using histograms, of the underlying data as the first step in EDA phase, which requires to pre-process all the

© The Author(s), under exclusive license to Springer Nature Switzerland AG 2023
J. Abdelnour Nocera et al. (Eds.): INTERACT 2023, LNCS 14145, pp. 557–562, 2023.
https://doi.org/10.1007/978-3-031-42293-5_72

dataset for providing the required visual summary views. In a VA tool providing support of EMA kind of workflow, users may need to go back multiple times to the EDA phase, which may involve adding new data [2] to the existing dataset for better model training. However, in the case of large dataset, as nowadays it can be millions of records, pre-processing all the data each time for providing the resulting summary view may require more processing resources and time, which can end up with slow interaction with the resulting visualizations.

To provide a better interaction in these VA tools during the EDA phase, we propose to use sampling techniques to show the data trends in the resulting summary view. In this case, VA tools do not need to pre-process all the data at EDA phase before showing the summary visualizations. The VA tools would use the sampled data to show the data trend in the resulting summary visualizations and then based on demand show the full summary visualization of the selected field(s) of the underlying dataset. This would enable these VA tools to provide the summary view in less time with better interaction.

For a proof-of-concept, we built a visualization tool, called **SamS-Vis**, that uses five sampling techniques to provide the summary view in histogram line-charts form for the numeric-based fields of a tabular dataset. The SamS-Vis also shows the full data summary view in histogram bar-chart of the selected field(s) based on demand. Although, different tools (e.g., voder [11], VisPilot [9], DataSite [3], Foresight [4], Quick Insights [5], etc.) have been developed in the past with the aim of showing auto-insight trends (e.g., from showing the outliers, trends, distribution, rank, etc.) in the underlying dataset [8] that can be used at EDA phase; however, our focus is on providing a quick data summary view to avoid using more pre-processing resources. We believe such a solution would be especially useful for VA tools (e.g., [1]) that support EMA kind of workflow, where users may need to go back to EDA phase many times.

2   SAMS-VIS: Sampling-Data Summary Visualizer

As a proof of concept, we developed a visualization tool, called **SamS-Vis** (**Sam**pling-Data Summary **Vis**ualizer), with the aim of showing the data trends in underlying data, but using the sampled data from each attribute in the dataset. The web-based client side was developed using HTML, CSS, and JavaScript. The visualizations were developed using the React-Vis with D3.js as the underlying visualization library. While the server side was developed using node.js.

SamS-Vis tools uses five data sampling techniques to select part of the data from each field in the data table. The tool uses these techniques to select 10% of the data sample in order to pre-process and provides the resulting summary view. Based on demand, SamS then pre-process the whole data of the selected data field(s) and then shows the summary view of the whole data of selected field(s). Following we briefly explain each of the used sampling technique:

- **Random Sampling:** This is a standard random picking [10] in which case SamS-Vis randomly picks 10% of the data of the underlying field. However, if one item was already picked then it is not picked up again.
- **Systematic Sampling:** The systematic sampling concept is taken from [13]. In this case, SamS-Vis loops through the whole data and based on sample size it calculates

an interval to choose a value to be part of the sample. For example, for choosing 10% of an attribute containing 100 entries, each 10th entry would be picked up in order to make sure that sampled data is taken evenly from the whole dataset.

- **Cluster Sampling:** In this case, we proposed a hybrid form of random sampling and systematic sampling. In this proposed sampling, we divide our data into smaller clusters based on interval and then choose a random value from all those clusters to get the final sampled data.
- **Reservoir Sampling:** This sampling techniques was initially proposed by Fan et al. [6]. In this case, the sampled data is collected from an input stream instead of first collecting the whole data.
- **Average Sampling:** In this case, SamS-Vis does not collect sampling data separately. In this case, all four above sampling techniques are processed and then the data value for each data point in the resulting histogram is taken as an average of all the four sampling techniques.

For the target dataset, SamS-Vis provides the option to load any tabular data stored in csv format. However, it also requires an attached JSON file for containing the metadata of all the fields in the dataset. Currently, the tool does the sampling of only those fields having numeric values and ignored those fields having other values. As a proof-of-concept VA tool, SamS-Vis uses histogram line-charts for showing the summary views of the sampled data of each field in the underlying dataset.

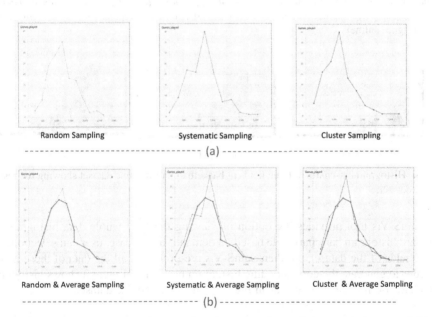

Fig. 1. (a) Three histogram line-charts using three sampling techniques for the same field of basketball hall-of-fame dataset. (b) The same three histogram line-charts in (a) alongside the line of average sampling technique (highlighted line) using the average of four sampling techniques.

Figure 1(a) shows the resulting histogram line-chart of the same field in a basketball hall-of-fame dataset using three of the sampling techniques. Figure 1(b) shows the same histogram line-chart of sampling techniques alongside the average of all four sampling techniques.

Figure 2 shows the histogram line-charts of three fields of the same dataset using all four sampling techniques (i.e., random, systematic, cluster, and reservoir) except the average one. SamS-Vis also provides cross-linking between the resulting histogram line-charts, so when user mouse hover a particular sampling technique's result line in one histogram, then this is highlighted not only in this histogram line-chart but the same sampling technique line is highlighted in all other attributes' histograms as well.

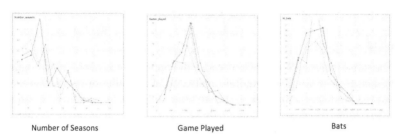

Fig. 2. Three histogram line-charts of basketball hall-of-fame dataset showing the results of four techniques; where light-blue line represents *random sampling*, green line represents *systematic sampling*, navy line represents *cluster sampling*, and orange line represents *reservoir sampling*. (Color figure online)

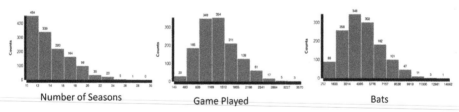

Fig. 3. Histogram bar-charts of three fields of basketball hall-of-fame dataset showing the result of full dataset.

SamS-Vis tool provides the option of viewing the field whole data histogram in standard histogram bar-chart style based on demand. In this case, user can select one of more fields of the dataset and then SamS-Vis pre-processes all the data of these fields in order to generate the corresponding histogram bar-charts. Figure 3 shows histogram bar-charts of three fields (same as in Fig. 2) of the hall-of-fame dataset.

3 Concluding Remarks and Future Directions

In this work, we proposed our approach of using sampled data rather than complete dataset for showing trends in data summary visualizations for larger datasets. We also presented our SamS-Vis visualization tool that currently uses five sampling techniques to collect sampled data for the resulting summary visualizations. The proposed approach would be useful in exploratory model analysis workflows targeting machine learning/deep learning models, where users may need to go back again and again to their data exploration view for generating better models.

In the future, we intend to investigate which of the used sampling techniques is useful for a particular kind of dataset. In such case, the system would analyze the underlying data field and will apply the appropriate sampling technique. We also plan to provide cross-linking between the data sampling histogram line-charts and the full data histogram bar-charts.

Furthermore, we would like to evaluate our approach and developed tool from the performance, accuracy and usability perspectives. In the case of performance, we intend to analyze our approach using different datasets to see how much it would save time in generating the resulting summary visualizations compared to generating summary visualizations of complete datasets. In the case of accuracy, we plan to evaluate our used sampling data approaches on different datasets to do comparison of the accuracy of sampled data trend behavior compared to the complete dataset trend behavior. Finally, we intend to do user study to evaluate our developed SamS-Vis tool from the perspective of common usability metrics (i.e., *effectiveness, efficiency*, and *user satisfaction*) to check whether users would be able to understand correctly data trends in the resulting sampled data summary visualizations. We would perform the user study in two settings using the *between-subjects* mode, where one group will work on sampled data summary view while the other group will work on the complete dataset summary view. The goal of this user study will be to analyze how users understand correctly the data trends in both settings and exploring if they face any difficulty while using the sampled data approach compared to complete dataset approach.

References

1. Cashman, C., et al.: A user-based visual analytics workflow for exploratory model analysis. Comput. Graph. Forum **38**(3), 185–199 (2019). https://doi.org/10.1111/cgf.13681
2. Cashman, D., et al.: CAVA: a visual analytics system for exploratory columnar data augmentation using knowledge graphs. IEEE Trans. Visual. Comput. Graph. **27**(2), 1731–1741 (2021). https://doi.org/10.1109/TVCG.2020.3030443
3. Cui, Z., Badam, S.K., Yalçin, A., Elmqvist, N.: DataSite: proactive visual data exploration with computation of insight-based recommendations. CoRR abs/1802.08621 (2018). arXiv: 1802.08621, http://arxiv.org/abs/1802.08621
4. Demiralp, C., Haas, P.J., Parthasarathy, S., Pedapati, T.: Foresight: Recommending Visual Insights. Proc. VLDB Endow. **10**(12), 1937–1940 (2017). https://doi.org/10.14778/3137765. 3137813
5. Ding, R., Han, S., Xu, Y., Zhang, H., Zhang, D.: QuickInsights: quick and automatic discovery of insights from multi-dimensional data. In: Proceedings of the 2019 International Conference on Management of Data (Amsterdam, Netherlands) (SIGMOD 2019), pp. 317–332. Association for Computing Machinery, New York, NY, USA (2019). https://doi.org/10.1145/3299869.3314037
6. Fan, C.T., Muller, M.E., Rezucha, I.: Development of sampling plans by using sequential (Item by Item) selection techniques and digital computers. J. Amer. Statist. Assoc. **57**(1962), 387–402 (1962)

7. Keim, D.A., Mansmann, F., Schneidewind, J., Ziegler, H.: challenges in visual data analysis. In: Tenth International Conference on Information Visualisation (IV 2006), pp. 9–16 (2006). https://doi.org/10.1109/IV.2006.31
8. Law, P.M., Endert, A., Stasko, J. T.: Characterizing automated data insights. In: 31st IEEE Visualization Conference, IEEE VIS 2020 – Short Papers, Virtual Event, USA, 25–30 October 2020, pp. 171–175. IEEE (2020). https://doi.org/10.1109/VIS47514.2020.00041
9. Lee, D.J., Dev, H., Hu, H., Elmeleegy, H., Parameswaran, A.: Avoiding drill-down fallacies with VisPilot: assisted exploration of data subsets. In: Proceedings of the 24th International Conference on Intelligent User Interfaces (Marina del Ray, California) (IUI 2019), pp. 186–196. Association for Computing Machinery, New York, NY, USA (2019). https://doi.org/10.1145/3301275.3302307
10. Meng, X.: Scalable simple random sampling and stratified sampling. In: Proceedings of the 30th International Conference on International Conference on Machine Learning, (Atlanta, GA, USA) (ICML 2013). JMLR.org, vol. 28, pp. III–531–III–539 (2013)
11. Srinivasan, A., Drucker, S.M., Endert, A., Stasko, J.T.: Augmenting visualizations with interactive data facts to facilitate interpretation and communication. IEEE Trans. Vis. Comput. Graph. 25(1), 672–681 (2019). https://doi.org/10.1109/TVCG.2018.2865145
12. Thomas, J.J., Cook, K.A.: Illuminating the Path: The Research and Development Agenda for Visual Analytics. National Visualization and Analytics CTR (2005). http://www.amazon.com/exec/obidos/redirect?tag=citeulike07-20&path=ASIN/0769523234
13. Tillé, Y.: Sampling Algorithms, pp. 1273–1274. Springer, Heidelberg (2011). https://doi.org/10.1007/978-3-642-04898-2_501

They Need to Know and Learn – Gamified Social Communication Framework for Adolescent Reproductive Health and Well Being

Debjani Roy[1]([⊠]) and Urmi Nanda Biswas[2]

[1] The Maharaja Sayajirao University, Vadorara, India
debjani.roy@manipal.edu
[2] Ahmedabad University, Ahmedabad, India
urmi.biswas@ahduni.edu.in

Abstract. Adolescence is a critical phase of life that establishes future patterns of health-promoting and health-compromising behaviours in a girl. The complications and issues women undergo manifest differently at different stages of their lifespan, emphasising the need to become vigilant and self-reliant towards one's health at an early age. The need to educate adolescents has been identified by encouraging them to take agency in their reproductive health. However, several countries' sociocultural and demographic settings still consider discussing such topics as a stigma and taboo. Several government and non-government organisations have taken the initiative to impart knowledge through awareness campaigns and programs. However, the discourse for "behavioural interventions" continues to follow a top-down paternalistic approach with little emphasis on making individuals self-reliant. This calls for reevaluating the current health communication frameworks, bringing diverse perspectives.

The article proposes a social communication framework underpinning psychological theories and concepts to make individuals self-reliant, taking ownership of their well-being. The proposed framework integrates Reflexive and Participatory Consciousness with Hard and Soft Nudges to create Risk Perception. Further, navigate an individual through the Transtheoretical Model or Stages of Change to attain self-goal. The proposed framework can be used as an aid by individuals to become self-reliant towards one's well-being, with an emphasis on meta-cognitive development and less on monitoring.

Keywords: Social communication framework · Adolescent reproductive health and well-being · Interventional model

1 Introduction

Our Bodies, Ourselves is a feminist movement that started in 1969 to encourage women to talk about their bodies rather than listen to experts [1]. The campaign focuses on personal experiences that provide valuable information for understanding one's body and related topics. This type of learning allowed women to be better prepared to identify

© The Author(s), under exclusive license to Springer Nature Switzerland AG 2023
J. Abdelnour Nocera et al. (Eds.): INTERACT 2023, LNCS 14145, pp. 563–568, 2023.
https://doi.org/10.1007/978-3-031-42293-5_73

institutions for their health needs. The inclusion of adolescent reproductive and sexual health in WHO's Sustainable Development Goals [2] acknowledges the fact that there is a need for discussions around reproductive health and well-being from an early age. It also highlights that although the topic's importance was recognised in 1960, awareness about the issue remains low in the mainstream. Most parts of the world staunchly continue to refuse, acknowledge, and accept adolescent sexuality. It is primarily discussed as a risk or problem to be avoided in disease pregnancy prevention and viewed as acceptable only in childbearing within marriage. Globally, adolescent girls possess little information regarding reproductive health and well-being, concurrent with cultural stigma and taboos. Despite significant research on menstruation and sexual health, reproductive health and its consequences on women's health are poorly understood [3–5].

For over a decade, health communication has been used as a medium for information seeking, creating awareness towards behaviour change. However, evidence suggesting consistent behaviour change having long-term effects is limited [6–8]. The discourse referring to "behavioural interventions" continues to follow a top-down, paternalistic approach with less emphasis on information-seeking, leading to self-reliance. The purpose of health communication models is to impart knowledge in a structured way. However, exploring psychological models that work at a metacognitive level towards behaviour change is still nascent. This becomes significantly important for adolescent girls as a mechanism needs to be devised that facilitates information seeking and knowledge building to speculate future implications of reproductive health and well-being. The need for long-term sustainable behaviour change requires reevaluating current health communication frameworks, further shifting focus towards social communication.

Social communication is a medium that has been able to positively influence sustainable behaviour change in social contexts at the population level. It has encouraged social reforms through songs, art, and street plays [9]. With the emergence of campaigns on family planning, HIV/AIDS awareness [10] and social media influence on topics like #MeToo and breast cancer, social communication has gained popularity as the information works at a metacognition level [11].

The article presented proposes a gamified social communication framework based on psychological theories for the psychoeducation of adolescent girls. The proposed framework works on discreetly building a safe space for information-seeking for teenage girls. Thus, promoting empowered choices and allowing self-devised approaches to self-management. The framework can be used as an intervention model to build technology interventions to speculate health and encourage self-management.

2 Components of the Framework

The proposed interventional module includes psychological theories and concepts of reflexive and participatory consciousness [12], trans theoretical model (stages of change) [13], nudge [14], and risk perception [15]. The section discusses the theories and concepts used in the framework and how they are integrated to bring about gamified social communication model (Fig. 1).

Fig. 1. Gamified Social Communication Model

2.1 Participatory and Reflexive Consciousness

Social evolution is an increasingly important concept with several models [16, 17]. The model used here was developed in 1997 and has been modified. It encompasses consciousness and all aspects of society, including the evolution of technology and social structure, thereby explaining the human species' scientific, humanitarian, and artistic advances. The model defines two complementary qualities of consciousness. Participatory consciousness is the sense of aliveness and belongingness to the world. In this mode, people relate to the world through intuition, art, religion, subjectivity, emotion, the body, and the immediate present. Reflexive consciousness is the ability to understand oneself and the world through factual, scientific, objective, and rational ideas; it allows accurate understanding and enhances the ability to control the environment [12].

It is essential to include this in the framework, as sociocultural practices substantially influence the formative years of an adolescent girl. It leads to conforming to rules, notions, or mindsets about reproductive health and well-being without questioning them. Triggering to ask questions to build knowledge can lead to self-awareness.

2.2 The Transtheoretical Model (Stages of Change)

The Transtheoretical Model (TTM) or Stages of Change Model [13] assumes people do not change behaviours quickly and decisively. Behaviour change, especially habitual behaviour, is an ongoing cyclical process comprising six stages: pre-contemplation; contemplation; preparation (determination); action; maintenance; and termination when a habit has been formed. Where the stages of change may remain constant, the time taken to shift from one location to another may vary from individual to individual. Once self-aware, individuals could be encouraged to take the initiative for behavioural change. Hence, for each stage of change, interventions promote cognitive, evaluable behavioural processes to help adolescents move from one location to another, leading to the maintenance of the ideal behaviour set.

2.3 Nudge

The concept of nudge has been used to influence freedom of choice in framing information. This can significantly influence behaviour without restricting choices [14]. In the proposed model, nudges traverse a spectrum from "hard" to "soft" nudges, where hard nudges are the realisation of consequences, working to create a dystopian fiction towards their health soft nudges are reminders, inspirations, and motivation. The former has been used in the framework to induce constructive fear, while the latter can probe towards self-management to promote health-protective behaviour.

2.4 Risk Perception

Risk perception varies by experience, age, gender, and culture [15]. An individual's perception of the risks is an essential protective behaviour determinant. Constructive fear created by risk perception can bring about health behaviour change [18]. The proposed model uses Risk Perception to let individuals speculate about their health and understand the repercussions of neglecting their health.

3   Gamifying the Framework

Gamification has been exponentially explored as a medium for building effective health interventions. Besides making content interactive and engaging, it allows the incorporation of psychological theories and concepts that can be used to devise health-promoting behaviour change mechanisms. The proposed social communication framework would make individuals conscious of their health choices through information seeking – knowledge building - self-maintenance - self-goal. The nudges would lead to risk perception, taking an individual from pre-contemplation to contemplation mode, where the individual receives a hard nudge with risk perception. This would progress to determination and action through self-attained knowledge. Soft nudges can be used for monitoring and management. In case of relapse, hard nudges are reinitiated (Fig. 2).

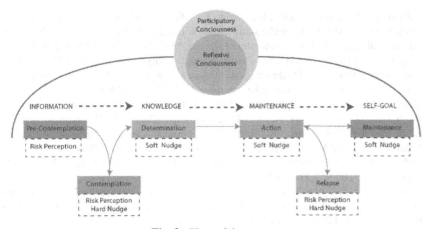

Fig. 2. Flow of the process

4 Implications and Future Work

The willingness to stay healthy and safe becomes the driving force for behaviour change [19]. The proposed framework can help promote well-being by informing, creating awareness, and devising a self-development mechanism based on informed choices. The framework could be used to build self-directed technological interventions, giving adolescent girls autonomy. Discussions around reproductive health and well-being are still considered a stigma in several parts of the world. Interventions based on the framework could empower adolescent girls to take ownership of their health and well-being.

Future work includes developing a toolkit in collaboration with NGOs and schools. Evaluate and validate it with experts in adolescent health and further deploy the toolkit in public domains.

References

1. Our Bodies, Ourselves. https://www.ourbodiesourselves.org/about-us/our-history/. Accessed 2023
2. WHO. Child and adolescent health: fact sheet on Sustainable Development Goals (SDGs): health targets. Geneva, WHO (2021). https://apps.who.int/iris/bitstream/handle/
3. Chandra-Mouli, V., et al.: Implications of the Global Early Adolescent Study's formative research findings for action and for research. J. Adolesc. Health. **61**, S5–S9 (2017). https://doi.org/10.1016/j.jadohealth.2017.07.012
4. Qiao, J., et al.: A Lancet Commission on 70 years of women's reproductive, maternal, newborn, child, and adolescent health in China. The Lancet (2021)
5. UNESCO. "Facing the facts: the case for comprehensive sexuality education." https://unesdoc.unesco.org/ark:/48223/pf0000368231
6. Scott, B.K., et al.: Advanced digital health technologies for COVID-19 and future emergencies. In: C.: Telemedicine and e-Health, pp. 1226–1233 (2020)
7. Sust, P.P., et al.: Turning the crisis into an opportunity: digital health strategies deployed during the COVID-19 outbreak: JMIR public health and surveillance (2020)

8. Kalhori, S.R.N., Bahaadinbeigy, K., Deldar, K., Gholamzadeh, M., Hajesmaeel-Gohari, S., Ayyoubzadeh, S.M.: Digital health solutions to control the COVID-19 pandemic in countries with high disease prevalence: a literature review. J. Med. Internet Res. **23**(3), e19473 (2021)
9. Wangui, C.M.: Graffiti as a source of social communication: case of Matatus Plying Nairobi CBD-Rongai Route (Ph.D. dissertation). Daystar University School of Communication (2022). http://repository.daystar.ac.ke/xmlui/handle/123456789/4065
10. Mishra, M., Goswami, P.: Perceptual defence of HIV and AIDS advertisement: a study on youth of India. Soc. Sci. Res. Netw. 1–19 (2008). https://doi.org/10.2139/ssrn.983464
11. Leiss, W., Kline, S., Jhally, S., Botterill, J.S.: Social Communication in Advertising: Consumption in the Mediated Marketplace. Routledge, Oxfordshire (2018)
12. Earley, J.: The social evolution of consciousness. J. Humanist. Psychol. **42**, 107–132 (2002). https://doi.org/10.1177/0022167802421006
13. Prochaska, J.O., Redding, C.A., Evers, K.E.: The transtheoretical model and stages of change. In: Glanz, K., Rimer, B.K., Viswanath, K. (eds.) Health Behavior: Theory, Research, and Practice, pp. 125–148. Jossey-Bass/Wiley, Hoboken (2015)
14. Thaler, R.H., Sunstein, C.R.: Nudge: Improving Decisions about Health, Wealth, and Happiness. Penguin Books, New York (2009)
15. Rimal, R.N., Brown, J., Mkandawire, G., Folda, L., Böse, K., Creel, A.H.s.l.: Audience segmentation as a social-marketing tool in health promotion: use of the risk perception attitude framework in HIV prevention in Malawi: Am. J. Publ. Health (2009)
16. Wilber, K.: Up from Eden: A Transpersonal View of Human Evolution. Anchor Press/Doubleday, Garden, New York (1981)
17. Whyte, L.L.: The Next Development in Mankind. Routledge, New York (2017) https://doi.org/10.4324/9781315133522
18. Maddux, J.E., Rogers, R.: Protection motivation and self-efficacy: a revised theory of fear appeals and attitude change. J. Exp. Soc. Psychol. **19**, 469–479 (1983). https://doi.org/10.1016/0022-1031(83)90023-9
19. De Bruin, W.B., Bennett, D.L.s.l: Relationships between initial COVID-19 risk perceptions and protective health behaviors: a national survey. Am. J. Prevent. Med. (2020)

Towards Cross-Cultural Assessment of Trust in High-Risk AI

Gabriela Beltrão$^{(\boxtimes)}$ ⓘ, Sonia Sousa ⓘ, and David Lamas ⓘ

Tallinn University, Tallinn, Estonia
{gbeltrao,drl}@tlu.ee

1 Research Problem and Goal

This study is the initial step of a research project investigating how different factors affect individuals' propensity to trust in high-risk Artificial Intelligence (AI). A series of mixed methods studies in different countries should achieve this goal [4]. Nonetheless, due to the nature and breadth of this inquiry, the data collection instrument requires special attention.

Existing research on trust in AI mainly focuses on specific types of systems (e.g., robots [2]). This variety of approaches, while aiming for accuracy, makes instruments context-bound and unsuitable for comparison. There is little consensus on how to measure trust in technology, in general, [10], and in AI [5]; thus, there is also an insufficient understanding of what affects it, despite the evidence that factors intrinsic and extrinsic to the users shape their trust [1].

In this research, high-risk AI refers to the European Commission's (EU) AI Act [3] risk-based classification. According to the document, Facial Recognition Systems (FRS) used for law enforcement fall under the high-risk category as they can impact individuals' safety or the fundamental rights of citizens.

As there is no robust instrument or method to assess trust in AI, this study focuses on developing and validating a protocol that enables the proposed investigation. We provide a detailed account of the procedures adopted for developing the studies' protocol, providing insights and recommendations for cross-cultural trust investigations.

2 Methods and Procedure

The current article is built upon systematic documentation of developing and implementing the data collection instruments, which follows three steps: (1) development of the instruments, (2) piloting, and (3) implementation in one country:

2.1 Development of the Instruments

The instruments include a scenario, a stimulus presented to the respondents in the survey and interview, the questionnaire, and the interview guide.

© The Author(s), under exclusive license to Springer Nature Switzerland AG 2023
J. Abdelnour Nocera et al. (Eds.): INTERACT 2023, LNCS 14145, pp. 569–573, 2023.
https://doi.org/10.1007/978-3-031-42293-5_74

To create the scenario, the authors extracted excerpts from two existing videos about two FRS, one from China and one from England. The short-video format was chosen to reduce the participants' efforts and ensure a higher engagement with the questionnaire.

The questionnaire has at its core the Human-Computer Trust Scale (HCTS) [6], a psychometric instrument designed to assess trust from a socio-technical perspective. The current validated scale (HCTS) has nine items measuring three constructs (Competence, Risk Perception, and Benevolence) on a 5-point Likert scale. For this work, three additional items were added to address a possible lack of the instrument's application in the context of AI. The items refer to the construct Social Capital [9]. In addition, the instrument included other variables that relate to other dimensions of cultural differences: the respondents' digital habits and belonging to minority groups (LGBTQ+ individuals, persons with disability, ethnic minorities, and immigrants), which little existing evidence indicates that they may have lower trust [12].

The interview guide was developed using principles from contextual laddering [7], aiming to identify what FRS' attributes and values the interviewees influence their trust in it.

2.2 Piloting

The questionnaire piloting included two phases, both with the support of students of a master's program in Interaction Design. The first phase involved collecting the students' responses and qualitative feedback. The second consisted of a home assignment in which the students used the instrument to collect data. In the first phase of piloting, the qualitative feedback received 20 responses and the survey 22. The second phase included additional 98 responses, resulting in 120. The interview guide was piloted in a focus group with five experts in Mozambique, who provided feedback on the format and clarity of the questions.

2.3 Implementation

Next, the first study was implemented in Mozambique. The questionnaire was in Portuguese, following a validated translation [8], completed online and in person, which collected 120 valid responses. 13 interviews were conducted in person with individuals of different profiles.

3 Results and Implications for Practice

3.1 Development, Piloting, and Implementation

In the pilot, the survey was mainly found adequate (N = 22) (scenario, understandability, and length). However, in Mozambique, most respondents considered the survey too long. The scenario presented in a video also constituted an obstacle, as it required that the respondents be in a setting in which they could watch and listen to it. Furthermore, online-only data collection was inadequate in Mozambique due to the population's limited access to technology. To overcome this issue, the authors adapted the survey into a version implemented in person with a tablet.

The systematic feedback collected during the pilot was helpful but not flawless. The comments were provided by respondents familiar with the topic, which may have facilitated their interpretation and positively affected their opinions. Consequently, unforeseen obstacles appeared when the study was implemented in Mozambique: the inadequacy of the online-only survey to the local context and difficulties for the respondents to interpret the questionnaire.

The interview guide was satisfactory in most cases but too complex for respondents with too low digital literacy, despite the support from the scenario. Alternative versions would be needed for more adequately include these respondents.

Overall, the results suggest that the protocol is adequate for its intended goals. Besides, adopting a systematic procedure for the initial stage of the work proved useful, as it enabled the authors to correct problems that could affect the data collection and, consequently, the results.

3.2 Preliminary Quantitative Results

We separately analyzed the responses from the pilot ($N = 120$) and the study in Mozambique ($N = 120$) to examine the procedure's effectiveness and potential. Thus far, the results are restricted to the quantitative data.

The pilot's respondents were 49.2% ($N = 59$) females, 50% ($N = 60$) males, and 0.8% ($N = 1$) non-binary. It included 17 countries, with most respondents coming from Europe (57.5%, $N = 69$). The data from the 9-item HCTS ($N = 120$) demonstrated good internal consistency [11], with Cronbach's alpha $= .796$. The scale using 12 items, including Social Capital, had a higher alpha, 0.835. Still, the analysis was done based on the validated (9-item) scale.

The difference in trust between genders was not significant, with females having slightly lower trust ($M = 2.617$, $SD = .622$) than males ($M = 2.743$, $SD = 706$). Individuals belonging to at least one minority group accounted for 40.6% ($N = 37$) of the participants and had a statistically significant lower trust ($M = 2.456$, $SD = .679$) than non-minority individuals ($M = 2.784$, $SD = .666$), $t(76.255) = -2.275$, p $= .013$.

In Mozambique, females accounted for 35.8% ($N = 43$), males for 63.3% ($N = 76$), and non-binaries for 0.8% ($N = 1$) of the responses. For this sample, a similar analysis of the HCTS revealed different results. The 9-item scale Cronbach's alpha was 0.627, below the recommended threshold [11]. On the other hand, the 12 items scale reached good internal consistency, with Cronbach's alpha $= 0.737$.

Females had higher trust ($M = 3.056$, $SD = .655$) than males ($M = 3.241$, $SD = .710$), and the difference was significant $t(93.261) = 2.056$, p $= .021$. 32.5% ($N = 39$) of the respondents reported belonging to at least one minority group and had slightly higher trust ($M = 3.350$, $SD = .704$) than the ones not belonging ($M = 3.324$, $SD = .700$), but the difference was not statistically significant.

Overall, the HCTS is a potentially useful tool for assessing users' propensity to trust. In its currently validated format, it may not sufficiently account for AI characteristics; However, including additional items is a possible fix for its adequacy to this and other interaction contexts. More studies are needed to identify the gaps and fixes to the scale, but efforts in this direction should be prioritized instead of the decentralized creation of more instruments. Assessment in varied cultures should also be prioritized.

Running the first study in Mozambique allowed the authors to identify critical aspects of the study and perform adjustments at the early stages. In addition, the preliminary results are encouraging: the differences between the pilot's and Mozambique's results reinforce the importance of broadening the scope and perspectives of trust assessment. Still, the quantitative data's depth is limited, so a qualitative phase is essential to clarify what, how, and why different factors affect trust in high-risk AI.

Finally, we present a set of recommendations for practitioners aiming for further cross-cultural understanding of trust or other endogenous concepts:

1. Prioritize the development of trust in technology assessment tools or protocols that can be applied in different contexts;
2. Ensure that the validation of instruments includes different cultures and users' profiles;
3. Include different methods to account for the multidimensionality of trust;
4. Adopt systematic procedures during the protocol development and piloting.

Acknowledgement. This study was partly funded by the Trust and Influence Programme (FA8655-22-1-7051), European Office of Aerospace Research and Development, and US Air Force Office of Scientific Research.

References

1. Bach, T.A., Khan, A., Hallock, H., Beltrão, G., Sousa, S.: A systematic literature review of user trust in AI-enabled systems: an HCI perspective. Int. J. Hum. Comput. Interact. 1–16 (2022). https://doi.org/10.1080/10447318.2022.2138826
2. Charalambous, G., Fletcher, S., Webb, P.: The development of a scale to evaluate trust in industrial human-robot collaboration. Int. J. Soc. Robot. 8(2), 193–209 (2016). https://doi.org/10.1007/s12369-015-0333-8
3. Commission, E.: E proposal for a regulation of the European parliament and of the council laying down harmonised rules on artificial intelligence(artificial intelligence act) and amending certain union legislative acts (2021). https://eur-lex.europa.eu/legal-content/EN/TXT/?qid=1623335154975&uri=CELEX%3A52021PC0206
4. Creswell, J.W., Clark, V.L.P.: Designing and Conducting Mixed Methods Research. Sage Publications (2017)
5. Gebru, B., Zeleke, L., Blankson, D., Nabil, M., Nateghi, S., Homaifar, A., Tunstel, E.: A review on human-machine trust evaluation: human-centric and machine-centric perspectives. IEEE Trans. Hum. Mach. Syst. (2022). https://doi.org/10.1109/THMS.2022.3144956

6. Gulati, S., Sousa, S., Lamas, D.: Design, development and evaluation of a human-computer trust scale. Behav. Inf. Technol. **38**(10), 1004–1015 (2019). https://doi.org/10.1080/0144929X.2019.1656779
7. Miles, S., Rowe, G.: The laddering technique. In: Doing Social Psychology Research, pp. 305–343 (2004)
8. Pinto, A., Sousa, S., Silva, C., Coelho, P.: Adaptation and validation of the HCTM scale into human-robot interaction Portuguese context: a study of measuring trust in human-robot interactions. In: Proceedings of the 11th Nordic Conference on Human-Computer Interaction: Shaping Experiences, Shaping Society, pp. 1–4 (2020). https://doi.org/10.1145/3419249.3420087
9. Putnam, R.D.: Bowling alone: America's declining social capital. In: The City Reader, pp. 188–196. Routledge (2015)
10. Söllner, M., Leimeister, J.M.: What we really know about antecedents of trust: a critical review of the empirical information systems literature on trust. In: Psychology of Trust: New Research. Nova Science Publishers, D. Gefen Verlag (2013)
11. Tavakol, M., Dennick, R.: Making sense of Cronbach's alpha. Int. J. Med. Educ. **2**, 53 (2011). https://doi.org/10.5116/ijme.4dfb.8dfd
12. Wilkes, R., Wu, C.: Trust and minority groups. In: The Oxford Handbook of Social and Political Trust, p. 231 (2018)

Towards Enhancing the Media Industry Through AI-Driven Image Recommendations

George E. Raptis[✉], Vasilis Theodorou, and Christina Katsini

Human Opsis, Patras, Greece
{graptis,vtheodorou,ckatsini}@humanopsis.com

Abstract. In a fast-changing media ecosystem, professionals and enterprises in the News and Media industry face new challenges that they should address to maximize their productivity and improve their services. The rise of alternative news sources, such as social media, the leading news source, especially for young people, has led to emerging requirements in the News and Media industry. A core requirement is publishing articles as fast as possible on various platforms, combining visual and textual content. Accompanying news with images raises the readers' interest, improves engagement, and recall. Therefore, the News and Media industry professionals must adapt their publication strategies to meet this requirement and the media consumers' expectations. However, the selection of the appropriate images is a time-consuming and manual task. Towards this direction, we propose VIREO, which addresses this challenge by providing professionals (e.g., journalists) with an integrated digital solution that automatically recommends a collection of images that could accompany an article. VIREO implements text and image analysis and matching processes leveraging AI techniques in real time to achieve this. VIREO aims to benefit both professionals (e.g., journalists) by suggesting appealing images that accompany the textual content of their articles and create breath-taking stories and the media consumers (e.g., readers) by delivering an enhanced reading experience, engagement, and recall.

Keywords: Image Recommendation · Artificial Intelligence · Image-to-text Matching · Content Creation · Media Industry · Computer Vision

1 Introduction

In recent years, the media ecosystem has changed due to emerging technological advances and the rise of social media. It is an increasingly evolving environment with the people working in it (e.g., journalists, content creators, authors, and news professionals) frequently facing new challenges. The rise of alternative news sources (e.g., social media being the primary news source, especially for young audiences) has led to several requirements in the media industry. Among them, a core one is the need for publishing as fast as possible on various platforms

© The Author(s), under exclusive license to Springer Nature Switzerland AG 2023
J. Abdelnour Nocera et al. (Eds.): INTERACT 2023, LNCS 14145, pp. 574–579, 2023.
https://doi.org/10.1007/978-3-031-42293-5_75

combining text and images to reach the target audience. Accompanying news with images that best depict the main content and keywords of the news, raises the readers' interest in the news and improves engagement [5]. Therefore, news and media industry professionals need to adapt their publication strategies to better meet these requirements and match the media consumers' (e.g., readers') expectations.

Considering that i) several tools that support cross-posting (i.e., sharing the same content across multiple platforms), such as Planable, eClincher, Buffer, and Hootsuite, are available in the market and save time and ii) professionals in the news and media industry have quick access to new information which they can check against fake news, hoaxes, and scams (e.g., eufactcheck.eu, IFCN, Google fact check tools, FactCheck.org), the burden falls into the need for quickly accompanying the article content (text) with related image(s). Therefore, the challenge is to deliver image recommendations based on text to create visually appealing stories and eventually save time for professionals in the news and media industry (e.g., journalists).

To this end, we propose VIREO, with the following objective: develop and evaluate an integrated digital solution to recommend a collection of images that could accompany an article, based on content analysis. The matching and the recommendation are based on applying artificial intelligence (AI) techniques and should be performed in close to real time. The project outcome should benefit both the authors (e.g., journalists) by enabling them to quickly select appealing images and create engaging and appealing stories and the media consumers (e.g., readers) by having an enhanced reading experience, engagement, and recall.

2 Challenges and Architecture

Research attempts have highlighted the importance of building tools to summarize news articles into images using AI techniques. Although they follow reliable methods, their performance and maturity level are limited [1,2,5,10]; therefore, there is room for improvement. The most common challenges in such works include the natural language understanding (NLU) to capture text concepts other than general [2,3,6] and the accurate image suggestion, focusing on eye-catching visual content that expresses diverse states (e.g., appealing, surprising, polarization, positive/negative) [4,8,9]. VIREO aims to overcome these challenges following a validated research framework [4] through a 3-step-and-innovation process: i) developing a mechanism that understands and represents article content in a machine-readable and understandable format, ii) developing a tool that supports accurate image caption embeddings processes, and iii) integration of these tools providing accurate and fast image recommendations.

Hence, VIREO consists of three main components: i) **Article Analysis** component that uses NLP techniques, such as tokenization, part-of-speech tagging, and named entity recognition, to analyze the text and extract relevant information; ii) **Image Analysis** component that uses computer vision techniques, such as feature extraction and image classification, to analyze the images and

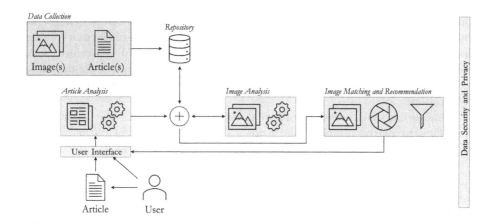

Fig. 1. The conceptual architecture of VIREO.

extract relevant information; iii) **Image Matching and Recommendation** component that uses AI techniques to match the images to the text (based on the extracted information) and recommend a collection of images that could accompany an article. Besides these, VIREO also has the following components: iv) **Data Collection** component that collects and preprocesses the text and image data, such as news articles and images, that will be used to train and test the system; v) **Repository** that stores the data and information used by the system, such as the text, images, and matching results; vi) **User Interface** that provides an interface for the users, such as journalists, to interact with the system and select the recommended images; vii) **Data Privacy and Security** that ensures compliance with data privacy laws and regulations and secure data handling. Figure 1 depicts the conceptual architecture of VIREO.

Next, we discuss the information flow for each component. For the Article Analysis component, after the author submits their article, the summarization of the article starts with the application of text processing techniques such as TextRank. The result goes through the keyword extraction process, which applies part-of-speech tagging, Lemmatization, Word frequencies, and similar techniques. The word embeddings generation follows, with Pretrained (transformer) models (e.g., BERT, GloVe, Word2Vec). The final step is the generation of MRU subspace vectors. The Image Analysis component follows a similar process. First, the image captions are generated through SAT, CNN, and RNN techniques. Then, the keywords are extracted, and word embeddings are generated along with the vector subspace in line with the processes presented before. This process is executed for all the available images in the collection before the article submission. The results are stored in the repository. Regarding integration, when an author writes an article, the text and image analysis tools run in the background, leading to matching between textual and visual content and, thus, recommending a collection of images that could accompany the article. A recommendation engine aggregates the outcomes of the afore processes. It provides the best-fitting image suggestions based on machine- and deep-learning techniques, such as classification, hierarchical analysis, CNNs, and cosine similarities.

3 Discussion

3.1 Impact on Media and AI Ecosystems

VIREO potentially impacts the media ecosystem, the broader AI ecosystem, and HCI. Regarding the media ecosystem, its impact may be materialized by improving the efficiency and effectiveness of the content creation process. Using AI to recommend images to accompany articles can help journalists quickly select appealing and relevant images that enhance the story and create a more engaging and memorable reading experience. This can improve the quality of the media content and increase audience engagement and retention. Additionally, automating the image selection process can save journalists time and resources, allowing them to focus on other aspects of their work. This could increase organizations' productivity and ultimately reduce costs. VIREO can also benefit the media industry by providing valuable insights into audience preferences and interests to inform content creation and advertising strategies. Using AI to analyze and match text with images can contribute to personalization, which can be used to create more tailored experiences for readers. Furthermore, by leveraging AI-driven image recommendation, VIREO has the potential to foster innovation in the media industry by enabling the exploration of new storytelling formats and creative approaches that captivate audiences in novel and immersive ways.

Regarding the impact on the broader AI ecosystem, NLP techniques can help improve and advance state of the art in this field. As more and more users use the system, the data collected will help to train and improve the NLP model, leading to better and more accurate results. Computer vision techniques can also improve and advance this field's state of the art. The system's ability to match images to text in real-time will generate more data and insights that can help to improve the understanding of images and improve the computer vision algorithms. Apart from that, VIREO's ability to understand and match images to text in real-time and deliver relevant images to the users will help to improve the understanding of the users' preferences, which can be used to improve the overall AI-human interaction. By providing a new way for media organizations to select images, VIREO can also open up new business models for the media industry (e.g., enable media organizations to create new revenue streams by licensing images, enable media organizations to offer personalized subscription plans or premium content tailored to the consumers' preferences).

3.2 Steps Towards Evaluation

VIREO could impact HCI, but to fully understand it, we should conduct evaluation studies with media producers (e.g., authors) and media consumers (e.g., readers). For media producers, the evaluation will focus on assessing the usability and usefulness of VIREO in the content creation process. Media producers will be asked to use VIREO to suggest images for their articles and provide feedback on the system's recommendations. They will be asked to evaluate the relevance, appeal, and suitability of the recommended images for their articles. Media producers' feedback will help identify any shortcomings in the image recommendation process and provide insights into how VIREO can be improved to better meet their needs. Additionally, the evaluation will gather data on time saved by media professionals when using VIREO compared to manual image selection processes, allowing for a quantitative assessment of its efficiency. For media consumers, the evaluation will focus on assessing the impact of VIREO on their reading experience, engagement, and recall. They will be provided with articles with images selected using VIREO and articles without recommended images. They will then be asked to read both versions of the articles and provide feedback on their overall engagement, interest, and recall of the content. Comparative analysis between the two groups will help determine how VIREO enhances the reading experience and captures readers' attention. Additionally, media consumers' feedback on the relevance and appeal of the recommended images will be collected to refine and optimize the image recommendation process further.

The evaluation process will include a combination of qualitative and quantitative methods. We will conduct surveys, interviews, and focus groups to gather qualitative feedback from media producers and consumers. Quantitative measures such as time saved by authors, click-through rates on articles with recommended images, and user engagement metrics will also be collected to provide objective insights into the system's performance and impact. In addition to evaluating the effectiveness and usability of VIREO, security and privacy aspects will be considered during the evaluation process. Advanced techniques like eye-tracking may gather data on users' security and privacy perceptions when interacting with the system [7]. We will implement stringent measures to ensure the privacy and confidentiality of users' data, including anonymization and secure storage protocols.

For the evaluation study, we will obtain user consent and research ethics regulations will be strictly followed to protect participants' rights and ensure a secure evaluation environment. We will take special consideration for managing the copyright of the images and text used by VIREO throughout the design and development process and ensuring compliance with research ethics regulations regarding the participation of adults in user studies. These would provide insights into the usability and user experience of the system and would help identify potential pain points or areas of improvement for the system, as well as provide feedback on the effectiveness of the image-to-text matching and delivery system. Such studies would provide insights into the impact of VIREO on the media industry and potential business opportunities.

Acknowledgment. VIREO has indirectly received funding from the European Union's Horizon 2020 research and innovation action programme, via the AI4Media Open Call #2 issued and executed under the AI4Media project (Grant Agreement no. 951911).

References

1. Chu, W.T., Kao, M.C.: Blog article summarization with image-text alignment techniques. In: 2017 IEEE International Symposium on Multimedia (ISM). IEEE (2017). https://doi.org/10.1109/ism.2017.40
2. Darimbekov, Z., Ubingazhibov, A., Serikbulatova, Z., Demirci, M.F.: News2Image: automated system of image recommendation to news articles. In: 2020 IEEE 4th International Conference on Image Processing, Applications and Systems (IPAS). IEEE (2020). https://doi.org/10.1109/ipas50080.2020.9334931
3. de-Lima-Santos, M.F., Ceron, W.: Artificial intelligence in news media: current perceptions and future outlook. Journalism Media **3**(1), 13–26 (2021). https://doi.org/10.3390/journalmedia3010002
4. Deldjoo, Y., Schedl, M., Cremonesi, P., Pasi, G.: Recommender systems leveraging multimedia content. ACM Comput. Surv. **53**(5), 1–38 (2020). https://doi.org/10.1145/3407190
5. Ha, J.W., Kang, D., Pyo, H., Kim, J.: News2Images: automatically summarizing news articles into image-based contents via deep learning. In: INRA@ RecSys, pp. 27–32 (2015)
6. Jere, R., Pandey, A., Shaikh, H., Nadgeri, S., Chandankhede, P.: Using machine learning for image recommendation in news articles. In: Shetty D.P., Shetty, S. (eds.) Recent Advances in Artificial Intelligence and Data Engineering. AISC, vol. 1386, pp. 215–225. Springer, Singapore (2022). https://doi.org/10.1007/978-981-16-3342-3_18
7. Katsini, C., Abdrabou, Y., Raptis, G.E., Khamis, M., Alt, F.: The role of eye gaze in security and privacy applications: survey and future HCI research directions. In: Proceedings of the 2020 CHI Conference on Human Factors in Computing Systems (CHI 2020), pp. 1–21. Association for Computing Machinery, New York (2020). https://doi.org/10.1145/3313831.3376840
8. Liu, F., Lebret, R., Orel, D., Sordet, P., Aberer, K.: Upgrading the newsroom. ACM Trans. Multim. Comput. Commun. Appl. **16**(3), 1–28 (2020)
9. Mohnish, S.P., Deepak, G., Praveen, S.V., Sheeba Priyadarshini, J.: DKMI: diversification of web image search using knowledge centric machine intelligence. In: Knowledge Graphs and Semantic Web, pp. 163–177. Springer, Cham (2022). https://doi.org/10.1007/978-3-031-21422-6_12
10. Svensson, P.: Automated Image Suggestions for News Articles: An Evaluation of Text and Image Representations in an Image Retrieval System. Master's thesis, Department of Computer and Information Science. Linköping University (2020). https://urn.kb.se/resolve?urn=urn:nbn:se:liu:diva-166669

Using Virtual Reality to Investigate the Emergence of Gaze Conventions in Interpersonal Coordination

Gregory Mills[1,2]([✉]) [iD] and Remko Boschker[2]

[1] School of Computer Science and Mathematics, Kingston University, London, UK
g.mills@kingston.ac.uk

[2] Centre for Language and Cognition, University of Groningen, Oude Kijk in't Jatstraat 26, 9712 EK Groningen, Netherlands

Abstract. Gaze plays a central role in regulating turn-taking, but it is currently unclear whether the turn-taking signals of eye gaze are static and fixed, or whether they can be negotiated by participants during interaction. To address this question, participants play a novel collaborative task, in virtual reality. The task is played by 3 participants, and is inspired by games such as Guitar hero, Rock Band, Beat Saber, and Dance-Dance Revolution. Crucially, the participants are not allowed to use natural language – they may only communicate by looking at each other. Solving the task requires that participants bootstrap a communication system, solely through using their gaze patterns. The results show that participants rapidly conventionalise idiosyncratic routines for coordinating the timing and sequencing of their gaze patterns. This suggests that the turn-taking function of eye-gaze can be flexibly negotiated by interlocutors during interaction.

Keywords: Dialogue · Transformed Social Interaction · Eye-gaze · Turn-taking

1 Introduction

When people speak with each other, they dynamically adapt their language to that of their conversational partner (Pickering and Garrod 2004; Clark 1996). A central finding in dialogue research is that the meanings of words and phrases used are negotiated ad hoc by participants. In addition to natural language expressions, face-to-face conversation is underpinned by myriad non-verbal signals which are used, inter-alia, to regulate procedural coordination in the interaction. For example, speakers tend to look away from their addressee when starting to speak, and then re-establish eye-contact at the end of their turn in order to yield the floor or signal the next speaker (Kendon 1967; Degutyte and Astell 2021). Although research has shown clear cultural differences in such gaze-behaviour (Rossano et al. 2019), it is currently unclear whether the communicative meaning of eye-gaze is static and fixed, or whether, like natural language, it might be dynamically negotiated by participants during interaction.

To address this question, participants play a novel collaborative task within a virtual reality environment which allows for testing whether and how idiosyncratic eye-gaze signals might emerge.

© The Author(s), under exclusive license to Springer Nature Switzerland AG 2023
J. Abdelnour Nocera et al. (Eds.): INTERACT 2023, LNCS 14145, pp. 580–584, 2023.
https://doi.org/10.1007/978-3-031-42293-5_76

Fig. 1. The view from each of the three participants' headsets (From left to right: Participants A, B, C).

Participants are rendered as virtual eye-balls. In this example, Participant A is assigned the role of Director, The target sequence of "look events" is displayed as a three-column table in the top-right hand corner of A's display. The table is read from top to bottom. The left-most column cells represent the actions to be performed by A. The middle column represents the actions to be performed by B, and the right-most column represents the actions to be performed by C. Each row describes a gaze configuration that must be achieved simultaneously by the triad. The target sequence represents the following sequence of actions: "*First A and B both need to look at C* (row 1) *Then C needs to look at A.* (row 2) *Then while C looks at A, B needs to look at A.* (row 3) *Then B needs to look at A* (row 4)". The task of the Director is to get the triad to perform this sequence of look events.

2 Methods

2.1 The Task

Groups of 3 participants play a collaborative task[1], in virtual reality, using Oculus Go headsets. Participants, who are rendered as "eye-ball" avatars, are placed equidistantly and facing each other in a virtual environment (see Fig. 1, above). The task is inspired by games such as Guitar Hero, Rock Band, and Dance-Dance Revolution. The three key differences are:

1. Instead of performing target sequences of musical notes or dance moves, each triad needs to perform, together, sequences of gaze events. For example, a typical target sequence might be: "*B must look at C. Then C must look at A. Then, while C continues looking at A, A and B must look at each other*".
2. On each trial, only one participant (the Director) sees the target sequence. This means that in order for the group to complete the target sequence, the Director has to instruct the other participants.
3. Crucially, the participants are not allowed to use natural language to communicate – they may only communicate by looking at each other.

---

[1] The source-code is available at https://github.com/gjmills/VRLookingGame.

Successfully solving target sequences requires that triads bootstrap an ad hoc communication system (see, e.g., Nölle and Galantucci 2022; Stevens and Roberts 2019) for instructing and taking turns, solely using their gaze patterns[2].

2.2 Manipulation

In order to test whether participants develop idiosyncratic signals for coordinating procedurally, the experiment was divided into a 25 min "training phase" followed by a 5 min "test phase". During the training phase, triads complete the task as described above. At the start of the test-phase, the identities of the participants were swapped: In Participant A's headset, Participant B's physical head movements are mapped onto Participant C's avatar, while Participant C's physical head movements are mapped onto B's avatar. Similarly, for B and C. This manipulation in the test-phase investigates whether participants within the triads develop a different communication system with each partner: participants are unaware that the identities of their partners are swapped, so if they have indeed established different systems, then, on entering the test phase, they will attempt to reuse a convention with the same partner (who is actually the other partner), leading to more errors and less efficient communication.

2.3 Hypotheses

The experiment tested two hypotheses:

1. During the training phase, participants will establish a communication system with each other that will allow them to collaboratively solve the target sequences.
2. In the test phase, the manipulation will cause participants to inadvertently use the wrong signals with each other, causing disruption to task performance.

3 Results

3.1 Training Phase

During the 25-min training phase, triads completed a mean of 20.5 sets (S.D. = 3.45). The most successful triad completed 27 sets. By the end of the training phase, triads were solving sets with a mean of 5.5 target items (S.D. = 1.2). The most successful triad completed sets containing 8 targets (see, e.g., Fig. 2 which shows a target set containing 7 "look events").

3.2 Test Phase

To test the effect of the intervention, we compared participants' performance in the 5 min preceding the swap with their performance during the 5-min test phase. We used two measures of disruption to task performance.

The first measure, task success, was modelled with a mixed binary logistic regression, using the lme4 package, which showed that triads solved significantly fewer games in

---

[2] See https://youtu.be/ctXXtFBr6Cc for a video of participants playing the game.

the test phase (b = −0.49, S.E. = 0.193, z = −2.54), p = 0.0111). The model predicts that triads successfully solve 66% [95% CI: 0.60, 0.72] of target sets in the training phase and 54% [95% CI: 0.48, 0.61] of target sets in the test phase.

The second measure recorded the number of "look events" per game, i.e., the number of times a participant selected a target. All things being equal, if participants are encountering more difficulties coordinating with each other, this will lead to them having to make more selections, i.e., expend more effort, to solve a set. A linear mixed model using the lme4 package showed that triads produced significantly more look events in the 5-min test phase than in the last 5 min of the training phase (b = 10.4, S.E. = 2.98, t = 3.5, p < 0.001). The model predicts 40 [95% CI: 36.2, 43.8] look events per game in the training phase, and 50.4 [95% CI: 45.5, 55.4] look events in the test phase.

4 Discussion

The results provide support for both hypotheses. The average sequence length at the end of the training phase suggests that the participants were solving the sets by communicating with each other, as opposed to solving via individual trial and error.

Moreover, the increased number of timeouts and look events in the test phase suggest that the manipulation disrupted participants' coordination. A plausible explanation for this pattern is that many participants communicated differently with each partner. This was confirmed by the participants themselves. On debriefing, we asked participants about the communication system they had developed. Some participants explicitly stated that they noticed that their partners communicated differently (e.g., using different signals for the same actions, or communicated faster/slower), which they had attempted to accommodate.

These findings are subject to a couple of important caveats: First, the participants' movements are severely constrained. The Oculus Go headsets only capture rotations around the x, y, z axes, but do not capture any change in location: throughout the experiment, the avatars are anchored at a fixed location. Second, the setup conflates "head gaze" and "eye gaze", as participants' head-movements are mapped onto their virtual eye-ball (see, e.g., Špakov et al. 2019).

Nonetheless, these findings suggest that the interactive signals that participants use to attract and direct another's visual attention can be flexibly negotiated during an interaction.

To conclude, these findings are of central importance for theories of Human-Computer Interaction. Research on dialogue has shown that in order for systems to converse naturalistically with humans, they must be able to dynamically adapt their vocabularies, ontologies, and emotional signals to their conversational partner (Healey et al. 2021; Mills 2014; Mills et al. 2021). The findings from the current experiment suggest that, in addition, technologies such as avatars, dialogue systems, as well as self-driving cars when communicating with pedestrians (Habibovic et al. 2018), need to be able to flexibly adapt their non-verbal and turn-taking signals to those of the user.

References

Clark, H.: Using language. Cambridge University Press, Cambridge (1996)

Degutyte, Z., Astell, A.: The role of eye gaze in regulating turn taking in conversations: a systematized review of methods and findings. Front. Psychol. **12**, 616471 (2021)

Habibovic, A., et al.: Communicating intent of automated vehicles to pedestrians. Front. Psychol. **9**, 1336 (2018)

Healey, P., Muggleton, S., Chater, N.: Human-Like Communication. Oxford University Press, Oxford, England (2021)

Kendon, A.: Some functions of gaze-direction in social interaction. Acta Physiol. (Oxf) **26**, 22–63 (1967)

Mills, G.J.: Dialogue in joint activity: complementarity, convergence and conventionalization. New Ideas Psychol. **32**, 158–173 (2014)

Mills, G., Gregoromichelaki, E., Howes, C., Maraev, V.: Influencing laughter with AI-mediated communication. Interact. Stud. **22**(3), 416–463 (2021)

Nölle, J., Galantucci, B.: Experimental semiotics: past, present and future. In Garcia & Ibanez. Routledge Handbook of Neurosemiotics (2022)

Pickering, M.J., Garrod, S.: Toward a mechanistic psychology of dialogue. Behav. Brain Sci. **27**(2), 169–190 (2004)

Rossano, F., Brown, P., Levinson, S.C.: Gaze, questioning and culture. Convers. Anal. **27**, 187–249 (2009). https://doi.org/10.1017/CBO9780511635670.008

Špakov, O., Istance, H., Räihä, K.J., Viitanen, T., Siirtola, H.: Eye gaze and head gaze in collaborative games. In: Proceedings of the 11th ACM Symposium on Eye Tracking Research & Applications, pp. 1–9 (2019)

Stevens, J.S., Roberts, G.: Noise, economy, and the emergence of information structure in a laboratory language. Cogn. Sci. **43**(2), e12717 (2019)

What's in a Name? How Perceived Music Playlist Personalization Influences Content Expectations

Bruce Ferwerda(✉)(iD), Nina Boksjö, Naomi Petricioiu, and Carolin Wollny

Department of Computer Science and Informatics,
Jönköping University, Jönköping, Sweden
bruce.ferwerda@ju.se

Abstract. With the vast amount of online content available to us, platforms are utilizing recommender systems to help their users in their decision making. By presenting content that is in line with the user's taste and preferences a personalized experience can be created. Platforms such as Netflix and Spotify have started to create an additional layer of personalization by framing of the content presentation through tailoring album art and titles towards the user. Even though all content in a user account is personalized, this additional layer of personalization creates a distinction between "regular" content and implied personalized content. In this work we explore how the textual framing (generic vs. personalized) of music playlists influences behaviors and content expectations. Our findings show that users mostly ignore the implied personalized playlists as they expect that it only consists of previously listened songs, while generic playlists are exploited to find new music to listen to.

Keywords: Personalization · Recommendations · Content Expectations

1 Introduction and Related Work

To help us navigate through an abundance of online content, platforms utilize recommender system algorithms to select relevant user items [3]. Although it is not explicitly mentioned, the use of recommendation algorithms is a form of personalization as the user items are adapted towards what is in line with user's behaviors, preferences, and/or needs. Platforms such as Netflix[1] and Spotify[2] have started to go beyond item personalization by also changing the item presentation through visual or textual adjustments. For example, Netflix personalizes the item artwork based on user preferences. This includes adapting the artwork to display familiar actors or certain scenes of the movie to make the item recommendations more attractive [1]. Spotify use titles for a portion of their recommended playlists to specifically address the user (e.g., "Made for *[username]*" and "*Your* top mixes") [2].

---

[1] https://www.netflix.com.
[2] https://www.spotify.com.

© The Author(s), under exclusive license to Springer Nature Switzerland AG 2023
J. Abdelnour Nocera et al. (Eds.): INTERACT 2023, LNCS 14145, pp. 585–589, 2023.
https://doi.org/10.1007/978-3-031-42293-5_77

Fig. 1. Example of a personalized title (left) and a generic title (right) [5].

This additional layer of personalization can create a cognitive bias by imply-ing that only specific content is personalized, while in fact all content in a user's account is personalized (e.g., Spotify would not recommend heavy metal music while knowing that a user likes RnB). The cognitive bias in this case can be referred to as a form of the framing effect in which decisions and attitudes are influenced in the way information is presented rather than how information is communicated [4]. The framing effect is in particularly present in the textual adjustments of Spotify's playlist titles that provide the explicit implications that certain playlists are specifically made for the user (i.e., personalized) whereby other playlists in a user's account are not personalized (see Fig. 1).

While there is much known on decision-making between different framing conditions, little is known how framing influences content expectations such as in recommendation lists. This work explores in a qualitative way how titles of recommendation lists influence the expectations of recommendation list content.

2   Method

To investigate how framing of recommendation list titles influences content expectations, we used Spotify as it has applied pronounced music playlist titles to imply personalization. We conducted semi-structured interviews among six participants ($F = 3$, $M = 3$, age 20–25) with each over 5 years of Spotify experi-ence. The interviews lasted ~30 min and were centered around the following two concepts: 1) how does implied personalization affect the content expectations of music playlists, and 2) how does implied personalization affect the satisfaction with the content of music playlists. All interviews were conducted in English. A framework analysis approach was used to analyze the interview data.

3   Results

At the start of the interviews, participants were asked about their general expe-riences with using Spotify. Participants thought that Spotify is a very useful service and were in general satisfied with the service. P4 said that they *"[...] took a break for maybe a year or two and then I'm still subscribed now."* What is considered as a great advantage of Spotify is the abundance of music content that is available on the platform: *"I can listen to all the songs that I want, or any song that I want...all my playlists are there and it's made it simple for me to keep going and adding playlists in one place"* (P2). Also the music recommendations that Spotify provides is seen as a good working and a useful feature: *"[...] all the suggestions it gives you for new music to listen to because sometimes I get stuck in the same music"* (P1). None of the participants indicate any extreme negative or positive Spotify experiences that could bias the interviews.

All participants indicated that they made their own playlists next to the recommendations of Spotify. P5 created and sorted playlists based on mood and scenario: *"playlists start with mood and then the whatever word related to the mood behind it...I have a bunch of playlists with guitar because I want to remind what to play."* It is important that the created playlists are given descriptive names to keep track of the content. P2 mentioned: *"When I hear a new song, I will put that into my playlist and I usually have different lists for example: digestive list, favorites, and so forth."* While others use a different way of naming their playlists: *"I don't name it so that it helps me remember the artists or genre because that's not helpful. I remember it by the season or the time"* (P3).

3.1 Generic Playlist Titles

Participants do not seem to be aware that playlists with a generic connotation (e.g., genre, artist, year) are still based on their preferences. Their perceptions and expectations of these playlists are that they are easy accessible and that they can be used for any occasion: *"When I want to find a very easy playlist in the background, probably with maybe some mates around. I don't want anything too weird to offend my friends"* (P2) or *"With people that I'm not entirely sure what they listen to and what they like, I will go for this directly"* (P6).

Because of the descriptive titles of these playlists, participants indicated that they use these playlists to explore and seek new music: *"If I become bored of my own music and kind of want to explore something new; not something I'm familiar with"* (P3). They also provide opportunities to discover new music within certain genres: *"If I was looking for newer rap music that I might not have heard yet...like a different vibe around music that I might not have a playlist for"* (P1).

When asked to listen to one of the playlists, the effect of the descriptive titles was seen in the satisfaction with the content. They all agreed that a descriptive title is very useful as *"it reflects the contents pretty well. New music and those songs... I think it's the perfect title"* (P5). Concerning the music content, P3 responded that the music in the playlist was *"Exactly what I expected, like I knew it would be those types of songs"*. For others the playlist exceeded expectations: *"The tone of this music was more chill, like laid back. However, it was not what I thought it was going to be, there was a bunch of older songs. I didn't expect that. And a bunch of songs that are in movies. It was a nice surprise"* (P4).

3.2 Personalized Playlist Titles

When usernames are displayed in playlist titles, it is clear that personalization is intended: *"Anything that says my specific name stands out to me and it is clear that the playlists are personalized"* (P4). However, they do not receive the same expectations as the general titles; caused by the non-descriptive titles: *"If it's like these weird names...I don't really care for those playlists because I don't know what's in them"* (P3). Additionally, personalization made participants think that the playlist consist of music that they already listened to before: *"Honestly, I've no clue about the content, but kind of sounds to me like it's more of the stuff I have already listened to, which is not what I'm looking for"* (P5).

When participants were asked to listen to one of the personalized playlists, they indicated that they were positively surprised by the content: *"think it was a bit better than expected. I listened to five songs and two of them were interesting to me"* (P5). P2 mentioned the diverse range of music in the personalized playlist: *"I liked what I heard because they had a little bit from everything here."* Although participants were positive about the content, they do seem to assess the content from the perspective that the playlist mainly consist of songs that they have listened to before: *"Pretty similar to the songs that I listen to in my spare time"* (P4) and *"Very accurate. I know all of these songs very well. Very much so...they are similar songs, fits my expectations"* (P3).

4   Discussion and Conclusion

We explored in a qualitative way how the framing of playlist titles (by implying whether they are personalized or generic playlists) in Spotify influence the expectations that users create on the playlist content. For Spotify generated music playlists, the titles of the playlists influence the expectations that users have on the content. The understanding that users have on personalized playlists is that it is a collection of songs that they have listened to before, while for generic titles, the understanding is that these are popular songs within a certain category (e.g., genre, mood, year). This understanding influences the expectations on the content. Whereas for the personalized playlists, users assess the content based on whether the content consist of songs that they have listened to in the past (i.e., familiarity), the generic playlists are assessed on the novelty of the content.

As expressed by the participants when creating their own playlists, it is of high importance that playlist titles are descriptive. This allows for easy recollection and findability. Participants expressed that the importance of descriptive titles also apply to the recommended playlists as they are important indicators of what music the playlist may consist of. Although personalized titles imply personalization, if they are not descriptive enough about the content that they posit, users tend to ignore them.

With this work, we made a first attempt at how titles of recommendation lists influences behaviors and expectations on the content, and thereby also the satisfaction. Although personalized titles create a new layer of personalization, it may backfire through the expectations that users create. For future work we plan to test our findings in a quantitative way through a user study by controlling the content of playlists and only manipulate the titles of the playlists that are presented. This allow us to be more conclusive on the impact of the titles on expectations and behaviors.

References

1. Amat, F., Chandrashekar, A., Jebara, T., Basilico, J.: Artwork personalization at netflix. In: Proceedings of the 12th ACM Conference on Recommender systems (2018)
2. Murphy, D.: Naming personalized playlists at spotify (2021). https://spotify.design/article/naming-personalized-playlists-at-spotify. Accessed 4 Oct 2022
3. Ricci, F., Rokach, L., Shapira, B.: Recommender systems: techniques, applications, and challenges. In: Recommender Systems Handbook (2022)
4. Scheufele, D.A., Iyengar, S.: The state of framing research: a call for new directions. In: The Oxford Handbook of Political Communication Theories (2012)
5. Spotify: The Spotify app [screenshot] (2023). https://www.spotify.com

Where Do All Stakeholders Find the Software Product Blueprint?

Shah Rukh Humayoun[1]([⊠]) [ID], Yael Dubinsky[2] [ID], Kerri Kariti[3], and Moshe Kariti[3]

[1] Department of Computer Science, San Francisco State University, San Francisco, USA
humayoun@sfsu.edu
[2] Kinneret Academic College on the Sea of Galiliee, Zemach, Israel
yael_dubinsky@mx.kinneret.ac.il
[3] Claritee LTD, Yavneel, Hazafon, Israel
{kerri,moshe}@claritee.io

Abstract. We present Claritee tool as part of the software development suite relating to the still existing problem of how to integrate the design specifications along the software development lifecycle. The tool aims at answering the stakeholders' need not just to view UI design artifacts but rather be able to on-going engage with the product blueprint, which reflects the concept that is evolved through whiteboarding. In the case of a change request, it is often crucial to be able to go back to the blueprint and make a collaborative documented conversation and decision over some components. We demonstrate the ability to create and maintain a formal product *blueprint deliverable* that is highly accessible to all the stakeholders and the whole team.

Keywords: blueprint · formal brainstorming deliverable · whiteboarding

1 Introduction

Software product design is used by development teams who implement different methods e.g., the Lean UX [1, 10], Design Sprint [12], the Double Diamond [7], and UCD [4]. In the last two decades, more and more development teams implement agile practices [3, 8], and during the years also the design practices were integrated with the agile practices to enable the notions of collaboration and the whole team [1, 9, 10].

Studying the integration between the agile methods and the design techniques [e.g., 1, 4], we can observe that all emphasize three main best practices with respect to the design that are 1) generate early and rapid design solutions, 2) keep meeting the stakeholders needs and expectations so the design fits the need, and 3) enhance collaboration so the whole team can be engaged with the evolution of the design. These three elements are reflected in contemporary tools like Figma, Sketch, Adobe XD [13].

Still, product stakeholders who are usually involved in the initial whiteboarding phases, feel disconnected later in the process when they can only view user interface (UI) artifacts and prototypes and do not have the ability to sketch on a formal artifact that the whole team can come back to when changes occur. We suggest a *blueprint*

© The Author(s), under exclusive license to Springer Nature Switzerland AG 2023
J. Abdelnour Nocera et al. (Eds.): INTERACT 2023, LNCS 14145, pp. 590–594, 2023.
https://doi.org/10.1007/978-3-031-42293-5_78

deliverable. The blueprint is the one artifact to go back in order to see the layout concept and what comes before the detailed design decisions and maintained along the process to accommodate changes. The whole team including the stakeholders can always come back to the blueprint to better understand and change things. The blueprint deliverable has some recommended content for the high-level design decisions that is provided as a kind of template e.g., a template for a store website.

Keeping this process in mind, we also present our tool, called **Claritee**, that provides the support to develop blueprint deliverables in a way that not only software development team (SDT) members but also all product stakeholders can contribute to these blueprint deliverables. Comments can be attached to the blueprint components in Claritee as well as documented conversations related to the decisions in hand. Furthermore, these would work as a central point for software product development and any changes in the software design will be reflected through these blueprint deliverables.

2   The Blueprint Deliverable as a Collaboration Point

In the last two decades, there has been a continuous search on what is the best way to integrate the software development process with the Human Computer Interaction (HCI) design practices, especially with the rise of the Agile paradigm that enhances the whole team notion [2, 5, 6, 9, 11]. Still, there is no agreement on the way such integration should be performed, how the integrative process looks like, and what are its deliverables. In the traditional approach, SDT works with product stakeholders (and sometimes with end users) and brainstorms the initial ideas through simple techniques such as whiteboarding. Based on these brainstorming whiteboarding sessions, designers and engineers in SDT work on a prototype tool (e.g., Figma, Sketch, Adobe XD, etc.) to create detailed UI design artifacts. However, due to the complex nature and the learning curve of these prototype/design tools, mostly non-technical product stakeholders do not participate or are not directly involved in creating UI design decisions. Many times, they see only the final results and need to communicate with the designers in order to provide feedback or suggest any changes to the underlying UI design artifacts.

In order to tackle the continuous challenges of collaboration between product stakeholders and SDT as well as within the SDT, we propose to introduce the **Brainstorming & Blueprint (B&B)** phase as an extension to the traditional whiteboarding phase (see Fig. 1). The result of this phase would be *blueprint deliverable*, which contains high-level system design decisions without having detailed UI design. We also propose the idea of offering tools that would provide an environment to create these blueprint deliverables and a place of collaboration between all stakeholders, irrespective of their background, as well as SDT members so they can work in a collaborative fashion while making all those high-level design decisions. Furthermore, we consider these blueprint deliverables as a central point to product development as any changes requested, either from stakeholders or any member of SDT, would be done through them.

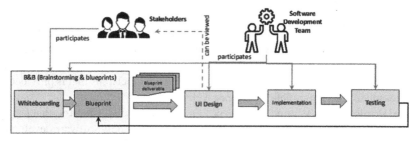

Fig. 1. The Brainstorming & Blueprint (B&B) phase as an extension to the traditional white-boarding phase.

3   The Claritee Tool for Blueprint Deliverable

Claritee[1] is a web-based tool developed using the Software-as-a-Service (SaaS) solution. It is served by cloud services using content delivery network (CDN) technique and secured APIs. Claritee aims at helping all the product stakeholders including SDT to participate actively in creating blueprint deliverables. It provides a platform for real-time collaboration amongst all stakeholders and SDT members. Claritee enables to move the focus from UI-centered flows to a content-centered flow approach, where all the change requests are made through the blueprint deliverables. It is important to note that Claritee was developed keeping in mind that non-technical stakeholders can also take part in making high-level design decisions directly through the blueprints or can request for it through blueprints. Claritee was developed to take part in building blueprint deliverables in the above-described extended process lifecycle.

Currently, Claritee provides the facility for creating blueprint deliverables for web apps (web and mobile browsers). It provides several templates to create the desired layout automatically, so users do not need to start from scratch, which saves their time. Users can also build interactive site map structures and product layouts simultaneously, which enables all the stakeholders to easily understand the project structure.

Claritee provides different elements and widgets to be used on each page in different categories (e.g., typography, forms, buttons, web components and graphs). These can also be searched on the left-side element panel. They can easily be edited and show the interaction (see Fig. 2), e.g., a list interactively shows all the possible options.

One of the main collaborative features in Claritee is the live collaboration between users in real-time when they are working on some blueprints. They can see who is currently online (through online user icon) as well as who is currently collaborating (live cursor), see Fig. 3. They can share conversations with each other through a think-out-loud approach using notes and conversation options on the canvas. In order to see the timeline activity of users on blueprints, Claritee provides the facility of recording users' actions with the option of searching the timeline activity. This is useful to search a specific activity by a particular user on a collaborative project. Due to space limitation

---

[1] https://claritee.io/.

in the paper, we demonstrate in a video[2] about creating blueprints in Claritee as well as users' interactive collaboration on a project task.

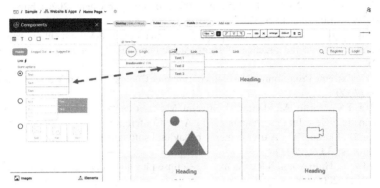

Fig. 2. Left-side figure shows how a user can provide possible options to a selection list, while right-side figure shows the resulting interactive options on the underlying blueprint.

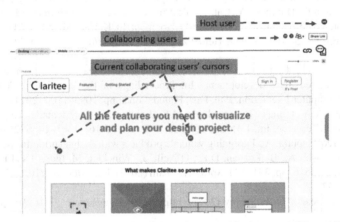

Fig. 3. On the top, the current user and collaborating users' icons are visible, while cursors of users who are currently working are also visible.

In order to share or discuss blueprint deliverables offline, Claritee provides the option to export these blueprint deliverables in pdf or PNG formats. These offline sharing options can also be emailed to other stakeholders or SDT members.

We believe that adopting the blueprint notion goes hand in hand with existing best practices and contributes to contemporary software development methodologies. Our future directions include the development of data driven techniques to predict development estimations that are based on the blueprint. This will increase the accuracy of the development plans. We also plan to develop automated transitions of blueprint deliverables to main UI design tools, so designers would need minimum efforts when building detailed design artifacts.

---

[2] https://youtu.be/ftInei2LPbs.

References

1. Aarlien, D., Colomo-Palacios, R.: Lean ux: a systematic literature review. In: Gervasi, O. (ed.) ICCSA 2020. LNCS, vol. 12254, pp. 500–510. Springer, Cham (2020). https://doi.org/10.1007/978-3-030-58817-5_37
2. Szabó, B., Hercegfi, K.: User-centered approaches in software development processes: qualitative research into the practice of Hungarian companies. J. Softw. Evol. Process **35**, 2 (2023)
3. Beck, K.: Extreme Programming Explained: Embrace Change. Addison-Wesley Professional, Boston (2000)
4. Da Silva, T.S., Martin, A., Maurer, F., Silveira, M.: User-centered design and agile methods: a systematic review. In: Proceedings - 2011 Agile Conference Agile, pp. 77–86 (2011)
5. Güncan, D., Durdu, P.O.: A user-centered behavioral software development model. J. Softw. Evol. Process **33**, 2 (2021)
6. Dubinsky, Y., Humayoun, S.R., Catarci, T.: Eclipse plug-in to manage user centered design. In: I-USED (2008
7. Gustafsson, D.: Analysing the Double diamond design process through research & implementation (2019)
8. Hazzan, O., Dubinsky, Y.: Agile Software Engineering. Springer, Heidelberg (2009)
9. Humayoun, S.R., Dubinsky, Y., Catarci, T.: A three-fold integration framework to incorporate user–centered design into agile software development. In: Kurosu, M. (ed.) HCD 2011. LNCS, vol. 6776, pp. 55–64. Springer, Heidelberg (2011). https://doi.org/10.1007/978-3-642-21753-1_7
10. Liikkanen, L.A., Kilpiö, H., Svan, L., Hiltunen, M.: Lean UX: the next generation of user-centered agile development? In: Proceedings of the 8th Nordic Conference on Human-Computer Interaction: Fun, Fast, Foundational, pp. 1095–1100 (2014)
11. Ogunyemi, A.A., Lamas, D., Lárusdóttir, M.K., Loizides, F.: A systematic mapping study of HCI practice research. Int. J. Human-Comput. Interact. **35**(16), 1461–1486 (2019)
12. Sari, E., Tedjasaputra, A.: Designing valuable products with design sprint. In: Bernhaupt, R., Dalvi, G., Joshi, A., Balkrishan, D.K., O'Neill, J., Winckler, M. (eds.) INTERACT 2017. LNCS, vol. 10516, pp. 391–394. Springer, Cham (2017). https://doi.org/10.1007/978-3-319-68059-0_37
13. UX Tools: Design Tools Survey (2021). https://uxtools.co/survey/2021/. Accessed 25 Apr 2023

Why Choose You? - Exploring Attitudes Towards Starter Pokémon

Toby Best[✉][iD] and Yu-Jhen Hsu[iD]

Queen Mary University of London, London, UK
{t.j.best,y.hsu}@qmul.ac.uk

Abstract. Non-playable characters (NPCs) are prevalent features of video games. Forming attachments with NPCs is often considered a core part of play. However, previous research suggests such relationships may vary drastically between players: some may view NPCs as important companions, whilst others consider them as mere gameplay tools. There is a gap in the knowledge base regarding the factors which may influence attachment. Specifically, it is unclear whether a player's attitude towards their own play corresponds to different levels of attachment. This report uses survey data from 8,371 participants from Pokémon communities to explore how players perceive attachment to in-game companions. We measured gameplay approaches (for example, if participants perceive themselves as competitive or casual players) and their attitude towards Starter Pokémon, ranging from the perception that they are the most important Pokémon in the game, to a gameplay burden. Initial exploratory results suggest that players may be more attached to a Starter Pokémon if they possess a more casual rather than competitive playstyle, and are playing for the first time over replaying with added challenges.

Keywords: Companion · Emotional Attachment · Non-Player Character · Parasocial Relationship · Starter Pokémon

1 Introduction

Non-playable characters (NPCs) are a vital component of both tabletop and video games, acting as gameplay elements for players to interact with the world. The literature contains significant theoretical speculation that players' social interactions with NPCs and their identity can influence a player's game experience [1], with the development of a strong bond between the player and NPCs considered to potentially bring richer game experiences [2]. Parasocial relationships, where players experience one-sided feelings of social intimacy with media characters, are proposed to result from repeated encounters with NPCs [3–6].

However, players may also experience negative emotions towards an NPC if they do not meet the player's expectations [7]. This may arise from ludonarrative dissonance between the narrative versus how the NPC acts in-game [8–10]. For

This work was supported by the EPSRC Centre for Doctoral Training in Intelligent Games and Game Intelligence (IGGI) EP/S022325/1.

© The Author(s), under exclusive license to Springer Nature Switzerland AG 2023
J. Abdelnour Nocera et al. (Eds.): INTERACT 2023, LNCS 14145, pp. 595–601, 2023.
https://doi.org/10.1007/978-3-031-42293-5_79

example, a companion NPC, who players must escort and protect in order to progress, may constantly put themselves in danger, with little regard for safety.

As stated by Warpefelt [7], attitudinal factors, such as a player's unbelief in an NPC's social aspect, may be in play when considering players' negative behaviours with NPCs. Recent literature work has focused on altering characteristics of games in attempts to improve believability through design. For example, by creating more convincing game environments [7] and more appealing characters [2,11], or giving NPCs their own background and motivation aligned with their story to enhance credibility in their actions [1,12].

Thus, prior research has explored features that may determine parasocial bonds developing with NPCs *between games*. A nascent literature has begun to investigate whether the motives players bring to a play experience contribute to such attitudes developing. For example, Milman [13] investigated whether different play motives (e.g. escape, coping) were able to predict parasocial relationships developing with in-game characters. However, relatively little work has explored how these relationships may vary *between players of a single game*, and how this variation may relate to the reasons for engaging with such a game.

2   Method

Design: We used a cross-sectional design to examine player attachments towards companion NPCs in **Pokémon**, and how this alters depending upon gameplay approaches. Since its release in 1996, the gameplay has remained fairly consistent over the years. The player takes the role of a Pokémon Trainer, who instructs their party of Pokémon on what attacks to use in turn-based battles. The Pokémon, meanwhile, act as companion NPCs that the player bears responsibility for. The player cannot progress without using their Pokémon to win the battles before them, and the Pokémon cannot act without the player's input.

In particular, we examined attitudes towards **Starter Pokémon**, who are the first Pokémon the player obtains in the game. The same three are available to choose from in every playthrough of a game, making them a consistent presence players must encounter. As a result, they are marketed as possessing higher narrative and gameplay importance over other Pokémon found in the early game.

10364 participants were recruited via advertisements in casual and competitive Pokémon communities on Reddit to answer our survey, and after cleansing erroneous and incomplete answers, 8371 responses were used in our analysis.

Measures: We recorded the following measures from participants. All measures involving Likert scales included questions asking *"How much do you agree with the following statement?"*, ranging from *Strongly Disagree* to *Strongly Agree*.

Attachment to Starter Pokémon: In order to provide a brief but interpretable measure of a player's attachment to their Starter Pokémon, we asked *"What best describes your relationship with your Starter Pokémon?"* Participants were given four options: *'I view my Pokémon as the most important*

Pokémon in the game' (12.5%), *'a special companion and part of the team'* (76.9%), *'no differently to any other Pokémon'* (9.7%), and *'a gameplay burden'* (0.8%).

Gameplay Purpose: The player's purpose for their most recent gameplay was also recorded, with three options given: *'first-time/brand new release'* (57.8%), *'replay for fun'* (23.0%), and *'replay with an additional challenge'* (19.2%).

Casual or Competitive: We asked *"Do you consider yourself more of a casual player, or a competitive player?"* 79.9% identified as casual, and 20.1% as competitive. We formed a composite index estimating if their playstyle is more casual

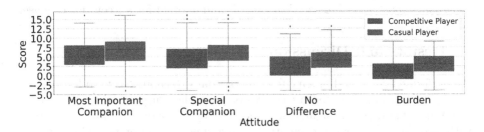

Fig. 1. Likert scale scores for questions on playstyle with Starter Pokémon, grouped by attachment levels and if players identified as casual (blue) or competitive (red).

Fig. 2. A word cloud of participants' considerations when choosing Starter Pokémon.

or competitive, with a Likert scale scoring responses to statements such as "*I have recreated my Starter Pokémon in Pokémon Showdown for online battles.*"

Perceived Usefulness: We formed a composite index estimating how important a Starter Pokémon's in-game usefulness is considered, with a Likert scale scoring responses to statements such as "*I will never replace my Starter Pokémon on my team with another Pokémon that shares the same type.*"

Design Appeal: We formed a composite index estimating how important a Starter Pokémon's appearance and design is considered, with a Likert scale scoring for statements such as "*I care more about how my Starter Pokémon looks than how strong they are.*" We also asked "*What considerations do you think of when you choose your Starter Pokémon?*", and allowed for a freeform response.

3   Results and Discussion

We performed some preliminary tests on our data to compare attitudes towards Starter Pokémon against both the players' gameplay purpose and approach.

Table 1 highlights a significant difference exists between players replaying with additional challenges compared to first-time players or replaying for fun. Table 2 suggests that players who replay with additional challenges are more likely to view Starter Pokémon indifferently or as a burden. Therefore the attachment between players and Starter Pokémon may drop significantly when self-enforced rules are introduced to make the game more challenging.

Meanwhile, Table 3 similarly highlights that competitive players overall are more likely to feel neutral or negatively towards their Starter Pokémon compared to casual players. This is shown in Fig. 1, where the median and interquartile lines for casual players tended to rank higher on the Likert scale for all four attitude groups compared to competitive players, suggesting more favourability.

Table 1. Dunn's Test on relations between player purposes, using attitude towards Starter Pokémon for comparison ($\alpha = .05$)

	First Time	Replay
Replay	0.2334	–
Replay + Challenge	$4.228526e^{-11}$	$3.037131e^{-06}$

Lastly, Fig. 2 shows the normalised answers from our wordcloud for what participants considered when choosing their Starter. Variations of 'design', 'look', 'type', 'cute', 'cool' and 'final evolution' were frequent responses, suggesting that appearance is an important factor to consider when examining how player attachments to NPCs are formed.

Table 2. Player purposes versus attitude towards Starter Pokémon ($X^2 = 61.1$, $\rho \approx 0$)

	First Time		Replay		Replay + Challenge	
	Real	X^2	Real	X^2	Real	X^2
Most Important	12.9% (626)	0.81	13.1% (252)	0.58	10.4% (167)	5.75
Special Companion	78.1% (3780)	0.93	76.2% (1467)	0.11	74.1% (1193)	1.68
No Difference	8.1% (392)	13.23	9.9% (191)	0.07	14.4% (232)	36.12
Burden	0.8% (39)	0.1	0.7% (14)	0.33	1.1% (18)	1.38

Table 3. Player types versus attitude towards Starter Pokémon ($X^2 = 136.09$, $\rho \approx 0$)

	Casual Player		Competitive Player	
	Real	X^2	Real	X^2
Most Important	13.0% (872)	1.67	10.3% (173)	6.66
Special Companion	78.3% (5241)	1.65	71.4% (1199)	6.58
No Difference	7.9% (529)	23.16	17.0% (286)	92.3
Burden	0.7% (50)	0.81	1.3% (21)	3.21

In conclusion, it appears lower attachment occurs more frequently for competitive players and those replaying to challenge themselves, whereas first-time and casual players were often more positive towards their Starter Pokémon.

4 Future Work

There are many potential avenues for future research to explore and consider, building upon the survey data used here. For one, not all of the questions answered by participants were considered in the current analysis. These include questions such as asking whether players find themselves talking to their Starter Pokémon as though they can hear them whilst playing, or how players feel about game features like **Pokémon-Amie** or **Pokémon Camp** which allow players to directly interact with their Pokémon. Exploring the relationships between these opportunities for parasocial interactions and how players approach the game will help to develop a greater understanding of how these attachments form.

There are some additional limitations within our survey that must also be acknowledged. Most notably, Reddit is but a small fraction of the Pokémon community - most participants generally came from countries that can understand or speak English (such as in Europe or North America), and all responses used for analysis were stated to be over the age of 18. Additionally, both participating subreddits (r/pokemon[1] and r/stunfisk[2]) have a good mixture of casual and

---

[1] https://www.reddit.com/r/pokemon.
[2] https://www.reddit.com/r/stunfisk/.

competitive users. Thus, results may have differed if participants were recruited from other parts of the wider Pokémon community and playerbase. For example, from younger users below 18 years of age, from alternative platforms such as Twitter, from more competitive communities such as Smogon University[3] or players participating in the official Pokémon Video Game Championships[4], or from non-English-speaking countries such as Japan and Korea.

Further studies should perhaps consider the attitudes and attachments of participants from other sections of the Pokémon community, in order to examine the emotional difference and attachments experienced by players from different countries, experiences and age groups, as well as further exploration on the attitudes held by groups of casual and competitive players. This could also explore scenarios where competitive players might have formed particular emotional attachments to Pokémon that they have found consistent success with, rather than those obtained during the main story's gameplay. Players may form attachments to the species of Pokémon rather than any specific individual of that species, which may be worth looking into as well.

Finally, it would be important to consider whether these findings still hold true for other games with more human-like NPCs who act independent of the players' actions, whereas Pokémon are more animalistic in design and in behaviour, and almost always require the player's input in order to act. One further research direction may be to understand players' emotional attachments between human-like and other types of NPCs when contrasted against how players approach their gameplay within different games.

Acknowledgement. We would like to thank our professor and lecturer, Dr. David Zendle, for his patience and guidance throughout this research, as well as the other students in our year's cohort at IGGI for their help and feedback with this project. Additionally, we would like to extend our appreciation to everyone who participated in our survey. We were simply overwhelmed with the amount of responses and feedback we received, and without the kindness of the r/pokemon and r/stunfisk communities, the Pokémon Society at University College London, and everyone who took the time to complete our questions, our research simply could not have happened. Thank you for everyone's kind words and support. Our full questionnaire is available to view here: https://osf.io/vahj2/?view_only=dcbceea1d2f74519a6f58929a3c774e8

References

1. Headleand, C.J., Jackson, J., Priday, L., Teahan, W., Ap Cenydd, L.: Does the perceived identity of non-player characters change how we interact with them?. In: 2015 International Conference on Cyberworlds (CW), pp. 145–152. IEEE (2015)
2. Bopp, J A., Müller, L.J., Aeschbach, L.F., Opwis, K., Mekler, E.D.: Exploring emotional attachment to game characters. In: Proceedings of the Annual Symposium on Computer-Human Interaction in Play, pp. 313–324 (2019)

---

[3] https://www.smogon.com/.

[4] https://www.pokemon.com/uk/play-pokemon/pokemon-events/pokemon-tournaments/video-game/.

3. Elvery, G.: Parasocial phenomena in video games. In: Lee, N. (ed.) Encyclopedia of Computer Graphics and Games, pp. 1–6. Springer, Cham (2022). https://doi.org/10.1007/978-3-319-08234-9_463-1

4. Liebers, N., Schramm, H.: Parasocial interactions and relationships with media characters-an inventory of 60 years of research. Commun. Res. Trends **38**(2), 4–31 (2019)

5. Horton, D., Wohl, R.R.: Mass communication and para-social interaction: observations on intimacy at a distance. Psychiatry **19**(3), 215–229 (1956)

6. Ivanova, T.: Attachment to fictional video game characters in Pokémon Sword and Shield (2021)

7. Warpefelt, H.: The Non-Player Character: Exploring the believability of NPC presentation and behavior (Doctoral dissertation, Department of Computer and Systems Sciences, Stockholm University) (2016)

8. Hocking, C.: Ludonarrative dissonance in Bioshock: the problem of what the game is about. Well Played **1**, 255–260 (2009)

9. Fantoli, D., Heinz, D., Wetzel, D.: Ludonarrative dissonance and gamification: a systematic literature review (2019)

10. Seraphine, F.: Ludonarrative dissonance: is storytelling about reaching harmony (2016)

11. Yee, N., Bailenson, J.: The Proteus effect: the effect of transformed self-representation on behavior. Human Commun. Res. **33**(3), 271–290 (2007)

12. Elvery, G.: Undertale's loveable monsters: investigating parasocial relationships with non-player characters. Games Cult. **18**, 475–497 (2022)

13. Milman, D., Mills, D.: The relationship between parasocial friendship quality with non-playable video game characters, gaming motivations, and obsessive vs harmonious passion. Telematics Inf. Rep. **10**, 100057 (2023)

Wokshops

Algorithmic Affordances in Recommender Interfaces

Aletta Smits[1]([✉]), Ester Bartels[1], Chris Detweiler[2], and Koen van Turnhout[1]

[1] HU University of Applied Sciences, Heidelberglaan 15, 3584 CS Utrecht, The Netherlands
`aletta.smits@hu.nl`
[2] The Hague University of Applied Sciences, Johanna Westerdijkplein 25, 2521 EN The Hague, The Netherlands

Abstract. Recommenders play a significant role in our daily lives, making decisions for users on a regular basis. Their widespread adoption necessitates a thorough examination of how users interact with recommenders and the algorithms that drive them. An important form of interaction in these systems are algorithmic affordances: means that provide users with perceptible control over the algorithm by, for instance, providing context ('find a movie for this profile'), weighing criteria ('most important is the main actor'), or evaluating results ('loved this movie'). The assumption is that these algorithmic affordances impact interaction qualities such as transparency, trust, autonomy, and serendipity, and as a result, they impact the user experience. Currently, the precise nature of the relation between algorithmic affordances, their specific implementations in the interface, interaction qualities, and user experience remains unclear. Subjects that will be discussed during the workshop, therefore, include but are not limited to the impact of algorithmic affordances and their implementations on interaction qualities, balances between cognitive overload and transparency in recommender interfaces containing algorithmic affordances; and reasons why research into these types of interfaces sometimes fails to cross the research-practice gap and are not landing in the design practice. As a potential solution the workshop committee proposes a library of examples of algorithmic affordances design patterns and their implementations in recommender interfaces enriched with academic research concerning their impact. The final part of the workshop will be dedicated to formulating guiding principles for such a library.

Keywords: User Interface Design · Recommender systems · Algorithmic Affordances · Example Library

1 Introduction

1.1 Transparent Recommender Systems

In the last twenty-five years, recommender systems have become an indispensable part of our daily lives, both personally and professionally [1–3]. They are widely used in various domains, including streaming services, web shops, dating apps, journey planners,

© The Author(s), under exclusive license to Springer Nature Switzerland AG 2023
J. Abdelnour Nocera et al. (Eds.): INTERACT 2023, LNCS 14145, pp. 605–609, 2023.
https://doi.org/10.1007/978-3-031-42293-5_80

and professional decision support systems [4, 5]. As recommenders can significantly impact people's choices, their omnipresence has societal implications [6, 7]. Therefore, it is crucial that their interfaces - the part of the system that facilitates communication between the user and the algorithm or, from a grander perspective, between society and algorithms - are well-designed, user-friendly, and transparent. Transparency is key to responsible and ethical design [8, 9], and it is critical for retaining human autonomy [10]. This workshop will explore how specific designs of recommender interfaces can promote transparency.

1.2 Explainable AI and Algorithmic Affordances

A well-researched approach to transparency is through explainable AI (XAI). Algorithm-focused XAI investigates how to extract explanations from black-box algorithms. In contrast, HCI-focused research examines the user-side of explanations: how explanations can aid users in comprehending the outcomes and decision-making processes of recommender algorithms [11]. It investigates how explanations help users build sounder mental models of the algorithm and how they contribute to transparency and to a better user experience [11–15].

Another approach to enhanced transparency involves algorithmic affordances [5], and it is those mechanisms that this workshop will focus on. Algorithmic affordances are interaction options that give users tangible control over the algorithm [5, 8]. Essentially, algorithmic affordances facilitate a two-sided communication process between users and algorithms. Users can 'talk back' to the algorithm or 'debug' the recommender's results [14]. While most people are familiar with some forms of algorithmic affordances, such as providing feedback on presented results, generating multiple profiles for different contexts, or choosing which data to include or exclude when calculating new recommendations (such as "exclude Friday night's listening history: my friends hijacked my account and were selecting tracks ironically"), academic literature describes more uncommon implementations. For example, He, Parra, and Verbert [8] describe a "talks recommender" for academic conferences that presents its suggestions in a network structure rather than a hierarchical list and allows users to manipulate combinations of parameters, so the network visibly restructures itself. Such examples have not yet been encountered outside of the academic realm.

In this workshop we will explore the means in which algorithmic affordances can be implemented in the recommenders' interface designs, both in real-live examples and in academic research. Specifically, we will examine how the various implementations might affect *transparency* and/or other interaction qualities (such as *fun, novelty, personalization*), and how those interaction qualities interrelate in designs. Participants are invited but not required to bring specimens of recommender design (whether encountered in real-live or developed for a case study) and/or research into this topic (published or in progress).

1.3 A Library of Enriched Examples

Despite the importance of implementing transparency in recommender interfaces, UX/UI practitioners often struggle to achieve these goals efficiently and elegantly, as indicated by a study involving over 200 designers worldwide [16]. Participants reported challenges such as determining how to design an effective rating process when users are tired of providing ratings, or balancing transparency with information overload in the presentation of recommendation results. To overcome these challenges, practitioners indicate they would benefit from having access to an extended set of examples of recommender interface design [17] including research that helps understand how small changes in their design might or might not affect transparency and users' sense of control.

The second half of this workshop focuses on providing a collection of such examples, not just geared towards practitioners, but also to researchers. Our applied universities plan to build a well-structured library of recommender system examples enriched with academic research on their effectiveness on interaction qualities. The design examples and quoted research are to align with real-life design challenges encountered by practitioners, and to be a valuable source of illustrations, research venues and references for academics. Our aim is for the example library to serve as a boundary object between practitioners and researchers, facilitating communication and collaboration. The explicit connection to examples that designers seek out, may serve as a way to cross the research-practice gap that otherwise prevents academic research into interface design to land in the design practice [17–19].

We will examine the fundamentals of such a library and address two key questions: 1) What are accessible and practical ways to structure examples of and research into algorithmic affordance in recommender interface designs?; and 2) How can academic research be presented in this library in a manner that reflects the complexity and nuances of research outcomes, while meeting the practitioners' need for solid information to inform design decisions?

2 Workshop Objectives

The objective of this workshop is firstly to explore means to design for algorithmic affordances that promote interaction qualities in recommender interfaces. We are interested in presentations and discussions of design examples (real-live or constructed for a research project), in research results, or research ideas on this topic and invite but do not require participants to bring their research. Secondly, we would like to examine the structuring principles of a library that includes examples of algorithmic affordances in design interfaces as well as research into these affordances. The library is to function as a boundary object between design and academia, as to promote the back-and-forth crossing of knowledge and inspiration.

3 Target Audience and Structure

Our primary target audience contains researchers with an interest in HCI and/or interaction qualities and/or design patterns. Additionally, we welcome UX/UI designers and information architects. The workshop will be open to 10–30 participants, who will alternate between presenting academic research, working in small groups, participating in plenary discussions, and presenting the results of their group's thinking. The workshop will take one full day, with the first half being dedicated to the exploration of algorithmic affordances in recommender interfaces, and the second half investigating structuring principles for a collection of examples and academic research on algorithmic affordances in recommender interfaces.

4 Expected Outcome

The workshop should result in

1. A deeper understanding of the wide range of implementations of algorithmic affordances in recommender systems, and how they can or could affect interaction qualities such as *transparency* and therefore *user experience*. For participants who brought their work in progress: insights in how to scope and/or direct their work as a result of the discussions.
2. Suggestions for how to structure a library with examples of and academic research on algorithmic affordances in recommender systems that functions as a boundary object between academics and practitioners.

The results will be transformed into a paper. Papers that have been brought to the workshop will be cited. Those interested are invited to participate in authoring the proceedings paper. Since one of the organizing research groups specializes in research into interface design of intelligent systems, papers that are still work in progress can be transformed into full papers. After passing a review, they will be published in a dedicated volume on recommender design.

5 Organization of the Workshop

The workshop will be organized by the research group Human Experience & Media Design (henceforth HEMD) (HU University of Applied Sciences Utrecht, The Netherlands), and the research group Philosophy and the Professional Field (The Hague University of Applied Sciences, The Netherlands). Chris Detweiler, professor at Philosophy and the Professional Field, specializes in the close reading of interface design. The participants from HEMD (Koen van Turnhout, Aletta Smits and Ester Bartels) specialize in research into interface design of intelligent systems.

References

1. Resnick, P., Varian, H.R: Recommender systems. Commun. ACM **40**(3), 56–58 (1997). https://doi.org/10.1145/245108.245121
2. Gunawardana, A., Shani, G., Yogev, S.: Evaluating recommender systems. In: Ricci, F., Rokach, L., Shapira, B. (eds.) Recommender Systems Handbook, pp. 547–601. Springer, New York, NY (2022). https://doi.org/10.1007/978-1-0716-2197-4_15
3. Jugovac, M., Jannach, D.: Interacting with recommenders—overview and research directions. ACM Trans. Interact. Intell. Syst. **7**(3), 1–46 (2017). https://doi.org/10.1145/3001837

4. Ghori, M., Dehpanah, A., Gemmell, J., Qahri-Saremi, H., Mobasher, B.: Does the user have a theory of the recommender? A grounded theory study. In: 2021 Adjunct Proceedings of the 30th ACM Conference on User Modeling, Adaptation and Personalization, pp. 167–174. Association for Computing Machinery, New York (2021). https://doi.org/10.1145/3511047.3537680

5. Hekman, E., Nguyen, D., Stalenhoef, M., Van Turnhout, K.: Towards a pattern library for algorithmic affordances. In: Joint Proceedings of the IUI 2022 Workshops, vol. 3124, pp. 24–33. (2022). https://ceur-ws.org/Vol-3124/paper3.pdf

6. Ngo, T., Kunkel, J., Ziegler, J.: Exploring mental models for transparent and controllable recommender systems: a qualitative study. In: Proceedings of the 28th ACM Conference on User Modeling, Adaptation and Personalization 2020, pp. 183–191. Association for Computing Machinery, New York, NY (2020). https://doi.org/10.1145/3340631.3394841

7. Februari, M.: Doe zelf normaal: Menselijk recht in tijden van datasturing en natuurgeweld. Prometheus, Amsterdam (2023)

8. He, C., Parra, D., Verbert, K.: Interactive recommender systems: a survey of the state of the art and future research challenges and opportunities. In: Expert Systems with Applications, vol. 56, pp 9–27. (2016). https://doi.org/10.1016/j.eswa.2016.02.013

9. Dietvorst, B., Simmons, J., Massey, C.: Overcoming algorithm aversion: people will use imperfect algorithms if they can (even slightly) modify them. Manage. Sci. **64**(3), 1155–1170 (2018). https://doi.org/10.1287/mnsc.2016.2643

10. Shneiderman, B.: Human-Centered AI. Oxford University Press, Oxford (2022)

11. Tintarev, N., Masthoff, J.: Explaining recommendations: design and evaluation. In: Ricci, F., Rokach, L., Shapira, B. (eds.) Recommender Systems Handbook, pp. 353–382. Springer, Boston, MA (2015). https://doi.org/10.1007/978-1-4899-7637-6_10

12. Zhang, Y, Chen, X.: Explainable recommendation: a survey and new perspectives. Found. Trends Inf. Retrieval **14**(1), 1–101 (2020). https://doi.org/10.1561/1500000066

13. Eslami, M., et al.: First I" like" it, then I hide it: Folk Theories of Social Feeds. In: Proceedings of the 2016 CHI Conference on Human Factors in Computing Systems, pp. 2371–2382. Association for Computing Machinery, New York, NY (2016). https://doi.org/10.1145/2858036.2858494

14. Pu, P., Chen, L., Hu, R.: A user-centric evaluation framework for recommender systems. In: Proceedings of the Fifth ACM Conference on Recommender Systems 2011, pp. 157–164. Association for Computing Machinery, New York (2011). https://doi.org/10.1145/2043932.2043962

15. Kulesza, T., Stumpf, S., Burnett, M., Kwan, I.: Tell me more?: The effects of mental model soundness on personalizing an intelligent agent. In: Proceedings of the SIGCHI Conference on Human Factors in Computing Systems, pp. 1–10 (2012). https://doi.org/10.1145/2207676.2207678

16. Smits, A., Van Turnhout, K.: Towards a practice-led research agenda for user interface design of recommender systems. In: Human-Computer Interaction–INTERACT 2023: 19th IFIP TC 13 International Conference, York, United Kingdom, 28 August–1 September 2023

17. Turnhout, K., Smits, A.: Solution repertoire. In: Grierson, H., Bohemia, R., Buck, L. (eds) Proceedings of the 23rd International Conference on Engineering and Product Design Education (2021). https://doi.org/10.35199/EPDE.2021.41

18. Höök, K., Löwgren J.: Strong concepts: intermediate-level knowledge in interaction design research. ACM Trans. Comput. Hum. Interact. (TOCHI) **19**(3), 1–18 (2012). https://doi.org/10.1145/2362364.2362371

19. Zielhuis, M., Visser, F., Andriessen, D., Stappers, P.: Making design research relevant for design practice: what is in the way? Des. Stud. **78**(101063), 1–21 (2022). https://doi.org/10.1016/j.destud.2021.101063

Co-designing Immersive Virtual and Extended Reality Systems for Remote and Unsupervised Interaction, Intervention, Training and Research

Wiesław Kopeć[1,5], Monika Kornacka[2], Grzegorz Pochwatko[3],
Cezary Biele[4], Anna Jaskulska[1,5], Kinga Skorupska[1,5(✉)],
Steven Barnes[2], Maciej Grzeszczuk[1], Tommy Nilsson[6],
Wladyslaw Fuchs[7], Jagoda Lazarek[1], Krzysztof Pijarski[8], and Gabriel G.
de la Torre[9]

[1] Polish-Japanese Academy of Information Technology, Warsaw, Poland
kinga.skorupska@pjwstk.edu.pl
[2] SWPS University of Social Sciences and Humanities, Warsaw, Poland
[3] Institute of Psychology Polish Academy of Sciences, Warsaw, Poland
[4] National Information Processing Institute, Warsaw, Poland
[5] KOBO Association, Warsaw, Poland
[6] European Space Agency (ESA), Cologne, Germany
[7] University of Detroit Mercy, Detroit, USA
[8] Lodz Film School, Łódź, Poland
[9] University of Cadiz, Cádiz, Spain

Abstract. We propose a one-day transdisciplinary workshop in the broad area of HCI focused on co-designing immersive virtual reality (IVR) for remote and unsupervised interaction, intervention, training and research. The development and deployment of such systems is a significant and important challenge. While remote and unsupervised systems are more accessible to a wider user-base, their design, implementation and deployment poses unique challenges, related to the need to involve truly transdisciplinary design teams, co-designing solutions with users, providing step-by-step interaction scenarios, and retaining user motivation and engagement over longer periods of time. Moreover, there are multiple ethical considerations related to both the inclusivity and accessibility of such systems and the security of data collected. Therefore, to facilitate the use of IVR systems in various contexts, ranging from unique interactions and research, through psychological interventions, to education and training, we propose to formulate a set of best practices. Taking into account the diverse aspects involved, we will formulate actionable guidelines for co-designing such solutions with users based on review of extant literature, expert knowledge, case studies and insights from the workshop.

Keywords: human-computer interaction · immersive virtual and extended reality systems · remote and unsupervised interaction · co-design · participatory design · transdisciplinary collaboration

© The Author(s), under exclusive license to Springer Nature Switzerland AG 2023
J. Abdelnour Nocera et al. (Eds.): INTERACT 2023, LNCS 14145, pp. 610–615, 2023.
https://doi.org/10.1007/978-3-031-42293-5_81

1   Theme and Topics

1.1   Theme

Virtual environments may be used in a variety of contexts. However in our workshop we would like to focus on four main areas of IVR applications: (1) research and development, (2) training and simulation, (3) healthcare and well-being and (4) entertainment and intersection with the arts. The entertainment domain excepted, the majority of IVR applications are typically deployed in lab settings for research purposes. For example, virtual environments to treat physical ailments like pain (e.g. in the context of pain management therapy with burn victims and cancer patients [6]) or psychological disorders, such as PTSD and phobias [1] (in the context of CBT and exposure therapy) have been tested in various studies and show promising results but are still not applied to everyday therapeutic practice. This is influenced by the limitations of IVR equipment and lack of know-how and established practices. Nevertheless, as VR hardware continues its rapid evolution, new application domains are starting to emerge, making the benefits of IVR available to research, training or entertainment activities outside the lab. Against this backdrop, designing complex solutions for remote and unsupervised operation is increasingly becoming the next frontier of IVR development.

One of the major challenges of these diverse IVR systems stems from the wide variety of contexts they may be applied to. They may be deployed as a part of therapy at mental health clinics. They can be used to conduct research in a network of laboratories across the globe or at home [3]. They can also find uses at hospitals during prolonged isolation to foster well-being (e.g. in patients with leukemia). They may be used for training at home, at the office or training centre or even in ICE (isolated, confined and extreme) conditions for training and simulations (e.g. Polar research stations, analog missions, ISS). They may also simply enable new ways of interaction with art via novel immersive artistic experiences or with educational content, such as architectural reconstructions and historical reenactments. The research potential of such activities and applications is massive, not only because of their wide-ranging applicability, but also their capacity to facilitate additional collection of quantitative data useful for research or to fine-tune interactive designs. A growing number of commercially available head mounted displays (HMDs) have in-built eye-tracking and data collection capabilities, allowing users and researchers to benefit from psycho-physiological insights. Additionally, such quantitative data can be simultaneously gathered and complemented by data from other devices, such as low-cost smartbands.

All of these contexts and opportunities present unique challenges and considerations related to the co-design of IVR systems that are to be used remotely, in an unsupervised way [4]. Therefore, during our workshop, participants and invited experts will contribute and discuss case studies, best practices and strategies for each aspect of designing IVR solutions. As an output of the workshop we will formulate guidelines for co-designing IVR solutions for remote and unsupervised use.

1.2   Key Workshop Topics

Although immersive virtual and extended reality systems may provide best quality of experience for use remotely in an unsupervised way [7], especially in the context of ecological validity, their design, development and deployment still pose a challenge. This workshop will focus on key aspects of designing remote and unsupervised virtual immersive systems for interaction, intervention, training and research. Preliminary interest areas are listed below.

Transdisciplinary Collaboration in the Design Teams. Combining competences from various disciplines to facilitate the process of designing such solutions is crucial for the development of research-informed applications for diverse uses. However, forming a team of experts with different backgrounds and skills can be challenging, especially as such teams ought to include artists, UX designers, engineers, computer scientists, and psychologists as well as facilitators.

Co-designing Solutions with Users. Directly involving users in designing solutions is crucial, especially if they are to be used in an unsupervised way. This is necessary to limit dropout. This means that users ought to be involved from the earliest steps of design, during the concept, flow, UI and prototype stages. While HCI provides a wide body of knowledge on co-designing solutions with users in general, IVR-specific guidelines for co-designing [2], especially taking into account unsupervised and remote use of applications, are lacking.

Users' Engagement, Motivation and Retention. Such unsupervised remote IVR applications offer access to a greater diversity of participants/users from across the globe. There is great potential to reach cohorts previously under-/unsupported with in-vivo provisions (e.g. in the context of mental health, anxiety conditions with high avoidance or MHCs with associated stigmas). To retain users to the end of expected immersive experiences in unsupervised contexts, such applications also ought to provide cognitive ease of use, and contain step-by-step use instructions and comprehensive interaction scenarios which are possible to complete in an unsupervised way. These solutions may also contain gamification or edutainment elements, to motivate users and prevent dropout.

Step-by-Step Study Design Considerations. Ecologically valid conditions are inherent to unsupervised remote studies, making insights gathered from them closer to real-life. However, considering the need to provide comparable experience, it is necessary to keep in mind diverse conditions of use, such as users' homes, therapy offices, hospitals or distributed living labs, which may differ in various aspects [5]. Another consideration is related to interaction length and schedule, both singular IVR session length and long-term commitment schedule as well as other aspects that may be relevant regarding the IVR purpose, target and application. Different methods of providing remote support to participants/users ought to be considered taking into account users' electronic literacy.

Limitations, Ethics, Inclusivity and Accessibility. When designing virtual systems for remote and unsupervised interaction, intervention, training, and research, it is important to consider limitations as well as ethical and social implications. We should consider potential risks and benefits, as well as how the system could differentially impact groups of people. We should also ensure that the system is accessible and inclusive to a diverse range of users.

Methods and Security of Data Collection. One of the crucial aspects of gathering representative data and ensuring continued use is keeping immersion in the system. It is especially important while gathering research and feedback data via in-IVR surveys, recording responses, recording various activities in immersive virtual environment. Another important aspect is the quality of data collection, potential for pushing study updates & adjusting experiences based on feedback/performance/use as well as available equipment and future device needs, e.g. high quality standalone HMDs. Another aspect is ensuring both the actual and perceived security of data collected in such remote studies and compliance of data collection methods with international and national law. This is important not only for scientific research but IVR application in general.

2   Organizers

Key organizers: Wiesław Kopeć, PhD, MBA, (Google Scholar Profile), Head of XR Center, Computer Science Department, Polish-Japanese Academy of Information Technology (PJAIT); **Monika Kornacka,** PhD, (Google Scholar Profile), Head of Emotion Cognition Lab, Institute of Psychology, SWPS University of Social Sciences and Humanities (SWPS); **Grzegorz Pochwatko,** PhD, (Google Scholar Profile), Head of Virtual Reality and Psychophysiology Lab, Institute of Psychology, Polish Academy of Sciences (IP PAS); **Cezary Biele,** PhD, (Google Scholar Profile, Head of Laboratory of Interactive Technologies, National Information Processing Institute (NIPI).

Program Committee: Anna Jaskulska, Kobo Association and Living Lab, XR Center PJAIT; **Kinga Skorupska**, PhD, XR Center PJAIT; **Steven Barnes**, PhD, Emotion Cognition Lab, Institute of Psychlogy, SWPS; **Maciej Grzeszczuk**, XR Center PJAIT; **Tommy Nilsson**, PhD, European Space Agency(ESA), European Astronaut Center (EAC), XR Lab, Cologne, Germany; **Wladek Fuchs**, PhD, Professor at the School of Architecture University of Detroit Mercy, International Programs Director and the President of the Volterra-Detroit Foundation; **Jagoda Lazarek**, PhD, Scholar and Entrepreneur, XR Center PJAIT; **Krzysztof Pijarski**, PhD, Lodz Film School; **Gabriel G. de la Torre**, PhD, Professor of Psychology, Neuropsychology and Experimental Psychology Lab, Vice-Dean for Academic Affairs, University of Cadiz, Spain.

3   Target Audience

We invite practitioners and researchers, in the broad area of HCI, who work with virtual immersive systems. These may be artistic or historical immersive systems meant to provide users with unique experiences, systems that aim to offer psychological interventions, training systems offering hands-on experiences of using complex machinery, or simulating unique work conditions. Finally, we welcome researchers who seek to design and use IVR technologies to facilitate delocalized research either outside of their laboratories or in cooperative networks of labs.

3.1   Expected Contributions

Each workshop participant is asked to prepare either:

- a short position paper (of 2–4 pages) bringing examples from their own practice related to designing and using virtual immersive systems for interaction, intervention, training or research, exploring challenges and opportunities of deploying them for use in an unsupervised and remote way,
- a short demo of a virtual immersive system or a presentation of prototype of a virtual immersive systems for interaction, intervention, training or research with a 1–2 page abstract situating the demo within the workshop theme.

4   Methods, Objectives and Expected Outcomes

4.1   Methods

We propose a one-day exploratory workshop. We aim to facilitate the exchange of best-practices in the form of interactive presentations, all in a friendly atmosphere, without strict presentation formats, where the participants may add their own topics of interest and expertise. In the course of the workshop our facilitators want to use some tools to aid free thinking, discussions and no-judgment brainstorming sessions, like mind-mapping or affinity diagramming. During the workshop we will also divide into topical teams based on their common experience and interests to work out specific considerations and insights, which at the end will be collected into a common matrix of guidelines.

4.2   Objectives

In organizing this workshop we have three key objectives:

- Establishing common ground and voice for the discussion of the challenges and opportunities related to the future broad use of immersive virtual and extended reality systems for remote and unsupervised interaction, intervention, training and research outside of research laboratories.
- Exchanging experiences and best practices for co-designing virtual immersive systems in transdisciplinary teams.
- Working out guidelines for co-designing immersive virtual and extended reality systems for remote and unsupervised interaction, intervention, training and research.

4.3   Expected Outcomes

We would like the outcomes to be applicable. Therefore, our key motivation is to discuss and generate practice-based guidelines for the design and co-design of virtual immersive systems for remote unsupervised interaction, intervention, training and research. These guidelines will form the basis for a post-workshop paper on the same topic, which will delve into the relevant related literature, and discuss insights gathered from experience-based cases presented by participants. This multidisciplinary publication will be disseminated to practitioners via a recognized research venue.

References

1. Jonathan, N., Bachri, M., Wijaya, E., Ramdhan, D., Chowanda, A.: The efficacy of virtual reality exposure therapy (VRET) with extra intervention for treating PTSD symptoms. Procedia Comput. Sci. **216**, 252–259 (2023). https://doi.org/10.1016/j.procs.2022.12.134
2. Kopeć, W., et al.: VR with older adults: participatory design of a virtual ATM training simulation. IFAC-PapersOnLine **52**(19), 277–281 (2019). https://doi.org/10.1016/j.ifacol.2019.12.110, 14th IFAC Symposium on Analysis, Design, and Evaluation of Human Machine Systems HMS 2019
3. Madshaven, J., et al.: Investigating the user experience of virtual reality rehabilitation solution for biomechatronics laboratory and home environment. Front. Virtual Reality **2**, 645042 (2021). https://doi.org/10.3389/frvir.2021.645042
4. Rivu, R., et al.: Remote VR studies - a framework for running virtual reality studies remotely via participant-owned HMDS, February 2021
5. Skorupska, K., et al.: All factors should matter! Reference checklist for describing research conditions in pursuit of comparable IVR experiments. In: Biele, C., Kacprzyk, J., Owsiński, J.W., Romanowski, A., Sikorski, M. (eds.) MIDI 2020. AISC, vol. 1376, pp. 125–133. Springer, Cham (2021). https://doi.org/10.1007/978-3-030-74728-2_12
6. Tantri, I., Tantri, A., Manggala, S., Firdaus, R., Pardede, T.: The role of virtual reality in cancer pain management: a systematic literature review. Bioscientia Medicina: J. Biomed. Transl. Res. **7**, 3018–3023 (2023). https://doi.org/10.37275/bsm.v7i1.752
7. Vlahovic, S., Suznjevic, M., Skorin-Kapov, L.: A survey of challenges and methods for quality of experience assessment of interactive VR applications. J. Multimodal User Interfaces **16**(3), 257–291 (2022). https://doi.org/10.1007/s12193-022-00388-0

Designing for Map-Based Interfaces and Interactions

Masood Masoodian[1]([⊠]) [iD] and Saturnino Luz[2] [iD]

[1] School of Arts, Design and Architecture, Aalto University, Espoo, Finland
masood.masoodian@aalto.fi
[2] Usher Institute, The University of Edinburgh, Edinburgh, UK
s.luz@ed.ac.uk

Abstract. Maps, in their many forms, have long been used to guide and coordinate different human activities, ranging from local to global, and small scale to large scale. As such, maps continue to play a central role as the basis for a wide variety of interactive tools and applications in our modern digital age as well. This workshop aims to bring together researchers, designers and practitioners interested in maps and map-like visualizations as the underlying physical, theoretical, or metaphorical framework for designing interfaces and interactions. This workshop will create a common ground and a collaborative space for sharing design, research, and practical expertise to aid its participants with creating novel future map-based designs in different fields, including visualization, visual design, interaction design, user interface design, and cartography.

Keywords: Map visualizations · map-like visualizations · visualizations · visual design · user interface design · interaction design · cartography

1 Introduction

"It [map] is a tool for geography, astronomy, and the many other studies and activities prompted by the momentous little adverb, 'where.' As the invention of tools is epochal in human history, the invention of the map, which is probably the first intellectual tool, is pre-eminent in human development." [3]

Maps, in all their varied forms [5], continue to play "pre-eminent" roles as "intellectual tools" in human development even in our modern digital age. They form the underlying physical, theoretical, or metaphorical basis for a diverse range of technologies, applications, tools and services necessary for effective functioning of our societies, and countless types of tasks we perform in our daily lives. Despite this, maps are often the unnoticed element of our many activities and tasks that heavily depend on them. This is perhaps because maps are so common that we take them for granted, and do not stop to even think about how valuable they are in our lives, or how challenging it is to design them to support different kinds of tasks.

© The Author(s), under exclusive license to Springer Nature Switzerland AG 2023
J. Abdelnour Nocera et al. (Eds.): INTERACT 2023, LNCS 14145, pp. 616–620, 2023.
https://doi.org/10.1007/978-3-031-42293-5_82

It is thought that the earliest maps in human history have been created to help people navigate and find their way, and by doing so *"reduce their fear of the unknown"* [8]. While maps still continue to be used for navigation in many cases, they can also act as visual tools for organizing information, visualizing knowledge, suggesting explanations, and inspiring us *"to ask more questions, [and] consider other possibilities"* [8].

To support such a wide range of tasks, maps, as "intellectual tools", are essentially a form of abstraction that generalize and simplify what they represent, thus compromising the reality of what they represent or parts of it [1]. Therefore, rather than even aiming to fully represent any reality [2], maps should instead be designed to support *"exploring data and seeing data in different ways"* [10]. This, however, is not such a simple task. Designing effective maps is in fact rather complex and challenging, requiring expertise in cartography, visual communication and graphic design, in addition to expertise in the specific areas of the underlying data being represented.

In addition, nowadays maps and map-like visualizations [4] form the underlying platform for a wide range of interactive digital tools and services. Therefore, such interactive maps [9] need to enable their users perform an even wider range of interactive "exploratory" tasks, *"far beyond what is possible with static maps"* [7]. This, in turn, requires that the design of interactive maps be guided by the expertise of interaction designers as well.

Currently there are no transdisciplinary venues that bring together design, research, and practical expertise from across all the different fields involved in designing for map-based interfaces and interactions. This workshop aims to address this challenge by providing such a transdisciplinary venue. It follows on from a successful previous MAPII workshop [6], which was held as part of the International Conference on Advanced Visual Interfaces (AVI 2022).

2   Objectives

The primary objective of this workshop is to create a common ground and collaborative space for sharing design, research, and practical expertise, practices, learnings, and experiences of its participants to help them with creating novel future map-based designs in different fields, including visualization, visual design, interaction design, user interface design, and cartography. Some of the main topics to be covered by this workshop include, but are not limited to, the following:

- research and design foundations of map-based interfaces and interactions.
- theories, principles and practices guiding the design of map-based interfaces and interactions.
- applications of map-based interfaces and interactions, in areas such environment, sustainability, epidemiology, healthcare, education, and entertainment.
- user evaluations of map-based interfaces and interactions.

3   Target Audience

This workshop is targeted at designers, researchers, and practitioners from across a wide range of related areas. The main audience is expected to be those interested in the design, development, deployment, and evaluation of maps and map-like visualizations used, for instance, in visual user interfaces and interactive tools, applications, and services.

Prospective workshop participants were invited to submit a short paper describing their interests and work related to the topics of this workshop. Numbers permitting, the workshop will be open to other participants without a contributing short paper.

4   Workshop Structure

This one-day workshop is informal and interactive, combining short presentations of the accepted workshop papers with group discussions, aimed at assisting the authors and other participants with developing their research and design ideas. The workshop also includes a hands-on group activity. As part of this, the workshop participants are invited to work in small groups to perform map-based tasks and create design sketches for an interactive application. The designs can then be shared at the INTERACT conference. The main components of this workshop are:

- short presentations of the accepted workshop papers.
- a group discussion to guide future related research and designs.
- a hands-on map-based group activity, facilitated by the workshop organizers.
- a group discussion on future collaborations and outcomes.

Further details on the full workshop program are available at the workshop website[1].

5   Expected Outcomes

In addition to sharing the accepted workshop papers with its participants, the authors are invited to submit extended version of their papers for inclusion in an edited volume, to be published by INTERACT 2023 organizers. Furthermore, as noted, the workshop includes a discussion session on future publications in, for instance, a special issue of an international journal and/or a co-authored report for dissemination of the workshop findings.

The workshop website (See footnote 1) is also being used for publicizing its aims and objectives, as well as disseminating its outcomes.

---

[1] http://avcd.aalto.fi/mapii2023/.

6   Workshop Organizers

Masood Masoodian (PhD) is a Professor of Visual Communication Design in the School of Arts, Design and Architecture at Aalto University. He leads the AVCD[2] research group in the Department of Art and Media. Prof Masoodian's research interests include visual design, interaction design and visualization. He often uses maps as the basis for the design of visualizations and user interactions in a wide range of areas, including health, environment, and sustainability. He was a co-organizer of the MAPII 2022 workshop[3] at the International Conference on Advanced Visual Interfaces (AVI 2022), as well as several INTERACT workshops and numerous other international conferences and workshops.

Saturnino Luz (PhD) is a Professor of Digital Biomarkers and Precision Medicine at The Usher, Edinburgh Medical School, The University of Edinburgh. His research interests include digital biomarkers for neurodegenrative diseases, precision medicine, and inference in high dimensional data sets and graphical models. His work on map-based interfaces includes visualization of human and environmental variables for modelling of infectious disease spread, and other applications in health care. He has organized, chaired and participated in the programme committees of several conferences, and served as associate editor in several journals. He was also a co-organizer of the MAPII 2022 workshop at AVI.

7   Program Committee

- Saturnino Luz *(The University of Edinburgh, United Kingdom)*,
- Masood Masoodian *(Aalto University, Finland)*,
- Shane Sheehan *(The University of Edinburgh, United Kingdom)*,
- Artemis Skarlatidou *(University College London, United Kingdom)*,
- Thomas Rist *(Augsburg University of Applied Sciences, Germany)*.

Acknowledgements. This workshop is supported by the IFIP TC-13 Working Group on Human-Centred Technology for Sustainability (WG 13.10). For more information about WG 13.10, see its website (http://it4se.hs-augsburg.de/wg13-10/).

References

1. Airikka, M., Masoodian, M.: A survey of the visual design of cartographic and other elements of illustrated tourist maps. In: Proceedings of the 23rd International Conference in Information Visualization - Part II, pp. 7–13. IV 2019, IEEE (2019). https://doi.org/10.1109/IV-2.2019.00011
2. Barber, P. (ed.): The Map Book. Walker Books (2005)

---

[2] http://avcd.aalto.fi/.

[3] http://avcd.aalto.fi/mapii2022/.

3. Greenhood, D.: Mapping. University of Chicago Press (1964)
4. Hogräfer, M., Heitzler, M., Schulz, H.J.: The state of the art in map-like visualization. Comput. Graph. Forum **39**(3), 647–674 (2020). https://doi.org/10.1111/cgf.14031
5. Luz, S., Masoodian, M.: Readability of a background map layer under a semi-transparent foreground layer. In: Proceedings of the 2014 International Working Conference on Advanced Visual Interfaces, pp. 161–168. AVI '14, Association for Computing Machinery, New York, NY, USA (2014). https://doi.org/10.1145/2598153.2598174
6. Masoodian, M., Luz, S.: Map-based interfaces and interactions. In: Proceedings of the International Conference on Advanced Visual Interfaces, pp. 88:1–88:4. AVI 2022, Association for Computing Machinery, New York, NY, USA (2022). https://doi.org/10.1145/3531073.3535258
7. Rist, T., Masoodian, M.: Interactive map visualizations for supporting environmental sustainable development goals. In: Ardito, C., et al. (eds.) Sense, Feel, Design, pp. 36–46. Springer International Publishing, Cham (2022). https://doi.org/10.1007/978-3-030-98388-8_4
8. Turchi, P.: Maps of The Imagination: The Writer as Cartographer. Trinity University Press (2007)
9. Tyner, J.A.: Principles of Map Design. Guilford Press (2014)
10. Tyner, J.A.: The World of Maps: Map Reading and Interpretation for the 21st Century. Guilford Press (2014)

Designing Technology for Neurodivergent Self-determination: Challenges and Opportunities

David Gollasch[1] , Meinhardt Branig[1] , Kathrin Gerling[2], Jan Gulliksen[3] ,
Oussama Metatla[4], Katta Spiel[5] , and Gerhard Weber[1 (✉)]

[1] Technische Universität Dresden, Dresden, Germany
{david.gollasch,meinhardt.branig,gerhard.weber}@tu-dresden.de
[2] Karlsruhe Institute of Technology, Karlsruhe, Germany
kathrin.gerling@kit.edu
[3] KTH Royal Institute of Technology, Stockholm, Sweden
gulliksen@kth.se
[4] University of Bristol, Bristol, UK
o.metatla@bristol.ac.uk
[5] TU Wien, Vienna, Austria
katta.spiel@tuwien.ac.at

Abstract. Technology for neurodivergent people has been developed in the past to align them with expectations by neurotypical people. Participants in the widest sense are encouraged to discuss the major challenges and opportunities in designing technology for neurodivergent persons in the context of education, work and for leisure. A key focus is to address knowledge acquisition, skill development, and joy from the perspective of a neurodivergent classmate, colleague, or teammates. At higher education institutions, accommodations are not common everywhere and mostly unknown to lecturers. In the workplace, management tools should respond to the requirements of an employee with autism or ADHD. Technology for leisure time is not designed for neurodivergent pleasure. Uptake of the findings are discussed with participants.

Keywords: Assistive Technology · Users with Disabilities · Neurodivergence

1 Introduction and Background

For neurodivergent people (people with atypical neurocognitive functioning, for example, autistic people, people with ADHD, people with anxiety or differences in sensory processing; see [4]) it is more difficult to access education, work, and leisure in a world that is designed for neurotypical people. For example, noisy environments such as public transport can be difficult to bear for some, others may not find themselves in a position to work efficiently in crowded office spaces that are shared with co-workers, and access to leisure can be restricted for some individuals because of specific social expectations.

© The Author(s), under exclusive license to Springer Nature Switzerland AG 2023
J. Abdelnour Nocera et al. (Eds.): INTERACT 2023, LNCS 14145, pp. 621–626, 2023.
https://doi.org/10.1007/978-3-031-42293-5_83

Research in Human-Computer Interaction has an extensive history of designing for neurodivergent people. A recent survey in Sweden has found, women with autism use the Internet more than any other group [8]. For example, there is a large body of work that seeks to teach neurodivergent children neurotypical social skills, and previous work has addressed symptoms of ADHD by targeting the individual. While technology certainly can serve as a tool to manage access needs (e.g., using noise-canceling headphones to avoid auditory overstimulation), there also is a risk that technology is leveraged as a shortcut to shape neurodivergent persons along normative expectations in an effort to make them appear neurotypical, limiting their agency rather than engaging with their needs, wishes, and desires for a fulfilled life [12]. A parody of assistive technology for autistic people is the design of FaceSavr, an intervention to help allistic (i.e., non-autistic) people reduce their need to mirror the emotions of those who surround them [9]. Likewise, we have seen a number of critical literature reviews that have drawn attention to the shortcomings of HCI research around neurodivergence, e.g., an intervention-driven research perspective [12] and a lack of meaningful involvement of the target audience [13]. We therefore want to turn to projects that are rooted in the experiences and perspectives of neurodivergent people, for example, in the context of neurodivergent work practices [4], or participation in enjoyable and playful leisure activities [16] and highlight the potential of technology to facilitate neurodivergent self-determination when designed with the target audience.

This workshop aims at how (1) neurodivergent people leverage existing technologies to address their needs, how (2) new technology should be designed to address issues relevant to them, and we intend to address (3) the design of technology that targets neurotypical people to increase understanding of the embodied experiences of neurodivergence, and create environments in which everyone contributes their share to inclusion. Thereby, we invite workshop participants to join us in critical reflection and conversation about the design of wearable assistive technology, self-determination, and the negotiation of individual access and societal responsibility.

2 Topic Areas

The workshop will address the most recent developments in designing technology in the context of neurodivergence, including systems for communication and collaboration in education, work and leisure time.

2.1 Neurodivergence in Education

Neurodivergence of pupils, students, and teachers can lead to segregation from the general education system in some countries; despite the UN convention on the rights of people with disabilities has determined that children and parents are free in their choice of the educational institutions. Additionally, free choice of a public school does not immediately imply the institution is ready and adapted to the needs of students; i.e. of those who can easily be distracted or overwhelmed by acoustic or visual stimuli, who may experience a crisis and need individual attention.

Research on inclusive education has addressed the need to change the educational practices and adapt the institution to the needs of students. The index of inclusion was demonstrated to be suitable for schools [2]. Inclusive pedagogy is only starting to train teacher students to address individual needs while becoming competent in the multitude of communication systems of students with a sensory disability and needs of someone who is neurodivergent. Problems are even more pronounced in higher education. The crowds in a lecture can be considerably bigger than a school class and create even more distraction. Quiet rooms for students are far away, if available at all. Accommodations for neurodivergent students to modify conditions of exams (such as remote, digital participation in exams) are not rooted in comprehensive legal frameworks in some countries, e.g., Germany. In general, adaptation of higher education institutions to neurodivergent students is more difficult than schools due to the size of the organization and lack of awareness by lecturers and administrators. Both top-down and bottom-up processes can help to promote changes [6]. Digitization can be a driver for a more hybrid teaching approach for asynchronous learning and place independence.

2.2 Neurodivergence at Work

Neurodivergent individuals often struggle to learn a profession and secure suitable job positions, leading to high rates of unemployment in the primary labour market [1]. Major challenges are verbal skills, personal organization, and sensory overload.

Effective verbal communication skills are highly valued by employers, especially for meaningful jobs [3]. However, neurodivergent individuals may exhibit diverse speaking abilities, ranging from no speech to inconsistent speaking behaviour. This can include difficulties with word finding, inconsistent speech, or challenges in understanding spoken words. Augmentative and Alternative Communication (AAC) tools provide additional information alongside verbal communication or substitutions for speech [7]. Assistive technologies, with speech synthesis or interactive communication alternatives, have shown promise in communication support for neurodivergent individuals [10]. Furthermore, to support individuals with autism spectrum disorder (ASD), feasible task and time management systems, as well as supportive workspace designs, are necessary.

Individuals with ASD may experience sensory overstimulation due to hypersensitivity. Assistive technologies such as noise-cancelling headphones can help cope with overstimulation in the workspace [15]. However, current strategies for ASD-specific stress management mainly focus on identifying stress levels [14], and enhancing awareness of stress factors caused by others in meetings [11].

2.3 Neurodivergence and Leisure

In leisure, there is opportunity for the design of technology that approaches neurodivergence from different perspectives. On the one hand, there is potential in technology that can help facilitate access to traditional forms of leisure (e.g., culture, sports, or play) by neurodivergent people, and research that examines how neurodivergent people appropriate existing technologies and systems to meet their needs. On the other hand, we would like to highlight the need to adopt a positive perspective on neurodivergence as a set of characteristics to design for (rather than to mitigate), exploring ways how we can design for neurodivergent pleasure, and how technology can be a tool to support and augment these.

3 Objectives

This workshop aims to foster discussions within the HCI research community about creating technologies tailored to neurodivergent persons. The goal is to facilitate their self-determined achievements and needs, empowering them to lead rewarding lives.

We aim to devise systematic design methods for diverse user groups, manage conflicting access needs, and involve neurodivergent individuals in research, ensuring shared power between users and teams.

Additionally, we hope to shift focus to critical reflection on our own positionalities, the theories that we draw upon in our work and their implications in the context of neurodivergence (e.g., autism) and empathy, [5] and the challenges that come with ensuring that technical artefacts do, in fact, support the intended target audiences rather than risking solidifying harmful stereotypes.

4 Key Organizers

This workshop is supported by IFIP Working Group TC 13.3 Human-Computer Interaction, Disability and Aging. WG 13.3 raises awareness about the needs of people with disabilities and older people, makes recommendations through guidelines for the design of technologies for the widest range of users possible, monitors the latest developments in HCI and their impact on accessibility and usability, and encourages the development of information and communication technologies and complementary tools which permit their adaptation to the needs of different users.

All organizers are experienced researchers in the field of accessibility of HCI for disabled people who have developed and evaluated research prototypes with disabled users in the past and in ongoing research projects.

David Gollasch is a PhD student at the TU Dresden, Germany with research interests in diversity-sensitive interaction design as well as structured methods and processes around software variability and AI to build adaptive user interfaces.

Meinhardt Branig is a PhD student at the TU Dresden, Germany with research interests in accessibility, data physicalization and tangible interaction with focus on user-group diversity.

Kathrin Gerling is Professor of Human-Computer Interaction and Accessibility at KIT, Germany, and a neurodivergent person. Her work aims to empower diverse audiences in the context of work, leisure, and wellbeing. It seeks to contribute to our understanding of the relationship between bodily difference, technology, and participation in society, and how technology can be employed by disabled people.

Jan Gulliksen is Professor of Human-Computer-Interaction and Vice President for Digitalization at KTH, Sweden and he does research on usability and accessibility, digitalization and digital work environments and user-centered systems design.

Katta Spiel is an FWF Hertha-Firnberg scholar at the HCI Group of TU Wien, where they work on the intersection of Computer Science, Design and Cultural Studies. They research marginalized perspectives on technologies to inform interaction design and engineering in critical ways, so they may account for the diverse realities they operate in and together with neurodivergent or nonbinary peers.

Oussama Metatla is a Senior Lecturer at the University of Bristol. As Co-Head of the Bristol Interaction Group, he and his team investigate inclusive technologies for disabled and non-disabled people. Current projects include interactive play technologies for autistic and non-autistic children, hybrid technologies for people with and without dementia, and education technologies for blind and sighted children.

Gerhard Weber is Professor of Human-Computer Interaction at TU Dresden, Germany. His interests are in multimodal interaction, non-visual interaction, tactile graphics, and teaching on accessibility. He is also liaison officer for students with a disability and leads a service centre for students with a disability.

5   Target Audience

The target audience for this workshop are researchers and designers working around neurodivergence, either through the lens of assistive technology or from the perspective of neurodivergent persons and their experiences with technology. We also invite the participation of lived experience experts (i.e., neurodivergent persons).

6   Expected Outcomes

Participants will discuss the major challenges and opportunities in designing for neurodivergent persons using interactive systems in various contexts to address knowledge acquisition, skill development, and joy from the perspective of both a neurodivergent person, classmates, colleagues, and teammates. As a follow-up to the call for papers on a website, a plain language summary will report the findings and results for sharing them with non-academic communities. Together with the participants, we will decide upon further avenues for dissemination, e.g., publication of the workshop papers, or work toward a jointly authored paper.

References

1. Bader, M., Labruier, M., Proft, J., Vogeley, K.: Menschen mit Autismus im Arbeitsleben – Informationen und Handlungsempfehlungen (2018). https://publi.lvr.de/publi/PDF/823-18_1040-Arbeitsheft-Autismus-im-Beruf-barrierefrei.pdf. Accessed 02 Sept 2021
2. Booth, T., Ainscow, M., Black-Hawkins, K., Vaughan, M., Shaw, L.: Index for Inclusion. Developing Learning and Participation in Schools, vol. 2 (2002)
3. Bryen, D.N., Potts, B.B., Carey, A.C.: So you want to work? What employers say about job skills, recruitment and hiring employees who rely on AAC. Augment. Altern. Commun. **23**(2), 126–139 (2007). https://doi.org/10.1080/07434610600991175
4. Das, M., Tang, J., Ringland, K.E., Piper, A.M.: Towards accessible remote work: understanding work-from-home practices of neurodivergent professionals. Proc. ACM Hum. Comput. Interact. **5**(183), 30 (2021). https://doi.org/10.1145/3449282

5. Fletcher-Watson, S., Bird, G.: Autism and empathy: what are the real links? Autism **24**(1) (2019). https://doi.org/10.1177/1362361319883506

6. Hähne, C., Marquardt, G., Rudolph, E., Schmidt, H.J., Weber, G., Wegner, G.: Inklusion benötigt verschiedene Prozesse: Aktivitäten und Strategien an der TU Dresden. Zeitschrift für Hochschulentwicklung **15**(3), 363–376 (2020)

7. Happ, M.B., et al.: Effect of a multi-level intervention on nurse patient communication in the intensive care unit: results of the SPEACS trial. Heart Lung **43**(2), 89–98 (2014)

8. Johansson, S., Gulliksen, J., Gustavsson, C.: Disability digital divide: the use of the internet, smartphones, computers and tablets among people with disabilities in Sweden. Univ. Access Inf. Soc. **20**(1), 105–120 (2021)

9. Kender, K., Spiel, K.: FaceSavr™: designing technologies with allistic adults to battle emotion echolalia. In: CHI Conference on Human Factors in Computer System. Extended Abstract, pp. 1–8 (2022)

10. Rispoli, M., Franco, J., Van Der Meer, L., Lang, R., Camargo, S.: The use of speech generating devices in communication interventions for individuals with developmental disabilities: a review of the literature. Dev. Neurorehab. **13**, 276–293 (2010)

11. Sanfilippo, F., Raja, K.: A multi-sensor system for enhancing situational awareness and stress management for people with ASD in the workplace and in everyday life. In: HICSS (2019). https://doi.org/10.24251/HICSS.2019.494

12. Spiel, K., Gerling, K.: The purpose of play: how HCI games research fails neurodivergent populations. ACM Trans. Comput.-Hum. Interact. **28**(2), 40 (2021), Article 11. https://doi.org/10.1145/3432245

13. Stefanidi, E., Schöning, J., Feger, S.S., Marshall, P., Rogers, Y., JNiess, J.: Designing for care ecosystems: a literature review of technologies for children with ADHD. In: Interaction Design and Children (IDC 2022). ACM, New York, NY, USA, 13–25 (2022). https://doi.org/10.1145/3501712.3529746

14. Tomczak, M.T., Wójcikowski, M., Listewnik, P., Pankiewicz, B., Majchrowicz, D., Jędrzejewska-Szczerska, M.: Support for employees with ASD in the workplace using a bluetooth skin resistance sensor–a preliminary study. Sensors **18**(10), 3530 (2018). https://doi.org/10.3390/s18103530

15. Wali, L.J., Sanfilippo, F.: A review of the state-of-the-art of assistive technology for people with ASD in the workplace and in everyday life. In: Pappas I.O., Mikalef, P., Dwivedi, Y.K., Jaccheri, L., Krogstie, J., Mäntymäki, M. (eds.) Digital Transformation for a Sustainable Society in the 21st Century. I3E 2019. LNCS, vol. 11701. Springer, Cham (2019). https://doi.org/10.1007/978-3-030-29374-1_42

16. Wyeth, P., Summerville, J., Adkins, B.: Stomp: an interactive platform for people with intellectual disabilities. In: Proceedings of the 8th International Conference on Advances in Computer Entertainment Technology (ACE 2011), pp. 1–8. Association for Computing Machinery, New York, NY, USA (2011). Article 51. https://doi.org/10.1145/2071423.2071487

HCI for Digital Democracy and Citizen Participation

Jose Abdelnour Nocera[1,2(✉)], Juan José Gómez Gutiérrez[3],
María Estela Peralta Álvarez[4], and Lene Nielsen[5]

[1] School of Computing and Engineering, University of West London, London, UK
Jose.Abdelnour-Nocera@uwl.ac.uk
[2] ITI/LARSyS, Funchal, Portugal
[3] Faculty of Philosophy, Universidad de Sevilla, Sevilla, Spain
[4] Universidad de Sevilla, Higher Polytechnic School, Sevilla, Spain
mperalta1@us.es
[5] IT University Copenhagen, Copenhagen, Denmark
lene@itu.dk

Abstract. This workshop will explore and discuss how Human Computer Interaction (HCI) as a field of knowledge and practice can contribute to develop platforms for digital democracy and participation. These issues are mainly seen at two levels: (1) the optimal design of the digital environment of citizen participation platforms, and (2) explore how HCI can contribute to the development of new trends in Political Science, such as e-democracy. The practice of designing digital platforms for citizen participation and democracy could benefit greatly from a multidisciplinary sociotechnical approach that incorporates into design reflection on issues of democratic theory and practice, legal and political science. Researchers have sought to articulate design patterns and evaluation tools for these platforms with general perspectives on the democraticity of the processes they sustain. But citizen participation systems give rise to specific problems related to usability and user experience. The user is both the institution, company, formal, and informal collective, as well as the subjects that interact with these platforms. This workshop proposes a multidisciplinary exploration and discussion about design of digital platforms for citizen participation and democracy, including issues such as the necessary digital and technological resources, typology of tools that allow communication (to share knowledge), create community (to find and integrate individuals into a collective) and cooperation between individuals (to achieve common community goals), legality of the decisions taken in these platforms or subjective trust in their general function.

Keywords: Sociotechnical · HCI knowledge · HCI practice · e-Democracy · Digital Platforms · Citizen Participation

1 Introduction

This workshop will explore and discuss Human Computer Interaction (HCI) as a field of knowledge and practice supporting digital democracy and participation processes. This support is mainly seen at two levels: (1) for the optimal design of the digital environment

© The Author(s), under exclusive license to Springer Nature Switzerland AG 2023
J. Abdelnour Nocera et al. (Eds.): INTERACT 2023, LNCS 14145, pp. 627–631, 2023.
https://doi.org/10.1007/978-3-031-42293-5_84

of citizen participation platforms, and (2) on how HCI can contribute to the development of new trends in political science, such as e-democracy.

Literature on the design of digital systems for citizen's participation and democracy (Bødker et al., 2000, Damodaran et al. 2005; Archibugi et al. 2011; Bjørn-Andersen and Clemmensen 2017 among others) seeks to articulate design patterns and evaluation tools for these systems with general reflections on the democracy of the processes they sustain. These patterns and tools connect democratic social theory and practices with the development of specific procedures and instruments for their furtherance.

Additional evidence of the multidisciplinary character of the design problems associated with these systems can be found, for example, in Nelimarkka's (2019) review, which conceives participatory design from the perspective of an array of deliberation, representation and decision-making procedures, which Vlachokyriakos (2013), for his part, associates with the institutional-political framework of contemporary Western democracies. Nelimarkka, however, does not exhaust the diversity of democratic procedures, their contextual adequateness, or the conditions for their implementation. Nor is the political-institutional dimension, studied by Vlachokyriakos, the only one in which democracy can be exercised. For instance, little attention has been paid so far to its practice in the business, professional and educational fields. And to this we add design issues associated with democratic practices in action (Kim 2012) resulting from the users' empowerment of platforms not intended for this purpose, such as social networks. Finally, citizen participation systems pose specific problems linked to usability and user experience, being the "user" both the institution, company, formal and informal collective, as well as the subjects that interact with these platforms. In this respect, issues such as the legality of the decisions taken and how to build up subjective trust in their general functioning are critical considerations for design.

With these ideas in mind, we conclude that, by its very nature, the practice of designing digital platforms for citizen participation and democracy could greatly benefit from a multidisciplinary sociotechnical approach, articulating the former with democratic theory and practice, juridical studies, and political science.

2 Workshop Objectives

In this workshop, we understand the above issues as sociotechnical in nature and aim to trace the cultural and political dynamics that drive the design of this type of platforms. More concretely, we solicit position papers that help us fulfil the following objectives:

- To help develop a framework of HCI to be applied in e-democracy and participatory processes.
- Collect examples and experiences of digital democracy platforms.
- Collecting examples and experiences that show that the field of HCI can be beneficial in the design and development of digital platforms for citizen decision processes
- Formulate a research agenda for future work on digital democracy research on HCI.

These four objectives are aimed at answering the following research questions:

- How can different approaches towards sociotechnical and interaction design promote or undermine democratic participation?

- What are the best design patterns and requirements that lead to effective platforms for Digital Democracy and Participation?
- How can digital democracy platforms be evaluated?
- What are the best tools and methods to support communication, community formation and deliberation in democratic processes?
- Design thinking and innovation: how the design process should be led by democratic requirements and not by technology affordances?
- How to identify forms of democracy and associated practices through the presentation of relevant case studies.
- How to identify and assess the nature and type of citizen participation in the process of design of these platforms.

3   Expected Outcomes

The workshop will produce a research agenda for studying the optimum development of digital platforms for e-democracy processes through a HCI lens, and how best to understand and analyze them. The aim with this research agenda is to stimulate further research interest and provide direction for critical research on HCI apply to design digital participatory platforms. In addition, extended versions of the workshop papers will be published by Springer in the LNCS series as a volume collecting papers from the INTERACT 2023 workshops and in a special issue in the Interacting with Computers journal.

4   Target Audience

The target audience for this workshop includes researchers and practitioners from different disciplines working on topics related to Digital Democracy and Citizen Participation in HCI. Early-stage researchers and PhD students are also encouraged to submit work-in-progress papers.

5   Organizing Committee

The workshop is organized by IFIP TC13 WG13.8 – Interaction Design for International Development. The organizers are:

José Abdelnour Nocera is professor in Sociotechnical Design and Head of the Sociotechnical Group for Innovation and User Experience at the University of West London. He is the current Chair for IFIP TC13 WG13.8 and the British Computer Society Sociotechnical Specialist Group. His interests lie in the sociotechnical and cultural aspects of stakeholder diversity in systems design.

Juan José Gómez Gutiérrez is Lecturer in Aesthetics and Art Theory at the University of Sevilla (Spain). His research focuses on art and politics, including critical urban theory, cultural policies, the high and the low in art and hegemony.

Estela Peralta is Senior Lecture in Design Engineering at the University of Sevilla (Spain). Her research focuses on development smart environment and products adapted to the human factor, considering biomechanical, cognitive, and environmental aspects, for any type of population, including people with special needs.

Lene Nielsen is associate professor at IT university Copenhagen (Denmark). She current research democratically owned enterprises, their use of technology, and the way they govern the business. As member of Forum on IT and Cooperative Governance (FITCG) she researched democratic entrepreneurship for the Danish Parliament that resulted in suggestions for new legislation to further cooperatives in Denmark.

Workshop Organization

The workshop is planned for a full-day workshop. The two main activities will be presentation/discussion of the participants' position papers and group work on a research agenda for studying the optimum development of digital platforms for e-democracy processes through a HCI lens, and how best to understand and analyze them. To make the workshop engaging and rewarding, we will emphasize discussion and group work over presentations. In outline form, the workshop program looks as follows:

- *Welcome* – introduction to the workshop
- *Presentation and discussion of position papers* – we will request brief presentations and instead focus on discussion. To facilitate this format, the position papers will be made available to all participants ahead of the workshop.
- *Group work to formulate a research agenda* – each group will be chaired by one of the organizers. In addition, material will be provided to inspire the groups and help structure their discussions.
- *Plenum discussion* – the groups report the results of their work.
- *Closing* – including the initial planning of post-workshop activities. The main post-workshop activity is that the organizers will invite the workshop participants to co-author a paper about the research agenda.

The call for papers for the workshop will be announced on the IFIP WG 13.8. In addition, we will post the call for papers on relevant mailing lists and on other HCI-related mailing lists. The organizers will also contact candidate participants – researchers as well as practitioners – in their network by mailing them directly to raise their awareness of the workshop.

Participation in the workshop requires the submission of a position paper. Position papers will be limited to a maximum of four pages in the INTERACT proceedings format. Each submission will be reviewed by two reviewers from. On the basis of the reviews, the organizers will make an accept or reject decision.

During the group work, the participants will produce posters. With the participants' permission, these posters will provide input for the formulation of a combined research agenda. Another source of input for this combined research agenda is the plenum discussion, which will be recorded if the participants consent to being recorded. The organizers will invite the participants to produce extended versions of the workshop papers to be published by Springer in the LNCS series as a volume collecting papers from the INTERACT2023 workshops and in a special issue in the Interacting with Computers journal (Oxford University Press).

References

Archibugi, D., Koenig-Archibugi, M., Marchetti, R. (eds.): Global Democracy: Normative and Empirical Perspectives. Cambridge University Press, Cambridge (2011)

Bjørn-Andersen, N., Clemmensen, T.: The shaping of the scandinavian socio-technical is research tradition. confessions of an accomplice. Scand. J. Inf. Syst. **29**(1), 4 (2017)

Bødker, S., Ehn, P., Sjögren, D., Sundblad, Y.: Co-operative design—perspectives on 20 years with 'the scandinavian IT design model'. In: Proceedings of NordiCHI, vol. 2000, pp. 22–24 (2000)

Damodaran, L., Nicholls, J., Henney, A.: The contribution of sociotechnical systems thinking to the effective adoption of e-government and the enhancement of democracy. Electron. J. e-Govern. **3**(1), 1–12 (2005)

Kim, M., Park, H.W.: Measuring Twitter-based political participation and deliberation in the South Korean context by using social network and Triple Helix indicators. Scientometrics **90**(1), 121–140 (2012)

Nelimarkka, M.: A review of research on participation in democratic decision-making presented at SIGCHI conferences: toward an improved trading zone between political science and HCI. In: Proceedings of the ACM on Human-Computer Interaction, vol. 3, no. CSCW, pp. 1–29

Vlachokyriakos, V.: Designing voting technology for participation. In: Proceedings of the 14th Annual International Conference on Digital Government Research, pp. 271–272 (2013)

HCI-E^2-2023: Second IFIP WG 2.7/13.4 Workshop on HCI Engineering Education

José Creissac Campos[1], Laurence Nigay[2], Alan Dix[3], Anke Dittmar[4],
Simone D. J. Barbosa[5], and Lucio Davide Spano[6(✉)]

[1] University of Minho and HASLab/INESC TEC, Braga, Portugal
[2] University Grenoble Alpes, Grenoble, France
[3] Computational Foundry, Swansea University, Swansea, Wales, UK
[4] University of Rostock, Rostock, Germany
[5] Pontifical Catholic University of Rio de Janeiro, PUC-Rio, Rio de Janeiro, Brazil
[6] University of Cagliari, Cagliari, Italy
davide.spano@unica.it

Abstract. This second workshop on HCI Engineering Education aims at carrying forward work on identifying, examining, structuring, and sharing educational resources and approaches to support the process of teaching/learning Human-Computer Interaction (HCI) Engineering. The widening range of available interaction technologies and their applications in increasingly varied contexts (private or professional) underlines the importance of teaching HCI Engineering but also the difficulty of taking into account changes and developments in this field in often static university curricula. Besides, as these technologies are taught in diverse curricula (ranging from Human Factors and Psychology to hardcore Computer Science), we are interested in what the best approaches and best practices are to integrate HCI Engineering topics in the curricula of programs in Software Engineering, Computer Science, Human-computer Interaction, Psychology, Design, etc. The workshop is proposed on behalf of the IFIP Working Group 2.7/13.4 on User Interface Engineering.

Keywords: Human-Computer Interaction · Engineering · Education

1 Workshop Topics and Scope

Engineering interactive systems is a multidisciplinary endeavour positioned at the intersection of Human-Computer Interaction (HCI), Software Engineering, Usability Engineering, Interaction Design, Visual Design, and other disciplines. The Human-Computer Interaction Engineering (HCI-E) field is concerned with providing methods, techniques, and tools for the systematic and effective design, development, testing, evaluation, and deployment of interactive systems in a wide range of application domains.

The aim of such contributions is threefold: i) improve the process of designing, developing, and evaluating interactive systems, ii) improve the quality of

© The Author(s), under exclusive license to Springer Nature Switzerland AG 2023
J. Abdelnour Nocera et al. (Eds.): INTERACT 2023, LNCS 14145, pp. 632–637, 2023.
https://doi.org/10.1007/978-3-031-42293-5_85

the user interface (UI) of interactive systems, including usability and user experience properties, and software properties (also known as external and internal properties, respectively [5] and iii) adapt these contributions to the specific requirements and needs of the various application domains.

In recent years, the range of interactive techniques and applications has broadened considerably and can be expected to grow even further in the future. While new interaction techniques offer the prospect of improving the usability and user experience of interactive systems, they pose new challenges, not only for methods and tools that can support their design, development and evaluation in a systematic engineering-oriented manner, but also to the designers developers who must use them. Examples of interactive applications include mobile systems, wearable medical devices, safety and mission critical systems, and AI-based systems. Such interactive applications require a broad range of HCI engineering (HCI-E) techniques, methods and tools.

These techniques, methods and tools, as well as many other novel forms of interaction, involve aspects that need to be adequately addressed in the curricula of programs in HCI, Software Engineering and Computer Science [1,4,6,8]. This begs the question of how best to address these topics in those curricula, and what the best approaches to address them are. When considering education about HCI Engineering, we need to think about who is being educated as there is likely to be different curriculum scope and educational methods for different types of learners. There are two main distinctions likely influencing these methods:

Technical vs non-technical. Students in Computer Science and similar areas are likely to be the main consumers of detailed HCI-E education. However, the creation of interactive applications "requires input from science, engineering and design disciplines" and multidisciplinary teamwork requires from participants an increased understanding and appreciation for other disciplines [7]. It is also important for those who are likely to have a more interface design or user research role to able to appreciate the limits of technology and the potential impacts of architectural design choices.

Student vs practitioner. It is likely that the primary interest of many participants will be university education. However, developers are often involved in lively online discussions about different frameworks, and even in the use of monads in interactive JavaScript. Interaction Design Foundation courses attract tens of thousands of UX practitioners worldwide, evidencing the desire of on-the-job learning in both communities.

Participants may target one or more of these types of learners, have interests that cover several, or indeed may address other groups.

1.1 Previous Workshop

The previous workshop at INTERACT 2021 [2] attracted contributions addressing a variety of educational settings for professionals and university students at various levels. The material described by participants ranged from relatively small units to full modules of various lengths. Many included project work of some kind but they also included more theoretical aspects such as user interface architectures. Motivation was also important, but varied greatly depending on the background of the students: computing students may need to be convinced that they need think about users at all, whilst those from a design/UX background might question why the need to know anything about the actual construction of user interfaces. There were also considerable differences in order, whether engineering/construction aspect should follow design, mimicking UX development practice, or whether engineering/construction aspects should come first in order to help students understand why user-centered design is needed.

In response to this range of settings, one of the workshop outcomes was to present a selection of educational resources (exercises and assignments) descriptions in relatively standard form, clarifying aspects such as objectives, and audience [3]. This has begun the process of creating a structure within which materials can be described and shared, and helped shape the goals of the present workshop.

1.2   Goals and Expected Outcomes

The workshop aims at identifying, examining, and structuring educational resources and approaches to support the teaching/learning of HCI Engineering. It aims to cover a range of areas from challenges related to novel forms of interaction to emerging themes stemming from new application domains. Another goal is to consider the variety of students' skills and experiences. For instance, how to incorporate and teach HCI Engineering in Computer Science curricula or in UI/UX Design curricula? How to teach HCI Engineering to students with different skills (e.g., engineers, designers)? The goal is also to consider different lecturing modalities, ranging from on-site lectures, project-based pedagogy to online/remote lecturing. The intended outcome of the workshop is a structured overview of educational resources, described in a common structure (see [3] for an initial definition of the intended structure). This overview will take the form of an online resource, built around a version control system, which will be made available to the community. We expect that, through this resource, educational materials (e.g., from slides and reference materials to exercises and exams) will be made available. In addition to the description of the educational resource itself, and for educators planning to use the resource, practical aspects and lessons from the experience of using the resource form a complementary part of the description of each resource. It is expected that the workshop will result in the first public instance of this resource and that this work will be continued in follow-up workshops, as well as in the context of IFIP Working Group 2.7/13.4 on User Interface Engineering[1]. Depending on the quality of the submissions and the workshop results, revised versions of the contributions will be considered for publication in the INTERACT 2023 post-proceedings. In addition, we will produce a journal paper summarizing and consolidating the contributions, in the form of an HCI Engineering Education roadmap. These results shall serve as a

---

[1] http://ui-engineering.org.

basis for drafting a roadmap for a curriculum for the engineering of advanced interactive computing systems and for identifying quality lecturing modalities.

1.3 Target Audience

Achieving the workshop's goals means bringing together experiences from people teaching HCI concepts impacting how we engineer interactive systems and from people working in HCI-E to identify topics and methods that should be included in teaching this subject. Besides the courses in HCI-E, interesting inputs may arrive from HCI courses outside the CS curriculum requiring to communicate engineering challenges, or from more general software engineering courses discussing aspects related to human factors. Hence, we will solicit contributions from the HCI-E-related communities, and we will be very interested in welcoming members of the educational community, for a fruitful discussion. To do so, we will dispatch the call to the usual channels, including announcements in mailing lists, conferences, and personal contacts.

1.4 Submissions

Position papers (6–10 pages in Springer format) must report experiences related to HCI Engineering education. Submissions could report software engineering units including some aspects of HCI-E, curricula or teaching units dedicated to HCI-E, case studies/projects demonstrating aspects of HCI-E, evaluation of students' skills related to HCI-E, training non-technical and mixed students in HCI-E, training appropriate aspects of HCI-E to professionals/practitioners, a new teaching modality promising for teaching HCI-E, introducing HCI-E into existing curricula, etc. Authors could also provide in their submission a short summary of their experience in the field and their motivation to participate in this workshop. Submissions will be processed via a web-based conference management system to be defined (e.g. Easychair). Position papers will be reviewed by a committee composed of members of IFIP Working Group 2.7/13.4, and participants will be invited to attend the workshop based on review results.

2 Workshop Structure

The workshop will last one day. We will start with a brief introduction to the workshop's goals, and a sequence of presentations of the different position papers in the first half. The second half will contain group activities aimed at the production of materials for the online resource mentioned in Sect. 1.2. The current version of the resource, resulting from the first workshop at INTERACT 2021, will be made available to participants in advance of the workshop.

We will organise the workshop in a hybrid mode. We will allow participants to attend the workshop in person, and we will also provide means for supporting remote participation for those unable to attend in person. The support for remote participation will consist of using a teleconferencing application (e.g., MS

Teams) streaming all the activities in the workshop room (e.g., presentations and discussions) during the first half of the workshop. We will use the workshop room facilities to broadcast the remote participants' activities on a shared screen and use loudspeakers. The second half of the workshop will make use of collaborative editing environment such as shared text documents (e.g., Google Docs), shared whiteboards (e.g., Miro), etc., to support joint work, regardless of the mode of participation. If necessary, we are ready to organise the workshop in a completely remote mode.

3   Organisers Background and Experience

The workshop is proposed on behalf of IFIP Working Group 2.7/13.4 on User Interface Engineering, and intends to further work ongoing within the group. WG 2.7/13.4 aims at advancing the state of the art in all aspects of designing, developing, and evaluating interactive computing systems with a particular focus on principled methodological engineering approaches. The scope of investigation comprises, among others: methods and tools for modelling, prototyping, developing, and evaluating user interfaces; quality models for interactive systems; and new interface technologies suitable to improve user interaction.

The WG understands HCI Engineering as the creation and application of scientific knowledge and systematic, structured design and development methods to predictably and reliably improve the consistency, usability, scalability, economy, and dependability of practical problem solutions. HCI Engineering addresses all aspects related to methods, processes, tools, technologies, and empirical studies involved in the invention, design and construction of interactive systems. The techniques addressed concern all types of applications, for example, business applications, social media, smart environments, medical devices, automotive and aeronautics applications, among others.

José Creissac Campos is the former chair of IFIP WG 2.7/13.4 on User Interface Engineering. He is an associate professor at the informatics department of the University of Minho, and a senior researcher at HASLab/INESC TEC. He has served in several organizing committees, including several IFIP TC13 INTERACT 2011, ACM SIGCHI EICS, and Formal Methods Week 2019. He regularly serves on the Program Committees of, INTERACT, EICS and IUI, among others.

Laurence Nigay is a full Professor (Exceptional class) in Computer Science at the University of Grenoble Alpes (UGA) and is also an elected senior member of the Academic Institute of France (IUF). She is the director of the Engineering Human-Computer Interaction (EHCI) research group of the Grenoble Informatics Laboratory (LIG). From 1998–2004, she was vice-chair of the IFIP working group 2.7/13.4. From 2005 to 2019 she was the director of the Masters of Computer Engineering at the University of Grenoble.

Alan Dix is Director of the Computational Foundry at Swansea University. He is author of one of the principle textbooks in Human Computer Interaction as well as many other research publications and a recent book on Statistics for HCI.

He was the general chair of HCI-Educators 2007 as well as several more recent workshops in the area, including a series of Covid-related virtual workshops on video in HCI education early in 2020. He has worked in a number of commercial roles in addition to his academic posts and contributes to courses at Interaction Design Foundation. Alan still designs and codes interactive systems.

Anke Dittmar is an associate professor at the informatics department of the University of Rostock. She is a long time researcher and teacher in human-computer interaction, software engineering, and interaction design. Anke is member of IFIP WG 2.7/13.4 on User Interface Engineering, and the current president of the European Association of Cognitive Ergonomics (EACE).

Simone Diniz Junqueira Barbosa is a professor in Computer Science at the Pontifical Catholic University of Rio de Janeiro, PUC-Rio. She is author of one of the main textbooks on Human-Computer Interaction in Portuguese and has for many years worked in projects with governmental and industrial partners. She is the Vice-chair for Working Groups at IFIP TC13, and has served in several conferences over the years in various capacities, including general chair of INTERACT 2007, EICS 2012, and CHI 2022, and full papers chair of INTERACT 2015.

Lucio Davide Spano is an associate professor at the University of Cagliari, Italy, since 2019. He is the chair of the IFIP Working Group 13.4/2.7 on User Interface Engineering. He has been a member of the Model-Based User Interface Working Group of the World Wide Web Consortium (W3C), paper-chair at IUI 2020, workshop chair at INTERACT 2021.

References

1. ACM/IEEE-CS Joint Task Force on Computing Curricula: Computer Science Curricula 2013. ACM Press and IEEE Computer Society Press, Tech. rep. (2013)
2. Baumann, K., et al.: HCI-E^2: HCI engineering education. In: Ardito, C., et al. (eds.) INTERACT 2021. LNCS, vol. 12936, pp. 542–547. Springer, Cham (2021). https://doi.org/10.1007/978-3-030-85607-6_74
3. Caffiau, S., Campos, J.C., Martinie, C., Nigay, L., Palanque, P., Spano, L.D.: Teaching HCI Engineering: Four Case Studies. In: Ardito, C., et al. (eds.) INTERACT 2021. LNCS, vol. 13198, pp. 195–210. Springer, Cham (2022). https://doi.org/10.1007/978-3-030-98388-8_18
4. Churchill, E.F., Bowser, A., Preece, J.: Teaching and learning human-computer interaction: past, present, and future. Interactions **20**(2), 44–53 (2013)
5. Cockton, G., Gram, C.: Design principles for interactive software. Springer Science & Business Media (1996)
6. Hewett, T.T., et al.: ACM SIGCHI Curricula for Human-Computer Interaction. Tech. rep. (1996)
7. Mackay, W.E.: Educating multi-disciplinary design teams. In: Proceedings of Tales of the Disappearing Computer, pp. 105–118 (2003)
8. The Joint Task Force on Computing Curricula: Software Engineering 2014: Curriculum Guidelines for Undergraduate Degree Programs in Software Engineering. ACM Press and IEEE Computer Society Press, Tech. rep. (2015)

Human-Centered Software Engineering: Rethinking the Interplay of Human–Computer Interaction and Software Engineering in the Age of Digital Transformation

Carmelo Ardito[1]([⊠]), Regina Bernhaupt[2], and Stefan Sauer[3]

[1] LUM Giuseppe Degennaro University, Casamassima, BA, Italy
ardito@lum.it
[2] Eindhoven University of Technology, Eindhoven, The Netherlands
r.bernhaupt@tue.nl
[3] Paderborn University, Paderborn, Germany
sauer@uni-paderborn.de

Abstract. Digital transformation is a fundamental change process for improving organizations, industries or society and redefining key values for its stakeholders. Digital transformation represents the transition process that has to be dealt with to innovate organizational processes, to improve their interaction with customers and to offer innovative services that are based on the intensive use of digital technologies. Digital transformation affects the life of end users who can access services in completely new ways, made possible by innovative technologies. Digital transformation is therefore a process of organizational, economic, social and creative change enabled by the adoption and development of digital technologies. Human-Centered Software Engineering (HCSE) as a research domain is thus more relevant than when it comes to the sole introduction of novel technologies in a socio-technical system. The interplay between human–computer interaction and software engineering needs to be rethought for a rapid response to the evolution of technologies, while also considering aspects such as greater agility in service development, sustainability, ethical considerations, cybersecurity, user mindset and awareness, to name a few. Beyond the traditional themes of IFIP WG 13.2 workshops, this edition promotes sharing of knowledge and experiences that address how to deal with the challenges of the digital transformation and its influence on human-centered socio-technical system design and development practices.

Keywords: digital transformation · sustainability · agile development · low-code development · digital twin · ethical considerations · cybersecurity

1 Overview and Goals

The Third Industrial Revolution had contributed to the spread of computers and the subsequent automation of many processes. The Fourth Industrial Revolution is characterized by a different – and exponentially enhanced – use of the tools designed during

© The Author(s), under exclusive license to Springer Nature Switzerland AG 2023
J. Abdelnour Nocera et al. (Eds.): INTERACT 2023, LNCS 14145, pp. 638–643, 2023.
https://doi.org/10.1007/978-3-031-42293-5_86

the Third Industrial Revolution. The Fourth Industrial Revolution is thus characterized by a process of technological transformation that is affecting the social structure across the globe. It has changed the way of shopping, of relating to others, of living. At the core of the process are technologies that generate important cultural impacts in our lives. In Europe, this process is differently named, depending on the different countries: digitisation, digital transformation, digital transition, etc. Here we call it digital transformation, but no matter how you name it, it has in fact revolutionized every market and company, as well as our life.

We follow the definition by Gong & Ribiere (2020) that states that digital transformation is a "fundamental change process, enabled by the innovative use of digital technologies accompanied by the strategic leverage of key resources and capabilities, aiming to radically improve an entity* and redefine its value proposition for its stakeholders" [1] (*An entity could be: an organization, a business network, an industry, or society).

Various technologies enable the digital transformation process: Mobile and Wearable Devices, Internet of Things, Cloud Computing, Big Data, Blockchain, Augmented, Virtual and Mixed Reality, Artificial Intelligence and Machine Learning, Digital Twin, Cybersecurity. However, while introducing undeniable benefits, they also bring some important issues.

Internet of Things (IoT), a leading technology of the digital transformation, empowers users to interact with the surrounding environment. IoT devices are becoming even more pervasive and social. However, there are still important issues to be solved to increase the adoption of such technologies: it is still hard for non-technical users to synchronize the behavior of multiple physical and virtual (i.e., software) resources, installed in the environment or embedded in tangible objects they have to manipulate. The opportunities offered by IoT can be amplified if new approaches are conceived to enable non-technical users to be directly involved in "composing" their smart objects by synchronizing their behavior. This leads to the need to provide non-technical users with innovative interaction strategies for controlling objects' behavior [2].

IoT also introduces issues from the cybersecurity perspective. Indeed, IoT has the unique capability of affecting both virtual and physical systems. Cyberattacks on IoT ecosystems could have far more unpredictable effects because they translate more easily into physical consequences, and users should also be aware of that.

The impact of Artificial Intelligence (AI) on human lives and the economy has been astonishing. However, it brings problems that need to be addressed, such as the required computing power, worry of how AI models predict the output (i.e., trust in AI results), data privacy and security, bias connected to the amount and quality of data the models are trained on, training data scarcity because of more stringent rules on their collection and storage imposed by some government to restrict unethical usage of user data.

Digital Twin (DT) [3] is another protagonist of the digital transformation process. It is a virtual replica of a real-world object that is run in a simulation environment to mirror its physical pendant, with digital and physical twins influencing each other including the ability to perform predictions. Some benefits of using digital twins consist of accelerated risk assessment and production time (since – with the help of a digital twin – companies can test and validate a product before it even exists in the real world); predictive maintenance; real-time remote monitoring. But despite the benefits, some challenges have slowed the widespread adoption of the digital-twin technology: for example, the initial investment (because you need sensors on the equipment, an infrastructure to allow them to communicate data, a computing and storage infrastructure); the lack of a clear business case; organizational silos.

We could continue with discussing benefits and issues of other technologies: usability of mobile and wearable devices, as well as of Augmented, Virtual and Mixed Reality; user awareness about the usage and the security of Cloud Computing, Big Data, Blockchain. What emerges is that Human-Centered Software Engineering (HCSE) is more relevant than ever. The interplay between human–computer interaction (HCI) and software engineering (SE) needs to be rethought and fortified for a rapid response to the evolution of technologies, while also considering aspects such as greater agility in service development, sustainability, ethical considerations, cybersecurity, user mindset and awareness, to name just a few. But also the approaches for addressing them have to be carefully considered. For example, some software development companies show an increasing interest in low-code development platforms to facilitate application development by domain experts without sophisticated software development knowledge, as a possible solution to the need of more agile, fast and also sustainable service development. Domain experts are, however, not trained in software development methods. This introduces a risk of domain experts creating unusable applications or exceeding the designated time frame of a project (or both) [4].

According to this picture, beyond the traditional themes of IFIP WG 13.2 workshops, this edition promotes sharing of knowledge and experiences that address how to deal with the challenges of the digital transformation and its influence on human-centered socio-technical system design and development practices.

This workshop is a follow-up of the successful workshops organized at INTERACT 2015 in Bamberg, Germany [5] INTERACT 2017 in Mumbai, India [6], INTERACT 2019 in Paphos, Cyprus [7], and INTERACT 2021 in Bari, Italy [8].

2   Target Audience and Expected Outcomes

This workshop is open to everyone who is interested in aspects of human–computer interaction from a development-oriented and/or user-centered perspective. Typical contributions to this workshop focus on methods, processes and approaches for designing, building and testing interactive systems. We expect a high participation of IFIP Working Group 13.2 members. We particularly invite participants to present position papers describing real-life case studies that illustrate how they rethought HCI's and SE's interplay in order to address aspects such as agile development, sustainability, ethical considerations, and cybersecurity. Any perspective and related aspects of user interface design are welcome. We are especially interested in work that deals with current trends that change the way humans use, interact and collaborate with technical components in socio-technical systems. We are also interested in methods, theories and tools for managing context of use at design and run-time. Position papers will be made available through the workshop website. Furthermore, extended version of selected papers will be considered for inclusion in a Springer LNCS post-proceedings volume published in conjunction with the other INTERACT workshops organized by the IFIP TC13 Working Groups.

3 Workshop Contributions

Ten contributions have been accepted for presentation at the workshop. They are briefly described in the following.

A Cross-Domain Investigation of Social Control Design Using Task Models presented by Melanie Berger, Harm van Essen and Regina Bernhaupt, reports an analysis of social control design for automotive and home domains to understand how task models can be used to support the development process.

A Roadmap for Digital Twin Design, presented by Regina Bernhaupt, discusses a set of key challenges for designing digital twins. Focus is how user-centered design has to be revisited addressing the particularities of digital twins, especially when it comes to their ability to monitor, simulate and predict.

Contextual Think Aloud: A Method for Understanding Users and Their Digital Work Environment, presented by Marta Lárusdóttir and Åsa Cajander, introduces a novel method called the contextual think-aloud method for understanding users' needs and work environment, which is crucial during software development, as it directly impacts their work engagement. The method was studied in an educational setting: involved students shared their experiences and provided feedback, highlighting the comprehensive approach of the method to examining the users' work situation.

Digital Twins for Sustainability Cities: A Research Agenda, presented by Hung Pham and Regina Bernhaupt, proposes a research agenda for digital twins when applied to the design of more sustainable cities.

Digitizing Processes in Manufacturing Companies via Low-Code Software, presented by Nils Weidmann, Jonas Kirchhoff and Stefan Sauer, addresses the shortage of experience reports on low-code development in small and medium manufacturing enterprises. It provides an overview of successful low-code utilization in the manufacturing sector, identifies suitable business processes, and discusses the selection of an appropriate low-code platform aligned with the company's digitization strategy. The opportunities and challenges of the low-code approach are explored through discussions with key users involved in implementation, emphasizing its significance for digitizing business processes in this context.

On Using the Task Models for Refinement and Validation of Requirements Generated through Co-creation, presented by Bilal Naqvi, Célia Martinie, Stepan Bakhaev and Kari Smolander, addresses co-creation as a commonly used approach for gathering software requirements, involving end users in the process. While it has merits, certain limitations exist. These include subjective judgment by analysts when translating user statements into requirements, and varying abilities of users to conceptualize systems during early development stages. To overcome these limitations, a three-step task model-based approach is proposed for validating and refining co-creation-generated requirements. The paper presents a case study on developing an e-ID scheme to illustrate the approach.

Supporting a Deeper Understanding of Users in Robot-Assisted Therapies by Two-Level Personas, presented by Peter Forbrig, Anke Dittmar and Mathias Kühn, describes insights and challenges from a project on robotic-assisted rehabilitation therapies. It is suggested to use two-level personas to better cover two groups of users in therapeutic sessions. Patients are end users of the therapeutic robots; they are assisted by therapists who should also be provided with means to act as designer-users. It is argued that proven user-centered design methods and representations need to be adapted or revised to better cope with the specific challenges of new technologies and consequences of their use.

Towards a Knowledge-Based Approach for Digitalizing Integrated Care Pathways, presented by Giuseppe Loseto, Giuseppe Patella, Carmelo Ardito, Saverio Ieva, Arnaldo Tomasino, Lorenzo E. Malgieri and Michele Ruta, discusses the utilization of knowledge representation techniques for digitalizing diagnostic and therapeutic care pathways. Clinical pathways, which guide the treatment of specific medical conditions, often rely on basic textual documentation, leading to inefficiencies in patient care. The research explores the application of knowledge representation techniques to annotate contextual data, patient information, and medical guidelines with a reference ontology. By creating a comprehensive knowledge graph, rule-based approaches can be used to support the patient care management process and provide valuable insights to physicians and medical practitioners regarding specific diseases.

Towards a Smart Combination of Human and Artificial Intelligence for Manufacturing, presented by Jan Van den Bergh, Jorge Rodriguez-Echeverria and Sidharta Gautama, addresses the manufacturing industry, which is moving towards increased automation and digitization, with data being collected from various sources. Despite this trend, human workers and their capabilities remain vital, as emphasized in the Industry 5.0 vision. However, concepts such as human-centricity and digital twin lack clear definitions in the context of complex manufacturing environments. The paper focuses on enhancing the Failure Mode and Effects Analysis (FMEA) process within quality management, proposing a framework and terminology to address challenges in Industry 5.0. The integration of human and artificial intelligence is explored to improve the FMEA process and enable continuous and actionable quality management.

Towards User Profile Meta-Ontology, presented by Ankica Barisic and Marco Winckler, suggests that improved development support is necessary for creating adaptable interactive systems to better cater to diverse user needs. Understanding user mindset and awareness is crucial, and user-centered design approaches and a strong connection between human characteristics and the application domain aid in comprehending user profiles and preferences. With the increasing availability of data on human activities, a meta ontology for user profiling is proposed to effectively leverage this data, enabling developers to model, reuse, and share user profiles. This standardized framework ensures interoperability and facilitates data federation, as detailed in this paper.

4   Workshop Format

This full-day workshop is organized around presentation of position papers and working activities in small groups. In the morning sessions, after welcoming the participants and setting the frame for the workshop, the selected position papers are presented. In addition, further position statements can be contributed by the workshop participants. Participants are also invited to comment on the propositions and case studies and to report similar experiences. Position papers and statements together are used to support the discussion that follows. The afternoon sessions are thus devoted to interactive sessions, where participants will be engaged to work in small groups, discuss and propose solutions to the identified challenges seen in the morning. Solutions proposed by the participants are compiled and compared. Based on the lessons learned, participants are encouraged to draft an agenda of future work that can be accomplished. The workshop is planned to be run onsite. If circumstances require it, we intend to switch to a completely digital format that will be run online.

References

1. Gong, C., Ribiere V.: Developing a unified definition of digital transformation. Technovation **102**, 102217 (2021). ISSN 0166-4972. https://doi.org/10.1016/j.technovation.2020.102217
2. Desolda, G., Ardito, C., Matera, M.: Empowering end users to customize their smart environments: model, composition paradigms and domain-specific tools. ACM Trans. Comput.-Human Interact. (TOCHI) **24**(2), 1–52 (2017). issn: 1073–0516
3. DIGITAL TWIN. TTW-Perspective Program cofunded by NWO. https://www.digital-twin-research.nl/
4. Kirchhoff, J., Weidmann, N., Sauer, S., Engels, G.: Situational development of low-code applications in manufacturing companies. In: Proceedings of the 25th International Conference on Model Driven Engineering Languages and Systems: Companion Proceedings (MODELS 2022), pp. 816–825. Association for Computing Machinery, New York (2022)
5. Winckler, M., Bernhaupt, R., Forbrig, P., Sauer, S.: IFIP WG 13.2 workshop on user experience and user-centered development processes. In: Abascal, J., Barbosa, S., Fetter, M., Gross, T., Palanque, P., Winckler, M. (eds.) INTERACT 2015. LNCS, vol. 9299, pp. 661–662. Springer, Cham (2015). https://doi.org/10.1007/978-3-319-22723-8_90
6. Winckler, M., Larusdottir, M., Kuusinen, K., Bogdan, C., Palanque, P.: Dealing with conflicting user interface properties in user-centered development processes: IFIP WG 13.2 + 13.5 workshop at INTERACT 2017. In: Bernhaupt, R., Dalvi, G., Joshi, A.K., Balkrishan, D., O'Neill, J., Winckler, M. (eds.) Human-Computer Interaction – INTERACT 2017. Lecture Notes in Computer Science, vol. 10516, pp. 521–523. Springer, Cham (2017)
7. Ardito, C., Bernhaupt, R., Palanque, P., Sauer, S.: Handling security, usability, user experience and reliability in user-centered development processes. In: Lamas, D., Loizides, F., Nacke, L., Petrie, H., Winckler, M., Zaphiris, P. (eds.) INTERACT 2019. LNCS, vol. 11749, pp. 759–762. Springer, Cham (2019). https://doi.org/10.1007/978-3-030-29390-1_76
8. Sauer, S., Bernhaupt, R., Ardito, C.: Human-centered software engineering for changing contexts of use. In: Ardito, C., et al. (eds.) INTER. LNCS, vol. 12936, pp. 548–552. Springer, Cham (2021). https://doi.org/10.1007/978-3-030-85607-6_75

Intelligence Augmentation: Future Directions and Ethical Implications in HCI

Andrew Vargo[1]([✉]), Benjamin Tag[2], Mathilde Hutin[3,10],
Victoria Abou-Khalil[4], Shoya Ishimaru[1], Olivier Augereau[6],
Tilman Dingler[7], Motoi Iwata[1], Koichi Kise[1], Laurence Devillers[3,8],
and Andreas Dengel[5,9]

[1] Osaka Metropolitan University, Sakai, Osaka 599-8531, Japan
awv@omu.ac.jp
[2] Monash University, Clayton, VIC, Australia
[3] Université Paris-Saclay, CNRS, LISN (UMR 9015), Orsay, France
[4] ETH Zurich, Zurich, Switzerland
[5] DFKI, Kaiserslautern, Germany
[6] ENIB, Lab-STICC (UMR CNRS 6285), Brest, France
[7] University of Melbourne, Parkville, VIC, Australia
[8] Sorbonne University, Paris, France
[9] University of Kaiserslautern-Landau (RPTU), Kaiserslautern, Germany
[10] F.R.S.-FNRS, Université catholique de Louvain, Louvain-la-Neuve, Belgium

Abstract. Intelligence Augmentation (IA) has long been understood as a concept that describes how human capabilities are enhanced by technologies to improve their intelligence (often in a collective sense), and therefore improve the outcomes of many tasks. While IA's goal is to keep the human in the loop and design technology around users, the future of IA as being universally beneficial for people has been widely questioned. As IA outputs are increasingly used to train Artificial Intelligence (AI) and AI is used to enable IA, new questions arise around the implications of integrating IA systems in the real world. These concerns span from autonomous agency, to privacy and ethics, workers' rights and the essence of ownership of cognitive output. This workshop seeks to explore the latest research on technologies and policies that allow IA to benefit individuals and groups, both in the private sphere and the workplace.

Keywords: intelligence augmentation · intelligence amplification · ethics

1 Introduction

Intelligence Augmentation (IA) is a term going back to Douglas Engelbart's early work at the Augmentation Research Center (ARC) at Stanford University [4]. While John McCarthy had just opened his Artificial Intelligence Laboratory on the other side of campus, the two approaches could have not been more different at the time. While McCarthy's goal was to replace the human through

© The Author(s), under exclusive license to Springer Nature Switzerland AG 2023
J. Abdelnour Nocera et al. (Eds.): INTERACT 2023, LNCS 14145, pp. 644–649, 2023.
https://doi.org/10.1007/978-3-031-42293-5_87

artificial intelligence (AI) technologies, Engelbart's vision involved the extension of human capabilities through technology as well as thinking about the ethics of these systems and the role of the people who would be collaborating with them.

IA has since been applied to a broad range of use cases. On one hand, (computational) tools have been developed that assist humans in performing cognitive tasks beyond their natural capabilities. On the other hand, applications have been devised that capture cognitive states from individuals to inform and build information producing platforms which are collectively made [6]. Thus IA can include basic usage of information technologies, such as the Internet, and AI systems that empower humans in the loop.

Part of what makes it difficult to grasp the domain of IA and Augmented Cognition [13], is that it encompasses such a great number of technologies. Some are very small and practical, such as collective scheduling tools [3], distance learning support approaches [12], physiological sensing techniques for individuals to support more effective study [10], more efficient crowdwork [9], and online peer-production systems [1]. However, these systems have flaws. For instance, peer-production systems suffer from intense power-law, which means few humans benefit from the process of knowledge creation and modification [15].

Automation and AI introduce ethical concerns for practitioners in Human-Computer Interaction (HCI) [2]. It could be argued that the overall goal of humankind is to use AI to facilitate IA [8], but it has been argued that this may not be desirable to all [5]. It can also be argued that IA is an alternative, replacement, or supplement for AI [14]. Regardless of which goal is chosen, we have to consider users, who could be individuals, communities, and workers. As they engage with different technologies, what rights and protections are owed to them? For example, should IA used to train AI require usage warnings? Do individuals deserve intellectual rights for collectively-produced content on IA platforms? Are workers prepared to work with machines and new platforms [7] and is there an ethical framework to support workers [11]?

These ethical concerns could be unsettling for some, as IA has traditionally inhabited a vaunted space. IA, at least in concept, has been responsible for many great achievements and advancements in the recent past and the aims of advancing human intelligence beyond the natural is certainly attractive. However, IA would have existed regardless of whether it had been formalized as a concept or not. The advantage in formalization of the concept is that we are in a position as a community to carefully consider ethics and to construct policies where needed. Without these steps, IA is merely an observation of human-machine interaction. In the tradition of a decades-long discussion, we think it is time to re-visit some of these themes of designing users into or out of systems. As AI is increasingly used by the HCI community as a design tool, this workshop intends to sharpen the collective thinking about the responsibilities of IA system designers that use AI with the potential to empower or patronize their users.

1.1 Workshop Objectives

There is a substantial corpus of works that center around Intelligence Augmentation (IA), the future of HCI and AI, and the role of humans in the future [2]. The goal of this workshop is to foster a community from both academia and industry that considers agency and ethics in IA on a practical level. That is, how and when do we present the scopes and limits of an IA application or system to users? This is a fraught question since informed consent initiatives can actually backfire, and not be indicative of an individual's real intentions.

- **Activate an Interdisciplinary Community Focused on Ethical Dimensions of IA in HCI**: Intelligence Augmentation is not new, but is continually evolving. The potential impact that new integrated systems can have demands attention. It is vital that a diverse community of experts is brought together to discuss practical and ethical issues that face end-users in all facets of IA. In this workshop, our focus in on working towards a code of ethics for designers and administrators.
- **Identify Network Externalities of IA**: It is often difficult for IA system designers to accurately predict how their technology will impact individuals and communities. We seek to hear from designers and practitioners who have observed and studied how IA is adopted, adapted, and even mitigated.

This workshop serves as a companion workshop for the Learning Cyclotron (LeCycl) Project[1] within the Tri-lateral AI[2] initiative between the Japan Science and Technology Agency (JST), the German Research Federation (DFG), and the French National Research Agency (ANR). It is also the a followup to the 2022 Ubicomp Lecycl workshop [16].

2 Organizers

- **Andrew Vargo** is a Research Assistant Professor in the Graduate School of Informatics at Osaka Metropolitan University. He focuses on supplements for learning via ubiquitous sensing technologies.
- **Benjamin Tag** is a Lecturer at Monash University. He researches Human-AI Interaction, Digital Emotion Regulation, and human cognition with a focus on inferring mental state changes from data collected in the wild.
- **Mathilde Hutin** is a Postdoctoral Fellow at the Institute Language and Communication (ILC) at Université catholique de Louvain in Belgium. She is also affiliated with LISN at Université Paris-Saclay, France. Her research focuses on variation in speech and their linguistic, communicative and cognitive implications.
- **Victoria Abou-Khalil** is a Postdoctoral Researcher at the Center for Project-Based Learning in the Department of Information Technology and

---

[1] https://www.lecycl.org.
[2] https://www.jst.go.jp/kisoken/aip/en/program/research/trilateral2020.html.

Electrical Engineering at ETH Zurich in Switzerland. She studies the effectiveness of different learning methods and technologies using mixed methods and multimodal data.

- **Shoya Ishimaru** is a Project Professor at Osaka Metropolitan University and a former Junior Professor at the University of Kaiserslautern-Landau (RPTU). He leads the Psybernetics Lab, an interdisciplinary and cross-country research group investigating human-computer interaction, machine learning, and cognitive psychology toward amplifying human intelligence.
- **Olivier Augereau** an Associate Professor in Lab-STICC and the director of the European Center of Virtual Reality. His research focuses on HCI and artificial intelligence for creating adaptive systems and improving interactions between users and systems through their mutual analysis.
- **Tilman Dingler** is a Computer Scientist and Senior Lecturer in the School of Computing and Information Systems at the University of Melbourne. Tilman's research focuses on cognition-aware systems, the detection of cognitive states, and adaptation of computing systems to aid their users.
- **Motoi Iwata** is an Associate Professor in the Department of Core Informatics, Graduate School of Informatics at Osaka Metropolitan University. His current research focuses on learning support system, educational technology, comic computing, digital watermarking, and data hiding.
- **Koichi Kise** is a Professor in the Department of Core Informatics, Graduate School of Informatics, and the director of the Institute of Document Analysis and Knowledge Science (IDAKS) at Osaka Metropolitan University, Japan. He is also the director of Japan Laboratory, German Research Center for AI (DFKI). He focuses on the analysis, recognition, and retrieval of documents, images, and activities.
- **Laurence Devillers** is Professor of computer science applied to humanities and social sciences at Sorbonne University, director of research of "Affective and social dimensions of spoken interactions with (ro)bots and ethical issues" at LISN-CNRS (Paris-Saclay). She specializes in machine learning, automatic speech processing and Human-Machine dialog, and affective computing.
- **Andreas Dengel** is the Executive Director at the German Research Center for Artificial Intelligence (DFKI) in Kaiserslautern and Head of the Smart Data and Knowledge Services Department at DFKI, as well as Professor at the Department of Computer Science at University of Kaiserslautern-Landau (RPTU). He focuses on the areas of machine learning, pattern recognition, immersive quantified learning, data mining, and semantic technologies.

3   Pre-workshop Plans

The primary goal for this workshop is to better understand how IA is being implemented for individuals and communities and, therefore, better understand potential outcomes and foresee ethical issues. We will encourage the submission of position papers, case-studies, and early-stage research papers that explore the topic area. The call for participation will request position papers and case studies within the following themes.

IA Output for AI Input: How is IA being used for training machine-learning and AI systems? How can we ensure that future IA systems benefit humanity? What responsibilities do designers and system engineers need to take?

Consent: How can individuals and communities give and withdraw consent from IA systems? When is consent important and when is it not?

Outcomes and Culture: What role does culture play in the development, testing, and implementing of IA? Are different cultures fairly represented in research and design?

The Question of Fairness: Do we need regulations such as for doping in sports for intelligence doping?

Physiological and Cognitive Implications: When are cognitive resources limited? When is augmentation too much?

Legal Framework: When should IA be introduced? Should it be early in life, late in life, or in specific situations?

Systems and Demos for Ethics IA: Novel IA systems with ethical frameworks that are works-in-progress will be welcomed.

Acknowledgements. This work was supported in part by grants from JST in Japan (Grant No. JPMJCR20G3), DFG in Germany (Project No. 442581111) and ANR (Grant No. ANR-20-IADJ-0007) in France. (20KK0235).

References

1. Adamic, L.A., Zhang, J., Bakshy, E., Ackerman, M.S.: Knowledge sharing and yahoo answers: everyone knows something. In: Proceedings of the 17th International Conference on World Wide Web, WWW 2008, pp. 665–674. ACM, New York (2008). https://doi.acm.org/10.1145/1367497.1367587

2. Dengel, A., Devillers, L., Schaal, L.M.: Augmented human and human-machine co-evolution: efficiency and ethics. In: Braunschweig, B., Ghallab, M. (eds.) Reflections on Artificial Intelligence for Humanity. LNCS (LNAI), vol. 12600, pp. 203–227. Springer, Cham (2021). https://doi.org/10.1007/978-3-030-69128-8_13

3. Dobrkovic, A., Liu, L., Iacob, M.-E., van Hillegersberg, J.: Intelligence amplification framework for enhancing scheduling processes. In: Montes-y-Gómez, M., Escalante, H.J., Segura, A., Murillo, J.D. (eds.) IBERAMIA 2016. LNCS (LNAI), vol. 10022, pp. 89–100. Springer, Cham (2016). https://doi.org/10.1007/978-3-319-47955-2_8

4. Engelbart, D.C., English, W.K.: A research center for augmenting human intellect. In: Proceedings of the December 9–11, 1968, Fall Joint Computer Conference, Part I, pp. 395–410 (1968)

5. Farooq, U., Grudin, J., Shneiderman, B., Maes, P., Ren, X.: Human Computer Integration versus Powerful Tools. In: Proceedings of the 2017 CHI Conference Extended Abstracts on Human Factors in Computing Systems CHI EA 2017, pp. 1277–1282. Association for Computing Machinery, New York (May 2017). https://doi.org/10.1145/3027063.3051137

6. Gill, Z.: User-driven collaborative intelligence: social networks as crowdsourcing ecosystems. In: CHI 2012 Extended Abstracts on Human Factors in Computing Systems, CHI EA 2012, pp. 161–170. Association for Computing Machinery, New York (May 2012). https://doi.org/10.1145/2212776.2212794

7. Harborth, D., Kümpers, K.: Intelligence augmentation: rethinking the future of work by leveraging human performance and abilities. Virtual Reality **26**(3), 849–870 (2022). https://doi.org/10.1007/s10055-021-00590-7
8. Hassani, H., Silva, E.S., Unger, S., TajMazinani, M., Mac Feely, S.: Artificial Intelligence (AI) or Intelligence Augmentation (IA): What Is the Future?, vol. AI 1(2), pp. 143–155. Multidisciplinary Digital Publishing Institute (Jun 2020). https://doi.org/10.3390/ai1020008, https://www.mdpi.com/2673-2688/1/2/8
9. Islam, M.R., et al.: Quality assessment of crowdwork via eye gaze: towards adaptive personalized crowdsourcing. In: Ardito, C., et al. (eds.) INTERACT 2021. LNCS, vol. 12933, pp. 104–113. Springer, Cham (2021). https://doi.org/10.1007/978-3-030-85616-8_8
10. Maruichi, T., Uragami, T., Vargo, A., Kise, K.: Handwriting behavior as a self-confidence discriminator. In: Adjunct Proceedings of the 2020 ACM International Joint Conference on Pervasive and Ubiquitous Computing and Proceedings of the 2020 ACM International Symposium on Wearable Computers, UbiComp-ISWC 2020, pp. 78–81. Association for Computing Machinery, New York (Sep 2020). https://doi.org/10.1145/3410530.3414383
11. Paul, S., Yuan, L., Jain, H., Robert, L., Spohrer, J., Lifshitz-Assaf, H.: Intelligence augmentation: human factors in AI and future of work. AIS Trans. Hum-Comput. Interact. **14**(3), 426–445 (2022). https://doi.org/10.17705/1thci.00174, https://aisel.aisnet.org/thci/vol14/iss3/6
12. Popova, O., Popov, B., Karandey, V.: Intelligence amplification in distance learning through the binary tree of question-answer system. Proc. - So. Behav. Sci. **214**, 75–85 (2015). https://doi.org/10.1016/j.sbspro.2015.11.597, https://www.sciencedirect.com/science/article/pii/S1877042815059522
13. Stanney, K.M., et al.: Augmented cognition: an overview. Rev. Human Factors Ergon. **5**(1), 195–224 (2009). https://doi.org/10.1518/155723409X448062
14. Szczerbicki, E., Nguyen, N.T.: Intelligence augmentation and amplification: approaches, tools, and case studies. Cybern. Syst. **53**(5), 381–383 (2022). https://doi.org/10.1080/01969722.2021.2018551
15. Vargo, A.W., Matsubara, S.: Editing unfit questions in Q&A. In: 2016 5th IIAI International Congress on Advanced Applied Informatics (IIAI-AAI), pp. 107–112 (2016). https://doi.org/10.1109/IIAI-AAI.2016.83
16. Vargo, A., et al.: Workshop on delivering sensing technologies for education and learning. In: Proceedings of the 2022 ACM International Joint Conference on Pervasive and Ubiquitous Computing (UbiComp/ISWC 2022 Adjunct), Ubicomp EA 2022, 11–15 September 2022, Cambridge, United Kingdom, New York pp. 1–5 (2022). https://doi.org/10.1145/3544793.3560373

Interacting with Assistive Technology (IATech) Workshop

Paul Whittington$^{(\boxtimes)}$, Huseyin Dogan , and Nan Jiang

Bournemouth University, Poole BH12 5BB, UK
{whittingtonp,hdogan,njiang}@bournemouth.ac.uk

Abstract. Assistive Technology (ATech) is designed to increase, maintain or improve the functioning of people with disabilities. These products can consider hardware, software or mechanical devices, such as a wheelchair. People with disabilities can have varying levels of ability and there cannot be a single technology solution to suit everyone. Therefore, a range of ATech products are developed to ensures that this user community is not marginalized and can interact in an inclusive society. One of the challenges of ATech is the awareness and for people with disabilities to know the products that are available to provide support. The Interacting with Assistive Technology (IATech) Workshop will proceed to Diversity, Accessibility and Inclusivity Workshops (DAI) held at BCS HCI 2021 and 2022 and will investigate the recent developments in the domain and the methods in which awareness can be increased developments that aim to ensure interactive solutions are accessible and inclusive to all users. The workshop will be a forum for researchers in the domains of accessibility, assistive technology, human computer interaction, human centered design and system of systems to discuss the challenges and solutions for interacting with ATech.

Keywords: Accessibility · Assistive Technology · Smart Homes · Universal Design · User Experience · Web Accessibility

1 Motivation

The Interacting with Assistive Technology (IATech) Workshop will follow the 1st and 2nd Workshops on Diversity, Accessibility and Inclusivity (DAI) held at British HCI Conference 2021 and 2022. These workshops resulted in informative discussions around the research themes, to determine a roadmap for ensuring inclusive cyber security. This is an important area of research as worldwide there are 1 billion people with disabilities, which account for 15% of the worldwide population [1].

The Organizing Committee of this Workshop includes Dr Dogan and Dr Whittington, who are academic representatives for the Smart Homes and Independent Living Commission that provides recommendations to the United Kingdom Government in relation to supporting adoption of smart home technology in social care.

The worldwide standard for measuring health and disability is the International Classification for Disability, Functioning and Health (ICF) Framework, developed by

© The Author(s), under exclusive license to Springer Nature Switzerland AG 2023
J. Abdelnour Nocera et al. (Eds.): INTERACT 2023, LNCS 14145, pp. 650–656, 2023.
https://doi.org/10.1007/978-3-031-42293-5_88

the World Health Organization [2]. The aim of the ICF is to define disability as "a complex interaction between the person and their environment" instead of characterizing individuals [3]. It is therefore important to promote assistive technology (referred to as ATech) to improve quality of life and ensure there are equal opportunities for user communities to access technologies; hence this is a continuously evolving market [4]. ATech can be defined as products to "increase, maintain, or improve the functional capabilities of persons with disabilities" [5]. People with disabilities often require more advanced interaction mediums instead of traditional touch-based interaction. Sip-and-Puff is a technology that sends signals to a device using air pressure by sucking in (sipping) or blowing out (puffing) on a straw or tube and used by people who have insufficient finger dexterity to operate a joystick [6]. Head-mounted displays can also be utilized as ATech.

A common challenge with ATech is awareness and for people with disabilities to know the products that are available to provide support. Whittington and Dogan [7], Organizing Committee members, developed the SmartAbility Framework and application as a solution to recommend ATech based on physical abilities, i.e. the actions that the user can perform. This challenge has been acknowledged by Policy Connect who operate the All-Party Parliamentary Group for Assistive Technology, through their events held in the United Kingdom Parliament.

People with disability can also experience difficulties with authenticating themselves online and this is recognized by Success Criterion 3.3.7 of the Web Content Accessibility Guidelines (WCAG) 2.2 [8]. One example is users who have learning disabilities being unable to complete cognitive function tests, e.g. Completely Automated Public Turing tests to tell Computers and Humans Apart (CAPTCHA). This can result in them being prevented from purchasing goods or accessing services. The World Wide Web Consortium [6] recommends accessible authentication to promote the inclusivity of technologies to users of all abilities. Alternative verification mechanisms should be provided, including at least one that does not contain a cognitive function test.

Throughout the recent COVID-19 pandemic, there has been a growing reliance upon ATech as this provides greater independence for people with disabilities. The utilization of such technologies can help to reduce inequalities and marginalization within this community and address the intersectional divide with able bodied users [9].

The IATech Workshop will examine current approaches along with lessons learned when developing ATech. It follows the organisation of workshops on Human Centered Design for Intelligent Environments (HCD4IE) at British HCI 2016 and 2018, as well as the Diversity, Inclusivity and Accessibility of Cyber Security at BCS HCI 2021 and 2022. Bournemouth University has also held two Assistive Technology Symposiums in 2018 and 2019 and planning to hold the BU-Dundee ATech Conference in June 2023 in collaboration with the University of Dundee and Policy Connect.

2 Topics

This Workshop aims to explore the application of solutions to promote the use of technologies that are inclusive for all abilities, as well as the challenges when developing ATech. It will culminate a range of topics, focused on six themes in relation to ATech:

- Diversity

  - Technology Acceptance
  - Technology Adoption
  - Technology Discrimination

- Inclusivity

  - Design for All
  - Inclusive by Design
  - Universal Design

- Accessibility

  - Accessible Authentication
  - Accessible Design
  - Usable Accessibility
  - User Experience
  - Visual Design
  - Web Accessibility

- Human Centered Design Approaches

  - Design Solutions and Evaluations
  - Heuristics
  - Multimodal Interactions
  - Participatory Design

- Application Areas

  - Aging Population
  - Ambient Assisted Living
  - Mobility
  - Smart Systems (homes, cities etc.)
  - Telecare and Telehealth
  - Industrial Case Studies
  - Education
  - ealth

3 Audience

The intended audience for this Workshop will be academics and industries involved in the development of ATech. This includes software developers, user experience researchers, healthcare professionals, social scientists, psychologists, and policy makers who contribute to the development of such interactive ATech solutions.

4   Organizing Committee

Dr Paul Whittington is a Lecturer in Assistive Technology at Bournemouth University. Dr Whittington's research focuses on Assistive Technology, Human Factors, Usability Engineering and Systems of Systems. Dr Whittington is an academic representative on the Smart Homes and Independent Living Commission and All-Party Parliamentary Group operated by Policy Connect. Dr Whittington was a member of the Organizing and Technical Committees of the 1st and 2nd DAI Workshop at BCS HCI 2021 and 2022, and a student volunteer at British HCI 2016.

Dr Huseyin Dogan is an Associate Professor in Computing at Bournemouth University and Co-Chair of the Human Computer Interaction Research Group (BUCHI). His research interests include HCI, Usability Engineering, Ubiquitous Computing, Assistive Technology, Soft Systems, Systems Design and Systems of Systems. He has been a reviewer for BCS HCI, IEHF, IEEE SMC, IEEE SoSE, IEEE Systems Journal and INCOSE. Dr Dogan was also the general co-chair for the 30th International British Computer Society Human Computer Interaction Conference (British HCI 2016) and on the Organizing and Technical Committees of the 1st and 2nd DAI Workshop at BCS HCI 2021 and 2022.

Professor Nan Jiang is the acting Head of Computing and Informatics and Professor in Human Computer Interaction. He has 10+ years of full stack web development experience as a freelance technical consultant and technical writer. Professor Jiang is specialized in web/mobile application architectural and interface design. He has provided consultancy for many organizations through national and international industrial and research projects, including European Commission Horizon 2020 (H2020), Higher Education Innovation Funding (HEIF) and Bill & Melinda Gates Foundation.

Professor Raian Ali is a Professor in Information and Computing Technology at Hamad Bin Khalifa University, Qatar. His research has an inter-disciplinary nature, with a focus on the inter-relation between technology and human requirements and behavior. Dr Ali has received the Marie Curie CIG grant and other grants from prestigious sponsors in the UK and Europe for work in software social adaptation and designing to combat digital addiction. He sits on the editorial board and organizing and program committees of leading international conferences and journals in the field of information systems, software engineering, and behavioral and social informatics.

Dr Dena Al-Thani is an Assistant Professor and the Director of Interdisciplinary Programs at the College of Science and Engineering at Hamad Bin Khalifa University, Qatar. Dr Al-Thani is now actively publishing papers in high-ranked journals, presenting her work at international conferences, as well as contributing book chapters to publications in her field. She serves as a part-time consultant for Research and Innovation at the Mada Assistive Technology Center, where she works with the innovation team. Dr Al-Thani actively participates as a keynote speaker and panelist in key world forums, including the annual meeting of the UN Council Working Group on Internet Policy Issues, the UN Human Rights Social Forum and the World Health Innovation Summit.

Dr Chris Porter is a Senior Lecturer with the Computer Information Systems department at the University of Malta's Faculty of Information Communication Technology. He has a PhD in Computer Science from University College London. Dr Porter's main research revolves around the study, development and adoption of techniques arising from the field of Human-Computer Interaction and Human Factors to domains such as accessibility (e.g. independence and efficiency), software engineering (e.g. mitigating risks arising from information anxiety) and information security (e.g. workload and risks).

5 Technical Committee

The following Technical Committee will review papers submitted to the Workshop.

- Dr Paul Whittington, Lecturer in Assistive Technology, Bournemouth University, UK
- Dr Huseyin Dogan, Associate Professor in Computing, Bournemouth University, UK.
- Prof. Nan Jiang, Professor in Human Computer Interaction, Bournemouth University, UK.
- Dr Dena Al-Thani, Assistant Professor and Director of Interdisciplinary Programs, Hamad Bin Khalifa University, Qatar.
- Dr Achraf Othman, Head of ICT Accessibility Innovation and Research, MADA Assistive Technology Center, Qatar.
- Dr Chris Porter, Senior Lecturer in Computer Information Systems, University of Malta, Malta.

6 Advisory Committee

The Advisory Committee will guide the selection process for submissions to the Workshop.

- Professor Raian Ali, Professor in Information and Computing Technology, Hamad Bin Khalifa University, Qatar.
- Mr Stephen Giff, User Experience Manager, Google, USA.
- Mr Robert McLaren, Director of the ATech (Assistive and Accessible Technology) Policy Lab, UK.

7 Expected Outcomes

The IATech Workshop will investigate the current development of ATech and will be a forum for researchers and academics, to discuss the challenges within the domain of assistive technology. The findings from the Workshop will be used to create a roadmap for promoting suitable ATech to people with disabilities, to ensure that inclusive access is provided. The Workshop will conclude with the Panel discussing potential solutions to increase awareness. This will help provide recommendations for the ATech domain in relation to developing new technologies. The motivation behind the IATech Workshop will be to improve quality of life for people with disabilities through the awareness and utilization of suitable assistive technologies.

IATech Workshop Organization

Workshop Format

The IATech Workshop will be a half day event with a Call for Papers. The schedule will be as follows:

09:00–09:30 Arrival and Welcome
09:30–10:00 Keynote Speaker
10:00–10:30 Paper Presentation 1
10:30 10:45 Break
10:45–11:15 Paper Presentation 2
11:15–11:45 Paper Presentation 3
11:45–12:15 Paper Presentation 4
12:15–12:30 Break
12:30–13:10 Panel and Research Agenda Discussion
13:10–13:15 Close

The Keynote Speaker is to be confirmed.

Workshop Facilitation

The submission deadline for Workshop papers will be Friday 9th June 2023 (23:59 AOE). All papers will be peer reviewed by the Technical Committee and decision notifications will be sent to authors on Thursday 29th June 2023. Camera-ready submissions will be required by Thursday 20th July 2023.

The IATech Workshop will be held as a hybrid Workshop at the University of York and online. The Workshop will be chaired in person by Professor Jiang and will commence with a 30 min presentation from a keynote speaker, followed by 10 min of Q&A. The keynote will focus on assistive technology and recent developments within the domain.

The Workshop will continue with paper presentations and each accepted paper will be invited to present for 25 min with 5 min for Q&A. The Workshop will conclude with a 50 min Panel discussion, focused on the main themes highlighted in the submissions and discussion on a future research agenda. The panelists will consist of, Professor Jiang, the keynote speaker and a selection of delegates, based on their papers.

Accepted submissions will be published in the Proceedings of Interact 2023.

References

1. Disability Inclusion. https://www.worldbank.org/en/topic/disability. Accessed 24 Feb 2023
2. International Classification of Functioning, Disability and Health (ICF). https://www.who.int/standards/classifications/international-classification-of-functioning-disability-and-health. Accessed 24 Feb 2023
3. Kostanjsek, N.: Use of the international classification of functioning, disability and health as a conceptual framework and common language for disability statistics and health information systems. BMC Public Health 11(4), 1–6 (2011)

4. Gallagher, B., Petrie, H.: Initial results from a critical review of research for older and people with disability. In: 15th ACM SIGACCESS International Conference on Computers and Accessibility, p. 53. ACM Press, New York (2013)

5. What is AT?. https://www.atia.org/at-resources/what-is-at/. Accessed 24 Feb 2023

6. Sip and Puff Switch Solutions. http://www.orin.com/access/sip_puff/. Accessed 24 Feb 2023

7. Whittington, P., Dogan, H., Phalp, K., Jiang, N.: Detecting physical abilities through smartphone sensors: an assistive technology application. Disabil. Rehabil. Assist. Technol. **17**(8), 974–985 (2022)

8. Understanding Success Criterion 3.3.7: Accessible Authentication. https://www.w3.org/WAI/WCAG22/Understanding/accessible-authentication. Accessed 24 Feb 2023

9. Rotarou, E.S., Sakellariou, D., Kakoullis, E.J., Warren, N.: Disabled people in the time of COVID-19: identifying needs, promoting inclusivity. J. Global Health **11** (2021)

On Land, at Sea, and in the Air: Human-Computer Interaction in Safety-Critical Spaces of Control
IFIP WG 13.5 Workshop at INTERACT 2023

Tilo Mentler[1]([✉]), Philippe Palanque[2], Kristof Van Laerhoven[3], Margareta Holtensdotter Lützhöft[4], and Nadine Flegel[1]

[1] Trier University of Applied Sciences, Trier, Germany
{T.Mentler,N.Flegel}@inf.hochschule-trier.de
[2] Université Toulouse III - Paul Sabatier, Toulouse, France
palanque@irit.fr
[3] University of Siegen, Siegen, Germany
kvl@eti.uni-siegen.de
[4] Western Norway University of Applied Sciences, Bergen, Norway
Margareta.Holtensdotter.Luetzhoeft@hvl.no

Abstract. In many areas, successfully deploying interfaces with high usability and user experience (UX) is crucial for people's safety and well-being. These include, for example, control rooms for emergency services and energy suppliers, aircraft cockpits, ship bridges, surgery rooms, and intensive care units. Information and cooperation needs are not limited to the users' immediate environment but often involve numerous actors in other places (regulators, field workers, shift supervisors, remote assistance, etc.). The specific aspects of Human-Computer Interaction (HCI) in such spaces of control are the subject of this workshop. This includes understanding and modeling routine and emergency operations, alarm management, human-machine task allocation and automation concepts, interaction design beyond graphical user interfaces, laboratory and field evaluations, and training approaches. In addition to addressing domain-specific issues (e.g., in healthcare, in aviation), cross-domain challenges and solutions will be identified and discussed (e.g., more flexible and cooperative ways of working with the aid of wearable and mobile devices). This workshop is organized by the IFIP WG 13.5 on Human Error, Resilience, Reliability and Safety in System Development.

Keywords: Safety-Critical Systems · Control Rooms · Cockpits · Usable Safety · Usable Security · Resilience · Dependability

1 Introduction

Whether in a fire department control room, on a ship bridge, in an aircraft cockpit or in an operating room, the well-being of many people every day depends

© The Author(s), under exclusive license to Springer Nature Switzerland AG 2023
J. Abdelnour Nocera et al. (Eds.): INTERACT 2023, LNCS 14145, pp. 657–661, 2023.
https://doi.org/10.1007/978-3-031-42293-5_89

on processes that should run in a structured manner and critical parameters monitored and controlled appropriately by skilled professionals. In such "location[s] designed for an entity to be in control of a process" [4], which will be collectively referred to as control rooms in the following, usable, dependable and safe human-computer interaction (HCI) is crucial.

However, limiting HCI-related research to control rooms, in terms of "place[s] with an associated physical structure, where the operators carry out [...] responsibilities" [12], is not sufficient. External (f)actors can be substantial:

- Field workers can provide data to operators or use mixed-reality solutions to integrate them into on-site operations [5].
- Smart environments, from solutions involving only a few sensors to whole infrastructures (e.g., smart cities), allow access to data and interaction capabilities that can be valuable to control room operators [7,9].
- In crisis situations that affect control rooms (e.g., power outages, technical problems, terrorist attacks), emergency control rooms must be operated or complement actual faulty ones [3]. Today, structures with control room-like functions are set up locally at scenes of an incident [11].
- Operators demand more flexible working models. For example, the German-language professional magazine "BOS-Leitstelle Aktuell" (Rescue Forces Control Rooms up to date) devoted an entire issue to the topic of "Home office & Co - Future Concepts for the Control Room"[1] in 2021.

While "understanding the physical space in which interaction takes place is central to providing a good UX" [1], a broader view and research approach from places to spaces of control seems appropriate. In the other direction, having a precise and detailed understanding of interactions is crucial to design and deploy efficient command and control systems.

Finally, "beyond the control room" [13] should involve looking beyond the actual process control. This is because the people who act and bear responsibility, the operators, have hardly been considered during the design and development of the technical solutions. If any, studies were conducted on hardware ergonomics (e.g., height-adjustable screen, cf. [10]). However, instead of being the "forgotten element[s]" [6] of process control, operators' health and well-being could be given the priority they deserve. Appropriate sensor technology and wearable devices could form the data basis. Brazier (2010) aptly puts it: "The important things to realize are that control rooms are not defined by their appearance or physical arrangements. Also, they are only a component and not a system in their own right" [2].

This workshop organized by the IFIP Working Group 13.5 on Human Error, Resilience, Reliability, Safety and System Development promotes sharing experiences in designing, implementing, and evaluating interactive systems in safety-critical control spaces. It follows INTERACT 2021 workshop on "Control Rooms in Safety Critical Contexts (CRiSCC): Design, Engineering and Evaluation Issues" [8].

---

[1] https://www.skverlag.de/rettungsdienst/meldung/newsartikel/homeoffice-co-zukunftskonzepte-fuer-die-leitstelle.html.

2 Structure of the Workshop

We propose a full-day workshop divided into 3 phases. Authors of selected contributions are invited to present their work at the workshop's morning session. Participants are invited to comment/discuss these contributions and report similar experiences. This is also intended to promote cross-domain "thinking outside the box."

The afternoon sessions are devoted to the issues raised by presentations and discussions in the morning. The work in small groups is moderated by the workshop organizers and supported with creative techniques. Proposed solutions will be compiled and compared. Based on the lessons learned, participants will draft an agenda of future work that can be accomplished.

3 Target Audience and Expected Outcomes

This workshop is open to everyone interested in the aspects related to the design, engineering, evaluation, deployment, training, maintenance, and certification of human-computer interaction in safety-critical spaces of control. We expect high participation of IFIP working group 13.5 members. We invite participants to present position papers describing real-life case studies that illustrate how a new technology would enhance operations in safety-critical spaces of control.

They could also highlight the trade-offs between two or more properties of interactive systems, such as user experience and dependability or usability and security. The way the new technology will be addressing some known or envisioned problem in control should be presented in the contribution. We are also interested in methods, theories, and tools for control room development if they address some user interface properties. Accepted position papers are published in INTERACT 2023 adjunct conference proceedings. We also expect to discuss how to disseminate individual contributions to the community in a special issue in a journal or edited volume at the workshop.

4 Workshop Organizers

Tilo Mentler is a professor of Human-Computer Interaction and User Experience at Trier University of Applied Sciences. His research is focused on human-centered design in safety-critical contexts (e.g. mobile devices and mixed reality in healthcare, novel approaches to critical infrastructure). Currently, he works on control rooms as pervasive computing environments and examines the role of user experience in safety-critical settings. Prof. Mentler chairs IFIP WG "13.5 on Human Error, Resilience, Reliability and Safety in System Development" and the Special Interest Group "Usable Safety & Security" within the German Informatics Society (GI). Furthermore, he is a member of the IFIP Advisory Board of GI, and has been the GI representative in the IFIP Domain Committee on IT in Disaster Risk Reduction.

Philippe Palanque is a Professor in Computer Science at the University of Toulouse 3, leading the Interactive Critical Systems research group. Since the late 1980 s, he has been working on developing and applying formal description techniques for interactive systems. He has worked on research projects at the Centre National d'Études Spatiales (CNES) for more than 10 years and on software architectures and user interface modeling for interactive cockpits in large civil aircraft (funded by Air-bus). The main driver of Philippe's research over the last 20 years has been to address usability, safety, and dependability in an even way to build trustable safety-critical interactive systems. As for conferences, he is the TPC co-chair of EICS 2021 and is a member of the ACM CHI steering committee. He is a member of the CHI academy and has been the chair of the IFIP TC 13 committee on Human-Computer Interaction.

Kristof Van Laerhoven is a Professor in Ubiquitous Computing at the University of Siegen, Germany. His research interests span the areas of wearable and distributed sensing systems that focus on machine learning challenges, such as recognizing what human users are doing, what they are focusing on, and how stressed they are. He is co-editor of Springer Adaptive Environments, editor for ACM IMWUT, and general co-chair for ACM UbiComp/ISWC in 2023. More information can be found on http://ubicomp.eti.uni-siegen.de.

Margareta Lützhöft is a master mariner trained at Kalmar Maritime Academy in Sweden. After leaving sea, she studied for a Bachelor's degree in Cognitive science and a Master's in Computer Science. In 2004 she received a PhD in Human-Machine Interaction and was associate Professor at Chalmers University of technology and Professor of Nautical Studies at the University of Tasmania, Australia. Presently, she is holding a position as Professor in the MarSafe group at the Western Norway University of Applied Sciences, and leader of the Mar-CATCH Research Centre. Her research interests include human-centered design and the effects of new technology, and she has published in these and other areas relating to maritime safety.

Nadine Flegel joined the Department of Computer Science at Trier University of Applied Sciences in 2020 as a research assistant in the project "PervaSafe Computing: Pattern-Based Wearable Assistants for Safety-Critical Human-Computer Interaction in Control Rooms" funded by the Deutsche Forschungsgemeinschaft (DFG, German Research Foundation). The project is part of the priority program SPP2199 Scalable Interaction Paradigms for Pervasive Computing Environments. She is doing her PhD in this field in cooperation with the University of Siegen.

References

1. Benyon, D.: Physical space. In: Spaces of Interaction, Places for Experience, pp. 29–36. Springer (2014). https://doi.org/10.1007/978-3-031-02206-7
2. Brazier, A.: Operations: a control room is only a component in a complex system. Article of AB Risk Limited Managing Risks of Control Room Operations (2010)
3. Fourmont, M., Prüfer, R., Meyer, D.: Das netzquartier: die neue zentrale des netzbetreibers 50hertz transmission gmbh in berlin: Die firmenzentrale besticht durch gestaltung, konstruktion und nachhaltigkeit. Stahlbau **87**(12), 1207–1213 (2018)

4. Hollnagel, E., Woods, D.D.: Joint cognitive systems: foundations of cognitive systems engineering. CRC Press (2005)
5. Lee, S.M., Lee, H.C., Ha, J.S., Seong, P.H.: Development of digital device based work verification system for cooperation between main control room operators and field workers in nuclear power plants. Nucl. Eng. Des. **307**, 1–9 (2016)
6. Li, X., McKee, D., Horberry, T., Powell, M.: The control room operator: the forgotten element in mineral process control. Miner. Eng. **24**(8), 894–902 (2011)
7. Liu, C., Ke, L.: Cloud assisted internet of things intelligent transportation system and the traffic control system in the smart city. J. Control Dec., 1–14 (2022)
8. Mentler, T., Palanque, P., Boll, S., Johnson, C., Van Laerhoven, K.: Control rooms in safety critical contexts: design, engineering and evaluation issues. In: Ardito, C., et al. (eds.) INTERACT 2021. LNCS, vol. 12936, pp. 530–535. Springer, Cham (2021). https://doi.org/10.1007/978-3-030-85607-6_72
9. Mentler, T., Rasim, T., Müßiggang, M., Herczeg, M.: Ensuring usability of future smart energy control room systems. Energy Inform. **1**, 167–182 (2018)
10. Osvalder, A.L., Andersson, J., Bligård, L.O., Colmsjö, A.: Ergonomic features of control room environments for improved operator comfort and support. In: Nordic Ergonomics Society 47th Annual Conference (NES 2015), Lillehammer, Norway (2015)
11. Rimstad, R., Njå, O., Rake, E.L., Braut, G.S.: Incident command and information flows in a large-scale emergency operation. J. Contingencies Crisis Manag. **22**(1), 29–38 (2014)
12. Santos, I.J., Fernandes, N., Santos, L.F.M.: Evaluation of performance mode of the operators of nuclear control rooms: an approach based on human factors. In: Proceedings of the INAC 2019: International Nuclear Atlantic Conference. Nuclear new horizons: fueling our future (2019)
13. Ulrich, T.A., Boring, R.L., Falls, I.: Beyond control room modernization-nuclear concept of operations development for novel systems using operator-in-the-loop control room simulations. In: Proceedings of the Human Factors and Ergonomics Society Annual Meeting, vol. 66, pp. 1737–1741. SAGE Publications, Sage CA, Los Angeles (2022)

Playful, Curious, Creative, Equitable: Exploring Opportunities for AI Technologies with Older Adults

Ewan Soubutts[1,5], Aneesha Singh[1,5(✉)], Bran Knowles[2,5], Amid Ayobi[1,5], Nervo Verdezeto Dias[3,5], Britta Schulte[1,2,3,4,5], Julia McDowell[2,5], Caroline Swarbrick[2,5], Andrew Steptoe[1,5], Jasmine Fledderjohann[2,5], Helen Petrie[4,5], Richard Harper[2,5], and Yvonne Rogers[1,5]

[1] UCL Interaction Centre, University College London, 66-72 Gower Street, London WC1E 6EA, UK
aneesha.singh@ucl.ac.uk
[2] University of Lancaster, Bailrigg, Lancaster LA1 4YW, UK
[3] School of Computer Science and Informatics, Cardiff University, Senghennydd Road, Cardiff CF24 4AG, UK
[4] University of York, York YO10 5GH, UK
[5] Bauhaus Universitat Weimar, Geschwister-Scholl-Straße 8/15, 99423 Weimar, Germany

Abstract. There has recently been much discussion around OpenAI, Generative AI, use of chatbots and the use of other immersive technologies in the mainstream. These developments have much to offer to older adults in terms of playful, accessible and creative ways to engage with technology in everyday life. In this workshop, we are interested in developing a research agenda for HCI research with older adults to explore, enjoy, build new and extend existing interactions with such technologies. What are the possibilities they offer simply for introducing creativity, playfulness, enjoyment and 'fun' for older adults in everyday life? Or are there other goals that older adults want to achieve using them, such as new ways of socially engaging with their grandchildren, developing hobbies and knowledge, or simply making their lives easier? Can these tools empower older adults to explore various interaction modalities to help them achieve their goals? Finally, what are the new ways that these tools can be used to engage with older adults in the research and design of new emerging technologies? In this workshop, we will aim to generate discussion, develop a community and a roadmap for older adults' use of technology that is playful, curious, creative and equitable. We will focus on five themes for the role of such technologies: (i) for enabling expression and creativity, (ii) as a catalyst for experience and action, (iii) for enabling reflection and awareness, (iv) for communication and (v) supporting the design process for (re) inventing new products and avenues for use. This workshop will feature co-creation and exploration of research methods and technologies, with panel and multidisciplinary discussions bringing together researchers who are interested in designing for and with older adults. We will explore new technology interactions including AI and immersive technologies within HCI; discussing methods, opportunities, and challenges in using these technologies and leveraging them for ideation, and form a multidisciplinary community for future synergies and collaborations.

© The Author(s), under exclusive license to Springer Nature Switzerland AG 2023
J. Abdelnour Nocera et al. (Eds.): INTERACT 2023, LNCS 14145, pp. 662–667, 2023.
https://doi.org/10.1007/978-3-031-42293-5_90

Keywords: OpenAI · Generative AI · Creativity · Fun · Play · Older Adults · Resources

1 Introduction

Artificial intelligence (AI) enabled technologies are being used to enable creative approaches in many different ways. Some notable examples recently have been AI generated art and music to create unique compositions; video creation by stitching together pre-existing footage or generating entirely new footage, writing poems and prose, answering questions and expanding knowledge on areas of interest. AI-enabled chatbots and voice interfaces provide interaction and fun in staying connected and also making it easier and more natural to engage with technology. There has been much discussion around the use of these technologies but most of the discourse has focused on younger people.

To re-contextualise this, our workshop particularly focusses on older adults, posing a range of questions, including: How do older adults perceive and experience AI-based technologies? How can these technologies empower older people and what are the possibilities and concerns? Can these technologies offer a playful and engaging way for older adults to stay connected and active? What roles can they play - as companions, mediators or just fun tools to allow people to engage with technology in new creative ways? Can these technologies also potentially help to engage older adults with the design and research process by supporting the generation of new and innovative ideas, and bring those ideas to life in ways that might not have been possible otherwise?

This workshop seeks to develop a 'roadmap' for researchers and practitioners within HCI and adjacent fields to explore technologies that are playful, creative and equitable in collaboration with older adults and discover what role they may play in everyday contexts. Whilst HCI has an extensive body of work investigating the ways in which technology can be designed creatively for older adults [3, 4, 11], there has been less of a focus on the ways in which older adults think or act creatively, much less the tools they use for creative ideation [1, 9]. Most of these endeavors have either focused on medical interventions [7, 8], the home [6, 12], or speculative but focused activities towards the design of a specific technology [2, 5, 10].

These efforts towards understanding creative practice through the lens of aging, have largely been tailored around specific empirical outcomes. What is needed, is a deeper conversation around how to enable and draw out individualised and unique creativity, stemming from older adults' diverse life experiences. There is potential, stemming from this, to build models based on playful approaches and leveraging older adults' creativity that can in turn, enable HCI researchers and practitioners' future investigations, allowing older adults greater creative freedom within technology studies, without the need to turn to conventional approaches to draw out people's creativity.

2 Workshop Objectives

This workshop has an open-ended exploratory tone and the starting point of our discussions include the following themes:

Experience: A detailed understanding of the AI needs of older adults is crucial to inform the design of agency and creativity supportive AI technologies.

- How do older adults perceive and experience different types of AI technologies, from voice-based user interfaces to generative AI design tools?
- What are the possibilities offered by new AI technologies for supporting creativity, playfulness, enjoyment and 'fun' for older adults in everyday life?
- What other roles can AI play in the lives of older adults?

Methods: We will reimagine how we can adopt and adapt human-centered methodologies to engage with older adults within the AI context:

- How can researchers and older adults be supported in collaboratively informing the design of AI technology?
- What methods and theories are particularly suitable to understand and support the AI needs of older adults?
- What key principles can be applied to support the agency and creativity of older adults throughout human-centered AI design processes?
- What are the new ways that these tools can be used to engage with older adults in the research and design of new technologies?
- Are these playful ways of creating content rich mediations (using AI-generation tools, for example) enjoyable for older adults?

Design: We will explore technology design to support the AI needs of older adults:

- How can AI tools be designed to empower older adults to leverage different interaction modalities in daily life?
- How can AI chatbots be designed to support how older adults intertwine digital and non-digital worlds?
- How can AI systems be designed to support older adults to creatively self-manage their lifestyles during a cost of living crisis?

3 Expected Outcomes

This workshop will produce discussions, understandings and methodological tools for identifying and conducting research with older adults using emerging AI technologies and services, such as OpenAI. The aim will be to enable research into older adults' creative practices and their sources of inspiration, and to derive methodologically rich insights for researchers conducting research with older adults in the future e.g. through co-design or participatory design workshops and interview studies.

4 Workshop Outline

The workshop will begin with introductions from the group and an outline of the workshop goals for the day by the organisers. Following this, we will lhave a round of 3 min presentations for 15 min by attendees before kicking off in full. These will be introductions to existing research or novel provocations around older adults and AI within HCI.

Interactive presentations by expert speakers for the workshop will follow this. Following this will be a facilitated panel discussion where presenters from the earlier presentations will be invited to present ideas around AI as a tool for older adults' creativity and as a way of scoping their needs. Participants will then break into groups to discuss the themes in the above sections. Lastly, we will wrap up the workshop summarising the day's discussion and outlining future directions and challenges and outlining future plans and actions including creation of an opt-in mailing list of the workshop attendees and discussing future collaborations.

5 Target Audience

The target audience for this workshop include researchers and practitioners working with older adults, those doing design research (e.g. co-design and research through design) and those working with OpenAI and other AI related, immersive and playful tools and technologies. We are interested in perspectives from people working in the social sciences, psychology, health and environment spaces. We encourage early-career researchers and PhD students to submit existing relevant work.

6 Organising Committee

Ewan Soubutts is a Research Associate in Human Computer Interaction for health and care at University College London. His research is interested in older adults and the study of health and wellbeing, in particular within the home. Ewan has published to venues such as ACM CHI and CSCW on topics such as emotional acceptance, social facilitation of smart home technologies and labour in shared care spaces.

Aneesha Singh is an Associate Professor in Human Computer Interaction at University College London. She is interested in the design, adoption and use of personal health and wellbeing technologies in everyday contexts. She has a broader interest in questions of identity and inclusion and how they (should) shape the technologies we use. Her research areas include digital health and wellbeing, ubiquitous computing, multisensory feedback and a focus on marginalised populations.

Bran Knowles is a Senior Lecturer in the School of Computing and Communications at Lancaster University. Her research explores the social impacts of computing, with a particular interest in trust, privacy, and ethics, including work exploring these issues at both ends of the age spectrum. Bran currently leads the EPSRC funded DigiAge project, and serves as a member of the ACM Europe Technology Policy Committee.

Amid Ayobi is a Lecturer in Digital Health at University College London. His work has included multidisciplinary projects aimed at supporting self-tracking in multiple sclerosis care, understanding the mental health needs of people from ethnic minority backgrounds, and developing machine learning models with clinicians, data scientists, and people with diabetes. His overarching research aims is to inform the design of agency and creativity supportive health and wellbeing technologies.

Britta F. Schulte is a postdoc at Bauhaus University Weimar. Their work explores our relationships towards technologies for elderly care and the ageing body, with a strong focus on intimacy and sexuality. In their works they often use speculative and creative approaches such as storytelling and design fictions in many forms.

Julia McDowell (PhD) brings over twenty years' experience as a researcher-practitioner in the fields of technology-enhanced learning, web programming and digital humanities. Her current interests centre around the cross-cutting and interdisciplinary themes emerging from the EPSRC-funded 'Equity for the Older: Beyond Digital Access' project, undertaking the day-to-day research to help improve understanding of structural contributors to older adult marginalisation in the digital economy.

Jasmine Fledderjohann is a Senior Lecturer in Sociology at Lancaster University. She holds a dual-title PhD in Sociology and Demography from the Pennsylvania State University and was a postdoctoral fellow in Sociology at the University of Oxford before joining Lancaster. She currently leads the Food Security for Equitable Futures project, a UKRI funded Future Leaders Fellowship. Her interest is in social inequities, including social justice in the design and application of digital technology, social causes and consequences of food insecurity, and reproductive justice.

Caroline Swarbrick is Director of Education and Senior Lecturer in Ageing in the Division of Health Research at Lancaster University and Senior Qualitative Methods Lead for the Research Design Service (Lancashire and South Cumbria). Her research involves working collaboratively with people living with dementia and care partners as co-researchers having co-designed the CO-researcher Involvement and Engagement in Dementia (COINED) model.

Nervo Verdezoto Dias is a Senior Lecturer in HCI and Digital Health and Lead of the Human-Centred Computer Research Unit at Cardiff University. His previous work has investigated how older adults and pregnant women use self-care technologies in everyday life and how these shape their everyday practices, clinical encounters and decision making. His recent work investigates socio-technnical healthcare infrastructures in the Global South (India, Ecuador, Peru, Ghana, South Africa, etc.). Research funded by GCR, MRC, AHRC, EPSRC, Newton Fund, GW4.

Helen Petrie is Professor Emerita of Human Computer Interaction at the University of York. She is a Chartered Psychologist and Associate Fellow of the British Psychological Society and has degrees in psychology and computer science She has been involved in over 30 British and international projects in this area, has published widely and provided consultancy to government and industry on accessibility and usability of new technologies She has received numerous awards for her work including a Social Impact Award from the ACM (2009), a Lifetime Achievement Award from the Royal National Institute for Blind People (2017) and a Fellowship from IFIP (2021).

Richard Harper is Professor of Computer Science and Director of the Institute for Social Futures at Lancaster University. He is a Fellow of the IET, Fellow of the SIG-CHI Academy of the ACM, Fellow of the Royal Society of Arts, and Visiting Professor in the College of Science at the University of Swansea, Wales. His research is primarily in HCI, though it includes social and philosophical perspectives. He has written 13 books and holds 26 patents. Prior to joining Lancaster he was at Microsoft Research.

Yvonne Rogers is a Professor of Interaction Design, the director of UCLIC and a deputy head of the Computer Science department at University College London. She was awarded the ACM SIGCHI Lifetime Achievement Research Award in 2022, "presented

to individuals for outstanding contributions to the study of human-computer interaction."
In the same year, she was elected as a fellow of the Royal Society as "one of the leaders
who created the field of Ubiquitous Computing".

References

1. Adams, P., Murnane, E., Elfenbein, M., Wethington, E., Gay, G.: Supporting the self-
   management of chronic pain conditions with tailored momentary self-assessments. In:
   Conference on Human Factors Computer Systems, pp. 1065–1077 (2017)
2. Desjardins, A., Viny, J.E., Key, C., Johnston, N.: Alternative avenues for IoT: designing
   with non-stereotypical homes. In: Proceedings of CHI Conference Human Factors Computer
   System, pp. 1–13 (2019)
3. Giaccardi, E., Kuijer, S.C., Neven, L.: Design for resourceful ageing: intervening in the ethics
   of gerontechnology. In: Proceedings of DRS 2016, Design + Research + Society Future Think
   (2016)
4. Harrington, C.N., Wilcox, L., Connelly, K., Rogers, W., Sanford, J.: Designing health and
   fitness apps with older adults: examining the value of experience-based co-design. In: ACM
   International Conference on Proceeding Series, pp. 15–24 (2018)
5. Jenkins, T., Vallgårda, A., Boer, L., Homewood, S., Almeida, T.: Careful devices, pp. 1–5
   (2019)
6. Kon, B., Lam, A., Chan, J.: Evolution of smart homes for the elderly. In: Proceedings of 26th
   International Conference on World Wide Web Companion, pp. 1095–1101 (2017)
7. Lasrado, R., et al.: Designing and implementing a home-based couple management guide for
   couples where one partner has dementia (dempower): protocol for a nonrandomized feasibility
   trial. JMIR Res. Protoc. 7(8), e171 (2018)
8. Procter, R., Wherton, J., Greenhalgh, T.: Hidden work and the challenges of scalability and
   sustainability in ambulatory assisted living. ACM Trans. Comput. Interact. 25(2), 1–26 (2018)
9. Salovaara, A., Bellucci, A., Vianello, A., Jacucci, G.: Programmable smart home toolkits
   should beter address households' social needs. In: Conference on Human Factors Computer
   System - Proceedings (2021)
10. Schulte, B., Hornecker, E.: Care stories: understanding people's hopes and fears for
    technologies of care through story elicitation, pp. 117–128 (2022)
11. Strengers, Y., et al.: "Isn't this Marvelous" supporting older adults' wellbeing with smart
    home devices through curiosity, play and experimentation. In: DIS 2022 – Proceedings of
    2022 ACM Design Interaction System on Conference Digital Wellbeing, pp. 707–725 (2022)
12. Zallio, M., Casiddu, N.: Lifelong housing design: user feedback evaluation of smart
    objects and accessible houses for healthy ageing. In: Proceedings of 9th ACM International
    Conference PErvasive Technology Related to Assistant Environment, pp. 70:1–70:8 (2016)

Re-contextualizing Built Environments: Critical and Inclusive HCI Approaches for Cultural Heritage

Linda Hirsch[1](✉)(iD), Siiri Paananen[2](iD), Eva Hornecker[3](iD), Luke Hespanhol[4](iD), Tsvi Kuflik[5](iD), Tatiana Losev[6](iD), and Jonna Häkkilä[2](iD)

[1] LMU Munich, Munich, Germany
linda.hirsch@ifi.lmu.de
[2] University of Lapland, Rovaniemi, Finland
[3] Bauhaus University, Weimar, Germany
[4] The University of Sydney, Sydney, Australia
[5] University of Haifa, Haifa, Israel
[6] Simon-Fraser University, Vancouver, Canada

Abstract. Cultural heritage is often questioned for its relevance or criticized for representing an incomplete picture of the past. Interactive technologies can bring up new viewpoints, and alternative narratives, or intensify or provoke the user experience when cultural heritage is accessed. They can be utilized in contextualized built environments, which foster meaningful experiences, understanding, and relationships. Our workshop aims at identifying design approaches from a Human-Computer Interaction (HCI) perspective for the re-contextualization of built environments through the discussion and co-design with participants. Furthermore, approaches should enable the critical discourse about and increase inclusive access and shaping of cultural heritage. The workshop targets HCI researchers focusing on cultural heritage and urban or human-building interaction design.

Keywords: cultural heritage · historical built environment · preservation · engagement · museum · public place · human-building interaction

1 Topic

Communicating and sustaining the significance of cultural heritage is a continuous challenge. One challenge derives from social and political movements that can lead to the complete demolition of historical buildings and monuments. For example, the Queen's Pier[1] in Hong Kong got demolished by the government for land reclamation. In the context of the *Black Lives Matter* movement[2], former

---

[1] www.shorturl.at/owyz8 movement, last accessed Jan. 19th, 2023.
[2] https://blacklivesmatter.com/, last accessed Jan. 19th, 2023.

© The Author(s), under exclusive license to Springer Nature Switzerland AG 2023
J. Abdelnour Nocera et al. (Eds.): INTERACT 2023, LNCS 14145, pp. 668–673, 2023.
https://doi.org/10.1007/978-3-031-42293-5_91

confederate statues and monuments to colonizers have been torn down[3], as a protest against the glorification of slavery. The built environment embodies different values for different sectors of society, and responses to it may vary from pragmatic, such as reclaiming the public space for other usage purposes [2], to social activism, such as narratives to historical events [7].

Cultural heritage is essential for the development of each individual and society [8]. Similarly, heritage artifacts are representations and symbols of a culture's identity and, thus, relevant for developing a local identity, understanding, and a sense of community [1]. This accounts for artifacts in everyday use, such as the Buddha statue placed in private households and artifacts displayed in museums. However, the meaning and perception of cultural heritage constantly change, leading to the challenges mentioned above. Therefore, it is required to identify design approaches that support critical discourses about cultural heritage sites and artifacts and make them relevant for diverse social and political groups through conversation with them. Designers should consider cultural sensitivities and ethics when designing in a specific cultural heritage context [9].

(a)   (b)

Fig. 1. Examples of built environments that foster interface contextualization: a) The floor in a museum (Finland) showing relevant natural components and resources linked to the Sámi culture, and b) artistic installation of empty birdcages hanging in the narrow space between two buildings.

In our workshop, we want to discuss and identify design approaches to (re-)contextualize built environments that open up critical discourse and include people from various (cultural) backgrounds and perspectives. With the contextualization of built environments, we refer to environments that foster sense- and meaning-making beyond onsite experiences [10]. It includes, for example, drawing relations from the experience to the surrounding physical environment or a certain event [4] through direct interaction with the built environment [10]. Figure 1 shows current examples of installations and interfaces that contextualize the built environment and make people reflect. The re-contextualization of cultural heritage sites can further increase the understanding of their meaning and significance [6] but is still under-explored. This also holds for built environments containing cultural heritage artifacts, such as museum exhibition pieces or statues in public environments.

---

[3] www.shorturl.at/goqGI, last accessed Jan. 19th, 2023.

This identifies a research gap and introduces two main questions for the workshop: First, what is the built environment's role? Should it be designed as a neutral medium or as a communicating and personified entity? Second, how can we, as HCI researchers, approach and design contextualized built environments to respond to the above mentioned challenges? In our workshop, we will discuss and develop approaches and concepts with and about interactive built environments for cultural heritage. The workshop will bring together experts from cultural heritage, urban interaction design, human-building interaction, participatory design, and critical computing.

1.1 Delimitation: What This Workshop Proposal Is Not

We want to emphasize that this workshop is not about the right and wrong of any social and political movements or situations. It is neither meant to find **the** solution for decolonization, although we welcome critical perspectives on the topic. In contrast, we aim to find approaches that foster meaningful exchange between people and address cultural heritage's challenges and sensitivity through (re-)contextualizing the built environment. This includes discussing and brainstorming HCI approaches that inform and engage people through meaningful conversations to share and learn about cultural heritage's many contexts, subtleties, complexities, interpretations, and controversies.

1.2 Goals

The workshop aims at connecting researchers across the areas of expertise to identify the potential for future collaborations, common topics of interest, and research ideas for follow-up projects. Furthermore, the workshop results initialize the design space for (re)-contextualizing built environments for cultural heritage. One of the workshop goals is for these findings to spark other researchers' interest and ideas to reshape the user-cultural heritage relationship and to counteract the challenges mentioned above.

2 Concept

Our workshop is planned in a hybrid format to include in-person and remote participants. We will recruit workshop participants through a variety of platforms and channels. We will distribute the call: i) using the internal channels of each research institution, ii) through e-mail distribution lists of the researchers' expert groups and professional networks, iii) through a website and iv) through social media. We will also ask all authors of accepted submissions to indicate their mode of participation, their timezone preferences if participating remotely, and whether they want to present a demo of their work. The workshop website is found at https://muittut.com/hci-for-cultural-heritage/.

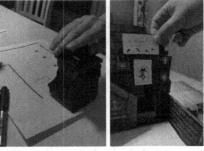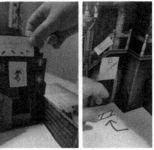

Fig. 2. Interactive sessions will utilize printed materials and cardboard models for group work. Photos from the organizers' prior concept and co-design sessions related to museum and historical contexts.

On the workshop day, we will have talks and interactive sessions. The talks are invited keynotes around social and moral challenges in the urban built environments as inspirational lightning talk and the presentation of accepted submissions by participants. During the interactive session, we plan to conduct an interactive co-design session with participants along with examples of contested heritage, culturally sensitive contexts, and behaviors. We will provide cardboard models or 3D-printed miniature replications of real-life buildings and monuments, printed maps of the surroundings, and additional prototyping materials; see 2 for examples. For remote participants, the interactive session materials include visual materials resembling the ones used in the physical sessions via the Miro board. Potential questions to participants go in the direction of the following examples:

- How could people equally participate in the critical discourse of cultural heritage through interaction with the built environment?
- What role would the built environment in the interaction have? Would it be a personified communication entity or a neutral interface?
- Applicable for both questions above: What could be pro-active or passive features from such environments?

After the workshop, we will share the accepted submissions and presentations on our website. Additionally, we will summarize and present the results from our interactive session. Lastly, we plan to propose a special issue to the ACM journal on computing and cultural heritage (JOCCH) (or similar journal) and invite the workshop participants to submit extended versions of their papers to the special issue.

3   Organizer Team

Linda Hirsch, main contact: is a Ph.D. student at LMU Munich, Germany, researching on the contextualizing of interfaces to foster sense-making and user engagement at public historical sites.

Siiri Paananen: is a doctoral student at University of Lapland, User Experience Design research group. Her research focuses on augmenting cultural heritage user experiences with interactive technologies, for example in Sámi museums.

Eva Hornecker: is Professor of HCI at Bauhaus-Universität Weimar. Her research lies at the intersection of technology, design and social sciences. She is an expert on visitor interactions with museum installations.

Luke Hespanhol: is a Senior Lecturer in Design at The University of Sydney. His research focuses on the intersection between technology, culture, society, cities and the environment. He has been commissioned by multiple local governments and public festivals to lead cross-disciplinary digital interventions on the built environment, investigating approaches to placemaking, community engagement and storytelling.

Tsvi Kuflik: is a professor of information systems at the University of Haifa, Israel. His research focuses on intelligent user interfaces and specifically on exploring the potential of novel technologies to enhance the experience of visitors to cultural heritage sites. He is the initiator and co-organizer of the PATCH (personal access to cultural heritage) workshop series, as well as numerous other events.

Tatiana Losev: is a Ph.D. student at the School of Interactive Arts & Technology at Simon Fraser University. She explores using data visualization and data physicalization for participatory engagement in community settings.

Jonna Häkkilä: is professor at University of Lapland, Finland, Faculty of Art and Design. She conducts research at the cross section of design and technology, and is interested in the user experience design of futuristic topics in human-computer interaction. She leads Lapland User Experience Design research group (LUX), and works, e.g., on HCI with Indigenous cultural heritage, local histories, and graveyards.

4   Call for Participation

Cultural heritage is often questioned for its relevance or criticized for representing exclusive perspectives of the past. Interactive technologies can be used to bring up new viewpoints, alternative narratives, or intensify or provoke the user experience when cultural heritage is accessed. In our workshop, **Re-Contextualizing Built Environments: Critical & Inclusive HCI Approaches for Cultural Heritage**, we invite you to identify approaches that support critical discourse and increase the inclusiveness of cultural heritage and computer mediated interaction with it.

We welcome research or position paper of 2–4 pages in ACM single column format[4] or a pictorial[5] of 4-6 pages through Easy Chair. Submission topics can include but are not limited to the following topics involving interactive technologies:

---

[4] https://chi2023.acm.org/submission-guides/chi-publication-formats/.
[5] https://tei.acm.org/2023/participate/pictorials/.

- Case studies of heritage sites.
- Approaches for dealing with layers of history and conflicting or historically shifting perspectives of historical sites and monuments.
- Concepts for participatory design approaches to engage people and citizens with diverse cultural backgrounds.
- Concepts for playful interactions with the physical environment to create contextualized built environments for cultural heritage.
- Approaches to design direct interaction with historical built environments or exhibition spaces and simulations.
- Critical Inquiries: cultural sensitivities and ethics.

Submissions should not be anonymized. The submission deadline is May 19th, 2023 (AoE). The workshop papers and presentations will be published on the web page[6]. At least one author of each accepted submission has to attend the workshop, and workshop participants must register for at least one day of the conference.

References

1. Campfens, E.: Whose cultural objects? Introducing heritage title for cross-border cultural property claims. Netherlands Internat. Law Rev. 67(2), 257–295 (2020). https://doi.org/10.1007/s40802-020-00174-3
2. Chen, Y.-C., Szeto, M.M.: Reclaiming Public Space Movement in Hong Kong (2017)
3. Grey, S., Kuokkanen, R.: Indigenous governance of cultural heritage: searching for alternatives to co-management. Int. J. Herit. Stud. **26**, 10 (2020)
4. Hirsch, L., Welsch, R., Rossmy, B., Butz, A.: Embedded AR storytelling supports active indexing at historical places. In: Sixteenth International Conference on Tangible, Embedded, and Embodied Interaction (2022)
5. Jones, S.: Wrestling with the social value of heritage: problems, dilemmas and opportunities. J. Comm. Archaeol. Heritage **4** (2016)
6. Nofal, E., Elhanafi, A.M., Hameeuw, H., Vande Moere, A.: Architectural contextualization of heritage museum artifacts using augmented reality. Stud. Digital Heritage **2** (2018)
7. Sanni, J.: The destruction of historical monuments and the danger of sanitising history. Philosophia **49** (2021)
8. Shirvani Dastgerdi, A., De Luca, G.: Specifying the significance of historic sites in heritage planning. Conserv. Sci. Cult. Heritage **18** (2019)
9. Suoheimo, M., Genc, C., Häkkilä, J.: Design sensibilities in a museum exhibition design process in indigenous context. In: The 11th Nordic Conference on Human-Computer Interaction: Shaping Experiences, Shaping Society (2020)
10. Wouters, N.: Contextualising Media Architecture: Design Approaches to Support Social and Architectural Relevance

---

[6] https://muittut.com/hci-for-cultural-heritage/.

Sustainable Human-Work Interaction Designs

Elodie Bouzekri[1]([envelope]) [iD], Barbara Rita Barricelli[2][iD], Torkil Clemmensen[3][iD],
Morten Hertzum[4][iD], and Masood Masoodian[5][iD]

[1] Univ. Bordeaux, Estia Institute of Technology, Bordeaux, France
elodie.bouzekri@estia.fr
[2] Università degli Studi di Brescia, Via Branze 38, 25123 Brescia, Italy
barbara.barricelli@unibs.it
[3] Copenhagen Business School, Howitzvej 60, Frederiksberg 2000, DK, Denmark
tc.digi@cbs.dk
[4] Roskilde University, Universitetsvej 1, Bldg 10.1, Roskilde 4000, DK, Denmark
mhz@ruc.dk
[5] School of Arts, Design and Architecture, Aalto University, 02150 Espoo, Finland
masood.masoodian@aalto.fi

Abstract. Sustainability is a multidimensional concept with dimensions intertwined. The field of sustainable HCI explores ways to design interactive systems in a more sustainable way and to make user behavior more sustainable. In addition, social justice and equity aspects became emergent domains in HCI during the last decade. To develop interactive systems for the workplace, research on Human Work Interaction Design integrated work analysis and interaction design methods from HCI. As little HWID research has so far addressed environmental, economic, and social dimensions of sustainability, this workshop is an opportunity to start a discussion on the subject. This workshop on sustainable human-work interaction designs aims to (a) investigate processes and methods for creating sustainable designs and workplaces, (b) collect case studies that analyze experiences with introducing and learning from sustainability at work, and (c) formulate a research agenda for future work on sustainable human-work interaction designs. The target audience for the workshop is researchers and practitioners working on topics related to work analysis, interaction design, green IT, digital transformation, slow design, craft design, system-organization fit, organizational implementation, benefits realization, and in-the-wild evaluation.

Keywords: Sustainable HCI · Human Work Interaction Design

1 Introduction

Human Work Interaction Design (HWID) focuses on establishing relationships between work analysis and interaction design from Human-Computer Interaction (HCI) domain to design and develop interactive systems for work environments.

© The Author(s), under exclusive license to Springer Nature Switzerland AG 2023
J. Abdelnour Nocera et al. (Eds.): INTERACT 2023, LNCS 14145, pp. 674–679, 2023.
https://doi.org/10.1007/978-3-031-42293-5_92

While contributions in this domain cover smart and pervasive workplaces, UX, ergonomic and motivating workplaces [11] at work, sustainability in the workplace could also benefit from HWID design methods and techniques. Sustainability can be viewed as *"a matter of what resources – natural resources, quality of the environment, and capital – we bequeath to coming generations"* [13]. Sustainable HCI (SHCI) is concerned with adding environmental issues to the design of interactive systems, whether in their manufacture or use [14]. Strategies proposed in this field deals with unsustainability of current interactive products or relies on persuasive technologies or ambient awareness in order to support a behavior change toward a more environmental one [7]. This latter strategy may have the aim to reinforce and measure users connectedness to nature [3] to make them more cognitively and emotionally connected to the environment. Another way to address the environmental issue is to rethink the economic processes of manufacturing. Favouring artisanal production, local resources or respect biodiversity are part of these sustainable economic processes. In addition, social justice in HCI that proposes to take more account of under-served populations and marginalised identities [2] can be viewed as contributing to sustainability strategies in HCI.

Then, building on the history of work analysis and empirical work-domain studies, the aim of this workshop is to investigate and discuss how HWID design methods can contribute to the implementation of shared environmental practices in the workplace, sustainable manufacturing processes, or socially fair systems and processes. To support this objective, participants can share their work on processes, methods as well as results of these to support digital sobriety, sustainable digitalization, users' experience in sustainable environment, or users' engagement in environmental behavior. Possible contributions are not limited to this list.

2   Workshop Objectives

The workshop on sustainable human-work interaction design has three main objectives:

1. To investigate processes and methods for creating sustainable designs and workplaces.
2. To collect case studies that analyze experiences - good and bad - with introducing and learning from sustainability at work.
3. To formulate a research agenda for future work on sustainable human-work interaction designs.

3   Designing for Sustainability at Work

Despite being discussed [13], sustainability is a multidimensional concept with three intertwined dimensions: social, economic, and environmental [10].

1. Environmental dimension:it deals with the relationship between humans and nature. Then, initiatives that address sustainable development (meeting current needs without compromising those of future generations) fall under this dimension.
2. Economic dimension: it deals with conflicting relationships between the survival of companies (profitability, productivity, and financial performance) and social and sustainability issues; for example slow design that enables sustainable production [9], or craft design that contributes to the circular economy [16].
3. Social dimension: it deals with social equity, such as social justice, distributive justice and equality of conditions, and social responsibility.

In the workplace, individual conduct toward sustainable behavior can be interpreted in terms of three dimensions: eco-initiatives (e.g., reusing paper), eco-civic engagement (e.g., participating in the organization's environmental events), and eco-helping (e.g., encouraging colleagues to adopt environmental behavior) [15]. To support such behavior, eco-feedback strategies have been proposed in Sustainable HCI (SHCI). Focusing on system usage, eco-feedback strategies that sense users' activities (e.g., driving to work) and feed related information back (e.g., resources consumed, waste produced, or resource status) [8] have been proposed. Several contributions have been proposed for the workplace to reduce energy consumption [12], focusing on reducing lighting consumption [5], reducing transport through hybrid work [1], or implementing an energy displacement strategy [6]. However, eco-feedback strategies have been criticized for being too individual-centered, for not designing with and for communities, and for not taking into account the complexity of context [4]. Then, the recent direction of the SHCI field is to move beyond individual behavior to community practices and reach decision makers [4]. From SHCI perspectives, Mankoff et al. [14] distinguish two approaches in order to tackle sustainability issues:

1. Sustainability *through* Design: This approach aims to influence users' decision-making and thereby foster more sustainable lifestyles.
2. Sustainability *in* Design: This approach mitigates software and hardware's material effects on the environment both directly and indirectly (in line with GreenIT approaches) and aims to reduce rapid product obsolescence cycles.

Focusing on this last dimension and from an economic point of view, slow design [9] proposes to take into account the heritage and history of communities, to feature biodiversity, and to transfer traditional techniques in the manufacture of products. This way, slow design seeks to reduce natural resources consumption and to connect products with producers and end users [9]. In addition, craft design [16] that requires manual skills and human energy can be a way to reconnect people with nature. From a social perspective, digital technologies can play a role by facilitating whistleblowing and allowing journalists to report human rights violations or by providing virtual meeting places for community action [2] for example.

As little HWID research has hitherto addressed the three dimensions of sustainability, this workshop is an opportunity to start a reflection on the subject.

By focusing on one or more of the dimensions of sustainability and sustainability issues, we propose to address the challenges and suggestions emerging from the integration of work analysis methods and sustainable HCI.

4   Expected Outcomes

The workshop will produce a research agenda for studying sustainable human-work interaction designs and how best to conceive, develop, and evaluate them. The aim of this research agenda is to stimulate further research interest and provide direction for HCI research that supports sustainability at work. At the workshop, the organizers will invite the workshop participants to co-author a journal paper that presents the research agenda and discusses it on the basis of the cases and insights contributed by the participants.

5   Target Audience

The target audience for the workshop on sustainable human-work interaction designs includes researchers and practitioners working on topics related to work analysis, interaction design, green IT, digital transformation, slow design, craft design, system-organization fit, organizational implementation, benefits realization, and in-the-wild evaluation. Participation in the workshop requires the submission and acceptance of a position paper, which is limited to a maximum of four pages. Early-stage researchers and PhD students are encouraged to submit papers describing work in progress.

6   Organizing Committee

The workshop is organized by IFIP TC13 WG6 - Human Work Interaction Design (https://hwid.unibs.it/).

The organizers are:
Elodie Bouzekri: Post-doctoral fellow at University of Bordeaux, ESTIA Institute of technology, France. Her research area, Human-Computer Interaction, focuses on analysis and design of interaction, with a particular interest in interactive automated systems.

Barbara Rita Barricelli: Associate Professor at the Department of Information Engineering of Università degli Studi di Brescia, Italy. Her research interests lie in the field of Human-Computer Interaction, and specifically: Human Work Interaction Design and End-User Development. She is Chair of the IFIP working group WG13.6 on Human Work Interaction Design.

Torkil Clemmensen: Professor at the Department of Digitalization, Copenhagen Business School, Denmark. His research interest is in psychology as a science of design. His research focuses on cultural and psychological perspectives on usability, user experience, and the digitalization of work. He contributes to Human-Computer Interaction, Design, and Information Systems. He is a co-founder of IFIP TC13 WG6.

Morten Hertzum: Professor of Digital Technologies and Welfare at Roskilde University, Denmark. His overall research interest concerns how information technology supports, and otherwise affects, human activity. He pursues this interest within human-computer interaction, computer-supported collaborative work, health informatics, and implementation studies.

Masood Masoodian: Professor of Visual Communication Design at Aalto University, Finland. He leads the Aalto Visual Communication Design (AVCD) research group. His research interests includes the design of interactive visualizations in health, energy, and sustainability areas. He is a co-founder and Chair of IFIP TC13 WG10: Human-Centred Technology for Sustainability.

References

1. Babapour Chafi, M., Hultberg, A., Bozic Yams, N.: Post-pandemic office work: perceived challenges and opportunities for a sustainable work environment. Sustainability **14**(1), 294 (2022)
2. Bellini, R., Leal, D.d.C., Dixon, H.A., Fox, S.E., Strohmayer, A.: "There is no justice, just us": making mosaics of justice in social justice human-computer interaction. In: Extended Abstracts of the 2022 CHI Conference on Human Factors in Computing Systems, CHI EA 2022. Association for Computing Machinery, New York (2022). https://doi.org/10.1145/3491101.3503698
3. Bouzekri, E., Rivière, G.: Choosing a questionnaire measuring connectedness to nature for human-computer interaction user studies: choisir un questionnaire mesurant le rapport à la nature pour des Études utilisateur en interaction humain-machine. In: Proceedings of the 33rd Conference on l'Interaction Humain-Machine, IHM 2022. Association for Computing Machinery, New York (2022). https://doi.org/10.1145/3500866.3516380
4. Bremer, C., Knowles, B., Friday, A.: Have we taken on too much?: a critical review of the sustainable HCI landscape. In: Proceedings of the 2022 CHI Conference on Human Factors in Computing Systems, CHI 2022, pp. 1–11. Association for Computing Machinery, New York (Apr 2022). https://doi.org/10.1145/3491102.3517609
5. Coutaz, J., et al.: "Will the last one out, please turn off the lights": promoting energy awareness in public areas of office buildings. In: Kameas, A., Stathis, K. (eds.) AmI 2018. LNCS, vol. 11249, pp. 20–36. Springer, Cham (2018). https://doi.org/10.1007/978-3-030-03062-9_2
6. Daniel, M., Rivière, G.: Exploring axisymmetric shape-change's purposes and allure for ambient display: 16 potential use cases and a two-month preliminary study on daily notifications. In: Proceedings of the Fifteenth International Conference on Tangible, Embedded, and Embodied Interaction, TEI 2021, Association for Computing Machinery, New York (2021)

7. DiSalvo, C., Sengers, P., Brynjarsdóttir, H.: Mapping the landscape of sustainable HCI. In: Proceedings of the SIGCHI Conference on Human Factors in Computing Systems, CHI 2010, pp. 1975–1984. Association for Computing Machinery, New York (Apr 2010). https://doi.org/10.1145/1753326.1753625

8. Froehlich, J., Findlater, L., Landay, J.: The design of eco-feedback technology. In: Proceedings of the SIGCHI Conference on Human Factors in Computing Systems, CHI 2010, pp. 1999–2008. Association for Computing Machinery, New York (2010). https://doi.org/10.1145/1753326.1753629

9. Gasparin, M., Green, W., Schinckus, C.: Slow design-driven innovation: a response to our future in the Anthropocene epoch. Creat. Innovation Manag. **29**(4), 551–565 (2020)

10. Giovannoni, E., Fabietti, G.: What is sustainability? A review of the concept and its applications. In: Busco, C., Frigo, M.L., Riccaboni, A., Quattrone, P. (eds.) Integrated Reporting, pp. 21–40. Springer, Cham (2013). https://doi.org/10.1007/978-3-319-02168-3_2

11. Gonçalves, F., Campos, P., Clemmensen, T.: Human work interaction design: an overview. In: Abdelnour Nocera, J., Barricelli, B.R., Lopes, A., Campos, P., Clemmensen, T. (eds.) HWID 2015. IAICT, vol. 468, pp. 3–19. Springer, Cham (2015). https://doi.org/10.1007/978-3-319-27048-7_1

12. Katzeff, C., Broms, L., Jönsson, L., Westholm, U., Räsänen, M.: Exploring sustainable practices in workplace settings through visualizing electricity consumption. ACM Trans. Comput.-Hum. Interact. **20**(5), 31:1–31:22 (2013). https://doi.org/10.1145/2501526

13. Kuhlman, T., Farrington, J.: What is sustainability? Sustainability **2**(11), 3436–3448 (2010). https://doi.org/10.3390/su2113436

14. Mankoff, J.C., et al.: Environmental sustainability and interaction. In: CHI 2007 Extended Abstracts on Human Factors in Computing Systems, CHI EA 2007, pp. 2121–2124. Association for Computing Machinery, New York (2007). https://doi.org/10.1145/1240866.1240963

15. Paillé, P., Boiral, O.: Pro-environmental behavior at work: construct validity and determinants. J. Environ. Psychol. **36**, 118–128 (2013). https://doi.org/10.1016/j.jenvp.2013.07.014

16. Zhan, X., Walker, S.: Craft as leverage for sustainable design transformation: a theoretical foundation. Des. J. **22**(4), 483–503 (2019)

Understanding HCI Approaches for the Metaverse in Education Applications for the Global South

Anmol Srivastava[1]([⊠]), Torkil Clemmensen[2], Pradeep Yammiyavar[3], and Pankaj Badoni[4]

[1] Department of Human-Centered Design, IIIT Delhi, New Delhi, India
anmol@iiitd.ac.in
[2] Copenhagen Business School, Frederiksberg, Denmark
tc.digi@cbs.dk
[3] IIT Dharwad, Dharwad, Karnataka, India
pradeepyammi@iitdh.ac.in
[4] University of Petroleum and Energy Studies, Dehradun, Uttarakhand, India
pbadoni@ddn.upes.ac.in

Abstract. The recent adoption of the Metaverse in various sectors indicates its potential for digital transformation. Technologies like XR, where X = Augmented/ Virtual/ Mixed Reality, will be its key enablers and can be powerful tools for developing nations' digital educational transformation. These developing nations are often categorized under the Global South. This workshop presents a first step toward the socio-technical Human-Computer Interaction (HCI) aspects of the Metaverse to understand its impact on education in the Global South. The socio-technical approach helps cover human, social, and organizational factors, leading to more acceptable systems for end users and stakeholders. With the Metaverse, students, and teachers can log in via different immersive devices and experience different virtual environments fabricated to their individual needs, learning, and teaching styles. It will open up possibilities to explore new situations and access facilities that might be impossible due to physical world constraints. Two key concepts will be covered – (i) A socio-technical HCI approach to the Metaverse and (ii) an Interaction Design perspective on Avatar representation and understanding of human work in the Metaverse. This workshop will initiate dialogs on questions: (a) What are the socio-technical issues of the Metaverse for education in the global south? (b) Are there any cross-cultural usability and interaction design concerns regarding digital avatar representation? (c) What considerations will be required for educational Metaverse human-work interaction design?

Keywords: Metaverse · Education · Global South

1 Introduction

This workshop aims to initiate dialogs on two key concepts - (i) A sociotechnical HCI [1] approach to the Metaverse for education in the Global South, and (ii) an Interaction Design perspective on Avatar representation and understanding of human work in

© The Author(s), under exclusive license to Springer Nature Switzerland AG 2023
J. Abdelnour Nocera et al. (Eds.): INTERACT 2023, LNCS 14145, pp. 680–684, 2023.
https://doi.org/10.1007/978-3-031-42293-5_93

the Metaverse. This workshop will address questions such as: (a) What are the socio-technical issues about the Metaverse for education in the Global South? (b) Are there any cross-cultural usability and interaction design concerns regarding digital avatar representation in the Metaverse? (c) What considerations will be required for educational Metaverse human-work interaction design?

Coined in 1962 by Neil Stephenson, Metaverse gained immense popularity - primarily after the social media giant 'Facebook' rebranded itself as 'Meta.' The Metaverse will be the next paradigm of the internet based on Web 3.0 – blockchain, immersive media, and decentralized networks. It promises many possibilities for digital transformation in various aspects of our physical lives. Although seen more as a virtual space, the Metaverses offer convergence possibilities for both physical and virtual worlds, giving rise to merged and perpetual worlds that coexist and influence each other [2]. It allows a gigantic unified immersive internet as a persistent shared realm. Recent adoptions of the Metaverse are seen in various sectors: like virtual embassies [3], real estate [4], and workplaces [5] that indicate its potential for policymaking, business, and computer-supported collaborative work [6]. Published articles have also identified its potential to transform the education sector [7]–[9]. The Metaverse also envisions an amalgamation of technologies such as XR (where $X = $ Augmented /Mixed / Virtual Reality (AR/VR/MR)) by combining all aspects of natural and virtual environments by utilizing various HCI modalities - such as haptics, wearables, and novel user interfaces. Users can access simulated digital ecosystems using their avatars under the duality principle [2]. However, as this field is still in its developmental phase, more insights are required to understand how it can improve the quality of education management in the Global South, especially from a socio-technical HCI perspective.

Metaverse for Education in the Global South: While current education relies on face-to-face teaching methods, it has certain shortcomings in exposing students to an international and multicultural environment [10]. This is mainly due to geographical limitations and the funds available with the institutes. With the Metaverse, this barrier can be reduced. Students and teachers can log in via immersive devices and experience different virtual environments fabricated to their needs, learning, and teaching styles. In addition, it will open up possibilities to explore new situations and access facilities that might not be possible due to physical world constraints.

In this regard, further understanding is on the impact of the Metaverse at an educational, organizational, and societal level. While many studies [6, 11] have shown the effectiveness of XR or virtual worlds in improving students' motivation, there is a lack of understanding of the broader impact of using such technologies in educational institutes and further regarding their implementation, especially in the Global South. For example, while effective, the Metaverse technologies also pose challenges at the organizational level for performance. These concerns go beyond the effectiveness of the technology and generally fall under the socio-technical implications of the use of technology.

Avatar Representation and Human-Work Interaction Design: Inside the Metaverse, students can experience various contexts and learning sessions and collaborate with other students globally via digital avatars or holographic telepresence. Avatars are a digital representation of users in the virtual environment via which they can interact with other users or computer agents. While there have been numerous studies on digital avatars, their influence on cultural usability remains, and students' perception remains arcane. These aspects are crucial to understanding the behavior and motivation of students to interact and engage with fellow peers in the Metaverse. Understanding the social and physiological impacts of the Metaverse and the digital avatars representation thus becomes essential. According to a detailed study on avatars [12], the design and appearance of DAs can influence users' perceptions. However, UX concerns such as cross-cultural usability [13] issues, *perception of gender* [12]*of digital avatars,* and its influence on presence [14] are yet to be understood fully from a sociotechnical HCI perspective. Further, how avatars influence human-work interaction design [15] also requires reconsiderations and re-thinking as the virtual world offers new affordances, paradigms, and work environments.

In addition to the UX mentioned above concerns, an important aspect is understanding how the Metaverse can capture the richness of vibrant cultures of the global south. As a diversified, multi-cultural hub, the global south is often viewed as a developing nation group. To capture the essence of the culture, traditions, values, and representations of the global south nations often remains arcane in Metaverse research for education. This concern will eventually gain traction with the formation of virtual communities and digital avatars in an immersive XR environment. Thus, we propose to also shed light upon this aspect of the global south nations to motivate and inspire researchers to consider investigations in this direction.

Figure 1 below presents the design concerns for this workshop.

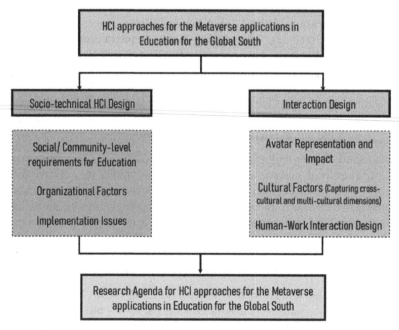

Fig. 1. Design considerations and aspects covered in this workshop

2 Workshop Objectives

This workshop is the first step towards spearheading research towards sociotechnical HCI aspects of the Metaverse to understand its impact on education in the Global South. The objectives of this workshop are to:

- Develop an understanding of the sociotechnical HCI issues about Metaverse for education in the Global South
- Collect examples, experiences, and interdisciplinary research work relevant to user experience and interaction design of Metaverse and digital avatars through a sociotechnical design lens.
- Formulate a research agenda for sociotechnical HCI research on the Metaverse.

3 Expected Outcomes

The workshop will produce a research agenda for designing Metaverse educational experiences in the Global South and provide future direction. In addition, it will help foster critical reflections on the Metaverse through a design lens and bring together researchers working in this area. Extended versions of the workshop papers will be published as workshop proceedings.

4 Target Audience

Designers, researchers, educational technologists, policymakers, and practitioners in socio-technical design, design psychology, HCI, and immersive experience design. Early-stage researchers, Ph.D. scholars, postdocs, and graduate students are also encouraged.

5 Organizing Committee

The following organizers will organize the workshop:

Anmol Srivastava is an Assistant Professor in the Department of Human-Centered Design at IIIT Delhi, where he has initiated an interdisciplinary Creative Interfaces Lab. His research interests are Sociotechnical design, XR, Metaverse, and Tangible Interaction Design. Before joining IIITD, he headed the User Experience & Interaction Design Program and co-founded the XR & IxD Lab at the School of Design, UPES.

Torkil Clemmensen is a Professor at the Department of Digitalization, Copenhagen Business School, Denmark. His research interest is in psychology as a science of design. His research focuses on cultural and psychological perspectives on usability, user experience, and the digitalization of work. He contributes to Human-Computer Interaction, Design, and Information Systems. He is a vice-chair of IFIP TC13 WG8.

Pradeep Yammiyavar is a Professor Emeritus and an Adjunct Professor at IIT Dharwad. He has been working in Creative Design, Innovation, Management & Human-Computer Interaction domains and holds an experience of 34 years. He is a Design Educator and mentor of National Eminence. He also established India's pioneering

UX-UE-UI-IxD HCI Research Lab. In addition, he initiated the Interaction Design specialization stream in IITG's B.Des program in 2003–04, which played a significant role in the success of the Department worldwide.

Pankaj Badoni is an Assistant Professor in the School of Computer Science at UPES, India. He is passionate about teaching game design and development to computer science students. He works in AR/VR, the Metaverse, and computer-generated graphics and imagery.

References

1. Abdelnour-Nocera, J., Clemmensen, T.: Theorizing about socio-technical approaches to HCI. IFIP Adv. Inf. Commun. Technol. **544**, 242–262 (2019)
2. Lee, L.-H., et al.: All one needs to know about metaverse: a complete survey on technological singularity, virtual ecosystem, and research agenda, vol. 14, no. 8, pp. 1–66 (2021)
3. Barbados Embassy Near You Could Soon Be the One on Metaverse - Bloomberg. https://www.bloomberg.com/news/articles/2021-12-14/barbados-tries-digital-diplomacy-with-planned-metaverse-embassy. Accessed 16 Mar 2022
4. Spanish Startup Gamium Announces the Sale of Land in its Metaverse By DailyCoin. https://www.investing.com/news/cryptocurrency-news/spanish-startup-gamium-announces-the-sale-of-land-in-its-metaverse-2785271. Accessed 16 Mar 2022
5. How the Metaverse Could Change Work. https://hbr.org/2022/04/how-the-metaverse-could-change-work. Accessed 28 Apr 2022
6. Suzuki, S., et al.: Virtual experiments in metaverse and their applications to collaborative projects: the framework and its significance. Procedia Comput. Sci. **176**, 2125–2132 (2020)
7. "Leveraging Existing Technologies," p. 135
8. Hirsh-Pasek, K., et al.: A whole new world: Education meets the metaverse February 2022 Policy brief (2022)
9. Facebook, the metaverse and the monetization of higher education - LSE Research Online. http://eprints.lse.ac.uk/113102/. Accessed 19 Apr 2022
10. Ortiz-Marcos, I., et al.: A framework of global competence for engineers: the need for a sustainable world. Sustainability **12**(22), 9568 (2020)
11. Radianti, J., Majchrzak, T.A., Fromm, J., Wohlgenannt, I.: A systematic review of immersive virtual reality applications for higher education: design elements, lessons learned, and research agenda. Comput. Educ. **147**, 103778 (2020)
12. Davis, A., Murphy, J., Owens, D., Khazanchi, D., Zigurs, I.: Avatars, people, and virtual worlds: foundations for research in metaverses. J. Assoc. Inf. Syst. **10**(2), 90–117 (2009)
13. Hertzum, M., Clemmensen, T., Hornbæk, K., Kumar, J., Shi, Q., Yammiyavar, P.: Usability constructs: a cross-cultural study of how users and developers experience their use of information systems, pp. 317–326 (2007)
14. Sah, Y.J., Rheu, M., Ratan, R.: Avatar-user bond as meta-cognitive experience: explicating identification and embodiment as cognitive fluency. Front. Psychol. **12**, 2669 (2021)
15. Katre, D., Orngreen, R., Yammiyavar, P., Clemmensen, T.: Human Work Interaction Design: Usability in Social, Cultural and Organizational Contexts, vol. 316. Springer, Heidelberg (2010). https://doi.org/10.1007/978-3-642-11762-6

VR Accessibility in Distance Adult Education

Bartosz Muczyński[2], Kinga Skorupska[1(✉)], Katarzyna Abramczuk[5],
Cezary Biele[3], Zbigniew Bohdanowicz[3], Daniel Cnotkowski[3],
Jazmin Collins[6], Wiesław Kopeć[1], Jarosław Kowalski[3],
Grzegorz Pochwatko[4], and Thomas Logan[7]

[1] XR Lab, Polish-Japanese Academy of Information Technology (PJAIT), Warsaw,
Poland
kinga.skorupska@pja.edu.pl
[2] Faculty of Navigation, Maritime University of Szczecin, Szczecin, Poland
b.muczynski@pm.szczecin.pl
[3] Laboratory of Interactive Technologies, National Information Processing Institute
(LIT, OPI PIB), Warsaw, Poland
[4] VR Lab, Institute of Psychology Polish Academy of Sciences (IP PAS), Warsaw,
Poland
[5] University of Warsaw, Warsaw, Poland
[6] Enhancing Ability Lab, Cornell University, Ithaca, USA
[7] Equal Entry LLC, New York, USA

Abstract. As virtual reality (VR) technology becomes more pervasive,
it continues to find multiple new uses beyond research laboratories. One
of them is distance adult education—the potential of VR to provide
valuable education experiences is massive, despite the current barriers
to its widespread application. Nevertheless, recent trends demonstrate
clearly that VR is on the rise in education settings, and VR-only courses
are becoming more popular across the globe. This trend will continue
as more affordable VR solutions are released commercially, increasing
the number of education institutions that benefit from the technology.
No accessibility guidelines exist at present that are created specifically
for the design, development, and use of VR hardware and software in
distance education. The purpose of this workshop is to address this niche.
It gathers researchers and practitioners who are interested in education
and intend to work together to formulate a set of practical guidelines
for the use of VR in distance adult education to make it accessible to a
wider range of people.

Keywords: Accessibility · Case studies · Distance education · Virtual
reality

B. Muczyński and K. Skorupska—Contributed equally to this study.

© The Author(s), under exclusive license to Springer Nature Switzerland AG 2023
J. Abdelnour Nocera et al. (Eds.): INTERACT 2023, LNCS 14145, pp. 685–691, 2023.
https://doi.org/10.1007/978-3-031-42293-5_94

1 Overview

1.1 Theme

Barriers to learning in distance education are long established, from the onset of the correspondence courses of the nineteenth century, through education via the radio in the twentieth century, to VR-mediated classrooms [1] that focus on teaching practical skills in the twenty-first century [4]. These barriers include, most notably, the absence of institutional support such as staff training, inadequate technological preparation and infrastructure, inadequate policies and negative stereotypes [6]. A recent large-scale exploratory study found "(1) administrative structure, (2) organizational change, (3) technical expertise, (4) social interaction and quality, (5) faculty compensation and time, (6) threat of technology, (7) legal issues, (8) evaluation/effectiveness, (9) access, and (10) student-support services" to be the ten key barriers to distance education [5]. Although the technology has developed in terms of extra-course factors, such as access, network stability, technological readiness, and the support policies of educational institutions, accessibility issues continue to hinder both virtual reality (VR) software functionality and VR instructional design. Many VR social applications lack accessibility features and support for educational settings, despite their use in education and the existence of VR-specific accessibility guidelines[1]. To address this niche during this workshop, we aspire to gather and analyze diverse perspectives, experiences, and approaches to VR distance education in the context of accessibility. We hope that the resulting practical guidelines for making VR more accessible in distance education will help researchers, practitioners, and educators to better design their VR-mediated distance learning experiences, and will provide a valuable perspective for software developers that will help them prioritize functional features that are crucial to the solutions' accessibility in VR distance education. This, hopefully, will serve as a step toward the application of Universal Design for Learning for new and for existing XR educational environments; that, in turn, will make those environments better not only for users with disabilities, but for all users (via so called curb-cut effect [3]). It is worth noting that in 2020 the Game Awards, which is the most prestigious and recognizable event in the video game industry, introduced the Innovation in Accessibility award to recognize achievements made by the largest game studios in making their games more accessible. This further demonstrates that VR education applications lag behind the entertainment industry in their support for diverse groups of users.

1.2 Target Audience

We invite researchers and practitioners who represent the fields of distance education, virtual reality, and accessibility, as well as those with combined experi-

---

[1] This includes the guidelines of W3C, available here: https://www.w3.org/TR/xaur/, guidelines for developers by Oculus https://developer.oculus.com/resources/design-accessible-vr/, and considerations related to professional settings https://xraccess.org/bcxr-report/.

ence in these areas. We encourage people that are interested in new forms of distance education to join our debate on the opportunities and challenges of the application of VR in their fields—even if they lack prior experience with the technology.

1.3 Contributions

Participants will prepare short abstracts (2–5 pages) containing:

- a short bio that includes the participant's experience in distance education, virtual reality, and accessibility
- at least one of the following topics:
  - Real-life examples of in-person or software-mediated educational situations in which specific accessibility features were absent or sorely needed.
  - The pros and cons of specific tools and applications (e.g. text, video, or VR) for distance education that the participant has used before. This point should be as detailed as possible with special attention paid to accessibility features.
  - Areas in which VR-based distance education can be more accessible than standard (in-person) or remote video education.
  - A description of powerful examples of VR accessibility features that the participant has used or encountered in the broad range of VR applications, including VR games and experiences.
  - An idea for a single new or modified software or hardware feature that could have a positive impact in the creation of an accessible VR-based distance course or lesson.
  - An idea for a course or lesson that the participant would like to conduct in VR, including the goal of the course or lesson, a detailed schedule (topics and number of hours), teaching methods and activities, forms of evaluation (e.g. assignments or tests/quizzes), and a reflection of challenges the participant might encounter while conducting it.

Participants may also consider situations in which, temporarily or permanently, not all attendees have access to VR headsets, which means that they must join using alternative means, such as voice, text, or video communication using a desktop or a mobile phone with limited data.

1.4 Topics

In this workshop, we are interested in the interplay of three key aspects:

1. Software solutions. Participants will consider a selection of major applications and platforms, such as Horizon Workrooms and Engage, as well as the influence of aspects such as environments, avatars, and available interactions in the VR experience [2]. This part will enable us to establish a set of features that are necessary for accessible distance education in the VR environment, optional features that impact the education experience positively, and features that could be implemented to enhance or extend education experiences.

2. Hardware and its capabilities. During the workshop, participants will identify the strengths and weaknesses of each major commercially available solution in the context of accessibility for distance education. Based on the identified weaknesses, participants will work to develop countermeasures that could be implemented in the next generation of VR hardware.
3. Instructional design for VR. Participants will evaluate how the design of courses for VR classrooms ought to differ from traditional learning, and from asynchronous and synchronous e-learning. This topic will be based on the findings of the sections above and will focus on interaction design guidelines.

2   Organisers

Katarzyna Abramczuk works at the Faculty of Sociology of the University of Warsaw. She is interested in research at the intersection of sociology, mathematical modeling of social phenomena, cognitive psychology, behavioural economics, and new technologies.

Cezary Biele is the head of the Laboratory of Interactive Technologies at OPI PIB. He is a human–technology interaction researcher with a background in psychology, psychophysiology, and computer science.

Zbigniew Bohdanowicz is a researcher at the Laboratory of Interactive Technologies at OPI PIB. He works on the social aspects of technology development—specifically, its impact on individuals and social networks.

Daniel Cnotkowski is a VR programmer at the Laboratory of Interactive Technologies at OPI PIB. He works on VR applications for researchers. He is interested in how VR can become a mainstream platform for research simulations.

Jazmin Collins is a PhD student at the Enhancing Ability Lab of Cornell University. Her research focuses on both the evaluation and the development of emerging VR/augmented reality (AR) technologies as accessible tools for blind/low vision communities. She is also a member of the XR Access organization, which promotes accessibility in VR/AR.

Wiesław Kopeć is a computer scientist and the head of XR Center at PJAIT and a member of Emotion-Cognition Lab at SWPS University. He also co-founded the transdisciplinary Human Aspects in Science and Engineering (HASE) research group and distributed LivingLab Kobo.

Jarosław Kowalski is an assistant professor at the Laboratory of Interactive Technologies at OPI PIB. He is a sociologist and research specialist. His areas of interest include User Experience studies, the sociology of innovation, and the social and psychological aspects of new technologies.

Thomas Logan is the owner of Equal Entry and has spent the past twenty years assisting organizations to create technology solutions that work for people with disabilities. He has delivered projects for numerous federal, state, and local government agencies as well as private sector organizations.

Bartosz Muczyński is a researcher at the Maritime University of Szczecin, Poland, where he leads the laboratory of VR and AR systems and serves as the head of the university's E-learning Center. He also works as a VR developer at OPI PIB.

Grzegorz Pochwatko is a leading expert in VR and psychophysiology. As the head of the Virtual Reality and Psychophysiology Lab at IP PAS, he has dedicated his career to exploring the interactions between virtual humans and co-presence in extended reality environments.

Kinga Skorupska is a researcher at the XR Center at PJAIT whose interests include UX Design and science communication. She conducts research in collaborative ICT solutions and technology enhanced learning.

3   Methodology

We propose a one-day remote hybrid VR and video workshop. The workshop will commence with a Zoom video call for introductions and ice-breaking. The participants will then share insights from their submitted abstracts, which contain specific cases and reflections they had on the subject. A discussion of recurring insights will follow. Participants will also be prepared for the next session, which will take place in a VR education environment. The organizers will explain how the participants should approach it, what to do in the case of any technical issue, and what the main goals of the experience are.

The second session, in Horizon Workrooms, will focus on the delivery of a hybrid VR/video experience to the participants. Although participants are encouraged to join using head-mounted displays, it will also be possible to use a desktop application to join the VR experience via video call. Having a part of the group joining the VR space via 2D video call will help expand the experience and perspectives of people that do not have access to VR headsets. Participants will be given a brief lecture on the W3C XR Accessibility guidelines, which will serve as an introduction to a group task in which each group will work with a few selected guidelines based on personas constructed previously from case studies gathered by the organizers. This will be complemented with a discussion and brainstorming session for all participants, during which all ideas will be compiled on a board.

In the next session, the participants will reflect on their shared VR education experience, and a facilitator will help them brainstorm insights that will later be categorized using affinity diagramming. The third session will focus on distance education functionalities, such as moderation for teachers, student evaluation, and note taking. Participants will discuss how the ideal education VR software should be designed to provide teachers with a set of features that support the teaching process and give due consideration to the accessibility features identified during the first session. The workshop will conclude with a discussion on a possible multi-author publication, a follow-up action plan, and a schedule for related activities (Fig. 1).

Fig. 1. We have selected Horizon Workrooms as our virtual venue for Sessions 2 and 3 of the Workshop to enable participants to experience distance education via VR, or, if impossible, by joining a predominantly VR session via a desktop application.

4 Expected Outcomes

The key outcome of the workshop will constitute a set of practical accessibility guidelines for the use of VR in distance education, which will assist developers, researchers, practitioners, and educators in better designing their VR-mediated distance learning experiences and applications. Although we expect these guidelines to be inspired by existing accessibility guidelines in VR and beyond, they may also draw heavily from both the diverse knowledge and experience of the participants, and relevant lessons highlighted in prior literature. Such guidelines will be particularly useful for practitioners of distance education who lack prior VR experience or expertise. The guidelines will be compiled in a post-workshop multi-author publication coordinated by the workshop organizers. The publication will be submitted to an ACM venue to ensure high visibility to other researchers. This justifies another connected outcome: the dissemination of accessibility concerns in connection to XR technology that is not limited to instructional settings. Both outcomes connect directly to the theme of this years conference, "Design for Equality and Justice".

Author contributions. Bartosz Muczyński and Kinga Skorupska–The first two authors contributed equally to this study.

References

1. Clark, J.T.: Chapter 62 - distance education. In: Iadanza, E. (ed.) Clinical Engineering Handbook, 2nd edn., pp. 410–415. Academic Press (2020). https://doi.org/10.1016/B978-0-12-813467-2.00063-8, https://www.sciencedirect.com/science/article/pii/B9780128134672000638
2. Harfouche, A.L., Nakhle, F.: Creating bioethics distance learning through virtual reality. Trends in Biotech. **38**(11), 1187–1192 (2020). https://doi.org/10.1016/j.tibtech.2020.05.005, https://www.sciencedirect.com/science/article/pii/S0167779920301268

3. Hesse, B.: Curb cuts in the virtual community: telework and persons with disabilities. In: Proceedings of the Twenty-Eighth Annual Hawaii International Conference on System Sciences, vol. 4, pp. 418–425 (1995). https://doi.org/10.1109/HICSS.1995.375707

4. Li, P., Fang, Z., Jiang, T.: Research into improved distance learning using vr technology. Front. Educ. **7** (2022). https://doi.org/10.3389/feduc.2022.757874, https://www.frontiersin.org/articles/10.3389/feduc.2022.757874

5. Muilenburg, L., Berge, Z.: Barriers to distance education: a factor-analytic study. Am. J. Distance Educ. **15**, 7–22 (2001). https://doi.org/10.1080/08923640109527081

6. Yeh, C.Y., Tsai, C.C.: Massive distance education: barriers and challenges in shifting to a complete online learning environment. Front. Psychol. **13**, 928717 (2022)

Author Index

© The Editor(s) (if applicable) and The Author(s), under exclusive license
to Springer Nature Switzerland AG 2023
J. Abdelnour Nocera et al. (Eds.): INTERACT 2023, LNCS 14145, pp. 693–697, 2023.
https://doi.org/10.1007/978-3-031-42293-5

Printed in the United States
by Baker & Taylor Publisher Services

Printed in the United States
by Baker & Taylor Publisher Services